D1189812

THE
CENTENARY HISTORY OF
KING'S COLLEGE LONDON

PRINT COMMEMORATIVE OF THE OPENING OF
KING'S COLLEGE

Fr.

THE
CENTENARY HISTORY OF
KING'S COLLEGE
LONDON
1828–1928

BY

F. J. C. HEARNSHAW M.A. LL.D.
FELLOW OF KING'S COLLEGE AND PROFESSOR OF MEDIÆVAL
HISTORY IN THE UNIVERSITY OF LONDON

GEORGE G. HARRAP & COMPANY LTD.
LONDON   BOMBAY   SYDNEY

U SCH Ottawa
PSYCH. ED. C

First published 1929
by GEORGE G. HARRAP & CO. LTD.
39-41 Parker Street, Kingsway, London, W.C.2

LF
435
.H4
1929

Printed in Great Britain at THE BALLANTYNE PRESS *by*
SPOTTISWOODE, BALLANTYNE & CO. LTD.
Colchester, London & Eton

PREFACE

THE celebration of the centenary of the inauguration of King's College in 1828, and of the acquisition of a Royal Charter of Incorporation in 1829, seemed to the present authorities of the college to call imperatively for the writing of a sketch of the history of the institution during the hundred years just completed. They felt that such a history would be of interest not only to all the past and present members of the college, but also to that larger public which is concerned with the development of English education during the nineteenth century.

They therefore requested the present writer, who since 1912 has been head of the department of history in the college, to make the required survey. They generously and unreservedly placed at his disposal all the minute-books and other records of the college, and left him wholly free to make such use of them as he should think fit. This unpublished and hitherto unexamined material has formed the basis of the narrative which he has constructed. The unique information supplied by the college records has, however, been supplemented from numerous printed sources, such as calendars, old newspapers, biographies, dissertations, and treatises. In collecting this scattered and miscellaneous material he has received invaluable aid from one of the distinguished students of the history department, Mr W. H. Wickwar, M.A., who has shown extraordinary diligence and skill in hunting out all conceivable authorities. Another very useful source of material has been numerous letters and memoranda from old students and former members of the staff who, in response to a widely circulated *questionnaire*, sent communications telling of what they have seen and known. Several of these are so interesting in substance, so authoritative, and so admirable in form that they are given as appendices to the narrative portion of this volume. Others would have been included had limits of space permitted. The writer wishes to thank most cordially all who have aided him in his work.

The writing of this history has been a labour of love; but

it has been a labour carried through in circumstances of exceptional difficulty. It has had to be achieved in the scanty leisure intervals of an unusually busy year. Shortness of time, together with multiplicity of other concerns, has prevented that concentration of attention, that thoroughness of investigation, and that maturity of judgment necessary to do justice to the theme. In particular, the writer feels that he has not had the freedom of spirit needed for the formation of balanced opinions on the many controversial questions which the history of King's College raises. He therefore wishes it to be clearly understood that the views expressed in this volume are his own personal views alone; that they do not bind anyone else in the college, still less the college as a whole. If he could have refrained from expressing opinions at all he would have been glad to do so; but the nature of the facts he has had to narrate precluded that possibility.

Since this history is a centenary history, it seemed proper to the writer to dwell with peculiar fullness upon the founding of the college a hundred years ago, and upon the story of its early developments. The story of the middle period is also related at as great a length as the limits of a single volume permit. The recent history of the college—that is, of the period since Dr Wace's retirement in 1897—is told in a more summary fashion. The time for a detailed treatment of events so well within living memory is not yet.

An attempt has been made in respect of the earlier periods to give, as an appendix to each chapter, a list of the more notable students who later attained to eminence. These lists, it is feared, are still very incomplete. The writer will be greatly obliged if readers of this volume will inform him, with as much detail and as many exact dates as possible, of any omissions they may note, in order that these omissions may be remedied in any future editions of this work that may be called for.

F. J. C. HEARNSHAW

UNIVERSITY OF LONDON
KING'S COLLEGE
March 1929

CONTENTS

PART I

THE GENESIS OF THE COLLEGE

PART II

THE SEMINARY OF RELIGIOUS EDUCATION

7

CONTENTS

9

APPENDICES

ILLUSTRATIONS

THE CENTENARY HISTORY OF KING'S COLLEGE LONDON

PART I

THE GENESIS OF THE COLLEGE

CHAPTER I

THE HISTORICAL BACKGROUND

§ 1. *The Condition of England in 1828*

I BEGIN to write this centenary sketch of the history of King's College at a quarter-past twelve on the twenty-first of June in the year 1928—that is to say, precisely one hundred years to the minute since the opening of the meeting in the Freemasons' Hall, Westminster, at which the foundation of the College was determined. Imagination tries to recover the scene and the circumstances of that notable day in 1828. Great Queen Street, on the south side of which the Freemasons' Hall and its associated tavern were situated, now hopelessly submerged by commerce, had not in George IV's time wholly lost evidence of the fact that in the seventeenth century it had been " one of the grandest and most fashionable parts of the town." Named after Queen Elizabeth, it had for two generations—roughly, 1603 to 1666—enjoyed the distinction of being in the heart of the aristocratic west end of the metropolis. Paulet House and Cherbury House, conspicuous in magnificence, had been only two among the many mansions of the nobility which had given it distinction. In this street, during the early part of the Stuart period, had dwelt, amid other notables, Lord Herbert of Cherbury, the Earl of Bristol, and Lord Chancellor Finch. In the time of Charles II it had housed men so eminent as the Dukes of Buckingham and Lauderdale, not to mention Edmund Waller, politician and poet. Its transformation from social to commercial importance dates from the Great Fire of London, which drove the business men out of the city, planted them in these purlieus of the aristocracy, and compelled the gilded throng to move farther west. In 1828 it was still in its intermediate or purgatorial stage, being largely peopled by artists and actors. The Freemasons' Hall had been opened in 1776, and until Exeter Hall was built (1830–31) it was the main centre of philanthropic and evangelical propaganda.

It is not difficult for us to picture with the mind's eye the scene on that midsummer day a hundred years ago when the leaders of church and state met to establish a college in which the pursuit of knowledge and the practice of religion should be joined in indissoluble union. We can see the great concourse of zealous clergy and pious laity—those from the city coming on foot, those from the country on horseback—drawn together by the summons of their bishops, rallied by the cry that the church was in danger, and attracted by the prospect of beholding and hearing the hero of Waterloo, now prime minister, who had promised to preside. We can catch in imagination the rumble of the episcopal chariots as they bring in swift succession all the most potent prelates of the realm. Finally, we can discern, vivid as though it were beneath our gaze, the arrival, punctual on the stroke of time, of the liveried equipage of the duke; we can watch the great man descend, make his way to the ante-room, and thence, accompanied by a splendid throng of bishops and nobles, enter the hall amid the enthusiastic plaudits of the assembled multitude. Such is the scene of a century ago which a moment's meditation re-creates.

Less easy, but incomparably more important, is it to call up again from the shadowy past the circumstances which led to the great gathering of June 1828, and to realize the conditions amid which the college had its start. Let us endeavour for a moment to evoke the spirit of that vanished Hanoverian world, even though to do so demands a wizardry more potent than that required to revivify ages far more remote in point of time. For the age of George IV, albeit it was the period in which our grandfathers flourished, is divided from us by an almost impassable barrier of unfamiliar institutions and alien ideas.

The decade 1820–30 was the climax or culmination of a long era of rapid and revolutionary change. The revolt against civil and ecclesiastical authority which had achieved its first triumphs in the Italian Renaissance and the German Reformation; which in the seventeenth century had displayed itself most effectively in Dutch Emancipation and English Rebellion; had in the eighteenth century made its main manifestations in France. Until the death of Louis XIV in 1715 the combined and overwhelming power of state and church had suppressed all symptoms of disobedience or dissent. But nowhere was scepticism more rife or desire for freedom stronger than in the cultivated but crushed society which impatiently endured the inquisitorial tyranny of the last days of the old king and Madame de Maintenon. The unfeigned and unconcealed joy with which the news of Louis XIV's death was hailed throughout France preluded an outburst of blasphemy and sedition which threatened to sweep away not only the abuses and oppressions of the old *régime*, but the very foundations of both religion and social order. The theories of Montesquieu undermined the bases of the Bourbon monarchy; the brilliant ribaldry of Voltaire poured contempt upon the Catholic church; above all, the fascinating speculations of Rousseau challenged, in the name of the sovereign people, all the peculiarities of the privileged classes. The clash of infidelity with obscurantism; of reason with passion; of irresponsible criticism with authoritative corruption and incompetence; of aggressive democracy with jealous aristocracy, finally came to a head in the French Revolution, during the flaming course of which all established institutions and all traditional creeds were thrown into the melting-pot. The ferment of revolution spread from France throughout Europe, and indeed throughout the world. In England particularly the seductive writings of men such as Thomas Paine and William Godwin, together with the formidable activities of numerous radical societies, menaced the stability of both throne and altar.

By the French Revolution were engendered the great wars which for nearly a quarter of a century (1792–1815) devastated the Continent, reaching their apogee in the terrific conflict between Napoleon and the Quadruple Alliance, whereof the culmination was the battle of Waterloo. Never had any preceding struggle caused so profound a social upheaval, or been accompanied by so vast an overthrow of ancient principalities and powers. In vain did the plenipotentiaries at Vienna in 1815 seek to obliterate the revolution and restore the ruins of the old order. In vain did the rehabilitated monarchs and the re-established hierarchies endeavour to reassert their ascendancy over the bodies and the souls of their subjects. In vain did the poets and the other visionaries of the Romantic reaction try to revivify and reincorporate the extinct spirit of the vanished middle ages. The new world of democracy and rationalism had come into inextinguishable existence, for ever disturbing the balance of the old world of loyalty and faith.

15

The disturbance coincident with the war, moreover, was enormously aggravated by the disorganization and distress caused by the conclusion of the peace—by the disbanding of colossal armies, the reduction of navies, the stoppage of military industries, the restoration of depreciated currencies, and so on. Few periods in our long history have been so painfully marked by misery, or so ominously characterized by agitation and unrest, as the thirteen years (1815-28) which preceded the inauguration of King's College. It was this period that saw the invention of the word 'socialism' and the first formulation of the communistic programme for the complete subversion of the existing order of things.

Further, the ferment due to revolutionary ideas, and the disorder resulting from prolonged war and injudicious pacification, happened, most unhappily, to synchronize with what would even in normal times have produced much social and economic dislocation—viz., the so-called Industrial Revolution. By this convenient but ambiguous name is connoted that great change in modes of production, distribution, and exchange which converted England from an agricultural to a manufacturing country; which caused the domestic system of hand-industry to be superseded by the factory system of machine-industry; which led to a vast exodus of population from the fields to the coalfields; which called into swift existence, as though at the fiat of a black demon, those hideous aggregations of hovels and gin-shops which constitute the major part of most of our larger industrial towns at the present day. Moreover, not only did population migrate and congregate, it also—thanks to the diminution of the death-rate at the hands of advancing sanitary science—steadily and rapidly increased: the census of 1801 showed the population of England and Wales to be under 9,000,000; that of 1831 revealed it as nearly 14,000,000. Most of this new population was entirely uneducated. Much of it lay wholly beyond the reach of the influence of the established agencies of the church; when, for instance, Dr George D'Oyly, prime founder of King's College, became rector of Lambeth in 1820 he found 54,000 people under his care; before he died in 1846 the number of his parishioners had risen to 130,000, and he had in vain striven to keep pace with the swelling flood by building thirteen new churches within the precincts of his vast domain.

§ 2. *Education in England under George IV*

Education and evangelization were felt to be the two great desiderata of this tremendous and unmanageable age. The two were not always desired by the same persons, nor were they by all thinkers regarded as compatible with one another. The Methodists, the great evangelizers of the period, and the Low Church party within the Establishment, which had caught the Methodist fervour, tended to regard the Gospel as sufficient for human need. Hence—although they had many highly educated men in their ranks—they were disposed to disparage learning, rejoicing that the weak things of this world were chosen to overthrow the strong, and the foolish to confound the wise. On the other hand, the Philosophical Radicals —sceptical, for the most part, in the matter of religion— regarded education as the one and only hope of humanity, believing that man is so constituted that as soon as he is convincingly taught that the way of virtue is the way of happiness, and the way of knowledge the way of virtue, he will believe, will do, and so will attain felicity and perfection. Midway between he Methodists and the Radicals—that is, between the pure evangelicals and the mere educationists—stood a large and diverse body of moderate and balanced opinion which repudiated the divorce between religion and science; which regarded both faith and knowledge as equally necessary for complete salvation; which felt that piety without mental discipline tended to degenerate into extravagance and fanaticism, while learning without devotion gave no security against the snares of the world, the lure of the flesh, and the wiles of the devil. Prominent among the members of this middle party was a group of eminent Anglicans, many of whom will later on come conspicuously before us as founders of King's College—*e.g.*, Hugh James Rose of Cambridge; Charles James Blomfield of London; Edward Copleston of Llandaff; Joshua Watson of Clapton; Henry Handley Norris of Hackney; John Lonsdale of Bloomsbury; and George D'Oyly of Lambeth, together with whom were associated for a time men such as Thomas Arnold and Richard Whately on the one side, John Henry Newman and John Keble on the other—the great Oriel fraternity.

There can be no doubt that round about 1828 the immense weight of influential opinion was on the side of education as opposed to mere evangelization—whether education freed from the fetters of theology as desired by Jeremy Bentham and James Mill, or education still closely associated with the national church as displayed in the universities of Oxford and Cambridge. The evangelical revival, indeed, both within the Church of England and among the Methodist sects, was distinctly on the wane. A new and less individualistic type of churchmanship was coming into dominance. The need of training and of discipline for the proper performance of both ecclesiastical and civic duty was generally recognized. All the prevailing modes of thought, indeed, tended at this time to emphasize the importance of education as the moulder of character and the determiner of destiny. The dominant psychology was still that of Locke, who had taught that the mind is at birth a *tabula rasa* upon which, throughout life, extraneous influences impress themselves with indelible effect. Eighteenth-century philosophers, strongly as some of them had dissented from Locke's *Thoughts concerning Education* in other respects, had entirely accepted his psychological assumptions. Rousseau, for example, who had introduced the cult of sentiment as a rival to Locke's cult of reason, had been wholly at one with Locke in regarding all men as originally equal and alike in empty innocence, and as differing from one another in their later days solely on account of different environments. Rousseau had attributed the evil of the world to civilization, and had striven to recall men to the simple environment of the primitive state of nature wherein the noble savage lived unspoiled. La Chalotais, writing specially of France, had maintained that the chief cause of his country's woes was that the education of its citizens was in the hands of the church and not of the state. Joseph Priestley (1768) and William Godwin (1793), both of them contemplating English conditions, had opposed the control of education by the state, contending that liberty and not authority is the essential requisite of progress. Adam Smith, Thomas Paine, Jeremy Bentham, all on the basis of the Lockian psychology, had stressed the fundamental importance of education. Above all, in the early nineteenth century, Robert Owen, whose name in the twenties was one to conjure with, held that character is wholly the creature of circumstances, and that among the circumstances which determine character none is so potent as early culture.

No wonder that in an age when so immense a consensus of opinion emphasized the influence of environment, exalting active nurture over passive and patient nature, great educational activity should have displayed itself. The devotees of every creed, and the propagandists of every party, felt that if only they could obtain an effective control of education they could confidently hope to convert the world to their mode of thinking and their way of life. Moreover, this same sense of the supreme potency of early instruction and discipline led them to oppose with implacable hostility and fiery zeal the educational enterprises of their enemies, and to employ every conceivable device to " confound their politics " and " frustrate their knavish tricks." Hence in this Hanoverian age the educational field was a battle-ground of contending enthusiasts.

From 1780 Sunday schools had been in energetic operation; in 1785 the Sunday School Union was instituted; and in 1828 nearly a million persons (by no means all of them children) were receiving from some 70,000 teachers instruction in the mysteries of reading and the rudiments of religion. In or about 1798 Joseph Lancaster opened an elementary school at Southwark, into which a few years later he introduced the monitorial system, the economies whereof being such that he was able to offer, to the children of the poor, instruction in the three R's at 4s. 2d. a year. The religious problem inseparable from elementary education he solved by a rigid undenominationalism which strictly excluded all inculcation of dogmatic religion. The Lancasterian scheme of undenominational education—which in practice meant secular education—received the enthusiastic support of the Philosophical Radicals, and spread throughout the country with amazing rapidity. In 1808 the Royal Lancasterian Institution—later renamed the British and Foreign School Society—was inaugurated, the governing body of which was soon joined by Henry Brougham, James Mill, and other leading utilitarians. The success of the Lancasterian experiment, combined with horror at its undenominational basis and its secularist tendency, stimulated a number of earnest church-people, with the active approval of the Archbishop of Canterbury (Dr Manners-Sutton), to found, under the management of Dr Andrew Bell, in 1811, a rival organization entitled the " National Society for promoting the Education of the Poor in the Principles of the Established Church throughout England and Wales." Prominent among the founders of this National Society were Joshua Watson and his wealthy Clapton associates—precisely the men who twenty years later took the lead in establishing King's College as an antidote to the secularist " University of London " of Brougham and his friends. Hence the battle which in 1828-31 raged on the heights of academic education was already joined between the same combatants in 1808-11 on the broad plain of elementary instruction. In the interval, moreover, the two identical bodies came into embittered conflict in the region of popular adult education—Brougham and his allies setting up the new Society for the Diffusion of Useful Knowledge (1827) as the antagonist of the old Society for the Promotion of Christian Knowledge (1698), which was showing great activity under the inspiring direction of Joshua Watson's intimate friend, Prebendary H. H. Norris, of Hackney. In short, a century ago a titanic struggle was in process in many quarters of the wide expanse of pedagogy between the champions of knowledge purely intellectual, scientific, utilitarian, and mundane, and the defenders of a knowledge which should train and develop character as well as intellect, which should foster culture as well as science, which should recognize the existence of usefulnesses beyond the limits of utility; a knowledge which, above all, should be imparted for the purpose not merely of securing for the recipient prosperity during his brief sojourn in this world, but for the immeasurably more important end of putting him in the way of attaining eternal felicity in the world to come.

In the sphere of secondary education the ascendancy of the Church of England was not as yet seriously challenged: all the headmasters of the public schools and of the local grammar schools were clergymen, and most of the senior members of their staffs were also in orders. The nonconformist academies, such as the famous Warrington Academy, in which Joseph Priestley had been taught, after a short period of prosperity had declined, together with the arid Unitarianism with which they were associated. The private schools which later—under the influence of the Edgeworths and on the model provided by the Hills of Hazelwood (1815-33)—were to become pioneers of progress were still in their infancy. But the public schools and the local grammar schools, although dominant and orthodox, were decadent and half dead. Their curricula, almost wholly classical, of the driest syntactical type, were mere relics of mediæval triviality, devoid of all relation to the ideas of the nineteenth century or the needs of industrial civilization. Their religion, moreover, was of the most deadly and depressing sort, mere mumblings of prescribed formulæ, powerless to convert the soul, impotent to restrain the grossest sensuality, ineffective in the face of violence, terrorism, and revolt. Nevertheless, before 1828 the day of reform had dawned. Faith in the power of education; consciousness of the defects of the old curricula; realization of the needs of the new life; and, above all, a quickened religious enthusiasm, had inspired men like Butler of Shrewsbury (1798–1836), Keate of Eton (1809–34), Russell of the Charterhouse (1818–32), and, *facile princeps*, Arnold of Rugby (1828–42) to amend discipline, to enlarge the syllabus, to improve methods of instruction, to reintroduce humanity, and to restore reality to worship.

§ 3. *The Universities in the Hanoverian Period*

The movement of new life which round about 1828 manifested itself in the dry bones of the ancient secondary schools of the country also, at the same time, displayed itself in the two venerable universities of Oxford and Cambridge. They too in the eighteenth century had touched their lowest depths of stagnation and inefficiency. Oxford sank rather lower than Cambridge; its persistent Jacobitism kept it aloof from the life of Hanoverian England; its religious exclusiveness was more extreme than that of Cambridge; its courses of study were more completely mediæval and unpractical. Cambridge to some extent accommodated itself to the Hanoverian *régime*; it imposed no rigid religious tests except on those who wished to take degrees, win prizes, hold fellowships, or fill offices; the influence of Newton sufficed to leaven the classical curriculum with mathematics and natural philosophy. Both Cambridge and Oxford, however, had practically ceased to be universities at all, and had become mere federations of colleges—seventeen in the one and twenty in the other—whose heads and fellows lived at ease on lavish endowments, doing little more than manage the college estates and maintain the reputation of the academic wine-cellars. In 1717 Toland, writing of Oxford, denounced its " proud, fierce, and unsociable spirit," its drunken teachers, its ignorant students, its lazy and tyrannical heads. Twelve years later Hearn remarked that " learning is at so low an ebb at present that hardly anything of that kind is sought after." In 1748 Humphrey Sibthorp was appointed Professor of Botany at Oxford; he held the post for thirty-six years, passing it on in 1784 as a comfortable sinecure to his son; during the whole period of his tenure of his office he delivered but a single lecture. Professor R. L. Archer, treating of 1760, says that " if we wish to picture Oxford in the year when George III ascended the throne, we must imagine a university in which professors had ceased to lecture, where tutors regarded an enquiring student as a nuisance, and where work was the last thing expected." In 1778 Vicesimus Knox made a devastating exposure of the procedure by means of which degrees were conferred: each candidate selected his own books (usually choosing the easiest) and his own examiner (naturally preferring the slackest); the examination was oral, it was held in private, it lasted but a few moments, its result was predetermined; it was followed by a jollification in an inn. It is on record that Lord Eldon qualified in Hebrew by answering correctly a single question which demanded a translation into the sacred tongue of the expression, so common in the everyday conversation of the Holy Land, "the place of a skull": in history the only question was "Who founded University College?" the answer expected and received being "King Alfred"! No wonder that Horace Walpole, writing on the eve of the French Revolution, should have asserted that at Oxford nothing was taught "but drunkenness and prerogative." Much the same is the burden of the well-known and damning indictments of the decadent university uttered by such eminent *alumni* as Joseph Butler (Oriel), Samuel Johnson (Pembroke), Adam Smith (Balliol), Jeremy Bentham (Queen's), Edward Gibbon (Magdalen). Cardinal Newman, who entered Oxford after reform had begun, admits that at the end of the eighteenth century the university "was giving no education at all to the youth committed to its keeping." Early in the nineteenth century the *Edinburgh Review*—and in particular those "three giants of the North," Lord Jeffrey, Professor Playfair, and the Rev. Sidney Smith—commenced a terrific attack upon the educational inefficiency and ecclesiastical exclusiveness of Oxford. By that time, it is true, some improvement on eighteenth-century standards had taken place. Under the reforming influence of John Eveleigh of Oriel, Cyril Jackson of Christ Church, and John Parsons of Balliol a more effective system of examinations had been inaugurated in 1800. Yet, Mr H. A. L. Fisher tells us, "When James Edwards Sewell of New College was examined for his B.A. degree in 1830, the examiners contented themselves with asking him to translate a few sentences of Livy, and to explain the fifth proposition in the first book of Euclid," and, he adds, "On that searching intellectual test Mr Sewell obtained his degree and a fellowship, and in due course proceeded to the doctorate of divinity and the office of warden of his college." New College, indeed, did not until 1851 surrender its right to confer degrees upon its *alumni* without any examination at all.

In 1831, the very year in which King's College was opened, Sir William Hamilton recommenced in the *Edinburgh Review*, the great organ of triumphant Whiggism, the fierce and not unjustified assault upon the obscurantism and inefficiency of the old universities, which effectively initiated their radical reconstruction and reform in the early years of Queen Victoria. He accused the colleges of having usurped the functions of the university; he condemned the instruction given by the tutors of the colleges as being merely a repetition of that imparted in schools; while admitting the right of the colleges, as private institutions, to exclude dissenters from their hospitality, he denied the right of the university to shut them out from its educational privileges.

The two main charges which Hamilton brought against Oxford and Cambridge in 1831 were (1) educational inefficiency—the curricula were antiquated, the standard of scholarship was low, many subjects of first-rate importance were ignored, and so on; and (2) religious exclusiveness. Hamilton's charges did not remain unanswered. The replies, however, were feeble and ineffective. The existence of the evils denounced was not seriously denied; controversy concerned itself almost entirely with the question, Who is to blame? Some attributed the fault to the colleges; others to the interference of the state; others, again, to the intolerance of the church. Some blamed the institution of celibacy, others traced the decline of the universities to the invention of printing and the rise of the text-book. Whilst, however, this controversy as to causes raged, in spite of the fact that the existence of abuses was admitted, resistance to reform was general and potent. Men like the venerable Dr Routh, a relic of George II's reign, President of Magdalen for sixty-three years (1791–1854), dreading radicalism and revolution as they dreaded the devil, steadily and conscientiously opposed all change, and possessed sufficient influence to make reform extremely slow. Gradually, however, the university curriculum was widened, new schools or triposes instituted, new chairs and lectureships founded. Still more slowly were religious tests relaxed. So far back as 1772 Parliament had been petitioned to remove the barrier which subscription to the thirty-nine articles placed in the path of matriculation at Oxford and graduation at Cambridge. Cambridge favoured the petition; but Oxford opposed it, and through its representative, Sir Roger Newdigate, secured its rejection. Sixty years later—under the influence of the repeal of the Test and Corporation

Acts, Catholic Emancipation, and Parliamentary Reform—the matter was mooted again at Oxford (1834-35). The abolition of the requirement of subscription was powerfully urged by the liberal Dr Hampden (later Bishop of Hereford), the darling of the Whigs. It was, however, successfully opposed by the Tories, prominent among whom were John Henry Newman (who had denounced Catholic Emancipation!) and Frederick Denison Maurice.

Hence it will be clear that in the reign of George IV the only two universities existent in England were, on the one hand, the close preserves of the Anglican church, and, on the other hand, were capable of providing little education that was of any use to anyone except a prospective clergyman who wished to give his congregation the benefit of original translations of the Greek Testament, or a budding Member of Parliament who wished (as was then expected) to sprinkle his orations with gems from the Latin poets. It was in these circumstances that in 1828 the " University of London " was opened, as the property of a joint-stock company, its purpose being, first, to supply an academic instruction available for Dissenters, Deists, and Jews, and, secondly, to provide a curriculum which in addition to classical literature should include such practical subjects as medicine, law, mathematics, natural science, and political economy. To the establishment of this great institution we must now direct our attention.

CHAPTER II

THE "UNIVERSITY OF LONDON" AND ITS CRITICS

§ 1. *The Founding of the "University of London"*

THAT until the year 1828 the metropolis of England, the wealthiest and most populous city of the world, should have had no university within its borders was an amazing anomaly. So far back as the Tudor period (1548) Sir Thomas Gresham, financier and philanthropist, founder of the Royal Exchange, had endowed seven chairs, corresponding roughly to the main subjects taught in the curricula of the mediæval universities—viz., rhetoric from the *trivium*; music, astronomy, and geometry from the *quadrivium*; with the three professional or doctoral studies of divinity, medicine, and law. He had, moreover, bequeathed his fine mansion in Bishopsgate to be the home of the seven professors and the seat of their edifying activities. He had omitted, however, to provide for his foundation, as was remarked in the seventeenth century, either " a common government " or " the protection of an honourable chancellor," with the result that his admirable scheme did not develop. The professors, in the absence of a disciplinary and co-ordinating authority, became (according to the habit of their species) apathetic in their duties and antipathetic toward one another. Their chairs degenerated into beds, and their activities declined into chronic lethargy. Only by their regularity in receiving their salaries and by the spasmodic energy of their periodical quarrels did they display evidence of their continued existence.

In spite, however, of the failure of the Gresham foundation to function as its originator had intended, it seemed possible to Sir George Buck in 1615 to contend that there actually was a London University in being, if only the world could be persuaded to believe it. The existence of the University of London, indeed, has always been a matter of faith rather than of sight. Even at the present day few things puzzle the omniscient metropolitan taximan so much as to be asked to drive his fare to the university, or to any of its constituent members: the only sure way to reach the desired destination

25

is to give the driver the name of the nearest large public-house. In 1615 Sir George Buck, in an appendix to a new edition of Stow's *Annals*, says that England possesses "three famous universities"—viz., Oxford, Cambridge, and London—and he proceeds to enumerate as the constituent members of the third university the following institutions : (1) the Gresham foundation, (2) the divinity Schools of Westminster and St Paul's, (3) the Inns of Court and of Chancery, (4) the College of Heralds, (5) the school of civil law at Doctors' Commons, and (6) St Paul's School. The very essence of a university, however, is corporate unity, and Buck's contemporaries, in common with all modern educationists, refused to allow the name of "university" to be applied to this unco-ordinated agglomeration of heterogeneous educational atoms. But Buck's contemporaries did nothing to remedy the defect which they were quick to perceive; nor were their immediate successors stirred to effective action either by Bacon's marvellous delineation of a metropolitan university in his *New Atlantis* (1627) or by Cowley's powerful and elaborately detailed plea for a great central college for the advancement of experimental philosophy, issued in 1661.

To the men of the early eighteenth century the function of a university appeared to be merely to provide parsons for the church and gentry for the state ; and this function—since it was unnecessary for either parsons or gentry to know very much—seemed to be adequately fulfilled by Oxford and Cambridge. The complaint, indeed, was made that these two ecclesiastical mills turned out parsons faster than the Establishment could absorb them. Toward the end of the century, however—amid the ferment of revolution, the transformation of industry, the expansion of commerce, the development of international finance, the movement of reform, and the revival of education—the idea of a university was enlarged. It was felt, first, that a university should provide universal knowledge, and not merely the limited pabulum of renaissance humanism ; secondly, that it should open its doors to all ranks and classes, irrespective of race or creed; thirdly, that it should prepare men for other careers than merely the church and the legislature; and, finally, that it should make charges for its services considerably less exorbitant than those extorted by the colleges of Oxford and Cambridge.

The demand for extended facilities for technical and higher education made itself heard persistently and imperatively, especially in London, during the decade which followed the close of the great war (1815–25). First and foremost, the skilled artisans, excited by the possibilities of the new machine-industry, eager to increase their mastery of their crafts, curious respecting the scientific principles involved in the novel inventions, stirred by political ambitions, puzzled by economic and social problems, clamoured for an adult education suited to their needs. A certain Timothy Claxton, responding to the call, opened in 1817 a so-called Mechanics' Institution. Its government, however, was too autocratic; its curriculum too narrow; its methods too academic: it faded away in 1820. Profiting by the lesson of Claxton's failure, and fortified by invaluable experience gained in Glasgow, Dr George Birkbeck, with the co-operation of the ultra-democratic J. C. Robertson and the almost anarchic Thomas Hodgskin, secured the establishment of the London Mechanics' Institution (now the Birkbeck College) in 1823. Its principles were self-government and the impartation of useful knowledge; its original purpose, as stated in its prospectus, was to enable artisans to make themselves "acquainted with the facts of chemistry and of mechanical philosophy, together with the science of the creation and distribution of wealth." Birkbeck's enterprise was triumphantly successful; in 1824 some 1300 students were entered in the books of the Institution; radicals such as Henry Brougham and Francis Place gave it enthusiastic support; the liberal Duke of Sussex, brother of King George IV, opened its lecture theatre in 1825, in which year, too, similar institutions were established in Spitalfields, Hackney, Deptford, Rother-hithe, Bermondsey, Hammersmith, and Chiswick. By 1850 there were 610 of these Mechanics' Institutions in existence throughout the country, with 102,050 students on their registers.

This spontaneous and spectacular movement for education among the masses put the middle class upon its mettle: the aristocracy had its exclusive foundations at Oxford and Cambridge; the democracy was creating its comprehensive institutions in all the great towns and cities; should the wealthy oligarchy remain unprovided with the means of the broader culture or the agencies of the higher utility? In 1825 this question was being asked in many quarters. But two separate and independent groups in particular were discussing it with a view to action. One was a group of cultivated dissenters headed by Edward Irving (then a Presbyterian) and Dr F. A. Cox (an eminent Baptist divine). The other was a group of resolute philosophical radicals, most of whom had passed beyond dissent into disbelief, including the aged Jeremy Bentham himself, his great successor, James Mill, John Austin, George Grote, and the youthful John Stuart Mill. With this group were associated the men who had the power to realize the project of a great non-episcopal utilitarian college: prominent politicians like Henry Brougham and Joseph Hume; opulent Jews such as Isaac Goldsmid; literary men such as Thomas Campbell.

To Thomas Campbell—then famous as the author of the now-forgotten *Pleasures of Hope*—is due the credit of precipitating action. He himself was a distinguished graduate of Glasgow University (of which he became Lord Rector in 1827). In 1820 he had visited and admired the newly founded University of Bonn. He came back to England burning with zeal to see established in London a university which should combine the admirable organization of Scotland with the wide liberalism of Germany. His comrade, Francis Place, early in 1825 wrote: " The establishment of an university in London has for a considerable time been a favourite object with my friend, Thomas Campbell. It is now more than a year since he first mentioned the project to me." Place approved of the project, but doubted the possibility of raising the necessary funds. Conversations which Campbell had, however, with Goldsmid, Brougham, Hume, and others tended to dispel Place's doubts and to warrant Campbell's indulgence in the pleasures of hope. Hence the poet formally launched his great idea in a two-column letter published in the *Times* on February 9, 1825. After speaking of the remarkable way in which desire for knowledge " has increased among the poor, and will increase," and after showing how agencies for supplying that knowledge are rapidly being provided, he goes on to urge the needs of the *bourgeoisie*. " The plan I suggest," he says,

> is a great London University . . . an institution for effectively and multifariously teaching, examining, exercising, and rewarding with honours in the liberal arts and sciences the youth of our middling rich people between the ages of 15 or 16 and 20 or later; an establishment availing itself of all the experience and experiments that can be appealed to for facilitating the art of teaching; an university combining the advantages of public and private education, the emulative spirit produced by examination before numbers and by honours conferred before the public, the cheapness of domestic residence, and all the moral influences that result from home.

Education, emulation, economy, and the ethics of the hearth—such are the harmonious notes of Campbell's song of appeal. He said little about the religious question, not wishing to rouse the furies; but it was clearly understood that the genius of the new university would be freedom from those theological tests which barred the way to the old universities, together with a breadth of curriculum which would include countless useful studies, such as sciences and modern languages, which were despised and neglected at both Oxford and Cambridge.

Campbell's appeal met with an immediate and enthusiastic response: it was, indeed, made in the fullness of time, and even before it was issued its success was assured. On February 14, 1825, Henry Brougham, James Mill, Joseph Hume, and John Smith (*magnum atque venerabile nomen*) met Campbell in order to discuss ways and means of realizing his idea. Within six months the sum of £110,000 was raised in the form of £100 shares, and the scheme was in full swing. During those fateful six months, however, several events of importance occurred. First, Thomas Campbell hurried off to the Continent in order to study on the spot the constitutions of the new universities of Berlin (1810) and Bonn (1818). Secondly, while he was away, the religious problem was raised in an acute form. The striking success of Campbell and the philosophical radicals stirred the political dissenters to action. In April a distinguished and determined company of them met at the King's Head tavern in the Poultry and appointed a provisional committee with an energetic secretary. It seemed probable that the secular university of Thomas Campbell would be confronted by a sectarian university under the auspices of Dr Francis Cox. This painful possibility was obviated (in the absence of Campbell) by the complacency of Henry Brougham and such of his associates as were politicians rather than philosophers. They secured a fusion of the Campbellites and the Coxites by means of a compromise: religion should *not* be excluded from the curriculum of the university; it should be admitted in two forms—viz., Anglicanism for the orthodox and Presbyterianism for the nonconformists. But this compromise, although it pleased Edward Irving and satisfied Dr Cox, roused a storm of opposition in other quarters. Many Anglican evangelicals, such as Lord Althorp and Zachary Macaulay, had given their support to Campbell's scheme because it offered instruction in technical and general knowledge useful for this world without attempting to encroach upon that sphere of moral and religious knowledge necessary for felicity in the next world, which was already filled by assiduous instruction in the home and the parish church. They threatened to secede if any theology other than Anglican were taught. On the other hand, the wealthy Jews, the powerful Benthamites, and the resolute secularists objected in the most vehement manner to the inclusion of any theology at all. Thomas Campbell, much perturbed by the repercussions of this triangular controversy which reached him on the Continent, hastened home, called the disputants together, and imposed his will upon them. The Anglicans really held the key of the situation. "Either the Church of England must predominate," they said, "or else there must be no Church influence at all." Their wealth and importance made it possible for them to insist on these alternatives. In vain did the dissenters plead the example of the new university of Bonn, where Catholic and Protestant chairs of theology were established side by side. The Anglicans would not hear of dualism; monism and nihilism were the horns of the dilemma which they offered to the followers of Irving and Cox. The latter could not conceivably permit the predominance of Anglican theology; hence nothing remained but the total exclusion of religious instruction from the university curriculum. Campbell powerfully urged this as the only practicable policy. He was able to quote the regulations of the university recently founded in the Prussian capital through the energy and genius of Wilhelm von Humboldt: "The University of Berlin shall be unattached to any particular creed or school of thought, and shall be devoted only to the interests of science and learning." He completely recaptured Brougham, Hume, and Smith to his nihilistic view. Finally, the dissenters came round to it. "Enough, enough," cried Edward Irving; "we are convinced, and concede the point that the university shall be without religious rivalship." This solution of the problem, eminently agreeable to the Philosophical Radicals, but acceptable only as a *pis aller* to either the Anglicans or the Dissenters, was ultimately embodied in the following statement issued by the council of the new institution:

> The council had many long and anxious deliberations upon this subject, which they felt to be of paramount importance; but they found it impossible to unite the principles of free admission to persons of all religious denominations with any plan of theological instruction or any form of religious discipline; and they were thus compelled by necessity to leave this great primary

object of education, which they deem too important for compromise, to the direction and superintendence of the natural guardians of the pupils,

adding that

parents will have the advantage of selecting for their sons a person of the same religious persuasion with themselves, as there will probably be such houses kept by persons of different religious opinions.

This statement is eloquent of embarrassment and regret. It shifts responsibility for the instruction of the students of the university in the " great primary object of education " to the Bloomsbury landladies! Sir Philip Magnus, speaking from the Jewish point of view on the occasion of the centenary of University College (April 27, 1926), argues that Campbell's solution of the religious problems in 1825 was a mistaken one. " As often happens," he says, " those who succeed at a conference in gaining the point which they regard as essential to their scheme often fail to secure the larger object for which they had fought," and he strongly holds that " some compromise might possibly have been effected by which the university might have escaped the taunt of being godless."

Be that as it may, the " no theology " policy was formally, firmly, and finally adopted, and on this basis the new university was founded. It was immediately and strikingly successful. Its offer of a wide education at a low cost made a powerful appeal to the members of the middle class. It easily secured the services of teachers of the highest eminence. Its £100 shares were taken up with eager avidity by the city magnates. An excellent site in Gower Street was secured through the agency of Mr Goldsmid. On December 19, 1825, a general meeting of subscribers was held, at which a governing body —a council with several committees—was instituted. Two months later (February 11, 1826) a deed of settlement was drawn up establishing " an association or institution "— legally a joint-stock commercial company—" under the name of the Proprietors of the University of London." The governing body specified in this deed of association included men so notable as Henry Brougham, George Birkbeck, Thomas Campbell, Isaac Goldsmid, George Grote, Joseph Hume, James Mill, and (rather incongruously) Zachary Macaulay. The foundation-stone of the Gower Street building was laid by the convenient Duke of Sussex on April 30, 1827. A warden (Mr Leonard Horner, F.R.S.) and various professors were appointed later in the same year. The university was opened in October 1828 with some 300 students, whose number had risen to 557 by February 1829. Strong efforts were made by Brougham and his colleagues to secure from the government a charter incorporating the university and authorizing it to confer degrees. At the time, however, these efforts—largely owing to the " godlessness " of the institution —were unavailing.

§ 2. *The Church and the University*

The early days of the new joint-stock company and its unchartered university, in spite of the numbers which flocked to its lecture-rooms, were not days of unmitigated felicity or undisturbed tranquillity. On the contrary, they shared to the full the unhappiness and turbulence of that agitated age. First, the students displayed more than the normal indiscipline of their kind, taxing beyond the limits of toleration both the patience of the professors and the piety of the Bloomsbury landladies. Secondly, the eminent warden manifested a tendency to autocracy which resulted before the end of 1829 in a revolt of the teaching staff that culminated in the warden's resignation and the suppression of his office in 1832. Thirdly, an embittered feud—known as " the battle of Gower Street " —broke out in the medical school during 1831 concerning an appointment to the chair of anatomy, and both governing body and proprietors showed themselves incapable of imposing peace. Fourthly, the council, filled with able and zealous educationists, kept so vigilant a watch over the doings and sayings of professors; exercised so irritating a control over them; insisted so inconveniently on punctuality, efficiency, and other *bourgeois* qualifications, that the harassed *savants* protested in the name of outraged liberty and academic right, and in many cases resigned. But finally, and worst of all, the university became involved in a disastrous controversy with the church over the question of the place of religion in education. At first the controversy was conducted with gravity and dignity on the high ground of principle; but soon the political and partisan press (already wrangling over religion in elementary schools) got hold of it and degraded it to the depths of scurrility. On the side of the non-theological university ranged themselves such liberal organs as the *Times*, the *Morning Chronicle*, the *Globe*, the *Examiner*, the *Sunday Times*, and the *Observer*; on the side of its assailants stood the *Standard*, the *Morning Post*, the *New Times*, and (*facile princeps* for violence of language) the ultra-tory *John Bull*.

So far as I have been able to discover, the first clear note in the great debate was sounded by the Rev. Hugh James Rose, Christian Advocate to the University of Cambridge, in a sermon which he preached at the university church on Commencement Sunday, October 1826. If this was the case it is an extraordinarily interesting and significant fact. For seven years later, at Hadleigh Rectory, in the study of this same Hugh James Rose—intimate friend of Keble, Newman, Perceval, Palmer, and Hurrell Froude—the plan for the publication of the famous *Tracts for the Times* was formulated. It is a remarkable circumstance, if true, that both the Oxford Movement and the movement to establish King's College should have had their source in the same seminal Cambridge mind. Of this noble and notable man, Hugh James Rose—scholar, orator, philosopher, theologian, and saint—much more will later have to be said ; for he was the second principal of King's College. Suffice it here to remark that but for his weak health and untimely death in 1838 at the early age of forty-three he would undoubtedly have risen to the highest eminence in the church, and would have exercised a dominant influence over its policy in the reign of Queen Victoria. In Archbishop Howley's deliberate judgment " he was the best preacher in England."

His Commencement sermon, which we are now considering, attracted much attention at the time. It was based on Eccles. iii, 2, and was printed and published under the title of *The Tendency of Prevalent Opinions about Knowledge Considered*. The eloquent preacher's theme was, on the one hand, the inadequacy of the intellect of man, unaided by divine revelation, to fathom the mysteries of the universe; and, on the other hand, the insufficiency of mere " useful information " to satisfy the soul of man. He denounced the dominant secularism and utilitarianism of the age, deplored the neglect of studies needed " to educate and form a moral and intellectual, a spiritual and eternal being," arguing that

> when we once admit the existence of God, and the continuance of the soul's existence to eternity, these two considerations at once impress a character of comparative insignificance on all that does not concern these great matters.

Hence he pleaded for the study of literature as a cultivator of the mind, and of theology as the indispensable nutriment of the soul.

C

The theme thus clearly sounded in the sermon of Hugh James Rose was taken up, after the manner of a fugue, by the *British Critic* in its issue of January 1827. This magazine was a quarterly (originally a monthly) theological review, owned by the devout Joshua Watson and his friend Prebendary Norris, and run in the interests of the National Society, the S.P.C.K., and sound churchmanship generally. The counter-theme which the *British Critic* introduced was the recently issued prospectus of the University of London. In a long article it contrasted the proposals of the prospectus with the principles of Rose's sermon, and strongly condemned the former. It appealed to the directors of the university to reconsider their prospectus, to recognize the truth of the proposition that while " education *with religion* is the greatest good which man can bestow on man, education unless grounded upon religious principles may be a curse instead of a blessing." It pointed out that they themselves admitted " the primary importance " of the subject, and therefore contended that it was highly illogical to omit it from the curriculum. It would be better, the *British Critic* continued, to have a defective or even an erroneous religion taught in the university rather than none at all :

> We would much rather see a Dissenters' University established in London in the next street to an University for members of the Church, and in open and fair opposition to it, or even a Deists' University instituted in the same way, than one like the present which professes to admit all other ingredients of knowledge, and rejects religion as something unwholesome and unpalatable.

And then it asked the significant question, which may be regarded as the first open hint of a possible King's College :

> We would ask why two or more collegiate institutions could not be founded in London, if the demand for a new university is so loud and general as has been pretended?

The provisional committee of the projected Gower Street academy, of course, showed not the slightest inclination to modify the non-theological platform which, as the result of a painful controversy, they had felt themselves compelled to adopt. Hence during the course of the year 1827, while the magnificent Bloomsbury building was rapidly rising and while its distinguished staff was being collected, much activity went on behind the scenes in high ecclesiastical circles with a view to the foundation of a rival college based on the twofold foundation of humane culture and divine philosophy. The very men who were supporting the Anglican National Society and its schools against the undenominational British and Foreign organization; the very men who had revivified the venerable S.P.C.K. and set it to counter mundane outpourings of the S.D.U.K.; these were the men who now, on a third field of educational conflict, prepared themselves to found, at enormous cost, a seminary of sound learning and religious education which should provide for Londoners an alternative to what they called the "godless" institution of Gower Street.

On November 26, 1827, the *Standard*, the organ of the rigid old-tory party, made the announcement :

> A rumour is very prevalent among the clergy that it is intended to make application to the legislature for the endowment of a college in the metropolis which, like the other great universities, shall be under the control of, and dedicated to the purposes of, the Established Church.

The rumour thus publicly—and perhaps prematurely—promulgated at once gave rise to an embittered newspaper war, the *New Times* and the *Morning Post* exulting in the prospect of the foundation of the new college, the *Globe* and the *Sunday Times* attacking it as unnecessary and impertinent. Before Christmas, however, the controversy died down, and both sides watched expectantly for the next move. They had not long to wait. The next move was made in February 1828, and the mover was the Rev. George D'Oyly, D.D., rector of Lambeth.

§ 3. *The Inauguration of King's College*

If to any one man more than to any other is to be assigned the distinction of bringing King's College into existence, that man is Dr George D'Oyly. On this point it may be well to quote here and now the resolution passed unanimously by the College Council on February 13, 1846, immediately after his death : resolved

> That a marble tablet be erected in the College Chapel to the memory of the late Dr D'Oyly, in order to commemorate not only his services to the College as a most zealous and active member of the Council, but also the acknowledged fact that the design of the Institution was originally conceived by him, and that, by giving the first impulse and direction to public opinion, he was virtually the Founder of the College.

The tablet thus resolved upon can still be seen on the outer wall of the chapel. A bust of Dr D'Oyly, moreover, adorns the college library. Since, then, Dr D'Oyly played so prominent a part in the establishment of King's College—a part similar to that of Thomas Campbell in the establishment of University College—it is proper to pause for a moment to ask who was this notable divine. The facts of his life can be found in the *Dictionary of National Biography*, or more fully in a memoir by his son, the Rev. C. J. D'Oyly, prefixed to a collection of his discourses (two volumes, 1847). Briefly, they were as follows : George, the fourth son of the Venerable M. D'Oyly, rector of Buxted in Sussex and archdeacon of Lewes, was born in 1778. He went to Corpus Christi College, Cambridge, in 1796, and had a distinguished university career : he was second wrangler and Smith's prizeman in mathematics (1800); Members' classical prizeman and fellow of his college (1801). In 1802 he was ordained, and for three years he served as curate to his father at Buxted. Then he returned to Cambridge, and there for nearly ten years (1806–15) he remained, showing much activity in many positions—lecturer, examiner, moderator, select preacher, Christian Advocate. In 1813 he was appointed chaplain to the Archbishop of Canterbury, Dr Manners-Sutton, and he soon became one of his most trusted friends and counsellors. In 1815 the archbishop recalled him to parochial life, and in 1820 made him rector of Lambeth. At Lambeth he continued for the rest of his life, declining in 1842 the deanery of Peterborough offered to him by Peel : at Lambeth he died on January 8, 1846. During the quarter-century of his service at Lambeth he did a prodigious work. In 1820 he found, as we have already remarked, 54,000 people resident within his parish; in 1846 he left 130,000. The old parochial organization was, of course, hopelessly inadequate to cope with this enormous influx. The most urgent need was for new churches, and into the task of providing them he threw himself with immense energy and capacity. Mainly by building, but partly by the purchase of derelict meeting-houses, he succeeded in establishing no fewer than thirteen new churches in South-east London. At the same time he was an active member of the governing bodies of the S.P.C.K. and the S.P.G., the author of a life of Archbishop Sancroft, and joint editor of D'Oyly and Mant's exceedingly solid *Commentary on the Bible*. Such was the man—scholarly, devout, business-like, energetic; the trusted adviser of the archbishop, the close and intimate associate both of Hugh James Rose and of the high anglican brotherhood which was maintaining the National Society and the S.P.C.K. as correctives of the prevailing undenominationalism and secularism of the day—such was the man who, at the beginning of

36

1828, took the first overt step toward the founding of King's College.

This overt step was the publication, under the pseudonym of " Christianus," of an open *Letter to the Right Hon. Robert Peel on the Subject of the London University* (pp. 40, February 1828, John Murray).[1] Sir Robert Peel, it may be remarked, had just returned to the Home Office in the ministry constituted by the Duke of Wellington at the end of January 1828 : he was known to be an earnest and enthusiastic supporter of the principle of the religious basis of education. The letter which Dr D'Oyly addressed to him can be summarized under five main heads. First, it points out the obvious need for more universities in England owing to (1) the increase in population, (2) the growth of a wealthy middle class, and (3) the spread of " a strong spirit of intellectual improvement." Secondly, it admits that the projected University of London will do something to supply this need, but expresses the opinion that any academic benefits which it may confer upon the youth of the metropolis will be more than counterbalanced by the moral and spiritual injury that it will inevitably inflict on them by " the entire omission of everything connected with Christianity " from their courses of study. Thirdly, it proceeds to discuss, on general lines— strikingly anticipatory of those followed by Cardinal Newman a quarter of a century later in his famous addresses on *The Idea of a University*—the place of religious knowledge in university education. It argues (1) that " the principle on which the London University is founded "—*i.e.*, the principle of the exclusion of religion—" is essentially different from that of every other public institution for the general education of youth in this kingdom," and that, consequently, " prescription and experience are against such a novel experiment." It contends (2) that the omission of so important a subject of study as theology is inconsistent with the title of " university," which the new institution has assumed : " By this very name, in the common and known acceptance of it, pretension is made to educate youth generally, and to form their minds to *all* useful and valuable knowledge." [2] It maintains (3) that the exclusion

---

[1] As to the authorship of this open letter, see C. J. D'Oyly's memoir of his father, p. xxxvi, and also an autograph letter of Dr D'Oyly to Peel, dated December 1, 1841, among the Peel Papers in the British Museum (Add. MSS. 40496, f. 130).

[2] *Cf.* Newman, *Idea of a University*, p. ix : " The view taken of a university in these discourses is the following :—That it is a place of teaching universal knowledge." Both D'Oyly and Newman are mistaken in their etymology. A university (*universitas*) means simply " a corporation," without any implication whatsoever as to the purpose for which it is established.

of religion from the university is morally harmful and spiritually pernicious; and it shows (4) that theology is so intimately bound up with many other subjects—*e.g.*, history and ethics—that none of them can be satisfactorily taught except on a theological basis.[1] The fourth section of Dr D'Oyly's letter proceeds to examine, on the principles just laid down, the *Statement* issued by the provisional committee of the projected London University concerning the exclusion of religious knowledge from the curriculum. It considers that the *Statement* fails to justify the exclusion, even on its own assumptions; for " it is as necessary for the Presbyterian and the Baptist, as for the member of the Church of England, to be acquainted with the evidences of Christianity, and with the general contents of the sacred volume on which their common faith is founded." But it further holds that even an undenominational H.C.F. of Christianity is unsatisfactory in England; for (1) " the British public are, in the main, sincerely attached to the Church of England " and would prefer to have its complete theology taught; (2) the Church of England " presents Christianity in its most pure and perfect form," and is therefore inherently superior to its rivals; and (3) " our Church, as by law established, forms part of the Constitution under which we live," and consequently the interests of the State, no less than those of religion, demand that Anglicanism should be officially recognized. The fifth and last section of the letter then goes on to formulate a practical programme. Dr D'Oyly urges three things, viz., (1) the enlargement and extension of the universities of Oxford and Cambridge ; (2) the founding of a new university in the North of England—a clear foreshadowing of the University of Durham instituted under the auspices of Bishop van Mildert, the last of the palatine counts, in 1832; and (3) the establishment in London of a second university

in which it shall be made, of course, an essential part of the education imparted, to imbue the minds of youth with the principles of Christianity, according to those sounder forms which are established in this kingdom; and in which the services of religion shall be performed as directed in our National Church.

It is evident that Dr D'Oyly is not merely flying a kite to test the direction of the wind, but is writing with the confident

---

[1] *Cf.* Newman, *op. cit.*, p. 69 : " To withdraw theology from the public schools is to impair the completeness, and to invalidate the trustworthiness, of all that is actually taught in them."

prescience born of much assurance of support, for he adds, respecting the suggested college :

> It is highly probable that His Majesty, whose attachment to the interests of religion and learning has been often and unequivocally manifested, might extend his gracious patronage to it, and even permit it to be called by his name; he might also be pleased to present a spot of ground for the site.

Hardly without royal approval would so bold an allusion to George IV's frequent and unequivocal manifestations of piety, his conspicuous love of learning, and his open-handed generosity have been made.

Dr D'Oyly's powerful letter, and the keen discussion to which it gave rise, had two notable results, one of them curious and unexpected. Among the members of the eminent staff appointed in 1827–28 to the new university in Gower Street were three clergymen of the Church of England—viz., the Rev. Thomas Dale, professor of English; the Rev. John Williams, professor of classics; and the encyclopædic Rev. Dr Dionysius Lardner, professor of natural philosophy. It occurred to these three that, although the university, as such, could not consistently with its constitution provide religious instruction, there was nothing to prevent its teachers in their private capacity from supplying the deficiency on behalf of such as desired for their young men more of the said instruction than they were likely to receive in their homes or their lodgings. Hence, with evangelical approval and support, they purchased an episcopal chapel in the neighbourhood of Gower Street and opened it in 1829 as a " theological institution," independent of, yet closely associated with, the new university. This evangelical lightning-conductor, however, on the one hand, was regarded with disfavour by the radical majority in the university, and, on the other hand, was not sufficient to divert episcopal fulminations from the institution to which it was informally affixed. It attracted theological storms, instead of providing security against them. Few students took advantage of its services; its founders were terrified or lured away; it was speedily and unostentatiously removed.

The second consequence of the publication of Dr D'Oyly's letter was the formal launching, at midsummer 1828, of the scheme for the establishment, on a definite anglican basis, of the new " King's College." Church and state were harmoniously, if not quite equally, combined in the venture. D'Oyly's great influence at Lambeth secured the Archbishop of

Canterbury's enthusiastic support for the project. That support was invaluable and decisive. Dr Charles Manners-Sutton, a grandson of the third Duke of Rutland, was the last of the aristocratic prince-primates of all England. The intimate personal friend of the royal family, the revered relative of many of the most powerful members of the old nobility, the confidential adviser of the heads of the high-tory party, the archbishop was able to secure, as no one else could have done, the patronage of the king, the co-operation of the whole episcopal bench, and the zealous aid of the clergy as a body. Peel and the archbishop together succeeded in persuading the prime minister (the Duke of Wellington), together with other prominent members of the cabinet, to favour and foster the design of the college. A great deal of preliminary work having been done, a prospectus was issued early in June 1828, stating the general principles on which it was proposed to found the new college, and inviting supporters to a public meeting to be held at the Freemasons' Hall, in Great Queen Street, Westminster, on Saturday, June 21, at a quarter-past twelve noon. The duke was to take the chair, and he was to be accompanied by both the archbishops, and by a distinguished assemblage of prelates and peers. The announcement was well received by the press as a whole : the tory papers hailed the prospect of the foundation of a " Christian university " in the metropolis ; and many of the liberal and radical periodicals generously admitted that in a population of a million and a half there was room for two universities, or even more than two, and expressed their good wishes for the success of the scheme.

§ 4. *The Meeting of June 21, 1828*

The great inaugural meeting in the Freemasons' Hall proved to be a spectacular success. " The company," says the *Standard* report of the same day, " was one which for rank and respectability was the most distinguished it has ever been our good fortune to meet." The duke was accompanied on to the platform by three archbishops, seven bishops, and " the principal nobility." The three archbishops were Dr Charles Manners-Sutton of Canterbury, the Hon. E. V. Vernon Harcourt of York, and Lord John George Beresford of Armagh, Primate of Ireland. The bishops included William Howley of London, Charles James Blomfield of Chester, and Edward Copleston of Llandaff, all notable men of whom more will have to be said in a moment. Who " the principal nobility " were we are not particularly told; but the reports state that while the meeting was in process two members of the cabinet, destined later to become prime ministers—viz., Peel and Aberdeen—entered the hall and promised large subscriptions. The audience consisted dominantly of clergymen in a state of high enthusiasm.

The duke opened the meeting with a brief explanation of the object for which it had been called. The constitution of this country, he said, is essentially protestant, and, since this form of religion is established in the land, it is proper that it should be at the basis of our national education. Education from which religious instruction is excluded is, he considered, worse than useless. He therefore cordially commended to the distinguished assembly before him the scheme formulated by the heads of the church for establishing in London a college in which practical instruction in the useful sciences and arts shall be combined with sound edification in the doctrines and duties of Christianity as taught by the United Church of England and Ireland.[1] He then put to the meeting the following resolutions, all of which were carried unanimously :

I. That it is the opinion of this meeting that a college for general education be founded in the metropolis, in which, while the various branches of literature and science are made the subjects of instruction, it shall be an essential part of the system to imbue the minds of youth with a knowledge of the doctrines and duties of Christianity as inculcated by the United Church of England and Ireland.

II. That the king having been graciously pleased to signify his approbation of the establishment of this college, His Majesty be most respectfully requested to take it under his royal patronage, and permit it to be entitled " King's College, London."

III. That the following be approved as the general outline of the plan on which the college is to be founded and conducted. [Here come seven stipulations respecting the curriculum, organization, and government of the college.]

IV. That a Provisional Committee of twenty-seven persons be now appointed which shall take all necessary steps for carrying these resolutions into effect, and prepare the details to be submitted to a future meeting. [Then follow the names of the twenty-seven, together with that of Mr Henry Nelson Coleridge, who was to act as secretary to the Provisional Committee.]

[1] *John Bull*, June 23, 1828, records : ". . . the electrical effect produced upon the meeting at hearing *that voice* which in times of national danger, and in the hour of battle, had so often been raised to animate our veterans to victory, now in the hour of peace and safety raised with equal energy in support of an establishment by which youth may be led to the attainment of worldly skill and wisdom, and to the knowledge and practice of pure religion as inculcated by the truly Apostolical Church of these United Kingdoms."

The funds necessary for the establishment of the college were to be raised partly by donations and partly by subscriptions in the form of £100 shares which were to carry a dividend not exceeding four per cent. : nothing was to be done until the total amount of donations and subscriptions combined should reach the sum of £100,000. A first list of donations and subscriptions was read out at the meeting, and additions were invited. Amid scenes of intense excitement the money poured in. Before the proceedings closed nearly £20,000 had been promised : a list published four days later shows a total—from 242 persons, of whom 88 were clergymen—of £30,794 (viz., £20,094 donations and 107 shares).

The rest of the meeting, with the exception of one incident, was formal. But that exception was important; for it raised what was the most burning and controversial question of the day—viz., the question of religious tests. " Who," it was asked, " were to be admitted to the new college? Was it to be closed to all who were not members of the Established Church? " To this inquiry a prompt and emphatic negative was given by Bishop Blomfield : " No question whatever as to religious opinions held by the student will ever be asked," he said, " and all that will be required of him is to conform to the rules of discipline which will be laid down on that head." This statement of the bishop was received with " loud applause," and the awkward subject was dropped, the " rules of discipline " of the college which should take the place of subscription to the creeds of the church being left for the moment undefined. The question was too thorny to be discussed on such an occasion. Enthusiasm having been restored, votes of thanks were passed with acclamation; congratulations were exchanged; and the company dispersed in high satisfaction.

The *Standard*, reporting the proceedings at the Freemasons' Hall, made " no attempt to hide its feelings of the most sincere exultation " at the success of the gathering. *John Bull* (June 30, 1828) is not content with rejoicing at the triumphant launching of the scheme for King's College; it is still more delighted because it believes that by the institution of King's College (in the elegant language of the day) " the finishing blow has been given to the stye of infidelity building at the end of Gower Street." It continues :

> Public indignation has at length been roused, and the greatest and best amongst us have rallied round the altar and the throne, in order to protect them from the destructive influence of an infidel rabble who are to be educated according to the rules of

This vigorous caricature is copied from a skit upon the projected college published in 1828, under the title "Lectures and Examinations for King's College Students." It refers to the supposed conflict between the radical founders of University College in Gower Street (then called the London University) and the reactionary promoters of King's College. The clerics represented are probably Archbishop Manners-Sutton, Dr D'Oyly of Lambeth, Bishop Howley of London, and Bishop Blomfield of Chester. Opposed to them are obviously Henry Brougham (waving the broom) and Jeremy Bentham (clad in dressing-gown); the other three may be Thomas Campbell, Joseph Hume, and Isaac Goldsmid.

modern philosophy, in perfect darkness as to the duties they owe to their God and their King.

It will be gathered from this select quotation that theological passion was running very high at the end of June 1828. Such was indeed the case. The party represented by *John Bull*— a Sunday paper dated Monday so as to avoid giving offence to sabbatarian sentiment—ultra-tory and ultra-protestant, was fighting desperately on two fronts against two very different foes. On the one hand, it was contending against the philosophical radicals and the dissenters, who were bent on establishing secular education throughout the land; on the other hand, it was resisting with embittered determination the efforts of the catholics to secure the removal of their religious and political disabilities. It welcomed King's College, therefore, on two grounds : first, because it was a definitely *Christian* institution, as opposed to " the infidel stye of Gower Street "; secondly, because it was a *Protestant* institution in " this essentially Protestant country." At the great meeting of June 21 there were distinctly two separate sections of supporters of King's College present. Since it might appear invidious to differentiate them as *Christians* and *Protestants*, we may perhaps be allowed to call them respectively the Anti-infidels and the Anti-catholics. When the establishment of the college was originally mooted, the Anti-infidel motive was dominant : Dr D'Oyly and his clerical friends were mainly concerned to counter secularism: the bishops, without exciting alarm, were sanctioning the repeal of the Test and Corporation Acts. But in June 1828 the catholic issue had suddenly come to the front. Toward the end of the preceding month Mr Huskisson had resigned the office of President of the Board of Trade and the Duke had appointed Mr Vesey Fitzgerald to succeed him. This appointment involved a by-election in County Clare, Ireland, Mr Fitzgerald's constituency. Instead of the " walkover " which Mr Fitzgerald expected, he found himself opposed by Mr Daniel O'Connell, the uncrowned king of Catholic Ireland, who was resolved to bring to a definite issue the question of the eligibility of catholics to sit in the parliament of the United Kingdom. At the very moment when the King's College scheme was being inaugurated in the Freemasons' Hall, a tremendous campaign of objurgation and violence was raging in Ireland—with noisy repercussions in Great Britain— between emancipationists and their opponents. In *John Bull* (June 30) the reports of the King's College meeting and of the

County Clare agitation appear in contiguous columns; and on the very day that the first list of subscribers to King's College was published began the County Clare election, as the result of which Daniel O'Connell was returned (July 4, 1828).

Now Wellington and Peel, the two principal ministerial patrons of King's College, were the leaders of that section of the tory party which was pledged to resist catholic emancipation, and they were at that very time engaged in clearing out from the cabinet all the Canningite tories who were not of their way of thinking. They had in their policy and proceedings the cordial support of the King, and the grateful approval of all the bishops who surrounded and applauded them in the Free-masons' Hall. Hence, as we have already seen, the first clear note sounded by the duke in his address on June 21 was the protestant note, and a large portion of the support which the college secured during the course of the great meeting came from men (such as the Earl of Winchilsea) who trusted the duke to resist the catholic demands to the end, and who looked to King's College to furnish a continuous supply of zealous protestants qualified to fill both parliament and the civil service, and to prevent the catholic invasion.

This is a fact important to remember, because it serves to explain how it came to pass that, when Wellington and Peel early in 1829 felt themselves compelled through fear of civil war to abandon their resistance to catholic emancipation, and to admit O'Connell to the House of Commons—it serves to explain, I say, why Winchilsea denounced Wellington in terms that led to a duel; why he and his friends withdrew their donations and subscriptions from King's College; and why consequently for many painful years the college was harnessed with a load of debt.

Not only, moreover, were Winchilsea and the ultra-protestants alienated from both the prime minister and the college which he had inaugurated; the bishops, also, found themselves constrained to oppose Wellington's policy of surrender, and to resist his Catholic Emancipation Act of 1829. The meeting of June 21, 1828, was, indeed, the last occasion on which it was possible for the leaders of the national church and the heads of the protestant state to unite in fraternal accord as joint representatives of the same supreme terrestrial authority. For not merely did catholic emancipation alter the basis of the Elizabethan constitution; it further caused a sharp antagonism to arise between the government and the episcopate. The most formidable opponents of Wellington's Emancipation Act, and later on the sharpest critics of his policy in respect of the Reform Bill of 1832, were precisely those great and able prelates who applauded him to the skies in the Freemasons' Hall on June 21, 1828.

With one exception, however. The venerable primate, Dr Charles Manners-Sutton, survived the inaugural meeting by only one month. He died on July 21, having lived just long enough to see the scheme for the college launched; to head the subscription list with a gift of £1000; to commend the college personally to the patronage of the King and the royal family, and to receive the gratifying assurance that its success was beyond doubt. He was happy in the occasion of his death. It would have deeply grieved his noble heart to see the unanimous assembly of June 21 broken up into three mutually suspicious groups—supporters respectively of Wellington, of the bishops, and of Winchilsea. After a brief interval the vacant see of Canterbury was conferred upon William Howley, Bishop of London, the metropolitan see being filled by the translation of Charles James Blomfield from Chester. These two notable prelates were the most prominent members of the provisional committee appointed on June 21 to establish King's College. We must now turn to the study of this provisional committee and its doings during the cardinal year of its existence (June 21, 1828–August 14, 1829).

CHAPTER III

THE FOUNDING OF " KING'S COLLEGE "

§ 1. *The Provisional Committee and its Work*

THE provisional committee nominated at the inaugural meeting consisted, as we have seen, of twenty-seven members. During the period of a little over twelve months which elapsed before it was able to hand over its authority to the council appointed under the charter of August 1829, it held thirty-four meetings in offices hired at 2 Parliament Street. In addition, it appointed finance and building sub-committees which did an immense amount of important preliminary work. Let us first note who were the members of this provisional committee— the corporate founders of the college; and then let us turn and examine the results of their devoted labours. Under the first head, it seems proper to deal with the members not according to their rank or extraneous position, but according to the number of attendances which they made at committee meetings.

In this order of merit, the REV. DR GEORGE D'OYLY comes easily first. He attended thirty-one out of the possible thirty-four meetings, on one occasion taking the chair. He was also an assiduous member of both the finance and the building sub-committees. Obviously he was the mainspring of the whole enterprise. We have already dealt so fully with him and his career that no more need now be said of him. A good second to Dr D'Oyly is DR WILLIAM HOWLEY, Bishop of London 1813–28, Archbishop of Canterbury 1828–48. He put in twenty-nine appearances, and on every occasion on which he was present he presided. He was a sound scholar and theologian; a man of cool judgment and equable temper; an excellent business man, although a poor speaker and unimpressive preacher; as a politician he was ultra-tory. Third in order of merit stands WILLIAM COTTON, with twenty-seven attendances. This devout layman, a resident at Leytonstone, was a wealthy manufacturer and a director of the Bank of England. He had widespread fame as a generous philanthropist and a builder of many churches in the East End of London. Next to him is another layman, EDWARD HAWKE LOCKER (twenty-three attendances),

46

commissioner of Greenwich Hospital and founder of the naval portrait gallery thereat; himself an artist, a man of science, and a writer—author of *Popular Lectures on the Bible and Liturgy*—a friend of Sir Walter Scott. Close after him comes another of his intimate friends, WILLIAM SOTHEBY (twenty-two attendances), a gentleman of substance, whose name stood high in the literary world of the time; an antiquary, a translator, a poet whose writings (now forgotten) were described by Byron as " sincere." Bracketed equal, with twenty-one attendances each, were three notable men—viz., DR CHARLES JAMES BLOMFIELD, Bishop of Chester 1824–28, Bishop of London 1828–56; SIR ROBERT H. INGLIS, M.P., a protestant of protestants, and a tory of tories; and the VENERABLE GEORGE OWEN CAMBRIDGE, Archdeacon of Middlesex, a prominent supporter of the National Society and the S.P.C.K. Of Bishop Blomfield more must be said; because not only was he one of the most influential and devoted of the founders of King's College, not only did he preach the sermon (a singularly eloquent and able one) at the opening of the college in 1831, but he remained for the first quarter-century of its existence its most faithful friend, the most eminent member of its Council, and one of the main controllers of its policy. Born in 1786, the son of a Suffolk schoolmaster, he had made his own way in life by means of high ability and an enormous capacity for work. Having entered Trinity College, Cambridge, in 1804, he had within five years achieved a scholarship, four university prizes, and a fellowship. Then he had set himself to edit Greek classics, and his laborious commentaries on the plays of Æschylus had brought him enduring fame among schoolmasters. Having taken orders, and having served various cures, he became successively chaplain to Bishop Howley (1817), Rector of St Botolph's, Bishopsgate (1819), Archdeacon of Colchester (1822), Bishop of Chester (1824), and Bishop of London (1828). He was an active supporter of the S.P.C.K. and the S.P.G.; an energetic builder of churches in his populous London diocese; and a man of unbounded generosity. " During his tenure of the see of London," says his biographer, " he must have given away not much less than £150,000." His dominant characteristic—apart from his ability, his diligence, his piety, and his lavish generosity—was his essential moderation. He shrank from extremes, and accordingly he suffered much from the assaults of all sorts of zealots, political and ecclesiastical : he favoured the repeal of the Test Act, but opposed catholic emancipation; he favoured parliamentary reform, but disapproved

47

of the Bill of 1832; he was in sympathy with the tractarians, but condemned and suppressed the practices of their more advanced representatives. The *Morning Post* (May 11, 1830) described him as "one of the brightest ornaments of our pure and heavenly church."

Next after the great bishop and his compeers comes SIR CHARLES PRICE (twenty attendances), baronet, a city magistrate, son of a former lord mayor; and then follows (with nineteen attendances) another bishop, a magnificent prelate, extremely eminent and influential in his day—viz., DR EDWARD COPLESTON, Bishop of Llandaff and Dean of St Paul's (1827-49), a great man, immortalized by Newman in his *Apologia*. Born in 1776, he was the son of the Rector of Offwell in Devonshire; a brilliant Oxford classic, one of the finest Latinists of his day; Fellow of Oriel, 1795; Vicar of the university church, 1800; Professor of Poetry, 1802-12; Provost of Oriel, 1814-27, and therefore the intimate associate of Newman, Keble, Hurrell Froude, Whately, and others who in their day made the college famous throughout the world; Dean of Chester, 1826-27; and then, for the rest of his life, Bishop of Llandaff and Dean of St Paul's. A man of keen intellect and gifted with a powerful literary style, he effectively championed the old universities with their religious and humane culture against the utilitarian attacks of the Edinburgh Reviewers (1810). No man brought to the councils of King's College a larger fund of trained wisdom and academic experience.

Close upon Bishop Copleston, with eighteen attendances—absent from the first seven meetings of the committee, but afterward very regular—was the REV. JOHN LONSDALE, a distinguished Cambridge classical scholar, destined to be third principal of King's College, and subsequently Bishop of Lichfield. Ordained at the age of twenty-seven (1815), chaplain to Archbishop Manners-Sutton (1816), at the date of the inaugural meeting he had just become rector of St George's, Bloomsbury. In intellectual power he was regarded as second only to the incomparable Thirlwall. Later, as Bishop of Lichfield (1845-67), he was described as "the best ever known."

Half the possible number of attendances (seventeen out of thirty-four) was the record of MR JOHN DISTIN POWLES, a city financier not unacquainted with the bankruptcy court, some of whose transactions are commented upon by Mr Monypenny in the first volume of his *Life of Disraeli*. Those who attended fewer than half the possible number of meetings, and whose influence upon the policy of the nascent college was therefore

48

intermittent and secondary, may be enumerated more briefly. They were LORD BEXLEY (sixteen), president of the British and Foreign Bible Society, better known as Nicholas Vansittart, Chancellor of the Exchequer for the first ten years of Liverpool's ministry (1812–22); ALDERMAN ATKINS, M.P. (thirteen), an influential city merchant; the MARQUIS CAMDEN (twelve), teller of the exchequer for sixty years (1780–1840), sometime Lord-Lieutenant of Ireland (1795–98), and Secretary at War (1804–5), a man in his seventieth year; MR (later Sir) BENJAMIN C. BRODIE (eleven), surgeon to King George IV and to St George's Hospital; SIR JOHN NICHOLL (eleven), Dean of Arches, Judge of the Prerogative Court of Canterbury, and M.P.; the HON. R. HENLEY EDEN (eleven), brother-in-law of Peel, Master in Chancery, M.P., later the second Baron Henley;[1] EARL BROWNLOW (seven); SIR HENRY HALFORD (seven), physician-in-ordinary to the king and president of the College of Physicians; SIR ASTLEY COOPER (seven), an eminent surgeon associated with St Thomas's and Guy's Hospitals; the MARQUIS OF BUTE (six); the SOLICITOR-GENERAL (Sir Nicholas Tindal), M.P. for Cambridge (three); the VICE-CHANCELLOR OF ENGLAND (Sir Lancelot Shadwell), the last holder of that office (two). Members of the provisional committee who never attended at all were the DUKE OF RUTLAND, MR W. R. HAMILTON, SIR JOHN RICHARDSON, a retired judge, and MR WILLIAM WARD, Director of the Bank of England, M.P. for the city, and father of W. G. Ward, the associate of Newman in the Oxford Movement and beyond.[2]

The secretary to the provisional committee was Mr Henry Nelson Coleridge, Fellow of King's College, Cambridge, nephew and subsequently son-in-law to Samuel Taylor Coleridge, whose literary remains and table-talk he edited. He was just thirty years of age when he was appointed; but he was delicate in health, and when the provisional committee completed its work he did not carry over his services to the new Council.

So much for the personnel of the committee. Let us now examine the work which it did during its strenuous year of existence. Its main tasks were five—viz., to frame regulations,

---

[1] Mr Eden was the twenty-eighth member of the provisional committee. His name had been inadvertently omitted from the list of June 21. He was subsequently invited to join the committee, and he began to attend at the sixth meeting (July 22, 1828).

[2] The members of the provisional committee, we may note, contributed in all £6100 (donations £4600, subscriptions £1500) to the inaugural fund of the college.

to raise money, to secure a site, to choose an architect and get him to draw up plans for a college building, and to obtain a charter from the government. In order to further these purposes sub-committees were appointed as follows : (1) trustees, empowered to collect funds, to invest them in exchequer bonds, and to make necessary payments : Alderman Atkins, Mr Cotton, Sir Charles Price, and Mr Ward; (2) finance committee, consisting of the four trustees, together with Messrs Locker and Powles; (3) a committee to frame regulations for the college : Bishops Blomfield and Copleston, Dr D'Oyly, and Mr Locker; and (4) a building committee, appointed on February 3, 1829, to consider the architect's plans for the college : Bishop Blomfield, Lord Bexley, Sir Robert Inglis, Dr D'Oyly, and Mr Locker.

§ 2. *The Framing of Regulations*

The sub-committee appointed to draw up preliminary regulations for the new college presented its report at the amazingly early date of July 1, 1828; its report was accepted, with two slight amendments, indicated below, and was at once issued to the world. The main matter dealt with was the vitally important question of the religious basis of the college : what students should be admitted to the college; what tests or obligations should be imposed upon them. The problem was an urgent one. It had been raised, as we have remarked, at the inaugural meeting. The fact that Bishop Blomfield was able to give an instant and emphatic reply to the inquirer, who was a member of the Society of Friends, clearly indicates that the question had already been carefully considered in the highest quarters, and that a definite policy had been framed. In substance the reply was : No inquisition into creed will be made; but conformity to college usages will be required. This reply was on the whole well received by the assembly, and it gave much satisfaction in nonconformist circles. The *Evangelical Magazine* (July 1828) said :

> No enlightened dissenter will quarrel with King's College because it ranks under the banners of the national church, provided he may send his sons to it without compelling them to profess themselves *ex animo* members of that church.

Satisfaction with this policy of the half-open door, however, was by no means universal. For instance, *John Bull* (June 30) devoutly trusted that " modern liberality would not be permitted to pass the threshold of the new establishment," and gave prominence to the letter of an anonymous correspondent who pleaded for the strictest exclusion of all save *bona fide* members of the anglican communion.

The regulations respecting this matter as framed by the provisional committee on July 1 were as follows : After rehearsing the "fundamental principle on which it is proposed to establish King's College "—viz., the indissoluble union of sacred with secular learning—they proceeded :

(1) In accordance with this principle, all the students who are MEMBERS OF THE COLLEGE, whether domiciliated or otherwise, will be required to attend the prescribed course of religious instruction, and to be present at divine service performed within the walls of the College, at such times and under such regulations as may be laid down by the Council.

(2) Persons who are not regular MEMBERS will be allowed to attend any particular course of lectures *in such numbers and* on such terms and conditions as the Council may from time to time prescribe.[1]

(3) It is not, however, intended that those persons who may avail themselves of this permission should be entitled to contend for prizes, to obtain certificates, or to enjoy any of the privileges and advantages which it may be thought expedient to confer on MEMBERS OF THE COLLEGE.

The practical effect of these regulations was to divide the students of the college into two classes : first, regular students, who—without being asked to make any profession of belief—were required to attend chapel daily and at least one lecture in divinity weekly; and, secondly, occasional students, who were free from these requirements, and who might therefore be Jews, Turks, infidels, or sectarians of any sort. In other words, " modern liberality " triumphed, and the entry into King's College was almost as unimpeded as was the entry into the " University of London."

Supplementary regulations on matters less urgent were considered at later meetings of the provisional committee, and were finally issued on December 30, 1828. The three following were the most important : (1) the principal of the college " must be a clergyman, having the degree of M.A. at least, in one of the Universities of Oxford, Cambridge, or Dublin "; (2) the professors " must all be members of the Church of

---

[1] The italicized words "*in such numbers and*" were added at the suggestion of Bishop Howley. Further, on his motion, the following words, included in the sub-committee's draft, were omitted at the end : " *and to such an extent as not to interfere with the instructions of the General Committee.*"

England, except in the case of the teachers of oriental literature and modern languages "; and (3) the college shall be organized in two departments, a higher department for students over sixteen years of age, and a lower department, or day school, for younger boys.

It was originally intended that the college should be in part residential, but ultimately it was found impossible to provide accommodation on the selected site. Hence, on July 3, 1829, it was decided that the college should, at any rate to begin with, be wholly non-resident, but that the professors and lecturers, together with other persons recognized by the council, should be authorized to take boarders and to subject them to the necessary supervision and discipline.

One further point is worthy of note. The provisional committee from the outset wished to have it " distinctly understood that no intention is entertained of erecting in the metropolis an university with the power of conferring degrees." [1] The purpose of the college was, on the one hand, to send young men, well trained and disciplined, direct into commercial and professional life, and, on the other hand, to prepare for the older universities such as desired degrees and ordination. All the early academic triumphs of King's College students were, as we shall later have occasion to note, as a matter of fact achieved at Oxford and Cambridge.

§ 3. *The Raising of Money : the Great Secession*

The second matter which engaged the attention of the provisional committee was the raising of the large sum of money required for the founding and equipment of the college. We have seen that the inaugurators of the scheme decided that no steps should be taken until £100,000 had been assured. We have further remarked that so great was the enthusiasm with which the scheme was welcomed that before the inaugural meeting itself closed nearly one-fifth of that amount had been promised, and that only four days later a list of subscriptions reaching a total of £30,794 was published. For several weeks the favourable flow continued. On July 17, 1828, an important meeting of city magnates was held in the Royal Exchange under the presidency of the Lord Mayor; resolutions were passed approving of the principles on which the college was to be established; and a special committee consisting of twenty-one

[1] Minutes of June 25, 1828, and public advertisements in the press of the following week.

important men was appointed to collect subscriptions in the city. Other meetings were summoned by the bishops and clergy. The provinces were stirred to activity : local committees sprang into existence at Ripon, Liverpool, Lynn, Norwich, York, Rochester, and Cheltenham. Donations and subscriptions poured in.[1] On August 19, 1828, the secretary, writing to Mr John Gladstone, the prime supporter of the college in Liverpool, was able to announce the fact that already £102,000 had been paid or promised. He added, however, lest his correspondent's energies should be relaxed, that at least a second £100,000 would be required to found and equip the college properly. His estimate, indeed, proved to be below rather than above the mark ; for when the Strand site was eventually selected, plans drawn up, and specifications obtained, it was found (May 1829) that no smaller a sum than £170,000 was needed for the preliminary outlay on buildings and furniture.

There can be little doubt that these large amounts would have been easily raised if the first flow of enthusiasm had been maintained, and if the happy harmony of church with state, which had marked the inaugural meeting, had continued. Unfortunately, however, enthusiasm was damped and harmony broken by those events in the political world to which we have already alluded. The catholic emancipation question divided the founders of the college, as it divided the tory party, into hostile and mutually suspicious sections. Wellington and Peel, in particular, hitherto the adored leaders of the anti-catholic die-hards, when, as a mere matter of political expediency, they decided to yield to the demand for emancipation, were not only regretfully opposed by the bishops, but were assailed with insolent invective by the ultra-protestant clergy and laity. They were denounced as traitors whose opposition to the catholic claims had never been sincere, and as conspirators who all along had been working in the interests of Rome. Peel lost his seat in the House of Commons, his place as member for the University of Oxford being captured by that prominent member of the King's College provisional committee, Sir Robert Inglis.

Profound suspicion of Wellington and Peel, generated by their tergiversation in the sphere of politics, soon involved the

[1] Reports laid before the provisional committee gave totals as follows :

July 8	.	.	.	.	£59,883
July 12	.	.	.	.	£68,839
July 24	.	.	.	.	" upwards of £77,000."

college, in the inauguration of which they had played so prominent a part. Was this also to be surrendered to catholics? Why had not more adequate means been taken to impose religious tests and to ensure the protestant ascendancy? Was Wellington at the inaugural meeting already meditating his great betrayal, and were his professed protestant sentiments mere snares for the over-trustful? Such were the questions asked by the ultra-protestants, and in particular by the Earl of Winchilsea, who had promised a donation of £50 to the college funds. On March 14, 1829, Lord Winchilsea sent a long letter to Mr H. N. Coleridge, secretary to the provisional committee, withdrawing his donation and giving his reasons for doing so. He further—a wholly unnecessary and entirely indefensible act—forwarded his letter to the press for publication. It appeared first in the *Standard* of March 16, 1829, and there Wellington read it. The length of the letter precludes its transcription in full; an epitome must suffice.[1] After intimating the withdrawal of his donation, the earl went on to say that he had objected to the founding of the University of London on a non-religious basis, and had cordially approved of the principles upon which the proposed King's College was to be established—viz., " the sound and scriptural doctrines of the Church of England." He confessed that the patronage of the Duke of Wellington had from the first caused him some misgiving, for the duke had not hitherto been known as " the public advocate of religion and morality." The subsequent behaviour of the duke in the matter of catholic emancipation had convinced him that " the whole transaction was intended as a blind to the protestant and high church party," under cover of which the duke might the more effectively " carry on his insidious designs for the infringement of our liberties and the introduction of popery into every department of state." His confidence in the protestant character of King's College was destroyed; he did not consider that in the matter of religion it was likely to be any better than the Gower Street institution; hence, he ended,

> I am under the necessity of coming to the conclusion that the principles likely to be inculcated at King's College may possibly be such as tend to produce an indifference to all religious creeds; they may, perhaps, be favourable to the tenets of the Roman Catholic Church, or they may border upon Socinianism

---

[1] The complete text of the letter will be found in Wellington's *Despatches, Correspondence, and Memoranda*, vol. v, pp. 526–527. The twenty pages following tell the story of the sequel.

or Infidelity; but that they will be truly religious, scriptural, or permanently Protestant, the premises I have stated forbid me to conclude.

If the college was disturbed by the loss of a large donation, which was likely to be followed by many other similar refusals to pay, the duke was naturally outraged by this public accusation of irreligion, immorality, and perfidy. He wrote to the earl demanding either the withdrawal of his imputation of " disgraceful and criminal motives," or else reparation for the insults and injuries which he had inflicted. Winchilsea— alarmed by the duke's fury, and strongly urged by friends who recognized the enormity of his offence—professed himself ready to withdraw his imputations provided that the duke would

> state on his part that at the time he came forward to preside at the meeting for the establishment of the King's College, he did not contemplate the measures which are now in progress for Roman Catholic Emancipation.

The duke, in view of the manner in which Winchilsea had chosen to initiate the controversy, emphatically declined to make the statement required, and regarded it as an additional insult that the earl should demand it. He claimed from the earl either unconditional withdrawal of his imputations or " reparation." The earl, in spite of great pressure brought to bear upon him, refused to withdraw his imputations unconditionally, and he accordingly had to accept Wellington's challenge. The Earl of Falmouth consented to act as Winchilsea's second; most unwillingly, indeed, for he considered that Winchilsea was wholly in the wrong, and " entirely disapproved of the publication of his letter, which indeed was indefensible." Sir Henry Hardinge acted for the duke. The meeting was arranged for 8 A.M. on Saturday, March 21, 1829, in the Battersea Fields, near the river. On the day before that of the duel Winchilsea, who probably had little expectation of survival, wrote a note in which he said :

> It is my determination not to fire at the duke, but after the first fire I shall offer the expression of regret which I shall then be ready to make. . . . I own I have been wrong.

Winchilsea's determination not to fire almost certainly saved his life; for when the word of command was given the duke was so amazed at the earl's immobility that his own aim was disarrayed and he shot wide. Then Winchilsea raised his arm above his head and emptied his pistol into the skies. He then

55

felt himself free to hand to the duke, through his second, an apology, which concludes as follows :

> I regret having unadvisedly published an opinion which the noble duke states in his memorandum of yesterday to have charged him with "disgraceful and criminal motives" in a certain transaction which took place nearly a year ago. I also declare that I shall cause this expression of regret to be inserted in the *Standard* newspaper, as the same channel through which the letter in question was given to the public.

Thus was honour satisfied in the days of George IV !

But, though Winchilsea withdrew his imputations, he did not renew his contribution to the funds of King's College. And, unfortunately, his example proved to be infectious. At nearly every subsequent meeting of the provisional committee numerous letters were read from quondam supporters announcing their determination to withhold their donations or subscriptions. In vain did the committee (April 22, 1829) frame a circular of appeal assuring the seceders

> that the system of education and government to be adopted in King's College will be strictly Protestant, according to the doctrines and duties of Christianity as inculcated by the United Church of England and Ireland.

In vain did the secretary write to the solicitor who was drafting the charter, asking him (May 19, 1829), if possible, to

> introduce into the charter after the words " the United Church of England and Ireland " the words following, or others to the like effect—viz., " *being of the Protestant Communion as now by law established.*"

Very few of the seceders were persuaded to return and renew their support of the college.[1] Others, too, seceded for different reasons : some because their shares did not at once begin to yield interest; some because they objected to the site chosen for the college ; and so on. Altogether it was a difficult and harassing time for the devoted members of the provisional

---

[1] See the *Times*, April 8, 1829. A week later the *Athenæum*, then edited by the Rev. F. D. Maurice, asked the question whether the secession of Winchilsea and his friends really injured the college, and it expressed the opinion that it did not. Of course it involved loss of money, but on the other hand it removed the influence of men narrow and intolerant—" men of sectarian principle and infidel spirit, ' anti-ists,'" who were " not churchmen but anti-dissenters ; not protestants but anti-catholics, not christians but anti-infidels." It considered that the purging was necessary and would be beneficial. This was the first, but not the last, occasion on which the views of F. D. Maurice differed from those of the governing body of the college.

committee. Expenses were much heavier than had been anticipated; the flow of donations and subscriptions was stopped, and even an ebb was evident.

At a general meeting of donors and subscribers held on May 16, 1829, with Archbishop Howley in the chair, it was announced that, as against an estimated preliminary expenditure of £170,000, the sum of £126,974 3s. 6d. had been paid or promised. This sum consisted of £54,074 3s. 6d. in donations, not all of which had actually been received, and subscriptions to 729 of the £100 shares, only £5 per share having as yet been called in.[1]

The first call, made on allotment, had naturally been very generally responded to; but the second call of £25 per share, made this same May 1829, was less successful. In spite of strenuous efforts made to placate the seceders, to remove their suspicions, and awaken them to a sense of their obligations, about a hundred and fifty of them remained obdurate. When, therefore, the provisional committee completed its task and handed over its functions to the duly constituted college council, it was compelled to report that donations to the amount of £4374 17s. 10d. remained unpaid, and that the subscriptions to the shares were £4560 in arrears. Thus the college was started in the midst of irritating controversy, and with a heavy financial handicap.

§ 4. *The Site Question*

King's College has nearly always been troubled by a site question. It took a long time a hundred years ago to decide where the college should be planted; the site ultimately chosen caused intense dissatisfaction in many quarters; periodically throughout its career efforts have been made to shift the college, some originating in government departments which coveted its situation in the Strand, others in circles whose desire has been to concentrate all institutions of a university rank in a university region in London. At present we are concerned only with the initial search for a site instituted by the provisional committee.

At the general meeting of donors and subscribers held on May 16, 1829, the committee reported that

after careful consideration of more than twenty proposed sites, they finally decided to make an application to His Majesty's Government for a grant of the vacant ground on the eastern side

---

[1] The subsequent calls were as follows : £25 in May 1829, £20 in February 1830, £25 in October 1830, and £25 in January 1831.

of Somerset House. This situation, from its position in the heart of the metropolis, and its facilities of access from every quarter, appeared to them to unite more recommendations than any other they were enabled to obtain.[1]

It will be interesting to trace the process by which they came to this decision, and to note some of the other sites suggested. The committee began the consideration of the question at its fifth meeting (July 16, 1828), when "the secretary stated a proposition by John Harrison Curtis, Esq., that Buckingham Palace should be bought for the purposes of the college." This was a hopeful start ! Unfortunately, the decorous silence of the minute-book does not tell us how the arresting proposal was received by the Bishops of London and Llandaff, the Vice-Chancellor of England, and the other eminent men present. One is left to imagine the scene. Certainly, however, the pursuit of Buckingham Palace was not taken up. Three other possible sites mentioned at the same meeting suggest that sudden descent described by Disraeli as " from the sublime to the ridiculous." After Buckingham Palace . . . the barracks and stables of the City Light Horse; or the plot of land between Gray's Inn Lane and Somers Town; or another plot between Oxford Road, Edgware Road, and New Road. None of these made any appeal. At the next meeting of the committee (July 22) a letter was read from Lord Kensington recommending the claims of Little Chelsea, and another from the Marquis Camden urging the advantages of North London. At the seventh meeting (August 1) more precise and practicable proposals were advanced; two sites in particular received careful consideration. One was in Lambeth, between Westminster Bridge and the Palace, presumably the site on which St Thomas's Hospital now stands. The Bishop of London was in favour of this site, and Dr D'Oyly was requested to make inquiries as to the possibility of securing it. The other site which received favourable consideration was Regent's Park, and in particular the portion of ground enclosed by the circular road. Mr Locker was commissioned to approach the government and see if there was any chance of a grant of this delectable spot. Four other sites were mentioned as having been recommended, the first in Paddington, the second in Southwark,

---

[1] They might also have added, if the information had not been perfectly familiar to their auditors, that Somerset House was at that time the headquarters of Science and of Art. Both the Royal Society and the Society of Antiquaries were established there. There, too, from 1780 till 1836 the Royal Academy held its annual exhibition.

the third near Kentish Town, and the fourth in Bermondsey. On August 12 the southern approach to Waterloo Bridge was suggested, and on September 30 the central portion of Lincoln's Inn Fields.

Whilst the provisional committee was busy discussing these varied possibilities and impossibilities, the newspaper press was active in the tendering of advice. The *New Times* thought that it would be an excellent thing if the college could be planted in the neighbourhood of an already existing hospital and church, and therefore suggested Smithfield Market (with the contiguous hospital and church of St Bartholomew) as an ideal situation. The *Morning Chronicle*, organ of the philosophical radicals, obviously anxious to keep the college as far as possible from Gower Street, thought that Southwark would be preferable, as St Saviour's (the present cathedral) could be used as the college chapel, and the hospitals of St Thomas and Guy (both at that time in the Borough) would provide practice for the budding medicos. The *Lancet* and the *London Medical Gazette*, indifferent to the church, but eager for the hospital, considered that Hyde Park Corner or Knightsbridge would be a good position, as St George's Hospital was so conveniently near. The *Literary Gazette* supported the proposal for a site in Regent's Park, because of the association of this park with the prince who, now the reigning monarch, was granting his gracious name and patronage to the college; as an alternative it suggested the Artillery Ground, near Finsbury Circus. The *Morning Journal* urged consideration of the advantages of the contiguous Bunhill Fields. The *Gentleman's Magazine*, maintaining that it was impossible to find any single central site easily accessible from all residential districts, suggested the desirability of hiring a number of houses in different parts of greater London, establishing a sort of federal college whose professors and lecturers would go round in weekly circuits. Such was the assistance kindly rendered by the press.

Of the twenty odd sites enumerated above, two alone, as we have observed, came in for serious consideration—viz., the Lambeth site and the Regent's Park site. Of these two the Lambeth site soon fell out of view. Presumably Dr D'Oyly's inquiries were unfavourable : the minutes contain no note of this result. In respect of the Regent's Park site, however, things went so far that at one time it seemed to be certain that there the college would be placed. Mr Locker presented his report to the committee on August 26. They were so favourably impressed by it that they passed the following resolution :

The committee are of opinion that, all circumstances considered, the Ring in the Regent's Park is the most eligible of the sites which have been proposed for King's College, and that enquiries should be made as to the terms on which the Government would be disposed to grant land to the College in that quarter.

Mr Locker was asked to convey the resolution to Lord Lowther, the first commissioner of woods and forests, and ascertain his views on the matter. On September 16 Mr Locker was able to make so satisfactory a statement that the Archbishop of Canterbury (Dr Howley) was requested to see the Duke of Wellington, and if possible conclude the business. On October 21 the matter appeared to be settled, when the committee learned that " The commissioners of His Majesty's woods and forests are prepared to receive an application from the committee for a site for King's College " within the circular road in Regent's Park—that is to say, the site now occupied by the Royal Botanical Gardens.

The matter seemed to be decided : but an unexpected obstacle arose. The inhabitants of the new suburb that was springing up round Regent's Park manifested the strongest objection to the proposal to plant a college in their vicinity, and a powerful section of the press took up their cause. Petitions were presented against the threatened alienation of public land. The right of the commissioner of woods and forests to make the grant was challenged. The injury which the establishment of a college in so select a suburb would inflict on both the persons and the property of its neighbours was lucidly depicted. Only that very year (spring 1828) the Zoological Gardens had been opened, thirty-four acres of the park having been cut off for the purpose of its establishment. Was another institution of a similar kind to be founded in the same region after so short an interval of time, at the cost of another huge slice of the scanty acreage of the park? It was preposterous ! Annual depredations on such a scale would soon leave nothing of the park at all for public use. Moreover, wrote a correspondent in the *Times* (December 24, 1828),

we all know what youths at college and boys at school generally are : inconsiderate, rude, and mischievous. Even if it were possible to enforce their orderly deportment, the very apprehension of insult would deter modest and timid females from choosing the park as a place of recreation. Maid-servants sent out with children for air and exercise would particularly be exposed to insult.

The editor agreed with the views of his correspondent : " A college in the park," he said, " would be much worse than the menagerie of wild beasts, unless the latter also were allowed to roam at pleasure."

Here, then, at Christmastide 1828, was an *impasse*. The government had virtually granted a magnificent site in Regent's Park, but the residents of the vicinity, supported by the radical press, indignantly protested against the grant. It is probable that the vehement opposition arose not merely or mainly in the interests of the maid-servants and other " modest and timid females " of the district; but rather from the supporters of the new " University of London " just opened in Gower Street. There would, indeed, inevitably have been a formidable and spectacular clash if the two institutions, at that time in embittered rivalry, had been planted within a thousand yards of one another. The government evidently came to realize that it would be inadvisable to complete the Regent's Park concession. But, having gone so far as it had, it could hardly withdraw without offering adequate compensation. Accordingly on December 30, 1828, and apparently for the first time in all the long discussions, the Strand site was suggested. It will be well to quote in full the minute of the meeting of the provisional committee held that day:

> The Lord Bishop of London stated that he had had a communication from Mr Peel, in consequence of which Mr Smirke had received directions to wait upon the Committee on that day. Mr Smirke was then introduced and—a great deal of conversation having taken place on the subject of the eastern side and wing of Somerset House, and Mr Smirke having retired—it was moved by Mr Locker and resolved, That his Grace the Archbishop of Canterbury be requested to communicate with the Lords Commissioners of His Majesty's Treasury as to whether an arrangement may be made for appropriating to the use of King's College the eastern side of Somerset House, together with the vacant ground lying between that building and Strand Lane, upon a beneficial lease from the Crown, in order that a building may be erected thereon to complete the original plan of Somerset House for the further service of King's College ; and, should His Majesty's Government consent thereto, that Mr Smirke be requested to prepare for the information of the committee a rough plan and estimate for completing the proposed works and for forming an opening from the Strand.[1]

---

[1] The Mr Smirke referred to in this minute was of course the famous architect, knighted in 1832, who designed the British Museum, the Royal College of Physicians, the Mint, the Carlton Club, and the General Post Office ; rebuilt Covent Garden Theatre ; erected the library and dining-hall of the Inner Temple ; and restored York Minster after the fire of 1829.

Archbishop Howley undertook the commission entrusted to him, and found that His Majesty's Treasury was entirely ready to receive and favourably consider an application for the suggested site. The building sub-committee (Bishop Blomfield, Sir Robert Inglis, Dr D'Oyly, and Mr Locker) unanimously recommended the making of the application. The provisional committee on February 17, 1829, adopting the report of the building sub-committee, accordingly resolved

> That the Lord Archbishop of Canterbury, the Lord Bishop of London, and the Lord Bexley, be requested to apply to the Lords Commissioners of H.M. Treasury for a specific grant of the ground to the eastward of the existing buildings of Somerset House, and for any part or parts of those buildings which they may at any time, or from time to time, be disposed to grant for the use of the institution.

A week later (February 24, 1829) it was reported to the committee that the Duke of Wellington, as First Lord of the Treasury, had acceded to the application; on March 12 the royal approval was announced.

So the problem of the site was settled. Difficulties, however, were by no means at an end. The site was encumbered by buildings and lumber; it was, moreover, devoid of any means of access to the outer world. The Somerset House officials, apparently by no means pleased at the loss of their backyard, were extremely slow in clearing off it, and a series of urgent requests had to be sent to the Treasury before they could be persuaded to move. Two houses occupying a portion of the site and facing into Strand Lane had to be purchased and pulled down, as also had two other houses in the Strand whose demolition was necessary in order to provide access to the college. The total cost of these four obliterated buildings, whose possessors had no desire to evacuate them, took £17,000 from the college's depleted funds. It was estimated, moreover, that the making of the river frontage of the college, with the accessories thereto, demanded by the government, but of no academical value, would run to another £16,500. Further, not only did the Somerset House site involve the college in enormous initial expenditure of an unexpected and unremunerative kind; it was by no means free from other objections. On the one hand it was too small—slightly under two acres: its acceptance rendered necessary the abandonment of all those plans for a residential college which had hitherto been cherished. On the other hand it was situated in a most unholy and unsavoury

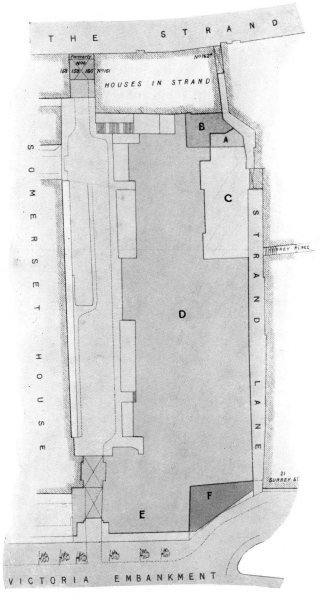

THE STRAND

Formerly
Nº6,
158 159 160 Nº161

Nº162

HOUSES IN STRAND

B

A

C

S T R A N D   L A N E

REY PLACE

D

21
SURREY ST

F

E

VICTORIA EMBANKMENT

SITE PLAN OF KING'S COLLEGE

A, B, site of houses in Strand Lane purchased in 1829. A, C, playground of King's
College School and later of the Strand School. D, main buildings of King's College.
E, principal's house. F, additional plot of land leased to the College after the
formation of the Embankment (1875) for the erection of the new physiological
laboratory.

62

neighbourhood. The peril would not be, as in Regent's Park, that the students should corrupt modest and timid nursemaids; it would be the peril that they should themselves be corrupted by actresses and other immodest and bold young persons who haunted the vicinity. A correspondent of the *Mechanics'* *Magazine* (November 14, 1829) wrote a letter to that periodical under the heading " The situation of King's College, bad, very bad ! " and he proceeded :

> In a moral point of view, the proposed site of the new college is probably the very worst that could have been selected in the whole metropolis or its vicinity. It is within about a five minutes' walk of *five* theatres, and of all the . . . other sinks of iniquity which derive their support from these celebrated schools of morality,

and he concluded by saying :

> No trifling benefit resulting from the royal grant of the land can for a moment be put into contrast with the awful and permanent evils which the council of the college will thus invite.

Two months, however, before this alarming letter appeared building had actually commenced, and it was not thought to be necessary to suspend operations.

§ 5. *The College Buildings*

The grant from the Crown of the land on which the college was to be built was signed by Viscount Lowther and Mr W. D. Adams on June 11, 1829. The chief conditions of the grant were three—viz., (1) That on the site should be erected

> a college in which instruction in the duties and doctrines of Christianity as taught by the United Church of England and Ireland shall be for ever combined with other branches of useful education;

(2) that the main buildings should be completed within ten years, and should be of such a nature as would not " injure the other buildings of Somerset House " ; and (3) that the south or river front of the college should be completed within five years, and should be such as would " form the eastern extremity of the present south front of Somerset House, built in strict conformity with the corresponding parts of the western end of the same front." Mr Smirke, the architect entrusted by the government with the charge of Somerset House, was obviously marked out as the designer of the new college buildings,

63

although his appointment necessitated the delicate and un-grateful task of declining a generous offer to act as architect without fee made by Mr John Nash, the eminent builder of Buckingham Palace and other enormities.

Long before the definite grant of the site was made, Mr Smirke, in confident anticipation of the concession, had been busy with his plans. So early as February 3, 1829, he had laid rough sketches before the provisional committee, and a special sub-committee had been appointed to go into details with him. By April 9, 1829, the plans and rough specifications were ready. The college when completed was to consist of (1) a chapel; (2) ten lecture-rooms to hold 2000 students in all; (3) twenty-eight rooms for professors; (4) schoolrooms in the basement for four hundred boys; (5) a large hall; (6) a residence on the river front for the principal; and (7) museums, etc. The total cost of the complete design was estimated at from £140,000 to £150,000. In the existing state of the finances the committee felt it to be rash to sanction so large an outlay. Hence they decided—subject to the cession of the site, the government's approval of their plans, and the consent of the donors and subscribers to the college—to commence operations by erecting (1) the chapel; (2) *six* lecture-rooms, to hold fourteen hundred students in all; (3) *eighteen* rooms for professors; (4) schoolrooms for four hundred boys; leaving the hall, the principal's house, and the museums for subsequent addition. It was estimated that these economies would bring down the immediate outlay to a sum of £115,000 or less. The general meeting of donors and subscribers, held on May 16, 1829, accepted the committee's recommendations; the transfer of the site was, as we have noted, completed on June 11; the provisional committee finally passed Mr Smirke's plans on July 17, and instructed him to set to work at once on the details of his scheme in consultation with the building committee, to which the Hon. R. H. Eden was added. That is as far as the provisional committee got.

Few sites in London can ever have presented to an architect more difficult problems than those which faced Mr Smirke when he surveyed the two irregular acres—encumbered by buildings, littered with lumber, hemmed in by tenements—on which he was commissioned to erect the new college. Not only was the site small in size and awkward in shape—its length (north to south) more than double its width (east to west)—it also was on a slope so steep that its frontage on the Strand was some thirty feet higher than its frontage on the Thames. Moreover, the proximity of the site to the river and the nature of the soil made it obvious that piles would have to be driven in before a foundation could be secured.

No sort of unity of design was possible : the college would necessarily consist of three distinct parts. The south front was doomed to be merely the appendix to Somerset House ;[1] the north front would consist solely of a narrow gateway, entirely isolated from the rest of the buildings, occupying the site of the two purchased houses, Nos. 159 and 160, the Strand;[2] the main block of buildings, over 300 feet in length, containing all the essential offices of the college, would have to lie along the eastern frontier of the site, abutting on Strand Lane. The building of the southern block, destined ultimately to house the principal, was for the time postponed, although the government grant required that it should be completed within five years— a nightmare both to the provisional committee and to the council which succeeded it ! The gateway, of course, had to be made at once. The purchase of the two Strand houses was completed in July; the edifices were demolished, and in their place was erected a massive circular arch over a central carriage-way, flanked by low, square-arched footways on either side. One of Smirke's critics (Mr A. W. Pugin) contrasted this gateway with that of Christ Church, Oxford, illustrating by means of the comparison the decay of taste in the nineteenth century ! He did not sufficiently allow for the difficulty of erecting any artistic monument in a narrow passage cut through a solid block of hideous tenements.

It was, however, on the central building that Smirke and the Committee concentrated their main efforts. They had an awkward site to deal with—long and narrow. They could not make the college impressive by means of height and ornamentation; for, on the one hand, that would have made it discordant with Somerset House, and, on the other hand, it would have been ineffective because invisible from the restricted quadrangle. Hence they had to seek distinction in length, and this distinction Smirke's design was admirably calculated to secure. The main building, although 304 feet long, was only three storeys

[1] The Radical papers—*Observer*, *Morning Chronicle*, *Times*, *Globe*—inimical to the College professed to regard the whole institution in this light. Said the *Observer*, for instance, January 31, 1830 : " The mere adjunct of a set of government offices is not the sort of habitation in which the men who have lived in Oxford, Edinburgh, Dublin, or even [*sic*] Aberdeen, would expect to see a British University located."

[2] The whole block of Strand houses up to Strand Lane ought to have been purchased, and no doubt would have been purchased but for the prohibitive prices—roughly £4000 each on the average—asked for them.

E

in height. The first storey consisted of one extensive arcade of twenty-five windows or doors; on the second and third storeys the sills of the windows formed continuous courses from one end of the building to the other. Although generally, as the official report stated, " designed in the same style of architecture as the other buildings of Somerset House," this treatment of the exterior marked a notable departure from the plan which Sir William Chambers had followed fifty years before (1776–86).

> Correcting the error into which Chambers had fallen by the too extensive rustication of the wall spaces, Smirke left the whole surface smooth, with the result that it maintains a general air of cleanliness as compared with the grimy appearance of the great quadrangle [of Somerset House] when seen in a dismal light. . . . There is a cold solemnity in its general aspect, and yet a suggestion of the massive grandeur which was afterwards so triumphantly achieved in his masterpiece, the British Museum.[1]

As to the internal arrangements. The ground floor, on the Strand level, was given up almost entirely to lecture-rooms and offices, apart from the great examination hall, which was left for the time as a mere shell. The second floor had the chapel (estimated to seat eight hundred students) as its central feature; on the north of the chapel were two large rooms, divided by a corridor, designed to accommodate the libraries of the institution; on the south were two similar rooms intended when completed to house the college museums. The third or top floor consisted primarily of "a suite of apartments for professors, extending along the whole western front of the building." The difference in elevation between the Strand on the one side and the bank of the Thames on the other made possible the construction of two semi-subterranean storeys; first, a basement which was considered a suitable habitation for a school of some four hundred boys; and, secondly, a sub-basement where stores (brought by river) were accumulated, and (when the medical school was started) corpses were anatomized. The fact that there was a river approach to the college was a considerable boon during the process of building. It was calculated that at least 5 per cent. (over £3000) was saved by bringing the stone used—Portland, Yorkshire, Scottish granite—by water rather than by land.

The main building, begun in September 1829, was roofed in before the end of 1830. The internal fittings of such parts as

---

[1] Needham and Webster, *Somerset House, Past and Present*, p. 372.

were included in the first specifications were completed in time for the college to be formally opened on October 8, 1831.

§ 6. *The Charter*

The last great task of the provisional committee—a task which occupied a large part of their attention during the period when they were also busy with the problems of the site and the buildings—was that of obtaining a charter for the college. *Without* a charter it would be at best a limited liability company administered under the principles of commercial law; *with* a charter it would become a full self-governing corporation, a legal person, capable of possessing property in perpetuity, competent to sue or be sued in the courts. *Without* a charter it would remain a private or proprietary institution; *with* a charter it would become a public or national institution. Above all, *without* a charter it would remain under the control of the donors and shareholders; *with* a charter a constitutional revolution could and would be effected by means of which absolute control over both the rules of the college and the appointments to its staff would be transferred to the dignitaries of the church—to the Archbishop of Canterbury, as visitor of the college, the Archbishop of York, as *ex officio* chairman of its council, the Bishop of London, the Dean of St Paul's, and the Dean of Westminster as perpetual governors, and eight life governors nominated by the primate.

Before the opening of King's College, the " University of London " in Gower Street applied in vain for incorporation by charter. In May 1825 a bill for the purpose was introduced into the House of Commons, but it was received so unfavourably that it was abandoned. Five years later, when the institution was in its second successful session, a petition was presented to the king begging him to grant the desired diploma : this time the open and energetic opposition of the old universities of Oxford and Cambridge caused the request to be refused. One of the prime reasons for the resistance to the Gower Street demand in both cases was the assumption by the new institution of the title " university," rather than the title " college." True, the difference between a " college " and a " university " was not very clearly apprehended at that time. The newspapers of the period, in their prolonged wranglings, spoke quite indiscriminately of the " two metropolitan colleges " and of the " two new universities." Both Thomas Campbell, on the one side, and Dr D'Oyly, on the other side, suffered from the

67

etymological hallucination which afflicted Newman thirty years later—viz., that a university is "a place of teaching universal knowledge"—an hallucination which made King's College, which did include theology in its curriculum, more truly a university than its rival, which did not include it. The lawyers, however, had a different and more businesslike conception of the difference between the two types of institutions: to them a "university" was an educational establishment which had the power to confer degrees; a "college" was one which did not possess that power. It was the degree-conferring power that the anglicans in parliament and the clerics at Oxford and Cambridge were determined, if possible, to withhold from the Gower Street institution, and the fact that from the very first King's College openly proclaimed that it entertained "no intention of erecting in the metropolis a university, with the power of conferring degrees" greatly facilitated its gaining of its charter. No doubt also it was immensely aided in its quest by the fact that it enjoyed the favour of the crown, the support of the ministry, and the patronage of the national church; whereas its rival was popularly identified with republicanism, radicalism, and dissent.

The following are the significant facts of the process by which the charter was secured, as they are recorded in the minute-book and the letter-book of the provisional committee. On August 1, 1828, it was resolved

> That the Lord Bishop of London [Dr Howley] be requested to ascertain from the Secretary of State for the Home Department [the Right Hon. Robert Peel] whether the Government will be disposed to grant a charter of incorporation to King's College.

Eleven days later the bishop reported that the Home Office desired to know details respecting the proposed constitution and organization of the college before committing itself to a promise. The matter seems to have rested there for some ten weeks, although no doubt much confabulation was going on in private. On October 21, 1828, however, Mr J. H. Markland, who had been appointed solicitor to the provisional committee, was asked to prepare the draft of a charter. He did so, and his draft was considered, amended, reconsidered, and reamended, in a series of meetings held successively on November 18, December 6, December 30, January 13, and January 19 (1829). On the last of these dates, when the draft was finally considered, amended, and approved, the Bishop of London (Dr Blomfield) was asked to draw up, and submit to the

Archbishop of Canterbury (Dr Howley) for his approval, a list of names to be sent up to the government, with the draft of the charter, as recommendations for the constitution of (1) the council and (2) the officers of the new college. This task having been completed, the whole was submitted to the Home Office for its decision on February 3, 1829. Subsequently (April 22 and May 19), in view of the agitation caused by Lord Winchilsea and his partisans, leave was asked—successful in the first case, but too late in the second—to add clauses guaranteeing the permanently protestant character of the college. There is no record as to the precise date on which the Government signified its willingness to grant the charter; but on May 16, 1829, on the occasion of the general meeting of donors and subscribers, the announcement was made that

> The Committee, aware of the importance of obtaining from His Majesty a Charter of Incorporation for the College, made application to His Majesty's Government for that purpose, and they have the satisfaction of stating that the Charter has received the approval of His Majesty's law officers. The Charter will be found to be framed in strict adherence to the Resolutions of the original meeting, and to the principles on which the College was founded as a seminary of sound learning and religious education, according to the doctrines of the United Church of England and Ireland. The Committee desire, in particular, to call attention to a special provision which it contains that no person shall be competent to act as a Governor of the College, or as a Member of the Council, or as Principal, or Professor, or Tutor (with the exception of the Teachers of Oriental or Modern Languages) who is not a member of that United Church.

The charter was sealed on August 14, 1829; it reached the college on Saturday, August 22; on Tuesday, August 25, the provisional committee held its last and purely formal meeting, its one and only business being to hand over its functions to the newly constituted council and, having done so, to expire.

CHAPTER IV

THE OPENING OF THE COLLEGE

§ 1. *The Provisions of the Charter*

THE Charter of 1829, under which the college continued to be governed until 1882, contained fifty-eight clauses. The more important of them can be summarized under the following ten heads :

I. *Preamble* in which His Majesty, King George IV, intimated that, in response to a petition from the Archbishop of Canterbury, the Duke of Rutland, and the Bishop of London, and " being desirous of maintaining indissolubly the connexion between sound religion and useful learning," he had consented to grant a charter to King's College, London.

II. *Perpetual Governors.* Nine great officials, four ecclesiastical and five lay, should by virtue of their offices be perpetual governors of the college—viz., the Archbishop of York, the Bishop of London, the Dean of St Paul's, and the Dean of Westminster; together with the Lord Chancellor, the Lord Chief Justice, the Home Secretary, the Speaker, and the Lord Mayor of London.[1]

III. The *Corporation* should consist of the aforesaid nine perpetual governors, together with the " proprietors " of King's College—the " proprietors " being the holders of the £100 shares in the college, or donors of not less than £50 to the college funds. The corporation, so constituted, should " have perpetual succession, a common seal," etc., etc.

IV. *Curriculum.* The subjects taught at the college should include (1) " the various branches of literature and science," and (2) " the doctrines and duties of Christianity, as the same are inculcated by the United Church of England and Ireland."

---

[1] A Supplementary Clause was added to the Charter at the request of the provisional committee on April 22, 1829—that is, during the ferment following the Catholic Emancipation struggle and the Wellington-Winchilsea duel. It had special relation to the perpetual governors. It ran : " That no person who is not a member of the United Church of England and Ireland as by law established shall be competent to act as governor by virtue of his office, or to be nominated as life governor, or to be eligible to any office in the College except to the professorships of Oriental and modern European languages."

V. *Visitor.* The Archbishop of Canterbury for the time being should be visitor of the college, " with authority to do all those things which pertain to visitors."[1]

VI. *Life Governors.* In addition to the nine perpetual or *ex officio* governors, eight life governors should be appointed by name, vacancies as they should subsequently occur being filled by the Archbishop of Canterbury, as visitor, out of the lay members of the corporation. The first eight life governors should be the dukes of Rutland, Northumberland, and Wellington; the marquises Camden, Bute, and Bristol; Earl Brownlow and Baron Bexley.

VII. *The Council.* The council—the active governing body of the institution—should consist of (1) the seventeen governors, perpetual and life; (2) the treasurer of the college; and (3) twenty-four members of the corporation—the first twenty-four being nominated in the charter.[2] Of these twenty-four six should retire each year, the vacancies so created being filled by election at the annual general meeting of the corporation from members of the corporation nominated by the governors—the retiring members being immediately eligible for re-election. The powers of the council, enumerated and defined in clauses 22–29, should include that of appointing, and " as they shall see occasion " dismissing, the principal, the professors, tutors, and masters, and the administrative officers of the college.

VIII. *The Annual General Court.* Every year, between January 31 and April 30, should be held a general meeting of the corporation of the college, the business of which should include (1) the election to vacancies on the council; (2) the appointment of the treasurer of the college and three auditors for the ensuing year;[3] (3) the reception of the council's report

---

[1] *Cf.* the archidiaconal functions of archdeacons.

[2] The twenty-four members of the Council named in the Charter consisted of (1) *Seventeen members of the old provisional committee*—seven other members of which were on the Council as governors. The seventeen were the Hon. R. H. Eden (Lord Henley, 1830), Sir L. Shadwell, Sir N. C. Tindal, Sir J. Nicholl, Sir R. H. Inglis, Sir C. Price, Sir H. Halford, Sir A. P. Cooper, Sir J. Richardson, Archdeacon Cambridge, Dr D'Oyly, Rev. J. Lonsdale, Alderman J. Atkins, B. C. Brodie, Esq., William Cotton, Esq., E. H. Locker, Esq., and W. Sotheby, Esq.; (2) *Seven others*—viz., Sir George T. Staunton, M.P. (one of the founders of the Royal Asiatic Society and one of the first translators of Chinese books into English), the Rev. George Shepherd, D.D., the Rev. Christopher Benson (Master of the Temple), the Right Hon. Henry Hobhouse (Under-Secretary for Home Affairs, 1817–27, Keeper of State papers, 1828–54), William Astell, Esq. (a director of the East India Company), John Drummond, Esq. (a banker), and William Manning, Esq., M.P.

[3] The first treasurer and auditors were appointed by the Charter—viz., treasurer: Alderman William Thompson; auditors: Henry Porcher, John Powell, and William Ward, esquires.

and the treasurer's audited balance-sheet for the preceding year.

IX. *Rules for the Keeping of Minutes*, etc.

X. *Regulations respecting Shares and Donations*, culminating in a notification that all subscribers and donors would lose their property and their privileges at the end of a thousand years !

Several points in this constitution are worthy of notice. First, the corporation of the college was mainly, but not wholly, a proprietary body, functioning through two organs, a general court and a council. In respect of this organization it resembled the " University of London " in Gower Street; and this common feature of the two metropolitan colleges was one which served as a model for most of the numerous new universities which were destined later in the century to be established widely throughout the provinces and the empire.

Secondly, in two important particulars King's College differed from its Gower Street counterpart—viz., (1) in having at its head an archiepiscopal visitor " with authority to do all those things which pertain to visitors," among which things was the nomination of successors to the original life governors; (2) in possessing a body of seventeen governors—nine *ex officio* and perpetual, and eight appointed for life—who not only constituted a large portion of the council of forty-two, but who exercised three functions not shared by other members of the council—viz., the power of vetoing any regulations of the council which they regarded as contrary to the fundamental principles of the college; the right of refusing to sanction any appointments or dismissals determined upon by the council; and, finally, the exclusive privilege of nominating members of the corporation for election by the general court to the council. Though normally the governors sat with the other members of the council and transacted business as members of council, nevertheless for the performance of their peculiar functions they were authorized to meet apart (three constituting a quorum), and when they thus met apart, they formed a sort of " house of lords " with very effective powers of veto. We have already noted that the seventeen governors included two bishops and two deans *ex officio*, and (after the deaths of the first life governors named in the charter) eight nominees of the Archbishop of Canterbury. Hence the clerical control of the college was as complete as was necessary.

Thirdly, the position of the " principal, professors, tutors, and masters " was an extremely unsatisfactory one. None of them had by charter any share whatsoever in either the government of the college or the determination of the curriculum. They had, moreover, no security of tenure, but were liable to be dismissed at any time, without cause shown, by a council on which they were not represented and before which they could not claim to appear. Only the principal of the college and the headmaster of the school were partially safeguarded by the possible veto of the governors.

Fourthly, at the time when the charter was originally drafted —*i.e.*, the autumn of 1828—the site of the college had not been determined; the Strand had so far as we know never been mentioned; the fine Regent's Park position was the one confidently anticipated. In these circumstances a college primarily residential was contemplated; indeed, in Dr D'Oyly's view one of the chief differentia of King's College from the " University of London " would be that the students of the one would grow up on the premises under the fostering vigilance of pious tutors, while the students of the other would be dissipated over the metropolis under the mercenary negligence of doubtful landladies. Hence the " plan for conducting this college " issued by the provisional committee on December 30, 1828, had definitely envisaged not only a resident principal, but also a group of resident tutors each in his house or hole :

> Tutors will be appointed by the principal with the approbation of the council. One or more of the tutors, under the direction of the principal, will reside in each house, or in each portion of the college allotted for the reception of students.

Similarly, the regulations for students had been divided into those for residents and those for non-residents. The substitution of the Strand site for the Regent's Park site—a descent which must at the time have filled Dr D'Oyly and his colleagues with despair—necessitated the temporary abandonment of the residential portion of the scheme. The retention of the word " tutors " represents its only survival in the charter itself. This, however, was perhaps enough to indicate that it had not wholly been given up. Its persistence was manifested later by the erection of a principal's house on the Strand site; by the provision of accommodation in the homes of tutors; and, finally, as we shall note in due course, by the conversion (in 1835) of the professors' attics into students' dormitories.

Finally, a large number of important matters were left to be decided at the discretion of the council. In particular (1) the application of the principles that all the officers of the college (except the professors of oriental literature and modern languages) should be members of the United Church of England and Ireland, and that the doctrines and duties of that Church should be taught in the college; (2) the establishment of a junior department or school, which is not specifically mentioned in the charter, although no doubt it is implied by the inclusion of " masters " and " headmaster " among the enumerated officials.

§ 2. The Preliminary Work of the New Council

Before King's College was actually opened, the council instituted by the charter had two years of strenuous and anxious work to accomplish (August 14, 1829–October 8, 1831). During this period it held twenty-six meetings, usually at 2 Parliament Street, but occasionally at Willis's Rooms. The active members of the council were in the main those who had been prominent on the provisional committee that preceded it. There was, however, one notable exception. Archbishop Howley, who had presided at twenty-nine of the thirty-four meetings of the provisional committee, on becoming " visitor " of the college had ceased to be a member of its normal governing body. The loss of his knowledge and experience was, however, found to be so serious that at the eighth meeting of the council (March 22, 1830) a resolution was passed that in future all notices of meetings should be sent to His Grace and that he should be invited " occasionally to favour the council with his presence." In response to this invitation, His Grace attended eight times during the months April 1830 to October 1831. The Archbishop of York, the chartered chairman of the council, never came at all; nor, apparently, did he pay any attention to the notices of meetings. In his absence, the Bishop of London, Dr C. J. Blomfield, usually presided : he was present at twenty-four of the twenty-six meetings, and he was in the chair at twenty-three of them. In all matters connected with the college he was extremely active and energetic. Dr George D'Oyly continued to be the bishop's right-hand man. Although, from some unexplained cause, he was not present at the first three meetings of the new council, he never missed another until the college was opened, and he was an indispensable member of every committee appointed. Archdeacon Cambridge attended twenty-one meetings; Mr William Cotton nineteen; the Hon. R. H. Eden (who in 1830 succeeded his father as Baron Henley) seventeen; Dr George Shepherd fourteen; the Rev. John Lonsdale thirteen; Sir Robert Inglis and Mr E. H. Locker twelve each; Sir Astley

Cooper and Mr W. Sotheby eleven each; Lord Bexley (a life governor) and Alderman Atkins ten each. Of the remaining twenty-nine members of the council of forty-two, ten (viz., five perpetual governors, three life governors, and two ordinary councillors) never attended at all, while nineteen put in attendances varying from one to nine. The only one of these usual absentees who calls for mention is Bishop Copleston of Llandaff, who sat on the council *ex officio* as Dean of St Paul's. He attended eight times, and was put into the chair on one of these occasions. No doubt he was prevented from attending more frequently by the claims of his Welsh diocese, where he was very active. He was, however, the most powerful member of the education committee of the council and, as such, he exercised a dominating influence in determining both the regulations of the college and the first appointments to its staff.

One pleasing episode, relating to the attendance at council meetings, is worth a passing notice. In November 1830 the Duke of Wellington's ministry gave place to that of Earl Grey, and the Lord Chancellor in the new Whig cabinet was no other than Henry Brougham, the leading promoter of the " University of London " and the chairman of its governing body. Thus under this charter the official head of the Gower Street College became *ex officio* one of the perpetual governors of King's College, and as such received the agenda of the meetings of the council. The situation was a delicate one, and it no doubt caused much speculation on both sides. On January 19, 1831, however, Lord Brougham addressed the following charming letter to the secretary :

SIR,
I have received one or two summonses to attend King's College meetings, and I have only abstained from a feeling that the connexion I have had and still have with the London University might give some jealousy to my colleagues of King's College. I am myself quite aware that such a feeling would be altogether groundless, and that none of themselves can have a warmer desire for the benefit of King's College than I have, and always have expressed publicly and privately. Nevertheless it is for them and not for me to decide whether I shall take any part in their deliberations. I tender my services. I have the honour to be, your obedient humble servant

BROUGHAM

The minutes record that

The Secretary was directed, in answer to the preceding letter, to convey the thanks of the Council to his Lordship for his obliging communication, and to say that the Council will feel honoured by his Lordship's presence whenever it may be convenient to him to assist at their deliberations.

So the matter ended. It apparently never was convenient to his Lordship to assist at the deliberations of the council of King's College, for the minutes give no record of his attendance. Nevertheless, this happy interchange of courtesies no doubt tended to lessen friction between the two colleges, and to foster those improved relations which (as we shall see) were among the most marked features of the ensuing years.

The first work of the new council was formal : it renewed the appointments of its predecessor—viz., Mr H. W. Smith as Secretary, Mr J. H. Markland as solicitor, and Mr Robert Smirke as architect; and it established four committees to deal respectively with buildings, finance, education, and by-laws.[1] The substantive concerns which occupied its main attention were : (1) the progress of the buildings; (2) the raising of funds; (3) the determination of courses of study; (4) the framing of by-laws under the charter; (5) the selection of a principal and a staff of professors; (6) the equipment of the various departments of the college; (7) the admission of students; and (8) the arrangements for the opening ceremony on October 8, 1831. Little need be said concerning the first four of these; the other four demand further treatment.

I. *Buildings*. The council at its first meeting (August 25, 1829) considered tenders for the construction of the " carcase or shell " of the new college buildings. Four had been submitted, the highest being £68,635 and the lowest—from Mr Thomas Martin, of Osnaburgh Street—£63,947. Mr Martin's tender was accepted, and work was actually commenced on September 10, 1829. The first task was to prepare the ground for building, and it proved to be a gigantic one. For more than three months some hundred and fifty men were employed levelling the site, driving piles, and constructing foundations. As the work dragged on they were put on overtime and even worked on Sundays, to the intense indignation of the stricter sabbatarians, who expressed amazement that the authorities of an institution established to promote Christian principles should permit so flagrant a violation of the decalogue.

---

[1] *Building Committee :* Blomfield, Bexley, Inglis, Eden, D'Oyly, Locker, Brodie.
Finance Committee : Price, Manning, D'Oyly, Drummond, Cotton.
Education Committee : Copleston, Hobhouse, D'Oyly, Shepherd, Halford, Lonsdale, Locker.
By-laws Committee : Shadwell, Richardson, D'Oyly.

THE GATEWAY FROM THE QUADRANGLE

THE OPENING OF THE COLLEGE

On March 2, 1830, when the preliminaries were completed, the building committee laid before the council Mr Smirke's estimates for the completion and internal fitting-up of the building, and announced that they would bring up the total cost to at least £100,000. The council, feeling that it could not at that time commit itself to so large an expenditure, indicated what portions of the college would be required from the first and what could be left over for a time, and asked Mr Smirke to revise his estimates accordingly. On April 1, 1830, Mr Smirke reported, through the building committee, that for £80,000 it would be possible

> to erect the carcase or shell of the building, according to the contract made with the builder, except the river front; to build and finish the anatomical theatre and dissecting-rooms; to furnish so much of the south wing as to provide four lecture-rooms capable of holding together about 1100 students, and to finish also two rooms for the chemical laboratory; to finish two rooms for the museum and two for the library; to finish in the north wing of the building the schoolrooms intended for the Lower Department, sufficient to receive from 300 to 350 boys; and to finish the entrance hall and the chapel in the centre of the building.

The council accepted Mr Smirke's revised estimates and instructed him to "complete such parts of the college" as were enumerated therein.

At the same two council meetings the question whether or not there should be a formal foundation-stone laying was considered. On account of "the great expense which would attend the ceremony" the council decided against it. There may have been other contributory causes : first, the King, who was the obvious person to perform the ceremony, was in rapidly failing health, having indeed but three more months to live; [1] secondly, the site in its raw condition, with its restricted area, its artificial surface, and its unfinished approach, looked so hideous that it was not desirable that more people than was necessary should see it; thirdly, the conflict over the Reform Bill was raging with so fierce an intensity in the world of politics that it may well have seemed hopeless to attract attention to a mere educational venture. In May 1830 the elevation and the plan were made public,[2] and by the summer it was evident

---

[1] The *Observer* remarked (January 31, 1830) with that touch of disrespect which at this date usually characterized the Radical press, "The ceremony called laying the first stone will be dispensed with ; the King, God bless him, has now become a little too ancient for feats of that class."

[2] See *Literary Gazette*, May 8, 1830, p. 306.

that King's College was to have an identity and a character of its own, and that it was not destined to be a mere annexe to a set of government offices. Before the winter of 1830-31 the " shell or carcase " was roofed in, and the work of internal finishing and fitting commenced. On February 7, 1831, plans for the gateway to the Strand were passed, the estimated cost being £2500. At the beginning of the autumn of 1831 all was ready for the opening ceremony.

II. *Finance.* Throughout the whole course of the building operations the council were desperately worried by the need of money. As the work of preparing the site and erecting the college proceeded, the bills poured in, those of the contractor being, of course, the heaviest.[1] Meanwhile, the flow of donations and subscriptions had almost entirely ceased; indeed, for various reasons, many of those who had originally promised to make gifts or take shares were trying to evade their obligations. It would be tedious to go through the details which month by month were reported by the finance committee to the council, or to transcribe the letters that were received and remitted. Suffice it to say three things : first, that the fifth and last instalment on the £100 shares was called in at the end of January 1831; secondly, that a collector was appointed, on a commission of 2½ per cent., to rake in arrears, and that he secured over £2200; and, finally, that when at the end of August 1831, just before the opening of the college, the finance committee and the council reviewed the situation they found that the total amount received to date had been £113,598 (donations £53,053, subscriptions £60,545); that the total amount expended had come to £85,889; and that consequently the balance in hand was no more than £27,709 (£27,000 in exchequer bills and £709 in the bank). Donations unpaid reached a total of £1935; while instalments still due on shares amounted to no less than £14,655—a gross deficit of £16,590. The matter of the shares occupied an enormous amount of time and attention, as well as a prodigious lot of book-keeping in the college office. It is interesting to note that the first transfer of a share recorded in the college register is (April 1830) from John Gladstone, Esq., of Liverpool, to his son "Mr William Ewart Gladstone, student of Christ Church, Oxford " : the transfer book contains the signatures of both father and son.

III. *Regulations.* The provisional committee, as we have

---

[1] Mr Thomas Martin's quarterly accounts for the first year were : December 1, 1829, £5136 ; March 1, 1830, £6158 ; June 1, 1830, £10,721 ; September 1, 1830, £13,221.

seen, had issued two statements respecting the organization and government of the projected college.[1] On July 1, 1828, it had formulated the religious principles on which the institution was to be founded; on December 30, 1828, it had published a plan for conducting the college, in which it had intimated, among other things, that the establishment would be divided into two departments, a higher department (primarily residential) for youths over sixteen, and a lower department (wholly non-residential), of a preparatory nature, for younger boys. Since the issue of these documents two things had occurred which rendered their revision necessary: on the one hand, the site had been fixed, and a residential college made impossible because of its smallness; on the other hand, the charter had been granted, establishing authoritatively some things mooted in the previous documents, but leaving the general course of study to be determined by the council. The education committee, therefore, set to work and laid before the council the following scheme, which the council accepted without amendment and ordered to be printed and circulated as the first prospectus of the college.

GENERAL COURSE OF STUDY

I. *Higher Department*

(1) The general course of education pursued at King's College will comprehend religion and morals, classical literature, mathematics, natural and experimental philosophy, chemistry, parts of natural history, logic, English literature and composition, the principles of commerce, and general history. To these will be added instruction in modern foreign languages, and in subjects connected with particular professions, as medicine and surgery, jurisprudence, etc.

(2) [Deviations from the general course of education will be permitted in certain cases.]

(3) At all public examinations enquiry will be made into the knowledge which the students may have acquired of the evidences of natural and revealed religion, and of the doctrines and duties of Christianity as taught in the Church of England; and every one will be expected to exhibit a certain degree of proficiency in these subjects.

(4) [The normal age for admission to the higher department will be sixteen.]

(5) The business of each day will commence with prayers in the college chapel, at which the attendance of the students will be required. Those who reside at a distance from the college will

---

[1] See above, pp. 50-51.

be permitted, under the sanction of the principal, to attend church on Sundays with their families; but whenever required by him they must attend the service at the college chapel.

(6) Students who are not admitted for general education, but who attend lectures with a view to particular professions, or for improvement in some single branch of literature or science, will be subject to such regulations as the college authorities may prescribe.

(7) It will be competent to any of the professors, and to such other persons as may be approved by the council, to receive students belonging to the college into their houses. Regulations will be laid down for the government of such houses, to which strict attention will be required.

II. *Lower Department*

(8) The lower department will consist of a school for the reception of day scholars. It will be totally distinct from the higher, and will afford an education preparatory to it. It will be placed under the separate management of a headmaster and a competent number of under-masters. The system of education will embrace a course of religious instruction suited to the age of the pupils, classics, elements of mathematics, arithmetic, English literature and composition, and some modern languages when desired, etc.

(9) Public examinations will take place at which prizes will be given.

Respecting this interesting document we may note, first, that the education offered in both the upper and the lower departments was unusually wide and comprehensive for that period, but that in both departments alike the affinities of King's College were with schools rather than with universities; it was concerned solely with the dissemination of existing knowledge and not at all with the extension of the bounds of knowledge; secondly, that clause 6 is the conscience clause which enabled nonconformists of all sorts to enter the college freely, without respect to the religious observances demanded from regular students; thirdly, that clause 7 provided the substitute for that much-desired residence within the college precincts which had had to be abandoned; fourthly, that the school envisaged in clause 8, together with the similar school attached to the " University of London " in Gower Street, was the model of a new type of secondary school destined to rise to great importance during the nineteenth century—a type intermediate between the great residential public schools and the old local grammar schools; finally, that the public examinations contemplated in clauses 3 and 9 are obviously oral examinations conducted in the presence of admiring parents and a critical world.

The principal function of King's College School was to act as a feeder for the higher department of the institution. It was not, however, to be the only source from which boys grounded in " sound knowledge and religious education " were to be drafted into the new college. On November 12, 1829, a highly important letter reached the council from the Rev. H. H. Norris of Hackney, the great educationist, reviver of the S.P.C.K., ally of Joshua Watson in the maintenance of the National Society. Mr Norris wrote as chairman of the committee of the Hackney Church of England School, and he addressed the secretary of King's College as follows:

> Sir,
> I beg leave to inclose for the information of King's College, London, the prospectus of a school about to be established in this parish. This school being established for the purpose of asserting the same principle which led to the formation of King's College, viz., the indispensable necessity of religious instruction forming a part of the general education of youth, I beg leave to inquire for the information of the committee whether any regulations have yet been adopted by the council by which such establishments can be taken into union with King's College. I have the honor [etc.]

The council, having given this letter their " mature consideration," decided to make a favourable reply to Mr Norris's letter, and " to encourage the formation of district or local day schools established in accordance with the principles of the intended school at Hackney." With this view, they drew up and published in the newspapers the following address:

> Public attention being now directed to the expediency of establishing local or district day schools for the purpose of affording a sound and liberal education at a moderate expense to the sons of professional and mercantile men and others, the Council of King's College, London, feel it to be their duty to impress in the strongest manner upon the contributors to such institutions the importance of founding them upon those principles which are embodied in the charter of King's College, as applicable to its Lower Department, and of making religious instruction according to the doctrines of the Established Church an essential part of their course of education. With this view the Council recommend that the more influential among the clergy and laity in the populous districts where schools of this description may be thought likely to succeed should take measures for their early

F

formation and place them, where it may be deemed expedient, in union with King's College, which will thus form the centre of a system of education for the middling classes of society, combining the advantages of a judicious and extended cultivation of the intellectual faculties with the careful inculcation of religious truths and moral duties.

The address then continued:

> The Council of King's College are ready to receive applications from district schools to be taken into union, and they trust that some plan may be devised for offering to pupils who shall have been educated at such schools certain facilities and advantages when they are admitted to the Higher Department of the College.

Applications for affiliation, or " union," with King's College, in accordance with the principles enunciated in this address, were, before the actual opening of King's College, received from the Hackney Church of England School; the Grammar School, Maidstone; the Woodbridge Grammar School; the Otford Grammar School; and the Kensington Grammar School.

IV. *By-laws.* The committee to frame the by-laws authorized by the charter, and necessitated by the scantiness of its stipulations respecting the internal organization of the college, consisted of three members only—viz., those two eminent lawyers Sir Lancelot Shadwell, the last vice-chancellor of England, and Sir John Richardson, formerly a judge in the court of common pleas, together with the Rev. Dr D'Oyly. They laid their draft of suggested by-laws before the council on December 1, 1829, and the council adopted it as it stood. The by-laws were twenty-one in number. For the most part they related to the formal procedure to be pursued in the administration of the college. It would be tedious and unprofitable to examine them in detail. The matters they treated of were as follows: (1) meetings of governors; (2, 3) meetings of the council; (4–6) appointment of committees; (7, 8) holding of general courts; (9, 10) payments of moneys; (11, 12) declarations of dividends; (13, 14) custody of the common seal and the books of the college; (15–20) business relating to donations and shares; (21) mode of amendment of by-laws in the future. The main item of constitutional importance was the second—viz.:

> That the council do assemble for the transaction of business not less than six times in every year, and that not more than two calendar months do elapse between any two meetings of the council.

§ 3. *The Appointment of Principal and Staff*

The question who should be the first principal of the new college was obviously one of first-rate importance. The " plan " issued by the provisional committee on December 30, 1828, had stated that

> the internal government of the college, and the general direction and superintendence of the course of education, will rest with the principal;

that

> he must be a clergyman, having the degree of M.A. at least, in one of the universities of Oxford, Cambridge, or Dublin;

and that

> it will be his duty to preside over the public examinations, to preach often in the college chapel, and to report from time to time the state of the college to the council and governors.

To this general statement neither the charter nor the subsequent regulations and by-laws of the council made any addition.

The first new reference to the principalship comes, as a report from the education committee, in the council minutes of April 1, 1830. The committee recommend, and the council concur in the recommendation, that

> a principal be appointed who, in addition to the general superintendence of the college, shall have the particular charge of the religious and moral instruction of the students, that his salary be £800 per annum,

and that

> private inquiries be made without delay for a person qualified to fill this situation with the greatest credit and advantage to the establishment.

Of the course of these private inquiries we have no official information, and the only item which I have been able to glean from unofficial sources is that the principalship was offered to the Rev. John Lonsdale, and that he, on this occasion, declined it.[1] The search for a suitable head of the college was extremely protracted, and must have been very difficult. For not until fourteen months had elapsed from the initiation of the quest

---

[1] E. B. Denison, *Life of John Lonsdale, Bishop of Lichfield*, p. 29. Mr Lonsdale, of course, accepted the principalship nine years later, and held it for five years, 1839–44.

did the council, on June 6, 1831, announce that " the Rev. William Otter, M.A., was appointed principal of the college and lecturer in divinity." On June 29

> the Rev. William Otter, M.A., attended the council and intimated his acceptance, subject to the approbation of the governors, of the situation of principal of the college.

The appointment was an extraordinarily late one; three years had elapsed since the inaugural meeting in the Freemasons' Hall; nearly two years since the determination of the site, the acquisition of the charter, and the commencement of building operations. The council had settled all the details of the organization of the college, the contents of its curricula, and even (as we shall see) the constitution of its staff, before Mr Otter appeared upon the scene and accepted the management of the going concern. And who was Mr Otter?

To say that Mr Otter was a man of eminent distinction would be an exaggeration. He was, however, a scholar and a gentleman whose qualities of mind and heart admirably fitted him to conduct the college through the anxious and difficult years of its early existence. Born in 1768, he was sixty-three years of age at the time of his appointment. He was a Cambridge graduate, having been fourth wrangler in 1790. After having taken his degree he had for five years held the headmastership of the Helston Grammar School. Then he had been recalled to Cambridge to act as fellow and tutor of Jesus College, where he had had as his colleagues and intimate friends E. D. Clarke, the noted traveller and antiquary, and T. R. Malthus, the notorious political economist—of both of whom he lived to write biographies. In 1804 he had left Cambridge to take up parochial work, and he had received successively the rectories of Colmworth, Sturmer, and Chetwynd. He had become closely associated with Dr George D'Oyly (whom he had probably known well at Cambridge) when Dr D'Oyly married his wife's younger sister. In 1825 Dr D'Oyly had placed him in charge of the newly erected church of St Mark's, Kennington, and it was from this rectory (which he held in conjunction with two of his former Shropshire livings *in absentia*) that he was called to the principalship of King's College. Among his recommendations for the King's College post were his marked moderation in both politics and religion, and in general his admirable sweet-reasonableness. He was a man excellently calculated to allay animosities, to close controversies, to soothe sensibilities, and to promote peace. It was an

WILLIAM OTTER
Principal 1831–36

84

advantage, too, that in politics his affinities were rather with the whigs than with the tories: hitherto King's College had been too closely bound up with toryism. He was intimate with the Benthamite circle who were running the "University of London"; one of his daughters married the reformer John Romilly (later Lord Romilly), another married the free-trader Edward Strutt (later Lord Belper). No one was in a better position to reconcile the conflicting principles, and harmonize the antagonistic interests, of the rival colleges of Westminster and Bloomsbury. Similarly, in religion, the fact that Mr Overton calls him "a sort of quasi-high-churchman" indicates that he was averse from extremes.[1] He was broad-minded, tolerant, easygoing; proud of the association of the church with the state; incapable of deviating from either orthodoxy or propriety; dignified, sedate; distrustful of enthusiasm, whether it took the form of the fervour of the evangelicals or the asceticism of the tractarians; thoroughly gentlemanly. No one was in a better position to prevent King's College at the outset of its career from being too closely associated with one particular section of the church. Undoubtedly his most lively interest centred in education. For five years he had been a schoolmaster in Cornwall; for eight years a tutor at Cambridge; in all his parishes the church schools had claimed his closest attention. Some one said of him that it was his "conviction that the welfare and very salvation of England depended mainly —under divine providence—on the improvement of education."[2] Here was the very man who seemed marked out for the principalship of the new institution. But probably of all his qualifications for the post none was more important than the charm of his character and disposition. The Rev. F. D. Maurice said of him that

> by a courtesy which made itself felt in all his words and acts, and which evidently proceeded from a divine root within, he caused men of the most opposite opinions to understand that they were parts of the same family.

Another writer, who knew him well, said that "in his whole temper of mind he was a man of peace, and above all things he yearned after the unity of the church"; while a third observer remarked that "there was a loveliness in his character which won every heart." His great powers as a reconciler and healer were, of course, specially manifested after he left King's College

[1] J. H. Overton, *English Church in the Nineteenth Century*, p. 291.
[2] *Educational Magazine* (1840), ii, p. 328.

(1836), when, as Bishop of Chichester, he ruled the church in Sussex. There his catholicity of temper was shown by his appointment of Julius Hare and Henry Manning as his two archdeacons; while his continued zeal for education was displayed in his foundation of an association for the building of church schools and in his establishment of a diocesan college for the training of clergy.

Long before Otter was appointed to the principalship the council had been busy in filling the professorial chairs. Almost as soon as reports of the inaugural meeting appeared in the press applications began to pour in; they are duly recorded in the minutes and summarized in a special book kept for the purpose. On April 1, 1830, the council, having decided what chairs were immediately to be established, decided to advertise the posts, and to fix June 1, 1830, as the date by which all papers should be sent in. There were to be three professors "for conducting the regular course of education"—viz., (1) classics, (2) mathematics, and (3) English literature and history. These three should be paid a certain proportion of the fees received from their students, but the college should guarantee that the total amount should not fall short of £200 each. There were to be, further, eight other professors, who also should receive a portion of their students' fees, but to whom the college did *not* guarantee any minimum. These less attractive chairs were (4) chemistry, (5) natural and experimental philosophy, (6) natural history and zoology, (7) law and jurisprudence, (8) anatomy and physiology, (9) theory and practice of medicine, (10) surgery, (11) principles and practice of commerce. We shall note that in the end the classification of chairs did not quite follow this original scheme.

The medical appointments received the earliest and most careful consideration of the council. Three of its members (who also had been members of the provisional committee) were, it will be remembered, medical men of the first rank—viz., Sir Henry Halford, president of the royal college of physicians; Sir Astley Cooper, and Mr (later Sir) Benjamin Brodie, two eminent fellows of the college of surgeons: they were connected respectively with Middlesex, Guy's, and St George's hospitals. On December 15, 1829, these three were requested by the council to consult together and " to report to the council as to the number and duties of the professors whom it will be expedient to appoint for carrying on the course of medical education in the college." Their consultations were probably numerous and prolonged; for medical education was at the moment passing through a crisis, and much would depend on the course pursued by the authorities of King's College. Hitherto the training of a doctor had commonly consisted of apprenticeship to a local practitioner, followed by a course of lectures at medical schools (some private, others connected with hospitals), and supplemented by a certain amount of specialized instruction provided by the royal colleges of surgeons and physicians; the usual qualification to practise had been the licence of the society of apothecaries. The unsatisfactory nature of this haphazard and unco-ordinated instruction had long been evident, and was precisely at that date the subject of a vigorous campaign conducted by the *Lancet*. The hopes of the reformers were centred in the new medical faculties just being set up in Gower Street and the Strand.

We have noted that on April 1, 1830, three medical chairs were ordered to be advertised—viz., those of anatomy and physiology, theory and practice of medicine, and surgery. When the applications in response to these advertisements were all in, they were remitted for report and recommendation to the same three advisers as before. On July 10, 1830, these advisers nominated Mr Joseph Henry Green to the professorship of surgery; Mr Herbert Mayo to that of anatomy and physiology; while they recommended the partition of the work of the chair of medicine between two professors—viz., Dr Bisset Hawkins, who should treat of the theory of physic, and Dr Francis Hawkins, who should deal with the practice. Before the college opened, two other medical chairs had been added, bringing the number to six—viz., midwifery (Dr Robert Ferguson, February 7, 1831) and forensic medicine (Dr Thomas Watson, June 29, 1831). These appointments were, on the whole, well received: good men had undoubtedly been chosen. A few words concerning them may be added.

(1) Mr J. H. Green (1791–1863) was particularly remarkable. A distinguished surgeon of St Thomas's hospital and lecturer at the Borough medical school, he was also a man of wide general culture. Not only was he a fellow of the Royal Society and eminent in anatomical science, he was also known as a philosopher. He had studied the Kantian system in Berlin and had come back as a champion of German idealism as against English utilitarianism. Thus he had been brought into touch with Samuel Taylor Coleridge and had become one of his closest and most sympathetic friends. Green's influence in King's College, therefore, was destined to extend far beyond

the limits of the medical school; he did much to keep its theology large and liberal. (2) Mr Herbert Mayo (1796–1852) was surgeon to the Middlesex hospital. He was an extremely capable anatomist and operator; he was not destined, however, to attain equal eminence as a teacher and lecturer. To his chair, as originally constituted, fell the task of giving instruction in not only anatomy, but also physiology and pathology, so that he had to deal with the whole field, both theoretical and applied, of the structure and the functioning (normal and abnormal) of the human frame. He appointed as his first demonstrator a man notable in King's College annals—viz., Richard Partridge, who, after assisting him for five years, succeeded to his office and held it till his death in 1873. (3) Dr Francis Hawkins (1794–1877) was likewise attached, as physician, to the Middlesex hospital. He was also one of the medical advisers to the royal family. He too was a man of general culture—a classical scholar of Oxford, and winner of the Newdigate in 1813. (4) Dr Robert Ferguson (1799–1865) was one of the most noted general practitioners and obstetrical specialists of his day. Among his ordinary patients he included many eminent political and literary men—*e.g.*, Sir Walter Scott. As a specialist he was physician to the Westminster lying-in hospital. In 1841 it was his distinguished honour to assist Queen Victoria to maintain the succession to the throne. He was founder of the *London Medical Gazette*. (5) Dr Thomas Watson (1792–1882)—destined to be the last survivor of the original staff of the college—was an old schoolfellow of Bishop Blomfield, a Cambridge graduate, and a physician to the Middlesex hospital. For a short time he had lectured in the " University of London." Later he rose to be president of the royal college of physicians. He attended the Prince Consort in his last illness; was made a baronet in 1866; and remained one of the most honoured and valuable members of the King's College council almost to the end of his long life.

So much for the medical appointments. The remainder can be treated more briefly. The applications received by June 1, 1830, were considered by the education committee, the active members of which were Bishop Copleston, Dr D'Oyly, and the Rev. John Lonsdale, who kept in close touch with Archbishop Howley and Bishop Blomfield. The council without demur accepted the committee's recommendation. Of the three professorships instituted " for conducting the regular course of education " only two were at this time filled. On July 10, 1830, the Rev. Thomas G. Hall, M.A., fellow and tutor of

Magdalene College, Cambridge (fifth wrangler, 1824), was appointed to the chair of mathematics, which he continued modestly, faithfully, and inconspicuously to occupy (rather than fill) for the next thirty-nine years. He wrote a few forgotten text-books, and rose to be a prebendary of St Paul's. The election to the chair of classical literature was not made until April 15, 1831. The choice was probably a difficult one, for the applicants were numerous and important—among them being John Allen Giles, of Corpus, Oxford, later headmaster of the City of London School, and a lavish benefactor of that large class of students who prefer to see their Latin and Greek authors not in the flesh, but in the Bohn; and Benjamin Hall Kennedy, the most brilliant Cambridge scholar of his day, destined to be the builder of Shrewsbury's classical fame (1836–1866) and then the regius professor of Greek at Cambridge (1866–89). The man, however, ultimately chosen was not unworthy to compete against such doughty rivals. This was the talented and spiritually minded Joseph Anstice (1808–36), of Christ Church, Oxford, cousin of Coleridge, fellow-student and intimate friend of W. E. Gladstone (whom he defeated in the contest for the Newdigate prize, 1828, the subject being Richard Cœur de Lion). Unhappily, he was frail in health, and he was able to hold his King's College post for only four years.[1] The third regular professorship—viz., that of English literature and history—was (no doubt for reasons of economy) left vacant. Its duties were divided between the professors of classics and mathematics. Professor Anstice was to lecture once a week on literature, his lecture to consist mainly of readings from edifying authors; Professor Hall was, similarly, to devote one hour a week to instruction in history, his text being Koch's *Revolutions of Europe*. This arrangement continued until Anstice's resignation in 1835.

The professorships whose holders were to have no guaranteed salaries, but were to be remunerated merely by a portion (usually three-fourths) of the fees received from their pupils, were filled as follows. (It is manifest that teachers so paid, whose salaries would frequently be only a few pounds per quarter, could be regarded as little more than visiting masters.) On November 26, 1830, Mr James Rennie (1787–1867), a master of arts of Glasgow University, was appointed professor of natural history and zoology. He was a lover of birds, a firm believer

---

[1] Anstice published a small volume of exquisite translations of Greek choric poetry in 1832; he also wrote a number of hymns, two of which are included in *Hymns Ancient and Modern*—viz., numbers 276 and 387.

in inductive methods of research, and a vehement denouncer (*e.g.*, in his King's College inaugural lecture) of the evolutionary hypotheses which were just then coming into vogue. In 1834 his chair was allowed to lapse. On January 30, 1831, four posts were filled. (1) The Rev. Henry Moseley, M.A. (1801–72), a Cambridge mathematician (seventh wrangler, 1826), was made professor of natural and experimental philosophy, including astronomy. He gave himself especially to mechanics, and particularly to problems connected with the stability of ships. He also wrote on astro-theology. (2) Mr John James Park (1795–1833), a distinguished barrister who had been compelled to abandon the law courts because of deafness, was placed in the double chair of English law and jurisprudence. He may have commended himself to the electors by the fact that he was a prominent opponent of Bentham (whose great disciple John Austin held the jural chair in Gower Street); he had effectively questioned some of Bentham's statements respecting foreign law, and he was an active antagonist of his grand panacea, codification. His brief two-year tenure of his post at King's was marked by the delivery and publication of some notable and timely lectures on " the theory and practice of the constitution." (3) A lectureship in the principles and practice of commerce was conferred upon Mr Joseph Lowe, whose views on currency and finance happily accorded with those of Bishop Copleston and Sir Robert Peel. (4) A chair of political economy had not been included in the original academic scheme, but when it was found that the eminent professor of the subject at Oxford, a close personal friend of Bishop Copleston, Nassau William Senior (1790–1864), was willing to come, no hesitation was felt in allowing him to establish his seat in the college and collect three-fourths of the fees of any students whom he might attract. He accepted the appointment, and actually prepared a course of lectures; but before the opening of the first session the government took him away to be a tithe-commissioner, and his lectures remained undelivered. A certain Rev. Richard Jones took up the subject in 1833.

On February 7, 1831, the professorship of chemistry was bestowed upon John Frederic Daniell (1790–1845), a fellow of the Royal Society, already eminent as a meteorologist, the inventor of the hygrometer still called by his name, an authority on the management of hot-houses. He was destined to do notable work at King's before his sudden death almost within the precincts of the college in 1845. Two months later (April 15) the chairs of botany and geology were filled. That of botany was conferred upon Mr Gilbert T. Burnett (1800–35), who, during the four years that remained of his short life, helped, by his work on the classification of plants, to prepare the way for the acceptance of evolutionary ideas. The chair of geology was assigned to a man even then well known as a man of science and an author, but destined later to rise to eminent fame as a pioneer of revolutionary ideas. This was Mr (later Sir) Charles Lyell (1797–1875), secretary of the geological society, an Oxford man whose liberalism was so pronounced that Bishop Copleston opposed his appointment to King's. He had been considered as a possible professor at the " University of London "; he was a friend of the first (and last) warden of that institution, Mr Leonard Horner, whose daughter he married in 1832. He had already published (1830) the first of the three volumes of his epoch-making *Principles of Geology*, in which he had made " an attempt to explain the former changes of the earth's surface by reference to causes now in operation "; but it was not until the appearance of the second volume—published in 1832, when he was a professor at King's—that his work was seen to be a direct challenge to Ussher's chronology, and to make havoc of the accepted cosmogony of current orthodoxy. He kept his chair at King's for two years only.

The chairs of modern languages were filled in June 1831. French went to L. T. Ventouillac, a convert to the Church of England, who had translated into his native tongue (and dedicated to Archbishop Howley) Bishop Watson's *Apology for the Bible*, an antidote to Thomas Paine's *Age of Reason*. German was assigned to Dr Adolphus Bernays, author of a *Compendious German Grammar*. Spanish went to a transient Don Pablo de Mendibil, who vanished from the scene within a twelvemonth. The Italian appointment was more noteworthy. It fell to Gabriele Rossetti (1783–1854), best known as father of the famous trio Dante Gabriel, William Michael, and Christina Georgina, all of whom were infants at the time of his election. He was a Neapolitan liberal, a vehement anti-papalist who had abandoned catholicism, though without openly abjuring it, and had become a freethinker. His presence at King's (1831–47) was an anomaly.

As to the junior department of the college: on November 26, 1830, the Rev. John Richardson Major, M.A., was appointed headmaster; on April 15, 1831, the Rev. Joseph Edwards, B.A., was selected as second master; and on July 15 Mr Ribbans was invited to teach writing and arithmetic as a visiting master.

That, apparently, was the whole staff of the school when it opened. As to remuneration: for the first three years the headmaster was to receive a capitation fee of £5 5s. per annum for each pupil (to be reduced to £4 4s. for all beyond the first hundred); the second master was to have £2 2s. per pupil irrespective of numbers (with a guaranteed minimum of £200); the writing master was to glean £1 1s. in respect of each of his victims. The early prosperity of the school rendered it possible for more satisfactory arrangements to be made in 1834.

§ 4. *Preparations for Opening*

The reason why the medical and scientific appointments were made so long—six to fifteen months—before the actual opening of the college was that the professors had to prepare an elaborate equipment in order to be able to start practical work together with their lectures. The council had to face formidable demands for money long ere any fees came in to reimburse them. Professor Mayo, the anatomist, was the most persistent and expensive. He began hopefully, on October 1, 1830, by asking for £900—viz., £250 for a small anatomical museum which he was prepared to sell to the college, £350 for the purchase of materials and specimens, and £300 for assistance: the council voted the whole sum. Just a year later, on the eve of the opening of the college, when finances were desperate, he came for another £100. He got it; but with an intimation that " no further grant can at present be made." Sir Henry Halford generously presented to the college his valuable cabinet of *materia medica* (November 26); hence Dr Bisset Hawkins required no more than £60 in order to complete the collection and provide drawings, etc. The other sums voted were: April 15, 1831, to Professor Daniell, for chemicals and apparatus, £300; April 27, £100 each to Professors Burnett and Lyell for botany and geology respectively; June 6, £100 to Dr Ferguson for obstetrical appliances and diagrams; and, July 19, £200 to Mr Moseley for the requirements of his department of natural and experimental philosophy, with an injunction " to use as much economy in the expenditure of the same as can be made consistent with the purposes of his lectures."

So far all was expenditure, and expenditure out of capital. On April 15, 1831, the council began to see the first definite prospect of some return; on that date, and regularly from that time onward, applications for admission both to the college and to the school were laid before the governing body, until, on October 1, the council decreed that in future " the principal be authorised to admit students conditionally on the subsequent sanction of the council." Nominations by proprietors and donors had precedence over applications from outsiders. It may be interesting to note that the first student admitted to the college was " Stapleton Cotton, aged 17 years, on the nomination of Mr Alderman Atkins," and that the first pupil accepted for the school was " R. Phillpotts, aged 13 years, on the nomination of the Right Hon. H. Hobhouse."

On August 30, 1881, the council considered recommendations of the education committee respecting the public opening of the institution. They resolved

> That the public opening of the college do take place on Saturday the 8th of October, and that His Grace, the Archbishop of Canterbury be invited to preside at the same; that the lectures in the medical department do commence on Monday the 10th, and that the several courses in the other departments open on Monday the 17th of the same month.

Further,

> The secretary was directed to intimate to the several professors that it is the wish of the council that they should prepare an introductory lecture to their respective courses with a view to the general attendance of the friends of the college at the said lecture.

§ 5. *The Great Day : October 8, 1831*

On October 8, 1831, the work of three laborious and anxious years was accomplished, and the college opened its portals to the world. As things turned out, a less auspicious day could hardly have been hit upon. For one thing, the weather was wet and cheerless, and a deep gloom hung over London and Westminster. For another thing, by a singular fatality, the preceding day (Friday, October 7) had been that on which, amid intense popular excitement, the House of Lords had been called upon to decide the fate of the second Reform Bill. The great debate had lasted all night, and at six o'clock on the morning of the very day on which King's College was to be opened the Lords had thrown the bill out by a majority of 41. Now in this majority of 41 there were 21 bishops, and it was thus obvious that if the episcopal bench had supported the measure, instead of almost solidly opposing it, the Reform Bill would have become law. Moreover, the speech which turned the balance against the bill was that of the Archbishop of

Canterbury. Hence, at the moment, of all persons in the Kingdom, the bishops—the founders, the patrons, the controllers of King's College—were the most intensely unpopular. For some days they went about in peril of their lives. The palace of the Bishop of Bristol was burned down by a howling mob. Dr Copleston noted in his diary that " the spirit of the populous towns is strong against the bishops." When at St Anne's, Soho, it was announced that Bishop Blomfield would preach on October 23, the parishioners told the rector that, if the bishop should attempt to do so, they would walk out of the church in a body, and so obvious was their intention of carrying out their threat that the rector begged the bishop to postpone his visitation. And Blomfield had not actually voted against the bill: he had absented himself altogether from the debate. But this did not mollify the reformers: " The Bishop of London," said the *Times,* " did not vote against the bill, but then he did not vote for it, and the nation will not be served by halves."

The prelates and peers, therefore, who made their way through menacing crowds and assembled at noon on October 8, 1831, in the unfinished hall of King's College to participate in the opening ceremony, made a very different appearance from the militant and enthusiastic throng who on June 21, 1828, under the presidency of a tory prime minister who seemed secure of a permanent dictatorship, had gathered in the Freemasons' Hall to launch the scheme. The attendance was thin, and the audience agitated and depressed. " We had to regret," said one of the reports,

> the absence of many noble and distinguished individuals, whom the very late debate in the House of Lords the same morning had prevented from attending; and the deep gloom and humidity of the day appeared to throw a damp over the whole proceedings.[1]

Bishop Copleston's diary gives us an interesting glimpse of the events of the day. " This morning," he wrote,

> about six o'clock, the House divided on the Reform Bill. I had been desirous of voting that the Bill might go into committee with a view to amendment; but the declaration of Lord Grey that no material amendment would be agreed to determined me and several others to vote against the second reading. Went to bed much exhausted at seven. I rose at nine to breakfast at Dr Hughes', where I met Sir Walter Scott, much recovered from his seizure but by no means what he was in his best days. At twelve I went to the opening of King's College, which lasted till four.

---

[1] *Gentleman's Magazine,* vol. ci, p. 349.

The main features of the opening ceremony, over which the Archbishop of Canterbury presided, were a sermon in the chapel at 1.30, by the Bishop of London, and, after a short interval, a lecture in the hall by Principal Otter. The sermon, which was subsequently printed and published, was one of remarkable eloquence and power. Taking as text 1 Corinthians xiii, 1-2, " Though I speak with the tongues of men and of angels," etc., Bishop Blomfield treated of that problem of the relation of religion to education the evasion of which was the main objection to the " University of London," the solution of which was the chief purpose of King's College. He advanced and maintained three theses : first, that knowledge of the material universe is good and necessary; that God has given us faculties by means of which that knowledge can be attained; and that these faculties should be used to the full; secondly, that the knowledge attained by man through the exercise of his faculties relates merely to processes and to secondary causes, never reaching to first causes or ultimate realities; and that knowledge of these mysteries can come only by way of divine revelation :

> There is something to be known above and beyond the universe and that is the nature and counsels of the Creator . . . and the nature and counsels of God are objects of knowledge only in so far as He Himself has been pleased to reveal them to us;

and, finally, that these matters of divine revelation are educationally incomparably more important than the discoveries of inductive science, for upon them depend man's character in this world, and his eternal destiny in the next. Hence,

> Every system of education which does not embrace instruction in the doctrines and duties of our holy religion is defective in that which alone can impart to human knowledge the principle of salubrity and life.

Wherefore, in King's College,

> Our desire is to erect the shrine of science and literature within the precincts of the sanctuary; to lay the foundations of public usefulness and individual happiness on the ground of right principle; and to promote the best interests of society by methods which tend to the glory of God.

The views expressed by Bishop Blomfield on this memorable occasion were precisely those which had been uttered by the Rev. Hugh James Rose in his great discourse before the University of Cambridge five years earlier; and they were precisely those which twenty years later were echoed before the new Catholic University in Dublin by Rose's quondam friend, Dr John Henry Newman, of the Oratory.

They were also, unhappily for the weary audience, precisely the same as those expressed by Principal Otter in a heavy lecture which filled out the remainder of the four hours. It was replete with classical references and poetical quotations; but it left the audience sleepy and dejected: it extended to the length, rather than rose to the height, of the occasion.

On the whole, the circumstances of the opening were not very cheerful nor the outlook of the college very hopeful. The pleasing unity of church and state which had marked the inaugural meeting was broken. Even the solidarity of the church was menaced by embittered faction. The flow of donations and subscriptions which had made 1828 so exhilarating had ceased, and the college opened altogether too near the verge of bankruptcy to be comfortable. The site which had been granted to the college was far less eligible both in size and position than had been anticipated, and its preparation had involved the council in ruinous expense. The college buildings were but half finished, and looming in the near distance lay the appalling obligation to finish off the river front in the style of Somerset House. Anxiety, rather than exultation, must have filled the minds of the founders of King's College as they made their way home amid the falling shadows of that wet and gloomy October Saturday. They were, however, brave and resolute men, full of faith and zeal, ready to face difficulties and turn adversity into success.

PART II

THE SEMINARY OF RELIGIOUS EDUCATION

CHAPTER V

THE STRUGGLE WITH ADVERSITY
1831–36

§ 1. *The Beginning of Work*

THE professors, as we have observed, had been warned that they would be expected to deliver inaugural lectures, each in his own subject, at the beginning of the session. These lectures were duly given; they were open to the public free of charge; and they drew large audiences of persons curious to see the new buildings and the strange performers. Six of these orations have been preserved to us in print. First, Professor Gilbert T. Burnett, on Tuesday, October 11, gave his " Introductory Lecture on Botany." The opening paragraph, containing the first recorded words of professorial wisdom ever publicly uttered in the college, must be quoted. It ran as follows:

> Gentlemen, meeting for the first time within these walls, for the first time treading on this now classic ground, it is natural to expect that the first thoughts conceived, the first words spoken, should be those of congratulation. Yes, now, if ever, may all concerned in the establishment of King's College be well permitted a moment's pause to indulge their feelings of honest pride in contemplating the progress of a work like this; a work so noble in its design, so grand in its execution, and so incalculably beneficent in its anticipated results. Based on the fear of God, and built for the love of man, we cannot doubt that with such a beginning, thus continued, our system of instruction will conduce to temporal good and tend to happiness eternal.

After continuing for some time on this exalted plane (although without so many unrelated participles), the professor descended to his main theme—viz., " What is a plant? What do we mean by the word vegetable?" This theme he discussed in a lecture which, if read as printed, must have exhausted two hours, and all its auditors, in delivery. Secondly, on the same day, Professor Daniell, the chemist, in a discourse of half the length and twice the pungency, criticized Charles Babbage's recent lament on *The Decline of Science in England*. Babbage had asked the chemists five rhetorical questions, of which the first was " Who among us has ever verified Ballard's and Serrulla's experiments upon brome? " and the last " Who can tell us anything of the sulpho-salts? " Professor Daniell gives him the required information, with compound interest, in each case, and concludes that the science of chemistry is not so decadent in England as the great mathematician would have us suppose. Thirdly, on Monday the 17th, Professor Anstice delivered a masterly and fascinating defence of the study of classical literature, dealing in turn with ancient history, ancient philosophy, ancient poetry, and finally the ancient languages themselves : it is a lecture of mature wisdom inspired by the enthusiasm of brilliant youth. Fourthly, on November 1, Professor Park, the jurist, discussed the uses of an academic, as distinct from a professional, study of law; contrasting the importance assigned to the theory of law on the Continent and in America with the exclusive devotion to practice evident in England.[1] Finally, the German professor, Dr Bernays, on November 2, and the French professor, M. Ventouillac, five days later, gave introductory surveys of the literatures of their respective countries.

Meantime, while these free oratorical displays to mixed audiences were taking place, the routine work of the college was slowly getting under way. It consisted of four different kinds—viz., in the higher department, or college proper : (1) the *general course*, consisting of divinity, taught by the principal; the classical languages, taught by Professor Anstice; mathematics, taught by Professor Hall; and English literature and history, divided (until 1835) between Anstice and Hall; (2) the *medical course*, an enormous and congested curriculum, framed to meet the requirements of the Society of Apothecaries and the College of Surgeons; it consisted of anatomy (Mayo and Partridge), botany (Burnett), chemistry (Daniell), *materia medica* (Bisset Hawkins), practice of medicine (Francis Hawkins), forensic medicine (Watson), midwifery (Ferguson), and surgery (Green) ; (3) *miscellaneous subjects*, such as law, political economy, geology, zoology, natural philosophy, and modern languages, unrelated to one another or to any systematic course of study

---

[1] Professor Park had over two hundred auditors at his (free) inaugural lecture. Of these, five only survived to continue the course. On the occasion of the third lecture the room was entirely empty !

at all, dependent for their continuance in the college curriculum, on the one hand, upon the attractiveness of the lecturer, and, on the other hand, upon the supply of " occasional students " sufficiently interested to keep up attendance; (4) the *junior department*, or *school*, down in the basement of the building; at first staffed by three teachers only—viz., the headmaster (Major), the second master (Edwards), and the writing master (Ribbans).

At first, probably, the work of teaching was not excessive in any section. Up to within seven days of the opening of the institution the council had admitted—if the minutes give a complete record—only nine to the college and twenty-seven to the school. But when the work was once going the numbers began to flow in rapidly, and before the end of the first session there were no fewer than 764 on the books. They were distributed as follows : in the higher department 66 regular and 149 occasional ; in the medical department 48 regular and 339 occasional ; and in the junior department 162.

The senior students, who took what was called the " course of general education," pursued the following curriculum : at 10 A.M. they all assembled in the college chapel for prayers, for which fifteen minutes were allowed; from 10.15 to 1 they devoted their time to classics and mathematics, except that on Tuesdays (10.15) they had an hour at English literature, and on Fridays (12.15) an hour at history—*i.e.*, at Koch's *Revolutions of Europe*. On Mondays at 1 the principal lectured on "the evidences of natural and revealed religion, and the doctrines and duties of Christianity, in conformity with the principles of the established church," and on Fridays at the same hour he examined his class on the same : the books studied in this divinity course were Paley, Butler, and the Greek Testament. Every Sunday morning, too, the principal preached in the college chapel, and all regular students in this department were expected to be present, unless they had obtained from the principal express exemption on the ground that they were going with their parents or guardians to some other place of Anglican worship. The afternoons of weekdays—Saturdays not excepted—were assigned to the non-compulsory subjects— *e.g.*, the sciences and modern languages. General students took as many or as few of these as, subject to the consent of the principal, they desired. The fees charged for this general course were £21 per annum to students who secured a nomination from a " proprietor " (*i.e.*, donor or shareholder); £26 5*s*. to those who did not.

U SCHULA U
PSYCH.-ED.

It will be observed that the education provided in this general course was of an order now regarded as proper to a school rather than to a university. It was based on text-books and did not seek to go beyond them; it was imparted by pedagogues and not acquired by independent effort. It was, indeed, precisely the same sort of education as was at that very time being imparted by Arnold to his sixth form at Rugby, and it was imparted for the very same reasons as those which inspired Arnold. The "senior department" of King's College at this date was indeed—apart from its medical and occasional activities—a finishing school for boys going into business, and a scholarship class for those destined for Oxford or Cambridge.

The medical curriculum was a frightful thing. The course usually lasted three years, and its content was determined by the regulations of the Society of Apothecaries (whose licence was needed by all who wished to act as general practitioners), supplemented by those of the Royal College of Surgeons. These bodies insisted that during the first session the young medical student should attend a hundred lectures in chemistry, a hundred in *materia medica*, fifty in botany, as well as a course in theoretical and practical anatomy. In the second session attendance at hospitals began; but with it went a hundred lectures on the theory and practice of medicine, and fifty lectures on forensic medicine, besides the courses on anatomy as before. Most of this continued in the third session, with the addition of a course of sixty lectures on midwifery. In order to pack this gigantic mass of cramming into the prescribed period abnormal hours were necessary. Every day at 8 A.M. for six days in the week Professor Burnett held forth on botany. Chemistry for the first year, principles and practice of medicine for the other years, ran from 9 to 10. Then came an interval of fifteen minutes, during which the students could, if they chose, go to chapel. From 10.15 to 11 anatomy was demonstrated; from 11 to 12 the courses on *materia medica* and midwifery were given. From 12 to 3 was an "interval for hospital attendance or practical anatomy"; the course on forensic medicine was delivered from 4 to 5; the principles and practice of surgery were expounded by Professor Green between 8 and 9 P.M. It is no doubt true that no individual student had in any one session to go through the whole of this appalling programme; but it is certain that all the medical professors—who were busy professional men with hospitals or private practices to attend to—were heavily overworked, and that all the students were enormously over-lectured, over-crammed, and over-examined. Religious observances were optional for medical students, and not compulsory as with students taking the general course. The prospectus ran :

> The council are aware that the great majority of medical students, during the time of their residence in the metropolis, have so many demands on their attention within the limits of their own peculiar pursuits, as to leave them but little leisure for other branches of study. They expect, however, that all who belong to the class of King's College Students of Medicine and Surgery will be regular in their attendance at divine worship in the college chapel on Sundays in the forenoon; and they hope that the students may be able to avail themselves, to a certain extent at least, of the opportunities of religious instruction afforded by the lectures of the principal.

Before long, as we shall later remark, special prizes were instituted to encourage piety in the profession.

The fee for the complete medical course was £50 to nominees; £54 12s. to others.

§ 2. *The Progress of King's College School*

Of all the sections of the college, the " junior department " or school was the one most immediately and strikingly success-ful. It supplied a pressing want—viz., a good day school for the sons of middle-class parents wherein not only classics and mathematics, but also modern languages and natural science could be studied. Its numbers went up by leaps and bounds, and for five years the council were constantly called upon to face urgent calls for increase of accommodation, enlargement of staff, dining-halls, recreation rooms, boarding-houses, and so on. The roll in 1832 showed an attendance of some 150; in 1833 the numbers had gone up to 319; in 1834 to 404. So embarrassing was this sudden influx that on February 1834 the council had to pass a resolution that

> in consequence of the rapid increase in the number of pupils in the junior department, no admissions be made after their numbers shall have reached 400, excepting upon the nomination of pro-prietors.

Nevertheless, in 1835 the names on the roll reached the total of 461.[1]

---

[1] Later years showed a slight diminution—viz., in 1836, 419, and in 1837, 380.

The teaching capacity of the three original members of the staff—Messrs Major, Edwards, and Ribbans—was, of course, soon exceeded. Assistant masters had to be secured in rapid succession. We need not record a number of temporary appointments. The more permanent additions to the staff were a "third master," the Rev. J. Fearnley (February 10, 1832); a "fourth master," Mr (later the Rev.) R. Hodgson (March 9, 1832); a "fifth master," Mr George Blake (December 14, 1832); and assistants for writing, drawing, fencing, French and German. The question of the payment of this large and varied staff caused the finance committee and the council much concern. At first they adopted the simple plan of a capitation fee: according to a scale adopted May 18, 1832, for every pupil in the school the headmaster was to receive £4 4s. (with an additional £1 1s. per head for the first hundred); the second master £2 2s.; the third master, the writing master, and the French master £1 1s. each per head. These payments exhausted rather more than one-half of the fees paid by the pupils, who were charged £15 15s. a year if nominated by a proprietor, or £18 15s. if not so nominated. There was obviously no margin left out of which to pay any further assistants who might be required: when, therefore, Mr Edwards asked for help, and Mr Hodgson was appointed, Mr Edwards had to provide his salary; similarly, Mr Blake was dependent on the headmaster. This was an unsatisfactory condition of things, even though it imposed no great hardship on Messrs Major and Edwards. For according to the 1832 scale, when the number of the school reached 404, the headmaster was reaping over £1800 in fees, and the second master nearly £850. When it is remembered that the principal of the whole college was managing the establishment, was preaching in the chapel, lecturing in divinity, and conducting weekly examinations, for a fixed stipend of £800, and when it is remembered, too, that the professors in the upper regions of the institution were conducting classes which yielded them sums varying from £400 a year down to nothing, it will be realized that the schoolmasters toiling like moles in the subterranean vaults of the building were the most prosperous persons on the premises. It is probable that the lowliest writing master in the school was making more than the most eminent professor in the college. In June 1834 the anomaly of the situation was such that the council drastically revised the mode of payment in the school. The normal number in the school was assumed to be 350: for any figure up to this 350, fixed salaries were to be paid as follows: the headmaster, £1050; the second, £500; the third, £300; the fourth, £200; the fifth, £150. For each boy in the school beyond the normal 350, capitation fees were to be paid at the respective rates of £2, £1, 15*s.*, 10*s.*, and 5*s.* The terms for the various assistants need not detain us.

If justification were needed for this revolution in the mode of remuneration, it would be found in the heavy expenses which were falling upon the council in respect of the increased accommodation required by the expanding school. The first demand for more rooms came before the council on January 13, 1832, and subsequent demands were incessant. In December 1832 a recreation room was fitted up in the basement, under the great hall, at a cost of £320. The provision of a refectory under the terrace on the river front was, later on, another big expense.

School hours at first were fixed at 9 A.M. to 3 P.M. in the winter, and 9 A.M. to 4 P.M. in the spring and the summer, with a one-hour interval for refreshment and recreation. The inconvenience of the change of time-table, however, was so great that in April 1836 the hours 9–3 were made uniform throughout the year, the interval being reduced to thirty minutes.

The main function of the junior department of King's College, as we have already noted, was to feed the senior department, and the headmaster was forbidden to accept as a pupil in his subterranean regions any boy over sixteen years of age, on the ground that his place was up aloft. But, although the school in the basement remained the principal feeder of the sons of light, it did not continue to be the only one. We have observed how, in response to a letter from the Rev. H. H. Norris of Hackney, the provisional committee in 1829 had instituted a system of affiliation by which schools that pledged themselves to the religious principles of King's College could be taken into " union " with the college. Before the college opened, five schools had applied for the privilege.[1] Other applications came in later; some were granted; others, after careful consideration of the adequacy of the religious guarantees, declined. At the end of the period that we are now concerned with, viz., the date of Principal Otter's resignation, August 1836, the following were the eleven " Grammar Schools in union with King's College " : (1) Hackney, (2) St Peter's, Eaton Square, (3) Kensington, (4) Stockwell, (5) Stepney, (6) the Philological School, Gloucester Place, (7) Camberwell,

[1] See above, p. 82.

103

(8) Blackheath Proprietary, (9) Forest, (10) West Ham, (11) Western. Beyond a certain prestige which these schools gained by affiliation, the only advantage which accrued to them was a common prize-giving in the great hall of the college when the Archbishop of Canterbury distributed the awards.

§ 3. *Changes in the Senior Department*

While the junior department of the college increased by leaps and bounds, swelling so far beyond the modest dimensions originally assigned to it that within three years of its opening a maximum limit to its expansion had to be assigned, the senior department of the college remained almost stationary in respect of regular students; and in respect of occasional students even tended to decline. During the five years under review (1831–36) the number of students taking the regular " course of general education " was, successively, about 64, 109, 104, 133, and 120; the number of occasional students fell from about 300 in the session 1831–32 to 105 in the session 1835–36. The stability, round about 100, of the numbers of regular students can readily be accounted for by the nature of the education provided in the " general course." It was, as we have seen, of the finishing school type; and the number of boys whose parents wished them to put in a couple or three years in a new institution between leaving their secondary school at sixteen and going either into business or to the university at eighteen or nineteen was strictly limited; it never at any time exceeded 156 (1848), and after 1854 it never again reached the normal 100. The decline in occasional students is probably explicable by the wearing off of the novelty of the new college; by the deaths or resignations of some of the more popular lecturers; and by the growingly academic nature of the courses given.

Changes in the staff were painfully frequent during these formative five years. Of the twelve original professors of the college (other than those of medicine) only five remained in 1836: no fewer than five had died; two of the most eminent had resigned. As to the deaths: the first to depart this life was Don Pablo de Mendibil, whose decease was reported to the council in January 1832: he faded away imperceptibly without leaving a single discoverable footstep on such portion of the sands of time as have accumulated in King's College. His place was taken (February 1832) by Señor I. M. X. de Alcalá, sometime professor of philosophy in the university of Seville. The second to go was Professor Ventouillac. He was soon followed by the able lawyer J. J. Park: on April 19, 1833, he was reported to be ill, and Mr H. N. Coleridge (quondam secretary to the provisional committee) was appointed to act as his deputy; on May 31 his death was announced, and on August 9 Mr John William Spurrier, of Lincoln's Inn, was elected to the vacant chair. Park, during his short tenure of his professorship, had done some excellent and valuable work; in particular he had delivered a well-arranged course of lectures on conveyancing law, and had published a masterly dissertation, marked by moderation of tone and maturity of judgment, on the burning question of the day—viz., constitutional reform. Mr Spurrier held the chair of law for only two years : in February 1835 the council accepted his resignation and in the following June appointed Mr Richard Preston, K.C., as his successor. The fourth death to be announced (August 1835) was that of the indefatigable Professor Burnett, the botanist. It must have been a strain to deliver lectures to medical students every day of the week, except Sunday, at eight o'clock in the morning; but probably what wore him out was the delivery of inaugural orations of inordinate prolixity— among the King's College papers are no fewer than four. He left a reputation as an enthusiastic teacher, and there can be no doubt that as the result of his life's labours the definition of the term " vegetable " was made more precise. Last of all came the tragic blow of the death of Professor Anstice at the early age of twenty-eight. He had been in failing health for some time, and in May 1835 he had felt compelled to resign his chair. In reply to his communication the following letter was sent :

> The Council of King's College have received with great concern from Professor Anstice the resignation of his professorship. They regret on every account the necessity of his retirement, and they desire to express to him the strong sense they entertain of the benefits which he has conferred upon the institution, as well by his zeal and ability in the discharge of his duties, as by the influence of his character and conduct upon his pupils and the other members of the college.

Early in 1836 he died, and on March 11 of that year it was resolved to set up a memorial to him in the college chapel. The Rev. Robert William Browne, M.A., Fellow and Tutor of St John's College, Oxford, was appointed to succeed him (June 27, 1836).

Some time before Professor Anstice's resignation, he and Professor Hall had asked to be relieved of their English teaching, and (January 1833) they had received permission to obtain assistance, provided they paid for it themselves. In June 1835, when the classical chair was vacant, the council decided to establish the long-projected chair of English literature and history, and they offered the post to the Rev. Thomas Dale, M.A.[1] We have already heard of Mr Dale : he had been the first professor of English at the " University of London " in Gower Street (1828–30) and as such had been the prime mover in the founding of that theological institution by means of which the anglican members of the staff had vainly tried to insulate the episcopal thunderbolts. In 1830 he had accepted an incumbency at Denmark Hill, and in that neighbourhood he had opened a school to which John Ruskin had been sent as a pupil. When, five years later, he was invited to King's College he had just been inducted into the important living of St Bride's in Fleet Street. The comparatively light supplementary work at King's, in a subject that he loved, suited him well.

---

[1] The following interesting letter, the original of which has been generously presented to the College by Professor Sir Israel Gollancz, indicates that Robert Southey, the poet laureate, was invited before Mr Dale to fill the chair.

> " 7 Bedford Square,
> "26 May, 1835

" My dear Friend,

" I do not forget our correspondence on the subject of the appointment of a Professor of English Literature at King's College, London, and the answer from you with which that correspondence closed, and, therefore, I ought perhaps to apologise to you for again giving you any trouble in the matter ; but the Council, though they cannot feel more strongly now than they felt before the advantage that the institution would derive from your acceptance of an office in it, yet believe themselves to be now so much more fixed in public opinion than they were at the date of my former communication to you, that they can hardly consider that the circumstances of the application are similar, or that your answer would necessarily be the same. I must preface my question with one further observation, namely that no appointment of a Professor of English Literature, as such, has ever yet been made by the Council. Under these circumstances, accordingly, the Committee of Education wish to submit to your decision the following proposal, namely, that you should, under the denomination of Professor of English Literature, give for the next three years lectures in English Literature in the King's College as follows, that is to say, twelve between Michaelmas and Christmas, and six between Christmas and Easter, or, if you would prefer it, between Easter and Midsummer ; that you should be assured in the receipt of two hundred pounds (£200) per annum, and, further, of a given proportion of the pupil fee above a given number, say £4 out of £6 to be paid by each pupil above 50, which, as the class would probably exceed one hundred, would be £200 more ; and, in addition, that, subject to the regulations of the College, you should be at liberty to receive in your lecture-room subscribers from the world at large. I need scarcely add that the lectures which you would deliver would be subsequently published, with probably more advantage than if they had not been so delivered.

> " Believe me,
> " Ever your obliged and faithful friend,
> " Robert Harry Inglis

" To Robert Southey, Esq., Poet Laureate "

He accepted the council's offer and joined the staff of the college, bringing Ruskin with him as a student. He was a churchman of the evangelical school, a preacher of great power and popularity. His coming was a notable indication that King's College was not to be identified with any one section of the establishment.

Besides the changes in the senior department caused by the five deaths just recorded, two others occurred as the result of resignations. The first calls for no comment : we have already noted that Mr Nassau Senior between the date of his appointment and the opening of the college was made a tithe-commissioner by the government. His formal resignation was received in March 1832; but not until January 1833 was the Rev. Richard Jones elected to succeed him. Mr Jones gave two courses of lectures, one on the wages of labour (1833) and the other on the progress of opinions on political economy in England (1834). In 1835 he was called to the East India Company's college at Haileybury, and the chair of political economy at King's College ceased to interest him. He did not resign it, however, until 1854.

The resignation of the great geologist, Professor Charles Lyell, was a more important and significant matter—a matter, too, not without its element of mystery. Of all the lecturers in the college Lyell was the most popular. He was a first-rate speaker; he had new material of the highest interest to lay before his hearers; he was a pioneer of revolutionary ideas which affected not only his own subject but also the current theology. The publication of the second volume of his *Principles of Geology* at the beginning of 1832 was an epoch-making event : it revealed an earth which had been countless millions of years in the making, as distinct from an earth created by a single divine fiat " on Sunday, October 23rd, B.C. 4004," as Archbishop Ussher had computed. It manifested to the astonished minds of men an infinity of time as difficult of harmonization with prevalent creeds as had been Copernicus's demonstration of the infinity of space with the mediæval cosmology. No wonder then that, when it became known that the substance of Lyell's third and concluding volume would be delivered at King's College in the form of popular lectures during the summer term of 1832, the learned world, together with its wives and daughters, pressed to hear the great man. The clerical governors of King's College also came, proud and gratified, but anxious and hesitant—Principal Otter, Dr D'Oyly, Archdeacon Cambridge, the Rev. John Lonsdale, together with the Rev. R. W. Jelf, a later principal of King's, always a pillar of orthodoxy, and a specialist on the approaching end of the world and the eternity of future punishment. Lyell recognized that he was skating on thin ice : " I worked hard," he tells us in his journal,

> upon the subject of the connection of geology and natural theology, and pointed out that the system which does not find traces of a beginning . . . is the most sublime ;

and he put himself in an impregnable position by quoting from Bishop Blomfield's magnificent inaugural sermon the passage :

> It is impossible that true religion can be injured by the ascertainment and establishment of any fact ; nor by any induction which may be legitimately drawn from facts.

He left his hearers to infer from these eloquent words the inevitable conclusion—extremely embarrassing at that time— that true religion did not involve the acceptance, in the literal sense, of the story of the creation as told in Genesis.

The situation was a delicate one. It was dealt with tactfully by the council. On May 18, 1832, according to the minutes of that body,

> it was resolved that the attendance of ladies be not permitted at any course of lectures to be hereafter read in the college, and that the several professors be made acquainted with this regulation.

Their wives and daughters thus being excluded, the learned world also stopped away, and Professor Lyell found his audience reduced to fifteen. He thus records the episode in a letter to his friend, Dr Fleming :

> The King's College governors determined this year that ladies should not enter my lecture-room, because it diverted the attention of the young students, of whom I had two. . . . My class being thus cut down to fifteen, I gave them a short course . . . but I would not give the time to such a class again.[1]

He resolved to depart from King's; but in carrying his resolution into effect he showed a tact not inferior to that of the council. He informed the principal that the task of preparing his great book for the press would be so heavy that he would not be able to spare any time for lectures for at least a year. " Otter," he told Babbage, " paid me the compliment of being

---

[1] *Life, Letters, and Journals of Sir Charles Lyell*, vol. i, pp. 396–397.

quite down in the mouth." [1] A harmless substitute was asked to take the lectures in the summer of 1833. On October 11 of that year Lyell's formal resignation came before the council :

> The principal having laid before the council a letter from Professor Lyell stating his inability to deliver any lectures during the next two years, and tendering the resignation of his professorship in consequence, it was resolved that the council in accepting the resignation by Professor Lyell are desirous to express to him their regret that any circumstances should have compelled him to resign an office which he has filled so highly to the credit of the college.

Only two further items of this edifying story need to be chronicled. (1) On June 8, 1832, the chairman of the council, the Bishop of Llandaff, appended a note to the resolution of the preceding month respecting the exclusion of ladies : " This resolution was not passed at the council of May 18, but was postponed." (2) Professor Lyell gave a highly popular course of public lectures before large audiences at the Royal Institution in the summer of 1833, in addition to a small class at King's College.

As one reads this record of tactful consideration, one is filled with admiration : the council had avoided the conversion of Lyell into Galileo, and Lyell had refrained from exhibiting the council as the inquisition. Nevertheless, the greatest geologist of the day was lost to the college, and in his place was seated (January 1834) a certain Mr John Phillips, who was permitted to hold the professorship at King's in conjunction with the curatorship of the museum at York. There was no need to make regulations as to who should, or who should not, attend his lectures.

Whilst the department of geology subsided into insignificance under Professor Phillips, the department of natural history and zoology expired under Professor Rennie. It seems to have languished from the first : in April 1832 the council declined to expend £20 on materials; on August 1, 1834, it resolved " that the professorship of natural history and zoology be discontinued, and that Professor Rennie be informed of such discontinuance." Apparently if he had not been informed of the fact he would not have become aware of it. His connexion with King's College having been severed, he migrated to Australia, where he spent the remainder of his life studying the habits of the strange birds that he found there.

[1] June 3, 1832. *Op. cit.*, vol. i, p. 387.

§ 4. *New Developments*

Whilst these changes were transpiring in the college, certain important new developments were taking place.

On June 8, 1832, the Rev. Michael Solomon Alexander was appointed professor of Hebrew and Rabbinical Literature to the college. He was a converted Polish Jew, and an active agent of the society for promoting Christianity among his people. On November 17 he delivered his inaugural lecture, in which he discussed, among other things, the problem whether or not Hebrew was the language spoken in the Garden of Eden.

In July 1833 Mr Felix V. Seddon was made professor of Oriental Languages. He seems to have been a man of enormous erudition, for his inaugural lecture on " The Languages and Literature of Asia," which, as printed, with notes, extends to sixty-seven octavo pages, is almost illegible to the ordinary Englishman by reason of the number and variety of its hieroglyphics. The study of the oriental languages was power-fully assisted in 1835 by the splendid gift of a fine collection of oriental books by Mr William Marsden.

Although Professor Alexander ultimately became Bishop of Jerusalem, and, as such, gave John Henry Newman the final push which sent him into the Church of Rome; and although Professor Seddon after four years returned to India as tutor to the Nizam, neither of these men can compare in importance with a colleague who joined them on the college staff in June 1834. For this was none other than Charles Wheatstone, a man whose name stands in the front rank among the discoverers and inventors of the nineteenth century; the man to whom were due many of the modern marvels of electric telegraphy, of stereoscopy, and of spectrum analysis. Hitherto the Rev. Henry Moseley had professed both natural and experimental philosophy, that is to say both theoretical and applied physics. Now the two subjects were separated. The minutes of June 20, 1834, record that

> The principal having communicated Professor Moseley's con-sent that a professor of experimental philosophy should be ap-pointed, he retaining the professorship of natural philosophy and astronomy, [it was] resolvedthat Mr Charles Wheatstone be accordingly appointed professor of experimental philosophy.

At the next meeting of the council £50 was placed at his disposal for the provision of apparatus, and on February 5, 1836,

The council approve of Professor Wheatstone's laying down a series of iron and copper wires in the vaults of the college for the purpose of trying some experiments in electricity on account and at the expense of the Royal Society.

Are there many earlier references to the electric telegraph?

It will be remembered that one of the original chairs established in the college was the chair of "the principles and practice of commerce," and further that a certain Joseph Lowe was appointed to fill the chair. That seems to have been the end of the matter. No classes appear ever to have been held, and Professor Lowe's name was quietly dropped from the prospectus. At the general court, however, held in April 1835, the council announced that they were "engaged in the consideration of a plan" for the revival of this commercial course, and in June of that year they formulated this scheme. It was as follows :

(1)	Christian instruction	*The Rev. the Principal*
(2)	General principles of trade currency, exchanges, mercantile accounts, geography, the history of commerce and commercial nations, and of foreign and domestic products	*Professor of the Principles and Practice of Commerce*
(3)	English literature and modern history	*Professor of English Literature*
(4)	French, and either German, Spanish, or Italian	*Professors of Modern Languages*

No new professor of commerce, however, was appointed until 1855, and for twenty years the scheme remained in abeyance.

A more effective piece of organization had taken place in the preceding year. For three successive sessions the "general course" of divinity, classics, mathematics, and English had been pursued, and it had become painfully evident that it started from nowhere and led to nothing. At best it was but a link between secondary school and university, and even so its length was undetermined. No one session's work had any necessary relation to the work of either the preceding or the succeeding session. Students drifted in at any time and dropped out at any other time, picking up whatever happened to be doled out in the interval. All was chaotic and aimless. Hence on December 13, 1833, the council appointed a committee consisting of Bishop Copleston, Dr D'Oyly, Dr Shepherd, and

Mr Lonsdale, to frame a consistent and continuous course. The committee reported on February 14, 1834, and the council accepted its report and ordered it to be published. The new scheme was headed " Senior Department in General Literature." The prospectus stated that the council " consider a period of not less than three years to be requisite for the completion of education in this department," and it sketched a three-year course of study : the basis each year was the old *quadrivium* of divinity, classics, mathematics, and English ; but in the second and third years other subjects, according to choice, were added. Finally :

> After the completion of a period of not less than three years, those students who shall have obtained testimonials from the principal and professors, stating that they have passed with credit through the course prescribed, and that their general conduct and attendance on the service of the college chapel have been satisfactory, will be entitled to a certificate setting forth these particulars and distinguishing them by the title of Associates of King's College (A.K.C.).

Thus did King's College take the first step toward educational independence, establishing a course of study which should be an end in itself, and not a mere means to an entrance scholarship at Oxford or Cambridge. It is interesting to note that the first person to receive the new A.K.C. certificate (May 15, 1835) was that same Stapleton Cotton who had been the first to be admitted to the college four years earlier.

One of the essential conditions of the acquisition of the A.K.C. was, it will be observed, regular attendance at the college chapel. Service was held every weekday at 10 A.M., and also on Sunday morning, when the principal preached a sermon. The first chaplain appointed (October 31, 1831) was the Rev. Professor Moseley, who held the post, at a salary of £105 per annum, for just over three years. Then, early in 1834, the Rev. John Allen—who had come to the college in 1833 as mathematical assistant to Professor Hall—received the appointment, which he continued to hold till 1846. He was a notable man, who became an intimate friend of Hugh James Rose and John Lonsdale. By the latter he was taken away in 1846 to the diocese of Lichfield and made examining chaplain and archdeacon. Outsiders were admitted to the Sunday services, and such as wished were allowed to acquire regular sittings at the rate of £1 1s. each per annum. Until the spring of 1835 the music in the chapel was provided by a barrel-organ hired from a certain Mr Bryceson for £21 a year. On March 13, 1835, however, the council resolved

> That the present barrel-organ in the chapel be removed, and that it be replaced by Mr Bryceson by a finger-organ, inclosed in the same case, to contain four stops, namely, open diapason, stopped diapason, principal, and chorus of three ranks, with a Venetian shell front, and two pedals for piano, the full compass of keys from double G to F in alt, 58 semitones with an octave foot-pedal; the cost of the said finger-organ not to exceed £110.

Mr Bryceson accordingly set to work to remove the mechanism and substitute the keyboard. Whilst he was at work, however, a generous medical student of the college, Terry by name, who happened to have an organ among his *bric-à-brac*, offered it to the council, who gratefully accepted it (April 27). Mr Bryceson was asked to desist from his transformation, and was compensated (£20) for his pain and loss. Mr Terry's organ was duly installed. On November 13, 1835, Mr Henry Bevington was appointed organist, the first to hold that office in the college, if we except the nameless executant who, before the days of the finger-organ, turned the handle, wound the key, or operated the levers which determined (within the limits fixed by the designer) the nature, the volume, and the duration of the melodies emitted by its predecessor.[1]

§ 5. *Troubles in the Medical School*

The institution of the A.K.C. in 1834 indicated that in the department of general education King's College was feeling its way toward individuality and independence. The same movement was evident in the medical school, where indeed the need of autonomy and self-sufficiency was even more urgent. The two great handicaps under which the school laboured were : first, the inability of its teachers to determine their own curriculum, and the difficulty which they experienced in satisfying the enormous requirements of the curriculum imposed upon

---

[1] It must have been just at this period of organic transmutation that Thomas Carlyle attended King's College chapel to hear John Sterling preach. " Another time—of date probably very contiguous—I remember hearing Sterling preach. It was in some new college-chapel in Somerset House—I suppose what is now called King's College—a very quiet small place, the audience student-looking youths, with a few elder people, perhaps mostly friends of the preacher's," etc. (Carlyle's *Life of John Sterling*, Part II, chapter iii.) Carlyle does not mention the music. It would be interesting to know whether or not he was able, by the light of his undoubted genius, to distinguish between a barrel-organ and a finger-organ.

H

them by the Society of Apothecaries and the College of Surgeons; secondly, the lack of a hospital wherein their students, under the direction of their teachers, could obtain the necessary training in the practice of medicine and surgery. This second handicap became an increasingly heavy one; for the great London hospitals—Middlesex, Guy's, St Thomas's, Westminster, Charing Cross—were all developing medical schools of their own, and were showing a diminishing willingness to admit students of another school which they came to regard as a rival. Most of the King's College medical professors were associated with one or other of these great hospitals, and they then found, not only their time occupied away from the college, but their allegiance divided. Friction, too, arose among members of the medical staff concerning the division of their duties and the partition of the fees, until in May 1836 the *London Medical and Surgical Journal* drew public attention to " the squabbling and quarrelling " that was going on in the college. It would appear, further, that some of the professors were inefficient: Mayo, though a good anatomist, could not lecture; Francis Hawkins, though admirable at the bedside of a sick patient, was helpless in the presence of a class. A letter to the secretary of the college, dated April 27, 1834, from Dr F. H. Ramadge, a noted physician of his day, spoke of the medical school as " reduced to zero," and mentioned the contempt with which the students regarded some of their teachers, saying in particular that

> the distinctive epithet of " Fanny Hawkins," given to one of your learned professors, shews the veneration with which your students must regard the diplomaed successor of Hippocrates and Galen.

In these circumstances the King's College medical school declined: its regular students sank from 77 in 1832–33 to 66 in 1833–34, and again to 42 in 1834–35. Nor did occasional students make up the deficiency—they too fell from 233 to 175 in the three years. Hence the school ceased to pay its way: on May 15, 1835, the council recorded the painful fact that

> in the investigation of the accounts they observe that—independent of any proportion of the general expenses of the college, rent, or repairs—the special expenditure of the medical school is estimated to amount to £1100 and the receipts to £820, leaving a loss to the college of £280.

They therefore informed the medical professors, first, that they must economize; secondly, that they must make good any final deficiency out of the proportions of the fees paid to them. The medical professors professed cheerfully to accede to this requirement; nevertheless, in spite of this expression of resignation, they incontinently began to resign. In the autumn of 1835 Dr Bisset Hawkins vacated the chair of *materia medica*; in May 1836 Mr J. H. Green surrendered the professorship of surgery, and Dr Francis Hawkins that of medicine; in August 1836 Professor Mayo found himself compelled to go. Sir Henry Halford, the intimate friend of the two Hawkins, feeling himself to be involved in the brawl, refused any longer to serve on the council. There was a general hullabaloo.

The council had the utmost difficulty in filling up the vacant professorships. Passion ran high. The friends of the recent holders refused to apply; many of those who did apply, and some who were actually invited to become candidates, were ultimately rejected because of their failure to pass the religious test—a certain Dr John Webster, for instance, who had actually deputized for Dr Bisset Hawkins for two whole terms, was refused appointment to the chair of *materia medica*, for which he was eminently qualified, because he was a presbyterian ! If, it was asked, the college accepts professors of modern languages even though they are nominally catholics and actually atheists, on what logical principle does it refuse to appoint a presbyterian to a medical chair? The problem of conformity was raised in an acute form, and a storm raged in the professional press. Ultimately, and after some rearrangement, the chairs were filled, but, with one outstanding exception, the new holders were markedly inferior to their predecessors. The faithful, capable, and popular Richard Partridge, already on the staff, succeeded Mayo in the chair of anatomy; Dr Thomas Watson was transferred from the chair of forensic medicine to that which Dr Francis Hawkins had vacated, a certain unknown and undistinguished Dr Fergus taking his former post; Dr Bisset Hawkins was succeeded by an equally obscure Mr J. F. Royle, a mere botanist, skilled in Indian vegetation. A surgeon to take Green's place was ultimately found in Mr J. M. Arnott of the Middlesex Hospital. Commenting on these new appointments the *London Medical and Surgical Journal* said (May 28, 1836):

> Lecturers of acknowledged talent, men of the first walk in their respective departments of science, applied for professorships. How were their applications treated? Why, rejected, refused; not because the candidates were incapable of filling the vacant offices, not because they had any stain upon their moral character.

No, but simply because they were not members of the Established Church of England. What results could be contemplated from bigotry and exclusiveness of this character? The council in their blindness expected that it would increase the prosperity of the school; they believed that the admission of such men as Faraday and Ritchie would be the means of withdrawing the patronage of many of the clerical and lay lords from the institution! The gentlemen named were not of the high-church party, and therefore could not impart knowledge to students professing that creed. And thus have the masters of King's College stultified themselves. They have educated pupils of all sects and denominations, in spite of the regulations they professed to start with; but they have rejected the very first men in science because they were not of a particular belief.

Five weeks later (July 2, 1836) it returned to the charge: " The directors of King's College," it said, with special reference to Messrs Royle and Fergus,

> have elected persons to the vacant offices who have little to recommend them except that they are either friends of some of the committee, or that they are of the right high-church party. Was it not possible to get men of some established reputation, known as scientific individuals, and capable of affording instruction to students? Or did every such person shrink from a connection with a half-ruined medical school? We fear that no one of an established reputation could be prevailed on to join it. There is no honour in being elected to a professorship in such an establishment, where the merits of the candidates are never considered, but where party feeling, politics, and a particular creed are looked upon as the necessary and highest qualifications.

This furious assault, which, though excessive in its violence, was not without justification, marks the darkest hour of the King's College medical school. The man, however, who was destined to restore its fortunes was among those appointed in the midst of this very crisis. On August 19, 1836, Dr Robert Bentley Todd was elected to a new chair, carved out of that composite professorship originally held by Dr Mayo—the chair of physiology and of morbid anatomy. He was a young Irish anglican who had already distinguished himself by his lectures at a private medical school, and by his demonstrations at the Westminster Hospital. A born organizer and pioneer, endowed with boundless energy and enthusiasm, he soon envisaged the need of the King's medical school and the sources of its weakness. With the cordial help of three great principals—Rose, Lonsdale, and Jelf—he set to work, first, to emancipate the medical staff from the excessive burden of religious tests; secondly, to secure for the college freedom from the fetters of the Society of Apothecaries; thirdly, to encourage medical education by means of scholarships; fourthly, to improve discipline and supervision of work by introducing the collegiate system; finally, and above all, to establish a King's College Hospital in the neighbourhood of the Strand wherein the students of the medical school of the college could gain their practical experience. On May 5, 1835, the minutes of the council record that

> The medical professors are of opinion that a hospital in the immediate neighbourhood of, and connected with, King's College, would offer the most effectual means of strengthening the medical school of that institution.

Once again, on June 12 of the same year, returning to the theme, and entering into more minute detail, the minutes state that

> The medical professors, considering a hospital to be of the utmost importance to the prosperity of the medical school of King's College, further believe that it should be placed in the immediate neighbourhood of the college, and are of the opinion that an application to the Government from the Council for a lease of a part of Somerset House would meet with success.

Apparently, whenever Somerset House was not trying to swallow King's College, the college was trying to swallow Somerset House! It was not there, however, that King's College Hospital was to be placed; but it was Dr Robert Bentley Todd who was destined to do more than any other man to realize the pious aspirations of his predecessors.

§ 6. *The Process of Building*

Before the question of the provision of a hospital in the vicinity of the college could be so much as considered, the completion of the college itself had to be taken in hand. Without endowments, unaided by government grants, with original funds depleted to the minimum, deserted by donors who refused to redeem their promises and by subscribers who declined to pay their contributions, burdened with a medical department which did not cover its cost, the council had to face the task of fitting up class-rooms, providing museums, equipping refectories, and, above all, of erecting the river front, including the principal's house. This last was the millstone round their necks; they were pledged by their bond to complete the work by June 1834, and the cost would be anything between £10,000 and £20,000. The funds were simply not there. The college was already living on its scanty capital: the £27,000 of exchequer bills with which it began its course in October 1831 had by May 1832 been reduced by repeated sales to £7000. The only source of income was the fees of the students, and during the first session (1831–32) these failed to cover the current expenditure by no less than £1420. Even without the incubus of further building, bankruptcy appeared imminent. Happily the rapid development of the junior department or school wiped off the deficit and for three successive years enabled current expenses to be met; but once again, in 1835, the decline of the medical faculty was expected to produce an adverse balance.

There was nothing for it but another call upon the generosity of pious benefactors. Early in 1832 a private appeal was made which by May, together with a legacy of £1000 which fortunately became available at the moment, produced nearly £4000. Sir Robert Smirke—he had just been knighted—was instructed to set to work on the river front, and do what he could for an outlay not exceeding £6000. Within a year rather more than this sum (£6339) had been expended, and the work was not quite half finished. The situation was desperate. No more money was available. Smirke was ordered (April 26, 1833) to suspend operations, and a special meeting of the general court of proprietors was summoned for May 31, 1833, to decide what should be done. The meeting was duly held in the great hall of the college under the presidency of the Archbishop; a full report on the situation was presented; the need of a further £8000 was announced; and the following resolution was unanimously carried:

> That it appears of essential importance that the works for completing the river front should be immediately resumed; that exertions should therefore be made by the friends of the institution to raise the necessary funds; that every proprietor be earnestly solicited to make an addition of *ten per cent.* to his former contribution, and to use his influence to obtain new subscriptions; and that the collector be authorised to wait upon such of the proprietors as are resident in or near the metropolis with a view of obtaining their concurrence and assistance.

Promises of £1149 were read out at the meeting; a committee of city men was appointed to promote further contributions;

118

Somerset House and King's College before the Thames Embankment was made

Sir Robert Smirke was authorized to resume work. At the next general court (April 30, 1834) it was reported that the special fund for the completion of the river front amounted then to £7423, and that the work was nearly finished. A year later (April 29, 1835) the council were able to make the following proud announcement:

> In regard to the buildings of the college, the council have the satisfaction of stating that the river front has been finished in accordance with the original design; and consequently the condition imposed by His Majesty's Government, when the grant of the site of the college was made, has been fulfilled. The house designed for the principal is now completed, and he will in future be constantly resident in the college.

It was a fine achievement, and its accomplishment speaks volumes for the energy and self-sacrifice of the devoted men who carried it through.

Other structural works effected at the same time gave a prospect of more pecuniary profit than did the grandiose river front. We have already noted the numerous new classrooms, the refectory, and the recreation hall required by the expanding school, as well as the museum accommodation demanded by the scientific sections of the college. Apart from these, the most important new development was the conversion of the attics originally intended for professorial meditations into apartments for the residence of students. Not much could be done: there were only fifteen rooms available. These in 1835 were fitted up and furnished at a cost of £3200, the money being raised by a special loan. Single rooms were to be let at a rent of £30 a year; double rooms at £36, £40, or £46 according to size; there was one suite of two rooms for which £80 a year was asked. The resident students were to be under the charge of the principal and a resident tutor. This provision of apartments was made specially in the interests of the medical students, many of whom came from the provinces.

§ 7. *The Problem of University Degrees*

The medical faculty of King's College, as we have had occasion to observe, had many other problems to face at this period besides those of finding lodgings for the remnant of their students, and of placing the morals and the manners of these lusty young men under tutorial supervision. Not less pressing was the problem of curriculum and degrees. The possibility of the school's expansion and development depended to no small extent on the gaining of independence and the acquisition of power to confer a diploma qualifying for practice. So early in the career of the college as November 16, 1832, the council received

> a memorial from the medical professors of the college suggesting certain improvements in the system of medical education, and expressing their wish that degrees in medicine should be granted in London.

The council appointed a committee of seven to consider the memorial—the Bishops of London and Llandaff, Dr D'Oyly, Sir Robert Inglis, and the three medical members, Halford, Cooper, and Brodie. The committee apparently failed to report; and a year later the question was again raised in a larger way. On November 8, 1833,

> the principal presented a memorial signed by the professors in the several departments of the college entreating the serious and continued attention of the council to the question of granting degrees, and calling upon them to aid by their powerful individual interest the plan of a university in London.

The council was evidently not greatly pleased by this officiousness on the part of the principal and professors; for it tersely resolved that " the said memorial having been read, it do remain for consideration." This resolution was equivalent to instant burial without even the formality of an inquest by a committee.

Probably one cause for the interest shown in this question of degrees by faculties other than that of medicine was the fact that the sister college in Gower Street was again moving in the matter. A whig ministry was now in power; the liberal Lord John Russell was Home Secretary; there was every probability that the charter (including the power to grant degrees) refused by the tory government of 1830 would speedily be bestowed. It was vitally important that King's College should not be left behind in the race for privilege. Since it was scarcely probable that any government would establish two degree-conferring institutions in the metropolis simultaneously, it seemed desirable to consider whether a scheme could be devised whereby some sort of joint university could be set up. Fortunately, thanks partly to Principal Otter's old and intimate friendship with some of the leading Benthamites, and partly to the fact that several of the professors at King's were on excellent terms with prominent members of the Gower Street staff (*e.g.*, Lyell with Leonard Horner, warden till 1831, to whose daughter he was engaged), the relations between the two colleges were much more cordial than they had been a few years earlier.[1] Hence, although the King's College council held aloof, the teachers of the two institutions, and particularly the medical men, met and discussed the possibility of joint action. The result was that in the spring of 1835—when the Government had virtually decided that a charter should be granted to the Gower Street college, and the Privy Council was considering its terms—the professors ventured once again to memorialize the council, definitely advocating a union of the two colleges for the purpose of the examination of students and the granting of degrees.

The response of the council to this bold proposal was not favourable : on April 10, 1835, it was resolved

> That the council are inclined to think that the union, suggested in the memorial, of King's College with the London University under one common authority for the purpose of conferring degrees would be inconsistent with the principles on which the college was founded. They are also of the opinion that the interests of the college cannot suffer by waiting until the report of the Committee of the Privy Council to His Majesty is made known before they take any steps for obtaining privileges similar to those applied for on the part of the London University. The council beg to return their best thanks to the professors for the attention to the interests of the college evinced in their memorial, and to assure them that they are most sensibly alive to the importance of the object which the professors have in view.

That is to say, the professors were told, in terms of studied politeness and old-fashioned courtesy, to mind their own business. Nevertheless, before the end of the month, the council addressed, through the secretary, the following letter to Lord John Russell :

> I have the honour by direction of the Council of King's College, London, to call your lordship's attention, on their part, to the subject of the charter which has been applied for by the London University, and respectfully to request that before that question is finally determined the council may have an opportunity of making a representation to your lordship and to his Majesty's Government.

[1] It will be remembered also that the chairman of the Gower Street Council, Lord Brougham, was, as Lord Chancellor, an *ex officio* governor of King's, as also was Lord John Russell, the Home Secretary.

To this communication Lord John Russell replied in a letter dated April 28, 1835, and signed, on his behalf, by Mr Charles Gore:[1]

> I am directed by Lord John Russell to acknowledge the receipt of your letter of the 22nd inst. requesting on the part of the council of King's College that he will give them an opportunity of making a representation to him and his Majesty's Government before finally determining upon giving a charter to the London University, and I am charged by his lordship to acquaint you that his unavoidable absence from town prevented his having the power to attend the meeting of the council held yesterday. Lord John Russell requests that you will move the council to send him in writing the representation they desire to make, which he will take into his consideration without delay.

This letter came before the council on May 5, and the Bishop of London and Dr D'Oyly were commissioned to draw up and send to Lord John the memorandum desired. The memorandum, dated the same day, was duly forwarded. As entered on the minutes it ran as follows:

> The council of King's College, London, although that institution has been incorporated by royal charter, have not been desirous of obtaining the power of conferring degrees as long as such power was not granted to any other institution in or near the metropolis. But in case His Majesty's Government should determine to invest any such institution with the power of granting degrees, the position of the college will be materially changed. It will obviously be placed in circumstances of comparative disadvantage, if so important a privilege should be withholden from it, and conceded to any other academical body. The council of King's College think it right to state that more than 100 students of the age of 16 and upwards are at this moment pursuing a regular course of study in general literature and science in the college, on a plan precisely similar to that which is followed in the universities of Oxford and Cambridge, and that these students will in due time be qualified to become candidates for a degree in arts, or in what are termed in academical phrase *literæ humaniores*, and as the council have reason to believe that no other metropolitan institution contains nearly so many students of this class, it appears to them that none can have a stronger claim than King's College to the privilege of conferring degrees. The council entertain, therefore, a confident expectation, that as King's College has been

[1] It is interesting to note that the writer of this letter—the Hon. Charles Gore, son of the third Earl of Arran—was father of the Right Rev. Bishop Gore, a distinguished and revered member of the King's College theological staff since 1919.

established at a great expense, and incorporated by royal charter for the express purpose of maintaining the connexion between sound religion and useful learning, His Majesty's Government will not sanction any arrangement which shall have the effect of placing it in a situation inferior to that of any similar institution as to the powers with which it may be endowed.

There, for the time being, the matter ended. Not for a year and a half (November 1836) was a solution to the problem found. Before that date arrived King's College had a new principal.

§ 8. *The Resignation of Principal Otter*

Of the activities of Principal Otter in King's College singularly little trace remains. His inaugural lecture, with all its ornaments of rhetoric, was never published. Of the weekly sermons that he preached in the college chapel on Sundays, and of the discourses in divinity that he delivered in the lecture theatre on Mondays, no record whatsoever survives. He was not a member of the governing body of the college, nor is it apparent that he was ever present at the deliberations of that body until August 19, 1836, when, we are told,

> The principal of the college, being present at the council, announced his intention of resigning his situation on being appointed to the Bishopric of Chichester, but expressed his readiness to retain it so long as the interests of the college might render it expedient that he should do so.

He held a " situation " more eminent in degree, but identical in kind with that of the porter. He served on no committees, nor is there any evidence that he was so much as consulted when the curriculum was being reorganized or the memorandum respecting degrees was being drawn up. He certainly exercised no sort of control over the policy of the college. Of his relation to the staff of the college, too, we have no record. On one occasion, however, we have seen him acting as the agent of the professors in conveying a memorial to Olympus. There was no professorial board; such discussions as the heads of departments had with one another or with the principal were informal; the teachers did not choose their own subjects of instruction, nor were they allowed to introduce any text-book to their classes until it had been approved by the council. The teachers had to do what they were told. It is amazing to find a man of the rank of Dr Thomas Watson—who held only a part-time post scantily remunerated by a portion of the fees paid by students—cancelling lectures which he had engaged to give in Liverpool and Manchester, at the fiat of the council; or to read in the minutes that when Professor Moseley, wishing to apply for a post in the Greenwich Naval School, asked for a testimonial, he was informed that the council had " come to a determination not to grant testimonials in any case."

Who were the effective members of this Olympic body, the real rulers of the college? Of the forty-two distinguished men who normally constituted the council, nearly one half never attended at all, only one-fourth were even moderately regular. The omnipresent and dominant triumvirate were the Bishop of London (Dr Blomfield), the Dean of St Paul's (Bishop Copleston), and the Rector of Lambeth (Dr D'Oyly). They were ably advised and supported by Archdeacon Cambridge, Dr Shepherd, and Mr Lonsdale. They had, too, a little band of loyal and obedient lay-followers, among whom Lord Bexley, Sir Robert Inglis, and Mr William Cotton were prominent. And behind them all, of course, loomed the impressive figure of the Archbishop of Canterbury, the visitor of the college, a never-failing help in days of trouble.

That Principal Otter worked for four years without serious friction in a situation of such servility is a striking tribute to that " loveliness in his character " on which his biographer laid stress. It is obvious that quietly, efficiently, faithfully, with complete devotion and entire self-effacement, he did his duty to the college and its council during the first four troubled years of its existence. On the other hand, it is doubtful whether the college and the council, by allowing him so little power, got from him all that he was capable of giving. Certainly, if in 1836 he had gone to Heaven instead of to Chichester, we should have felt compelled to regard him as a sweet, meek man, rather dull and commonplace, willing to serve, but incapable of initiative. But the record of his brief episcopate at Chichester proves that we should have been entirely wrong. He was sixty-eight years of age when he was made bishop, and he had but four more years to live. Nevertheless, in that short span of time—no longer than that which he had spent at King's—he left an indelible impress upon his diocese. Not only did he show himself to be, as ever, a man of peace, yearning after the unity of the church; he also displayed high powers of organization and enterprise. In educational activity he was especially laborious—founding schools, training teachers, preparing clergy for their high responsibilities. The Otter

Memorial College, erected in his honour, is a permanent tribute to his greatness.[1]

NOTE

The following is a table showing the number of students in the college during this period. It is compiled from the reports presented to the General Court at the end of April each year.

I. NUMBER OF STUDENTS, 1831–37

| | STUDENTS | | | | | |
| SESSION | SENIOR | | MEDICAL | | JUNIOR | TOTAL |
	Reg.	Occ.	Reg.	Occ.		
1831–32	66	149	48	339[2]	162	764
1832–33	109	196	77	233	319	934
1833–34	104	171	66	175	404	920
1834–35	133	104	42	175	461	915
1835–36	120	105	80	100	419	824
1836–37	118	54	65	108	380	725

II. DISTINGUISHED STUDENTS

Among the students who entered the college during the period 1831–36 were the following who afterward achieved fame. Whenever they formally " signed on " at the beginning of their course the date is given in brackets.

Delane, John Thadeus (April 16, 1833). Editor, the *Times*, 1841–77.

Dasent, George Webbe (October 1, 1833). Assistant-editor of the *Times*, 1845–70; civil service commissioner, 1872–92.

Simon, John (October 2, 1833). First medical officer of health in the city of London; K.C.B., 1887.

Goldsmid, Frederick John (October 6, 1834). Delimiter of the Persian boundary, 1871; controller of crown lands in Egypt, 1880–83; K.C.S.I., 1871; major-general, 1875.

[1] After the death of Bishop Otter the report of the Council to the General Court of King's College contained the following notice, expressed with the felicity characteristic of Early Victorian eulogy : " To the affectionate solicitude with which this excellent person watched over the infancy of the College, as its first principal, much of its present welfare may doubtless be attributed."

[2] This very high figure in 1831–32 includes 222 medical students from schools where the professors had been previously lecturing, who were allowed to attend in order to complete their courses.

Cayley, Arthur (October 8, 1835). Senior wrangler, 1842; Sadlerian professor of pure mathematics at Cambridge, 1863–93.

Ruskin, John (February 4, 1836). An occasional student in Professor Dale's classes before going to Oxford.

Edwardes, Herbert Benjamin (February 11, 1836). Major-general; did much important service in India; knighted, 1860.

Tomes, John (September 29, 1836). Noted dental surgeon; inventor of the modern forceps; initiator of the use of gas for extractions; founder of Odontological Society, 1856, and the Dental Hospital, 1858.

McDougall, Francis Thomas (November 11, 1836). Medical missionary in Sarawak, 1847; first bishop of Labuan, 1855–68.

Plumptre, Charles James (1836). Barrister; editor of *County Courts Chronicle*; lecturer in evening classes at King's.

CHAPTER VI

A PERIOD OF EXPANSION

1836–43

§ 1. The Second Principal : the Rev. Hugh James Rose

PRINCIPAL OTTER's main distinctions were gained after he left King's College and when he was a septuagenarian. His successor, a comparatively young man, came to the college as already one of the most famous and influential of the clergy of the day. We have already had occasion to mention more than once the Rev. Hugh James Rose. He it was whose sermon at Cambridge in 1826 had initiated that movement for the reunion of sound learning with religious education which had resulted in the founding of King's College itself. He, too, it was who had gathered in his rectory at Hadleigh seven years later that little band of devoted anglicans, the nucleus of the Association of Friends of the Church, the fruit of whose deliberations and labours were the epoch-making *Tracts for the Times* (1833–44). In the spring of 1836, only a few months before the principalship of King's College fell vacant, had occurred that cardinal correspondence between Rose and Newman (arising out of Tract No. LXVI) which marks the divergence of the paths of the tractarians (*e.g.*, Rose, Keble, Pusey) who remained within the Church of England, and the other tractarians (*e.g.*, Newman, Ward, Faber) who seceded to Rome. Hugh James Rose, then, although little beyond forty years old, was one of the pioneers of the anglican revival, an outstanding leader of the most vigorous party in the church, a champion of the independence of the spiritual power, a vehement opponent of subversive liberalism in both politics and religion. But for a frailty of health which hampered him from infancy and ultimately brought him to an early grave, he would undoubtedly have risen to the highest offices in the Church of England, and would have occupied a place in the ecclesiastical history of the nineteenth century not less eminent than (though assuredly very different from) that of John Henry Newman himself. "He was," said Archbishop Howley, "the best preacher in England." "Had

127

this noble man lived," said one of his tractarian colleagues, the Rev. W. Palmer, " he would have been the greatest ornament and the most trusted leader of his church," adding that he was " a profound scholar, an eloquent orator, a deep thinker, and an admirable theologian." Dean Burgon, his biographer, who was closely connected with him,[1] wrote of him :

> His personal aspect was certainly most striking : his figure tall and commanding—a grand ecclesiastical presence, as one of his pupils remarked—a singularly intellectual brow, a wondrous grave and thoughtful countenance.

Newman, while still a clergyman of the Church of England, dedicated to Rose, then actually principal of King's College, the fourth series of his sermons in these words :

> To the Rev. Hugh James Rose, B.D., Principal of King's College, London, and Domestic Chaplain to the Archbishop of Canterbury, who, when hearts were failing, bade us stir up the gift that was in us, and betake ourselves to our true Mother, this volume is inscribed by his obliged and faithful friend.

What had been the previous career of this notable man who in October 1836 was called upon to succeed Bishop Otter as principal of King's ?

Born in 1795, at Little Horsted in Sussex, where his father was curate, he was soon removed to Uckfield, whither his father was called to assist the Rev. Dr D'Oyly, at that time rector of Buxted-cum-Uckfield. In spite of chronic ill-health, the boy showed a remarkable precocity in scholarship. Sent to Cambridge in 1813, he carried all before him : he was Bell Scholar, 1814; Scholar of Trinity, 1815; fourteenth wrangler and first chancellor's medallist, 1817; member's prizeman, 1818. Ordained by Howley in December 1818, he returned to Buxted as curate to Dr D'Oyly. In 1821 he was made vicar of Horsham, and in a few years he caused a remarkable religious revival in his parish. But, alas, his health gave way, and in 1824 he was compelled to take a prolonged holiday in Germany. Such was his courage and energy, however, that he used the opportunity which necessity forced upon him to acquire a thorough command of the German language, and to make a profound study of German theology (or " neology," as he preferred to call it). The result of his research was, on his return to England, the delivery, in the Cambridge University church, of some sensational

---

[1] Burgon's sister married Rose's brother.

HUGH JAMES ROSE
Principal 1836–39

128

Discourses on the State of the Protestant Religion in Germany (published 1825), in which he denounced the rationalism which prevailed in the Lutheran communion—a rationalism which he attributed to the lack of episcopal discipline, the absence of binding articles of belief, and the want of a liturgy such as that of the English Church. The discourses made a considerable stir both in England and in Germany. In England they were answered, somewhat vehemently, by the learned E. B. Pusey, who had not at that date become a puseyite. In Germany they led the pious minister Bunsen and the incalculable prince who in 1840 became King Frederick William IV ardently to desire for Prussia, as a prophylactic against revolution, the advantages of episcopacy, a prayer book, and the thirty-nine articles.

In 1830 Archbishop Howley—who was Rose's devoted admirer and cordial friend—conferred upon him the delectable rectory of Hadleigh, in Suffolk, hoping that the change of climate would benefit his health. Unfortunately, however, it did not do so, and in 1833 he was moved to Fairsted, in Essex. Thence he was speedily summoned by the bishop of Durham, who persuaded him to accept the chair of divinity in the newly founded university of the palatinate. Here he gave one memorable course of lectures, the burden of which was " back to the middle ages." But the rigour of the northern air was more than he could stand. So serious and persistent now was the asthma from which he suffered that London alone seemed to hold out hope of alleviation. Hence in 1834 he came south; was appointed domestic chaplain to the archbishop, and in 1835 perpetual curate of St Thomas's, Southwark. The change appeared to be justified. He rallied in a marvellous manner, and threw himself with all his old energy into countless notable enterprises. He closely associated himself with Joshua Watson and his educational organizations; he edited the *British Magazine of Ecclesiastical Information*; he took over the control of the new *Encyclopædia Metropolitana*, projected by Coleridge; he planned a great biographical dictionary, which after his death was completed by his brother and Mr T. Wright, and published in twelve volumes (1848). He became the very life and soul of the " Canterbury Party "— that is, of the great central body of churchmen who, under the lead of Archbishop Howley and Bishop Blomfield, were steering a middle course between catholicism and nonconformity; who, while strongly asserting their protestantism, were restoring the Elizabethan ritual; who, while clinging to their connexion

I

with the state, were asserting the claims of ecclesiastical independence. So closely was Rose associated with Howley and Blomfield, and so completely was he in harmony with them, that the three may almost be said to have formed a ruling triumvirate in the church. No wonder that the visitor of King's College and the chairman of its council wished to have Rose as principal of the institution in which they were so much interested. Should we be thought to attribute too much diplomacy to these eminent and saintly prelates if we were to suggest the possibility that Principal Otter's elevation to the see of Chichester was the consequence, rather than the cause, of their desire for the appointment of Rose to the principalship of King's College? At any rate, Dean Burgon tells us in his biography of Rose that "without candidature, much less solicitation of any sort on his part, he was proposed as principal in August [1836]."[1] Now Otter became bishop of Chichester on October 2, and his formal letter of resignation, dated October 20, came before the council of King's College on October 21. The council accepted his resignation, offered him their "cordial congratulations upon his elevation to a high and important office in the government of the church," and alluded appreciatively to " that spirit of conciliation and kindness which has secured to him the confidence and regard of every member of the college." Then, without further to-do, and without any hesitation or delay,

> it was proposed by the Lord Bishop of London and seconded by Lord Bexley and unanimously resolved that the Rev. Hugh James Rose, B.D., be appointed principal of the college in the room of the Bishop of Chichester.

It is obvious that all was prearranged.

Of the first principal of the college no more is heard in the extant records of the institution. It was never proposed that he should become a member of the council; there is no indication that he was ever consulted concerning any problems that arose; he was not present at any courts or prize-givings; he does not seem to have felt it necessary to make any contribution to the urgent appeals for funds which were issued by the council during the four years of his episcopate. There is, in short, a slight veil of mystery pendent over the departure of Principal Otter and the appointment of his successor.

---

[1] J. W. Burgon, *Lives of Twelve Good Men*, p. 234.

§ 2. *The Charter of the University of London*

Almost the first problem which faced the new principal of the college and the council was that caused by the issue of a charter, dated November 28, 1836, establishing a degree-conferring university in London. The problem was one in which Rose was intensely interested: its crux was that very question of the place of divinity in general education with which he had dealt in his great Cambridge sermon of 1826; the very question which had divided the utilitarians of Gower Street from the idealists of the Freemasons' Hall in 1828. In January and February 1836, when the matter of the charter was still under consideration by Melbourne's government, the *British Magazine*—founded by Rose in 1832 and edited by him until his death—had published two uncompromising articles in which the appointment of examiners by the Home Office was ridiculed, and the exclusion of religion from the syllabus (and even the abolition of doctrinal tests) was denounced. He came, then, as principal to deal with the charter problem as a man whose mind was already made up; and the attitude that he assumed was far less conciliatory than that of the philo-Benthamite Otter.

We have traced the history of the charter problem up to May 1835.[1] It will be remembered that the proprietary " University of London " in Gower Street, disappointed in its application for a charter in 1830, had renewed its request more hopefully in 1833 when the reformed parliament was in session, and a whig government in power. It will be further recollected that in the spring of 1835, when the Privy Council was actually considering the terms of the proposed charter, the authorities of King's College had petitioned the Home Secretary, asking that no privileges and powers, such as that of conferring degrees, should be bestowed upon any metropolitan institution to the detriment of King's College. To the suggestion, made by the professors, that the two institutions in Gower Street and the Strand should in some way be united or federated for examining and degree-conferring purposes— a suggestion strongly supported by the *London Medical Gazette* and by the *Athenæum*—the council had returned the answer that it was inconsistent with the fundamental principles of King's College. This intransigent attitude, which was probably as little agreeable to Principal Otter as to the professors of the college, left the government with but one course to

[1] See above, pp. 120–123.

pursue. King's College would not combine with its undenominational fellow to form a single degree-conferring university; the government could not contemplate the absurdity of setting up simultaneously two degree-conferring universities in the metropolis; the only possibility, therefore, was to withhold the privilege of conferring degrees from both of them, and to establish a separate and independent degree-conferring authority whose diplomas would be open to either. Proposals to this effect were submitted by the government to Gower Street in August 1835, and after much debate were accepted by the proprietors of the " University of London." Their acceptance involved some exceedingly disagreeable consequences; but the advantage of securing London degrees at all (and particularly in medicine) seemed to outweigh the drawbacks. The disagreeable consequences were these: first, the Gower Street institution had to drop its title of the " University of London," and to take the more lowly designation of " University College "; secondly, it had to surrender its control over its own curricula and its own examinations, and to subject itself to courses of study imposed by an external authority and to examinations in which its teachers had no voice; thirdly, it had to see established under its own old title, the " University of London," a body that was neither a university nor metropolitan, but a mere government department established to conduct examinations—examinations open not only to students of University College and King's College, but to those of any other " bodies for education " in Britain or abroad which might " from time to time be named by the crown."

The authorities in Gower Street having intimated their acceptance of the government's terms, the government issued two charters simultaneously on November 28, 1836. One of them conceded to the Gower Street institution, under the title of " London University College," the incorporation which it had so long sought. The other set up, under the title of " the University of London," a new body of " persons eminent in literature and science, to act as a board of examiners, and to perform all the functions of the examiners in the senate-house of Cambridge." The governing body of this new examining " university " was a senate nominated by the crown. Its members were men of the highest eminence. At the head, as chancellor, was the Earl of Burlington (afterward seventh Duke of Devonshire), and with him were associated Sir John W. Lubbock (vice-chancellor), three enlightened lords (Brougham, Macaulay, Monteagle), four liberal bishops Maltby), Otter, Stanley, Thirlwall), Sir G. C. Lewis, Dr Arnold of Rugby, and Mr George Grote. It will be noted that among the members of this distinguished governmental committee, or senate, were two prominent representatives of University College—viz., Brougham (its president) and George Grote—but that King's College—some of whose rulers were almost certainly invited—was unrepresented. It will be noted, further, that among the bishops who lent their sanction to the new university was " that excellent person " the ex-principal, Dr Otter—another indication that at this juncture his policy diverged seriously from that of the council of King's College.

The council of King's College, indeed, looked with most unfriendly eyes upon the new examining university; and probably, but for the urgent needs of the medical department, it would have had nothing to do with it at all. At a meeting held a few weeks after the publication of the charter (January 20, 1837) it passed the following resolution and ordered it to be printed and circulated:

> His Majesty having been pleased to incorporate a university in London by a charter which includes the students of this college in the number of those who may be candidates for degrees, the council of the college think it right to make a declaration of their adherence to the principles upon which the institution confided to their management was founded and has been conducted. The council retain, unqualified and unmodified, their deep and thorough persuasion that there is no other sure foundation for national education than the doctrines of the Christian religion. . . .

Now the basis upon which the new chartered university was established was that its degrees should be open " to persons of all religious persuasions, without distinction and without the imposition of any test or disqualification whatever." As the *British Magazine* lamented, its examinees could not even be asked whether or not they believed in " another state and in a God." Nay, it was not by any means certain that divinity of any sort would be included in its examination syllabus.

That was a problem which agitated the new senate of the university during the whole of the year 1837, when the examination syllabuses were being framed. Within the senate, Arnold of Rugby led a powerful group which wished to make a knowledge of the Greek Testament and Scripture history compulsory for an arts degree. He was vehemently opposed by the Benthamites. Lord John Russell, Home Secretary, when

133

appealed to as head of the department of which the senate was a committee, said that he had no objection to the inclusion of the Greek Testament, etc., in the examination syllabus, provided it were put in as an optional subject, but that he would veto any attempt to make it compulsory. The council of King's College held majestically aloof from the brawl; but it entered upon its minutes (February 9, 1838) the following letter, dated January 30, sent to the chancellor of the university over the signatures of Principal Rose and Professors Hall, Browne, and Dale:

MY LORD,

Being desirous of communicating with the senate of the University of London, we think it most respectful to your lordship and to that body to request that you will lay before them the following statement: We have learned from public sources of intelligence that the faculty of arts of the University of London have had under their consideration a recommendation that as a general rule the candidate for the degree of B.A. shall pass an examination either in one of the four Gospels or the Acts of the Apostles in the original Greek, and also in Scripture history; that remonstrances against the adoption of this proposal as a regulation have been made by the United Committee of Dissenters and the Council of the University College; and that in consequence the Secretary of State for the Home Department has written a letter to your lordship requiring your lordship to bring this matter again before the senate, and implying his disapproval of the regulation.

We are ourselves the officers of a body named in the charter of the university, and have the charge of that department of King's College from which all students wishing to gain the degree of B.A. would proceed. We have been for several years engaged in the education of young men under various circumstances, and have consequently both been led ourselves to a frequent consideration of the question of academical degrees, and have had constant opportunities of knowing the opinions of large numbers of persons whose sons are likely to desire them.

Knowing, therefore, how constantly the silence of those whose duty it may be esteemed to speak is misconstrued, we trust your lordship will excuse us for taking this opportunity of declaring distinctly that after considering the royal declaration in the charters, that their Majesties' object in founding the new university was "the holding forth encouragement for pursuing a regular and liberal course of education," we are of opinion that no system of examination which should positively exclude the subjects named in the proposed regulation could possibly be said to give encouragement to a "regular and liberal course of education," but must from whatever point it may be viewed, or whatever its merits in other regards may be, be considered as greatly defective. It is consequently our opinion that the introduction of the subjects in question would be, to say the least, essential to the efficacy of any such examination, and we can add that we have every reason to believe that it would be most acceptable to a very large and influential class of the community.

We are desirous to add that on this occasion we are speaking only our own sentiments and must not be understood as in any way conveying the opinion of our college council (which does not indeed meet until after the period fixed for debating the question in the university), and with respect to ourselves we beg most distinctly to say that we do not in any way intend or profess to deliver our opinion on any question whatever connected with the metropolitan university, except that particular one which is the special subject of this communication.

> We have the honour,
> [etc.]

This emphatic utterance was reinforced by a vehement open letter addressed by Professor Dale to " a Member of the Senate of the University of London," and published as a pamphlet (Seeley, 1838). It contends in a series of highly coloured sections that the exclusion of Greek Testament and Scripture history from the B.A. examination is not legal, not honest, not just, not liberal, not even—the prime matter with the Benthamites—expedient. The letter concludes by saying to the member of the senate:

> if you exclude divinity from your syllabus, you will compel Christianity to march against you with the banner of the Cross unfurled, and the sword of the Bible unsheathed,

adding that

> thus encountered, the University of London will become, from the moment of passing the fatal resolution, an object of suspicion to the wise and of abhorrence to the good.[1]

The " fatal resolution " nevertheless was passed. Arnold, who believed as strongly as Rose or as Newman that religion

---

[1] Another passage from Professor Dale's pamphlet, significant of the attitude of King's College to the new University at this date, runs as follows. Writing of the exclusion of divinity, Dale says : " It is peculiarly unjust in reference to King's College. The terms of your charter have pressed that institution into a forced and uncongenial connection with you, like a woman who is wedded against her will. . . You waited neither for her consent, nor for that of her lawful guardian, the council. You dragged her not to the altar, but to the registration office," etc.

is the only sound basis of national education, resigned from the senate. King's College held indignantly aloof from the arts degrees of the new university, encouraging the brilliant boys in the school and the general students of the senior department to pass on to Oxford or Cambridge rather than seek the godless diplomas dispensed as the result of extremely difficult examinations by the nominees of the Home Secretary established (in exasperating contiguity to King's College) in Somerset House. Only gradually, as King's College students insisted upon taking advantage of the opportunities and privileges open to them, was the boycott broken down.

Early in 1838 the University of London issued its first detailed syllabuses. In view of the wide divergence of the present-day syllabuses from this original model, a few outstanding features may be noted. The university offered degrees in three faculties only—viz., arts, laws, and medicine. In the case of arts and laws the first, or bachelor's, degree was to be obtainable by means of two examinations, the matriculation and the final: there was to be no intermediate examination. The matriculation, common to all faculties, was to be held once a year, in October; the fee was to be £2, and it was to be returned intact to all candidates who failed to pass; there were to be only three subjects for examination, all compulsory—viz., (1) *mathematics:* arithmetic, algebra, euclid; (2) *chemistry and natural history*; (3) *classics:* Greek, with the history of Greece, Latin, with the history of Rome, English history, with the outlines of geography. The pass lists should be issued four days after the close of the examination, and candidates who satisfied the examiners could proceed at once to sit for a further examination for honours. The second, or degree, examination could not be taken until two years after the passing of the matriculation. For the B.A. the candidate would have to satisfy the examiners in (1) *mathematics and natural philosophy:* arithmetic, geometry, trigonometry, mechanics, hydrostatics, astronomy; (2) *chemistry, physiology, and botany*; (3) *classics:* the Greek and Latin languages, Greek and Roman history, English history, and either French or German; (4) *logic and moral philosophy*. Apart from the choice between French and German, there were to be no options: all the subjects would have to be taken, and in all simultaneously the examiners would have to be satisfied. The examination would be held once a year, in May or June; the fee would be £10, returnable to failures. Those, and those only, who obtained the pass degree could proceed to honours in mathe-
136

matics or classics, either the same or the following year. One year after taking the B.A. the candidate could proceed to M.A. by further examination in classics, or mathematics, or moral philosophy. Similar regulations applied to the degrees of LL.B. and LL.D. In medicine evidence of practical work and hospital experience was to be an indispensable preliminary to the M.B. and M.D. degrees. Moreover, there were two examinations to be passed before the M.B. degree could be secured.

In the report presented by the council of King's College to the general court on April 27, 1839, the following reference to the new university was made:

> Since the last report the senate of the university of London have put forth their plans of examination for matriculation and degrees. At present only a few students of King's College have been admitted at this university, the greater part of those who were desirous of academical honours having preferred to enter their names at Oxford or Cambridge, where, as is well known, many of them have obtained considerable distinction.

But though King's College thus held aloof, the privilege of affiliation to the new university was eagerly seized by a number of colleges and schools in the provinces, and particularly by those institutions wherein catholic priests and dissenting ministers received their training. Within five years no fewer than sixteen educational establishments, besides University and King's Colleges, had been authorized by the crown to issue certificates of attendance and good conduct qualifying their holders to sit for degrees in arts and in law. The number of recognized medical schools was greater still. Hence the University of London became not a teaching institution for the metropolis, but a board of examiners for the empire.[1]

§ 3. Revival of the Medical School

We have remarked that, apart from the needs of the medical school, King's College would probably have had little or nothing to do with the new London University, whose senate was seated next door to the college, in a spare room of Somerset House. For arts degrees the professors of King's College preferred to send their students to the still uncontaminated universities of Oxford and Cambridge; and these universities

---

[1] The matriculation list for 1840 shows 69 passes, of which King's College has 9 and University College 26. The B.A. list for 1841 shows 35 passes, of which King's College has 3 and University College 8.

welcomed the excellently trained and admirably disciplined students from the Strand. Magdalene College, Cambridge, indeed, in 1836 instituted a scholarship of £40 a year specially for members of King's College, one of the first recipients of which was Charles Kingsley (1838). As to law degrees, no one at King's College wanted them at all. The department of law languished to such an extent that on September 13, 1838, Professor Preston wrote to the council saying that he was " ready to make a vacancy in the professorship for any gentleman who can secure a class." As a matter of fact, both the Inns of Court and the Law Society were developing their own schools of jurisprudence, and they held aloof (as they still hold aloof) from the university faculty of law. With respect to medicine, however, the case was different. In this faculty it was of the utmost value to the college to be associated with an institution authorized to confer the degrees of M.B. and M.D., even though until 1854 these degrees were not coupled with the qualification to practise physic and surgery. Nevertheless, even here, so strongly was the council prejudiced against the new university, that it was not until April 26, 1839—two and a half years after its establishment—that, in response to an urgent communication from the medical professors, the council agreed to apply for the recognition necessary for the admission of King's College students to its medical examinations. And even then, for a long time the number of King's College graduates in medicine at London University remained small. The first King's College student to take the London doctorate was W. A. Miller (destined to spend the whole of the remaining forty years of his life in the service of the college) : in 1841 he alone represented King's College in the final M.B. examination, as against nine from University College; in 1842 he was again alone at the M.D., and although he obtained a certificate of special proficiency in the examination, he was beaten by Quain of University College for the gold medal. So late as 1843 the *Lancet* (September 2) denounced in no measured terms the " hold-backism of the college of theologians and conservatives " in the matter of London medical degrees.

The *Lancet*, however—a distinctly radical journal at that date—had always been ill-disposed to King's. In 1836 it had characterized its medical school as " next to the worst in London." Nor can it be denied that there was some justification for its strictures at that particular period. It will be remembered that in 1835 the number of students in the school had fallen to 42 ; that the expenses of the school had exceeded its revenue by £280; that dissensions had been rife; that in 1836 nearly half of the medical professors had resigned their chairs, and that the council had found the utmost difficulty in securing successors who combined scientific efficiency with religious orthodoxy.[1]   So bad, indeed, did things become that on December 8, 1837, the council felt it necessary to issue a formal denial of a persistent rumour that the medical school was to be closed down altogether.   It will also be recalled, however, that precisely when things were at their worst a *restitutor reipublicæ* was found in Dr R. B. Todd, who had been appointed (August 19, 1836) to the chair of physiology and morbid anatomy.[2]   " This great friend of medical science and progress," says Mr Lionel S. Beale in a notable eulogy,

> laboured vigorously and incessantly to advance medical work, and to raise the college he loved so well as a place of medical education. He endeavoured to encourage his pupils in every way in his power to press forward into the very centre of the stream of active work and thought. . . . Todd was a man who was ever moving onwards, and therefore he was accused of restlessness, and was regarded by some as a disturber of the peace and too fond of change.[3]

He found, too, in the new principal of King's, the Rev. Hugh James Rose, an active and devoted ally. Rose, as perpetual curate of St Thomas's, Southwark, had had Guy's Hospital (as well as St Thomas's) within his parish. Here he had got to know Frederick Denison Maurice, then chaplain of Guy's, and had been much impressed by the notable educational and religious work he was doing among the medical students. Rose opened the columns of the *British Magazine* to Todd, and, beginning in March 1837, published a series of powerful articles from his pen treating of the reform of medical education. Those who had regarded King's College as the home of reaction had to revise their judgments, and rather to protest against the spirit of revolutionary innovation which seemed to have taken possession of its medical department!

The first matter that aroused Todd's and Rose's concern was the question of the social and religious training of the youthful doctors of the land:

> Are the future medical men of this country to be brought up radical in politics and indifferent in religion? . . . If infidelity and radicalism prevail among the medical profession, they will

---

[1] See above, p. 115.   [2] See above, p. 116.
[3] L. S. Beale, *On Medical Progress*, p. 10.

have a ready access to the rich man's castle and the poor man's cottage.

King's College did not avowedly intermeddle with the politics of its medical students; but their religion had always been its peculiar care. They were encouraged to attend chapels and divinity lectures; in 1834 annual prizes were instituted by Mr S. H. Leathes to go to two medical students " for their proficiency in religious knowledge and for their general good conduct "; in 1838 Dr S. W. Warneford bestowed £1000 upon the college, the proceeds of which were to go year by year as rewards for essays by medical students on

> the evidences of natural religion from the facts and laws of the physical universe, more especially those parts of it which are connected with medical or anatomical studies.

Todd and Rose did everything in their power to instil religious principles into the students placed under their charge.

The second matter to which Todd turned his attention was the professional education of the medical students, and here his great achievement, in conjunction with his fellow-professors and the council of the college, was the establishment of a system of scholarships, conferred exclusively for merit and attainable solely by examination. The subject was first mooted early in 1838; by March 1839 the scheme was complete. The medical professors themselves offered two scholarships, each of the value of £40 and tenable for three years; the friends of the college subscribed for a third. In order to re-enforce the religious basis of medical education, it was provided that

> none can be a candidate for these scholarships but those who have passed a previous examination in the Sacred Scriptures, the Church Catechism, and Butler's Analogy.

Our present-day familiarity with scholarships must not blind us to the fact that these King's College open medical scholarships were the first of their kind.

The third subject of Todd's solicitude was the discipline and moral supervision of the medical students. For the most part, as we have observed, these students came up from the provinces, having served an apprenticeship to a local apothecary; they lived in unregulated lodgings and too many of them tended to live unregulated lives. Todd felt strongly that the only remedy for the serious evils which existed was to establish hostels, bring the students into residence, develop the collegiate system on the Oxford and Cambridge model, with its tutors, its scheduled hours, its dinners in hall, its chapels, its general supervision. The minutes of the council for the years 1839–42 are filled with memoranda from Todd individually, and the medical professors collectively, on this important topic; the council is continually urged to extend the residential and tutorial departments of the college. In April 1842 Todd addressed an extremely able and powerful open letter—a thirty-two page pamphlet—to the principal of King's College on the question. In that year the council, moved to action in spite of its poverty, actually sounded Somerset House to see if it would hand over part of its east wing as a boarding-house, and, on receiving a reply in the negative, next turned its eye upon Surrey Street and secured estimates for the purchase of houses, and their connexion with the college by ways over Strand Lane. But the expense was prohibitive, and the collegiate scheme had to be suspended. Only the fourteen sets of rooms provided in 1835 remained available. Two frag-ments of Todd's large plan, however, were put into operation. (1) On June 10, 1842, it was decreed that each of the medical professors in turn should serve as dean of the faculty, with general supervision, under the principal, of the manners and the morals of the medical students. (2) In November 1843 the council appointed George Johnson—the holder of the first medical scholarship, a brilliant student who had just carried off the gold medal in physiology at the London M.B. examina-tion—to be "resident medical tutor whose special duty it is to superintend the studies and conduct of medical students." These two innovations were valuable, but they were the merest fringe of Todd's large design. Todd, in his conception of collegiate discipline for youthful medicos, was again a notable pioneer; but it was to the great hospitals, and not to King's College, that the honour accrued of realizing his idea.[1]

The last of Todd's seminal ideas was that which resulted in the opening of King's College Hospital in 1840. This, how-ever, is so big and important a matter that it must have a section to itself. Suffice it here to say that Todd's initiative and energy, combined with the loyal co-operation of his colleagues, the vigorous support of Principals Rose and Lonsdale, and the cautious acquiescence of the council, resulted in the complete resuscitation of the medical school. Its numbers went steadily up from 42 in 1834–35 to 131 in

[1] St Bartholomew's Hospital opened a hostel for its students in 1843. See *London Medical Gazette*, June 16, 1843.

1843–44; it began once more to pay its way; peace and prosperity reigned within its borders.

The period under review of course saw some changes on the staff. Early in 1838 Dr J. F. Fergus, professor of forensic medicine, died, and on June 8 Dr W. A. Guy, eminent as a medical statistician, was elected in his place. In August 1838 John Simon and Francis Thomas McDougall were made demonstrators in the department of anatomy, the first students to be appointed to the staff; each was destined to distinction in later life, the one as first medical officer of health to the city of London, the other as medical missionary and first bishop of Labuan. The founding of the hospital in 1840 involved the resignations of Professors Watson (medicine) and Arnott (surgery), concerning which more anon. Their chairs were filled (March 13, 1840) by Drs George Budd and William Fergusson respectively. Budd was a young Cambridge physician who had distinguished himself by his study of epidemics. Fergusson came from Edinburgh, where he had learned surgery under Syme, the greatest conservative operator of his day. Fergusson was destined to remain at King's College for thirty-seven years, and to win a world-wide reputation as a surgeon. On his retirement in 1877 he was succeeded by another of Syme's pupils, even more distinguished than himself—viz., Joseph Lister.

§ 4. King's College Hospital

We have already noted [1] that one of the heaviest handicaps of the King's College medical school in its early days was the lack of a hospital wherein the teachers of the college could exemplify to their students the principles which they were propounding in the lecture room. The medical students of the college were expected to "walk the wards" in some hospital or other. Until 1836 the Middlesex hospital (near Tottenham Court Road), with which several of their professors were connected, provided for most of them the required perambulation; but, first, the distance of this hospital from King's College was inconveniently great; secondly, it became increasingly evident that mere "walking," if unsupplemented by clinical instruction, was insufficient to qualify a young man to practise on the bodies of his majesty's subjects; finally, in 1836, partly as a consequence of the brawls which arose around and within the King's College medical school, the Middlesex

[1] See above, pp. 114–115.

hospital started a school of its own under ex-professor Mayo, and made things unpleasant for King's College students. Hence in June 1837 the medical staff of King's College laid before the council a plan for establishing a special connexion with the Charing Cross hospital (then recently rebuilt). But, although some interchange of services was arranged, it was found that Charing Cross hospital could not possibly provide all that was desired of experience and training. Once more, therefore, in April 1839, the medical professors approached the council, urging the importance of having a hospital definitely connected with the college, and informing them that the workhouse of the St Clement Danes' parish, situated in Portugal Street, would be vacant in the summer of that year, and that it could, without excessive expense, be converted into the required institution. They themselves promised generous contributions toward its conversion. The council seized the opportunity with alacrity, appointed a committee at once to open negotiations with the parochial authorities, and were able to announce to the general court held on April 27, 1839, that they

> have long felt the great importance of attaching to the medical school of the college a hospital where the students might have the advantage of attending clinical lectures under their own professors. They have never lost sight of this object ; and they now have the satisfaction of announcing to the general court that circumstances have very lately occurred which open a prospect of procuring a suitable building for this purpose in the vicinity of the college.

Arrangements with the parish of St Clement Danes were speedily concluded: the college hired the workhouse for a term of sixty years at a rent of £300 a year. Then arose the problems of equipment and maintenance on the one hand, government and administration on the other hand. As to finance, the college possessed no spare funds; so a new levy had to be raised. As to control, it was decided that, since in finance the two institutions would be separate and distinct, so in government they must remain apart. Hence on May 10, 1839, the council issued the following address:

> The council of King's College, having been long anxious that a hospital should be attached to their medical school, have now before them the immediate prospect of seeing their wishes in this respect realized. An agreement has been entered into with the parish of St Clement Danes for a long lease of a building in Portugal Street, Lincoln's Inn Fields, which has been hitherto

occupied as a workhouse, but which is now no longer wanted for that purpose. The building has been carefully inspected and found to be capable of containing at least 250 beds and well adapted to the purposes of a hospital.

Upon the immense advantages which would result to the medical students of King's College from witnessing the medical and surgical practice, and receiving the clinical instruction of their own professors, in a hospital connected with the college, and in its vicinity, it is unnecessary to enlarge; nor are the advantages which would accrue to the public from the establishment of the proposed hospital less evident. For although there are at present several large hospitals in London, the fact is but too certain that great numbers are refused admission into them from want of the necessary accommodation. Any institution, therefore, which will increase the means of affording to the suffering poor that medical and surgical assistance which hospitals alone can supply must be a most important addition to the general good. And it should be observed in particular that the district in which the building now intended to be converted into a hospital is situated is at a considerable distance from any of the existing hospitals. . . .

As King's College does not possess any funds applicable to the establishment and support of the proposed hospital, and as the hospital, although in immediate connexion with the college, must be under separate management, it will be necessary to make provision for the requisite outlay from other sources.

Under these circumstances, the council of King's College express their earnest and confident hope that the friends of the college in particular, and the public in general, especially the wealthier inhabitants of the neighbourhood which will be more immediately benefited, will readily come forward to supply the means of carrying into effect so benevolent and useful a design.

The council decided (May 24, 1839) that every donor of thirty guineas to the hospital should become a life-governor of the institution, and every subscriber of three guineas a year should be a governor so long as he should continue to subscribe. The general administration of the hospital should be in the hands of a " committee " elected by the governors; but

> in order to preserve the connexion between the hospital and King's College, the power of nominating all the medical officers of the hospital and the chaplain shall be vested in the college council.

This was a very formidable reservation, which from time to time greatly strained the relations between the hospital governors who paid the piper and the college council who, from the other side of the Strand, called the tune.

A PERIOD OF EXPANSION

The response to the appeal for funds for the new hospital was generous: within twelve months nearly £10,000 was raised, and promises of annual subscriptions amounting to £540 made. But the adaptation of the building to its new purpose cost £3776, and expenses for furnishing and equipment accounted for a further £3100. Hence the hospital was opened, on April 15, 1840, with a capital sum of little more than £3000, and the prospect of a wholly inadequate annual income. At first only 120 beds were provided; but it was hoped that soon the number would be increased: the Royal College of Surgeons, in fact, required 150 as a condition of its recognition.

If the use to which a hospital is put is a criterion of its success or failure, the new institution speedily justified itself. At the end of the first twelve months (April 15, 1841) the committee reported that 1109 in-patients and 6576 out-patients had received attention. The annual subscriptions, however, still came to no more than £700, and it was found that an income of no less than £3500 would be necessary for efficiency. By the end of 1841, although the claims on the services of the hospital were continually increasing, it seemed probable that the institution would have to be closed as a bankrupt concern: a special report to the council showed a deficit on the eight months' working (April–December 1841) of £512. The council as a body could render no assistance, but many of its individual members lent generous aid, and the crisis was tided over. It continued to recur, however, annually with monotonous iteration, until in 1845 heroic measures had to be taken. By this time, too, it had become necessary to extend the hospital. Hence, a large public meeting was called in Willis's Rooms, presided over by the Duke of Buccleuch, and addressed by the Bishops of London and Lichfield, Lord John Russell, Mr W. E. Gladstone, and others. The report laid before the meeting stated that since the hospital had been opened (April 15, 1840–December 31, 1844) it had relieved 5650 in-patients and 47,636 out-patients; it was, however, unable to meet its expenses, still less to expand; £15,000 was required to put it on a sound basis. A subscription list was opened which Queen Victoria headed with a donation of £100; before the meeting closed over £2000 had been raised, while £52 10s. had been promised in annual subscriptions. Before the end of April 1845 the donations amounted to £2594, and the new annual subscriptions to £99 10s. For a time the financial pressure was relieved.

One difficult problem raised by the opening of the hospital

K

remains to be recorded. The fundamental principle of the hospital was that it should be staffed by the medical professors of King's College, who should be thus enabled to demonstrate in its wards the theories which they enunciated in the college lecture-rooms. Now two of the most eminent of the King's College medical professors, viz., Dr Thomas Watson and Mr J. M. Arnott, were prominent luminaries of the Middlesex hospital. They could not serve two hospitals; they were not willing to sever their connexion with the Middlesex hospital; hence they were compelled to resign their professorships. The matter came before the council first on November 29, 1839, and for four months a keen controversy raged. Letters, memorials, petitions, protests poured in. Finally, however (March 15, 1840), the council came to the decision that

> (1) No physician or surgeon shall hold any appointment in the hospital (except an honorary one) who is not at the same time a professor in the college; and when he shall cease to hold his professorship in the college, he shall cease at the same time to be a medical officer of the hospital.
>
> (2) No medical professors of King's College shall belong to any other medical school, or to any hospital to which a medical school is attached.

Professors Watson and Arnott, therefore, had to go. Fortunately the parting was extremely amicable. The council on the one side expressed its deep gratitude, profound regret, etc.; the two professors gracefully accepted the honorary positions of " consulting physician " and " consulting surgeon " respectively on the staff of the King's College hospital. Further, Dr Thomas Watson (who was made a baronet in 1866) later consented to join the council of King's College, and he remained one of its most honoured and influential members almost to the time of his death, at the age of ninety, in the year 1882. The admirable lectures which he had delivered at King's College on the *Principles and Practice of Physic* were published in book form in 1843, and for some thirty years they held their place as the standard authority on the subject.

§ 5. *The Department of Engineering*

The same period as saw the revival of the medical school and the founding of the hospital saw also another development of a widely different kind, but one not less interesting and important, viz., the organization of the department of

146

engineering. The decade 1830–40 was one of great engineering activity throughout the country: new macadamized roads, new canals, new factories, new buildings of many kinds, new coal- and iron-mines, above all, new railways, were in ubiquitous process of construction. The demand for trained mechanicians, surveyors, architects, and designers was vast, far exceeding the supply. In these circumstances it occurred to some unrecorded idealist on the staff of King's College that among the scattered and unconcatenated scientific departments of the institution were, already existent and operative, the main elements necessary for the construction of an effective faculty of engineering. Perhaps the idealist was the principal, Hugh James Rose, himself: he was fruitful of large conceptions. Certainly it was from him that came the first reported word on the subject. On April 26, 1838, he informed the council that " arrangements for a class of civil engineering were in process," and gave them details of the scheme. The second word came two days later in the annual statement of the council to the general court of proprietors. It ran as follows:

> The council have lately had under their consideration the expediency of instituting a class for instruction in civil engineering and mining, which, from the peculiar circumstances of the country, is particularly called for at the present time. They hope at an early period to give public notice of the proposed plan, in order that students desirous of attending such a course may be prepared to commence it after the next summer vacation.

Three weeks later (May 19, 1838) the first prospectus was issued. The subjects of instruction were as follows:

(1)	Mathematics	. . .	Professor	T. G. HALL
(2)	Mechanics, etc.	. . .	,,	H. MOSELEY
(3)	Chemistry, etc.	. . .	,,	J. F. DANIELL
(4)	Geology, etc.	. . .	,,	J. PHILLIPS
(5)	Electricity, etc.	. . .	,,	C. WHEATSTONE
(6)	Machine-drawing	} . .	*Masters to be appointed*	
(7)	Surveying, etc.			

The course was to extend over two or three years, and the fee was to be £10 10s. a term. Detailed syllabuses were issued in the autumn, from which we find that Mr Joseph Bradley had been appointed to teach mechanical drawing, and Mr James Tennant to assist Professor Phillips (who suffered from the inconvenience of living in York) in mineralogy.

The department was opened in October 1838 with 31 students, and the numbers rose to 50 in 1839, and 58 in 1840.

Gradually, as new calls made themselves heard, the scope of the department was widened. In May 1839 arrangements for instruction in surveying were made with Mr H. J. Castle; next month Mr Cooper was appointed " lecturer in manufacturing art and machinery "; in July " regulations in respect to certificates " in engineering were formulated and issued. The year 1840 saw still more substantial developments: a workshop was opened in the basement and " a skilful and experienced workman appointed to direct and assist the labours of the students "; a junior class of civil engineering was formed in order to give prospective students in the department an adequate grounding in mathematics, mechanics, drawing, and composition; but above all—a departure in which King's College was again a pioneer—architecture was added to the syllabus, and Mr William Hosking, one of the leading hydraulic architects and railway engineers of the day, was persuaded to accept the chair of " the arts of construction." In 1841 it was suggested to the council that military engineering might with advantage be dealt with, and the council was advised to secure a professor of fortification and gunnery; but the council (June 11) did not at the moment " think it expedient to establish such a professorship." The young idea was left to find out for itself how to shoot. The council, however, generously provided £200 for the fitting up of the workshop. The various extensions of the scope of the department involved successive changes in its name; a series of cumbrous combinations terminated in 1844 in the simple title, Department of General Instruction in the Applied Sciences.[1]

It was to this new and growing engineering department that in September 1841 Queen Victoria graciously presented

> a large and very valuable collection of instruments of experimental philosophy formed in the Observatory at Kew under the immediate direction of his Majesty George III.

Before November 12 the whole of the collection had been " safely brought from Kew and deposited on the college premises," and the council, obviously embarrassed by the magnitude of the benefaction, appointed an eminent committee to discover what to do with it. To increase their perplexity, one of the proprietors of the college, Mr H. Pownall,

---

[1] The preceding titles were : (1) Civil Engineering and Mining (April 1838). (2) Civil Engineering and Science as applied to Arts and Manufactures (May 1839). (3) Civil Engineering and Architecture, and of Science as applied to Arts and Manufactures (June 1840). (4) Engineering, Architecture, Arts and Manufactures (July 1841).

148

added as "a suitable appendage to the recent gift of her Majesty to King's College, a marble statue of his late Majesty George III by Turnerelli." The committee finally recommended the conversion of one of the two libraries of the college into the "George III Museum," and in this the collection was housed. "The expense of the work has been great," lamented the council to the court of proprietors, "but the council feel that it is more than justified by the occasion." On June 22, 1843, the Prince Consort visited the college, formally to open the museum. He was received by the lords of the council; he attended demonstrations by the various professors and lecturers of the department of engineering, architecture, arts, and manufactures; in particular he adjourned to the terrace of Somerset House to see Professor Wheatstone fire a cannon placed on the top of the shot tower on the south side of the river by means of a spark from a galvanic battery situated in the college. From some unexplained cause the cannon refused to perform; but the prince graciously perceived the idea of the thing.

Professor Wheatstone, we may remark, was at this time making a great sensation in the world of science and technology by his amazing discoveries and inventions in electricity. He had wholly ceased to give lectures to students, and was entirely engrossed in fruitful research. He was the first of a notable series of great men associated with King's College who gradually converted the institution from a mere higher grade school, concerned only to purvey existing knowledge, into a true university wherein not only is the known imparted, but the unknown explored. Bishop Copleston has left so striking a tribute to Wheatstone in his diary (under the date February 2, 1840, his own sixty-fourth birthday) that it is worth transcribing in full:

Last night I was hardly able to sleep from the strong impressions made on my mind by the stupendous discoveries and results of experiments by Mr Whetstone [sic] in electricity and his most ingenious mechanical apparatus for an electric telegraph. He had kindly met me by appointment in the lecture-room of King's College, and for an hour and a quarter was incessantly occupied in explaining to me alone the whole doctrine and the admirable application of it to this purpose of a telegraph. The velocity with which the communication takes place is almost inconceivable. By some curious experiments, however, he seems to have ascertained that it travels 160,000 miles, or more than eight times the circumference of the globe in one second; and, what is more wonderful still, he speaks of this not as denoting *instantaneous* or *immeasurable*, but he has contrived to measure a subdivision of time equal to one-millionth part of a second, and he speaks of this *one second* as a portion of time ascertained, so that it might take *two seconds* to travel 400,000 miles, and so on. Gas and steam have done much, but this agent is destined to do much more, and to work an incalculable change in human affairs. It far exceeds even the feats of pretended magic, and the wildest fictions of the East. This subjugation of nature and conversion of her powers to the use and will of man actually do, as Lord Bacon predicted it would do, a thousand times more than what all the preternatural powers which men have dreamt of and wished to obtain were ever imagined capable of doing. Happy am I in having commenced my sixty-fifth year with this bright vision, which promises to introduce a wonderful reality, and an accession to our intellectual dominion boundless both in extent and in value.[1]

§ 6. *The Third Principal : the Rev. John Lonsdale*

The engineering department in its earlier days had been an object of peculiar care to Principal Rose; and, his biographer tells us, one of his last acts at the college was to make provision for " the geological lectures required by the engineering class." [2] This was in the autumn of 1838, when he had been principal for just over two years. At the time when the council confirmed the appointment of his nominee—Mr James Tennant—as lecturer in geological mineralogy—viz., November 16, 1838—he had but five more weeks to live.

For the first three months of his principalship all had gone well. He was able to continue his many and varied labours—to minister at St Thomas's; to run the *British Magazine*; to edit the *Encyclopædia Metropolitana*; to plan his *New Biographical Dictionary*; to attend the committees of the National Society—and at the same time to manage the heavy business of the numerous departments of King's College; to preach regularly in the college chapel; and to begin a remarkable course of Monday lectures on the evidences of the Christian religion. In February 1837, however, he fell a victim to influenza, of which there was a severe epidemic that year. Already a sufferer from chronic asthma, he never completely recovered from this illness. For the remainder of the session the college saw very little of him. The summer he spent in the Isle of Wight. When the long vacation was over he was still not

---

[1] W. J. Copleston, *Memoir of Edward Copleston, D.D., Bishop of Llandaff* (1851), p. 169.
[2] J. W. Burgon, *Twelve Good Men*, p. 259.

JOHN LONSDALE
Principal 1839–44   150

strong enough to return to the Strand: so the archbishop
invited him to Addington and lodged him in his own house,
where he could keep in touch with affairs. Here during the
winter he wrote a course of lectures on ecclesiastical history
which were read at King's College on successive Mondays by
the Rev. John Allen. All through the summer he was very
ill, and on October 4, 1838,

> the chairman having stated to the council that in consequence
> of the precarious state of the principal's health it was deemed by
> his medical advisers absolutely necessary that he should pass the
> ensuing winter in the south of Europe, it was resolved that leave
> of absence for that purpose be given to the principal, and that the
> chairman be authorised to make the necessary arrangements for
> supplying his place during the time of such absence, subject to
> the approval of his grace the visitor.

At the next meeting of the council the chairman announced
that the Rev. John Lonsdale—a member of the council itself,
and of the provisional committee before it—had agreed to
perform the duties of principal during Mr Rose's absence.

Mr Rose, alas, never came back. He left England on
October 13, hoping to reach Rome. With much difficulty
and with many delays he got as far as Florence by the
middle of November. There dropsy set in, and he died on
December 22, 1838. He was buried at Fiesole, where an
altar-tomb—inscribed with a Latin epitaph from the pen of
the Rev. John Lonsdale—still keeps alive his memory. For the
college chapel Bishop Copleston wrote the Latin memorial.
Mr Rose's death was not only an irreparable loss to the college;
it was a tragedy for the church, and it was an intense personal
bereavement for Archbishop Howley and Bishop Blomfield.
The primate, to whom he had been domestic chaplain, said to
Joshua Watson: "I do not ask for a man to supply Mr Rose's
place; that is impossible; it can never be supplied. But he
must have a successor." What was true of the chaplaincy
was true also of the principalship of the college. But here,
happily, there was no uncertainty as to who should succeed
him. For the whole of the term the Rev. John Lonsdale
had acted as his deputy. In January 1839 he was formally
invited to accept the office, the functions of which he had so
admirably discharged, and on the 29th his formal acceptance
was announced. In a letter to a friend he wrote:

> The unanimous and cordial expression of the council of the
> college, and the advice of friends in whom I could not but

151

place confidence, have weighed with me much in my determination, notwithstanding my misgivings, to accept the office of principal. It may be that I have determined unwisely. All I can say is that it shall be my daily endeavour and prayer to discharge my duties here faithfully.[1]

Of the Rev. John Lonsdale, B.D., third principal of King's College, something has already been said in this book; for he was one of the original promoters of the college.[2] Since 1828 he had been rector of St George's, Bloomsbury, the parish church of the lawyers; in 1836 he had been elected preacher of Lincoln's Inn. Trained at Eton and at King's College, Cambridge, he was a finished scholar, one of the most polished Latinists of his day. In character he was eminently modest and retiring, always preferring others to himself, tending to shrink, not from work, but from prominence and responsibility. He won his way by sheer kindliness, devotion, and ability. Had he cared to push his claims in the smallest degree it is probable that he could have been Provost of Eton in 1840, and Archbishop of Canterbury in 1848. One who knew him well at King's said of him later:

> I was first struck with his marvellous kindness. I felt that I had never known one who showed so much sympathy, so much consideration for others.

In similar strain another wrote:

> A playful gentleness of manner, remarkable simplicity of character, and unexpected kindness to everyone with whom he had to do, could not but win hearts. . . . He was absolutely without party spirit. . . . Above all things he was a lover of good men.[3]

Fortunate indeed was it for the college that so fine and noble a man—and one who was so familiar with its history and its needs—should have been prepared to assume the burden of the principalship at the time of the premature death of Hugh James Rose. One advantage, it should be remarked, Principal Lonsdale enjoyed over and above his predecessors. He was a duly elected member of the council, and as such he continued to attend all its meetings, sit on its committees, and really share in the control of the institution. To him it fell to complete the organization of the department of engineering; to aid in

---

[1] E. B. Denison, *Life of John Lonsdale* (1868), p. 29.
[2] See above, p. 48.
[3] The *Guardian*, October 23, 1867.

the establishment of the hospital; and to do what in him lay to keep going the " senior department " of the college, which tended to languish for lack of definite function.

§ 7. *The School and the " Senior Department "*

Of the two departments of the college which purveyed general information—divinity, classics, mathematics, history and literature, with a modicum of science, modern languages, and drawing—the "junior," or school, flourished, while the " senior " did not. The majority of the boys who wanted this type of middle-class training were destined for commercial careers in the city, and they had had enough of it when they emerged from the top of the school at the age of sixteen. The number of those who wished to continue it till eighteen or nineteen in the airier amplitudes of the professorial lecture-rooms was small; although it included an unusually large proportion of youths of character and ability who were destined to attain eminence in the church and the world. In the " senior department," as we have already observed, the main purpose of the instruction given was to prepare the students for entry to the universities of Oxford and Cambridge. For many years the college looked askance at the godless University of London; published with reluctance the notices of its examinations; and discouraged its students from sitting for its degrees. It tried to make its A.K.C., of which religious knowledge was the basis, the equivalent of the London B.A. ; but the world refused to accept the valuation.

The council, it will be recollected, regarded 350 as the normal number of boys in the school; and it had passed a resolution that only in exceptional cases was the number to exceed the maximum of 400. In 1837 the actual figure on the rolls was 380, and by 1839 this had risen to 396; in 1840 the four hundred limit was passed, and so great was the pressure to enter the school that in 1841 (September 17) the regulation as to limit was formally suspended. New rooms were added, new teachers secured, and nature was allowed its course. By 1843 the names on the register all but touched 500. The council, indeed, had cause to be profoundly thankful for the prosperity of the school. Had it not been for the congestion of the infernal regions, amid whose gloomy vaults the *impubes* were grounded in the rudiments of learning, the regions of light wherein professors pointed the way to the altitudes would have had to close their portals. The minutes of the council at this date do not give many details of finance; but they do happen to contain the estimates for the year 1838–39, from which it appears that out of an anticipated income of £3310, no less than £2520 was expected to be derived from the council's share of the school fees.

Much of the success of the school was undoubtedly attributable to the energy and high ability of the excellent headmaster, Dr J. R. Major, who continued to rule it—under the principal and the council—for the protracted period of thirty-six years (1831–67). He was faithfully and efficiently assisted by a staff which in its higher grades was almost as stable as himself—in particular, the Rev. J. Edwards (second master, 1831–52), the Rev. J. Fearnley (third master, and later vice-master, 1832–67), the Rev. R. Hodgson (fourth master, 1832–49), and the Rev. T. O. Cockayne (1837–69). All of these diligent pedagogues employed their none too ample leisure in producing text-books which increased both their own emoluments and the notoriety of the institution to which they were attached. In January 1837 a slight modification in the school hours was made: the school was to meet from 9 A.M. to 3 P.M. all the year round, a break of fifteen or twenty minutes being allowed toward the middle of that six-hour period to the classes one by one: it was impossible to have four or five hundred boys all at once crowding the narrow corridor, the inadequate gymnasium, and the restricted playground. In June of the same year it was ordered by the council

> that a book be provided and kept in the custody of the school porter, and that every master upon entering or leaving the school each day do write his name and the exact time of entering or leaving the school in the said book.

In December 1841 the school had to be closed because of an outbreak of fever. Until Principal Rose's time a single prize-distribution had served for the general senior department and for the junior. But Principal Lonsdale separated the two; partly because the growth of the school strained the utmost capacity of the college hall; partly because the smallness of the higher department was thrown into painful relief by the magnitude of the lower; and perhaps also because scenes such as the following, however pleasing to fond parents, tended to dim the dignity of the professors. "It was indeed gratifying," said the *Literary Gazette*, in reporting an early prize-giving,

> to witness the exhilaration of a tiny infant of not more than eight or nine years old—who, it was stated, could read Cornelius

An Early Victorian Prize-giving in the Large Theatre

Nepos—standing on tiptoe to receive at the hands of the highest dignitary of our church the reward to which his good conduct and assiduity had entitled him.

Whilst the numbers of pupils in the school thus went up by leaps and bounds, those of the students who attended the general course in the senior department tended to diminish. We noted that they reached their high-water mark in 1834–35 with a register of 133; in 1836–37 this had fallen to 118; by 1841–42 it had sunk to the low level of 84. The causes of the decline have already been suggested. After 1842 there was a temporary revival, probably owing, on the one side, to the growing fame of some of the professors at King's, and, on the other side, to a series of striking successes which old students of the college achieved at Oxford and Cambridge. The reports for the five years beginning 1840 show that at Cambridge among the students sent up by King's College were eight scholars, twenty-five wranglers (including Arthur Cayley, 1842, one of the most brilliant senior wranglers ever known), five firsts in classics (including Charles Kingsley), twelve fellows of colleges; while at Oxford simultaneously old King's men secured six scholarships and one fellowship. The teachers whose labours bore these remarkable fruits were primarily Professors Hall (mathematics), Browne (classics), and Dale (English). The two former continued to labour at the college until the sixties; but Professor Dale, vicar of St Bride's, Fleet Street, a popular preacher of great repute, found it necessary to resign his chair in 1840. A few years later he became vicar of the vast and populous parish of St Pancras, which, before he left it, he succeeded in dividing up into no fewer than twenty incumbencies. He ended his strenuous career as Dean of Rochester (1870).

Dale's successor was a man notable in the history of King's College, and in the religious history of nineteenth-century England, viz., the Rev. Frederick Denison Maurice, who was appointed by the council on June 13, 1840. Born in 1805, the son of a unitarian minister, he had studied law at Cambridge and practised journalism in London before, in 1830, he found his way to orthodoxy, went to Oxford, and began to read for orders. When ordained in 1834 he was already known in academic and ecclesiastical circles as a man of remarkable metaphysical ability, high individuality, fine character, and humble piety. The publication in the same year of his first theological work, *Subscription no Bondage*, a defence of religious tests at the universities, strongly commended him to the tractarians, won the approval of the council of King's College, and secured the friendship of Hugh James Rose. The powerful influence of Rose helped to obtain for him in 1836 the chaplaincy of Guy's Hospital, which was situated in Rose's Southwark parish. He was still chaplain at Guy's when appointed to succeed Dale at King's College; and since his work as professor involved no more than the delivery of two afternoon lectures a week—one in history, one in literature—for thirty weeks a year, he was able to retain his chaplaincy. In 1839, moreover, he had become editor of a new *Educational Magazine* which was energetically opposing the state-inspection of elementary schools, and was ardently contending that the task of educating the people is the proper function of the national church. This also was doctrine delectable to the council of King's. There was, indeed, at this date, little except obscurity (which was regarded as superior profundity) to distinguish the utterances of Frederick Denison Maurice from those of John Henry Newman. On October 13, 1840, Professor Maurice delivered his inaugural lecture, which was published in the next number of the *Educational Magazine*. It must have given great satisfaction to the authorities. The end of education, it said, is moral and religious; it consists in the formation of character; in the preparation of man for life and immortality. The prime means for the attainment of this end is, of course, theology, which imparts knowledge of God; but valuable adjuncts to theology are classical literature, which reveals the nature of man, and mathematics, which gives the key to the science of the universe. History and English, the subjects of the lecture and of the courses which are to follow it, cannot claim the eminence of any one of these three protagonal subjects; but they have their uses. Their main purpose is to reveal the workings of divine providence, and interpret the ways of God to the human race. The courses thus introduced by Maurice consisted, on the one hand, of a survey of English history to the time of Henry VIII, and, on the other hand, of a detailed study of the *Prologue to Chaucer's Canterbury Tales*. They were rather fantastic courses, tending to bewilderment, their method being the elucidation of truth by the elimination of fact. "I never," said F. W. Farrar, who attended the lectures a few years later, when the method had been matured, "I never in my life attended any history lectures which dealt so little with facts." At first the students strove to follow: "The lads," wrote Maurice to his wife on October 20, 1840, "sit with their desks before them and write after me." This was penned at the close of the first lecture of the history course. As the other lectures succeeded, and comprehension failed, the lads first ceased to write, and then ceased to sit. Chaos supervened, and Maurice, who had as little ability to inflict temporal punishment as he had to imagine eternal punishment, was helpless. "I do not know why that gentleman is doing what he is doing," he said on one occasion respecting a conspicuous disturber of the peace, "but I am sure it is for some great and wise purpose; and if he will come here and explain to us all what it is, we shall be delighted to hear him." Delicate irony of this kind was lost on the hobbledehoys; so the wiser students who wished to hear the lecturer's lofty speculations, together with the more humane students who realized that even professors have feelings, formed a band of informal monitors, pledged to suppress the wilder manifestations of barbarism. The monitors had their reward. The professor, says Farrar, "inspired us with a lifelong sense that history was one of the grandest of human studies"—history, of course, when freed from the debasing limitations of facts; and "interesting and valuable to those who could appreciate them as were the lectures on history, those on English literature were even more so." [1]

Other changes on the staff must be chronicled more briefly. In October 1836 Professor Seddon resigned the chair of oriental languages, and was succeeded (April 1837) by Mr Duncan Forbes. In December 1838 Mr Edward Bullock followed Professor Preston, who had been unable to form a class, in the chair of law and jurisprudence. In April 1839, on grounds of health, Dr R. W. Higgs was compelled to vacate the classical lectureship, combined with librarianship, which he had held for four years; he had as his successor a notable scholar and great teacher, destined to remain within the college in various offices for nearly forty sessions—a man whose skilled labour on the state-papers of Henry VIII made him the pioneer of the modern scientific study of the Tudor period— the Rev. John Sherren Brewer. In 1840, when geology had become part of the engineering course, the absentee Professor Phillips had to give way to the more accessible Professor D. T. Ansted. The same year an interesting innovation was attempted; Mr William Dyce of the Royal Academy, an early pre-raphaelite, an accomplished painter and a devout high churchman, was appointed professor of the theory of the fine

[1] F. Maurice, *Life of F. D. Maurice*, vol. i, pp. 288–318.

arts. Nothing, however, came of the appointment, and the professorship unostentatiously expired. In October 1840 Professor Angel de Villalobos succeeded Professor Alcalá in the chair of Spanish. At the end of 1841 Professor David Don, the botanist, died, and his chair was conferred (1842) upon Mr Edward Forbes. A simultaneous change which caused a great stir in the world was that due to the elevation of the Rev. M. S. Alexander to the protestant episcopate of the United Church of England and Ireland in Jerusalem (November 7, 1841). Of this and its consequences more in a moment. At present it is enough to note that the bishop was succeeded in the chair of Hebrew and Rabbinical literature at King's by Dr Alexander M'Caul.

The organization of the departments of medicine and engineering made the title " senior department," as applied to the section of the college in which the humanities were studied, inapplicable. On June 13, 1840, accordingly, the council resolved to drop the term altogether and to substitute for it the title "department of general literature and science." A year later the professors of French and German tried to get their subjects raised from the rank of optional and secondary studies to the rank of compulsory and primary studies; but the council refused to accede to their request.

During this period death was busy among the older members of the college council: in 1840 the Marquis Camden passed away; in 1841 Lord Henley, Sir Astley Cooper, Sir John Richardson, and Archdeacon Cambridge. Among the new members selected to fill vacant places were Mr W. E. Gladstone in 1838, Earl Howe, Lord Francis Egerton, and Mr Justice Coleridge in 1841, and Lord Radstock in 1842.

Two new college prizes were instituted—viz., the (Sir George) Stephen Prize (1840)—the annual interest on fifty guineas— for an English essay; and the Ireland Bequest (1842)—a legacy of £1000 from the late dean of Westminster, the proceeds of which were to go

> for the support and promotion of the principles of the Established Church of England in connexion with the literature and science taught within the said college.

In 1838 the first Worsley Scholar, Mr Henry von Dadelszen, completed his course of study, was ordained, and was sent under the auspices of the S.P.G. as a missionary to Madras. In 1838, too, was inaugurated one of the first students' societies to be established in England—viz., the King's College Medical

and Scientific Society—a society still extant, although connected now with the hospital rather than the college, and
renamed the Listerian Society. Three years later a small
group of students, headed by Henry Morley, started a monthly
King's College Magazine. Its literary quality was unusually
high, but it did not pay, and it was dropped after a run of
eighteen months (July 1841 to December 1842).

In 1841 the seats in the chapel were rearranged. On May 14
the council

> considered the desire expressed by the principal for an alteration
> in the present very inconvenient arrangement of the sittings of the
> chapel, and directed that Sir Robert Smirke should be requested
> to submit a plan and estimate of the expense of the alteration
> proposed.

On July 11 the council authorized the carrying out of the
suggested rearrangement at a cost not to exceed £300. At the
same time it was ordered that " a new access be made to
the organ gallery, and that the projection at the entrance
into the chapel be removed."

§ 8. *The Bishopric of Jerusalem*

On November 7, 1841, in the chapel of Lambeth Palace, the
Rev. Michael Solomon Alexander, professor of Hebrew and
Rabbinical literature at King's College, was by the Archbishop
of Canterbury, assisted by the Bishops of London and Rochester,
consecrated first Bishop of the United Church of England and
Ireland in Jerusalem. This was a strange event, and it had
unexpected consequences both in the world at large and in the
college. It was strange; for there was not a single anglican,
whether clerical or lay, within the circuit of the new bishop's
jurisdiction. It had unexpected consequences; for it was a
prime cause, on the one hand, of John Henry Newman's
secession to Rome, and, on the other hand, of Frederick
Denison Maurice's fatal transference from the chair of history
to the chair of divinity in King's College.

The circumstances which led to this ecclesiastical aberra-
tion were partly political and partly religious. First,
and apparently entirely irrelevantly, the cabinet wished to
strengthen the ties between Great Britain and Prussia.
Secondly, and not much more obviously to the point, the new
king of Prussia, Frederick William IV, and his friend Baron

von Bunsen, both sincere Christians and ardent protestants, wished to strengthen both church and state in their dominions by uniting Lutherans and Calvinists under a common episcopacy. Thirdly, Britain and Prussia, as the leading protestant powers in Europe, wished, as protectors of protestants, to claim the same rights of supervision in the Turkish dominions as were enjoyed by Russia as protector of Greek Christians, and by France as protector of Latin Christians. Fourthly, the anglican bishops, and in particular the Archbishop of Canterbury and the Bishop of London, were anxious to introduce protestantism into the Holy Land, to convert Jews and Arabs to Christianity, to enter into fraternal relations with Lutherans and Calvinists, and into patronal relations with Armenians, Jacobites, Maronites, Nestorians, Monophysites, and any other sectaries who were not orthodox Greeks or catholic Romans, and to weld them all into a solid third party around the sacred sepulchre. Finally, they were not unwilling by a display of cordial co-operation with Lutheran Prussia to dissociate themselves emphatically from the promulgators of the recent notorious Tract No. XC, who spoke of Lutheranism as "a heresy repugnant to scripture," and repudiated protestantism in all its forms.

Hence when in July 1841 Baron von Bunsen came on a special mission from the King of Prussia to discuss the matter of the bishopric he received a cordial and sympathetic welcome from the leaders of both church and state. The matter was soon arranged: Prussia and Britain should share the expense; the two governments should nominate to the office alternately, Britain (as already possessing bishops) starting off, Prussia taking second turn, and thus getting the thin edge of episcopacy into the Lutheran system. Lutherans and Anglicans were to enjoy equal status and privileges, the thirty-nine articles being remitted in the case of the former, the Augsburg Confession in the case of the latter. It was a triumph of compromise and concession.

Preliminaries having been thus amicably and accommodatingly arranged, Parliament passed an Act (October 5, 1841) authorizing the new bishop, when consecrated, to

> exercise spiritual jurisdiction over ministers of British congregations of the United Church of England and Ireland, and over such Protestant congregations as may be desirous of placing themselves under his authority.

A month later, as we have seen, the Professor of Hebrew at

King's College was consecrated to this unprecedented post in the presence of a congregation which included

> his Excellency the Chevalier Bunsen, as representative of the King of Prussia; Sir Stratford Canning, her Majesty's ambassador extraordinary to the Porte; the Baron Schlemitz, Prussian *chargé d'affaires*; the Prussian consul-general Hebeler; Lord Ashley; the Right Hon. W. E. Gladstone; the Right Hon. Sir John Nicholl; Sir R. H. Inglis; the Rev. Dr Abeken, chaplain to the King of Prussia; and many of the clergy in their robes.

The clergy in their robes, however, did not comprise any of the tractarians. These were horrified at the whole procedure: the dominance of the state over the church offended them; the fraternization of Anglicans with Lutherans scandalized them; the relaxation of the formularies of the church outraged them; the patronage bestowed upon heretics and schismatics such as Nestorians and Monophysites filled them with loathing; the ostentatious antagonism to Rome displayed by the thing with its flaunting protestantism caused them intense annoyance and pain. Newman, as is well known, sent (November 11, 1841) his tremendous protest to the Bishop of Oxford and prepared to pack up for the journey which he eventually took in 1845.[1] The Rev. W. Palmer, one of those who had helped to plan the *Tracts for the Times* in Hugh James Rose's Hadleigh Rectory in 1833, wrote a ferocious pamphlet which not only denounced the Anglo-Prussian evangelical alliance, but made a general attack on protestants and protestantism. This furious tractarian assault irritated and alarmed the Anglican episcopate. They were, therefore, immensely grateful when Professor Maurice came forward and in three unanswerable, because incomprehensible, letters—one on the name Protestant, the second on the Church of England, and the third on the Jerusalem bishopric—repelled the tractarian onslaught. Maurice's repute as a theologian was confirmed when a little later the Archbishop of York, together with the Bishop of London, appointed him Boyle Lecturer for 1845, and when, almost simultaneously, the Archbishop of Canterbury conferred upon him the Warburton Lectureship. No one could possibly hope to receive higher credentials. When, therefore, in 1846 three theological chairs were established at King's College, his appointment to one of them was obvious and almost inevitable. But that is a story which belongs to the next chapter.

Before this chapter closes, however, one further episode,

[1] See Newman's *Apologia pro Vita Sua*, pp. 141–146.

L

arising out of Jerusalem, must be recorded. On February 2, 1842, the King of Prussia, who had come over to England to act as sponsor to Albert Edward, Prince of Wales, visited King's College, to behold the sacred spot from which the first Anglo-Lutheran Bishop of Jerusalem had been elevated. The council presented to him the following address:

> The Governors and Proprietors, Council, Principal, Professors, Masters, Associates, and Students of King's College, London, approach your Majesty with the expression of the humble and grateful feelings of their hearts.
>
> The members of this institution, which is founded on the principle that " the fear of the Lord is the beginning of wisdom," and which is connected in its administration with the doctrine and discipline of the Church of England, cannot but regard with especial interest the arrival on these shores of a monarch who has long been eminent for his attachment to literature and science, and above all to religion; and in particular who has lately selected the Apostolical Church of England as the means of reviving in the East the knowledge and practice of the Gospel in that which they believe to be its purest form; and with a view to the permanence, as well as the growth of true religion, has munificently led the way to the endowment of a bishopric of that church in Jerusalem.
>
> Interested as all true sons of the Church of England are in everything which promotes her influence in the world, those who are connected with King's College trust that they may be permitted to express to your Majesty a more than ordinary and almost personal sense of your Majesty's liberality towards the Church in Jerusalem, when your Majesty shall be pleased to recollect that one of their own body, their Professor of Hebrew and Rabbinical Literature, has been appointed to fill in the first instance the episcopal chair of that Church.
>
> While they thus express their special interest in the occasion which has recently called forth your Majesty as one of the nursing fathers of the Church in a distant land, they do not the less share in the feeling of thankful respect with which the religious purpose of your Majesty's visit to our beloved Sovereign has been regarded by all classes here; and they pray that the Royal Infant, for whom at his admission into the Church, your Majesty has been pleased to appear in person as sponsor, may, as he grows in years, grow in wisdom and grace, and be the instrument in God's good providence of extending and strengthening the Christian relation which has been formed between the Royal Houses of Prussia and England, and that the two greatest Protestant Sovereigns of Europe may be permanently united in the maintenance of Christian liberty and true religion to the good of mankind and to the glory of Almighty God.

A PERIOD OF EXPANSION

NOTE

I. Number of Students, 1836–43

| Session | College | | | | School | Total |
| | Regular | | | Occa-sional | | |
	General	Medical	Engineer-ing			
1836–37	118	65	—	162	380	725
1837–38	116	60	—	143	346	665
1838–39	120	65	31	137	396	749
1839–40	112	81	50	102	432	777
1840–41	87	88	58	116	462	811
1841–42	84	93	53	112	471	813
1842–43	106	115	37	113	497	868
1843–44	130	131	33	80	465	839

II. Distinguished Students

Among those who entered the college in the period 1836–43, and later became famous, were the following :

Kingsley, Charles (January 24, 1837).[1] Notable novelist, social reformer, and divine.

Bowman, William (June 6, 1838). Eminent ophthalmic surgeon; pioneer in the training of nurses; joint-professor of physiology at King's College, 1848–55; surgeon at King's College hospital, 1856–62.

Morley, Henry (October 2, 1838). Evening lecturer in English at King's College, 1857–65; professor of English at University College, 1865–94; noted writer and editor.

Miller, William Allen (October 5, 1838). The first student of the college to take the London M.D. degree (1842); spent the whole remainder of his life at King's College; professor of chemistry, 1845–70.

Johnson, George (1839). Eminent pathologist; one of the most brilliant of King's College medical students; first resident medical tutor, 1843; physician to King's College hospital, 1856; professor at King's College, 1857–86; knighted, 1892.

Galton, Francis (October 4, 1839). Pioneer in the study of heredity and in the advocacy of eugenics; went on to Cambridge, 1840; knighted, 1909.

[1] The dates in brackets are those of " signing on." The month and day are given when these are ascertainable.

Plumptre, Edward Hayes (October 4, 1839). Fellow of Brasenose College, Oxford, 1844–47; chaplain at King's College, 1847–1868, and professor in the theological department, 1853–81; Dean of Wells, 1881–91.

Rogers, J. E. Thorold (April 28, 1841). Pioneer in the economic interpretation of history; professor of economics at King's College, 1859–90; liberal M.P. for Southwark and Bermondsey, 1880–86.

Barry, Alfred (October 4, 1842). Took seven prizes in 1843; went to Cambridge, where he was fourth wrangler and seventh classic in 1848; principal of Cheltenham College, 1862–68; principal of King's College, 1868–83; Bishop of Sydney and Primate of Australia, 1884–89.

Burges, William (April 21, 1843). Noted architect; designed cathedrals at Lille (1856), Brisbane (1859), and Cork (1862).

Boyd, Andrew K. H. (October 2, 1843). Famous presbyterian divine and writer; minister of first charge St Andrews, 1865–99; entered King's College from King's College School.

CHAPTER VII

PEACE AND PROSPERITY

1843–53

§ 1. *The Fourth Principal : the Rev. Richard William Jelf*

FAITHFULLY and well for nearly five years (January 1839–December 1843) did the Rev. John Lonsdale serve the college as principal. Avoiding controversy, holding aloof from the enthusiasts of all political and religious parties, he gave to the college a catholicity and comprehensiveness, an urbanity and sweet reasonableness representative of the Church of England at its best. Himself a moderate and loyal anglican, of the school of Hugh James Rose, he worked in the most cordial harmony with evangelicals such as Thomas Dale, and latitudinarians such as Frederick Denison Maurice. On the council he helped to keep the peace between crusted low church tories like Sir Robert Inglis and volcanic high church peelites like Mr W. E. Gladstone. His character, his deep and genuine piety, his scholarship, his outstanding abilities, his powers of organization, his capacity for winning affection and for drawing out the best in his associates, had long marked him out for preferment. In 1842 he had become Archdeacon of Middlesex, and at the end of 1843 he was nominated to the bishopric of Lichfield.

On November 10, 1843, the Bishop of London announced to the council " the elevation of the principal to the see of Lichfield," and the council unanimously passed a resolution of congratulation, gratitude, and regret, specially emphasizing

> the advantages which the college has derived during the last five years from the rare combination of learning and judgment, of firmness and gentleness, that has marked his [the principal's] administration of its discipline.

On December 8 a letter of acknowledgment from the newly consecrated bishop was read, in which he speaks with evident emotion of

> the unwavering countenance and support of the council; the most cordial co-operation on the part of the professors and

165

masters; the never-failing respect and attention from the students; and the uninterrupted prosperity of the institution.

"I have," he says, "had everything to make my office pleasant to me." He left the college to his successor in an admirable condition of tranquillity and successful activity. His departure, however, did not, as had been the case with Bishop Otter, mean the severance of his connexion with the college. Far from it. Not only did he continue for the whole remainder of his long life a member of the council; he was a member unusually regular in attendance. He must frequently have come to London from the Midlands for no other purpose than to further the interests of King's. In his eightieth year, the year of his death, 1867, he presided at the annual general court of proprietors—the last survivor of the provisional committee which forty years earlier had effected the foundation of the college. He died, October 1867, after a laborious and strikingly fruitful episcopate of nearly a quarter of a century, "the best loved bishop in the land."

A not unworthy successor to this estimable man was found in the Rev. Richard William Jelf, D.D., Canon of Christ Church, and sometime Fellow of Oriel College, Oxford.[1] The appointment was made at a special meeting of the council on December 15, 1843, and, subject to confirmation by the governors, was to take effect on December 22.[2] The confirmation was readily and promptly given, and early in 1844 the new principal came into residence. His principalship at King's was destined to last even longer than Dr Lonsdale's episcopate at Lichfield. Not until 1868 did he retire. Hence, of the hundred years that are surveyed in this volume almost exactly one-fourth is comprised in the reign of Dr Jelf. This protracted period, however, as we shall see, has to be divided for descriptive purposes into two parts. The first ten years—a normal and natural continuation of Principal Lonsdale's halcyon rule— were years of peace and prosperity. The last fifteen years, on the other hand, were years of controversy, conflict, discord,

---

[1] Julius Hare had strongly urged F. D. Maurice to apply for the vacant principalship. But Maurice had prudently declined to allow his name to be put forward. "I have not the slightest talent for government," he had modestly and truthfully said. "I have not succeeded in procuring the least respect from the body of the pupils, and very imperfectly the attention of my own class—rather a bad omen for a future principal." (F. Maurice, *Life of Frederick Denison Maurice*, vol. i, p. 355.)

[2] A significant resolution, passed at the same council meeting, December 15, ran: "That until further directions to the contrary, the secretary invite the principal to be present at the meetings of the council and the committee of education and buildings."

RICHARD WILLIAM JELF
Principal 1844–68

and decline. And the cause of the lamentable change was to no small extent the work of that saintly and devoted man who, toward the end of his days, said, and said sincerely: " The desire for unity and the search after unity both in nation and church have haunted me all my days." [1] So little do man's intentions affect the consequences of his actions! A premature passion for unity is a sure precursor of a new schism; and no one is more likely to originate a novel sect than an enthusiast for comprehensiveness who would obliterate or amalgamate all the existing sects.

Dr Jelf, when he assumed the principalship of King's College, was forty-six years old. The son of a Gloucestershire knight, he had been educated at Eton and Christ Church. At Oxford he had made his mark by scholarship and character, and in 1821 had been elected to a fellowship at Oriel, during the great provostship of Edward Copleston—whose recommendation no doubt did much to secure his appointment to King's in 1843. At Oriel he had found himself a member of that marvellous (if theologically mixed) company which included Whately, Keble, Hawkins, Hampden, Thomas Arnold, J. H. Newman, and (Jelf's old schoolfellow) E. B. Pusey. He had left Oxford for a time in 1826, before the acids and the alkalis in the Oriel mixture had begun seriously to effervesce: he had left in order to become tutor to Prince George, heir-apparent to the Hanoverian throne.[2] He remained in Germany, with intervals, for thirteen years, and when he came back to Oxford in 1839 to take up residence as canon of Christ Church—again in association with Pusey—he brought with him a thorough knowledge of the German language, an intense detestation of German theology, and a German countess as his wife. His absence from England during the period of the embittered controversies that had raged round Catholic Emancipation (1829), University Tests (1834), and Tract No. LXVI (1836), combined with his well-known moderation and integrity, caused him to be regarded as an arbiter in the war between the evangelicals and the tractarians which he found in process on his return. Newman addressed an open letter to Jelf stating the anglo-catholic case, and to him Newman's opponents made their reply. His judgment was eminently balanced and sane; he disliked equally the

[1] F. Maurice, *op. cit.*, vol. ii, p. 632.
[2] Jelf's former pupil, when King of Hanover, attended a prize-giving at King's College on June 27, 1853, and addressed to the students " gracious words of warning and encouragement."

narrowness of the low church, the looseness of the broad church, and the Romeward inclination of the high church. His sympathies undoubtedly leaned to the tractarian side, and in 1841 he cordially joined his old Oriel friends, Pusey, Newman, and Keble, in founding the Library of Anglo-Catholic Theology, instituted for the purpose of republishing the obsolete works of a large number of long-defunct divines—works "maintaining and inculcating the doctrines and discipline of the Anglican branch of the Catholic and Apostolic Church"; and for this enormous series he himself edited several cubic feet (about twenty pounds avoirdupois) of the writings of Bishop Jewell (eight volumes, 1848). In 1842, however, he preached a characteristic and decisive sermon before the University, entitled *Via Media, or The Church of England our Providential Path between Romanism and Dissent.* Next year, as the authoritative exponent of the *via media*, he was called upon to perform the first of a series of painful tasks of one and the same kind—viz., to act as assessor or inquisitor to the vice-chancellor in examining the sermon for which Pusey, his old schoolfellow and colleague, was ultimately suspended from preaching in the university. Jelf's prominence and importance were immediately recognized by his appointment as Bampton Lecturer for 1844, and he was busy preparing his discourses on *The Means of Grace, their Mutual Connection and Combined Use,* when he was called to the principalship of King's.[1]

As to the personality of the new principal, nothing better could possibly be written than the noble tribute paid to it in King's College chapel twenty-seven years later by Professor E. H. Plumptre, brother-in-law of Maurice, and colleague of Jelf from 1847 onward. Dr Jelf, said the preacher, had lived

> a singularly happy life . . . free from most of the anxieties and cares of earth, happy in the work given him to do, and in being allowed to witness its results.

He then continued:

> It was a life unshaken by the storms of passion, free from the unrest of the tempest-winds of doubt. Others who have fought

---

[1] Cf. *Life of F. D. Maurice,* vol. i, p. 363 : "It would scarcely have been possible for the governing body of King's College—anxious above all things to avoid the falsehood of extremes—to hit upon a man more marked out by circumstances as *par excellence* the representative *via media* man. His natural kindliness of disposition, and strict conformity to the current opinions of the day, were qualities that greatly enhanced his qualifications for the post."

and conquered, passing through the surging waves and the clouds of darkness till they find themselves in the haven where they would be, and under the clear light of heaven, may gain by that experience greater insight into the spirit of the age in which they live, greater power to sympathise with and help those who are in danger of making shipwreck of the faith; but as regards the happiness of life, we cannot doubt that it is on the side of the clear, untroubled, unwavering faith, of which our friend's life was an example. To him, that which he read in the Bible, that which had been handed down from the first ages of Christendom, that which is embodied in the prayers, creeds, articles, of our church, were as the appointed witnesses to the truth, and humbly and reverently he accepted their guidance. . . .

A character formed on such a basis presented, as might be expected, two aspects: on the one side, the humility which enters into the Christian life in proportion as a man realises his own need of forgiveness for the past, and of a strength higher than his own for the future; on the other, the firmness which will not surrender one jot or tittle of what he holds to be the truth of God. . . .

True to his conviction that the path of safety was the middle way between opposite extremes, he entered his protest against movements that seemed to him to be carrying us back to superstition, or throwing us upon a merely subjective and emotional religion, or drifting into the shoreless sea of doubt. . . .

The earnestness of that sincerity was always tempered by the courtesy and the humility which were ingrained in his nature, and it never passed into bitterness. It was saved from that peril, so proverbial in the disputes of theologians, precisely because it was, to the very root of it, sincere. From first to last, it was the part of a man who never wilfully misjudged or misrepresented, and therefore was always able to carry on controversy without personal resentment.

It is difficult to conceive two persons more diametrically different from one another than this pillar of orthodoxy and monument of unquestioning faith, this supporter of tradition and maintainer of convention—whose creed, in whatever age of the world's history he had happened to be born, would have been determined by the place of his nativity and the circumstances of his education—and his distinguished professor of English literature and history, the extremest of individualists, who, having already made the protracted journey from Unitarian dissent to Anglican conformity, was busy examining the novel and unfamiliar sanctuary in which he found himself, in order to discover as many secret passages, unsuspected hiding-places, and emergency exits as possible. Jelf was the tory, Maurice the radical; Jelf the serene believer, Maurice the restless inquirer; Jelf the refurbisher of the old, Maurice the pioneer of the new. They can have had no moral or intellectual communion whatsoever. Nevertheless there would probably have been no overt clash between them had the college remained constituted as it was when Jelf became principal; or had Maurice continued in the position in which Jelf found him. But early in Jelf's career as principal a new department was instituted in the college, viz., the department of theology, and in this new department Maurice was installed as one of the three professors of divinity. *Hinc illæ lachrimæ.*

§ 2. *The Department of Theology*

It may seem strange at first sight that in a college specially founded for religious purposes, and largely governed by bishops, there should have been no department of theology until 1846. Yet the apparent anomaly is easily explained. The universities of Oxford and Cambridge were the special nurseries of the church, and until the beginning of Queen Victoria's reign they seemed capable of supplying both the quantity and the quality of clergy required. Hence when King's College was founded, and the sanction of the old universities was imperatively necessary for the success of the new venture, the promoters of the college had expressly repudiated the desire, on the one hand, to grant degrees, and, on the other hand, to train candidates for ordination. King's College was intended to receive boys from school at the age of sixteen, to give them two or three years' drill in the higher departments of classical literature and mathematical science, and then send them on to Oxford and Cambridge to obtain their diplomas and receive their theological training. The new institution was to be the feeder, not the rival, of the old universities. Dr D'Oyly in his open letter to the Right Hon. Robert Peel, 1828—the letter which initiated the movement to found King's College—said:

> I would mention my entire acquiescence in that which is stated at the beginning [of the London University manifesto]—viz., that the universities of Oxford and Cambridge supply ample means of educating the clergy of the Established Church,

and he explicitly added that the arguments of his letter applied " solely to those students who are destined for lay professions."

Since 1828, however, circumstances had changed. On the one hand, the number of young men going to Oxford and

Cambridge with a view to entering the church had begun to decline: ferocious theological controversy was alienating them; other professions were drawing them. On the other hand, it had become evident that it was desirable to open the doors of the ministry to numerous young men of piety and ability who by reason of poverty were not in a position to incur the heavy expense of the Oxford or Cambridge curriculum. The grave social unrest of the chartist era, and the growing antagonism of the working-class to the establishment, indicated the importance of breaking down the barriers which had tended to make the clerical profession the preserve of the aristocracy and gentry, and of welcoming the entry of worthy representatives of the middle and lower orders. Hence in 1846 the bishops received with ready favour the suggestion that a new department should be established in King's College to prepare for holy orders men who would otherwise find themselves debarred from the necessary training. Two other considerations also weighed with the council of the college: first, they felt, and rightly felt, that the existence of a theological department would strengthen the languishing department of general literature and science, for the classical course would be the natural and nominal precursor of the theological course; secondly, they were confident that

> one portion of the college being devoted to divinity as a distinct object of study, must act favourably upon all the branches of instruction, and impart to the whole something of the ennobling, elevating, and sacred character which belongs to divinity itself.[1]

The new department would not injure the older universities; it would benefit both the church and the world; above all, it would advance both the material and the moral well-being of the college.

The first formal proposal for the new department was made in a communication laid before the council by Dr Jelf on January 3, 1846. It is entitled *A Plan for the Establishment of a Theological Department in King's College, London, submitted to His Grace the Visitor by the Principal.* It had received the " general approval " of both the Archbishop of Canterbury and the Bishop of London. In it the principal stresses the need of the church for more clergymen, due particularly to " the multiplication of small benefices "; he points out that the three years' course at King's leading up to the A.K.C. is quite equal in standard to the ordinary degree course at the older

---

[1] *Annual Report*, 1846.

universities; he urges the desirability of providing a theological course as an appropriate sequel to it, and he roughly sketches the details of the proposed course, which, he says, could be provided by the college—a vital matter—at very little additional expense. The council received the suggestion favourably, and referred the principal's plan to the education committee for consideration and report.[1]

The committee reported within a week (January 9, 1846), and the council accepted its recommendations, which differed in some secondary details from the principal's original plan. It was resolved: (1) that a theological department should be established, to commence operations at Easter 1846; (2) that the persons eligible for admission should be associates of King's College, graduates of Oxford or Cambridge, or other persons recommended by a bishop and approved by the principal; (3) that all on admission should sign the thirty-nine articles; (4) that the course of study should extend over two years, and should comprise Christian evidences, Hebrew Old Testament, Greek New Testament, the articles, the prayer book, ecclesiastical history, and " the theory and practice of the pastoral office "; (5) that theological professors and tutors should be appointed by the council, subject to the approval of the visitor; (6) that opportunities for district visiting and Sunday school teaching should be provided for the students of the department; (7) that instruction in singing and in public health should be given; (8) that the fees should be £4 13s. on entrance, and £12 12s. a term; (9) that certificates should be granted by the principal to successful and satisfactory students qualifying them to apply for ordination; (10) that such and such salaries should be paid; (11) that any surplus of receipts over expenditure should be set aside to provide a residence for theological students, or to found theological fellowships; and (12) that a certain number of free places should be reserved for impecunious students.

On February 13 the council were informed that twenty-three bishops had agreed to accept King's College certificates in

---

[1] It may be noted in passing that this question of the theological department was the last big matter connected with his beloved college that came within Dr George D'Oyly's ken. For some time his health had been failing ; his last council meeting had been that of June 26, 1845 ; he died on January 8, 1846. Before his death he signified his approval of the new departure.

On February 13, 1846, the Council passed the resolution quoted on page 35 above, in proposing which the Bishop of London " reminded the Council that King's College owed its existence to Dr D'Oyly ; that he was the first person to suggest its institution, to point out the necessity which required it, and to indicate the principles on which it should be established."

theology in lieu of university degrees—a number later increased to twenty-six—only the bishops of Ely and Bangor, for local reasons, holding aloof. The council, too, at this same meeting were called upon to consider another communication from the principal, urging the importance of establishing a hostel for the theological students, since many of them (like the medical students) would come from homes in the provinces: the matter was referred to the education committee. The question of class-room accommodation also came up for discussion and the Bishop of London was " requested to make an application to her Majesty's Government for the use of a portion of Somerset House "!—an application the response to which, whatever reverberations it may have produced in the Strand at the time, has left no echo in the minute-book. Finally, it was decided that three theological professors should be appointed without delay, and a committee consisting of all the clerical members of the council was appointed to make recommendations.

On February 27, 1846,

> upon the recommendation of the committee of the clerical members of the council, the Rev. Alexander M'Caul, D.D., the Rev. Frederick Denison Maurice, M.A., and the Rev. Richard Chenevix Trench, M.A., were appointed professors of divinity in the college

and

> the secretary was directed to obtain the consent of the Right Reverend the Diocesan and of his Grace the Visitor to these appointments.

The appointments involved the minimum of change in the college: Dr M'Caul was already there teaching Hebrew; Mr Maurice had been for six years trying to get a hearing for English and History; only Mr Trench was new. His appointment was an ideal one. Born at Dublin in 1807, educated at Harrow and Trinity, Cambridge, he was a man of the highest cultivation and character. Having entered the church, he had served as curate to Hugh James Rose at Hadleigh, and to Samuel Wilberforce at Alverstoke; hence his attachments were obviously to the high anglican party. His *Notes on the Parables* (1841) had given him fame; he had been chosen as special preacher at Cambridge in 1843 and Hulsean lecturer in 1845. When summoned to King's College he was rector of Itchen Stoke in Hampshire, and was on the point of publishing his *Notes on the Miracles*. He was a poet of no mean order, a disciple of Wordsworth, a friend of Tennyson, a kindred spirit with Keble. His later writings, *The Study of Words* (1851) and *English Past and Present* (1855), composed while he was still at King's College, marked him out as a pioneer in popular philology. The council in selecting their three professors would appear to have kept in mind the existence of three main parties in the church, and to have displayed their catholicity by giving each a representative: M'Caul was low; Maurice was usually regarded as broad, although no one, not even himself, was quite sure about it; Trench was high. It was unfortunate that the functions of the three were not defined: they were all called " professors of divinity." If it had been clearly stated that M'Caul taught the Old Testament, that Trench taught the New, that Jelf himself lectured on the Articles, while Maurice merely dealt with ecclesiastical history, much trouble might have been avoided. Because it does not matter what a professor of history believes, or what he says— even when he *can* keep order in his class. Maurice simply had no occasion or opportunity directly to teach theology, orthodox or heterodox, to his students; nor is there any evidence that he ever sought occasion or opportunity to do so. When, therefore, later on he published *Theological Essays*, and they appeared over his name as " professor of divinity at King's College," the religious public was unnecessarily bemused. The *Essays* were not his professorial utterances at King's College; they were sermons delivered at Lincoln's Inn. His lectures at King's College had dealt exclusively with the history of the church, and had displayed nothing more alarming than a kindly sympathy with Gnostics, Origenists, Nestorians, Monophysites, Apollinarians, Pelagians, and heretics generally. But we must not anticipate the tragedy of 1853: suffice it here to note that the root of it lay in Maurice's appointment to an undifferentiated chair of divinity in February 1846.

The theological department began work on April 21, 1846. During the first session 33 students were enrolled; during the second session 55; during the third session 66; and in the seventh session (1852–53) the number reached 78. The report for this last year stated that up to that date 106 certificates had been given, and that most of the recipients had been ordained and were doing good work. In 1847 (May 14) Professor Maurice sent a letter to the council strongly urging the establishment of a theological hostel, and indicating the possibility of securing a house contiguous to the college (No. 162

The Strand) for the purpose. The council took the matter up, secured the house on a twenty-one years' lease at £250 a year, and furnished fourteen sets of rooms for divinity students, with a common library and reading-room on the ground floor. The Strand entrance was closed, an approach from the college premises was constructed, a resident censor, the Rev. E. H. Plumptre, was installed (October 1847). The same year a preparatory " class for theological candidates " was instituted, intended to give such persons of twenty-one years of age and upward as were not graduates or associates of the college a grounding in the rudiments of necessary learning. For the benefit of the same class, on April 7, 1848, the council made it possible for the A.K.C. to be obtained on the results of the final examinations in the theological department.

On that same April 7, 1848, another letter was read to the council from Professor Maurice, asking that, in view of the great increase in his classes both general and theological, he might be allowed to have an assistant in the department of English history and literature. On April 12 Maurice took Charles Kingsley to Jelf and recommended him for the appointment. Jelf received him kindly and apparently favourably. But in between those two contiguous dates—viz., on April 10— the great Chartist demonstration had taken place, and " Christian Socialism " had been born. The association of Maurice and Kingsley with the new movement on the one hand caused the rejection of Kingsley's application for the English lectureship, and, on the other hand, almost caused Maurice's expulsion from his theological professorship. The trouble, however, was smoothed over, and no ripple of the upheaval was allowed to ruffle the superficial serenity of the college. More will have to be said about the matter later on.[1]

Before we leave the newly constituted department of theology we may note: first, that a new and superior organ was installed in the chapel in 1845; secondly, that, in November 1848, at the request of the theological students, evening services were commenced in the college chapel; thirdly, that, in order to provide a better choir, twelve choral scholarships were established in the school in December 1848, and that, in February 1849, Mr W. H. Monk (later the musical editor of *Hymns Ancient and Modern*) was elected to the office of director of the choir; and, finally, that on November 9, 1849, the council decided to add instruction in elocution to the theological curriculum, and that in due course they appointed the

[1] See below, pp. 213–216.

Rev. A. S. Thelwall (son of the once formidable revolutionary agitator, John Thelwall) to the office of "lecturer in public reading."

§ 3. *The Military Department*

The theological department was peculiarly the creation of Dr Jelf; he gave an immense amount of thought and care to its institution and development; he lectured laboriously to it, year in and year out, on the thirty-nine articles; he was exquisitely sensitive to anything that threatened to cause it harm. But if the theological department was his first-born and best-loved child, it was by no means the only institution in King's College of which he could claim the paternity. He was in these early and happy days full of energy, eager for development, overflowing with zeal. Second only to the welfare of the church did he place the security of the state. Hence, having established the department of theology, he supplemented it in 1848 by instituting a department of military science.

The year 1848, the *annus mirabilis* of the nineteenth century, was pre-eminently the year of revolution in Europe. Naples, Piedmont, France, Austria, Hungary, Bohemia, Prussia— every country in the Continent, in fact, except Russia and Belgium, saw a violent challenge to government. Not even Britain was unaffected: a rebellion in Ireland and the chartist uprising in England caused widespread agitation and alarm. The whole state system of Europe seemed to be crashing, and there were few publicists who thought it possible that a general Continental war could be avoided. In these circumstances there was great military activity in this country, and an urgent call for young officers. The resources of Sandhurst were quite unequal to the emergency, and it seemed to Dr Jelf that good service could be rendered by opening in King's College a class for cadets. He hoped, moreover, that even in normal times there would be wide appreciation of military education provided in

> a college possessed of all the resources of instruction, and conducted upon principles harmonising with our other institutions in church and state.

The college already possessed instructors in most of the subjects that would be required—Mr Plumptre could teach the young men divinity; Professor O'Brien, who was rather short of work, astronomy; Professor Browne, Latin; Professor Angelo,

176

fencing, and so on. Only one new teacher, indeed, would be necessary—viz., a professor of fortification and military tactics. On October 13, 1848, the principal laid his suggestions before the council, and on November 10 the council gave their sanction to the scheme.

The proposed course of military education was to consist of three parts: the first concerned with divinity, mainly the Bible and the Catechism; the second with general knowledge—viz., history, geography, literature, Latin, French, German, mathematics, and natural philosophy; the third with direct professional studies—viz., strategy, tactics, fortification, military surveying, etc. It was the third part of the course that necessitated the special teacher, and the council at once proceeded to seek for him. On December 8 they appointed a certain Captain Manly Dixon of the Royal Artillery as professor of military science. They had, however, reckoned without the Master General of the Ordnance, who informed Captain Dixon that his acceptance of the professorship would involve the loss of his rank in the army. A second appointment was similarly blocked, and not until March 27, 1849, were the council able to find a competent military man who was free to occupy their chair. On that day Captain William Walker of H.M. 69th Regiment (whose papers had been approved by the Lord Bishop of London) was elected professor.

The department did not flourish as had been anticipated. The army authorities, apparently, were not enthusiastic for a military training conducted, independently of themselves, by clergymen. There were 20 students in the first session; 11 in the second; and only 10 in the third. It was thought that perhaps the curriculum had been a little overloaded with divinity and general information; hence in June 1851 the burden was reduced, and the fees brought down from thirteen guineas a term to ten. At the end of 1852 Captain Walker resigned his chair, and Captain Frederick Augustus Griffiths, R.F.P., Royal Artillery, was appointed in his place. "The council entertain no doubt," they inform the proprietors at the general court of 1853, "that his great energy and talent will enable them to realize the expectations which led to the formation of this department." But no lightening of syllabus, reduction of fees, or change of staff sufficed to infuse life into this moribund limb. Not even the Crimean War, with its huge demand for officers, was an effective stimulus. Captain Griffiths did his best. He accumulated round himself an enormous collection of " cannon balls, bullets, and shells of every description,"

M 177

together with " all kinds of models of fortifications and useful plans." He earnestly invited inspection. But the War Office held aloof; parents were unimpressed; students did not come. The department, as we shall see later, ultimately had to be abandoned.[1]

§ 4. *The Department of General Literature and Science*

One of the causes which led Dr Jelf to suggest the establishment of the theological department was the hope that its existence in the college would increase the numbers of students in the department of general literature and science, the work of which (culminating in the A.K.C. diploma) was the normal preliminary to the specialized studies of the school of divinity. One of the causes, too, which led him to promote the institution of the military department was the expectation that the task of imparting general information to cadets would provide work (and therefore fees) for partially unemployed professors of arts and science. Both these anticipations were, in different degrees, realized. True, the increment from the military section did not amount to much; the stimulus, however, given to the old general department by the new theological school was considerable. The numbers leaped up from 121 in 1846-47 to 156 in 1847-48; professors in several cases had to divide their classes, and ask the council for assistance.

We have seen how, in April 1848 (an unlucky moment), Professor Maurice begged for aid in his English classes and recommended the young Charles Kingsley as lecturer. Probably never before or since has the question of appointing an assistant lecturer in the college caused so much commotion. A special committee was nominated by the council to deal with the matter, and it held no fewer than three meetings. At three meetings of the council, too (one of them a special meeting), was the problem discussed. Finally, on June 9, Maurice was allowed to have an assistant, but *not* Charles Kingsley, who was acquiring a notoriety most displeasing to many members of the council as " Parson Lot," the Christian Socialist. A certain Mr J. J. Stutzer was appointed, who held the post until, in November 1851, he was succeeded by the admirably efficient Rev. J. S. Brewer (already an assistant in the classical department).[2] Assistants were

See below, p. 260.
[2] We have an interesting note concerning the history classes at King's about this time from the pen of C. H. Pearson : " Professor Maurice kept order badly,

178

installed in various other departments without causing any perturbation.

Several important changes in the professorial staff occurred during the decade 1843–53. Taking them in order of time, we note the following. First, Professor Moseley (January 1844) resigned the chair of natural philosophy, which he had held since the opening of the college, in order to take up the work of H.M. Inspector of Schools; he was succeeded (March 1844) by the Rev. Matthew O'Brien, fellow and assistant tutor of Gonville and Caius College, Cambridge. Secondly, a year later (March 13, 1845) the great Professor Daniell, the notable chemist and electrician, died suddenly in the council room of the Royal Society, Somerset House, immediately after the performance of his usual college duties. His invaluable services to the college were in due course commemorated by the erection of a marble bust in the library, and by the foundation of a chemical scholarship of the annual value of £25. His worthy successor was his brilliant pupil and assistant, Dr W. A. Miller (June 1845), who brought in J. E. Bowman as his demonstrator (July 1845).[1] One of Professor Miller's first pieces of work was the institution of a new department of analytical chemistry, toward the equipment of which the council granted £250. Thirdly, in May 1847 Professor Gabriele Rossetti—another of the original members of the staff, a distinguished man and the father of three still more distinguished children—had to resign because of failing eyesight:[2] his place was taken by Signor Valerio Pistrucci (June 1847). Fourthly, in November of the same year the Spanish chair became vacant through the return of Professor Villalobos to his native land: after his departure the scanty duties of his office were performed, and its scanty emoluments received, by Mr Robert Lott (1847), Signor J. A. Curtoys (1851), and the Rev. Juan Calderon (1852)

though I do not know that the signs of it were worse than remiss attendances and a disposition to riotous applause. Professor Brewer, on the other hand, had his classes completely in hand, and you might have heard a pin drop while he was speaking. If a pupil was inattentive or lazy, Brewer drove him summarily out of the class. The dread of this was a very strong motive for work, partly because dismissal from lecture would lead to awkward questions at home, and partly because we all knew Brewer to be an incomparable teacher." (W. Stebbing, *Charles Henry Pearson*, pp. 31–32.)

[1] It appears that Sir Benjamin Brodie and the college professors wished to see Liebig, the famous German chemist, appointed as Daniell's successor, but that Bishop Blomfield and Archbishop Howley refused to sanction the appointment of a Lutheran. Professor W. A. Miller, however, had for a time studied under Liebig without contracting his Lutheranism. *Cf.* T. Holmes, *Sir B. C. Brodie*, pp. 79, 232–234.

[2] He died on April 26, 1854.

in turn.[1] Fifthly, the almost sinecure and honorary position of professor of law was vacated by Mr E. Bulloch in December 1849. The council, much disappointed that the legal department of the college had made no progress whatsoever, appointed a committee consisting of Mr Justice Coleridge, Mr Justice Patteson, and Mr Frere, to consider the problem and report. These eminent men evidently felt that the matter was not one of any urgency; for they did not present their report until January 1851. Their report, when it came, was a valuable and interesting document: the vital section was the following:

> The law as a profession cannot properly be taught by lectures alone, nor does it fall within the scope of any university, properly so characterised, to attempt to qualify young men for it as a profession. What should be aimed at is to give to *all*, whether intended to be practical lawyers or not, such sound elementary information as may make the former more fitted to enter readily and usefully on a strictly professional course of study; and to give to the latter that acquaintance with the constitution of the country and the spirit and outline of its legal system without which no gentleman or member of any profession can be considered completely educated. The college is to teach law as a part of education, not of professional instruction, and so considered it is certainly an essential step in the course of any university.

The council, therefore, decided to revive the professorship, which had now been in abeyance for over a year, and in due course they appointed an eminent barrister, Mr G. K. Rickards, counsel to the speaker of the house of commons, to the vacant post (March 1851). Mr Rickards, however, never lectured. Before the end of the year he found that his parliamentary duties were increasing so rapidly that he was compelled to send in his resignation: Mr James Stephen was elected in his place (November 1851).

Four new chairs were established during the decade under review, viz., the chairs of Chinese (1847), International Law (1848), Landscape Drawing (1851), and Practical Chemistry (1851). A word as to each in turn. (1) On February 13, 1846, Sir George T. Staunton, a member of the council, laid before his fellows a memorial urging the importance, mainly for missionary purposes, of spreading a knowledge of the Chinese language in this country, and suggesting the founding of an

---

[1] In 1849 Professor Lott was lost for about three months without anyone suffering much inconvenience. After his chair had been declared vacant he was discovered at Boulogne and, on his return to London, reinstated.

endowed chair. The council agreed, provided funds could be raised. Sir George set to work and within six months had got together nearly £2000. The council considered that the interest on this sum, supplemented by fees, would provide adequate remuneration. Hence they proceeded to seek for a professor. At first an effort was made to secure the services of Dr Hoffman of Leyden, but he required a larger guaranteed salary than the council could offer. Finally Dr S. T. Fearon was appointed (March 1847), succeeded by Mr James Summers (December 1852).[1] (2) Dr Jelf, when in October 1848 he had suggested the institution of the military department, had also intimated the desirability of forming a class in diplomacy. It appeared that there were a number of Egyptian students—sent over by Lord Palmerston's old friend Mehemet Ali—attending the college under government auspices, as occasional students, and anxious for courses in practical politics. At first Dr Jelf contemplated a complete new department of diplomacy; but the council, being well acquainted with Old Testament history, prudently declined to put its trust in Egypt, and ended by merely establishing a chair of the " law of nations " and getting Dr Travers Twiss to fill it (January 1849). He held it for six years and then, on his becoming regius professor of civil law at Oxford, it was allowed to lapse. No good thing had come out of Egypt. (3) In January 1851 the council decided to supplement the teaching of drawing which was given in the school, and in the engineering and military departments of the college, by founding a professorship of " landscape drawing and perspective." Mr Henry Worsley was appointed to the post. (4) In March of the same year Mr J. E. Bowman, who since 1845 had been a demonstrator in chemistry, was made the first professor of practical chemistry. He was destined, alas, to hold the post for little more than three years, as he died in 1854 at the early age of thirty-five. The college lost in him a teacher and investigator of brilliant promise.

The students of the department of general literature and science still considered it to be their main function to secure scholarships and exhibitions at Oxford and Cambridge. Comparatively few of them sat for the examinations of the University of London, to the syllabuses of which the King's College course was not well adapted. At the older universities, however, the successes of the King's men continued to be conspicuous both

[1] In February 1853 Sir George Staunton purchased from Professor Summers and presented to King's College a library of about 600 Chinese books.

in numbers and in quality. It would be tedious to enumerate them in detail as they were read out year by year to the gratified governors and the proud proprietors at the general court. The following summary may suffice. In the ten years 1843–52 no fewer than fifty-one old King's students at Cambridge became wranglers, including the senior wrangler of 1846 (L. Hensley) and the second wrangler of 1850 (H. W. Watson), while in the year 1853 all previous records were broken when thirteen of the wranglers and nine of the senior *optimes* hailed from the Strand. Classical successes at Cambridge were not so numerous: but in the decade 1843–52 seven firsts were secured. During the same period twenty-six old King's men were elected to Cambridge fellowships: in 1851 it was announced that " there are at the present time ten fellows of Trinity College, and one conduct-fellow, who were formerly students of King's College, London." This is a record that few institutions can have approached. Not so many men, apparently, went to Oxford as to Cambridge, but within the ten years under consideration old King's students secured six open scholarships, nine first classes, and five fellowships. Among the students who thus distinguished themselves and brought credit to their college were Alfred Barry, the Hon. E. H. Stanley, E. H. Plumptre, G. W. Kitchin, C. H. Pearson, and W. Stebbing. In London University Frederick William Farrar headed the honours list in classics at the final B.A. examination of 1852, and carried off the university scholarship.

In March 1851, as the result of a memorial presented by Professors Hall, Browne, and Maurice, and supported by the principal, French and German, hitherto optional, were made compulsory subjects in the general literary and scientific course.

We are fortunate in having pictures of the life of the students in this department of King's College at this period from the pens of four men who later rose to eminence—viz., Sir Leslie Stephen, in his *Life of Sir James Fitzjames Stephen*; Charles Henry Pearson, in the memorial volume edited by W. Stebbing; F. W. Farrar, in a letter contributed to Sir Frederick Maurice's *Life of F. D. Maurice*; and Sir Edwin Arnold, in a communication printed in R. Farrar's *Life of Dean Farrar*. Two quotations must suffice. (1) Sir Leslie Stephen says, respecting his brother, who came to King's from Eton in 1845, at the age of sixteen:

The two years he spent at King's College were most happy. He felt himself changed from a boy to a man. The King's

College lads, who indeed called themselves "men," were of a lower social rank than the Etonians, and, as Fitzjames adds, unmistakably inferior in physique. Boys who had the Strand as the only substitute for the playing-fields were hardly likely to show much physical prowess. But they had qualities more important to him. They were industrious, as became the sons of professional and business men. Their moral tone was remarkably good: he never knew, he says, a more thoroughly well-behaved set of lads. . . . But the great change for him was that he could now find intellectual comradeship. There was a debating society in which he first learnt to hear his own voice, and indeed became a prominent orator. . . . The lads discussed politics and theology and literature, instead of putting down to affectation any interest outside of the river and the playing-fields. Fitzjames not only found himself in a more congenial atmosphere, but could hold his own better among youths whose standard of scholarship was less exalted than that of the crack Latin verse-makers of Eton, although the average level was perhaps higher.

(2) James F. Stephen went from King's to Trinity, Cambridge, in 1847. In April of the same year Charles H. Pearson came to King's from Rugby, at the age of seventeen. He left in 1849 for Oxford, where he secured a first in classics in 1853 and an Oriel fellowship in 1854. The fourth chapter of his story of his life (pp. 30–46) is devoted to a vivid description of his experiences at King's during the critical period of the chartist agitation. He tells, for example, how a number of the students of the college used to sign the great chartist petition twice every day, under different names, as they passed to and fro; and how, in spite of this revolutionary activity, as the critical tenth of April approached, every individual in the college save one (who was a philosophical radical) enrolled himself as a special constable. The following passages relate more particularly to the college life:

To King's College I owe everything that can be derived from a place of education. I think the system was thoroughly good; I am sure it suited me. In place of the puritanism of my home, and the mechanical discipline of Rugby, I found a rule of the largest liberty compatible with common order. We were allowed to choose our own lectures with the consent of our guardians; punishments were almost unknown; and the assumption throughout was that we were to be influenced through our own sense of honour and duty. . . . It was considered bad form to be idle, and disgraceful to tell a lie. Though a good deal of this spirit was attributable to home influences, I believe it was mostly due to the tradition of the place, which had been created by principal and professors. Dr Jelf, the chief for more than twenty years, was a gentleman of the old school, who was incapable of supposing that anyone would lie to him, and indisposed to track any but the most obvious charge home. It was an accepted maxim that no one could tell a lie to the principal, because he always believed what was said. . . . In another respect King's College was above the moral standard even of Rugby. Foul language and coarse wit were absolutely repressed by public opinion. . . .

It is an eminently pleasing picture of King's and its men that Mr Pearson presents. Those of Dean Farrar and Sir Edwin Arnold are not quite so attractive.

§ 5. *The Medical School and the Hospital*

Throughout the whole of the ten years under review Dr R. B. Todd continued his successful labours on behalf of the King's College medical school and its appendant hospital. He was loyally assisted by a body of unusually able colleagues—*e.g.*, Professors Partridge, Budd, R. Ferguson, Royle, W. Fergusson, Rymer Jones, Guy, and Farre, with Messrs Bowman, Simon, and Lee—and was effectively supported by the medical members of the council—Sir Henry Halford, Sir Benjamin Brodie, Mr J. H. Green, and (from 1844) Dr Thomas Watson. That Todd, however, was the leader of the devoted company was indisputable: he had an intelligence quick to perceive necessities, an enthusiasm eager to surmount difficulties, and a will capable of achieving impossibilities. The three great tasks accomplished during this decade were, first, the improvement of the discipline of the medical students; secondly, the provision of residences for them; and, thirdly, the extension and equipment of the hospital.

(1) The discipline of the medical students had from the first been a source of trouble. A tradition had established itself in London that it was proper for youthful medicos to be gay and festive, and journals like the *Lancet* encouraged them to resist any attempt at restraint. Hence they were irregular at lectures, and when they attended they were rowdy; while, out of college, they tended to all kinds of brawls and dissipations. The only grave cases of indiscipline that came before the council at this period, in fact, arose in the medical school, and several students (one of whom had landed himself in prison) had to be expelled. We have already noted [1] that two steps

[1] See above, p. 141.

had been taken in Principal Lonsdale's time for the better maintenance of authority: in 1842 the office of dean had been instituted, the professors taking it in turn, a year at a time; in 1843 Dr George Johnson had been appointed resident medical tutor. These measures had their due effect, and the council were able to report year by year a steady improvement. In the summer of 1849 the annual dean gave place to a permanent dean—a sort of vice-principal for the medical department—and Dr W. A. Guy was appointed to the post. The results during the ensuing session (1849–50) were so markedly satisfactory that Dr Jelf addressed a letter to the council on October 11, 1850, in which he said:

> I think it my duty to call your special attention to the eminent services of Dr Guy as permanent dean of the medical department, and to the very inadequate remuneration which he receives. His attendance daily at the college during the past year has been most exemplary and unremitting. He is generally at the morning service in the college chapel, and he remains in the Marsden Library one, two, or three hours to receive the medical students, to regulate their studies and professional duties, to offer them advice in professional matters and with respect to their moral conduct, and to watch over their interests in every way. His punctual daily attendance is *known* to the students, and is regarded by them as most valuable. As a member of the board of discipline, also, Dr Guy has been most zealous and judicious, in repressing the first germs of evil, in warning the indolent, and in encouraging the industrious and well-conducted student. He has also taken great pains in organising a complete system of discipline with respect to the residence of all those students who appeared to require such surveillance. The result of these exertions, which I cannot fully describe in this letter, has been a most marked and visible improvement in the deportment and industry of the whole body of the medical students. . . .

One of the features which signalized the general tightening up of medical discipline in the college was the establishment of the system of marking attendances not only at lectures, but also at the demonstrations given at the hospital. In July 1850 Dr William Brinton succeeded Dr George Johnson as resident medical tutor. In October 1851 the Rev. Dr S. W. Warneford presented to the college the sum of £5000 for the establishment of medical scholarships (each £25 a year for four years), the essential qualification for which should be the passing of a satisfactory examination in divinity.

(2) Dr Todd was firmly convinced that no completely adequate system of medical discipline could be instituted until

residences should be provided for the students and the full collegiate organization introduced. He therefore laboured incessantly during this period to secure some sort of hostel accommodation in or near the college, to supplement the insufficient fourteen rooms which since 1834 the medicals had shared with the other sections of the college. No fewer than four proposals did he lay before the council: two came to nothing at all, one was tried and immediately abandoned as a failure, one was carried through as a partial success in 1848. Dr Todd's first proposal was an extremely ambitious one (July 1843): it was to close the Strand entrance to the college altogether, build in its place a hostel for twenty-eight students, and get the Somerset House officials to allow the college traffic to pass through their precincts. The estimated cost of this undertaking, £8500, caused the council to reject it at once, without troubling the Somerset House officials to express their emotions respecting its implications. Two years later (August 1845) Dr Todd, on behalf of the college, entered into an agreement, terminable at short notice, with a Mr Kent, of 32 Norfolk Street, to use his furnished house as a hostel at a rent of £42 a month. This high rent made it necessary to charge so much for rooms in this house that only seven students came into residence in October, and the place was given up at Christmas. Dr Todd's third suggestion (November 1845) was that fourteen more sets of rooms should be superimposed on those already existent in the college; but it was found that this erection would destroy the symmetry of the building, and that the expense (£4500) would be too great; hence for some months the problem was allowed to lie in abeyance. But Dr Todd was not to be deterred by failures, by conciliar coolness, or by architectural sensitiveness. He secured private promises of £1300 toward the cost of building; he got an architect of his own to come and survey the college premises, and finally (January 8, 1847) he came before the council with a wholly novel plan. He proposed to erect an entirely new structure on the unoccupied south-east corner of the site, abutting on the river end of Strand Lane; his architect assured him that a building to house twenty-eight students could be put up for £5500. The council asked their own architect, Mr Smirke (son of Sir Robert), to examine the proposal. He did so and reported that it was quite feasible, but that it would cost nearer £15,000 than £5500. Dr Todd, however, was not discouraged by a little discrepancy such as this. His architect procured estimates, and got a builder

THE SOUTH-EAST BLOCK

to undertake to put the place up for £5449. Mr Smirke thereupon withdrew, and expressed his willingness to allow Dr Todd's architect to do it. The council, seeing that Dr Todd would not be happy till he got it, and that until Dr Todd was happy they would have no rest, gave their consent to the carrying out of the plan. Accordingly in the summer of 1847 the jerry-building at the back of the college began. Things went on merrily until August 19, when

the secretary laid on the table a letter which he had received from Messrs Fen and Co., the solicitors to His Grace the Duke of Norfolk, in which they threatened proceedings in the Court of Chancery against the college on account of the new buildings now being erected for the residence of medical students.

The trouble arose from the menace which the new building presented to the " ancient lights " of the duke's property in Surrey Street, just across Strand Lane. The story of the ensuing conferences and correspondences is too long and complicated here to tell. Enough that in the end the matter was referred to arbitration, and that the arbitrator decided that the college must reduce the proposed height of the new building from 95 feet to 72, and that it must pay three-fourths of the duke's legal expenses, together with one-half the expenses of the award. This award was given in November 1847; meantime, building operations had been suspended for three months. This suspension involved new demands for compensation from architect and builder; new threats of litigation; new arbitration; new awards; new expenses. The council had a time which, in twentieth-century phraseology, is commonly called "hectic." One can imagine the " affected smile " on the face of Mr Smirke! Ultimately the place was finished (1849); but it was smaller than had been originally planned. It contained an anatomical theatre in the basement, and fourteen (instead of twenty-eight) sets of rooms above. Still, it was better than nothing; and Dr Todd had to rest content.

(3) One reason why the council had to be so very cautious in launching upon building schemes on their own premises was that they were forced by circumstances into heavy outlays in respect of the hospital in Portugal Street. The new institution supplied so urgent a need in the crowded parish of St Clement Danes and the contiguous regions that the old workhouse building soon proved to be hopelessly inadequate. The report of April 1843 stated that during the preceding

year 1290 in-patients and 11,138 out-patients had been relieved. It was imperative in the interest both of the patients and of the medical school to increase the accommodation and improve the services of the hospital. At first it was suggested that it would be best to move the hospital altogether, and, of course, Somerset House presented itself as a suitable spot for a new building. The council actually decided on January 20, 1843, to ask her Majesty's Government to grant them the then unoccupied piece of land fronting upon the east side of Wellington Street. Her Majesty's Government did not see their way to make the desired concession; so nothing remained save to enlarge the already existing hospital, and to purchase the necessary land. On April 16, 1844, Professors Todd, Fergusson, and Partridge sent a memorial to the council informing them that land contiguous to the hospital was for sale, and urging its acquisition. The council, unfortunately, had no money to spare; the committee of the hospital so far from having funds for any extensions had to face annual deficits which rarely fell below £600. Hence, as we have already observed,[1] a special appeal had to be launched which yielded about one-sixth of the £15,000 asked for. This sufficed to meet the current expenses of the hospital for a time, but left no surplus for building. In the circumstances the physicians and surgeons of the hospital themselves nobly came to the help of the institution, and in order not to lose the option of the site needed for the proposed extension, made themselves responsible for the £3400 required for its purchase. Further appeals for funds were then issued, and by April 1847 about £4000 had been raised. That, however, was not enough to warrant the making of a start, and the slow work of accumulating money had to be resumed. Meanwhile the pressure on the hospital accommodation increased year by year: in April 1845 the report stated that nearly 20,000 patients had been relieved during the preceding twelve months. When things were getting desperate, in December 1849, an anonymous "Friend of the College" (who proved later to be the generous Rev. Dr Warneford) made a conditional offer of £3000 and propounded an ingenious and admirably devised scheme by which £50,000 could, it was hoped, be raised. One part of the scheme was that the council itself should guarantee £1000 a year for five years, and this, after much hesitation, the council finally agreed to do. The situation was now completely changed;

[1] See above, p. 145.

money once more began to flow in; and in April 1850 the council were, with great satisfaction,

> able to add that the funds for promoting this work [of building] have been rapidly increasing until, on the day on which this court is assembled, upwards of £25,000 have been subscribed.

It was possible then to begin operations. In order to get over legal difficulties respecting the holding of property, the hospital was incorporated by Act of Parliament (August 1851). Tenders for new buildings—a portion only of the complete design—to the amount of £19,131 were accepted, and on June 17, 1852, the foundation-stone was laid by the Archbishop of Canterbury (Dr J. B. Sumner).

Changes in the staff of the medical department and the hospital were singularly few during this notable decade. In May 1844 Dr Robert Ferguson resigned his professorship of midwifery, and Dr Arthur Farre, who had been associated with him in the chair since June 1841, took sole charge of the subject. In August 1847 the extremely able and efficient Dr John Simon announced his intention to leave the college in order to take up the work as first medical officer of health for the City of London which was destined to give him worldwide fame and (1887) a knighthood; he was succeeded as demonstrator in anatomy and assistant surgeon at the hospital by Dr William Brinton and Mr Henry Lee respectively (1848). In 1848, also, Mr William Bowman, who had been for nine years in the college as a demonstrator in anatomy, was associated with Professor Todd in the chair of physiology. This joint arrangement went on for five years—Professor Todd lecturing from October to Christmas only, and Professor Bowman completing the session. On January 11, 1853, however, Dr Todd addressed the following letter to the council from his house, 3 New Street, Spring Gardens:

MY LORDS AND GENTLEMEN,
After much consideration and reflection I have come to the conclusion that the time has now arrived when I ought not to hold any longer the professorship of physiology and of general and morbid anatomy in King's College. In consequence of increasing engagements of other kinds, I find myself unable to devote to the onerous duties of that chair all the time and attention which are necessary for the good of the pupils and the interests of the college. In thus resigning into your hands the trust with which you honoured me so long ago as 1836, allow me to offer you my most respectful and cordial thanks for the kindness

189

which I have ever experienced from you, and let me again assure you that it is only a strong sense of duty that has impelled me to loosen my connexion with King's College, an institution in which I have always taken the warmest interest. I am, [etc.]

It was as though the mainspring of a clock had asked permission to retire. The council were greatly perturbed; they appointed a special committee to consider the situation. Dr Todd's eight colleagues presented a memorial on the questions raised by his resignation. What was done we must see later.

§ 6. *The Department of Engineering*

The department of engineering—called from July 1844 onward the "department for instruction in the applied sciences including natural philosophy, manufacturing arts, engineering, and architecture"—demands but little attention in respect of the decade under review. For the first half of the period it continued to flourish exceedingly, the number of students steadily rising from 33 to 71. Then came the time of the great railway slump, with a deep, though merely temporary depression in all departments of engineering. Numbers sank to 39 in 1851, when once again they began to go up. In 1846 the engineers asked that they, like the doctors, might have a dean; the council replied that they might have one with pleasure, provided they would pay for the luxury themselves. This they were happy, or at any rate willing, to do. In 1849 the offices of curator of the George III museum and superintendent of the engineering workshop—hitherto held by the same person—were separated. Mr J. E. Cook, the former dual holder, continued in the museum, with instructions to demonstrate to students the meaning of the mysteries under his care. Mr G. A. Timme was placed in charge of the workshop, and to the workshop was assigned the useful duty of keeping the college in repair.

The museum, it may be remarked, was proving—as museums usually do—a magnet which tended to draw to itself all those pieces of large lumber in London and the provinces which private persons find too good to destroy, inconvenient to keep, impossible to sell, and unsuitable for wedding-presents. The biggest white elephant, however, dumped down upon the college during this period was Babbage's calculating machine. And this came not from a private person but from the government. It was deposited in the George III museum in March

1843 by the Office of Works, the government retaining property in the thing. As its value was estimated at £7000, a special insurance had to be effected upon it at an abnormally high rate of premium. When the Office of Works was asked to assist the college in paying this premium,

> the board conveyed their best thanks to the council for their communication, but stated that it was not the custom of their department to effect policies of insurance from fire.

The department suffered one grave loss during this period in the unexpected death, October 1852, of Mr Edward Cowper, professor of manufacturing art and machinery since the year 1839. His work was undertaken, almost at a moment's notice, by Mr T. M. Goodeve of the mathematical department, and so efficiently did he discharge his extempore duties that in December—although there were several strong candidates for the post—he was made permanent professor. Mr Cowper during his twelve years of service had got together a large collection of valuable diagrams and models. They were his own property, although he used them freely in his departmental work. In order that the students might not lose the advantage of this collection—which outside purchasers were eager to secure—the council sought to buy it for £229 (January 1853).

§ 7. King's College School

For several years after Dr Jelf's installation as principal the subterranean department of King's College, otherwise termed the school, continued to flourish like a healthy potato plant. It reached its maximum of luxuriant prosperity in the year 1846. Its numbers stood at just over 500; two new classrooms had had to be placed at its disposal; a new master had had to be appointed—the Rev. J. R. Major, B.A., of Exeter College, Oxford (May 1846). Not only, moreover, were the numbers high, but the quality of the pupils was unusually good. At this time there were together at the school many remarkable boys who gave distinction to the institution while they were in it, and reflected glory upon it in later years—e.g., H. P. Liddon (1841–46); Algernon Borthwick, later Lord Glenesk (1842–46); Frederic Harrison (1843–48); William Stebbing (1843–48); Martin H. Irving, son of Edward Irving (1843–49); F. G. Fleay (1843–49) ; and Walter W. Skeat (1845–47). Two things, however, are to be noted concerning these eminent youths: first, most of them stopped at the school beyond the normal age of sixteen; *e.g.*, Harrison got the first classical prize when he was seventeen, and Irving the first mathematical prize at eighteen. Secondly, many of them passed straight from the school to Oxford or Cambridge without "going upstairs" into King's College at all. In other words, the school in its upper ranges was becoming a rival to the college rather than its feeder. It is not in the least surprising that an increasing number of parents preferred to leave their sons in a school where they were being excellently and continuously taught, rather than send them up aloft where for a considerably higher fee—£9 8s. 6d. a term, as against £6 15s. 2d.—they were merely being intermittently lectured at. The senior department of King's College—the department of general literature and science—began to suffer from the fact that it was neither school nor university, but merely something purgatorial in between. The departments of medicine, engineering, theology, and military science were all ends in themselves; the department of general literature and science was only a means to an end—viz., the scholarships and degrees of Oxford and Cambridge. And these scholarships and degrees were found to be even more readily attainable from the sixth form of the school than from the lecture-room of the college. Thus, as we shall later see, it became necessary for the college to reconsider its attitude of aloofness from the University of London, and to begin to avail itself more freely of its privilege of sending its *alumni* in for the London arts degrees.

After 1846 the numbers in the school began slightly to decline, until in 1850 they stood at 463. The council took the matter seriously into consideration in the autumn of that year, and came to the conclusion that part of the losses could be accounted for by the fact that a large number of new schools of a similar type had been started in more salubrious regions; but that part was probably due to the fact that the dominantly classical curriculum of King's College School did not suit the needs of the growing number of boys who wished to pass from the school not to the college, or to a university, but to business. There were, indeed, in the school at the time no fewer than sixty boys who, having been withdrawn from Latin or Greek, or from both, were pursuing a "modern" education for which the school was not adequately equipped, and by the informal provision of which the school time-table was much disarrayed. In December 1850, then, the council took the heroic resolve to divide the school formally into two sections, one classical and the other modern. The modern side was placed under the immediate charge of the Rev. John Fearnley, with the title of vice-master of King's College School. The division took effect in January 1851, and the modern side opened with 128 names on its roll. The unity of the school was still symbolized by the general assembly for prayers in the college chapel at 9 A.M. This general assembly had, in January 1847, taken the place of prayers in the separate classrooms, which had up to that date prevailed.

The principal changes in the staff were as follows. In March 1847 Mr W. Hayes, master of the lower sixth form, died, and Mr (later the Rev.) Thomas Markby was appointed to succeed him. At the same time a middle sixth form was created—mainly drawn from the headmaster's upper sixth form, which contained the excessive number of 50 boys—and the Rev. William Webster, sometime fellow of Queens' College, Cambridge, was placed in charge of it. In future, it was decreed, the headmaster's class should not contain more than 24 boys. At the end of 1848 the Rev. R. Hodgson left to take a cure of souls in Westmorland. There was a general move up of the junior staff, Mr Hodgson's place in the upper third being taken by the Rev. T. O. Cockayne. The lower first, ultimately left vacant, was assigned to a new master, the Rev. George Rust. In 1852 Professor Henry Angelo, master of fencing, caught off his guard by death, passed away, and his son, Henry Charles Angelo, fenced in his stead. *Non Angli, sed Angeli*, no doubt the clerical members of the council murmured. Toward the close of the following year a still more notable mastership came to an end. The Rev. Joseph Edwards, second master for twenty-two years, sent in his resignation, and was succeeded by Mr J. J. Heywood, scholar of Trinity College, Cambridge. Mr Edwards had vigorously opposed some of the recent changes in the school, which had altered his position for the worse, and he was glad to get away.

Since the present seems to be the proper moment for raking over the dust-heaps of the Dickens family, we may perhaps be permitted to note that on March 26, 1847,

> an application was received from Mr Charles Dickens requesting that the fees paid for his son's education in the school for the next term should be returned on the ground of ill-health,

and that the council " resolved to return to Mr Dickens the sum of £6 1s. 2d." The name of the son is not given, but presumably it was Frederick C. Dickens, who was in the fifth form at the time.

N

§ 8. *General Progress*

Besides the matters relating to the various departments of the college that have been dealt with in the above sections, a few connected with the college as a whole remain to be mentioned. The most important are: (1) the introduction of a general scheme of scholarships in 1846; (2) the institution of honorary fellowships in 1847; (3) an experiment at evening classes in 1848; (4) various manifestations of student activity; (5) the struggle to put the finances of the college on a sound basis; (6) changes in the governing body of the college—visitor, governors, council, secretariat.

(1) With a view both to attract students to the college and to stimulate students already in the college to competitive energy, Dr Jelf, on November 14, 1845, laid before the council a proposal to establish a system of scholarships throughout all the departments of the institution. The council asked for full details of the plan, and they were provided on December 12. The principal suggested the offer of no fewer than forty-two scholarships ranging from £40 a year for three years down to £6 a year for two years; they were to be apportioned as follows among the departments: general literature, 10, engineering, 4, divinity, 1, medicine, 7, the school, 20. The total cost would be £872 a year, and the money was to be raised by (1) a diminution of the deductions from the ordinary fees granted to nominees of proprietors; (2) a small terminal levy on each pupil in the school and college—2*s.* 6*d.* in the first case, 5*s.* in the second; (3) profits on the bookshop. The council accepted the scheme, which seemed likely to be self-supporting, and formulated rules for the examinations on the results of which the scholarships should be awarded.

(2) The proposal to establish honorary fellowships in the college came from Bishop Blomfield. On January 8, 1847, he raised in the council, over which he was presiding,

> the question of instituting a class of honorary fellows of King's College with the view of electing into it those connected with the college as professors or otherwise who may be thought worthy of such a distinction.

On February 19 the council, on the recommendation of its education committee, accepted the proposal; decreed that each honorary fellow should pay £2 2*s.* for his diploma; and elected the Rev. John Allen, late chaplain of the college, as the

first of the new order.[1]   Among the honorary fellows elected
1847–53 were Alfred Barry, Arthur Cayley, J. A. Frere,
Lewis Hensley, George Johnson, G. W. Kitchin, Henry Moseley,
E. H. Plumptre, J. E. Thorold Rogers, John Simon, the Hon.
E. H. Stanley, William Stebbing,[2] and R. B. Todd.

(3) On December 8, 1848, "the subject of giving lectures in
the evening at the college by some of the professors in turn"
was brought before the council.   It appeared that five gentlemen were ready to give during the next term one lecture each
per week to continue through ten successive weeks from eight
to nine o'clock in the evening—viz.,

Professor	Cowper,	on Monday,	on	Manufacturing Art
"	Guy	" Tuesday	"	Public Health
"	Miller	" Wednesday	"	Chemistry
"	Ansted	" Thursday	"	Descriptive Geography
"	Bell	" Friday	"	Natural History

at a cost of 10s. 6d. each course or £2 2s. for the whole; the
college to receive one-sixth of the entire sum.   The object
sought to be obtained was "the opening of the benefits of King's
College to a different class of men from those who now attend
—viz., those who are employed during the whole day in offices of
various kinds."   The professors believed that much good might
be done in this way, and accordingly proposed making the
experiment for one term, suggesting that if it then succeeded
it might be continued the following term by another course
differing from the first.

> The principal having stated his general acquiescence in this
> plan, and that he did not anticipate any difficulties from this
> opening of the college in the evening, the council sanctioned the
> experiment being made.

So runs the entry in the minute-book.   It is interesting: for
it fixes the date of the inauguration of the King's College
evening classes seven years earlier than the date usually assigned
to it—viz., 1855;   and four years earlier than the commencement of F. D. Maurice's working-men's evening lecture courses
—viz., 1852.   The course was actually given, being inaugurated
(January 1849) by the principal with a lecture on "the relation
which scientific pursuits bear to our holy religion."   Eighty-
three students attended some or all of the classes provided.
There the experiment seems to have ended.   Another course

---

[1] The exaction of a fee from the fellows ceased from June 13, 1850.
[2] Mr William Stebbing, elected 1853, held his fellowship until his death, at the
age of ninety-five, in May 1926—a record that will not easily be broken.

was projected for the Michaelmas term of the same year; but apparently it was never given. No mention of it occurs in minute-books, report, or calendar; and no evening students figure among the " occasionals " for the session 1849-50.

It may be noted also that about the same date—the beginning of 1849—the students of the theological department, with the permission and aid of the vicar of St Martin-in-the-Fields, set on foot an evening school for the indigent children and adults of the great and thickly populated region round Trafalgar Square. The students took it in turn to attend and conduct the institution. This institution seems to have lasted about five years. The regulations for the theological department mention it annually until 1854, saying that " every student is required to give his services as a teacher." After 1854 it drops out.

Professor Maurice and his friends were also busy, in their private capacities, at this time, in many notable and praise-worthy educational ventures, in all of which they received valuable assistance from the staff and students of King's College —in opening a night school in St George's parish, Bloomsbury; in establishing classes for shop-assistants in the city; and above all in founding Queen's College, Harley Street, for the higher education of women (1848). In this last important and successful enterprise Professor Maurice was supported by Professors Hall (mathematics), O'Brien (natural philosophy), Brasseur (French), Bernays (German), and Hullah (vocal music), all of whom lectured during the first term. The Rev. Charles Kingsley—rejected by the council of King's College— was appointed to profess English composition and literature at Queen's. It is conceivable that Dr Jelf and the council of King's College did not like this independent venture on the part of Maurice and his colleagues—a venture which distracted the energies of the staff, and one over which neither they nor the bishops had any control. It cannot, moreover, have been altogether pleasing to them to witness the founding of a college with a royal title, even if only for women, wherein any sort of doctrine might be taught, and to whose staff actually were appointed persons whom they had rejected, and persons whose views were so obnoxious to their chairman, the Bishop of London, as to cause him to prohibit their holders from preaching in his diocese.

(4) The students of King's College during this early Victorian decade showed a good deal of energy and initiative, and it is clear that a university or corporate consciousness was

196

beginning to manifest itself among them. We have already observed that a *King's College Magazine* came into existence in 1841 and expired in 1842.[1] Six years later, Professor C. H. Pearson tells us in his autobiography,

> There was some talk of establishing a magazine for college and school. The representatives of the school on our provisional committee were Frederic Harrison, Martin Irving, and F. G. Fleay, who has since taken high rank as a Shakespearian critic. I was one of the representatives of the college, but oddly enough cannot remember who were associated with me. Fitzjames Stephen had left the college, and Edwin Arnold had not yet joined it; but besides Edward Dicey and Leslie Stephen, whom I have mentioned, we had two students who have since won their spurs in literature, viz., Henry Kingsley, the first novelist who made Australian life a theme of romance, and D. C. Lathbury. . . . However, we were none of us destined to break ground in a magazine of our own founding. It was thought necessary to obtain leave from the principal before we issued it; and Dr Jelf discouraged the idea courteously but decisively. I do not remember that he absolutely forbade it; but as we were not strong in funds, and perhaps not very confident of our literary powers, we allowed our chief's disapproval to settle the matter for us.[2]

A third attempt, made in 1849, had more success. In June of that year a Fleet Street bookseller, Mr George Bell, began to publish an ambitious quarterly entitled the *King's College Literary and Scientific Magazine*, of which five numbers were issued. It was highly academic, excessively technical, and deadly dull. Its prose related to mathematics, mechanics, history, and philology. Its verse—which included contributions from F. W. Farrar and Edwin Arnold—was rigidly classical in both form and substance. It ceased to depress the spirits of its readers and deplete the funds of its publishers in June 1850.

Four months later a fourth venture was launched, apparently under the editorship of Thomas Macknight, the biographer of Bolingbroke, Burke, and Disraeli, and for over thirty years editor of the *Northern Whig*. He was a student in the medical department, and the magazine under his control was much less theological and much more radical than its quarterly predecessor had been. It was entitled the *King's College Magazine : A Literary, Scientific, and Collegiate Journal*; and it was published monthly, at the price of 1*s.*, by Messrs Wickam and Yelland, booksellers in the Strand. Its liveliness and variety did not

---

[1] See above, p. 159.
[2] W. Stebbing (editor), *Charles Henry Pearson : Memorials*, etc., pp. 37-38.

suffice to make it pay: it saw the session through (October 1850–July 1851), but the following session it did not reappear.

Student societies of one sort and another seem to have been numerous and generally ephemeral. The more permanent and important were: (1) The *Literary and Scientific Union* formed

> for the purpose of promoting the circulation of the literary and scientific periodicals of the day amongst the members, and of holding weekly meetings at which papers are read on topics of general interest in literature and science.

In 1850 it held a *conversazione* in order to offer " to its members and other students of the college an opportunity of meeting their professors without the necessary restraint and formality of the lecture-room." (2) The *King's College Medical Society*, a serious professional organization, dominated by the senior members of the medical department: it held weekly meetings for the discussion of technical subjects, and every year it offered a prize for an essay on a topic chosen by the dean of the medical faculty. (3) The *King's College Discussion Society* and a schismatical offshoot thereof (1847) which called itself the *King's College Athenæum*, two debating societies at whose weekly meetings views on the political and social questions of the day were freely expressed and freely criticized. The opinions current seem to have been mainly different varieties of conservatism. " Edward Dicey was," says C. H. Pearson, " our nearest approach to a liberal."

(5) The struggle which college magazines and student societies had to wage in order to keep themselves afloat was a pale reflection of the conflict with bankruptcy in which the college council and the hospital committee were constantly engaged. The hospital, of course, could not meet its own current expenses; every year it had to look to charity to wipe off a deficit of some £600. The college, on the other hand, thanks mainly to the prosperity of the school, was as a rule easily able to pay its way, apart from fresh demands for heavy capital expenditure. But no sooner did its finances begin to show signs of stability and solvency than some gigantic call for new buildings, extensive alterations, or enlarged equipment brought back the old trouble.

It would be tedious to enter into minute detail concerning the receipts and expenditure of the college at this time. Two statements, one from the finance committee to the council on November 10, 1848, the other from the council to the annual general court on April 29, 1851, will probably give as much information as is necessary. (1) In 1848 there was a favourable balance on the current account, that is of receipts over expenditure, of rather more than £700. But

> it appeared that since January 1845 to the present time there had been an extraordinary expenditure for new buildings, fitting and furnishing—including the promised loan of £1000 to the hospital —of the sum of £18,212.

Toward this large sum a special fund of £6293 had been raised, leaving £11,919 to be met out of ordinary revenue. Of this £11,919 about £8000 had actually been paid out of current income: but the finance committee had to recommend the raising of a fresh loan of £4000, " to be paid off from time to time out of current income," in order to clear off the remainder of the debt. (2) At the annual general court of 1851 the council reported as follows:

> They regret to state that the funds at their disposal, derived as they are without exception from the fees of students, by no means keep pace with the increase of the demands made upon them. It must always be borne in mind that with the exception of four small endowments, given for the establishment of particular prizes, King's College, unlike other large collegiate establishments, has no funded or other property of any kind. Hence it is that the expenditure of each year has to be defrayed wholly out of income derived from fees. The council would also remind the court that the annual income has had to bear a very large portion of the expense of fitting up the college. The accounts laid upon the table to-day show that the gross expenditure incurred up to the 31st December last, upon buildings, fittings, furniture, etc., including £4000 still due to King's College Hospital, amounted to £165,584 3s. 8d., the only portion of which producing any direct return is that spent on students' rooms, from which a profit of £234 16s. was derived last year. To meet this very large outlay of £165,584 3s. 8d. the council have received (a) from shares £68,356, (b) from donations £65,502 12s. 4d., leaving to be paid out of income £31,725 11s. 4d. Looking at this statement, the council cannot but congratulate the court that in this the twentieth year of the existence of the college the amount of their liabilities has been reduced to £13,358 4s. 3d., the sum of £18,327 7s. 1d. having been already paid out of income. In connexion with this statement, the council think it right again to remind the court that no less than £11,474 has never been paid by the originally subscribed capital, and this arising from defalcations on shares only, without including the loss of donations. The payment of this sum would go far towards covering the present deficit. The net income

of the college during the past year has only exceeded the necessary and current expenditure by £304 4s. 6d. This is a less favourable statement than the council have usually been able to make. . . .

There was some trouble during this period from a number of shareholders who persisted in asking when they were going to receive dividends on their investments. The secretary was compelled in a series of soothing circumlocutions to convey to their minds the meaning of the word "never." The majority of the shareholders, however, making a virtue of necessity, began to convert their shares into donations. The movement—cordially welcomed and fostered by the council—began on a large scale in June 1846, and at the annual court of 1847 it was announced that £12,000 had been so commuted. This movement foreshadowed the ultimate abolition of nominations, the extinction of the court of proprietors, and the elevation of the institution from a joint-stock company into a university college.

(6) The ten years 1843–53 saw some important changes in the governing body of the college. First and foremost, the official visitor, the Archbishop of Canterbury, Dr William Howley, passed away on February 11, 1848. He had been one of the original founders of the college, one of the most generous subscribers to its funds, and throughout the whole of the twenty years of his primacy one of the most laborious workers on its behalf. He and his friend the Bishop of London had, above all others, determined the policy of the college since its foundation, and controlled the appointments to its staff. Dr Howley's place as visitor was, of course, taken *ex officio* by his successor in the primacy, Dr J. B. Sumner (whose brother, Dr C. R. Sumner, Bishop of Winchester, was already an active member of the college council and education committee). The new archbishop played his appointed part in distributing prizes and confirming appointments; but, naturally, he could not act with the personal authority and intimate knowledge of the old archbishop. Bishop Blomfield was left for the remaining eight years of his episcopate in a position of undisputed ascendancy.

Apart from the Bishop of London the only official governor of the college who made any pretence of exercising his functions was the Dean of St Paul's, Dr Edward Copleston, who was also (and primarily) Bishop of Llandaff. We have noted his invaluable services to the college in its early days. He continued, so long as his health and strength endured, to attend its councils and committees with exemplary regularity. His last appearance at the council was on May 11, 1849, and he died on the following October 14. The council passed a resolution of profound regret at his irreparable loss, and of warm appreciation of his devotion to the interests of the college for more than twenty years. He was a noble man; one of the greatest scholars, wisest statesmen, and finest gentlemen of his day and generation. His successor in the deanery, and therefore on the council of King's, was the rector of St Margaret's, Westminster, Dr Henry Hart Milman. Of the eight nominated life governors in office in 1843, four died before 1853—viz., the Duke of Northumberland (1847), the Marquis of Bute (1848), Lord Bexley (a very regular attendant at councils, and generous contributor of money) in 1851, and the Duke of Wellington (who since his duel with Lord Winchilsea had had little or nothing to do with the college) in 1852. Their places were filled respectively by Lord Radstock (a member of the council since 1842, who became one of the most active and influential of the rulers of the college until his death in 1857), the Marquis of Cholmondeley, Sir Robert Inglis, and the Earl of Harrowby. Of the ordinary elected members of the council the following passed away: Sir Henry Halford (1844); the Rev. Dr George D'Oyly (1846); Sir Charles Price and Sir Nicholas Tindal (1847); the Rev. Dr George Shepherd (1849); Sir Lancelot Shadwell, last vice-chancellor of England (1851); and the Rev. J. E. Tyler (1851). All save Mr Tyler, minister of St Giles-in-the-Fields, were original members of the council. It is needless to recall here how great was the debt of the college to all of them, and in particular to Dr D'Oyly, the prime founder of the institution. Among the new members of the council elected to fill the vacant places were Dr Thomas Watson, Archdeacon Harrison, the Rev. J. S. M. Anderson (preacher of Lincoln's Inn), and the Rev. Dr S. W. Warneford (generous founder of scholarships).

The last change to be noted is one of great importance. In July 1845 the very competent and trusty secretary, Mr H. Smith, announced the necessity of his resignation. For twenty-five years he had been treasurer to the trustees of Morden College, and the recent reconstitution of that charity by Act of Parliament meant that his treasurership would occupy the whole of his time. The council passed a vote of cordial thanks to Mr Smith for his devotion and efficiency during seventeen years, and begged his acceptance of £100 as a mark of their esteem. There were thirty-three applicants for the post: five were interviewed by a special committee; further consideration reduced the five to three; out of the three, after long deliberation, the council selected Mr John William Cunningham. The choice was a singularly prudent and fortunate one. Mr Cunningham remained secretary for nearly half a century (1845–95), and in course of time he became an incomparable permanent head of the executive of the college, serving the institution with exemplary devotion and ability, visiting the visitor, governing the governors, counselling the councillors, and keeping a long succession of principals and professors in order.

NOTE

I. Number of Students, 1843–53

| | COLLEGE | | | | | | SCHOOL | TOTAL |
| SESSION | REGULAR | | | | | OCCA-SIONAL | | |
	Gen.	Med.	Eng.	Theo.	Mil.			
1843–44	130	131	33	—	—	80	465	839
1844–45	125	152	30	—	—	71	471	849
1845–46	122	192	54	—	—	85	502	955
1846–47	121	182	71	33	—	94	500	1001
1847–48	156	137	71	55	—	85	460	964
1848–49	132	151	55	66	—	137	466	1007
1849–50	120	159	42	54	20	79	463	937
1850–51	111	196	39	54	11	94	449	954
1851–52	111	199	44	68	10	96	447	975
1852–53	106	199	41	78	13	76	469	982

II. Distinguished Students

Among those who entered the college during the period 1843–53, and subsequently became distinguished, were the following:

Stanley, Honourable Edward Henry (1843–45). Came from Rugby *æt.* seventeen; proceeded to Cambridge, where he obtained a first in classics; later Earl of Derby and secretary for foreign affairs under Disraeli, 1874–78.

Brinton, William (1843–47). Physician; M.B., 1847; M.D., 1848; demonstrator in anatomy at the college, 1848; resident medical tutor, 1850–53.

Harrison, Frederic (1843–49). Entered the lower division (school) of King's College in 1843, and left as head boy in 1849, to go to Wadham College, Oxford; became fellow and tutor of

Wadham, 1854–56; called to the bar, Lincoln's Inn, 1858; prominent lawyer, publicist, positivist, and literary man; died January 14, 1923, at the age of ninety-two.

Kitchin, George William (1844–46). Churchman; double first at Oxford, 1850; student of Christ Church; dean of Winchester, 1883–94; dean of Durham, 1894–1912.

Watson, Henry William (1844–46). Mathematician; second wrangler and Smith's prizeman, 1850; fellow of Trinity; master at Harrow, 1857–65.

Church, Alfred John (1844–47). Classical scholar and popular writer; later professor at University College.

Stephen, James Fitzjames (1845–47). Jurist; came to King's from Eton *æt.* sixteen; proceeded to Cambridge, where he read law; professor of Common Law at the Inns of Court, 1875–79; judge of the High Court, 1879–91; knighted, 1877.

Brodribb, William Jackson (1845–48). Classical scholar; proceeded to Cambridge; first in classics, 1852; fellow of St John's College; vicar in Wiltshire, 1860–1905.

Eade, Peter (1845–48). Physician and surgeon; physician to Norwich hospital, 1856–1903; three times mayor of Norwich; knighted, 1885.

Lathbury, D. C. (1846–48). Literary man and high churchman; editor of the *Economist,* of the *Guardian,* and of the *Pilot;* compiler of *English Hymnal,* 1906.

Wood, John (1846–50). Surgeon; gold medallist in anatomy, 1848; demonstrator at King's College, 1850; professor of clinical surgery, 1871–89.

Ayerst, William (1847–49). Churchman; founder of Ayerst Hall at Cambridge, 1884.

Pearson, Charles Henry (1847–49). Classical scholar and historian; came from Rugby; proceeded to Oxford, where he secured a first in classics and a fellowship at Oriel; professor of History at King's College, 1855–65; professor at Melbourne University, 1874; minister of education in Victoria, 1886–90; author of *National Life and Character,* etc.

Kingsley, Henry (1847–50). Literary man; younger brother of Charles Kingsley; proceeded to Oxford; then to Australia to hunt for gold, which he found indirectly by writing novels concerning Australian life.

Beale, Lionel Smith (1847–51). Surgeon and microscopist; professor of physiology at King's College, 1853–69; of pathological anatomy, 1869–76; and of medicine, 1876–96.

Dicey, Edward J. S. (1847–51). Journalist; proceeded to Cambridge; president of the Union; on the staff of the *Daily Telegraph,* 1862–70; editor of the *Daily News,* 1870, and of the *Observer,* 1870–89; author of numerous books on foreign affairs.

Farrar, Frederick William (1847–51). Classical scholar and churchman; proceeded to Cambridge; first in classics; fellow of Trinity; headmaster of Marlborough, 1871–76; rector of St Margaret's, Westminster, 1876–95; dean of Canterbury, 1895–1903; author of numerous imaginative works.

Hastings, Graham (1848–50). Eminent lawyer; student in the department of general literature and science; passed on to Worcester College, Oxford; called to the bar, 1854; K.C., 1875; bencher of Lincoln's Inn, 1877.

Stephen, Leslie (1848–50). Literary man; younger brother of James Fitzjames Stephen and cousin of Edward Dicey; came from Eton *æt.* sixteen; proceeded to Cambridge; fellow of Trinity Hall, 1854; in holy orders, 1855–75; edited the *Dictionary of National Biography*, 1882–1904 (wrote 378 articles himself); author of *History of English Thought in the Eighteenth Century* and many other important works; knighted, 1902.

Stebbing, William (1848–51). Scholar, historian, and journalist; came from Westminster and King's College School; proceeded to Oxford; double first; fellow of Worcester College; for nearly thirty years assistant-editor and leader-writer of the *Times*.

Bensly, Robert L. (1848–52). Orientalist; fellow of Caius College, Cambridge; lecturer in Hebrew, 1861–89; professor of Arabic, 1887–93; member of the Old Testament revision committee.

Probyn, Dighton Macnaghten (1849). A student in the short-lived department of military science; entered the army in 1849; served in India during the Mutiny, 1857–58, where he gained the V.C.; in China, 1860; and on the North-West Frontier in 1863; attached to household of King Edward VII when Prince of Wales, 1872, and remained in his service till the latter's death in 1910, when he was keeper of his privy purse; comptroller to Queen Alexandra from 1910; K.C.S.I., 1876; K.C.B., 1887; General, 1888; G.C.V.O., 1896; privy councillor, 1901; G.C.B., 1902; G.C.S.I., 1911; died, at the age of ninety-one, in 1924.

Macknight, Thomas (1849–51). Journalist; editor of the *Northern Whig*, 1866–98; author of Lives of Bolingbroke, Burke, and Disraeli.

Liveing, Edward (1849–53). Student in the medical department of King's College; proceeded to Caius College, Cambridge; M.B., 1859; M.D., 1870; fellow of the Royal College of Physicians, 1874, and registrar, 1889–1909; fellow and member of the council of King's College, and assistant physician to the hospital.

Arnold, Edwin (1850–51). Journalist; on the staff of the *Daily Telegraph* from 1861; editor, 1873; author of *The Light of Asia*, etc.

Godson, Augustus F. (1850–52). Barrister and politician; M.P., 1886–1906; knighted, 1898.

Lias, James John (1850–52). Entered as a student in the general literature and science department; secured foundation scholarship in mathematics at Emmanuel College, Cambridge; B.A., 1857; M.A., 1861; ordained, 1858; minor canon of Llandaff Cathedral, 1868–71; professor of modern literature at St David's College, Lampeter, 1871–80; chancellor of Llandaff Cathedral.

Fawcett, Henry (1851–52). Came up from King's College School; proceeded to Cambridge; fellow of Trinity Hall, 1856; professor of political economy at Cambridge, 1863–84; Postmaster-general, 1880–84.

Heath, Christopher (1851–53). Surgeon and anatomist; came up from King's College School; professor of clinical surgery at University College, 1875–1900.

Stebbing, Thomas R. R. (1852–53). Naturalist; brother of William Stebbing; fellow and tutor of Worcester College, Oxford; authority on Crustacea; took orders, 1858, but wrote *Faith in Fetters*, 1919; died the same year as his brother—viz., 1926—aged ninety-one.

Bowen, Edward E. (1852–54). Schoolmaster; joined the military department of King's College, but changed to the general; after a brilliant career at King's, proceeded to Cambridge, where he took a first in classics and secured a fellowship at Trinity; master at Harrow, 1859–1901; wrote that most dismal of school songs, *Forty Years On*.

Lambert, Brooke (1852–54). Vicar of Greenwich, 1880–1901; authority on poor-law administration.

PART III

THE UNIVERSAL PROVIDER

CHAPTER VIII

CONTROVERSY AND DECLINE
1853–68

§ 1. *The Dismissal of Professor F. D. Maurice*

THE first ten years of Dr Jelf's long reign were, as we have just seen, years of remarkable development in King's College. They saw, in particular, the establishment of the theological department—a department as directly due to Jelf's personal initiative as had been the hospital in the preceding period to Todd's. But, besides this, they were marked by the institution of the military department; by the introduction of a wide and generous scheme of scholarships; by an extension of the facilities for students' residence; by great improvement of the college buildings; and by the complete reorganization of the school.

The one thing that they did *not* see, however, was the placing of the finances of the school and college on a sound basis. The liabilities of the institution—roughly equivalent to the amount of the defalcations of the seceders of 1829—hung like a millstone round the necks of the council. In vain did they struggle to free themselves from the incubus of debt. For current expenses, and for sinking fund also, they had to depend, in the absence of all endowments, solely on fees; and not infrequently these fees wholly failed to meet the requirements of the case. Hence the debt tended rather to increase than to diminish, and on occasions, as we shall later see, desperate and deplorable means had to be adopted to stave off bankruptcy and keep the doors of the college open.

The effects of this financial stringency were in the main bad. The college was undermanned; the staff was underpaid and overworked; its members were compelled to supplement their inadequate incomes by doing much extraneous drudgery; the classes were kept too large; apparatus and equipment were frequently insufficient and out of date; a general air of poverty and depression brooded over the dingy scene. One

206

effect, however, must be placed on the other or credit side of the account. The urgent need to secure new sources of supply made the principal, the secretary, the staff, and the council quick and eager to discern new educational demands, and to start new activities in order to satisfy them. Hence gradually King's College came to be a sort of " universal provider "— *i.e.*, not so much a single institution as a composite educational emporium; a bundle of institutions, almost separate and distinct from one another, serving a great variety of ends, held together only by their existence in one and the same building, by their subordination to a common authority, and by their recognition of a single unifying religious principle. The watchword of the period was " elasticity ": again and again that very word or some equivalent phrase appeared in the annual reports of the time, as some new department was projected, or some novel development adumbrated.

This " elasticity " of function was imperatively demanded by the steady and apparently inevitable shrinkage of all the three great departments with which the college had opened in 1831: the department of general literature and science fell from 106 in 1853 to 66 in 1868; the medical department from 199 in 1853 to 130 in 1868; the school from 469 in 1853 to 344 in 1868. The causes of decline were not far to seek: the demands of industry and commerce called young men away from classics and mathematics; the new hospital schools of medicine proved formidable rivals to the medical departments of King's and University Colleges; the cult of the boarding-school and the passion for playing-fields, which began to seize the middle class about this date, drew many possible pupils away from urban day schools which taught in cellars, exercised in sunless backyards, and promenaded in sinful streets.

The very continuance of the college depended upon its capacity to strike out in new directions and to meet new wants as they displayed themselves in society. It was imperative, also, when a new department was opened out, that everything possible should be done to foster it, so that it might become a support to the college, instead of a burden upon its straitened resources; and that nothing should be done to bring it into doubt or disrepute. This is a circumstance that must be borne in mind when the story of the unhappy controversies which gathered round the devoted head of the Rev. F. D. Maurice is investigated. The storms which his utterances and activities generated did not rage within and around an old and wealthy institution (such as either Oxford or Cambridge University) which could be trusted to weather any tempest of criticism, and to withstand any cyclone of public disapprobation; they raged within a department which had only just been erected, and around a college the designs of whose founders were still uncompleted. In so far, also, as they were theological storms, they involved every department of the college in their fury; for the very *raison d'être* of the whole institution was the intermingling of sound religion with every branch of secular education. Any suspicion of connivance with heresy on the part of the authorities would have depleted the college of students, would have dried up the sources of supply, and would have involved the ultimate closing of the doors. In particular, any taint of condoned heterodoxy in the theological department would have meant the withdrawal of the bishops' licences, and the extinction of the department: it was, in fact, the bishop of London's intimation in 1853 that so long as Professor Maurice taught divinity at King's he would decline to recognize the certificates issued by the college that brought matters to a head, and made it necessary for Maurice to depart. The council and the principal, in combating Maurice's opinions and evicting him from his chair, were fighting not so much for orthodoxy as for existence. It was immediate bankruptcy rather than eternal perdition of which they were afraid.

Professor Maurice, in spite of his angelic appearance, his saintly character, his noble enthusiasms, and his high abilities, had from his first appointment in 1840 been a very doubtful asset to the college. He could not keep order; he was unable to make himself intelligible; he had no affinities with the young; he was entirely devoid of humour; he was shy, sensitive, reserved, preternaturally solemn. He inspired profound respect, of course, in the better students—such as Leslie Stephen, Edwin Arnold, F. W. Farrar, and C. H. Pearson—who came away from his history lectures with a vague sense of awe at the mysterious workings of Providence, although with empty notebooks. But his lofty speculations concerning the ways of God with Man were lost upon the generality, who desired, and did not get, precise information respecting such mundane things as the Norman Conquest and the Glorious Revolution. "At one time," says C. H. Pearson,

the inattention displayed at his lectures was so marked that Professor [then Mr] Brewer, with characteristic loyalty, came in to sit as a student and take notes, as a sign of the value he attached to Maurice's thoughts. It was very much Brewer's private

208

influence with the leading students that changed the tone of the history lecture-room. For myself, I must confess with humiliation that, though I was interested in the subjects taught, and took the highest prize in history, I never really valued Maurice's teaching at the time. It seemed to me vague and made up of sonorous words and meaningless generalities. I still think that Maurice was not in his element as a teacher of boys.[1]

In 1846, however, when the theological department was inaugurated, the fact that Maurice as a teacher of history was far from a success did not deter the council from adding to his secular duties the profession of divinity. It was Jelf's policy, dictated by the urgent need of economy, to construct his new departments out of existing materials; and it was to him a matter of legitimate pride that he was able to create a complete faculty of theology by the addition of but a single member (Professor R. C. Trench) to the staff of his arts department. Maurice was giving only three arts lectures a week: it would be no burden to him to add a few lectures on ecclesiastical history to those which he was giving on secular history, especially as he did not recognize any distinction between things sacred and profane. So convinced was he of the unity of knowledge that all his arts lectures were leavened with divinity, and all his theological lectures with profanity (in the proper sense of the term). At the time, moreover, when Jelf was collecting his theologians Maurice was in high favour with both the bishops and the anti-catholic laymen of the council. On the one hand, he had fought hard in his *Educational Magazine* and elsewhere against the state control of education, denouncing the new government inspectorate of schools, and contending that it was the peculiar function of the national church to provide the early instruction of the nation's children: this was precisely the view of Archbishop Howley, Bishop Blomfield, and the council of King's College generally. On the other hand, in his *Three Letters to the Rev. W. Palmer* (1842), arising out of the Jerusalem bishopric controversy, he had vigorously vindicated the protestantism of the Church of England, and had maintained the entire propriety of her close association with the Lutheran Church of Germany: and this had greatly gratified the bishops (who had been amazed and alarmed at the tractarian attack on the Anglo-Lutheran see of Jerusalem), and had immensely pleased Sir Robert Inglis, Lord Radstock, and other pious evangelicals on the council,

---

[1] W. Stebbing, *Charles H. Pearson*, pp. 35–36.

who dreaded the anglican drift toward catholicism. His appointment in August 1845 by Archbishop Howley as Warburton Lecturer seemed to set the seal upon his orthodoxy, and marked him out as a representative man. When, therefore, six months later he was transmuted into a " professor of divinity " no one appeared to be apprehensive.

The appointment, nevertheless, was highly injudicious, and entirely inexcusable. It was highly injudicious; for Professor Maurice was an intense individualist, restless under any sort of restraint, incapable of accommodating himself to any system; a free-lance who even when he reached orthodox conclusions reached them in a heterodox way; an original and dissatisfied thinker, the contents of whose creed were in a constant state of flux. It was also entirely inexcusable; for in numerous publications Professor Maurice had expressed views substantially identical with those for which he was ultimately condemned and dismissed. Bishop Blomfield and Dr Jelf had either read or not read his *Kingdom of Christ* (second edition, 1842), his *Christmas Day and other Sermons* (1843), his Warburton *Lectures on the Epistle to the Hebrews* (1845), and, above all, his *Two Letters to a Non-resident Member of Convocation* (1845). If they had *not* read them, they are to be severely blamed for appointing a professor of divinity without finding out from readily accessible sources what sort of divinity he professed. If they *had* read them, they ought for ever to have kept silence respecting anything that Maurice said in his *Theological Essays* of 1853. For there was nothing in these essays that had not been stated or implied in his earlier works, published before his appointment in 1846. In particular, he had in the *Two Letters* of 1845, issued exactly twelve months before his election to the divinity chair, expressed, with as little ambiguity as in 1853, precisely that conception of " eternal life " for maintaining which he was expelled; that is to say, the view that it consisted essentially of knowledge of God, and had no relation to duration of time. Maurice, however, was not (and is not) easy to read; and it is clear that neither Blomfield nor Jelf had read him. Not until the religious press began to clamour, and began to question not only the orthodoxy of Maurice, but also the soundness of King's College theology generally, did the chairman of the council and the principal turn their august attention to the writings criticized. When they did so they were astonished and horrified.

As for Professor Maurice, many a time and oft must he have regretted his elevation from the obscurity and irresponsibility of a chair of history to the lofty prominence and dangerous authority of a chair of divinity. When he was merely an historian and educator, few persons had perused his writings, still fewer had troubled to unravel their meaning, and scarcely anyone had bothered whether they were orthodox or not. When, however, he had become an accredited theologian and a trainer of candidates for the ministry, his words and deeds had acquired a new and embarrassing importance. From 1846, indeed, he had no peace. The controversy of 1853 which ended in his dismissal was no less than the sixth in which he had become involved with the urbane and long-suffering Dr Jelf, who probably would have avoided them all had it not been for the goadings of the sectarian press, the agitations of the evangelical laymen on the council, and the trepidations of the Bishop of London. The details of these unedifying brawls can be found in the *Life of F. D. Maurice* by his son (2 vols., Macmillan, 1884), and it fortunately is not necessary here to recapitulate them. It will be enough to mention the causes of dissension in the order in which they arose. (1) In the autumn of 1847 the election of a Rothschild as member for the city of London raised the question of the admission of Jews into parliament: the authorities of the college were solidly opposed to the concession; Maurice ardently advocated it. (2) About the same time a great agitation sprang up respecting the consecration of the latitudinarian Hampden to the bishopric of Hereford: the high church party vehemently denounced it; Maurice strongly supported it. Hence in January 1848 Jelf addressed the first of his protestant epistles to Maurice—an epistle eminently mild and wholly free from menace—in which he begged him in his zeal for persecuted humanity not to forget the college upon which he was conferring an unfavourable notoriety. Maurice replied in a letter which must have imposed a severe strain on Jelf's temper: it was slightly sarcastic; it expressed no regrets; it made no concessions; it showed no recognition of Jelf's point of view; it held out no hope of any amendment in the future. At no time, indeed, in any of his controversies did Maurice display the slightest concern for the welfare of the college which he was involving in ruinous conflict. He was fighting for what seemed to him to be great causes; but he regarded the college as a mere blockhouse in which he happened to be entrenched, and concerning which on its own account he felt no interest at all. (3) The third dispute followed a few months later (May 1848), when Maurice tried to secure the appointment of

Charles Kingsley as his assistant in English. Of Kingsley's qualification for the post there could be no question: he was an old King's student, of brilliant literary gifts, who had just obtained a first in the classical tripos at Cambridge. But he was becoming notorious as a sympathizer with chartists, and as a popular agitator who under the pseudonym of " Parson Lot " wrote highly inflammatory articles in *Politics for the People*. Hence, to Maurice's intense chagrin, the cautious and conservative council decisively turned him down, and appointed a safe nonentity. (4) In 1849 Maurice became involved— together with Julius Hare, Samuel Wilberforce, R. C. Trench, and many other eminent clergymen—in the furious wranglings that raged round the tomb of that ordained freethinker, John Sterling; and Maurice, as Sterling's brother-in-law and the associate of his last days, was not far from the centre of the cyclone. The orthodox press—the *English Review*, the *Christian Observer*, the *Record*, the *Morning Herald*—formed a pack to hunt Hare and Maurice, and the name of King's College became involved in wild and whirling charges of heresy and infidelity. Jelf was in despair: he wrote again to Maurice protesting and imploring: Maurice replied in an interminable rigmarole (March 14, 1849) which yielded nothing and promised nothing. He seemed to regard Jelf's agitation with contemptuous amusement: on March 17 he wrote to the lady whom he afterward married:

> My foolish business is, so far as I know, at an end for the present. I am afraid it has done my good friend Dr Jelf more harm than me. He is ill in bed, and I am afraid I have some of his nervous feelings to answer for. One is sorry to be the cause of keeping worthy people in a fever, but that comes of their inviting such dangerous explosive reformers to enter their quiet orthodox schools.[1]

It did not seem to occur to him that King's College, no longer either quiet or orthodox, was not in a condition to stand an incessant series of explosions within, combined with assaults from without. Before twelve months had elapsed, however, reverberations more sonorous than ever before informed the world that a new battle was raging.

(5) In January 1850 Maurice's noble-minded and devoted friend, J. M. Ludlow, in the hope of finding a way of emancipation for enslaved and downtrodden artisans, began to establish co-operative workshops. It was an experiment well worth trying, and, although it proved in the end a costly failure, it

[1] *Life of F. D. Maurice*, vol. i, pp. 525–526.

taught valuable lessons as to what could not, and what should not, be done in industry. Maurice took up the co-operative cause with enthusiasm, his first contribution to it being to find for it the wholly inappropriate and entirely damnatory title of "Christian Socialism." There was nothing in the movement distinctively Christian; there was nothing whatever in it properly Socialistic. The name, which Maurice had intended to be an *eirenicon*, became a battle-cry; and amiable, if extremely incompetent, co-operation, masquerading as "Christian Socialism," was attacked as dangerously revolutionary by Christians, and as a piece of pious humbug by Socialists. In November 1850 the *Christian Socialist*, to which Maurice occasionally contributed, and over which he exercised a controlling influence, was started, and in the Christmas vacation of the same year Maurice and his friends went on a propaganda tour in Lancashire. Then the hurly-burly began. First, the philosophically radical *Edinburgh Review* made a direct personal assault upon Maurice's collectivism (January 1851); then the high church *Guardian* in three successive weekly issues denounced both the economics and the theology of the "Christian Socialists" (February 19–March 5). The cry was taken up by organs so diverse as the cobdenite *Daily News*, the catholic *Tablet*, and the nonconformist *Eclectic Review*. Finally came, in September 1851, a terrific onslaught in the pontifical *Quarterly Review*—an onslaught in which King's College was involved. The assailant was John Wilson Croker, then a power in conservatism and anglicanism, though now best known through the immortal caricatures of Macaulay and Disraeli, both of which masters of invective he succeeded in making his implacable enemies. Croker had no love for King's College; he was one of those original defaulters who had steadily refused to pay the subscriptions they had promised, and whose names had finally been displayed by the angry council on a conspicuous notice board in the entrance-hall of the institution. He had no love for Maurice, with whom he had been in conflict on educational matters so far back as 1840. Hence his attack was inspired by a double malignancy. He expressed surprise

> to find the reputed editor of *Politics for the People*, and the avowed author of other works, theological as well as political, of a still more heterodox character, occupying the professorial chair of divinity in King's College, London.

The council of the college became agitated, and poor Dr Jelf had to commence another of his harassing correspondences with his elusive insubordinate.[1] When the unsatisfactory collection of epistles was laid before the council, a clerical committee was appointed (November 14, 1851) to investigate the matter and report.[2] The committee presented its report on December 12, and the council decided to hold a special meeting on the 19th to consider it. The report declared (1) " Christian Socialism," apart from its name, to be innocent, (2) Maurice, apart from his associates, to be respectable, and (3) his recorded utterance, although injudicious, not heretical. It therefore recommended that he should be cautioned, but allowed to continue to profess divinity. The practical conclusion of this report was extremely unwelcome to many members of the council—especially the conservative laymen— and no fewer than three special meetings[3] had to be called before finally the report was accepted (January 23, 1852). An amendment, " That the council feel that it is their duty to declare the chair of the theological department occupied by Professor Maurice vacant," was only just lost.[4] Maurice was saved for the moment in spite of himself; for on December 30 he had written a letter to Jelf in which—as Jelf pointed out— he had expressed no sort of regret for the disturbance he had caused; had held out no hope of caution in the future, and, above all, had shown not the smallest regard for the interests of the college. Jelf had implored him, but wholly in vain, to add some phrase indicative of his intention " to bear in mind the duty and importance of not compromising the college." He was too honest to promise what he did not propose to perform; he would not add a word calculated to " remove the impression felt by some " that he was " too proud or too obstinate to condescend to allay the just apprehensions of the council."[5] He himself had expected to be dismissed, and,

[1] See *Life of F. D. Maurice*, vol. ii, pp. 78–102.

[2] The committee consisted of the Bishops of London and Lichfield, the Dean of St Paul's (Milman), Archdeacon Harrison, and the Preacher of Lincoln's Inn (Anderson). Lonsdale, Milman, and Anderson were distinctly well disposed toward Maurice.

[3] December 19, 1851, January 9 and 23, 1852.

[4] The vote is not recorded, but I speculate that it was as follows : for Maurice, Bishop Blomfield, Dean Milman, Archdeacon Harrison, the Rev. J. S. M. Anderson, Mr Justice Patteson, Sir Benjamin Brodie, Mr J. H. Green ; against Maurice, Earl Howe, Lord Radstock, Sir R. H. Inglis, Sir G. Staunton, Mr W. Cotton, Mr E. Wigram. It should be carefully noted that the amendment did not propose to deprive Professor Maurice of his chair of history and English. It merely moved for his deposition from his dangerous eminence as professor of divinity, and his restriction to his former lowly sphere, in which he could not possibly do any harm.

[5] Jelf's letter, January 17, 1852, quoted in *Life of F. D. Maurice*, vol. ii, p. 98.

although he had for the time being escaped, he felt that the respite would not be for long. In the circumstances it would have been infinitely better both for himself and for the college if at this point he had sent in his resignation. He determined, however, to stay and to let things take their course.

(6) The inevitable sequel was not long delayed. During Lent 1853 he preached in Lincoln's Inn chapel a series of sermons which in the ensuing summer were published under the title of *Theological Essays*, " by the Rev. F. D. Maurice, M.A., Professor of Divinity in King's College." In these essays he assailed or questioned many of the doctrines of current orthodoxy, and in particular the prevalent interpretation of the doctrine of eternal punishment. If the Essays had been issued as the work of a mere professor of history, or even of ecclesiastical history, though no doubt they would have been severely criticized, they would not have involved the college. Even if they had been entitled *Lincoln's Inn Sermons*, and if Maurice had described himself simply as " Chaplain to Lincoln's Inn," they might have been regarded as utterances concerning no one but himself and the patient lawyers. To issue them, however, as *Theological Essays* by a (or the) " Professor of Divinity in King's College " was deliberately and wantonly to implicate the college in the promulgation of views which were not being inculcated in the college, and which he knew were regarded with horror by his principal, his theological colleagues, and the overwhelming majority of the members of the council. If it were suspected that these strange doctrines were the things that were being taught to theological students in King's College by a professor of divinity, the bishops would be compelled to withhold their licences, the pious would cease to send their sons for training in theology, the theological department would have to close down, the college would in all probability become bankrupt. The council had no option but to act, and the need for action became urgent when, on the one hand, the religious press began to attack the college with unprecedented ferocity,[1] and, on the other hand, the Bishop of London—who regarded the theological department of King's as his diocesan college— expressed his inability to recognize the certificates issued by Dr Jelf so long as Maurice remained a professor of divinity.

There were two possible ways of bringing Professor Maurice to book. The first was to charge him with abusing his position

---

[1] *Cf.* especially *Morning Advertiser* (July 21, 1853) ; *Record* (" Theology of King's College," July 25 and August 4, 1853) ; *Christian Observer* (August 1853) ; *Guardian* (August 10, 1853).

as a professor of divinity in the College, and with doing things likely to inflict irreparable injury upon the institution which he was employed to serve; the second was to accuse him of heresy. The first method of procedure was the proper method for the council to adopt, and Professor Maurice (who was throughout actuated by the highest principles) clearly intimated that if and when the authorities of the college should inform him that his continuance on its staff was injurious to the interests of the college he would without demur resign. The second method of procedure—viz., by inquisition for heresy—was one wholly improper for the council to adopt. But the attack upon Maurice and the college, in the *Record* and the other so-called religious papers, was wholly on the ground of heterodoxy, and the Bishop of London's refusal of recognition was entirely due to the supposed subversiveness of Maurice's neology. Moreover, the evangelical members of the council of King's College—especially Lord Radstock and Sir Robert Inglis—were at the moment more alarmed by the peril of Maurice's teaching to immortal souls than by the effect of his actions on the college finances. Hence, in a fatal moment, they incited the Bishop of London to incite the unhappy Dr Jelf to start another and æonian correspondence with the painful professor respecting his alleged erroneous doctrines.[1] Poor Jelf soon became entangled in a hopeless and endless logomachy with his protean opponent respecting the meaning of the word αἰώνιος in the New Testament.

If the council, the bishop, and the principal managed their case with execrable ineptitude, Maurice, on his side, did little better. Instead of taking his stand on the simple and decisive fact that he had uttered nothing in his *Theological Essays* to which he had not given public and published expression before he was appointed a professor of divinity, he followed Jelf's lead into the mazes of theological terminology, wherein speedily both of them were eternally lost. But as to this he was resolved: having been accused of heresy, he would not resign, but would wait to be expelled. He felt that the cause of truth and freedom was at stake, and he was prepared, in the spirit of a Christian martyr, to immolate both himself and the college rather than yield an inch. So the controversy dragged on its dreary length from the beginning of July to the end of October 1853.

[1] The correspondence is printed in full in a sixty-four-page pamphlet entitled *Grounds for laying before the Council of King's College, London, certain statements*, etc., by R. W. Jelf (1853), and it is supplemented by a forty-page pamphlet by Maurice on *The Word "Eternal"* (1853). See also *Life of F. D. Maurice*, vol. ii, pp. 163–209.

Meanwhile the heathen continued to rage, and the ecclesiastical press to fulminate. The college was torn by rival Jelf and Maurice factions; even the church was menaced with schism. When, after the long vacation, on October 14, 1853, the council met for the first time in the new session, it was evident that decisive action would have to be taken. Hence a special meeting was summoned for October 27. At this meeting, " after long and anxious deliberation," the following resolutions were moved by Bishop Blomfield and seconded:

The council having taken into consideration an essay lately published by the Reverend Frederick Maurice, Professor of Divinity in King's College, and also a correspondence between the principal and the professor on the subject of the said essay, and having been informed by Professor Maurice that he does not wish to make any statement in addition to his *answer to the Principal's final letter*, resolve:

(1) That in their judgment the opinions set forth and the doubts expressed in the said essay, and re-stated in the said answer, as to certain points of belief regarding the future punishment of the wicked and the final issues of the day of judgment, are of a dangerous tendency, and calculated to unsettle the minds of the theological students of King's College.

(2) That the council feel it to be their painful duty to declare that the continuance of Professor Maurice's connection with the college as one of its professors would be seriously detrimental to its usefulness.

(3) That the council, while it laments the necessity which constrains them to adopt this resolution, are bound in justice to Professor Maurice to express the sense which they entertain of the zealous and able manner in which he has discharged the duties of the two offices which he has held, and the attachment which he has at all times manifested to the college.

Of these three resolutions the third was obviously a mere emollient. The second was the operative resolution which the bishop was justified in putting, and which the council had no option but to pass. The first was a sop to Cerberus—viz., to the *Record* and the fanatical rout that followed it upon its heresy hunt. It was highly improper for the council to consider it at all, as it was not for the administrative body, the executive agent of a limited liability company, to convert itself into an inquisitorial court and sit in judgment on the opinions of its servants. And if the court itself was *ultra vires*, still more was its mode of procedure irregular and indefensible. Of the fourteen members present, only two (Bishop Blomfield and Archdeacon Harrison) were clergymen. The accused was not summoned to appear, nor was any opportunity given to him to make a defence. Four members of the council, however, alone protested against the arbitrary action of the majority : Mr W. E. Gladstone proposed, Mr Justice Patteson, Sir Benjamin Brodie, and Mr J. H. Green supported the following amendment to the first resolution:

> That the Lord Bishop of London be requested to institute an examination into the question how far the writings of Professor Maurice, or any propositions contained in them, which have been brought under the notice of the council, are conformable to or at variance with the three creeds and the formularies of the Church of England, and to make a report thereupon, and that the Lord Bishop be requested to communicate the results of this examination to the council.

But the Lord Bishop of London had no intention whatsoever of instituting any investigation into the creeds or formularies of the Church of England. He was well aware that any such investigation would have the most embarrassing results. In his refusal to accept the amendment he was supported by all the members of the council present except the equitable four— viz., by Archdeacon Harrison, the Marquis of Cholmondeley, Earl Howe, Lord Radstock, Lord Calthorpe, Dr Watson, Mr Wigram, Mr Twining, and Mr Cotton. They felt instinctively (and rightly) that it was expedient and indeed necessary that Maurice should depart. They realized that they had got into a horrible theological and judicial muddle, and that if they began to institute examinations of the tangle they would never get out of it at all. Hence they decided—no doubt with many qualms of conscience—to discard procedure and display arbitrary will. By dabbling in doctrine they had put themselves hopelessly in the wrong. When Professor Maurice, on being informed of the decision of the council, wrote formally and said:

> I think it due to my own character as a clergyman, to the interests of the college, and to the liberties of the English Church, that I should call upon the council, if they pronounce a theological sentence upon me at all, to declare which article of our faith condemns my teaching,

all the puzzled inquisitors could say was that " they did not think it necessary to enter further into the subject." They unquestionably thought it extremely necessary *not* to enter further into the subject.

The consequence of this badly bungled business was that a large section of public sympathy veered to Professor Maurice's

218

side; that King's College passed under a cloud; that its council obtained a name for obscurantism and tyranny; and that Dr Jelf—the kindest and most patient of men—was denounced as a persecutor and an oppressor. For both Maurice and Jelf the path of ecclesiastical preferment was closed. Every calamity, however, has its compensations. On the one hand Maurice secured much-needed emancipation from restraint; on the other hand Jelf was strengthened and confirmed in his belief in the eternity of future punishment.

§ 2. *The Reconstruction of the Theological Department*

In the unhappy and disastrous Maurice controversy both sides were right; that is to say, both sides were wrong. On the one hand, Maurice—who had an infinite capacity for believing what he liked and for doing what he did not like— was fighting for great and noble causes with a sublime disregard of consequences. He was fighting for a larger and more liberal theology than that dominant in his day; for the right of private judgment in the interpretation of the Bible, the articles, and the creeds; for the priceless privilege of ambiguity; for academic freedom. On the other hand, the council and Jelf were struggling for the continued existence of the college; for the salvation of the theological department from imminent ruin; for the right to prevent professors from abusing their official position by taking advantage of it to further their personal ends, when these personal ends were gravely injurious to the college. Maurice had made his position as a professor an impossible one by the reckless manner in which he dragged the college into one public brawl after another; by his total disregard of all warnings or appeals; by his open contempt for the wishes of both principal and council. It was said of Rousseau that he was one of those philanthropists who know how *chérir tout l'univers excepté leurs enfants*. It might equally truly be said of Maurice that he was devoted to the service of all men, except those who paid him. Even his best friends on the council were unable to acquit him of fault: Sir Benjamin Brodie, for example, wrote to Archdeacon Hare (Maurice's brother-in-law): " I must also say that I am not a little vexed with Professor Maurice that he should have brought us into this difficulty," and added the opinion that " a little worldly wisdom " would have obviated the crisis. Maurice was, however, wholly devoid of worldly wisdom; and so he had to go. The council would have failed in their duty if they had not secured his departure. But they did their duty in the worst conceivable manner. They made their fatal mistake when they forsook administration for inquisition; abandoned discipline for dogma; left the solid ground of academic order and embarked on the seething sea of theological controversy. When once they had set the faithful Jelf on to Maurice, and had got the two fairly involved on the tossing floods in the battle of αἰώνιος—a battle which clearly was likely to be one of endless duration, and inconclusive—nothing remained for them but to terminate the conflict by means of an Olympian thunderbolt; and, when Maurice (his blood thoroughly up) challenged them all to come on, they could only say with agitated emphasis that "they did not think it necessary to enter further into the subject."

No wonder that a section of public sympathy veered round to the side of the undefeated champion of liberty and liberality; that congratulatory letters poured in upon the evicted professor; that the lawyers of Lincoln's Inn and the scholars of Queen's College presented addresses; that dissenters and co-operators continued to celebrate their hero; that Tennyson, the new poet laureate, dedicated to him a copy of verses, promising him a welcome to his island home,

> Should eighty-thousand college-councils
> Thunder 'Anathema'

at him. The press, however, on the whole was on the side of the council. The *Daily News*, the *Examiner*, the *Spectator*, and the *Globe* were almost alone in condemning the censure and dismissal. The *Times* was all but silent: it mentioned the case but once (November 11, 1853). The rest, including even the unitarian *Inquirer* and the anti-Christian *Reasoner*, held that Maurice's dismissal was (since he refused to resign) proper, necessary, and inevitable.[1]

All the same, the painful episode caused a tremendous upheaval, and it shook the college to its very foundation. In particular, the theological department, deprived of one of its leading teachers at the beginning of a new session, and torn by schism, instantly and urgently called for reorganization and reconstruction.

Immediately upon receipt of the sentence of dismissal (October 27, 1853), Professor Maurice wrote to Dr Jelf to

---

[1] The wisest and kindest words on the whole unfortunate controversy are probably those uttered by Professor E. H. Plumptre in his *Sermon in Memory of R. W. Jelf* (1871), pp. 11–12. The passage is too long for quotation here. It holds the balance true between the Platonic Maurice and the Aristotelian Jelf.

inquire whether or not he should continue his work in the college until a successor should be appointed. Dr Jelf replied that in order to spare Professor Maurice the painful experience of appearing as a censured and evicted teacher before his classes, he would make arrangements for others to take them over at once. The council approved Dr Jelf's action, and voted to Professor Maurice, in lieu of notice, the share of fees (£120 17s. 8d.) which he would have received for his term's work had he performed it—a share which he emphatically refused to accept. Three of Maurice's colleagues—M'Caul, Browne, and Hall—agreed in the emergency to divide his work among them. Dr Jelf, in commending their devotion, spoke of them to the council as "distinguished ornaments" of the college. Had trade-union principles been more widely recognized at the time, they might have found themselves described as "blacklegs," with other adjectives besides "distinguished" prefixed to the term. When more permanent arrangements came to be considered Dr Jelf was able to formulate a scheme which not only reduced the types of divinity taught in the college from three to two, but effected a pecuniary saving of £140 a year. Dr M'Caul, who already professed Hebrew and Old Testament exegesis in the college, agreed to add ecclesiastical history to his programme, provided he could have the assistance of a new Hebrew lecturer. This condition was readily agreed to, and (January 13, 1854) Mr J. J. S. Perowne, of Corpus Christi College, Cambridge—later eminent as vice-principal of Lampeter, dean of Peterborough, and bishop of Worcester—was elected to the new post. On the same occasion, moreover, a significant change in the titles of the chief teachers in the theological department was effected. It was clearly recognized that one of the main sources of all the trouble respecting Maurice was due to the fact that he had unfortunately been called a "professor of divinity." Under almost any other title he would have been innocuous: as professor of history indeed he had actually for five years talked and written all sorts of things, later denounced as heretical, without anyone paying the slightest attention to them. Not even the bishop and the principal were aware of them. But to profess divinity is a serious matter; it invests a mortal man with a prerogative almost pontifical, conferring upon him a kind of *jus respondendi ex auctoritate ecclesiæ*. His words become weighty and oracular. The college, no doubt, hoped to bestow dignity upon its teachers of Old Testament Hebrew, New Testament Greek, and Ecclesiastical History by calling them "professors of divinity." But it bestowed too much dignity upon them; it made them dangerously important; it endowed them with too great a power. Even a single professor of divinity was probably more than so small a college as King's was capable of sustaining. What then can be said of the policy which placed within its walls simultaneously no fewer than three, especially when no two of the three professed precisely the same sort of divinity? It was as though there had been three independent and rival oracles at Delphi. No wonder that tumult and controversy supervened, and that both the college and the religious world at large were riven by the conflict. Much is in a name; and heresies are never formidable until they are propounded by bishops or professors of divinity.

Recognizing, too late, this cardinal truth, in January 1854 Dr Jelf addressed to the lords and gentlemen of the council the following letter:

It has appeared in the course of the late discussions respecting the arrangements of the theological department that some ambiguity exists as to the titles assigned to the professors in that department. Ever since the foundation of the department the professors have been entitled "professors of divinity" without any special designation with reference to the particular branch of theology taught respectively by each. There has been an understanding, however, that to each was entrusted a special duty.

(1) I have taken upon myself what is tantamount to dogmatic theology.

(2) Dr M'Caul teaches Hebrew and the exegesis of the Old Testament.

(3) Mr Maurice taught ecclesiastical history.

(4) Mr Trench the exegesis of the New Testament.

(5) Pastoral theology, so far as it has been attended to, has been assigned to Mr Plumptre in his capacity as lecturer in divinity.

I am inclined to think that henceforth it may be advisable to discontinue the title of "professor of divinity," and to give to each professor the proper designation to distinguish his particular branch of instruction—e.g., professor of Hebrew and of the exegesis of the Old Testament [etc.].

The council heartily concurred with the principal's proposal, Mr Plumptre was elevated to professorial rank, and the prospectus of the theological department was revised and reissued as follows:

The Rev. A. M'CAUL, D.D.
- *Professor of the Exegesis of the Old Testament*
- *Professor of Hebrew and Rabbinical Literature*
- *Professor of Ecclesiastical History*

CONTROVERSY AND DECLINE

The Rev. R. C. TRENCH, B.D.   *{ Professor of the Exegesis of the New Testament*

The Rev. E. H. PLUMPTRE, M.A.   *Professor of Pastoral Theology*

The Rev. J. J. S. PEROWNE, M.A.   *{ Lecturer in Divinity, including the " Evidences " Lecturer in Hebrew and Rabbinical Literature*

During the period under review (1853–68) several notable changes occurred in the distinguished staff of the theological department. (1) In October 1856 Professor R. C. Trench was appointed dean of Westminster—a position that made him *ex officio* a member of the college council. He announced his willingness to continue his professorial work at King's, and he did so for two sessions. In June 1858, however, the pressure of his decanal duties—and especially of the evening services in the nave which he had inaugurated—compelled him to resign. He remained an active member of the council until his elevation to the archbishopric of Dublin in 1863. His place as professor of the exegesis of the New Testament was taken by that eminent scholar the Rev. C. J. Ellicott, fellow of St John's College, Cambridge, whose commentaries on the Pauline Epistles had already made him famous. (2) In the autumn of 1860 Mr Ellicott was made Hulsean professor at Cambridge, but with some help from his devoted colleague Mr Plumptre, he managed to keep the two chairs going. Nay more; even when he was appointed dean of Exeter in 1861 he did not resign, but made arrangements to come up to London for a mid-week every fortnight. This he continued to do for more than a year; but neither his own constitution nor that of the college could stand the racket of this incessant oscillation between Devonshire and Middlesex, and in November 1862 he resigned. Professor Plumptre was transferred to Ellicott's chair, and a new professor of pastoral theology was found (February 1863) in the Rev. S. Cheetham, fellow and late assistant-tutor of Christ's College, Cambridge, vice-principal of the theological college at Chichester. (3) In June 1862 Mr J. J. S. Perowne became vice-principal of Lampeter College; his post as lecturer in Hebrew and Divinity was conferred upon the Rev. Stanley Leathes, of Jesus College, Cambridge. (4) In November 1863 the threefold professor of Hebrew (since 1841), Old Testament exegesis (since 1846), and ecclesiastical history (since 1853), Dr Alexander M'Caul, closed his laborious existence. The council resolved (November 24) to redivide his work, and accordingly

(December 23) they promoted Mr Stanley Leathes to the chair of Hebrew and Old Testament, and appointed the Rev. J. C. Robertson, canon of Canterbury, to the chair of ecclesiastical history. Thus in 1868 Jelf was lecturing on the thirty-nine articles (although he rarely managed to deal with more than four of them in the course of the session); Plumptre on the New Testament; Leathes on the Old; Robertson on ecclesiastical history; and Cheetham on pastoral and liturgical theology.

In spite, however, of the labours of these sound, if not very lively, divines, the theological department did not prosper. In 1853, at the time of the Maurice controversy, the number of its students had been 78; ten years later they had sunk to 41. Dr Jelf professed to think that the department was hampered, in competition with the older universities and with Durham, by its inability to confer degrees in divinity. He, therefore, on July 10, 1855, addressed a long letter to the council urging that a supplementary charter should be sought from the government conferring the requisite powers. The council concurred; the archbishop's aid was secured; the government was approached; but all in vain. For nearly eight years the matter continued to be mooted; but to no purpose. The old universities were unfavourable; if King's College had secured the privilege, there were numerous other theological colleges, anglican and nonconformist, that were determined to follow suit; above all, the London University did not think it proper that one of its affiliated colleges should exercise independent degree-granting functions, even in a subject outside its own sphere of influence. So King's College had to be content with its A.K.C., and had to concentrate its efforts upon the task of keeping the standard of that diploma high, and making it generally known and respected.

If, however, divinity degrees remained beyond the reach of the young theologians of King's, such was not the case with hoods. For, it appeared, the right to concede the privilege of wearing a hood inhered in the Archbishop of Canterbury, as a university sole. He had, indeed, recently conferred upon the *alumni* of St Augustine's College an adornment so radiant that it was possible to argue that Solomon in all his glory was not arrayed like one of these. Hence, with sober confidence, on March 24, 1862, Dr Jelf addressed an enormous letter to Archbishop Sumner, stating under six heads why King's College theologians desired hoods, and begging him to exercise his prerogatives of pity and power on their behalf. At present, he said:

they are restricted to the use of a *tippet*, which simply identifies them with a few individuals who are confessedly inferior to university men. The consequence of this academic contrast between them and their brethren in the ministry is a certain degree of depreciation in their social status. They are undeservedly looked upon as an inferior class, and it is no disparagement of their more than ordinary zeal in their Master's service to say that they feel a certain amount of discouragement which tends to depress their energies.

The archbishop, anxious that nothing which he had the ability to remove should continue to depress the energies of these more-than-ordinarily zealous young men, promptly replied from Lambeth (March 26):

MY DEAR PRINCIPAL,
I think that the proposal contained in your letter embodying the feelings of the students of King's College is very natural and legitimate, and, happily, one which can be complied with without hesitation or scruple. I am not aware that any formal measures are necessary in order to give authority for such a measure as a distinctive hood. In the case which you mention of St Augustine's, I remember nothing further than such a letter from the principal as you have sent to me, to which I sent the same reply as that which I am now writing. Should anything further be required I shall readily concur in it, and remain, my dear principal, very sincerely yours [etc.].

Nothing could have been simpler, or less hampered by formalities: he spake and it was done. The council, thankfully welcoming the proffered boon, resolved (May 9, 1862):

That the favour granted by his grace the Archbishop of Canterbury at the principal's request, viz., that associates of the theological department of this college be henceforward allowed to wear a distinctive hood, be gratefully accepted; that the pattern of such hood be fixed by the principal; and that it be issued through the college office to all associates of the theological department who may be in holy orders, at such price as shall be arranged.

Thus it came to pass, when Dr Jelf had completed his survey of silks and satins, and had decided upon the shape and hue of the new vestment, that, freed from the degrading tippet and arrayed in the resplendent hood, the A.K.C. no longer felt himself inferior to the B.A. of Oxford or Cambridge, but moved with a confident sense of equality among the rabbit-skins; and that, with his more than ordinary zeal still further stimulated, he threw off the discouragement which the tippet

P

had engendered, and entered upon his career with nothing to depress his energies beyond the normal wickedness of mankind, and the deplorable indifference of the masses both to the clothes that curates wore and the sermons that they preached.

While Dr Jelf was devoting his intellectual powers and æsthetic gifts to the settlement of the great problem of the hood, Professor E. H. Plumptre, the faithful chaplain of the college, was keenly concerned to secure for the college a chapel more in keeping not only with the hood but with the whole character of King's. On October 11, 1859, he addressed to the principal a letter, which the principal laid before the council, and the council ordered to be printed for circulation. He argued that the chapel was wholly unworthy of the college; that its " meagreness and poverty " were even " at variance with the principles which the college was founded to assert "; that its seats and kneeling-boards were " absolutely uncomfortable "; that few went to it except under compulsion; and that " no local memories and affections " gathered round it. He himself offered £100 toward the cost of reconstruction, and volunteered to assist in the raising of such further funds as should be necessary. The council at a special meeting (December 9) adopted Professor Plumptre's proposal, and decided to get Mr (later Sir) G. Gilbert Scott, the great restorer and renovator—the indirect and unwilling founder of the Society for the Protection of Ancient Buildings—to examine the chapel and present a report. The report, dated December 22, 1859, ran as follows :

I send you herewith a plan and an internal sketch showing what I would suggest as the best means of improving your college chapel.

There can be no doubt that, in a classic building, the best mode of giving ecclesiastical character is the adoption of the form and, in some degree, the character of an ancient basilica. It is at once the original ideal of a classical Christian church, and the groundwork on which the majority of those in subsequently developed styles have been founded; and, though the earliest idea struck out for a large church, it possesses so much intrinsic dignity and solemnity of character that it has never since failed in exciting the respectful admiration which it at first inspired. Such being the case, I have always felt convinced that when the adoption of the classic style is imperative, this is the model we ought to adopt.

The existence of two ranges of iron columns in the room below the chapel offers facilities for carrying out the idea I have

King's College Chapel

226

suggested. It is true that we cannot safely erect massive stone columns, but I would in their place suggest double columns of metal (iron decorated with brass) in their form, not unlike those in the cloister of St John Lateran. These might carry a light clerestory with an open roof, slightly decorated with colour, as in the basilica of S. Miniato at Florence.

The great difficulty is the erection of the semicircular apse, which is essential to the basilican form; but I see the means of effecting this by bracketing out with iron brackets etc.

The present large windows must be divided by a columnar mullion, and should be filled with stained glass, and the chapel of course decorated in a simple and appropriate manner, and be fitted up in a style suited to its general design.

I think that the cost would be about £3800 or £4800.

The council accepted Mr Scott's report, commissioned him to carry out the work, and appointed a committee of forty—twelve from among its own members, fifteen from the staff of the college, and thirteen old students—to find ways and means of raising the required funds.

The task of reconstruction and refitting proved to be a much bigger and more expensive one than had been anticipated. Not even at the end of ten years had it been wholly completed, and by that time over £7000 had been expended, of which £6264 had been raised by donations. A report presented by the committee in June 1868 sufficiently indicates the process of the work:

In the summer of 1861, they [the committee] erected an apse, and inserted new windows. In August 1863 they gave orders for proceeding with the remaining alterations of the structure, including a new roof and the clerestory. In March 1864 arrangements were made for putting in the clerestory windows, for finishing the walls and the apse, for reseating the whole chapel (except the stalls at the west end for the principal, the head-master, etc.) and for throwing out an apse at the west end as a site for the organ. . . . Many portions of the building are still incomplete, and special donations will be gratefully received for special works, such as the inlaying of the remainder of the roof, the carving of the windows, the internal decoration, and the stalls at the west end for the principal and professors.

The stained-glass windows were the gifts of generous donors as follows:

North Aisle

1.[1] Timothy	Rev. J. R. Major, D.D.
2. St James and St John	William Bowman, Esq.

[1] Beginning from the east end.

3.[1] St Matthew and St Luke   T. G. Sambrooke, Esq.

4. St Mark and St Peter   { Edward Wigram, Esq., in honour of Rev. R. W. Jelf, D.D.

Apse

1.[2] Our Lord sitting amongst the Doctors } The Earl of Powis

2. Our Lord in the Carpenter's Shop } Rev. T. A. Cock, M.A.

3. Our Lord bearing the Cross   J. W. Cunningham, Esq.

4. Our Lord healing the Sick

5. Our Lord teaching in the Synagogue } The Earl of Powis

South Aisle

1.[3] Samuel   Rev. J. Fearnley, M.A.

2. Abraham and Isaiah   Rev. Professor Hall, M.A.

3.[4] Moses and Aaron   { The friends of the late Rev. A. M'Caul, D.D.

4. David and Solomon   { The friends of the late Joseph Henry Green, Esq.

The enlarged and beautified chapel suggested the need for a new and better organ. In February 1864 the council received a letter from Mr W. H. Monk (who in 1854 had succeeded Mr Bevington as organist) " asking the permission of the council to sell the old instrument which was never very fit for the purpose, but which in the new building would be wholly inadequate." He offered " with the assistance of Dr Lavies, an old student of the college," to raise the necessary funds. The council readily gave the desired permission.

In June 1864 the work of reconstructing, refitting, and redecorating the chapel was so far advanced as to make it possible to use the building once again for worship. It was formally reopened, on the 19th of the month, by the bishop of London, Dr A. C. Tait, who preached the sermon.

One further matter remains to be mentioned before this long section on the theological department is closed. The residence for theological students adjoining the college—162 The Strand—did not pay its way.[5] In June 1857, therefore, the council decided to sublet the front room on the ground floor at a rent of £150 a year. Even so, however, the house could not be made self-supporting: in March 1858 a statement of accounts showed a loss on the preceding year's working

---

[1] Marble columns given by Messrs Jackson and Shaw.
[2] Beginning from the north side.   [3] Beginning from the east end.
[4] Marble columns given by the subscribers to the window.   [5] See above, p. 175.

of £210 2s. 4d. and a total deficit on the four years 1854–57 of £786 7s. 4d. The council, therefore, reluctantly decided to close the residence altogether. They had the house on their hands, at a rent of £250 a year, for another ten years. But they readily found a tenant who was prepared to pay them £285 a year for it. So all was well financially. Nevertheless, they regretted the loss of the hostel, and looked forward hopefully to a future day when their theological students should attain to an ampler and more enduring abode—a hope that was destined to be realized in 1902. Two rather deplorable results flowed from the closing of the Strand hostel: first, the evening service in the college chapel was abandoned; and, secondly, the Rev. J. J. S. Perowne, who had acted as censor to the resident theologians, was informed by the council that, as he was *functus officio*, he could no longer have his meals in college free of charge.

§ 3. *The Medical School and the Hospital*

One reason why Mr Perowne had to be deprived of free food; why the theological residence had to be closed; and why the most stringent economies of all sorts had to be enforced, was that exceptional and exceedingly heavy expenses had to be incurred in respect of the medical department and its appendant hospital. The hospital, of course, had its own administrative committee, but on that committee representatives of the council had a dominant voice; the council itself was the original lessee of the hospital buildings; the council appointed all the major officials; and the medical school of the college depended for its continued existence upon the maintenance of the hospital. Hence the council was deeply committed to whatever expenditure was required to keep the hospital efficient.

We have already noted [1] that, the old St Clement Danes workhouse having become totally inadequate to the growing needs of the neighbourhood, a special building fund—toward which the council promised to contribute £5000 out of college revenue—had been opened in 1849, and that when a year later a sum of over £25,000 had been assured, the erection of a new wing adjacent to the converted workhouse had been decided on. Of this new wing the foundation-stone was laid by Archbishop Sumner on June 17, 1852; and the wing was completed and opened in October 1854. The total cost—

[1] See above, pp. 187–189.

including £20,650 for the site—came to over £46,000.[1] It had been confidently expected that the new building, which provided extensive accommodation for out-patients, as well as seven more wards for in-patients, would meet the demands of the vicinity for many years to come. But that expectation was not realized: with increased supply came a more than proportionately increased demand. The number of out-patients treated during the year rose from 22,813 in 1853 to 43,166 in 1862; while the tale of in-patients simultaneously increased from about 1250 to about 1700. The inhabitants of the two contiguous parishes of St Clement Danes and St Mary-le-Strand would appear to have acquired the hospital habit; to have made the waiting-rooms of the out-patients' department a social club, and the pleasant young assistant physicians and surgeons their father confessors. In a normal year (1854 *et seq.*) the numbers from these two parishes of those whose names appear on the hospital registers amount to two-fifths of the entire population.

Hence within three years of the opening of the new wing—*i.e.*, in 1857—urgent necessity compelled the hospital committee and the college council to face the task of another appeal and resumed building. It was decided to clear the old workhouse away altogether, and to put a completely new and much loftier structure on the site; to purchase three contiguous houses in Grange Court; and to facilitate approach from the Strand by acquiring and demolishing Nos. 39 and 40 Clement's Inn. The total cost of these demolitions and constructions was estimated at some £40,000, and efforts were at once commenced by a special committee to raise this formidable sum—the college council advancing on loan £2500 (June 1858). Within a year £27,605 was raised; in 1859 the fund was closed, the council making itself responsible for any further amount that might be required up to the estimated £40,000. The new and complicated work was at once put in hand; during the summer of 1861 it was completed and the great central block of the hospital opened. " The portion then opened," says the report of 1862,

> comprised, in addition to the new wards, an entrance hall and business offices, the great staircase with its provisions for warmth and ventilation, the kitchen, and similar accommodation for the nursing sisters and the resident officers.

[1] Full particulars respecting the site, the buildings, and the finances are given in the *Annual Report* of April 30, 1853. There is also an enthusiastic account of the new wing, after it had been opened, in Dickens's *Household Words* for December 15, 1855.

A third, or west, wing of the hospital was projected; but funds being exhausted, its erection was postponed to a future indeterminate date. As a matter of fact it was never put up; for when, forty years later, the extension of the hospital had once more become urgent, the council came to the revolutionary decision to move the whole institution bodily to Denmark Hill in Camberwell.[1]

It will be observed that in the quotation from the 1862 report given above mention is made of " nursing sisters." This term contains a reference to one of the most novel and interesting experiments associated with King's College Hospital. It might be tersely described as the supersession of Mrs Gamp by Miss Florence Nightingale. In 1848—largely through the influence of R. B. Todd, William Bowman, Lionel Beale, and other King's men—had been founded at St John's House, Queen's Square, Westminster, a training institution for nurses on a definitely religious basis. Details of its early years are lacking, but at the time when King's College Hospital became formally associated with it there were within its walls a lady superintendent, seven honorary lady sisters, and thirty-five paid nurses. All were taught " to regard their work as a holy function; not as a mere trade, but as a dignified office." For eight years the St John's institution and King's College Hospital had no formal connexion with one another apart from the fact that the same medical men were interested in both. During this period (1848–56), however, the nursing at the hospital was far from satisfactory; too many women of inadequate skill, coarse manners, low character, and bibulous tendencies found their way into the wards, to the distress of the patients, the despair of the doctors, and the demoralization of the medical students. Hence in 1853 Miss Florence Nightingale herself was invited to institute a training school for nurses in connexion with the hospital. Before, however, she had time to do anything, the Crimean War broke out, and her energies were diverted into another direction. To the Crimea she took with her many of the nurses from St John's House. On the conclusion of the war the hospital authorities opened negotiations with the St John's House committee, and on March 31, 1856, an agreement was reached according to which all the nursing in the hospital was to be placed in the hands of the institute. At once a vast improvement both in the quality of the nursing and in the ethos of the hospital took place. On the occasion of the first annual meeting of the

[1] See below, p. 419.

institute held after the amalgamation, Dr Jelf commented on " the inestimable influence of the presence of these ladies upon the character of the medical students," and Dr R. B. Todd followed more felicitously in the same strain: " There are no persons," he said,

> connected with our hospital, who would come forward more warmly, more cordially, I may say more vociferously, and would cheer the ladies more heartily than our medical students, and that I think is strong practical testimony to the great and important value of the fusion of these two establishments.

Another experiment made a few years later, in which King's College Hospital was again a pioneer, was not so successful. In October 1861 a lying-in ward containing ten beds was opened for the double purpose of ministering to the needs of the poor married women in the neighbourhood, and of providing a training for maternity nurses. It was equipped at the cost of the Nightingale fund, and was placed under the general superintendence of Miss Nightingale herself. For six years it continued to do its best: but at this date antiseptics were unknown; puerperal fever raged; and the mortality rate in the ward was so high that in 1867 it had to be closed. Its main permanent result was Miss Nightingale's famous *Introductory Notes on Lying-in Institutions* (1871).

In the interval between the initiations of the two important and unprecedented experiments just recorded, viz., on January 30, 1860, the great Dr R. B. Todd had passed away. Something remains to be said respecting the last seven years of his energetic and influential life. It will be remembered that in January 1853 Dr Todd had resigned the chair of physiology which he had held since 1836. This involved the resignation also of his position as physician to the hospital, since the office of physician to the hospital was attached to the college professorship. So strong, however, was the desire on the part of both college council and hospital staff to retain Dr Todd's services as physician that, on February 25, 1853, the rule tying the two posts to one another was rescinded, and Dr Todd, though released from the college, was retained for the hospital —the popularity of which, no doubt, was greatly increased by the frequency and freedom with which he prescribed brandy for his patients. Professor W. Bowman, who for five years had been associated with Dr Todd in the teaching of physiology, was invited to take over Dr Todd's college lecturing. He was unable, however, to add to his duties. Hence the vacant chair had to be filled from outside. The question of the appointment

232

was one that caused Dr Jelf much concern. On April 8, 1853, he addressed to the council a voluminous letter on the subject; it began as follows:

MY LORDS AND GENTLEMEN,

The importance of the present crisis in the medical department will plead my excuse for submitting to you some of my thoughts respecting the election of a fitting successor to Dr Todd. Assuming that the resolution of the committee in favour of dividing the chair of physiology is adhered to and confirmed by the council, two questions arise, viz., first, what sort of person it is desirable to associate with Professor Bowman, and, second, what are the best measures to ensure the appointment of such a person.

The council are doubtless aware that, of all the subjects taught in this college, physiology is the one which requires the most delicate handling. Everything depends upon the *spirit* in which it is treated. It may be made the vehicle for scepticism, disguised or undisguised, or else be turned to the glory of Almighty God. I do not hesitate to say, therefore, that here, if anywhere, the great principle of the whole college should be kept steadily and primarily in view—the principle of considering the religious element as paramount to every other in the candidate's character; that of allowing no powers, no acquirements, no plausibility, no facility of lecturing, to outweigh the one grand question " Is the man in life and conscience, as well as in profession, a good Christian man, a sincere member of the Church of England? "

After enlarging on this theme at prodigious length, Dr Jelf intimated that he knew a physiologist of sufficient piety for the post, and recommended his appointment. The council, while thoroughly concurring in Dr Jelf's principles and thanking him for his recommendation, decided to advertise the chair in the usual way, confident in their ability to detect sceptics, even if disguised, and to exclude doubtful characters, however plausible. From among the applicants four were selected by the committee as possessing that harmonious combination of science and religion so necessary for the " delicate handling " of physiological truth in the college. One of the four was Thomas Henry Huxley, aged only twenty-eight, but already an F.R.S. and noted for his investigations relating to hydrozoa. That he was not the candidate finally chosen must not be regarded as any slur upon either his orthodoxy or his efficiency. His successful rival, Lionel S. Beale, had over him the immense advantage of being an old student of the college, a member of the medical staff, and an assistant-physician at the hospital. Professor Beale proved to be an eminently sound and safe physiologist; but, in spite of his great and faithful services to the college, one cannot help feeling a certain regret that Professor Huxley was not appointed. If he had been appointed, and had remained on the staff till Dr Wace's time, what powerful allies they might have been in the struggle against agnosticism ! [1] In July 1855 Professor Bowman resigned his share in the teaching of physiology, and Professor Beale became sole occupant of the chair. The precedent established in Dr Todd's case was followed in 1855 : Dr Bowman remained a surgeon at the hospital, twelve beds being assigned to him, in spite of the fact that he had severed his connexion with the college. In 1856 Dr Royle vacated the chair of *materia medica* which he had held for twenty years, and was succeeded (February 1857) by Dr George Johnson. No further changes of first magnitude occurred for the next six years; but in 1862 a batch of resignations, due to mere coincidence and not to controversy, caused a crisis almost as grave as that of 1836. First, Dr Bowman surrendered his position as surgeon at the hospital, which he had held since its initiation (June); secondly, Dr Budd retired from the professorship of medicine and the office of physician to the hospital which he had held since 1840 (July); thirdly, Dr Farre resigned his chair of obstetrics after twenty-one years' service (January 1863). Dr Bowman's place was not filled; Dr George Johnson succeeded Dr Budd in the chair of medicine, thus vacating the chair of *materia medica*. To this post, after much consideration and long delay, was appointed (November 1862) Dr A. B. Garrod, professor of *materia medica* in University College—an admirable appointment, made on the special recommendation of Dr Thomas Watson and Mr Joseph Henry Green, but one that caused much heart-burning among the junior members of the college and hospital staff who had looked upon the chair as their rightful inheritance. In February 1863 Dr Farre's vacant chair was assigned to Dr W. O. Priestley. Two new chairs were instituted during this period—viz., that of dental surgery (Mr Samuel Cartwright) in 1860; and that of ophthalmology (Dr J. O. Wells) in 1865.

During this period, too, the medical staff became involved in three serious controversies which must be mentioned. First, in July 1854, Dr Todd laid before the college council a vigorous memorandum respecting clinical instruction in the

---

[1] In November 1864 Professor Beale wrote to Dr Jelf offering to deliver in the college hall a course of lectures " tending to establish the harmony between revelation and science." Dr Jelf was asked by the council to consult the bishops of London, Winchester, and Lichfield, together with Mr W. E. Gladstone and other pious laymen, as to the advisability of accepting the offer. Presumably their opinion was unfavourable, for nothing seems to have happened.

hospital, in which he complained *inter alia* that "inasmuch as a physician and a surgeon attend daily at the same hour, a student desirous of watching the practice of both cannot do so," and he urged a drastic revision of the time-table. An address in opposition to Dr Todd's criticisms and proposals was presented by Professors Budd, Fergusson, and Partridge, and the council had to appoint a special committee to adjust the differences between these eminent and voluble men. They decided, however, in the main to adopt Dr Todd's suggestions, and accordingly (October 1854) a new time-table of hospital attendance was drawn up, medical practice being fixed for the hour 1–2 P.M., surgical practice for the hour 2–3. Apparently the professors who did not like the new arrangement (which must have interfered with their dinners and their afternoon naps) manifested their displeasure by coming to the hospital late. Hence in March 1856 a system of fines for unpunctuality was instituted by the medical board, an exception being made in favour of the professor of obstetrics, whose times, it was realized, were inevitably determined rather by the laws of nature than by the regulations of men.

The second controversy, which occurred in 1857, related to the government of the medical department. All the professors of that department, except Dr Guy (dean), together with three medical men of the hospital (Todd, Bowman, Lee), presented a strongly worded memorial to the council, dated May 8, complaining that the control of the department had been usurped by the secretary of the college, Mr J. W. Cunningham, who was drawing up prospectuses, issuing advertisements, admitting students, and generally managing the department without consulting the dean or any one else. They begged the council (1) to restore control to the board of professors; (2) to allow them to elect their own dean annually; (3) to consult them more frequently respecting the filling of vacancies on the medical staff; and (4) to modify some of the college regulations concerning medical students which experience showed to be working badly. A special committee, with the bishop of Lichfield at its head, was appointed to consider the memorial and report. The committee, guided by Dr Lonsdale's urbane and skilful hand, drew up an eminently conciliatory reply in which a number of minor concessions under (3) and (4) were granted, but no surrender made on the major matters of (1) and (2). This reply the council adopted in its entirety on July 10. The professors were far from satisfied; the secretary was confirmed in his autocracy;

and, consequently, within six months the quarrel flared up again. In February 1858 the secretary, with the approval of the principal, and the subsequent concurrence of the council, but without consulting any of the medical professors, admitted to a Warneford scholarship a student whom the medical board had rejected. After much palaver, Dr Guy, as dean, wrote to the council a letter (July 8) in which he formally complained of the tendency of the secretary " to transfer the initiative in matters nearly affecting the interests of the medical department from the dean and the medical board to himself," adding, with regard to the particular matter at issue:

> I desire to add the expression of my entire concurrence in the views of the board and my personal regret that the secretary of the college should have displayed so grave a want of courtesy and consideration for the office I have the honour to hold.

Dr Jelf, who was evidently very angry, defended his action in a letter so energetic that the council had to tone it down before conveying its substance to the irritated doctors: he accused the medical board of conspiring to set up an *imperium in imperio*. The council, though realizing that the medicos had some cause for complaint, were unable to rescind their resolution respecting the Warneford scholar. Hence Dr Guy sent in his resignation as dean (July 20), and it was clear that no other professor would accept the vacant deanship as a nominee of the council. Hence the council were compelled to yield the point so long contended for—viz., the election of the dean annually by the board of medical professors. They accompanied the surrender, however, with the proviso that a permanent sub-dean should be appointed by themselves and that in his hands all the routine work of the department should reside. On October 8 it was announced that the medical professors had elected Professor Partridge as their dean for the session 1858–59; the council, thereupon, appointed Mr John Harley as sub-dean. The new system worked execrably badly; there was friction between the dean and the sub-dean; Professor Partridge by his unbusinesslike habits reduced the organization of his department to chaos. On May 11, 1859, Dr Jelf, in the course of an enormous and detailed communication to the council, said:

> I regret to have to report that the experiment so far as it regards the office of the annual dean has resulted in the most signal failure—a failure which has been doubtless mitigated in its consequences by the perfect success of the experiment so far as the new office of sub-dean is concerned—but a failure so complete

as to suggest the question whether the new system can as a whole, as at present constituted, be made to work satisfactorily.

Jelf evidently hoped that the council would rescind their concession of 1858, and would resume the practice of appointing a dean whom the principal could control. But the council felt this to be impossible. They had to leave the medical professors to restore order in their department. This their own interests compelled them to do. They did not re-elect Professor Partridge, and, after various experiments, in 1863 they found the right man in Professor Bentley, the botanist, and, having found him, they elected him year after year until his retirement in 1883. The permanent deanship was virtually re-established, although of a representative and not of a bureaucratic type. In 1864 the office of sub-dean was abolished. The relations between the dean of the medical department and the secretary of the college had been regularized by the council in 1861, when a set of rules had been framed requiring the secretary to consult the dean before framing prospectuses and issuing advertisements, and providing for an appeal to the council in cases where they could not agree.

The third controversy of the period raged from 1859 to 1863, and it related to the tenure of office for the assistant-surgeons and assistant-physicians of the hospital. On December 9, 1859, the council resolved that in future these appointments should be for four years only, and that at the end of that time the holders should not be eligible for re-election. They also made it abundantly clear on several occasions about this date (particularly in 1862) that tenure of a junior post gave no claim to preference when a senior post happened to fall vacant. Hence seething discontent, vehement protestations, and numerous resignations on the part of the junior staff, which, coupled with increasing difficulty in getting first-rate men to apply for these temporary and unhopeful posts, forced the council (June 13, 1864) to revise their rules and decree that:

> For the future all assistant-surgeons and assistant-physicians of the hospital be appointed for four years, but in every case they be eligible for re-election.

On the whole, then, this was a stormy period for the medical department, and Dr Jelf in particular must have come to dread the sight of physicians and surgeons. The numbers of students in the department also declined: they were 199 in 1853, only 130 in 1868. The finances, moreover, were so unsatisfactory

237

that in most years a serious deficit had to be met by deductions from the professors' fees.[1]

One incidental matter seems worthy of note in this section. On November 14, 1862, an application came before the council

asking that permission might be granted to Miss Lucy Sewell, a young lady who had obtained the degree of M.D. at Boston, U.S.A., to attend the clinical lectures on the diseases of women and children at the hospital.

All that the minutes further record is, "Application declined."

§ 4. *Department of General Literature and Science*

The decline in the theological and medical departments was paralleled by a still more serious falling off in the department of general literature and science. The numbers in the department diminished steadily, though with minor fluctuations, from 106 in 1853 to 66 in 1868, the lowest point touched being 58 in 1866. And, what was still worse, the quality of the students sank even more rapidly than the numbers. The professors complained that too many of the youths who entered were devoid of all accurate knowledge of even the rudiments of classics and mathematics, and that consequently they were totally unfit to follow the courses of instruction provided. The long lists of honours gained at Oxford and Cambridge dwindled: the thirteen wranglers of 1853 declined to two in 1867[2] and none in 1868. The principal and the council were much troubled by this deplorable decadence; for the department of general literature and science was the original nucleus of the college; and the education which it supplied was regarded as that type of culture best fitted to produce the ideal Christian gentleman in which the college specialized. In the report of 1855 the council expressed their firm adherence

to the old opinion that there is no basis of education so universally secure and lasting, or so well calculated to enlarge the mind, as that of a careful training in classics and mathematics, and that there is no one of the higher callings of life which is not furthered as well as adorned by such studies.

When they came to examine into the causes of the lamentable decline, they arrived at the conclusion that they were three in

---

[1] It may be noted in passing that the finances of the hospital were most seriously affected from 1865 onward by the fact that—owing to a decision of the House of Lords in the case of Jones *v.* The Mersey Dock Company—parochial rates had to be paid on the institution.

[2] One of the two wranglers of 1867, however, was W. K. Clifford—second wrangler and Smith's prizeman. Moreover, the Evening Department of King's College produced two more—viz., C. J. Lambert (third) and W. H. Grove.

number—viz., first, that the standard of classical teaching in schools was markedly lower than it had been in earlier days; second, that the public schools, including King's College School, tended to keep their boys beyond the age of sixteen and to send them up at the age of eighteen or nineteen direct to the universities; and, third, that the allurements of business and the attractions of the new civil service examinations were drawing young men away from the academic into the practical life, and were causing the classics, together with the abstract mathematics, to be deserted in favour of more modern and utilitarian studies. We shall note shortly how this last conviction led to a starting of a civil service department at this juncture, and also to a revival of the dormant professorship of commerce.

The first effect, however, of the council's investigations into the causes of decline in the department of general literature and science was an attempt to revive the department by a reorganization of its curriculum and time-table. The principal and professors devised, and the council approved, a scheme whereby: (1) the teaching of classics and mathematics should be restricted to the mornings; (2) on four afternoons a week a class should be held in English composition—" a branch of instruction hitherto wholly unprovided for in this college, and, with a few insignificant exceptions, elsewhere "; (3) the hours devoted to history and literature should be increased from two to four a week; (4) the periods assigned to French and German should be so rearranged as not to clash with one another. These administrative reforms, however, although they involved the expense of a new lecturer, did not stem the ebb of the tide. On March 29, 1860, Dr Jelf addressed a voluminous letter to the council, beginning as follows:

My Lords and Gentlemen,
  I beg leave to lay before the council a few remarks on the present state of the department of general literature and science, in the hope that they will be willing to lend their aid in devising a remedy for an acknowledged evil. I have for some time been much struck with one peculiarity in the department alluded to: the *entrances* generally have been very good, so much so as to remind me sometimes of its junior prosperity. But the number of those who *remain* under our care has been generally speaking diminished, several students taking their departure after one term's tuition; so that the average number in class does not bear any due proportion to the number of new students.

The cause of this curious phenomenon he conceives to be " the lamentable deficiency in grammatical teaching which may be

239

detected in many of the preparatory schools"; and as a remedy he proposes the institution of a new and more elementary class in Latin and Greek wherein the neglected foundations of the study of these languages may be relaid. He ends by recommending the appointment of the Rev. J. J. Heywood, master of the lower sixth form in the school, to the new post. The council (April 13, 1860) accepted the principal's proposal and recommendation. But still there was no improvement; rather, on the contrary, an accelerated decline. In 1866, when the numbers had fallen to 58—about one-half of what they had been in 1853—the teachers in the department remaining fairly constant round about 20, the council positively groaned in their annual report:

> The numbers in the department of general literature and science have fallen off considerably since last year, and the intellectual standard in general appears not to be high.

It was obvious, however, by that time, that the old position of the department as a half-way house between the public schools and the universities could never be recovered. Necessity compelled the council to call a new world into existence to redress the balance of the old. Before, however, we pass on to treat of the institution of the civil service department, the revival of the chair of commerce, the reorganization of the oriental language school, and—*facile princeps*—the establishment of the evening class department, we must note some important changes in the staff which occurred during the period under review—*i.e.*, the last fifteen years of Dr Jelf's principalship.

(1) Mathematics remained stable. Professor T. G. Hall, now a prebendary of St Paul's, continued until 1869 to hold the chair to which he had been appointed in 1830, although his interest in his work had languished. Classics, however, saw a complete change of personnel. In 1853 the two teachers were Professor R. W. Browne and Mr J. S. Brewer. In 1855 Mr Brewer was transferred wholly to English, in which for three years he had been giving assistance; he was followed as classical assistant by a succession of brilliant young men, fresh from the older universities, whose tenures of office were, from one cause or another, very brief. Professor Browne was, toward the end of 1860, appointed archdeacon of Bath. In conveying to the council the news of his elevation, however, he informed them that his new archidiaconal duties could well be performed during the intervals when his services were not required by the college. He was, with much hesitation, permitted to

become a dualist, the council expressing the strong opinion that he would find that his new office would make " more serious claims upon his time " than he seemed to anticipate. He somehow managed to serve two masters until Easter 1863, but then, having been further inducted into the rectory of Weston-super-Mare, he was reluctantly compelled to vacate his chair.   It was advertised, and out of eleven candidates Mr J. G. Lonsdale, fellow of Balliol, the brilliant son of the Bishop of Lichfield, was chosen—Mr Robinson Ellis, fellow and tutor of Trinity, being second on the list.

(2) The combined chair of English literature and modern history, vacated by Professor F. D. Maurice in October 1853, next calls for attention.   It was advertised, and from among the applicants Dr G. W. Dasent, Magdalen College, Oxford— an old King's College student,[1] and since 1845 assistant editor of the *Times*, was selected as the most highly qualified.   He was not appointed, however, until he had undergone a double inquisition; first at the hands of a committee, which made " certain inquiries " concerning doubtful opinions which he was suspected of holding, and secondly at the hands of the council, under the chairmanship of the Bishop of London, to whom he gave a " satisfactory explanation of his views " (December 1853).   Dr Dasent, however, did not keep his place as a professor for long.   After a little over a year he became involved in a terrific brawl with the secretary of the college, Mr Cunningham, as the result of which he sent in his resignation on March 30, 1855, adding:

Nothing can induce me to retrace this step, but if you wish to know the grounds on which I have taken it, I shall be ready to state them ;

and further expressing

sincere regret at being obliged to sever myself from an institu- tion in which I was mainly educated, and which I shall always regard with deep affection.

The council naturally desired to be informed precisely as to what all the pother was about, and they appointed a special committee to receive the statements of the disputants.   On receiving the committee's report, and " after much delibera- tion," they resolved to

accept the resignation of Dr Dasent, and express their regret that such a disagreement should have taken place between one of the professors and the secretary of the college.

[1] See above, p. 125.

Q

241

Dr Dasent's vacation of his composite professorship enabled the council to separate the teaching of language and literature from the teaching of history. The Rev. J. S. Brewer, freed from his lectureship in classics, became professor of the English language and literature. The brilliant C. H. Pearson, old student of King's College and fellow of Oriel, who had just returned (March 1855) to King's as a lecturer in English, was made professor of modern history. " I found my class at first," he says in his autobiography,

> in a high state of disorder. Dasent had been unduly gentle with them, and Hyman, my old tutor, who had succeeded Brewer as classical lecturer, was an active element of demoralization.

He himself, however, was, like Brewer, a strong disciplinarian and a stimulating teacher. He soon secured order, and he gave his students lectures of so striking a power and originality that they had no desire to play the fool. Among his abler pupils, who never forgot the lessons he taught them, were Henry Wace and W. K. Clifford. The general decadence of the department, however, meant that his classes were small, and that his emoluments as professor never reached the sum of £200 a year. But his work at King's left him—in common with most of his colleagues—ample leisure for other pursuits, and he became a frequent contributor to the *Saturday Review*, the *Continental Review*, and the *Spectator*. For one year (1862–63) he actually edited the *National Review*. In February 1864 his health broke down, and he received from the council a year's leave of absence in order to visit Australia and live an open-air life. In March 1865 he announced his intention to remain in Australia, and accordingly resigned. The chairs of English and history were reunited under Professor J. S. Brewer. A valuable incentive to the study of English and history in the college was the founding of the Inglis studentships in memory of Sir Robert H. Inglis, one of the founders of the college, who died May 5, 1855. Over £3000 was raised and invested, the annual proceeds being divided between the two subjects. It may be further noted here that in February 1854 the council received from a private source the offer of £100 a year for the endowment of a new chair of " British History and Archæology," the offer being coupled with the condition that the donor should nominate the first holder of the chair. The council accepted the offer, but when the name of the gentleman designated as the first professor was submitted to them, boggled at the condition. The generous donor then modified his condition and agreed to send in three names, any one of which could be chosen. Once more the council concurred, and once more, when the three names came before them, revoked. Dr Jelf was very angry, and in a letter of unwonted pungency expressed his views respecting the vacillation of "my lords and gentlemen." In the end an *impasse* was reached; the scheme had to be abandoned; the money was lost. The council, indeed, in this business acted with a most amazing ineptitude. At the meeting in which the final breakdown of negotiations was announced (June 27, 1854) it was resolved " that all future meetings of the council shall be commenced with prayers."

(3) In February 1854 the Rev. Richard Jones, who had slept in the chair of political economy since 1833, woke up and announced his wish to retire. The council placed no obstacles in his path, and expressed no thanks for his inactivities. They advertised the vacant place, and four applications came in. None of the applicants, however, " appeared to have sufficient merit to justify the committee in making any recommendation to the council," so (May 1854) the professorship was allowed to lapse, and

> what gave rise to no little surprise,
> Nobody seemed one penny the worse!

Five years later, however, when commerce was in the ascendant, when the call for a business education was clamant, when Cobden was at the height of his influence, and the principles of free trade triumphant,

> a letter, dated 14 March, 1859, was received from William Newmarch, Esq., secretary of the Globe Insurance Company, enclosing certain resolutions adopted by a committee appointed to raise a subscription in honour of the personal character and the services rendered to science by the late Thomas Tooke, Esq., of 31 Spring Gardens, and proposing to found with this object, under certain conditions, a professorship of economic science and statistics in this college.

Mr Thomas Tooke (1774–1858) whom it was thus proposed to honour was a prominent merchant, financier, and economist; eminent as the promoter of the sensational free-trade petition of 1820 which inaugurated the successful attack on the corn laws; a stalwart opponent of the Bank Charter Act of 1844; a pioneer in the economic interpretation of history. The council thankfully accepted the offer of the Tooke committee, and it was speedily settled (1) that L. and N.W. Railway debenture stock sufficient to yield £50 a year should be transferred to the governors and proprietors of King's College; (2) that a Tooke professor of economic science and statistics should be elected by the college council, subject to no restrictions save membership of the Church of England; (3) that the professor should deliver at least twenty lectures a year, and that at least ten of them should be in the evening; (4) that the tenure of the office should be limited to a period of five years, but that the holder should be eligible for re-election ; and (5) that, in addition to the £50 endowment, the professor should receive the usual proportion of the students' fees. The post was at once advertised, and from among the applicants the Rev. J. E. Thorold Rogers was unanimously chosen. Professor Rogers, who held the post by successive re-elections until his death in 1890, valiantly maintained the Tooke tradition. He was a militant free-trader, the friend and brother-in-law of Cobden; a strong radical individualist; a powerful exponent of the economic interpretation of history.

(4) When in 1859 Professor Rogers began his work as an economic historian in King's College, he found already established within its walls a congenial colleague and cordial ally—Cobdenite and radical—in Dr Leone Levi, professor of commerce and commercial law. The story of Levi's appointment is a curious one, illustrative of the difficulties under which the council laboured owing to the strict ecclesiastical requirements of the twenty-fifth clause of the charter.[1] Early in 1853 the demand in the college for the teaching of commercial law became so insistent that the council felt it necessary to make some provision to meet it. Now the obvious and only person to invite was Mr Leone Levi, whose great work on the subject, recently published (1850–52), had placed him in a class above all rivals. But, unfortunately, although a naturalized British subject and a convert to Christianity he was not a member of the Church of England. Consequently he was ineligible for office in King's College. The council got over, or round, the obstacle, by inviting him as an outsider to give a course of lectures within the sacred precincts. This he did, with such conspicuous success that on the termination of his course (March 15, 1853) his grateful and enthusiastic students presented a memorial to the council in which they

---

[1] " Provided always that no person who is not a member of the United Church of England and Ireland, as by law established, shall be competent . . . to fill any office in the college, except only the professorships of oriental literature and modern languages."

ventured to urge that august but embarrassed body " to institute a permanent chair in the college for this important and hitherto neglected branch of study "—viz., commercial law. In reply to this memorial the council resolved (April 8)

> that they considered it inexpedient to comply with the wishes of the memorialists, particularly as they would be unable to appoint Mr Leone Levi to the proposed professorship, he being a member of the Free Church of Scotland.

Mr Levi, therefore, continued to lecture as a pariah " by permission of the council " for another session, drawing highly important and influential audiences of " bankers, shipowners, general merchants, underwriters, commission agents and clerks." In January 1854, as he was doing more than the work of an ordinary professor, and as the demand for his services was likely to continue, he wrote begging for permanent appointment. Knowing the nature of the only barrier that blocked his way, he condescended to make the following explanation of his religious position:

> From what I learned, the only objection to such a step is a personal disability from my not being in immediate connexion with the Church of England, as I am in the practice of attending Dr Hamilton's Scotch Church. By the gracious leading of Providence since my arrival in this country, I met with friends in that church whom I esteem highly and with whom I associate in works of Christian fellowship and philanthropy. I occasionally attend the Established Church, whose liturgy I prize, and, in so far as I am conversant with its tenets, they are all but uniform with those of the Church of Scotland, whilst I have unfeigned respect both for the institution and members of the Church of England. If these expressions are sufficient to remove the apparent barriers to the appointment, I shall feel myself highly honored.

These expressions, however, were obviously not sufficient to satisfy the requirements of clause twenty-five of the charter. If only he could have proved that commercial law was a modern language or a branch of oriental literature all would have been well. But it was not enough for him to assert that, so far as he could see, there was no appreciable difference between an English episcopalian and a Scottish presbyterian. The council, therefore, inevitably " resolved, with much regret, that they were unable to accede to Mr Leone Levi's request " (February 1854). Hence he had to continue to lecture on the old permissive, occasional, and unofficial basis. Before the end of the following year, however (October 1855), he had evidently reconsidered the question in the spirit of Henry of Navarre, and when the Earl of Harrowby brought up once again in the council (November 16, 1855) the question of his election to the professorship of commerce and commercial law,

> the principal bore high testimony to Mr Levi's character, and stated that the only objection which was made when the same proposal was before the council on the 10 February, 1854, viz., that Mr Levi was not in communion with the Church of England, had since been removed. The principal also stated that the subject of Mr Levi's lectures had become of great public interest, and that he considered the filling up of the vacant professorship a matter of considerable importance.

Mr Leone Levi, therefore, having duly made his submission, was on November 30, 1855, formally installed as professor of the principles and practice of commerce. The chair thus secured was retained by Professor Levi until his death in 1888. He conferred distinction upon it by the publication in 1872 of his great and wholly orthodox *History of British Commerce*.

(5) The ecclesiastical barrier which so long blocked Professor Levi's pathway to his chair of commerce seemed at one time likely to cause an even more troublesome obstruction in the department of geology. For geology, since the establishment of Sir Charles Lyell's principles, was a subject far more suspect than commercial law; and most of the leading geologists assumed a worse-than-presbyterian attitude toward the cosmology of Moses, the catastrophe of Noah, and the chronology of Ussher. Hence, when in March 1853 Professor D. T. Ansted, owing to the pressure of business engagements, resigned the chair which he had held inoffensively since 1840, much anxiety was felt respecting the appointment of a successor. Dr Jelf's inevitable letter to the council (May 13, 1853) stated that, although some of the professors thought that "a fit and safe man" might be secured by advertisement, there were others, including himself, who were "so much impressed with the risk of dangerous or indiscreet teaching incidental to this science" that they considered it the more prudent course to confer the chair upon "the present excellent, indefatigable, and competent professor of mineralogy," Mr James Tennant, who, they knew, regarded geology wholly from an engineering and not at all from an anti-biblical point of view. The council, in spite of the principal's preference, decided to run the risk of advertisement. In the end, however, as the safe person selected was an inspector of coal-mines who was unable to secure the government's consent to his acceptance

of the chair, the professorship of geology passed into Mr Tennant's possession and was annexed to his chair of mineralogy.

(6) The chair of natural philosophy—primarily physics and astronomy—passed through some important changes during this period. In October 1854 the Rev. Matthew O'Brien, professor since 1844, sent in his resignation on his being appointed to the chair of mathematics in the Royal Military Academy at Woolwich. Dr Jelf in a letter of prodigious prolixity, dated November 2, 1854, suggested to the council that they might further the causes both of unity and of economy by amalgamating the professorship of natural philosophy with that of manufacturing art and machinery held since 1852 by Mr T. M. Goodeve, concerning whose " zeal and assiduity " he spoke in terms of the warmest eulogy. The council agreed, and Mr Goodeve was duly established in the two offices. He held them for six sessions, and then, like his predecessor, was lured to Woolwich by the superior emoluments which the government could offer. The council decided (July 1860) to separate the two chairs once more, and, advertisements having been issued, appointed Mr C. Percy Bysshe Shelley—*magni nominis umbra*—to the professorship of manufacturing art and machinery, while the professorship of natural philosophy was conferred upon Mr James Clerk Maxwell, late fellow of Trinity College, Cambridge, and later professor in the University of Aberdeen. Clerk Maxwell was undoubtedly one of the most distinguished of all the great men associated with King's College. His investigations into the nature of the ether and his theories respecting the electric field, indeed, place him among the foremost of the pioneers of nineteenth-century science. As a teacher of raw youths, however, he did not prove to be a success. " He was," says one who knew him, " a quiet and rather silent man, and it seems not unlikely that the students were too much for him." [1] Almost certainly, then, it was not excess of work, but excess of disorder that caused the council in October 1863 to appoint Mr W. Grylls Adams, of St John's College, Cambridge—brother of J. C. Adams, the great astronomer, discoverer of Neptune—to be lecturer under him in natural philosophy, so as to relieve him of the presence of the more turbulent of the disturbers of the peace. Things, however, did not greatly improve, and there was obviously not

[1] Letter to the writer (February 15, 1927) from the Rev. Canon Richard Abbay, who in July 1868 was appointed lecturer and demonstrator in physics at King's College.

enough going on, apart from noise, to give employment to two teachers; hence early in 1865, it would appear, an intimation was conveyed to Clerk Maxwell that he should resign.[1] At any rate, on February 10, 1865, his resignation came before the council and was accepted, the council resolving

> that in accepting Professor Maxwell's resignation they desire to convey to him their best thanks for the services which he has rendered to the college, and to express their high appreciation of his talents and attainments

—a resolution which is as eloquent in its omissions as in its expressions. Mr W. Grylls Adams, an excellent lecturer and strong disciplinarian, keen on laboratory work, was promoted to the vacant chair, and the lectureship which he had held under Clerk Maxwell was abolished.

(7) Several modern language chairs changed their occupants during the fifteen years under review. First, early in 1854, the Rev. Juan Calderon, professor of the Spanish language and literature, died, and his chair was allowed to remain vacant (till 1891). Secondly, in June 1856, Monsieur Brasseur terminated by reason of age and infirmity his twenty-two years of faithful and efficient service as professor of French. The council passed a cordial vote of thanks to him, and elected him an honorary fellow. Monsieur Mariette, who for two years had assisted Professor Brasseur as lecturer, was promoted to the vacant chair. Thirdly, in April 1863, Dr Bernays, one of the original members of the teaching staff of the college, brought to an end his thirty-two years' labours as professor of German. He too received from the council the same marks of appreciation as had been voted to his French colleague. The appointment of a successor, however, was not quite so simple a matter. The chair was advertised, and there were five excellent applicants, all of them doctors of philosophy, and most of them political refugees. The one most eminent at the moment was Dr J. Gottfried Kinkel—ex-theologian, poet, art critic, rebel and revolutionary—who had escaped to England

---

[1] Canon Abbay further writes: "It was difficult to keep order in the class in those days, especially when the blackboard was much used ; but probably the disorder led to the greatest scientific discovery of the century. It was believed by scientific men that the Governors asked Clerk Maxwell to resign his professorship of physics because he could not keep order ; that then he went back to Cambridge and quietly worked out his theory of the aether." In a later letter (February 18, 1927) Canon Abbay adds : "It was Professor Clifton who told me—I think in 1869—that he had heard that Clerk Maxwell had been asked to resign because of the disorder at his lectures," and he goes on to point out that Clifton was in a position to know.

in 1850 from the Prussian prison to which he had been condemned for life because of his share in the Heidelberg uprising of 1849. The committee appointed to consider the applications for the German chair reported (July 3, 1863)

> that amongst these candidates Dr Kinkel stands pre-eminent in literary distinction, that he has already secured the highest reputation both at home and abroad as a scholar and a teacher, and that on almost every ground his election would add greatly to the reputation of the college. The only reason that the committee have for not recommending him is that his name seems to be universally connected with all that is most ultra-liberal both in politics and religion in Germany, and although the committee are far from believing that he would introduce into his professional work anything opposed to the religious teaching of the college, or anything which would raise doubts in the minds of the students, yet they entertain grave fears (which are shared by the principal) as to the wisdom of electing to this professorship one who is looked upon with considerable suspicion by all who know them [*sic*].

In the circumstances, the committee recommended the appointment of Dr C. A. Buchheim, an excellent scholar and teacher, who continued to hold the chair with conspicuous success until 1900, when it passed to its present holder, Professor H. G. Atkins.[1]

(8) The changes in the section of oriental languages were more marked and revolutionary than those in modern languages. This was owing, on the one hand, to the abolition of the East India Company and the establishment of the Indian Civil Service, and, on the other hand, to the opening up of China and the immense demand for interpreters. Dr Duncan Forbes, who had been professor of oriental languages and literature since 1837, although he had an amazingly wide acquaintance with the diverse tongues of India, could not cope with the new demands, particularly as his health was failing. Hence, in October 1861, he resigned, and his work was portioned out to no fewer than three new professors, viz., Dr James Ballantyne (Sanscrit and Bengali); Mr S. Slater (Hindustani); and Mr T. Howley (Tamil and Telugu). To these was added next year a professor of Indian jurisprudence in the person of the erudite Dr Fitzedward Hall, the great philologist, then librarian at the India Office. At the same

---

[1] In no other case have three tenures covered without a break the whole course of the century of the history of the college. It may be noted, further, that Professor Buchheim's daughter still holds the post of lecturer in German at King's.

time the lectureship in Arabic, which Dr G. W. Leitner had held with much acceptance since 1859, was raised to a professoriate. Chinese continued to be taught by Professor James Summers, who had succeeded Dr Fearon in 1852.[1] Thus a strong and well-equipped Oriental section of the department of general literature and science was formed, and successes in the I.C.S. began to compensate, to some extent, for the falling off of distinctions at Oxford and Cambridge. But the section was not quite so prosperous as the council had hoped it would be, and in 1866 they joined the governing body of University College in asking the India Office for more consideration and support. The personnel of the section, too, caused an unusual amount of trouble. The professors were all of them busy men whose main centre of activity lay elsewhere—e.g., the India Office or the British Museum. The fees from King's College did not suffice to keep them from accepting anything else that offered. Hence changes were constant: there were ten within the years 1862–68. One transient holder of the chair of Sanscrit, for instance, got lost for many months and had to be advertised for. He was discovered at Munich and brought back; but ten days after his return to college he once more silently vanished, and "under these circumstances the council resolved to declare the professorship of Sanscrit to be vacant."

One further matter relating to the department of general literature and science must be noted before this long section is closed. In February 1858 the standard of the A.K.C. was raised. Hitherto it had been, in this department, a certificate of moral inoffensiveness and religious regularity rather than of intellectual eminence. The qualifying requirements had been three—viz., (1) nine terms' attendance as a matriculated student; (2) good behaviour; (3) a satisfactory number of appearances at chapels and divinity lectures. Dr Jelf, in a letter to the council, urged that in future, "without in any way lessening the standard as to character, it might be well to give greater prominence to intellectual exertion." The council agreed, and ordered the rules to be amended accordingly.[2]

[1] In 1854 the Secretary of State for Foreign Affairs asked the college to nominate a supernumerary Chinese interpreter for Hong-Kong. The college did so, with results so satisfactory that the request was repeated within a few months, and within five years twenty-one nominees of the college were in Government employ. This was an immense stimulus to the study of Chinese in the college.

[2] The amended rules for the general (as distinct from the theological) A.K.C. are given in the Calendar for 1859–60, pp. 73–74.

§ 5. *The Civil Service Department*

The overcrowding of the learned professions, the rush of young men to enter government service, the probable wide extension of the examination system recently established in respect of Indian appointments—all these circumstances led the observant and resourceful Dr Jelf to compose a letter to the council in February 1854. It began as follows:

> MY LORDS AND GENTLEMEN,
>
> Since the last meeting of the council an announcement has been made in Her Majesty's speech to the effect that the appointments in the chief public offices will be bestowed according to ascertained merit. It has long been my opinion that a section of some one of the existing departments might be advantageously devoted to preparation for the public service, and I think the time is now come when the feasibility of such an addition to our educational resources, and the best means of carrying a well-digested scheme into effect, ought to be seriously considered. An opportunity is now offered to King's College for enlarging its usefulness such as if neglected may never recur again.

The principal then proceeded at prodigious length to develop his ideas. He showed that the new department would display the characteristic elasticity of King's; would require no new equipment and but small addition to the staff; and would possibly revive the moribund military department and, amalgamating with it, constitute a combined " public service department." He concluded with a draft syllabus and time-table, of which the following is the skeleton:

I. *Combined Civil and Military Divisions*
   Chapel, divinity, Latin, mathematics, history, geography, French.

II. *Military Division only*
   Plan-drawing, fortification, ancient history, fencing.

III. *Civil Division only*
   Law, political economy, English composition, German, arithmetic and book-keeping.

The council (February 10, 1854) referred the principal's important communication to the education committee for consideration and report, and that committee held no fewer than three protracted meetings before it was prepared to present its findings. They were, however, ready to be submitted to a special assembly of the council summoned for March 24. The committee had no hesitation in recommending the council to adopt the principal's proposal; the difficulties had related solely to administrative details respecting staff, fees, salaries, and curriculum. It did not advise, however, the suggested union with the moribund military department. A separate curriculum was framed; students were to be admitted at the age of fifteen; fees were to be £12 12s. a term; new instructors in English and French were to be appointed. The council approved the scheme; the necessary arrangements were made; the course was widely advertised; and in October 1854 the new department was inaugurated.[1]

It disappointed the principal's sanguine expectations. Only ten students made their appearance. In the annual report presented April 1855 the council had to confess:

> The department of civil service and commerce, the opening of which was announced in the last report, has not hitherto attracted much notice. The contemplated arrangements with respect to the examination of candidates for admission into the public offices are still in abeyance; but the council feel confident that, whether the proposed examination be altogether open or limited only to those who have received provisional appointments, the system laid down in this department for the preparation of candidates will be found admirably suited to its purpose. The friends of those who have already joined the classes speak with great satisfaction of the progress made in the prescribed studies.

The satisfaction of the friends, if great, was short. The confidence of the council was not justified. The department at the end of its first session vanished into thin air, and Dr Jelf had to write a black-edged letter to the council respecting its decease (November 16, 1855). He attributes its failure to two main causes—viz., (1) a defective curriculum which did not as a matter of fact meet the requirements of students; (2) an impossible time-table, since most of those who desired a training in civil serviceableness and commercial morality could attend only in the evening. Hence, on November 30, 1855, the council resolved "that the department of civil service and commerce be suspended for the present and omitted from the prospectus." If Dr Jelf had been asked to translate the resolution into Greek he would probably have turned the phrase "for the present" into some form of the word αἰώνιος. But councils cultivate euphemisms.

§ 6. *The Evening Class Department*

One of the indirect and unexpected results of the civil service department's unsuccessful struggle for existence had

[1] Details of the new department are fully set forth in the King's College Calendar for 1854–55, pp. 195–202.

been the revelation of a great and growing demand on the part of many varieties of people for systematic education in evening classes. It will be remembered [1] that in the spring of 1849 an interesting experiment in evening work had been made in the college, but that the experiment, although by no means a failure, had, for some reason or other, not been repeated. The lectures, however, delivered in 1849 had been rather of the popular type intended to attract the man out of the street. The demand now came from the youth in the office or the shop, the clerk in the bank, the incompletely qualified teacher in the day school; and what he wanted was not an intellectual pastime but a serious and sustained course of properly organized instruction culminating in a diploma or degree.

Mr J. W. Cunningham, the energetic and resourceful autocrat of the college office, seems to have been the first to grasp the significance and importance of the new demand. He found an enthusiastic supporter in Professor E. H. Plumptre, who expressed his willingness to teach divinity after dusk free of charge. Dr Jelf, ever eager for elasticity and expansion, took up the idea, and on June 13, 1854, attended a meeting of the education committee of the council, and

> brought before them the subject of opening the college for evening classes, stating that from time to time he was in the habit of receiving communications strongly pressing the point upon his attention, and that he was himself disposed to believe that the subject was highly deserving of attention, and that the experiment might be fairly tried with the existing staff of teachers and without any large outlay of money.

The council received the committee's report sympathetically, and requested Dr Jelf to submit, after consultation with the professors, a definite scheme. The following session (1854–55) was devoted to the maturing of the scheme; and during its course the decline of the civil service department, largely because students could not attend in the day-time, emphasized the urgency of the need for evening instruction. During the long vacation of 1855 arrangements were completed, and the evening department was opened experimentally in October of that year. Classes were offered in sixteen subjects, and would-be entrants were informed that "if any number of gentlemen not less than ten shall wish for instruction in any subject not named in this list, arrangements will if possible be made to meet their wishes." The consequence of this liberal provision was that before long twenty-one subjects figured on

[1] See above, pp. 195–196.

the prospectus. In order to attract students, fees were made very low: a single course for the whole session (October to March) was only a guinea and a half; any four classes could be taken for five guineas. These fees were less than one-half the corresponding fees for classes in the day-time conducted by the same teachers. For, at first, there was no separate evening staff. The professors and lecturers in the dwindling day classes were generally glad to supplement their exiguous earnings by pickings in the evening. No wonder then that from the start the new department was a most exciting success —in striking contrast to the languishing failures of the civil and military departments. So early as November 16, 1855— when the classes had been opened a few weeks only—Dr Jelf was able (and therefore eager) to write a letter to the council giving particulars of the amazing influx. "The number of distinct individuals who have entered," he triumphantly reported, "is 175." Some were taking one class only; others two, three, or four classes. The classes actually in operation, with the numbers on the register, were as follows: Old Testament, 56; New Testament, 52; Greek, 7; Latin, 34; French, 64; German, 19; English, 32; History, 19; Mathematics, 37; Commerce, 10; Drawing, 9; Chemistry, 6. Not only, moreover, were the classes well attended; the students " in point of punctual attendance, diligence, and decorous conduct " far surpassed the average of the riotous hobbledehoys who, under parental compulsion, constituted the day classes. The evening students were older, more serious, more eager to secure the education which the lecturers were ready to impart. One of the lecturers, writing in 1861, when the classes had had a six years' run, used the following remarkable words:

> The earnest, independent purpose that brings our younger fellow-students into the class-rooms animates them throughout their attendance. They mean work, and they do work. There is literal truth in the assertion that, since the evening classes at King's College were established, no lecturer has once been met with inattention, or has received from any student even the most insignificant discourtesy. Classes of this character offer, of course, an Elysium to the teacher. All the professors and lecturers testify that the work refreshes and enlivens them, and that they go out of the lecture-room less weary than they were when they went into it.[1]

This is saying a good deal; and its significance will be duly realized when it is noted that the hours of the evening classes

[1] H. Morley, *Account of the Evening Classes at King's College* (1861), p. 11.

were 7.30–9.30 P.M. Few people in London or elsewhere at that date who returned to their homes after 9.30 P.M. " refreshed and enlivened " were able to exculpate themselves by saying that they had been delivering lectures.

After the evening classes had been in operation two years, the numbers in attendance became so great that it was necessary in some cases to appoint special teachers. For the session 1858–59, when the names of 378 evening students were on the registers, Mr Henry Morley was engaged to take over the teaching of English, and Mr William Stebbing that of history. Both these able men, former students of the college, were earning their living as journalists in London, and they were glad to devote an evening a week to lecturing. Mr Morley, in particular, proved to be a great and inspiring teacher. Gradually education drew him away from journalism, until in 1865 he was called from the evening department of King's to the distinguished position of professor of literature in University College. At this date the numbers attending the evening classes had risen to the remarkable figure of 654; two years later they were to touch their maximum in 674. The evening department had come to a point at which it very nearly equalled in magnitude all the day departments of the college put together. Its striking success served to conceal, and partly to compensate for, the insidious decline evident everywhere else. To some extent, indeed, it helped to accelerate that decline. For persons who could get excellent instruction in orderly and serious classes in the evening were not infrequently willing to submit to the inconvenience of late hours rather than pay more than twice the amount in fees to attend disorderly or moribund classes, taught in most cases by the same teachers, during the hours of daylight.

This evening work at King's College was pioneer work, and it was one of the most notable contributions that the college made to the educational institutions of the nineteenth century. True, there was evening teaching of various kinds carried on in London at earlier dates—as, for example, at the Mechanics' Institution; at Crosby Hall; at Mr Maurice's Working Men's College in Great Ormond Street ; and by the Y.M.C.A. But it was teaching of a different sort; not systematic education of a university type, and of a diploma or degree standard, pursued continuously through a period of three or four years. The seal was set upon the new institution when—a thing without precedent, at any rate in Britain—the council decided to throw open, under strenuous and stringent conditions, the

A.K.C. certificate, and all possible college prizes, to properly qualified students of the evening department. On December 11, 1857, having considered a voluminous and detailed communication from Dr Jelf, they framed the regulations which determined the novel and revolutionary departure. They are printed in full in the Calendar for 1858–59 (pp. 232–234). Here it may be sufficient to note that the requirements for the A.K.C. were, summarily: (1) attendance at four courses a year, for three consecutive years, or three courses for four years; (2) attendance at divinity lectures and at college chapel; (3) good conduct; and (4) successful passing of examinations, together with attainment of prizes or certificates. It was the setting of so high a standard for the evening A.K.C. that made it necessary for the council to screw up the requirements for the A.K.C. in the day department of general literature and science, adding a demand for intellectual respectability to the demand for moral excellence and religious regularity which had hitherto sufficed.[1] In a short time, too, external examination successes began further to justify and stimulate the new department: in 1867, for instance, it was reported that two wranglers at Cambridge, together with three successful candidates for the I.C.S., were products of the evening department; and in 1868 that another ex-evening student

after distinguishing himself highly in an examination for a scholarship at Magdalen College, Oxford, passed for the I.C.S., having received the highest marks in classics in the whole number of candidates except one.

In so far as the striking success of this new department—which contrasted so sharply with failure elsewhere—was due to the efforts of the college officials, two men in particular have claims to recognition—viz., Mr J. W. Cunningham, the secretary of the college, and the Rev. E. H. Plumptre, who acted as dean of the department, and delivered free lectures on divinity to its members. Dr Jelf also took a great interest in the department, personally registering all entrants, and giving them gratuitous tuition in the thirty-nine articles, or as many of those articles as limitation of time permitted.

Dickens's *Household Words* (December 18, 1858) contained a glowing account of the evening work at King's. "It was," it said,

an opening not only of college doors, but of doors into a higher life for hundreds of men who have since shown how prompt and how able they were to pass over the threshold when the bolts were once withdrawn.

[1] See above, p. 250.

Among those who availed themselves of the open door in these
early days were Thomas Hardy and Edward Clarke. Hardy,
when studying architecture under Bishop Blomfield's distinguished son, attended evening classes in modern languages
at King's during the session 1859–60. Clarke, then on a
junior stool in the India Office, entered the college about the
same time (October 1859) as a matriculated student, and took
a full course for two years. He won two prizes (1861) before
he left in order to begin his eminent career at the bar.[1] He
was particularly attracted and impressed by Henry Morley as
a teacher, and he has given in his *Story of My Life* a pleasing
picture of the cordial relations which existed between that
notable man and his pupils.

> He was one whose friendship was so delightful a privilege that
> I have been thankful all my life for having been brought under
> his influence. If in my own life there have been times when
> voices of self-interest have tempted me to be unfaithful to the
> truth as I saw it, the inspiration of the teaching and example of
> Henry Morley have, I trust and believe, helped to keep me to
> the path of duty. He gave me his kindest friendship. I used—
> often with another of his pupils at King's College, who was a
> fish salesman at Billingsgate Market, a man of fine literary taste,
> and himself a writer of some pleasant poetry—to go and spend a
> Sunday evening now and then with him at Upper Park Road,
> Hampstead, and there saw a vision of perfect domestic happiness
> which could not fail to elevate and teach.[2]

When in 1866 [3] Henry Morley went from his lectureship at
King's College to his professorship at University College, he
was succeeded by George Macdonald the novelist and poet,
who at that time was at work on *Robert Falconer*, one of his
earliest stories of Scottish working-class life. He had been
attracted into the Church of England by F. D. Maurice (the
model of *David Elginbrod*). But Macdonald's theology was
too nebulous to be confined to any single ecclesiastical organization, and in 1867 he was actually caught preaching in a conventicle! Professor Plumptre, dean of the evening classes, was
horrified, as he had actually seen Macdonald communicating
in Maurice's church in Vere Street. Dr Jelf, however, before

[1] Sir Edward Clarke always retained, and still retains, a kindly and generous
interest in his old college. He became a fellow in 1880 ; took a prominent part
(as Q.C., M.P.) in the Jubilee celebrations of 1881 ; presided at the old students'
dinner of 1887, and, after many subsequent manifestations of loyalty, made a
delightful speech at the centenary dinner of June 21, 1928.

[2] Pp. 51–52 and pp. 71–72.

[3] Mr Henry Morley's resignation came before the council on December 8,
1865 ; he, however, by special request, continued his work in the evening classes
until March 1866.

whose presence Macdonald was summoned to appear, was not so severe as might have been expected. He had no desire to become involved in another controversy with the elusive Maurice and his latitudinarian disciples. So he came to an understanding with the offender. He might continue his irregular practices unmolested, provided he would undertake that "in any public announcement of his engagements to preach he should refrain from mentioning his connection with King's College." [1] This undertaking he readily gave; but at the end of the session (March 1868) he resigned his lectureship. He was succeeded by the scholarly and able John Wesley Hales, M.A., fellow of Christ's College, Cambridge, whose distinguished association with the college was destined to continue for nearly half a century, during the whole of which long period he was never known to enter a conventicle, or do anything so likely to compromise the reputation of a college dedicated to religion as preach.

§ 7. *The Department of Applied Science and Engineering*

The vitality and energy of the evening department were in marked contrast with the stagnation and depression that characterized the majority of the day departments during the closing years of Dr Jelf's *régime*. The department of engineering, however, although it showed none of the exuberance of the former, somehow managed to escape from the blight which settled on the latter. It succeeded, indeed, in recovering some of its pristine prosperity. The demand for engineers in connexion with the Crimean War; the call for the construction of railways in Russia during the period following the war; the opening up of India, Canada, Australia, and South Africa to British enterprise; the desire of Continental countries to learn the secret of British prosperity—all these causes tended to stimulate the department in which Professor Hosking taught the arts of construction and Professor Goodeve the arts of manufacture. Beginning the period (1853), during the great slump, with only 41 students, it ended (1868) with 88. Apart

---

[1] Greville Macdonald, *George Macdonald*, pp. 366–367. It is interesting to note that shortly before this Professor C. H. Pearson had gone to Dr Jelf to make a confession of latitudinarian views. He tells us in his *Memorials* (p. 103) : " I said I had no intention of ever concealing my opinions, but would resign my professorship without noise or publicity if he desired it, so that the college might avoid such another scandal as had attended the retirement of Maurice. Dr Jelf replied, saying that he thought I was entitled as a layman to great latitude of opinion, that he would not accept my resignation, and that he was prepared to take his chance of anything I might publish."

from the inevitable changes of staff which any term of fifteen years must display, the main feature of the particular period under consideration was the effort—in accordance with the principle of elasticity—to enlarge the scope of the department, and to include within it other applied sciences besides those of engineering and architecture.

First (December 19, 1856), the council decided to provide instruction in the art and craft of photography. For this purpose they voted £350, and procured the services of Mr T. F. Hardwick, "formerly Daniell scholar of the college, for three years demonstrator of chemistry, and now one of the most distinguished photographers of the day." For four years Mr Hardwick taught his mysteries in the dark subterranean regions of the college with such effect that for the first time in the history of the institution we are able to acquaint ourselves with the appearances as well as with the deeds and works of the prime movers of affairs. We can gaze on the countenances of professors who obviously needed feeding, of lecturers who obviously needed exercise, of students who obviously needed shaving, and of people at large—early Victorians—who, great as were their virtues, were obviously deficient both in smartness and in humour. In October 1860 Mr Hardwick resigned, recommending as his successor Mr Thomas Sutton, late scholar of Caius College, Cambridge. Mr Sutton, who lived in Jersey, accepted the post; but at the end of his first session, having found it difficult to combine working in London with residence in the Channel Islands, he resigned (October 1861). He was succeeded by Mr George Dawson, who dwelt no farther away than Bath. Perhaps the quality of early Victorian photographs rendered it unsafe for the operator to live within the hundred-mile radius of his victims.

Secondly, the council informed the proprietors in April 1857 that

> a course of lectures on practical farming by Mr Lockhart Morton has just been opened with an introductory lecture attended by a large number of noblemen and gentlemen,

adding that

> as this is a subject of great present interest, and strictly within the sphere of this department, the council hope that it may lead to the furtherance of practical agriculture.

Whether it did so or not we have no means of knowing; but the subject did not become one of those permanently included in the list of the applied sciences taught in the college.

259

Thirdly, the military department, having failed to stand alone, and having been rejected as the Siamese twin of the civil service department, was reduced to the rank of an applied science and placed under the tutelage of the engineers. In December 1857 its curriculum was remodelled on more modest lines; in November 1859 it lost its independent status; in November 1864, " the principal having stated that the special class called the military section of the department of the applied sciences was now no longer required," the council decided on its complete abolition. What happened to Captain Griffiths, with his large and varied assortment of bullets, shells, cannon-balls, and fortifications, does not appear.

Fourthly, drawing was raised to the rank of an independent " applied science " by the appointment of a professor of free-hand drawing (Mr W. J. Glenny, November 1864) to be the colleague and assistant of Mr Thomas Bradley, professor of geometrical drawing.

Finally, engineering itself considerably extended its sphere and enlarged its equipment. In 1856 Professor Goodeve asked for, and secured, at a total cost of £435, a four-horse-power steam-engine and a planing machine. In 1868 the council voted £520 for the enlargement and re-equipment of the workshop.

As to changes in the personnel of the department, the two most important were as follows. In July 1860 the highly efficient and ingenious Professor T. M. Goodeve, on his appointment to Woolwich, resigned his chair of manufacturing art and machinery (together with that of natural philosophy in the general department). Professor C. Percy Bysshe Shelley took over the engineering portion of his work, while, as we have seen, Professor Clerk Maxwell became responsible for investigations into the nature of the universe. During the long vacation of 1861 the eminent professor of the arts of construction, Mr William Hosking, famous as the designer of the reading-room of the British Museum, passed away, after twenty-one years' devoted service to the college. His daughters asked and received permission to place a stained-glass window to his memory in the chapel. The appointment of his successor raised the familiar religious difficulty. From among the applicants for the post the education committee selected Mr Robert Kerr as the most suitable. They reported, however, that

it appeared from Mr Kerr's application that he was a presbyterian by birth, and was now holding sittings in the Scottish Church in the Regent's Park, but that he had constantly attended the services of the Church of England, that his family were baptized and educated in its communion, and that sooner or later he meant to attach himself to one of the churches in his own neighbourhood; and that Mr Kerr had further stated that he was willing to declare his adhesion to the Church of England in any proper form.

Finding the prospective professor of the arts of construction in so hopeful a religious frame of mind, the committee felt that they " might lawfully recommend " him to the council for election, provided he could give satisfactory proofs of the genuineness of his conversion. Dr Jelf was therefore instructed to institute an inquisition into this vital matter. This he did, and he was happily able to report to the council that

> having sent for Mr Kerr, he had read to him the resolution passed by the committee of education, and that in reply Mr Kerr had stated explicitly that he was very glad of taking the present opportunity for becoming, as he had long contemplated, a regular attendant upon the services of the Church of England.

In these gratifying circumstances " the council resolved to elect Mr Kerr to the post of professor of the arts of construction " (November 15, 1861).

§ 8. *King's College School*

The school during the period 1853–68 shared in the decline of numbers which marked all the departments of the college except the new evening department and the department of applied sciences. It had reached its maximum in or about 1846, when at one moment 518 names had been on its roll; in 1853 the number had fallen to 469; by 1868 it stood at no more than 344. No longer did the surplus revenues of the school suffice to make good the deficits of the college; no more were the lecture-rooms of the arts professors upstairs fed by a supply of well-trained sixth-form boys from the basement. For the fall in numbers and the decline of quality were both displayed most conspicuously on the classical side of the school, where Dr Major continued to preside with failing powers. In 1856 one assistant-master (Mr T. S. Carr) was transferred from the classical to the modern side; in 1863 the upper and lower classical fifth were amalgamated into a single form, and in 1866 a similar amalgamation was effected in the classical sixth; so that the classical staff was reduced by three. The modern side, although it maintained itself better under the Rev. J. Fearnley's vigorous and masterful rule, could not keep its classrooms full; still less could it compensate for the decline on the other side of the school. The truth was that, apart altogether from the growing antiquity of Dr Major and the rapid diminution of his efficiency, the day was passing when parents were willing to send their sons to be educated by gas-light in the subterranean vaults of an urban college, where no pure air could be obtained, whence no playing-fields could be reached, and wherein the healthful discipline of sports was an impossibility. In vain (June 1862) did the council vote £10 per annum for three years for the encouragement of cricket; for where could cricket be played except in a sloping backyard hemmed in by window-panes? Good as the education still continued to be in parts—and specially the lower parts—of the school, it ceased to attract parents who thought more of health than of wisdom and piety for their boys, and preferred the introduction to life provided by the boarding-house system of the public schools to the mixed culture of home and day school (to say nothing of street and train) which attendance at King's College School involved.

The decline in numbers and the consequent diminution in revenue tempted the council to adopt various expedients for securing increased payments from boys who continued to attend. For example, in July 1853 the council decided to pro-vide all the text-books required in the school and to make a charge, varying from 10s. to 16s. 8d. per term, to each boy for the use of them. In February 1857 the benign practice of allowing each professor and lecturer in the college to have one son at a time in the school free of charge was—on account of the increasing number and fruitfulness of these gentlemen—abandoned. In May 1860 the charge for books was raised to £1 per term all round. In January 1861 the entrance fee was raised from 21s. to 31s. In November 1866 the tuition fees were increased from £6 15s. 2d. to £7 per term; and four months later the entrance scholarships were abolished (March 8, 1867). These growing exactions and dwindling concessions no doubt tended to accelerate the slump in numbers.

Another thing, too, which must have been most prejudicial to the prosperity of the school was the prodigious number of changes in the staff which occurred at this time. Of the twenty-three masters, regular and occasional, of 1853, only six remained in 1868; and several posts had changed hands several times. It would be wearisome and unprofitable to give particulars of all the changes—forty-two in number—which transpired. The following were the most important:

three assistant masters secured headships and resigned;[1] one absconded;[2] three died in office;[3] six terminated their teaching careers by reason of old age and infirmity.[4] In this last-named group by far the most noteworthy were the Rev. Dr Major, headmaster of the school since its initiation in 1830, and the Rev. John Fearnley, appointed as third master in 1832 and raised to the position of vice-master in charge of the modern side in 1851. Dr Major during the early part of his long headship had done exceedingly well, and had made an income for himself far exceeding that of the principal of the college.[5] Year after year the reports to the proprietors had spoken of him as " able and indefatigable " and had described in glowing terms the triumphs of his pedagogy. But after 1853 the note of gratulation was muffled, and the tendency to criticize became clear. Dr Major, waiting for ecclesiastical preferment which did not come, grew slack and apathetic. His teaching declined in efficiency; above all, his discipline went to pieces, and even in his own diminished upper sixth form chaos and disorder prevailed. Hence in March 1866 a special committee (of which more anon) " appointed by the council on the 9th of February 1866 to inquire into the whole state of the college and school," after presenting a damning report on the condition of the classical side of the school, expressed the emphatic opinion that " the time has come when a gentleman who took his degree forty-seven years ago ought to be relieved from the duties of teaching." The council adopted the report of the committee (April 1866) and deputed their chairman, the Archbishop of York (Dr W. Thomson), to break to Dr Major the painful information that they would expect to receive his resignation without delay. It was intended at first that it should take effect at Christmas; but

---

[1] January 1854, Rev. T. Markby, St John's Wood Proprietary School; March 1857, Rev. J. R. Major, Thetford Grammar School; August 1864, Rev. J. D. Kingdon, Sutton Valence Grammar School.

[2] On April 11, 1856, "a letter was received from the Rev. J. Fearnley, officially stating that Mr Thomas Hutton, assistant arithmetical and writing master in the school, had not attended since Easter. The secretary stated that there was ground for believing that Mr Hutton had left England on Easter Monday or Tuesday for Australia, and under these circumstances he had felt it to be his duty, with the full sanction of the principal, to issue the usual advertisement."

[3] Mr J. W. La Jeune, writing master, December 1864; Professor Angelo, fencing master, March 1865; Mr T. S. Carr, third master on the modern side— after thirty-one years' service in the school—September 1865.

[4] M. Gassion, 1853; Mr J. Hann, for seventeen years mathematical master, 1854; Professor Brasseur, 1855; Dr Major and Mr Fearnley, 1866; Dr Wintzer, 1868.

[5] In 1866 it was recorded that " Dr Major receives £1050 in fixed salary, and at present from £70 to £100 extra in fees, which have been much more."

he himself asked to be allowed to retire at the end of the summer term. The council granted him a pension of £300 a year.[1]

Mr Fearnley had passed through the ordeal of examination by the committee unscathed. But just at this time, most unhappily for the school, his health broke down. Hence on May 14, 1866, he wrote to the council:

MY LORDS AND GENTLEMEN,

In consequence of the heavy affliction with which it has pleased God to visit me during the last six months, I feel myself unable to continue my labours in the school of King's College. I therefore beg to resign [etc.].

The council accepted the resignation with a regret that amounted to consternation; for Mr Fearnley would have been the obvious successor to Dr Major. They passed a most cordial vote of appreciation and sympathy, and set aside fifty guineas with which to provide a suitable parting gift.

Among the new assistant-masters who had joined the staff of the school during this changeful period was the Rev. George Frederick Maclear, a first-class honours man of Trinity College, Cambridge, who, at the age of twenty-seven, had come to take charge of the lower fifth form in 1860. He had shown himself to be a good scholar, an excellent teacher, an adequate disciplinarian, and an orthodox divine. His text-books on Bible history and his writings on Christian missions had attracted the favourable attention of the evangelical world. In 1864 (when Mr Kingdon went to Sutton Valence) he was promoted to the mastership of the lower sixth. Here, again, he did as well as the circumstances allowed, helping to check the anarchy which radiated from Dr Major's upper sixth and the Rev. T. O. Cockayne's upper fourth. Hence in July 1866, when Dr Major begged for immediate release, he was appointed as " acting headmaster " until the end of the year. In the autumn the vacancy was duly advertised, and on November 16, out of seven candidates, Mr Maclear was selected as the most suitable for the position, his only serious rival having been the Rev. C. Matheson.

Mr Fearnley's vice-mastership had already been filled. On June 30, 1866, from among eighteen applicants, the Rev. John Twentyman, late fellow of Christ's College, Cambridge, and for the previous three years one of the masters at Cheltenham College, aged twenty-eight, was chosen.[2] Messrs

[1] Dr Major died in the early part of 1876.

[2] Mr Twentyman, who continued to be vice-master of the school until 1889, is still, at the time of writing, in the land of the living, aged ninety. His son, Mr A. E. Twentyman, late of the Board of Education, is on the present staff of the college as director of researches into the history of education.

Maclear and Twentyman at once commenced the work of reorganizing and revivifying the school. The details of their doings, however, had better be reserved for the next chapter.

To conclude the present chapter: What of the pupils of the school during this decade and a half of disorganization and decline? It is astonishing to find how many of them continued to do well, and even to achieve eminent successes. Apart from the distinctions won by pupils of an older day, such as William Stebbing, who attained firsts in classics and history, 1853–54, with a fellowship at Worcester; M. H. Irving (son of the apostolic Edward), who was appointed professor of classical literature at Sydney in 1857; and Monier-Williams, who became professor of Sanscrit at Oxford in 1860, many boys of this later period brought credit to the school and laid the foundation of enduring reputations. The annual reports mention the following among others: 1854, L. O. Pike, scholarship at Brasenose; 1855, F. Harrison, fellowship at Wadham; 1856, H. Fawcett, seventh wrangler; 1859, I. Bywater, scholarship at Queen's, followed by a long series of classical triumphs culminating at the end of five years in a fellowship at Exeter; 1860, A. V. Dicey, the Arnold Prize at Oxford; 1861, Charles Taylor, scholarship at St John's, Cambridge, leading to a fellowship and ultimately the mastership; 1862, W. S. Lilly, Indian Civil Service; 1863, George Saintsbury, postmastership at Merton; 1864, W. T. T. Dyer, studentship at Christ Church; 1867, A. K. Rollit, gold medal in London LL.D. It is notable, too, that most of these brilliant scholars of the fifties and sixties had gone straight to the universities from the school without passing through the intermediate stage of the college. The original purpose of the founders of the duplex institution was frustrated by the unwillingness of the schoolmasters to lose their best pupils at the age of sixteen, and by the disinclination of parents to pay appreciably higher fees for a doubtfully better form of instruction.

The tendency to keep boys in the school up to the university age was recognized and strengthened by the valuable Forest Bequest of £3000 announced to the council on October 11, 1861. Out of the interest on this sum (invested in Consols) three scholarships were provided, each of £30 a year and tenable for three years. The age limit was fixed at eighteen, and the scholarships could be held either at Oxford or Cambridge, or at King's College, London. The last named, however, came in for very few of them.

§ 9. *The Decline and Fall of Dr Jelf*

In the present concluding section of this bloated chapter three things will demand such attention as our limited space will permit—viz., first, the government of the college during the period 1853–68; secondly, the finances of the institution; and finally, the circumstances which led to Dr Jelf's resignation and departure.

I. *Government.* One of the most notable features of this term of fifteen years is the disappearance of the last relics of the original governing body of King's College. It will be remembered that according to the charter of 1829 the administration of the institution was placed in the hands of a council consisting of nine official governors, eight life governors, a treasurer, and twenty-four councillors. Of the first forty-two, named in the charter, twelve still survived and continued their work for the college in 1853, nearly a quarter of a century after their original appointment.[1] By this date, however, they were all of them elderly men, and before 1868 every one of them had passed to his long rest. The first to go (March 1854) was Alderman Thompson, the treasurer, who bequeathed £500 to the college. He had scarcely ever attended a council meeting, and had entirely lost touch with the course of college affairs. His place as treasurer was taken by the devoted and assiduous Mr William Cotton, who held it, to the comfort of the council, till his own death twelve years later, at the age of eighty. The next notable death was that of Sir Robert Inglis, in May 1855. He, in virtue of his wealth, his high character, his ability, and his extremely reactionary principles, had played a dominant part in guiding the policy of the college along the strait and narrow way of evangelical orthodoxy: to him more than to any other single individual had been due the eviction of Professor Maurice. His great services to the college for twenty-seven years were recognized not only by a cordial resolution of appreciation and regret entered on the minutes of the council (May 11, 1855), but by the founding on the part of his friends and admirers of an Inglis Fund, amounting to £3455 16s., from the proceeds of which scholarships and studentships have continued to foster the pursuit of

---

[1] These survivors were as follows :

Official Governors, one—viz., the Bishop of London (Dr C. J. Blomfield).
Life Governors, three—viz., the Duke of Rutland, the Marquis of Bristol, and Earl Brownlow.
The Treasurer—viz., Alderman W. Thompson.
Councillors, seven—viz., Sir Benjamin Brodie, Mr William Cotton, Mr Henry Hobhouse, Sir Robert Inglis, the Rev. John Lonsdale (Bishop of Lichfield), Sir Charles Price, and Sir G. T. Staunton.

history and literature in the college. In October 1856 Bishop Blomfield's resignation of the see of London carried with it the vacation of his seat as one of the official governors of the college. He was at the earliest possible moment (April 1857) restored to the council as an elected member; but his health was broken and he never attended again. His death was reported to the council in October 1857. The immense influence which, as acting chairman of the council for more than a quarter of a century, he had exerted in determining the constitution and controlling the destiny of the college was recorded in a touching and sympathetic minute drawn up by his old friend and colleague the Bishop of Lichfield. His place as official governor passed to Bishop A. C. Tait, who on February 20, 1857, was formally welcomed to the council and placed in the chair. But though he attended from time to time, and when present usually presided, he never acquired a tithe of that autocratic power that Bishop Blomfield had exercised. If any one man can be regarded as Blomfield's heir, that man was Lord Radstock, who seems to have made the college business the main concern of his later years; but he died on May 10, 1857 (two days after presiding at a meeting of the college council), and authority was in the future more widely distributed.

Last of all the original members of the council to pass away was the saintly and scholarly John Lonsdale, Bishop of Lichfield, the perfect exemplar of the King's motto, *Sancte et sapienter*, the Sir Bedivere among the courageous band of those who forty years before had started on the venture which resulted in the founding of the college. The death of the venerable Mr William Cotton at the end of 1866 had left him for nearly a year the sole survivor of the founders. He continued to the last to show his devotion to the institution with which he had been associated for one-half of his long life. On April 12, 1867, he presided at the council, and on the last day of the same month he took the chair at the annual meeting of the court of proprietors. He was then seventy-nine years of age, and his strength was waning. As he looked round the familiar hall, which he was never to see again, was it once more peopled to his mind's eye with his friends of long ago? No doubt he recalled them with affectionate regret. But we may be sure that he did not allow his thoughts to dwell exclusively upon the past. For he saw around him new colleagues full of energy and hope, and before him a company of young men eager to carry forward the torch of knowledge and of faith. Six months later he died; and with him the first age of the college definitely

267

came to an end. It was the age of its government by bishops
—Howley, Blomfield, Copleston, Lonsdale, Sumner—men of
high character, cultivated intellect, strong conviction, serene
faith, and in the main men of a larger liberality and a more
tolerant charity than the worthy laymen with whom they were
associated. In a few moments we shall have to consider a
report on the condition of the college, signed, with one exception, exclusively by laymen. It was marked by a severity,
almost a brutality, of tone that would have been inconceivable
in any report drawn up by the urbane and courtly clerics of
the earlier days. For better or worse, however, the conduct
of the college passed from the control of the bishops—not
through any change in constitution, but simply because they
let it go—into the hands of the pious laity. The new men who
were appointed or elected to the council between 1853 and
1868 included the Duke of Cambridge, the Earl of Carnarvon,
the Earl Powis, Lord Feversham, Sir William Heathcote,
Mr A. J. B. Beresford-Hope, and Mr W. H. Smith. They
were generous and devoted supporters of the college. And
there was need of all their generosity and devotion, for the
finances of the institution were in a bad way.

II. *Finances.* When the year 1853 opened the college was
burdened with the formidable debt of over £16,000, on which
interest amounting to some £400 per annum had to be paid.
Further, there was the obligation which the council had
undertaken of contributing £1000 a year for five years
(1850–55) toward the new hospital. And so far from there
being any balance of profits out of which to meet these obligations and pay off the capital debt, there had been on the
actual working of the college during the calendar year 1852
a deficit of nearly £600. The situation was plainly desperate.
Immediate needs were met by the raising of a loan of £1600;
but the restoration of a condition of solvency was attained only
by the deplorable expedient of a levy of 2½ per cent. on the
already exiguous salaries of the staff. Next year the situation
was even worse; for the deficit on the working of the college
during the twelve months ending December 1, 1853, was
(including the £1000 claimed by the hospital) over £2084.
Hence the deduction from salaries had to be repeated; and
repeated it was annually for six years, until in 1860 rigid
economies had succeeded, although at a grave cost of comfort
and efficiency, in making ends meet. By that time the staff
contributions had amounted in all to £2474, and the capital
debt on the college had been reduced to £11,649. In normal

years the total income of the college and school was round about £22,000, the whole of which (except a few hundreds which accrued from special scholarship funds, rents, book-stock, etc.) was derived from fees. Out of this sum, if no unusual outlay for building or equipment was necessary, some £600 or £700 could be counted on in prosperous times as profit on the year's working. From this slender margin of profit the council made it a rule to set aside £500 for the diminution of the capital debt. Thus even in prosperous times a merely minute fund was available from which to meet extraordinary calls. If any section of the institution—*e.g.*, the school or the medical department—declined, then, as we have seen, the council was at once confronted by insolvency. When any big new venture was initiated, such as the rebuilding of the chapel, a special fund had to be raised by widespread and pertinacious begging. So much, indeed, was begging the order of the day that in 1864 the council evinced no surprise or disapprobation when they were informed that the organist with the assistance of an old student of the college had on his own account, and apparently without consulting anyone, started to raise a fund for the purchase of a new organ. The friends of King's College were provided with many opportunities for the exercise of the Christian grace of generosity.

By 1860 the finances of the college had temporarily so far improved that the council not only remitted the 2½ per cent. levy on the salaries of the staff, but even listened sympathetically to a long letter from the principal in which he set forth five urgent needs of the building—viz., (1) a students' cloak-room; (2) a students' common room; (3) new lecture-rooms; (4) a waiting-room near the principal's office; and (5) further improvements in the chapel. The sum of £1750, supplemented next year by another £750, was voted for the carrying out of these developments. As an aid toward the provision of the money, the insidious expedient was adopted of increasing matriculation fees from £4 15s. 6d. to £5 15s. 6d. These constant additions to charges—here ten shillings and there a pound—without any immediate and obvious additions to the amenities of the college, must have had the effect of accelerating that decline in numbers which was the prime cause of the council's embarrassment. In any case, by 1865 the condition of things was worse than ever. There was a deficit of £1060 on the previous year's accounts, and in order to meet it the council had to sell some of its property, to raid the library and machinery funds, to let the catering in the dining-hall for £200 a year (to a person whose dinners were so bad that he had soon to be evicted and compensated), and, finally, to revive the levy on the salaries of the staff, this time at the rate of 3 per cent. On this occasion the levy was met by vehement protests, and by strong assertions that the decline of the college and its finances was due in no small a degree to the defective administration of Dr Jelf above and Dr Major below. In those circumstances the council (February 9, 1866) appointed a strong committee "to investigate the state of all the departments of the college and school."

III. *The End of Dr Jelf's Régime.* The committee set to work at once with extreme vigour, summoning before them all and sundry—and particularly Dr Jelf and Dr Major, who were put through an examination so searching and unsympathetic as to rouse in their aged breasts the most intense indignation and resentment. Dr Major, as we have seen, was soon disposed of: he was obviously past his work, and the council without hesitation asked for his resignation and pensioned him off. Dr Jelf was harder to deal with. Although sixty-eight years of age, he showed no signs of failing powers. He was still able to potter about as usual; his letters displayed no diminution either in length or in frequency; if he did not preach quite so often as of old, he preached as often as anyone wanted to hear him; his lectures on the first four of the thirty-nine articles spread as of yore with unabated prolixity over the whole college session; he could sustain any interview with a student or a visitor for two or even three hours while a queue waited in his new anteroom; he regularly sat to register new students, and did masses of routine work which any less conscientious principal would have remitted to a junior clerk or an office boy. Moreover, he was kind to all. It was a difficult case. But the committee, and the council with them, came to the definite conclusion that his activities were not worth the £1250 a year which his salary and his house together extracted from the scanty resources of the college. They did not like drastically to impose a new way of life on so venerable and respectable an antiquity, so they contented themselves with resolving that every future principal should do more teaching and less office work; should be paid on a lower scale; and should retire at the age of sixty-five. The implied vote of censure on Dr Jelf's conduct of affairs was so severe that his immediate resignation might have been expected. But his fighting spirit had been roused; he felt that he had been " treated in the course of his examination with less respect than was due to his high office "; he wrote, and circulated in print, a sixty-nine-page reply to the " hasty and ill-considered report " of the committee; and (although he surrendered £200 of his salary) he refused either to budge or to carry out the committee's recommendations. Hence the committee continued to sit and to report, expressing regret at the principal's refusal to co-operate with them in effecting the reforms and economies which they and the council considered necessary. This condition of friction and non-co-operation could not continue indefinitely, and it was a matter of intense relief to all concerned when, December 20, 1867, Dr Jelf, a few weeks before his seventieth birthday, sent in his letter of resignation, which was to take effect at midsummer 1868. The council accepted the resignation, and passed a generous resolution expressive of their appreciation of the old gentleman's " courtesy and kindness " and of the good work that he had done twenty years before in founding the theological department.

On July 3, 1868, Dr Jelf made his last appearance before the council and bade its members farewell. He retired to his canonry at Oxford; for three years, in academic tranquillity, he continued his investigations into the thirty-nine articles, then caught measles and died (September 19, 1871).

NOTE

I. NUMBER OF STUDENTS, 1853–68

SESSION	COLLEGE							SCH.	TOTAL
	REGULAR						OCC.		
	Gen.	Med.	Eng.	Theol.	Mil.	Evening			
1852–53	106	199	41	78	13	—	76	469	982
1853–54	105	191	47	76	10	—	85	473	987
1854–55	89 [1]	178	42	71	6	—	91	433	910
1855–56	84	172	58	73	6	322 [2]	94	435	1244
1856–57	89	158	57	74	5	184	85	426	1078
1857–58	92	158	65	59	3	164	66	404	1011
1858–59	81	161	51	63	3	378	59	370	1166
1859–60	83	166	66	71	—	549	66	402	1403
1860–61	84	156	86	71	—	648	51	410	1506
1861–62	73	147	83	66	—	618	48	405	1440
1862–63	95	144	74	48	—	578	44	426	1409
1863–64	76	153	71	41	—	639	50	418	1448
1864–65	72	130	84	52	—	661	78	413	1490
1865–66	58	140	86	51	—	654	65	384	1438
1866–67	69	140	88	51	—	674	54	370	1446
1867–68	66	130	88	50	—	630	55	344	1363

[1] Including 10 in the short-lived Civil Service Department.
[2] Including 110 in a special course of lectures on commerce.

II. DISTINGUISHED STUDENTS

Among those who entered the college during the period 1853-68, and subsequently became distinguished, were the following:

Ainger, Alfred (1853-56). Canon of Bristol and Master of the Temple; gained mathematical prize at King's College, 1854, proceeded to Cambridge; ordained, 1860; Master of the Temple, 1894-1904.

Wace, Henry (1853-56). Entered King's College from Marlborough and Rugby; secured five prizes during his course at King's College; proceeded to Oxford, 1856; returned to King's College as evening lecturer in history, 1860-62; professor of ecclesiastical history, 1875-83; principal, 1883-97; then succeeded Farrar as Dean of Canterbury.

Gilbert, William Schwenck (1853-57). Author; collaborator with Sir Arthur Sullivan in production of comic operas; B.A. London, 1857; passed from King's College into the education office of the Privy Council by examination; knighted, 1907.

Besant, Walter (1854-55). Novelist; secured mathematical scholarship at King's College, 1855; proceeded to Cambridge; eighteenth wrangler, 1859; professor in Mauritius, 1861-67; fellow of King's College, 1882; knighted, 1895.

Smith, Horace (1854-56). Metropolitan police magistrate; entered King's College from Highgate Grammar School; proceeded to Cambridge, 1856; called to the bar, 1862; appointed magistrate, 1888; voluminous writer on law.

Treloar, William Purdie (1854-58). Pupil of King's College School; Lord Mayor of London, 1906-7; knighted, 1900; baronet, 1907.

Benham, William (1855-57). Ecclesiastical historian and biographer; popular writer under the pseudonym " Peter Lombard "; theological student at King's College; rector of St Edmund's, Lombard St, 1882-1910; honorary canon of Canterbury, 1888.

Browne, Richard Charles (1855-57). Literary man; contributor to the *Dictionary of National Biography* ; editor of Milton's poetical works in the Clarendon Press series.

Hudson, William Henry Hoar (1855-57). Mathematician; senior mathematical scholar, 1857; proceeded to Cambridge; third wrangler, 1861; fellow of St John's College, 1862-75; professor of mathematics at King's College, 1882-1903.

Mackay, Æneas James George (1855-58). Lawyer and historian; secured five scholarships and six prizes at King's College; later studied at Oxford, Heidelberg, and Edinburgh; professor of constitutional history and law at Edinburgh, 1874-81; sheriff of Fife and Kinross, 1886-1901.

Symes-Thompson, Edmund (1855–59). Physician; medical student of King's College; gained seven prizes; London M.B., 1859; M.D., 1860; assistant-physician to King's College Hospital, 1860–63; physician to Brompton Hospital for Consumption, 1863–90.

Fox, Charles Douglas (1856–58). An occasional student; past president of the Institution of Civil Engineers; J.P. London, Kent, and Surrey; knighted, 1886; fellow of King's College, 1887.

Worms, Baron Henry de (later Lord Pirbright) (1856–60). Politician; entered engineering department of King's College; on his departure presented model engine which he had constructed; fellow of King's College, 1863; called to the bar, 1863; M.P., 1880; secretary to the Board of Trade, 1885 and 1886–88; under-secretary for the Colonies, 1888–92; hereditary baron of the Austrian Empire; raised to the peerage of United Kingdom, 1895.

Macnamara, Nottidge Charles (1857–61). Student in the medical department; F.R.C.S.; professor of ophthalmic medicine, Calcutta; founder of the Mayo Hospital, Calcutta; later consulting surgeon to the Westminster Hospital; fellow of King's College, 1884.

Thiselton-Dyer, William Turner (1857–63). Pupil of King's College School, where he was first mathematical scholar; proceeded to the medical department of the college, where he remained till 1863, when, at the age of twenty, he passed to Christ Church, Oxford, and took up the special study of botany, in which he was destined to attain the highest eminence; professor of natural history at Cirencester, 1868; professor of botany in Royal College of Science, Ireland, 1870; assistant-director of Kew Gardens, 1875–85; director, 1885–1905; fellow of King's College, 1886; K.C.M.G., 1899.

Liveing, Robert (1858–61). Specialist in diseases of the skin; student in medical department, having already graduated in mathematical honours at Cambridge (where he was a scholar of Christ's College); physician to the Middlesex Hospital; Gulstonian Lecturer, 1873; fellow of King's College, 1888.

Arber, Edward (1858–63). English scholar; evening class student at King's College; secured five prizes; lecturer at University College under his old King's College teacher Henry Morley, 1878–82; professor of Mason College, Birmingham, 1894.

Hardy, Thomas (1859–60). Novelist; evening class student studying modern languages.

King, Thomas (1859–60). Senior chief inspector of schools; junior mathematical scholar at King's College, 1860; proceeded to Cambridge; ninth wrangler, 1864; fellow of Jesus College, 1864–71; inspector of schools, 1871–1903.

Caldwell, Robert Towsley (1859–61). Master of Corpus Christi College, Cambridge; gained two mathematical scholarships

S

at King's College; proceeded to Cambridge; tenth wrangler, 1865; fellow of Corpus, 1865–1906; master, 1906–14.

Clarke, Edward G. (1859–61). Eminent lawyer and statesman; evening class student; two prizes; clerk in India Office, 1859; called to the bar, 1864; M.P., 1880–1906; Solicitor-General, 1886–92; knighted, 1886; P.C., 1908.

Harrison, William English (1859–61). Eminent lawyer and one of the most devoted and loyal of all the sons of King's College; student of the general literature and science department; called to the bar, Middle Temple, 1867; Q.C., 1897; Commissioner of Assize for Stafford and Birmingham, 1899; for many years a regular and invaluable member of the council and the delegacy; fellow of King's College, 1925.

Bryne, Edmund W. (1860–63). Chancery Judge; called to the bar, 1867; Q.C., 1888; M.P., 1892–97; Judge, 1897; knighted, 1897; member of the council of King's College, 1898–1904.

Clifford, William K. (1860–63). Eminent mathematician and physicist; gained five prizes at King's College; proceeded to Cambridge; second wrangler, 1866; fellow of Trinity; professor of mathematics and mechanics at University College, 1871–79.

Doughty, Charles Montagu (1861). Distinguished traveller; author of *Arabia Deserta*, etc.; occasional student of King's College in mathematics, 1861; later honorary fellow of Gonville and Caius College, Cambridge; D.Litt.; etc.

Lyall, Charles James (1861–63). Indian administrator; entered King's College from King's College School; proceeded to Balliol College, Oxford; Indian Civil Service, 1867; K.C.S.I., 1897; fellow of King's College, 1900; life-governor of King's College; vice-chairman of the theological committee, 1910–19; fellow of the British Academy.

Cox, Arthur Frederick (1861–68). Pupil of King's College School, 1861–66; passed to the general literature and science department of the college; entered I.C.S., 1869; retired, 1906; Kaiser-i-Hind Medal, 1900; C.S.I., 1901.

Neville, Édouard (1862–63). Distinguished Egyptologist; student in the general literature and science department for four terms; fellow of King's College, 1894.

Chalmers, Mackenzie Dalzell (1863–65). Permanent under-secretary of state for the home department, 1903–8; student in the general literature and science department; proceeded to Trinity College, Oxford; I.C.S., 1869–72; counsel to Board of Trade, 1882; Chief Justice, Gibraltar, 1894; C.S.I., 1899; K.C.B., 1906.

Curnow, John (1864–68). Anatomist; medical student at King's College; gained two scholarships at King's, and three gold medals in London University examination; professor of anatomy at King's College, 1873–96; assistant-physician of King's College Hospital, 1874–90; physician, 1890–1902; professor of clinical medicine, 1896–1902.

Garrod, Alfred H. (1864–68). Anatomist; medical student of King's College; gained four scholarships; proceeded to Cambridge; senior in natural sciences tripos, 1871; professor of comparative anatomy at King's College, 1874–79; F.R.S., 1876.

Gow, James (1864–72). Pupil of King's College School; proceeded to Trinity College, Cambridge; third classic and chancellor's medallist, 1875; fellow of Trinity, 1876; D.Litt., 1885; master of the High School, Nottingham, 1885–1901; headmaster of Westminster School, 1901–19.

Allen, John Romilly (1865–66). Engineer and archæologist; builder of railways in Persia and docks in Britain; Celtic archæologist; F.S.A., 1896.

Upcott, Frederick Robert (1865–66). Student in the applied science (engineering) department for five terms; public works department, India, 1868; consulting engineer to Madras Government, 1892; director-general of railways in India, 1896; fellow of King's College, 1902; K.C.V.O., 1906.

Broadbent, Benjamin (1866–68). Student of the general literature and science department; Mayor of Huddersfield, 1904–6; pioneer in the movement for the prevention of infant mortality; C.B.E., 1918; fellow of King's College, 1923.

Perks, Robert William (1866–69). After early education at Kingswood School, attended King's College as an occasional student for classics, mathematics, and modern languages; railway lawyer, 1878–92; later constructor and director of railways; M.P., 1892–1910; created baronet, 1908.

Stern, Edward David (1866–72). Entered King's School, 1866, and proceeded thence to the college as an occasional student; graduated B.A., 1878; High Sheriff of Surrey, 1904; knighted, 1904; lieutenant-colonel of the third battalion Surrey Volunteers; fellow of King's College, 1920.

Garstin, William Edmund (1867–68). Came from Cheltenham College as a student in the general literature and science department; Indian public works department, 1872; inspector-general of irrigation in Egypt, 1892; K.C.M.G., 1897; G.C.M.G., 1902; fellow of King's College, 1903; adviser to ministry of public works in Egypt, 1904; British director of Suez Canal Company, 1907; G.B.E., 1918.

Rose, William (1867–71). Distinguished student of the medical department; M.B. and F.R.C.S.; appointed professor of surgery in King's College, 1888; fellow of King's College, 1888; member of the council of the college till his death in 1910.

CHAPTER IX

THE TURN OF THE CENTURY
1868–83

§ 1. *The Fifth Principal: the Rev. Alfred Barry*

WITH the departure of Dr Jelf in the summer of 1868 we pass from the inquisitorial Middle Age of the college into the larger liberality of its Renaissance and Reformation. Never in the history of the institution has a change of man involved a more marked change in spirit and in tone. On the one hand, the committee of inquiry and the council obtained the opportunity they had long desired of altering the position and powers of the principal. In a printed document issued to all applicants for the post they intimated that in future the principal would be expected to act as chaplain, to lecture frequently, to summon and preside at staff meetings periodically, to accept a salary of £500 with a capitation fee of £1 per student, and to retire at the age of sixty-five. In a resolution passed on June 12 they decided

> that the principal be always informed beforehand by the secretary of the meetings of the council; that for the first portion of their time the council sit alone, and that at any convenient break in their proceedings a messenger be sent to the principal to request him to give his attendance.

All these things were eloquent of a determination on the part of the council never again to allow things to sink into the condition of pottering and bickering that had marked the last days of the *ancien régime*. On the other hand, they chose as Dr Jelf's successor a man as different from himself as, within the limits of the Anglican clergy, they could possibly find.

There were ten applicants for the principalship, eight of whom were men of high academic distinction. The four selected for interview were (1) the Rev. George Rawlinson, Camden Professor of Ancient History in the University of Oxford; (2) the Rev. E. H. Plumptre, Professor of New Testament Exegesis in the College; (3) the Rev. John Hannah, Warden of Trinity College, Glenalmond; and (4) the Rev. Alfred Barry, Headmaster of Cheltenham College. A first

276

ALFRED BARRY
Principal 1868–83

vote eliminated the two professors; a second vote gave Dr Barry a decisive majority over Dr Hannah (who later became vicar of Brighton and archdeacon of Lewes).

Alfred Barry, born 1826, was the second son of Sir Charles Barry, the eminent architect, among whose many and important buildings are the Travellers' Club and the Reform Club in Pall Mall, Bridgewater House, King Edward's School, Birmingham, the Halifax Town Hall, and, *facile princeps*, the Houses of Parliament at Westminster. Two of Alfred's younger brothers also rose to distinction—viz., Edward Barry the academician and John Wolfe Barry the civil engineer, designer of the Tower Bridge (not to mention the bridge at Charing Cross, of which he has to share the guilt with Sir John Hawkshaw). Alfred himself was an old student of King's College,[1] where his career had been one of conspicuous brilliance: in 1843 he had carried off no fewer than seven of the college prizes. At Cambridge he had more than fulfilled the bright promise of his King's days: in 1848 he had been seventh classic, fourth wrangler, and second Smith's prizeman; he had become Fellow of Trinity, 1848; M.A., 1851; B.D., 1860; and D.D., 1866. A man of great physical vigour and of restless energy, scorning to live at ease on his fellowship, he had taken up teaching as a career. Hence he came to King's in 1868 with nearly twenty years of varied and invaluable experience behind him. He had served in turn as sub-warden of Glenalmond (1849–54), headmaster of the Leeds Grammar School (1854–62), and principal of Cheltenham College (1862–68), which, like King's College, was a proprietary institution. At Cheltenham he left permanent memorials of his brief headship in the junior school, the gymnasium, and five boarding-houses. Interested in institutions rather than ideas, an educationist rather than a theologian, he was admirably fitted to begin the transformation of King's College from a seminary dominantly ecclesiastical to a school of learning of university rank. The motto of the college—*sancte et sapienter*—indicates with admirable brevity and completeness the fundamental principle of the college—viz., the indissoluble union of religion and science. Different spokesmen for the college, however, have expressed different conceptions of the relation between the two constituent elements of faith and knowledge. To some they have appeared as two distinct things kept, with some difficulty, in harmonious combination. To others—men of more penetrating vision and loftier outlook

---

[1] See above, p. 164.

—they have seemed to be one and the same thing seen in different aspects. Dr Jelf had represented the first view; Dr Barry represented the second. Dr Jelf, a timid and conventional thinker, had lived in constant dread of the outcome of the conflicts between Genesis and geology, Moses and Darwin, and so on. Hence he had, especially in making appointments, tended to emphasize the *sancte* and to let the *sapienter* take care of itself. Indeed, if one had to find a single word to express the spirit of his *régime*, one would invent the word *sancte*-monious. Thus he had succeeded in gathering round him a group of men obviously orthodox and eminently respectable, many of whom were nonentities in the world of advancing knowledge. Dr Barry, changing the stress from *sancte* to *sapienter*, recognized the fact that if the college wished to succeed it must get teachers of the highest qualifications as specialists, and that if it wished to get the best specialists it must not pursue too far the inquiry as to where they sat on a Sunday morning. He was a broad churchman, a friend of Charles Kingsley, a disciple of Frederick Denison Maurice, a man who believed that every party in the Anglican communion, and almost every sect outside it, was divinely instituted to emphasize some partial truth necessary for the perfection of the whole; a man who had faith enough to believe that every demonstrated truth of science, however incompatible it might be with current orthodoxy, could not be inconsistent with essential religion. Hence he relaxed to the extremest possible limits the rules of conformity, freely gave exemptions from chapel and divinity lectures to conscientious objectors, even for a time (until pulled up) threw open the A.K.C. to Dissenters, co-operated with non-Anglicans (such as the Unitarian Miss Anna Swanwick) in the founding of a college for women, secured fellowships in King's College not only for Charles Kingsley (whom Dr Jelf had refused to admit to the staff, and to whom Bishop Blomfield had closed the London pulpits), but also for Henry Fawcett, Walter Besant, and James Fitzjames Stephen, all of whom had wandered far beyond the pale of even the broadest Anglicanism. Barry, in short, recognized that although, no doubt, in the high realms of the absolute, *sancte* and *sapienter* connote the same reality, they present different appearances behind the desk of a college lecture-room. In other words, he recognized the fact that, if you made religious conformity the prime qualification for the holding of office in King's, you might have to put up with a second-rate man of science; while, if you made scientific eminence your main concern, you might have to be content with a merely formal adhesion to the Anglican communion. He was, of course, thankfully aware that it might, in the order of providence, come to pass that in appointing a man of piety you might secure a St Thomas Aquinas, or that in appointing a man of science you might obtain an Isaac Newton; but he was conscious that such happy coincidences were of the nature of uncovenanted mercies which could not be counted on. Nevertheless, broad as was his tolerance, and strong as was his emphasis upon sapience as phenomenally (albeit not essentially) distinct from sanctity, he was kept within limits by the charter, by the by-laws, and by the venerable resolutions of the council. Thus when he began to recommend dissenters for the A.K.C. it was demonstrated to him that divinity was of the essence of that diploma; and when (November 1882) a Quaker—who " was not aware until after the election that it was necessary for all members of the staff to be members of the Church of England " —had been actually installed as demonstrator in physiology, the Quaker was compelled to resign, the council thanking him "for his willingness to join the college staff had it been possible."

To Barry, with his twenty years' experience at Glenalmond, Leeds, and Cheltenham, nothing at King's College seemed more anomalous than the omnipotence of the council and the impotence of the staff. Apart from the medical professors, who met from time to time, and had a dean through whom they could give utterance to their emotions and ideas, there was no sort of organization of the college staff. Now Barry's formal exclusion from the council, except when at a " convenient break " he was sent for by a messenger, just as the gate-keeper might be sent for, caused him strongly to stress his position as head of the staff, and made him see things from a professorial rather than from a conciliar point of view. Principal Lonsdale had been pre-eminently a member of the council; Dr Jelf had oscillated hesitantly from one side to the other; Dr Barry was wholly the chief of the staff. And under him the staff began quite definitely and decisively to take the lead in determining the educational policy of the college. The original council had wholly vanished away; the great bishops who *ex officio* took the places of such men as Howley, Harcourt, Blomfield, Copleston, and Lonsdale rarely attended council meetings and never got that hold of the college organization which the founder-prelates had secured and retained; the conduct of college business passed into the hands of smaller men, laymen, busy politicians and professional men, who generously gave their time and money, but who did not command the awe and reverence which had made their predecessors all-powerful. They were, moreover, aware that they did not possess that intimate acquaintance with the changing world of education which the needs of the college required. Hence they were glad to accept the advice of the staff, although very jealous of any encroachment on their ultimate powers of jurisdiction.

Accordingly, a year after his assumption of office—viz., October 7, 1869—Dr Barry held a great confabulation with his educational staff, and as the outcome addressed a strongly worded memorial to the council, the gist of which was expressed in the words:

> Considering that the income of almost all the members of the staff is directly dependent on the success of the college, and liable to deduction beyond its proper standard in case of deficit, it is but reasonable that the teaching staff should have in some way, directly or indirectly, but at any rate substantially, some share in the government of the college, and some knowledge of its educational and financial administration.

A committee of the agitated council was appointed to parley with the insurrectionists, and a long negotiation took place, into the details of which we have no space to enter. Perhaps it was a mere coincidence that during its course the college showed signs of subsidence, that numerous and ominous cracks displayed themselves in its walls, and that (December 6, 1869) the roof of the dining-hall collapsed with a crash that involved the hall itself and the kitchen beneath it in a £1700 ruin. Be that as it may, early in 1870 an agreement was reached, and on March 11 new "regulations for establishing departmental and general boards" were ordered to be circulated to all members of the academical staff. First, each department of the college, including the school, was to have its board of teachers presided over by a dean, who should be its medium of communication with the council, and it was empowered to express itself freely on educational matters. Secondly—and this was the vitally important innovation— a general board was instituted to consist, (*a*) " as to the college, of the dean and one representative of each department to be chosen annually out of their own body by the educational staff of that department," and (*b*) " as to the school, of the headmaster, the vice-master, and one representative to be chosen annually out of their own body by the other masters." This impressive representative general board was to communicate with the council through the principal. Although it had no executive power, and although its advice was restricted to educational matters, this general board at once began to take an active part in the determination of college policy, and before the end of Dr Barry's principalship it had acquired a controlling influence within its own sphere of operation.[1] We shall have to note in due course how Dr Barry, at the head of his various departmental and general boards, during the fifteen years of his principalship, improved the technical education of the college; reorganized the curriculum of the department of general literature and science; revolutionized the medical school and the hospital by the installation of Joseph Lister and his antiseptic surgery; established an evening school in theology; attached to the college a large second-class civil service department; connected the college with the "science and art" movement centred at South Kensington; vastly improved relations between King's College and London University; and, above all, laid the foundations of King's College for Women.

So effective and successful, indeed, was Barry that one is tempted to ask whether in any respect he fell short of perfection as a principal. Such were his capacity, energy, versatility, that it was commonly said among his staff that "Barry could do anything."[2] Perhaps the one trait that displayed his affinity with ordinary mankind was a certain pushfulness and ambition on his own behalf. He tended to regard the college too much as "a stepping-stone to higher things." He was too ready, in the exuberance of his powers and his desire for honours and emoluments, to take upon himself extraneous work that deprived the college of time and attention that it had a right to expect. In 1871 he became a residentiary canon of Worcester, which meant that he was compelled every year till 1881 (when he was made a canon of Westminster) to ask for two months' leave of absence; in 1875 he accepted a chaplaincy to the queen, and from 1876 to 1878 he was Boyle lecturer. In 1872 he was invited to add to the principalship of King's College the principalship of Queen's College in Harley Street, coupled with the obligation to give a course of twenty lectures each year. He was anxious to accept the invitation, but the council kindly but firmly said (November 8) that "they

---

[1] The members of the first "general board" appear to have been: (1) Theological, Professors Plumptre and Leathes; (2) General Literature, Professors Brewer and Mozley; (3) Applied Science, Professors Hall and Miller; (4) Medical, Professors Bentley and Gay; (5) Evening Classes, Professors Levi and Adams; (6) School, Dr Maclear, Mr Twentyman, Mr Rust.

[2] Letter from the Rev. Canon Richard Abbay, of Earl Soham, February 15, 1927.

thought it better that the principal should not undertake any more extraneous duty." The matter of salary, too, was one that frequently occupied his attention. The pittance assigned to him on his appointment, he said, proved to be wholly insufficient for the maintenance of himself, his family, and his position. Hence he gradually screwed it up until (December 1879) it reached the Jelf level. Then there was the principal's house. This was (and is) an elegant structure picturesquely and delightfully situated on the bank of the Thames, but internally characterized by every inconvenience that man has ever devised to reduce woman to despair. Having lived in it for five years, Dr Barry (May 1874) came before the council with the request that (on account of his children's health) he might be allowed to leave it and take up his residence elsewhere, with a compensating addition to his stipend. He suggested that

> under the present difficulty of obtaining space in the college, and especially the want of class-rooms, it might be of more advantage to use the house for educational purposes than to devote it to the residence of the principal.

The science professors, indeed, and especially Professor Grylls Adams, the physicist, were eager to get hold of it and convert it into laboratories. The council granted the principal's request for permission to remove his household into the country, provided that his attention to his college duties was in no degree relaxed. But they did not accept his suggestion that the house should be incorporated in the college—that was left for 1920. Nor did they make any proposal to contribute to the upkeep of his rural establishment. Hence (June 12, 1874) Dr Barry approached them once more with the information that the Statistical Society had made him an offer for the use of the house (less two upstairs rooms) of £200 per annum. This offer the council allowed him to accept, and accordingly the Statistical Society was installed, within the academic precincts, on the Embankment.[1] There it remained for precisely ten years—viz., until July 31, 1884.

§ 2. *The Problem of Finance*

If finance bothered Dr Barry, not less did it bother the council of the college. We have noted that heavy annual deficits

---

[1] The Embankment had been constructed 1864–70, and in July 1870 the college had received permission from the First Commissioner of Works to open an entrance therefrom.

were the prime cause of Dr Jelf's decline and fall.[1] The first three years of Barry's *régime* showed but little sign of improvement: in order to cover expenses and enable £500 per annum to be contributed to the sinking fund, levies on the pittances paid to the staff had to be made at the rates of 1½ per cent. in 1869, 3 per cent. in 1870, and 1½ per cent. (which ought to have been 3 per cent.) in 1871. The chronic destitution of the college was at this time, moreover, greatly aggravated by the catastrophe which has already been alluded to. At a council meeting on December 10, 1869,

> The secretary reported that an alarming accident had occurred at the college on Monday, December 6. At 8.15 on that morning the entire roof of the dining hall under the terrace fronting the Thames fell in with a loud crash, carrying with it the floor below and burying the kitchen in ruins.

There can be little doubt that the immediate cause of the collapse was subsidence due to the making of the Metropolitan Railway beneath the new Embankment. The experts (Messrs F. J. Bramwell and J. Wolfe Barry) called in to investigate the matter, however, reported that structural defects, in particular inadequate and badly cast cross-girders, were in part to blame. Hence the council had to face the whole £1700 required to re-edify the hall and kitchen without the aid of any compensation. In these desperate circumstances (February 11, 1870),

> Mr Robert Cheere brought before the notice of the council some letters which he had received from members of their own body on the subject of endeavouring to raise a large sum of money for the purpose of paying off the debts of the college and securing an endowment fund.

A special meeting was summoned, and thereat it was resolved

> That an effort be made to raise the sum of £30,000 for the purpose of discharging the debts of the college and providing for its efficient management and necessary extensions from time to time.

A form of appeal was drawn up, in which the heavy liabilities of the college were attributed to (1) the defalcations of 1829, estimated at £15,000; (2) the expenses involved in the equipment and maintenance of scientific laboratories; (3) the dining-hall catastrophe; and (4) donations to the hospital. The appeal was duly launched in the spring of 1870, the members of the council themselves generously starting it with donations amounting to more than £3000, the underpaid and heavily taxed staff following with another £700. But there

---

[1] See above, pp. 269–270.

was practically no public response. The college was too ecclesiastical to attract the wealthy layman, and no longer sufficiently ecclesiastical to draw the subscriptions of the zealous churchman. It was in the awkward and unprepossessing stage of transition from the Anglican seminary to the university college; it was falling between the two stools of Church and State. Circumstances, too, were against the success of the appeal. On the one hand, the Franco-Prussian war was filling the world with a sense of insecurity; on the other hand, the new radical Education Act was concentrating the attention of the faithful upon elementary instruction, and was demanding every penny that they could spare for the support of the church schools. At the end of a year scarcely £1000 beyond the contribution of the council and the staff had been promised, and still less paid. Hence it was decided to hold a great public meeting to further the appeal. The meeting took place in Willis's Rooms on May 10, 1872. The Archbishop of Canterbury (Dr A. C. Tait) presided, and speeches in varied types of eloquence were made by the Prime Minister (Mr Gladstone), the Bishop of Peterborough (Dr Magee), and others. The archbishop struck the true baritone note when he said in his opening remarks that " while King's College is a thoroughly Church institution, it is at the same time, and in the best sense of the word, a liberal institution." It was, indeed, as we have just remarked, too " thoroughly Church " to please the liberals, and too " liberal " to satisfy the " thoroughly Church." In vain, then, did Mr Gladstone descant at length on the harmony of science and revelation as manifested in its curriculum; in vain did Bishop Magee plead " in the name of religious education, of definite dogmatic teaching, and of broad catholicity of view " for contributions to the special fund. Once again the bulk of the giving fell to the lot of the council and the staff, and, even so, at the end of 1872 the total amount raised was no more than £8145. Hence in 1873 a renewed attempt was made to soothe the suspicious Church and stir the apathetic world, and for the third time the council and the staff nobly responded.[1] Finally, in 1876, after half a dozen years of laborious and rather humiliating mendicity, the fund was closed, only £11,000 out of the desired £30,000 having been raised. Before this date—viz., June 11, 1875—the council had given the secretary authority to sell such silver spoons and forks as the college possessed, and to procure electroplate instead.

[1] See subscription list in the Calendar of 1873-74, p. 68.

It is true that under the energetic and enlightened rule of Dr Barry in the college, and of Dr Maclear in the school, the income from fees steadily and even rapidly increased. But expenses advanced with a more than proportionate acceleration. A mysterious fire which broke out in the refectory during the small hours of Sunday, January 27, 1878, caused much damage before it was discovered by a passing policeman and extinguished; in 1880 a formidable addition was made to the rates demanded by the Strand Union; [1] several professors of the college and masters of the school, having reached the limit of senility, and being impecunious, had to be pensioned off; the remarkable recovery of the school (which rose from 344 in 1867 to the record number of 631 in 1879) necessitated the making of four new classrooms in the basement; [2] the development of the medical school required the building of new physiological laboratories on the Embankment at a cost of some £7000; above all, the growth of applied science and engineering put an intolerable strain upon the college finances. It was impossible for the council out of current income to buy the machines and apparatus necessary for an efficient technological institute.

In these circumstances of extreme need—fees being wholly inadequate and private charity running dry—invaluable first-aid was rendered by two of the great and venerable city companies—viz., the Clothworkers and the Drapers. The generous and timely action of the companies was not, perhaps, wholly disinterested. The government of London was in process of reconstitution, and formidable inquiries were being made as to how the twelve city companies were employing the revenues that accrued from their properties, which were estimated to be worth a capital sum of £15,000,000. With a haste that showed some signs of trepidation they began to buy less turtle, and to endow schools, colleges, chairs, and charities. [3] In November 1874 the Clothworkers' Company placed £50 a year at the disposal of the council for the founding of an exhibition, and a few years later (1878 and 1880) they added two further exhibitions of £25 each, together with a number of prizes. They also furnished the engineering department

---

[1] The rateable value of the college premises, which had been assessed at £1650, was suddenly raised to £3850. A compromise was eventually effected at £2500. Even so, however, about £850 a year was added to the burdens of the council.

[2] Two were cut off the gymnasium, and the other two were newly constructed at the extreme north end of the basement corridor.

[3] *Cf.* Royal Commission to inquire into the foundation and objects of the City Companies, 1880 (*Report*, 5 vols., 1884).

with a slotting machine (£70) in 1878, and a testing machine (£200) in 1881. The Drapers' Company equipped a new metallurgical laboratory in 1879 at a cost of £500. In 1874, moreover, it seemed possible that a new and unexpected source of revenue would be opened up. For

> the secretary reported having received on February 17 last a registered anonymous letter containing £30 enclosed in an envelope bearing the words " An act of restitution from a penitent sinner."

It was hoped that other sinners, the number of whom was believed to be large, would become penitent, and would display their contrition in the same commendable manner. The movement, however, unfortunately did not spread. Perhaps it might have been assisted by a little judicious advertisement.

But not even lavish donations from wealthy city companies, supplemented by acts of retribution on the part of penitent sinners, could suffice for the permanent needs of a college rapidly advancing toward university rank. From public funds alone could adequate supplies be looked for. But the receipt of public money involved public control, and the establishment of public control meant the abolition of the control of both the proprietors and the church. The council cared nothing for the proprietors, who, after half a century's attrition, were negligible and for the most part undiscoverable. But the question of church control was another matter. The very essence of the college was at stake. The problem was first brought before the council on November 12, 1874, by the Rev. William Ince, sub-rector of Exeter College, Oxford, and later canon of Christ Church and regius professor of divinity. He drew the attention of the council to the recently issued fifth report of the Devonshire Commission on scientific instruction, and proposed a resolution to the effect that inquiries should be made as to the conditions, if any, on which grants would be made by the government to the college— (*a*) toward capital expenditure and (*b*) toward annual charges. At first Mr Ince could not secure a seconder to his motion; but later the matter was reopened and a committee of seven (two clergymen and five laymen) appointed to consider and report upon the matter. On December 11, 1874, the committee laid before the council for their approval the following conditions on which a government grant, if offered, would be accepted:

> (1) That, should Her Majesty's Government before making any grant to King's College insist upon the college cancelling

the proprietary rights of its shareholders, an endeavour should be made to effect this object.

(2) That a deputation should be appointed to wait upon the Lord President of the Council, and that such deputation should be instructed to adhere to the existing practice as to the admission of students and the exemptions from attendance on religious teaching, as well as to those conditions of the charter which require professors, with certain exceptions, to be members of the Church of England.

In other words, the proprietors should be thrown to the wolves, but a resolute effort should be made to preserve the ecclesiastical control. The council adopted the report, and appointed the deputation, which was duly received by the Lord President, the Duke of Richmond, on February 11, 1875. The Bishop of London (Dr Jackson) presented the case for the college, and he was supported by Earl Powis, Mr Thomas Webster, Q.C., and Dr Barry. The duke listened with sympathy when the bishop told him that " the college's great difficulty had been its poverty " and that it " had been in debt from the time of its birth "; nor does his sympathy seem to have been in any way diminished when the bishop got mixed in his statistics and put the liabilities of the college at £6000 instead of £16,000, and the total amount expended on buildings at £20,000 instead of £200,000. Finally the duke, who was evidently an expert at the receiving of deputations, dismissed his distinguished visitors with the utmost affability, asking them to furnish him with more precise information as to their needs and aspirations, concluding, " I can only promise to refer the matter to my colleagues, because it is one that will have to come before the cabinet." [1]

As a matter of fact, nothing whatever resulted from this palaver, and during the whole of Dr Barry's principalship, and for long after, the college had to do the best it could with hopelessly inadequate funds drawn from the old sources of fees and donations. The last annual reports drawn up by Dr Barry are eloquent of continued financial stringency: in 1882 he said:

pressure on the council for large outlay to keep the college in an efficient state and to meet the ever increasing demands for extension becomes greater every year;

in 1883 he lamented that

the receipts have only just met the expenditure, leaving no surplus for the extinction of debt;

[1] Report of the visit of the Deputation, *Daily News*, February 12, 1875.

in 1884 he deplored the fact that

> pressing wants for additional apparatus and enlarged accommodation are coming before the council at every meeting, and they have unfortunately no funds at their disposal for new developments of any kind.

The college, indeed, was living a hand-to-mouth existence, with no reserves to tide it over any emergency; with no resources out of which to make imperative advances; with no funds for the payment of adequate salaries, or the provision of necessary pensions. It was impossible to expect anglican piety to supply all the vast sums required for the equipment of the new technological departments that were constantly being called for. The only question was whether the college could maintain itself in a sufficient state of efficiency to be qualified to receive the government grants when they should become available, and whether the college would so modify its constitution as to make it possible for the state to contribute to its needs. Dr Barry and his devoted colleagues took care that the first part of the question should be answered in the affirmative: it is amazing what they did with the scantiest resources. The second part of the question had to be left for a later generation to answer.

§ 3. *The Development of Applied Science*

The most pressing of the demands for new money came from the department of applied science, and in particular from the engineering section thereof. At the moment when Dr Barry assumed office the council was expending £520 in the enlargement and re-equipment of the workshop, and this outlay proved to be but the beginning of recurring and increasing charges. On the one hand, the improvements in the process of the manufacture of steel due to the discoveries and inventions of Bessemer (1856) and Siemens (1859), supplemented by those of Thomas and Gilchrist twenty years later (1878), made possible a wholly new range of mechanical tools and engines. On the other hand, the development of electricity for heating and lighting opened up for engineering a vast and wholly novel field of operations. Hence the demand for fresh apparatus and for specialist teachers was insistent.

Another circumstance, too, must be borne in mind. Until this third quarter of the nineteenth century Britain had fairly well maintained her monopoly as the manufactory of the world. But from this period the rivalry of other countries began to be formidable. In particular America started to develop her limitless resources; while, after 1871, the newly founded German Empire employed the milliards of the French indemnity to plant and foster the industries which, according to the accepted principle of List, a well-balanced and wholly autonomous state required. Britain, then, found her industrial supremacy seriously menaced, and began to realize (a little late) that if she were to maintain her place in a world becoming keenly competitive, it could be only by means of a marked improvement in her scheme of technical education.

In 1868 Sir Joseph Whitworth, the great mechanical inventor and wealthy steel manufacturer, wrote to Disraeli, then for the first time prime minister, and offered to found thirty scholarships—each worth £100 a year and tenable for three years—in order to encourage the scientific education of those who would become masters, managers, and foremen in British industrial concerns. The offer was, of course, promptly accepted by the alert and far-sighted prime minister, and the scholarships were thrown open to public competition. King's College was one of the first educational institutions in the kingdom to recognize the importance of the new departure, and to make provision for the training of would-be Whitworth scholars. This involved, of course, the equipment of physical and chemical laboratories open to students. In November 1868 Professors Grylls Adams and Miller laid before the council a request for some £300 for the purpose. The request was granted in December, and early in 1869 the laboratories were in working order. They claimed to be the first of their kind—i.e., open to students—outside Paris. Mr Richard Abbay of Exeter College, Oxford, was placed in charge of them. " In taking these steps," said the council in its report of April 23, 1869, " they have had especially in view the great impetus given to technical education by the noble provisions of the Whitworth Scholarships." The college speedily had its reward. In the report of the following year (May 13, 1870) the council was able to announce that King's men had carried off two of the first ten Whitworth scholarships awarded. So pleased was Sir Joseph Whitworth at the manner in which the college entered into the spirit of his great design that in 1875 he chose King's as one of three institutions where a further experiment should be tried. The report of April 16, 1875, runs:

> The council have the pleasure of announcing that Sir Joseph Whitworth has promised a sum of £100 annually, for four years

at least, to found three exhibitions, each tenable for two years, with the special object of encouraging young men who show mechanical aptitude, and are already possessed of a certain amount of manual dexterity, to perfect themselves in theoretical study so as to be fit competitors for the Whitworth Scholarships, and to be prepared to hold positions which require theoretical knowledge and practical experience of engineering.

In 1877 the workshop was further enlarged at a cost of £700, and Sir Joseph Whitworth at the same time gave £200 for the provision of new tools.

During this period, too, other incentives toward the development of the applied sciences came from many quarters. (1) In 1870 a "royal commission on scientific instruction and the advancement of science" was appointed, and its reports (1872–75) held out hope of government grants.[1] (2) In 1871, through the kind offices of Mr Anderson, a former student of the college, Messrs Easton and Anderson established the so-called "Easton Prize," which consisted in the admission of one duly selected student of the college each year, for the seven years 1872–79, as an apprentice to the Erith Works, without the payment of the five hundred guineas normally demanded for apprenticeship. (3) In 1875 the great Sir Charles Wheatstone passed away. For forty-one years he had been nominally professor of experimental physics in the college. After his first session, however, he had done no lecturing, but had devoted himself (presumably without salary) to his researches in electricity, and to his inventions in telegraphy, magneto-electrical machines, and recording instruments. On his death he left a will in which he bequeathed to the corporation of King's College all his scientific books and apparatus, all his medals and diplomas, together with the sum of £500 to be expended in laboratory equipment. The books numbered 1500; the apparatus, which included much of that with which Sir Charles had made his pioneer experiments, was estimated to be worth at least £1000. The council gratefully accepted the generous bequest, decided to erect a special gallery in the George III museum to receive and display the apparatus, and, having spent the monetary portion of the legacy on scientific equipment, named the physical laboratory in which it was placed the "Wheatstone laboratory." (4) The London livery companies, which in 1877 appointed a committee to prepare a scheme for the furtherance of technical education, established

[1] Evidence for King's College was given before the commission by the principal, the secretary, and Professor Grylls Adams. See *Second Report* (1872), Cd. 536, xxv.

in 1878 a " City and Guilds of London Institute " with large funds, under Mr Philip Magnus as organizing director. Ultimately—viz., in 1884—the institute set up a college of its own in South Kensington—now a constituent member of the Imperial College of Science; but meantime it gave valuable assistance to colleges already engaged in technical instruction. In 1879 the Institute agreed to place £400 per annum, under certain conditions, at the disposal of King's College for the founding of two new and important technical chairs—viz., those of metallurgy and practical fine art. The Drapers' Company supplemented this generous grant by giving £500 for the equipment of the metallurgical laboratory, while the City and Guilds (April 1880) added a further £200 for the provision of the necessary fittings and appliances in the department of practical fine art. The first professor of metallurgy was Mr A. K. Huntington, of the Royal School of Mines; to the chair of practical fine art Mr S. H. Delamotte, who for a quarter of a century had been teaching landscape drawing in the college, was elevated. (5) In January 1882 Dr (afterward Sir) C. W. Siemens intimated his wish to give to the council a sum of money sufficient to provide an annual medal and prize, each of the value of £10 10s. " with the object of stimulating the students of King's College, London, to a high standard of proficiency in metallurgical science." The council received " with warm thanks the proposal made to them by Dr Siemens " and framed regulations accordingly. The study of metallurgical science, indeed, was at that date of vital importance for the future of the British iron and steel industry. The discovery in 1878 by Thomas and Gilchrist of the process by means of which phosphorus (which the Bessemer process did not touch) could be eliminated from iron ore, enabled the steel of Lorraine for the first time to come into serious competition with British steel. The increasing stress of foreign competition was the main cause of the appointment of a new " royal commission on technical instruction," which in 1882 again heard evidence concerning the doings and the needs of King's College. The case of the college was stated by Professors Adams and Shelley, with Mr David Walker, the superintendent of the workshop. Their evidence, too, was supported by that of Dr Siemens, who employed many old King's men, and of Mr William Anderson, of Messrs Easton and Anderson, himself a former student of the college and the originator of the " Easton Prize " already noted. King's College, it appeared, was far ahead of most of its rivals in the equipment of its laboratories, and in the practical nature of its engineering education. Still, however, the much-needed government grants failed to arrive. The fame of the laboratories and workshops, nevertheless, spread far and wide, and the numbers of engineering students went up by leaps and bounds. From 55 in 1871 they reached 69 in 1881; then in 1882 they jumped to 91, and in 1883, for the first time in the history of the college, exceeded the hundred.

A few other changes, besides the doubling of numbers, have to be chronicled. First, the department twice (1871 and 1874) changed its name. The designation " applied sciences," after a clumsy compromise in 1871, finally became " engineering and applied sciences," often shortened simply to " engineering." Secondly, several of the old—very old—teachers of the department passed away. In 1869 Professor T. Bradley ended a period of thirty-one years' instruction in geometrical drawing: the professor of architectural drawing (W. J. Glenny) took over his work. The same year Professor James Tennant resigned the chair of geology, in which he was succeeded by Dr P. M. Duncan. He continued, however, to hold the chair of mineralogy (which he had received in 1838) until his death in 1881, when Professor Duncan assumed its duties also. In 1880 another veteran, by resignation after forty years of service, passed from the precincts of the college: this was Mr H. J. Castle, the professor of surveying. To his post Mr Henry Robinson was appointed. Under these younger men the rejuvenated engineering department made rapid headway. The council's report in 1884 is eloquent of progress and prosperity. It ends as follows:

> The condition of this department is a matter for special congratulation, and the council have reason to believe that it commands in an eminent degree the confidence of the important profession which it serves.

§ 4. *The Medical School and the Hospital*

Another department that made great progress during this period, but also at the cost of much expenditure and not a little friction, was the department of medicine with its appendant hospital. Its numbers, which in 1868 were low—viz., 130—ran up to 223 in 1883; and, what is more important, its reputation became world-wide through its association with Joseph Lister and his new antiseptic surgery.

As in the engineering department, so here, the period of

Dr Barry's rule saw an almost complete rejuvenation of the staff. First, on September 30, 1870, passed away Dr W. A. Miller, who for thirty years—five as demonstrator and twenty-five as professor—had taught chemistry in the college. The circumstances of his death were dramatic and pathetic. He had, from a strong sense of duty and much against his inclination, gone to the Liverpool meeting of the British Association in order, if necessary, to combat the agnosticism of Professor T. H. Huxley, president for the year. The excitement of preparing for the battle proved too much for a highly nervous and emotional nature, and he died on his arrival at Liverpool, from a cerebral seizure. His chair was amalgamated with that of " practical chemistry," which Professor Bloxam had held since 1856. In order to assist Professor Bloxam in his double duties, Mr W. N. Hartley was appointed demonstrator (December 1870), and Mr John Millar Thomson—still happily with us as a distinguished emeritus professor—as assistant-demonstrator (February 1871). Secondly, on March 25, 1873, died the last of the original members of the staff, the notable Richard Partridge, appointed demonstrator of anatomy in 1831 and professor five years later. From 1840 to 1870, moreover, he had been surgeon at the hospital; but, though an admirable dissector, he was nervous and hesitant as an operator upon a body that was not already a corpse. His strength lay in his lectures, his brilliant and artistic diagrams, and in his masterly demonstrations. He was a great teacher, who left a permanent impress upon the medical school of King's. During the course of his long career at the college he collected and stored in a retentive memory an immense number of anecdotes, many of them of so intimate and confidential a character that they brought a blush to the cheeks of even medical students. His favourite poem was Butler's *Hudibras*, from which he freely and effectively quoted in his lectures.[1] Dr John Curnow, one of the ablest of the pupils of Partridge, demonstrator in anatomy since 1870, succeeded him in the chair. Thirdly, Dr Rymer Jones, for thirty-eight blameless years professor of comparative anatomy,

---

[1] Two remarkable episodes in Professor Partridge's career were: (1) his discovery of the murder of an Italian boy, whose body was brought to his dissecting-room in 1831, and his consummate skill in aiding the police to capture the two murderers, one of whom was handed over to the college (after the law had finished with him) for dissection ; (2) his call to Spezzia in September 1862 to examine Garibaldi, who had been badly wounded in the ankle the preceding month at Aspromonte. Full particulars of these episodes are given in *King's College Hospital Reports*, vol. vi (1900).

sent in his resignation (May 1874) in order to enjoy a few years of comparative tranquillity. He was succeeded by Mr A. H. Garrod (son of Sir A. B. Garrod, the physician), an old King's man, who had just completed a distinguished course at Cambridge by securing a first in the natural sciences tripos and a fellowship at St John's College. He was a man, says his friend Curnow, " of indomitable energy, and singular originality of thought." After doing excellent work for four years, however, his health most lamentably broke down. He had to obtain leave of absence in October 1878; the following March he resigned, and on October 17, 1879, died. His successor was Mr F. J. Bell, of the zoological department of the British Museum. Fourthly, on February 10, 1877, the eminent Sir William Fergusson passed away at the age of sixty-nine. Since 1840 he had been surgeon at the hospital, where his amazing skill, self-possession, and resourcefulness had won for him the reputation of " the greatest practical surgeon of the day." He had introduced operations hitherto regarded as impossible; had triumphantly revived operations abandoned as too dangerous; and had achieved results in such ordinary operations as those for harelip and cleft palate which were the admiration and despair of less perfect practitioners. As a lecturer he was not a success; his fumbling ineptitude with words was in striking contrast to his deft precision with the knife. Nevertheless, he professed surgery at King's College from 1840 to 1870, when he handed over his functions to Mr Henry Wood, a highly competent practitioner of the old school, who had held minor posts in the college and hospital expectantly for some twenty years. Since 1870 Fergusson had borne the title of " professor of clinical surgery," and had limited his oratory to (most inadequate) explanations of his performances at the hospital, given in that building to students walking the wards. The death of Sir William Fergusson opened the way for the coming of Professor Joseph Lister to King's College Hospital; but that was so important an event that I must postpone treatment of it for a moment. It remains first to chronicle a few further changes in the medical department of the college. Fifthly—to resume the series of deaths and resignations under Dr Barry—in November 1871 Dr W. A. Guy resigned the professorship of forensic medicine which he had held for thirty years, retaining, however, a professorship of hygiene (which had been created for him in 1869) for another seven years. Dr (later Sir) David Ferrier succeeded to the forensic chair in 1872, and Dr Charles Kelly to the hygienic one in 1878. Sixthly, and last, Dr Soelberg Wells, the ophthalmologist since 1865, died at the end of 1879; and early next year Mr M. M. McHardy was appointed in his stead to give sight to the blind.

Besides the six changes just noted, a bewildering number of permutations and combinations within the medical circle—shiftings and shufflings that recall the old game of family coach or the tea-party of Alice in Wonderland—took place. Most of them were due to the desire of busy physicians and surgeons, such as Mr Lionel Beale or Dr George Johnson, to escape from the burden of lecturing at regular hours in the college, and restrict themselves to practice and clinical instruction at the hospital. To record all these kaleidoscopic rearrangements would be tedious: can they not be discovered by the curious from the annual reports of the college and the hospital? One of them, however, had causes and consequences too important to be omitted. In April 1869 Mr Lionel Beale announced his wish to vacate the chair of physiology which he had held for sixteen years, but expressed a desire to retain his beds at the hospital. In order to enable him to do so, the council created for him the ornamental chair of " pathological anatomy." No doubt the cause of his desire to be freed from physiology was the fact that the Royal College of Surgeons at this time was beginning to insist on a practical training in the subject that involved equipment of a students' laboratory, and an immense addition to professorial toils and responsibilities—a far bigger addition than any medical man in full practice could possibly undertake. The vacant professorship of physiology, with its new burdens, was offered to, and accepted by, Dr William Rutherford of Edinburgh, who for five years devoted abilities of the highest order, and exceptional skill as a teacher, to the development of his department. He constructed a marvellous series of diagrams; he invented novel experiments; above all, he set his students to work to prepare microscopical sections and carry out the simpler manipulations of the laboratory. By 1871 the activity of the department had become so great that a demonstrator had to be appointed to assist the professor: singular good fortune enabled the council to secure the services of Dr David Ferrier for this post (February). Very soon after this, the need for further accommodation for practical work in physiology became urgent. On June 9, 1871, a letter from Professor Rutherford pressed the council for the provision of a new laboratory—a request repeated with added emphasis six months later. The council proceeded to take action; but owing to difficulties respecting site and finance its movements were very slow. Letters from Professor Rutherford became chronic. In November 1872 Her Majesty's Office of Works agreed to grant the college a small additional plot of land, created by the embankment of the Thames, at the south-east corner of the original site.[1] On July 11, 1873, plans for a physiological laboratory on this new plot were passed—plans which had to be revised and materially altered because of disputes concerning ancient lights in 1874. Not until 1875 was the laboratory completed and opened. By this time—viz., in October 1874—Dr Rutherford had returned to Edinburgh, and Dr G. F. Yeo reigned in his stead.

The period during which the college was struggling to provide the professor of physiology with his new laboratory was also the period during which an awkward and formidable quarrel broke out between the committee managing the hospital and the committee of St John's House, which "nursed the hospital." The dispute arose respecting the sister-in-charge, and related at first to such minor administrative matters as cooking and washing. It culminated at the end of 1873 in a demand on the part of the hospital committee (carried by a bare majority) that the sister-in-charge should be removed and a new one sent. With this demand the executive of St John's House refused to comply, and appealed from the committee of the hospital to the council of King's College. The council (December 17, 1873) was compelled to come to the conclusion that " the agreement between the two bodies does not entitle the committee of the hospital to require from St John's House the withdrawal of the sister-in-charge." The hospital committee (again by a bare majority) gave notice on February 1, 1874, that in six months it would terminate the existing agreement and organize its own system of nursing. Then began a furious controversy within the hospital and the college, as well as in the public press. Drs George Johnson and Lionel Beale openly sided with St John's House; the *Times*, adopting the same view, denounced the majority on the committee as an obscurantist body which wished to restore the *régime* of Mrs Gamp. The council and court of King's College once again intervened between the two exasperated committees. The points at issue were ultimately referred to the arbitration of Lords Hatherley and Selborne (two legal members of the council), and as a result of their judicious mediation a working compromise was attained: on the one

[1] See illustration opposite p. 62.

hand, the specific difficulties relating to cooking, washing, and the like were removed; on the other hand, an arrangement was made by which the council of King's College (but not the committee of the hospital) could require the removal of any offensive sister. The particular offensive sister, however, concerning whose procedure the trouble had arisen, remained in possession of the field. Not in vain had she been trained in the school of Florence Nightingale and Sister Dora. The majority of the committee, who had demanded her removal, recognized her victory by resigning. Both the hospital and the medical school suffered from this embittered wrangle. The funds of the hospital sank to a very low ebb; the numbers of medical students declined steadily from 161 in 1874 to 121 in 1877. It was at that unhappy juncture that Sir William Fergusson died, and that the suggestion was made that Professor Joseph Lister should be invited to come from Edinburgh to London.

Sir William Fergusson, as we have already noted, died on February 10, 1877. For some months he had been unable to attend the hospital, and his work there had fallen upon Messrs John Wood and Henry Smith. His death or resignation, then, was not unexpected, and much discussion had taken place as to how his post should be filled. Messrs John Wood and Henry Smith, venerable and respectable *alumni* of the college, who had plodded on year after year in patient expectancy, claimed the inheritance. The physicians of the hospital, the professors of the college, and those two important medical members of the council Sir Thomas Watson and Mr (later Sir) William Bowman—while anxious that the worthy Messrs Wood and Smith should secure well-earned promotion —felt that every possible means should be employed to bring Lister to the hospital. Since 1865, first at Glasgow and then at Edinburgh, he had been developing and demonstrating his new antiseptic treatment of surgical cases. His immense success in reducing mortality had caused an unprecedented sensation throughout the scientific world, and hospitals all over the country and on the continent were struggling to adapt themselves to his methods. London, almost alone, remained faithless and unbelieving, continuing as of yore to let its hospital patients perish, after quite successful operations, of septicæmia, pyæmia, gangrene, or other bacillary plagues. The antiseptic treatment, with its constant reek of carbolic acid, said the conservative surgeons of the metropolis (as they put on their clotted operating coats, sharpened their unsterilized knives, and spread out their germ-laden sponges), may be useful in insanitary towns like Glasgow, or in dirty countries like Germany, but in a clean place such as London it is wholly unnecessary. Hence Lister was as anxious to come to London as St Paul had been to go to Rome—the headquarters of resistant heathendom. In 1866 he had applied for a vacant post at University College; but a worthy on the spot, who had been waiting for the place eighteen years, got it. At first it looked as though the same fate would meet him at King's in 1877.

Immediately after Fergusson's death Lister was informally sounded—apparently by Sir Thomas Watson—as to his willingness to come to King's. He replied on February 18, 1877, expressing his readiness to accept the chair of clinical surgery on certain conditions. Unfortunately, news of this tentative negotiation leaked out, and the press prematurely announced the prospect of the great surgeon's departure from Edinburgh. This announcement painfully perturbed the medical students who were working under Lister in Scotland, and on February 22 his class presented a memorial to him begging him not to leave them in order " to occupy the vacant chair of clinical surgery at King's College, London." Lister in his unpremeditated reply to his students let fall some pungent words respecting the benighted condition of the London hospitals which (to his amazement and horror) were reported in next day's *Times*. Not unnaturally, these were resented in London, and an inflamed correspondence broke out which for some weeks illuminated the pages of the *Lancet* and other periodicals. The pitch, then, was very badly queered when, on March 9, 1877, the council of King's College met, for the first time after Fergusson's death, to receive the formal notice of his decease, and to decide on the mode of filling his chair. A report was read from the medical committee in which recommendations were made that studiously omitted any mention of Lister. The committee advised: (1) that Mr John Wood should be appointed professor of clinical surgery at the hospital in place of Sir William Fergusson; (2) that the professorship of surgery at the college, which Mr Wood would vacate, should be advertised; (3) that Mr Henry Smith should be made a full surgeon at the hospital. Before the council voted on these recommendations a letter from Sir Thomas Watson was read in which he urged that, instead of advertising the professorship of surgery at the college, the council should offer it to Lister. The council accepted the recommendations of the medical committee with Watson's amendment, and accordingly Mr John Wood was appointed professor of clinical surgery at the hospital, while Lister was invited to accept the chair of surgery at the college with its appendant surgeoncy at the hospital.

This offer he quite emphatically declined. He had not, he said, done any formal lecturing on surgery for eight years, and he had no intention of resuming it. He must have a clinical professorship, or none at all. Mr Wood was then sounded as to his willingness to have Lister as a fellow-professor of clinical surgery at the hospital. At first he was implacably hostile to the idea, and the council, with great reluctance and regret, felt compelled (March 27) to revert to the proposal to advertise the vacant professorship of surgery at the college. Before, however, any advertisement was issued, a memorial was presented to the council from the medical board of the college, signed (say the minutes) " by all the staff of the medical department with the exception of the surgeons and assistant surgeons and one unimportant professor," [1] strongly urging the acceptance of Lister's terms, and emphasizing the extreme importance of securing him. The council, therefore, on April 20, called the obstructive Mr Wood before them and he " was informed that they were very anxious to secure the services of Professor Lister, and was asked whether he could suggest any mode of effecting this object." Thus driven to explain and expose himself he made a very poor display. The only objections to Lister's appointment which he ventured to bring forward were the two difficulties of (1) providing systematic lectures on surgery in the college, he himself refusing any longer to give them, and (2) finding beds for an extra surgeon in the hospital. The objections when thus reduced to concrete form were soon disposed of: Mr Henry Smith, although hitherto he had been regarded as inadequately qualified for the post, was made professor of surgery at the college, and the number of beds in the hospital was increased from 172 to 205. Hence, on May 11, 1877,

after full consideration, the council resolved (1) to create an additional chair of clinical surgery, and (2) to elect Professor Lister

[1] The contradiction in terms with which this extract from the minutes closes indicates the agitation caused by this acrimonious dispute. The seventeen signatories of the memorial were George Johnson, Lionel S. Beale, I. Burney Yeo, A. H. Garrod, David Ferrier, Soelberg Wells, S. H. Cartwright, Gerald F. Yeo, W. A. Guy, C. L. Bloxam, A. B. Duffin, E. B. Baxter, W. S. Playfair, Urban Pritchard, John Curnow, T. C. Hayes, and Robert Bentley. The surgeons at this date were Messrs John Wood and Henry Smith ; the assistant-surgeons Messrs H. R. Bell and W. Rose ; the " unimportant professor " . . . but, no, such a being is inconceivable.

a professor of clinical surgery and a surgeon of King's College Hospital.

Lister did not accept the offer until he had laid down conditions, which included the bringing with him from Edinburgh his own house-surgeon, clerk, and dressers, trained in his methods. His conditions were readily accepted, and on June 8, 1877, the business was completed.[1]

Lister, when he came to King's College Hospital, was in the main received with the respect and cordiality which his character and achievements commanded. His inaugural lecture at the beginning of October, delivered in the large theatre of King's College and attended by many of the most eminent men of science then living, was a brilliant oratorical success: its subject was "the nature of fermentation." His courtesy, his modesty, and the obvious soundness of his principles gradually won over his fellow-surgeons: even the resistant Professor Wood became a convert to the antiseptic method, and invoked Lister's aid in some peculiarly critical operations. Lister's position, however, was not without its difficulties. In particular, the examination system was against him, and it kept his classes depressingly small: students found that it did not pay to attend his clinic, and that it was positively fatal to mention antiseptics to some of the more elderly surgical examiners. Then again, he had much trouble at first with the haughty and independent nurses of St John's House, who either could not understand or would not carry into effect the new method.[2] It became increasingly evident that Sir William Fergusson and the hospital committee had been right when they had contended that it was absolutely essential that the nurses and the doctors—to say nothing of the cooks and the charwomen—should be under one and the same authority. In spite of difficulties, however, Lister made good. His wards in King's College Hospital became a centre of interest to surgeons and men of science all the world over: in 1881 they were visited by the great international medical conference, whose members included both Koch and Pasteur. Lister himself was made a baronet in 1883; in 1895 he was

[1] Some three years later, March 1880, another battle royal raged between the septics and the anti-septics when Lister's nominee Mr (now Sir) William Watson Cheyne was appointed assistant surgeon in the hospital and demonstrator of surgery in the college, in preference to a local candidate whose " claims to succeed to the vacant office " were pressed by Messrs Wood, Smith, Bell, and Rose.

[2] For some amazing examples of sisterly non-co-operation see Sir R. J. Godlee's *Lord Lister*, pp. 409–412.

elected president of the Royal Society, and two years later he was created a peer. The order of merit and the privy council followed in 1902. Meantime his system of surgery had made itself universal throughout the world, and its adoption had rendered possible hundreds of operations undreamed of before. Among the benefactors of the race few stand so high as he. His association with King's College Hospital is one of its imperishable glories.[1]

Two further developments of the medical school during this period remain to be noted. In March 1871, on the recommendation of the medical board, the council established a chair of " psychological medicine," otherwise mental pathology or lunacy, and appointed to it an old student of the college, Dr Edgar Sheppard, medical superintendent of Colney Hatch. Thus was forged a new link between the educational institutions of the metropolis. Then, secondly, in 1874, in order to complete the curriculum required by the Royal College of Surgeons for their dental diplomas, a new assistant dental surgeon, Mr S. H. Cartwright, was appointed to give an annual course of lectures and demonstrations in " dental mechanics." Thus was forged a new link between the medical and engineering departments. It is clear that the idea of the unity of the college was gaining ground, and that the conception of a federal university for London was in process of incubation.

§ 5. *The General Literature and Science Department*

Meantime the department which should have been the centre of the college, and the nucleus round which all the constituent schools should gather, was languishing into insignificance. Its numbers, only 66 in 1868, had fallen to 39 in 1884. The eminent professors lectured to half-empty classrooms; their fragments of fees were so small as to render it hardly worth while for them to come to collect them. Seated round their board, with Dr Barry at their head, they debated often and anxiously the means that should be adopted to revivify their department and enhance their inadequate remuneration. The root cause of their trouble was, they felt, the rivalry of the schools—and, not the least formidable, of King's College School itself. Instead of continuing, as in old days, to send

---

[1] Lister held his position at King's for fifteen years (1877–92), at the end of which period, when he was sixty-five years old, he had to retire under that rule of the age limit which had been passed as a perpetual memorial to Dr Jelf.

their best boys at the age of sixteen to be prepared at King's College for Oxford and Cambridge, they preferred to keep them themselves, and to win for themselves the credit of exhibitions and scholarships secured. In general, only the less efficient schools now passed on their ill-trained products to the literature and science department, with the result that not only the numbers but also the quality of the students lamentably declined.

The remedies for this state of things variously suggested were as follows. First, the equalization of school and college fees. This suggestion the council declined (December 1873). Secondly, the establishment of attractive entrance exhibitions, the staff of the department offering to combine in the institution of three, worth respectively £40, £30, £30: this prudential proposal the council graciously adopted (June 1876). Thirdly, the enlargement of the curriculum by the inclusion of several new subjects (*e.g.*, ancient history and moral philosophy), and the granting of a larger liberty of choice to students in their selection of a course: such enlargements took place notably in 1878 and 1880. Under this head, also, may be included the institution of a special class for the training of candidates for the Indian Civil Service, placed under the charge of Mr G. C. W. Warr, in July 1876. Fourthly, and closely akin to the last, the relaxation of the demand for the classical languages. So early as 1869 Dr Barry (who had recently instituted a " modern " side at Cheltenham) secured from the council permission to divide the general department into two sections—viz., a " classical division " and a " modern division," in the second of which French and German should take the place of Greek and Latin. In 1877 the " modern division " was remodelled on scientific lines with a view to the requirements of the London B.Sc. examination. Here we see the origin of the present-day faculty of science as distinct from the faculty of arts. Fifthly, the affiliation of the college to the universities of Oxford and Cambridge. In November 1873 the departmental board devised a scheme according to which duly qualified associates of the department would be allowed to enter Oxford and Cambridge as second-year men—the college offering to Oxford and Cambridge graduates reciprocal concessions in their technical departments. The council approved of the scheme and submitted it for consideration to the authorities of the old universities. Cambridge promptly rejected it. Oxford discussed it more sympathetically for a couple of years, but finally, in May 1876, turned it down.

Sixthly, the placing of an age limit on the boys at the school, compelling all boys who attained "a certain fixed age" (presumably sixteen), if they wished to continue their education, to pass on automatically to the college. This proposal was formally made by the professors of classics and mathematics in May 1880, and a special committee was appointed by the council to consider it. The committee, however, came to the conclusion that such a rule would gravely injure the school without proportionately benefiting the college (June 11, 1880). Their report ran:

> The committee do not think it advisable that any new rule should be made with reference to the age at which boys should be compelled to leave the school. They doubt whether the effect of a limit would be to bring any more students to the general literature department of the college, and it would certainly diminish unnecessarily the number of the boys remaining in the school who are not intended for the universities or the higher professions.

The headmaster of the school, Dr Maclear, also expressed his opinion of the proposal in a letter dated June 30, 1880, which in points of clarity and emphasis left nothing to be desired.

All these expedients and suggestions having proved ineffective, there remained but one thing to do to prevent the old department of general literature and science from dying out from mere inanition. That one thing was to abandon the attitude of aloofness from the University of London which had (except in respect of medicine) been maintained for nearly half a century, and frankly to make preparation for its degrees in arts and science the prime function of the department. During that half-century the University of London had undergone one important change. In 1858 the practice of affiliation had been dropped, and the examinations of the university—hitherto restricted to students of affiliated institutions, of which King's College was one—were thrown open to the whole world. In other words, the university had become a mere examining body, exercising no control over teaching apart from the framing of examination syllabuses, and making no inquiry as to how the candidate for its diplomas (those in medicine excepted) had acquired their knowledge. King's College had strongly opposed the policy of disaffiliation, and on the failure of her opposition had refrained even more ostentatiously than before from encouraging her students to compete with the world for distinctions devoid of divinity. In sublime indifference, however, to the aloofness of King's, the University of

London had won its way to the very front of degree-granting institutions; and its certificates, awarded on the results of examinations which for stringency, impartiality, and equity far exceeded anything hitherto known in the world, were generally regarded as among the surest of all guarantees of capacity. In particular, its degrees in science, in which it did not compete with Oxford and Cambridge, had a quite unique value in the educational world. Here, then, was a sphere in which the old and dying department of general literature and science could find rejuvenescence and vitality. Dr Barry, a great educationist, admirably free from prepossession and prejudice, was the very man to take advantage of the opportunity. As we have seen, the curriculum of the department was remodelled so as to make it fit the requirements of the London syllabuses. In his 1881 report he was able to say: "The number of candidates for the London University examinations, both for matriculation and for the B.A. degree, is increasing," and later reports successively laid more and more stress upon successes achieved in the London honours lists.

Not that successes in the older universities wholly ceased. Far from it, although they became less numerous as the years went on. It was in this very period, for instance, that Alfred Milner gained distinctions as brilliant as any that had been attained by his predecessors in the palmiest days of the department. Having entered the college in 1869, during the next three years he carried off almost every prize in classics, history, and literature open to students of the department. Then in 1872 he won an open scholarship to Balliol College, and went into residence at Oxford, under the discriminating eye of Jowett. At Balliol, as at King's, he carried all before him by sheer ability and a limitless capacity for work. Year after year the King's College reports chronicled his triumphs—Hertford scholarship, Jenkins exhibition, firsts in mods. and greats, fellowship at New College, Craven scholarship, Derby and Elton Law scholarship—an amazing record of sustained and brilliant achievement extending over ten years (1869–79). Nor did Milner's record stand alone. Not unworthy to be compared with it were the records of A. Goodwin, Ireland scholar and fellow of Balliol, and P. Lyttelton Gell, scholar of Balliol and Annan prizeman.

It is possible that, in so far as the success of these eminent students was due to anything beyond their own abilities and labours, it was attributable to the fact that the smallness of the classes enabled the King's College teachers to give an unusual amount of individual tuition to their more promising pupils. Another factor, however, may have contributed to the result. In this department, as in others, the old and weary aboriginal professors were being superseded by younger and more up-to-date men. (1) In 1869 Professor T. G. Hall, who since the opening of the college in 1831 had taught mathematics within its walls, sent in his resignation. He had long been apathetic and devoid of active interest in either his subject or his pupils. His place was taken by the Rev. H. W. Drew, of St John's College, Cambridge, eighth wrangler in 1849, who held the chair of mathematics with admirable efficiency until 1882, when, his health having broken down, he was succeeded by Mr W. H. H. Hudson, of the same college, a man of immense vivacity and energy, an old student of King's and third wrangler in 1861. During Mr Drew's tenure of the chair one of the antiquated assistants in the department, concerning whose neglect and incompetence repeated complaints had been made, was requested to resign, " it being the wish of the council to provide Professor Drew with a younger and more able colleague "! (2) In 1870 the Rev. James G. Lonsdale, the scholarly son of the third principal of King's, accepted the offer of the living of South Luffenham in Rutlandshire, and in consequence vacated the chair of classical literature which he had held since 1863. He was succeeded by the Rev. J. B. Mayor of St John's College, Cambridge, an eminent Grecian and ancient philosopher. At the end of seven years (December 1877) Professor Mayor, anxious to be relieved of part of his work, suggested the division of his chair into two separate professorships, one Latin, the other Greek. When the council rejected his proposal, he begged (February 1878) that he might be allowed to make arrangements for assistance in his work with " Mr Alfred Milner, a former highly distinguished student of the college." To this request the council gave its consent for the remainder of the then current session. Next session, however (May 1879), he resigned the classical professorship altogether, and took instead of it a new professorship of moral philosophy, which involved the giving of no more than one lecture a week, intended primarily for theological students. The classical chair was filled by the appointment of Mr G. C. W. Warr, late fellow of Trinity College, Cambridge, who since 1874 had been an extremely efficient lecturer in the department. (3) On December 8, 1871, Mr Samuel Rawson Gardiner, late student of Christ Church, Oxford, was elected lecturer in history, to assist Professor Brewer, who, since

C. H. Pearson's departure in 1865, had taught both history and literature. Gardiner's appointment, an excellent one, suggests that the religious tests at the college were being applied with considerable laxity; for Gardiner was a son-in-law of Edward Irving, and until 1866 he had been a deacon in the Catholic Apostolic Church. He was, however, rapidly establishing his reputation as the greatest living authority upon the men and movements of the early seventeenth century. At the end of five years (November 1876) he was made full professor of history, Mr Brewer having resigned the historical portion of his work on his appointment to the crown living of Toppesfield in Essex. At the urgent request of the council Mr Brewer consented to continue for a time his professorship of English; but at the end of twelve months he found that the task of coming in weekly from his remote and inaccessible parish was more than his strength could stand. Hence, on October 12, 1877, he laid his resignation before the council, and severed a connexion with the college that had lasted for thirty-eight years. The council, in a resolution of exceptional cordiality, expressed their regret at his departure, and their appreciation of his invaluable services.[1]

Mr John Wesley Hales, sometime fellow of Christ's College, Cambridge, since 1867 a master in the school, and for a short time (1868–69) lecturer in the evening classes, was appointed professor of the English language and literature in his room. In commemoration of Professor Brewer's long and faithful service to the college a sum of £130 was collected, the interest on which was to go to provide an annual prize of books " for the best work in modern history throughout the preceding academical year." The first award went to Thomas Bailey Saunders in 1879.

§ 6. *The Evening Class Department*

The same energy and resource as Dr Barry showed in reviving the department of general literature and science, and in turning its activities into new directions, were displayed in maintaining and extending the flourishing evening class department. Dr Jelf had made it his practice to sit and see the evening students as they arrived at the beginning of each

---

[1] Mr Brewer, unhappily, was not destined to enjoy his rural leisure for long. He caught a chill when attending a sick parishioner in February 1879, and after a three days' illness died of heart-failure. An excellent memoir by his colleague, Professor Henry Wace, is prefixed to his memorial volume entitled *English Studies* (1881).

session. Not content with this inaugural inspection, Dr Barry himself commenced to teach in the department. On October 8, 1869, he opened the winter's work by delivering a noteworthy lecture, which was printed and published at the request of the staff, on *The Relations of Technical to General Education.* In this lecture he emphasized the growing importance of technical education, expressed the opinion that " the day is coming, or come, when no man ignorant of physical science will be called a thoroughly educated man "; but contended, all the same, that, as the life is more than meat and the body than raiment, so the culture of the mind is even more essential for the development of personality than the training of the hand; concluding that " technical education should not be predominant or exclusive, but should grow out of general education." The same session (1869–70) Dr Barry began to give regular instruction by taking over from Professor Plumptre the Wednesday evening divinity lectures: he commenced with a course on " the authorship, general subjects, and internal connexion of the books of the New Testament."

More important, however, than the direct instruction that Dr Barry gave in the evening department was his complete and masterly reorganization of the whole curriculum. This reorganization was rendered necessary partly by the immense and chaotic variety of subjects that had come to be included in the syllabus, and partly by the increasing rivalry of polytechnics and other evening institutes, largely modelled on King's College, whose attractions caused a marked diminution in the numbers attending the classes of the department. First, the teachers of the department were constituted a board, with Professor Leone Levi as dean. Secondly, through the instrumentality of this board, the subjects of instruction were classified into four groups—viz., (1) law; (2) civil service; (3) commerce; (4) practical arts and crafts—in each of which diplomas and honours certificates could be attained, and for proficiency in which a number of prizes were—largely through private beneficence—instituted.[1]

The reorganization here indicated was effected at the very beginning of Dr Barry's principalship: it was reported as in full and successful working at the general court held on

---

[1] For example, in 1872, the council announced a £10 prize in commerce from Messrs Duncan and Co., and a £10 prize in law from Messrs Matheson and Co.; in 1873 the Lord Chancellor gave £10 for a special prize in law ; in 1874 the National Provincial Bank instituted prizes in banking ; in 1878 and 1880 the Clothworkers' Company established scholarships and exhibitions in applied science; and so on.

May 13, 1870. During the remaining thirteen years of his rule no fewer than eight further developments of the evening department took place, bringing, in the aggregate, over 1400 additional students to the college every year. Two significant features of these novel departures have to be noted: first, some of them were so elementary in standard and so non-academic in character that they had to be described as extra-collegiate—*i.e.*, held in the college, but not of it; secondly, one of them involved the bringing of women as students within the sacred precincts. A table showing these new classes with the numbers attending them year by year will be found at the end of this chapter. A few words concerning each of them, taken in chronological order, must be given here.

I. *Gilbart Lectures in Banking.* On February 9, 1872,

> an offer was received from the trustees of the late Mr Gilbart offering to present to the college the sum of £1250 L. and N.W. Railway Debenture Stock for the purpose of providing an endowment for an annual course of lectures on the subject of banking.

The " Mr Gilbart " referred to in this communication was Mr James William Gilbart, F.R.S., one of the pioneers of joint-stock banking in the metropolis, manager of the London and Westminster Bank 1833–59, and author of several standard treatises on banking. The council accepted the offer, and agreed to arrange an evening course of six lectures each year between January and June (every lecture to be commenced with a reading from one or other of Gilbart's scriptures), open without fee to all interested enough to come, and civilized enough to behave themselves. The first Gilbart lecturer appointed was Professor Leone Levi, and he worked off his course between February and April 1872. This course, says the report of April 15,

> was attended by fully 300 students, about 50 of whom afterwards voluntarily attended an examination on the subjects of the course. The council also received gifts of money from Mr Gilbart's trustees, and from the managers of the London Joint Stock Bank, to be distributed in the shape of books as prizes to the most deserving of the students attending these lectures.

Other banks later followed the example of the Joint Stock Bank, and offered prizes to their own clerks who attended the course and passed the examination.

II. *The Home Civil Service.* In 1875 the Government extended the examination system from the appointment of first-grade clerks to the appointment of the limitless second and third grades. A certain Mr William Braginton, a man of energy and initiative, had started as a private venture various classes for the training of candidates for these competitive tests. In March 1875 he wrote to suggest the connexion of these classes with the college: he wanted the use of the college rooms and the prestige of the college name. The council left the matter in Dr Barry's hands, and without a moment's hesitation Dr Barry closed with Mr Braginton's offer. During the first session (1875–76) 172 young men of the clerkly class came to the college to be crammed; in the seventh (1882–83) so successful was Mr Braginton's machine and so widespread the fame of its products that no fewer than 866 youths submitted to its operations. A further development occurred in 1881, of which more anon.

III. *Workshop*. In 1875 an evening workshop class was instituted. It began with thirty students, and it rarely drew more than that number. The Clothworkers' Company showed interest in it, encouraging it by offering prizes for metal-work and woodwork, and by providing it with a testing-machine worth £200 in 1880.

IV. *London University Examinations*. By 1876 the number of evening students preparing for London University examinations was sufficiently great to warrant special mention in the annual report, the examination specially in vogue being apparently the teachers' diploma in the theory and practice of education.

V. *Extension Lectures*. This same year, 1876, saw the formation of the *London Society for the Extension of University Teaching*, of which the Right Hon. G. J. Goschen (later Lord Goschen) was president. King's College was invited to send a representative to the council of the society, and Dr Barry was appointed. Neither Dr Barry nor the governing body of King's College was very keen on the new movement. They felt it to be a rival to the King's College evening classes. The report of 1879 contains the significant passage:

> In relation to the movement which has this year been going on for the extension of university teaching to those engaged in London in various forms of business, the council feel with much satisfaction that this is in great degree the work which King's College has been successfully doing in its evening classes now for many years, and to many hundreds or even thousands of students. While they will be glad to see new centres of usefulness created for this important work, they at the same time believe that it may be carried out in very great measure by a simple use of the

machinery already existing and in efficient action at King's College and elsewhere.

What this naïve utterance ignores is the fact that extension lectures were open to women, while King's College evening classes were not. How long would it be possible for the college to show itself oblivious to the existence of half the human race? One effect of the extension movement on the college was, probably, some diminution in the number of men attending the evening classes: the figures steadily fell from 630 in 1868 to 384 in 1883. Extension fees were lower than those of King's College; extension courses were more popular and less severe in character; extension lecturers carried culture to the suburbs, and did not require suburbans to travel to the Strand.

VI. *Public Lectures.* It was probably the popularity of the extension courses on social and political problems that caused the college council to entertain suggestions that popular public lectures should be given in the large theatre from time to time to audiences of working men and others. In 1876 and again in 1877 Professor Leone Levi delivered, on Saturday afternoons, free of charge, courses on *Work and Wages.* Professor Levi's views—which were those of Cobden and Mill—apparently did not accord with those of some of his audience, for on April 28, 1876, a letter was sent by Mr Hodgson Pratt, vice-chairman of the working-men's club, asking permission to give in the theatre a series of counter-lectures on the same theme.

> The council resolved to inform Mr Pratt that, Professor Levi being a professor of the college, they had allowed him to deliver within the college a course of lectures to working men, but they were unable to lend their rooms for general controversial discussions.

VII. *Practical Art.* The establishment by the government of the Science and Art Department at South Kensington, with its large scheme of local instruction and central examination, led the council to institute in 1879 an evening school of practical art, which was placed under the superintendence of Mr W. J. Glenny, professor of geometrical drawing in the engineering department. During the first session thirty-one students attended, the majority of whom secured prizes or certificates. Never again, however, during Dr Barry's principalship, was the number quite so high. In 1880 Messrs Liberty and Co. presented to the school seventy-five specimens of Eastern art for its comfort and encouragement.

VIII. *Female Clerkships.* In 1881 the council was compelled to face in a small preliminary way the problem of the admission

310

of women to the college buildings. The government, through Mr Henry Fawcett, was offering positions in the post office, attainable by competitive examination, to those proud and perfunctory young ladies who maintain the traditions of the civil service in respect of the distribution of stamps. Hence, on June 17, a letter from Mr Braginton came before the council expressing the opinion that

> it was desirable that classes should be at once formed in connection with the college in preparation for the examinations.

He added, however, that

> having been informed that such classes would not be allowed within the walls of the college itself, he had ascertained that for a moderate sum the necessary accommodation could be secured at Exeter Hall.

He therefore asked the council's permission to make the requisite arrangements. The council sanctioned the proposal made by Mr Braginton. The duplication of classes, however, and the consequent dissipation of energy, was extremely irritating and wasteful. Hence, on October 14, 1881, the secretary, Mr J. W. Cunningham, greatly daring, and drawing on the treasury of merit accumulated during thirty-six blameless years, ventured to make to the council

> a proposal to allow Mr Braginton to conduct his evening female post office clerkship classes in the classrooms of the school, the pupils to enter by the school door and to be entirely cut off from the remainder of the college.

This audacious suggestion obviously deprived the council of breath. Although, as we shall see in a moment, one slight concession to women had already (March 1880) been made to women in another department, this demand opened up possibilities too appalling to be settled off-hand. So the matter was adjourned to a special *ad hoc* meeting of the council to be held on November 11. At this meeting, after long and solemn debate,

> it was resolved to allow as an experiment the civil service women's class (candidates for post office appointments) to be held in one of the classrooms of the school instead of at Exeter Hall as at present, the young women to enter by the separate school entrance and to be entirely cut off from the college.

Thus, in the autumn of 1881, through the agency of the young women attending the " evening female post office clerkship classes," was the exclusive masculinity of King's College sapped from a schoolroom in the basement. So, significantly, was the second half-century of the history of the college inaugurated.

§ 7. *"Lectures for Ladies"*

Although the first definite breaches in the exclusive masculinity of King's were made in 1880 and 1881, precisely at the time when the college was celebrating its jubilee, powerful attacks from the feminist forces had been going on for a considerable period. A detailed account of them need not here be given, for they are set forth in an appendix by the authoritative pen of Miss Hilda Oakeley. A summary, however, is necessary in order to complete the record of Dr Barry's notable innovations.

From very early days King's College, although unofficially, had been interested in women's education. Members of the college staff in general, and F. D. Maurice in particular, had played a prominent part in the foundation of Queen's College in 1848, and they had greatly assisted in the establishment of Bedford College in 1849. The association of these two women's colleges with King's still continued. During the period under review Professor Plumptre was principal of Queen's (1875-77), Dr Barry and Professor Leathes served on its council, while several members of King's staff regularly lectured to its students. As to Bedford College, no fewer than six teachers of King's—Gardiner (history), Hales (literature), Buchheim (German), Seeley (geography), Hullah (harmony), and Monk (singing)—figured on its professoriate. These two institutions, humbly housed in Harley Street and Baker Street respectively, had for over twenty years unostentatiously imparted to young ladies an elegant education of the finishing-school type, when an immense stimulus to the feminist movement was given by the Education Act of 1870 (which recognized no sex distinction whatsoever) and by the discussions and controversies that arose out of it. Secondary educationists took up the challenge thrown down by the radical pioneers of elementary education for all. Old endowments long appropriated for boys' schools were claimed as equally available for girls'; and in many cases were secured. In 1872 the Girls' Public Day School Trust was founded. The improvement of girls' secondary education gave rise to an imperative demand for the provision of facilities for the higher culture. Hence Girton College was established at Cambridge in 1873 and Newnham in 1875. The medical profession was thrown open to women in 1876; and, most important of all, in 1878 the University of London secured a supplementary charter which enabled it to admit women to its degrees. Hence during the seventies numerous new verses had to be added to that famous old poem which begins:

> Common are to either sex
> *Artifex* and *opifex*.

It was, further, mainly in order to meet the demand for the higher education of women that during the same period—viz., in 1873 at Oxford and three years later in London—the University Extension movement was inaugurated.

No one was more keenly alive to the significance and importance of this social revolution than was Dr Barry. He was a devoted disciple of F. D. Maurice, that zealous pioneer of the higher feminism; at Cheltenham he had witnessed the growth of a notable " ladies' college," and had had as his own vice-principal the husband of Josephine Butler. At King's he found a number of his staff actively engaged in teaching women, at Queen's College and at Bedford College, in their unregulated leisure hours, and he encouraged them to continue. He himself was, as we have seen, actually invited (November 1872) to combine the principalship of Queen's with that of King's, and would gladly have done so if the council of King's College had allowed him. His, distinctly, was the initiative which led, in the spring of 1871, to the experimental institution of " a course of lectures for ladies in Richmond and Twickenham in connection with King's College, London." It was a most interesting early manifestation of the " extension movement." Dr Barry received the cordial support of such college lecturers as J. B. Mayor, who acted as secretary, and such masters of the school as the Rev. J. Twentyman. Richmond and Twickenham were chosen as the sphere for this missionary effort, not because their inhabitants were abnormally benighted, but because the principal lecturers happened to reside in the neighbourhood. Barry himself delivered the inaugural lecture on May 13, 1871, taking as his subject *The Higher Education of Women*. The lecture is well worth reading, but it is too long to summarize. Three points only can be noted: first, he contended that " higher education cannot stand still while elementary and secondary education are going rapidly ahead "; secondly, he argued that women can claim the higher education because, on the one hand, many of them have to earn their own living, and because, on the other hand, all of them have

313

divinely bestowed faculties to develop; thirdly, he expressed the confident hope that, "although at present they are shut out from King's College, that exclusion will soon be abolished." He well understood that "the inconveniences of access through the bustle of the Strand would prejudice any attempt to open its teaching to ladies," but he indicated that the construction of the new subway from the Thames Embankment would remove this objection. Meanwhile, "if the ladies could not come to King's College, the college itself should show its elasticity of system, and courtesy of tone, by coming to the ladies." Still that blessed word "elasticity"! Lest the ladies of Richmond and Twickenham should be alarmed, a local committee of respectable matrons was established, and it was decreed that "a member of the ladies' committee shall be present at each lecture." Anxious parents were further invited to send chaperones with their daughters, and for these formidable females "general tickets admitting to all the lectures" were provided at a nominal charge. Thus securely safeguarded, the ladies of Richmond and Twickenham ventured to approach the tree of—judiciously pruned—knowledge.

One course of these miscellaneous extension "lectures to ladies" seems to have sufficed to satisfy the cravings of the fair denizens of Richmond and Twickenham. Not until 1875 does any further attempt appear to have been made by Barry and his colleagues to lighten the darkness of the female sex ; and then not Richmond but Kensington was the object of their solicitude. The movement was inaugurated by a memorial from the general board to the council, in response to which the council (June 11, 1875) appointed a committee "to confer with the board on the question of the desirability of giving instruction to women, in connexion with the college, either in the college buildings, or elsewhere." Of the result of this conference I have not been able to find any record. But it is obvious, first, that Barry did not secure permission to admit women into King's College, even by the southern subway; and, secondly, that the committee declined to recommend the college to extend its activities by undertaking the education of women "elsewhere." For the next move, made two and a half years later (November 1877), was an entirely private one, initiated by Dr Barry and Professor G. C. W. Warr, in conjunction with the vicar of Kensington (the Rev. W. D. Maclagan, afterward bishop of Lichfield and archbishop of York) and a number of local ladies, among whom Mrs Spottiswoode, Miss Shirrett, and Miss A. Swanwick were prominent.

On November 19

> the principal having asked whether the council would object to himself and the professors organising a series of lectures to women at South Kensington, it was resolved that the subject be postponed for the principal to prepare the details of the scheme.

On December 14

> the principal laid before the council a scheme which was proposed for delivering, chiefly by the staff of the college, a series of lectures to ladies on divinity, modern languages, classics, geography, and some of the sciences. . . . Most of the lectures were to be given in the Kensington Vestry Hall, but it was desired that those in chemistry and physics should be given at the college, where a laboratory and all necessary apparatus would be at hand. The principal asked the council (1) to consent to the publication of the scheme in the name of the principal and professors of King's College, London; (2) to allow the lectures on chemistry and physics to be given at the college between 11 and 2 on Saturdays. The council assented to the principal's first proposal, but declined admitting ladies to the college.

The principal and professors, then, duly went ahead. An inaugural meeting was held in the Kensington Vestry Hall on February 6, 1878, and during the succeeding months lectures in divinity, and in various branches of arts and science, were delivered. The venture was eminently successful : " the attendance exceeded all expectations, averaging 500 throughout the year "—whatever that may mean. Hence in 1879 the unofficial committee resolved to hire a house of their own, and found one in Observatory Avenue, Kensington. In March 1880 Professor Delamotte asked to be allowed to admit ladies on Saturday mornings to the sacred precincts of King's College for the purpose of teaching them fine art. The matter was long debated, but finally (a triumph for Dr Barry) " the council by a majority of votes sanctioned the experiment being tried for one year," provided that at the end of that time the professor would " give an honest report on how the plan had worked." This was the first breach in the sex-exclusiveness of King's. The second came, as we have seen, next year in connexion with the civil service classes. The third was not long delayed. On November 10, 1882,

> the principal made application in the name of the college staff who were giving science lectures in the ladies' classes at Kensington for leave to hold classes for ladies at the college on Saturdays, and stated that in the two cases in which the council had already permitted ladies to attend at the college—viz., to Professor

Delamotte for Saturdays, and to Mr Braginton for evening work—no difficulty of any kind had arisen, but that everything had worked satisfactorily.

Though this request had been before declined, there is no indication that it was now even debated. Mrs Partington recognized at last that her mop was an inadequate implement with which to check the inflow of the ocean, and, without further to-do, " the council granted the application."

Between the admission of lady art students to King's in 1880, and the admission of lady science students in 1882, some extremely important events had taken place both at Kensington and in the Strand. On November 12, 1880,

> the principal reported that in consequence of the great success of the King's College lectures for ladies it was intended to attempt the establishment of a permanent college for the higher education of women at Kensington, and that the name of *King's College for Women* had been suggested for the new college. It was intended that the principal of King's College, London, should be *ex officio* chairman of the council of the new college, having the power of nominating teachers for the approval of the council, and that one-third of the members of the council should be taken from the academical staff of the King's College, London.

The council postponed decision of this important matter for a month, and then (December 10, 1880), after discussing it " at much length, partly in the presence and with the assistance of the principal, and partly in his absence," resolved: (1) to " decline to allow the name of King's College to be used in the designation of the proposed college "; (2) to permit the principal to act in his private capacity, provided that (3) the scheme of the new college should be such as to meet with the council's approval.

This limited concession did not satisfy Dr Barry and his colleagues. During the Christmas vacation eighty of them presented a strongly worded memorial to the council begging that body to give its official sanction to the scheme, to associate it with King's College, and to make the extension of the college type of education to women the outstanding feature of the jubilee year, 1881. They were not content merely to be allowed to found another " Queen's College " out in the wilds of Kensington; they wanted a new-model institution which should be an integral part of King's, even if separated from it by sex and site. The council, impressed by the power and passion of the octogint, appointed a committee (January 14, 1881) to consider the problems raised. Sex and site were the difficulties, apart from disinclination and prejudice. Did the charter of King's College authorize the council to furnish instruction to women, or to erect buildings elsewhere than in the Strand? On February 11 the committee reported (1) that they considered it " desirable if possible to extend to women higher education upon the same principles as those which govern King's College " and (2) that they were of opinion that the council themselves should undertake the scheme for the extension, provided they could secure legal powers and adequate funds. This report came before a special and largely attended meeting of the council on February 25, 1881, and

> after full discussion it was resolved unanimously that it is desirable to establish a department of King's College, London, for the higher education of women, to be conducted on the same principles as the existing departments of education at this college, provided (1) that the sum of £25,000 be raised in the first instance for the purpose of providing suitable buildings, furniture and apparatus, and (2) that the necessary statutory powers be obtained.

The founding of the women's department of King's College at Kensington thus became the central feature of the celebrations of the jubilee year, 1881. Dr Lightfoot, Bishop of Durham, made it the burden of an important section of his jubilee sermon, preached in Westminster Abbey on June 21. A great meeting was held under the presidency of the archbishop of Canterbury, Dr A. C. Tait, three days later, for the purpose of inaugurating a special fund. On July 2 the Prince and Princess of Wales attended the prize-giving in the college and blessed the proposal. Meantime steps were taken to secure the necessary statutory powers, and these were ultimately obtained by means of an Act of Parliament—drafted by Sir Edmund Beckett, afterward Lord Grimthorpe—which received the royal assent on May 19, 1882.

Money, however, as was usually the case with King's College appeals, came in exceedingly slowly. Although the principal and staff of King's College contributed £1250; although members of the council of the college added another £1000, and although the Clothworkers' Company gave £500, after two years of effort the total amount raised was barely £6000, out of the £25,000 aimed at. Hence the idea of erecting a fine collegiate building on a new site had to be abandoned, and the council had to be content to purchase a modest mansion in Kensington Square. A decision to make this purchase was taken on December 10, 1882; but difficulties supervened, and before they were removed Canon Barry had ceased to be principal.

The work at Kensington, however, continued to go on vigorously and successfully in the temporary buildings, the staff of the college showing much zeal and self-sacrifice in their missionary labours. For instance, on February 9, 1883,

> an application was received from Professor Warr asking for the sanction of the council to the organization of about six dramatic performances for the benefit of the fund being raised for the department for the higher education of women, the entertainment to consist of scenes and tableaux from Homer, and to be given in the large hall of the college, the parts to be taken as far as possible by students or ex-students of the classes at King's College and at Kensington, with help where needed from the outside. After long discussion, the council resolved to comply with Professor Warr's wishes, provided ladies took no share in the acting and their parts were taken by men.[1]

§ 8. *The Theological Department*

The experiment of providing "lectures for ladies" was not the only notable innovation made by Dr Barry during this period of enterprising elasticity. Almost equally remarkable was his expansion of the theological department to include men of mature years still occupied in the affairs of the world, but cognisant of the call of the church. On his arrival in 1868 the theological department excited his intense interest; but its condition and its prospects caused him much apprehension. As a disciple of Maurice, and a man deeply concerned with social problems, he was profoundly impressed by the advantages of a training in theology carried on, not in the abnormal seclusion of a diocesan college, but amid the bustle of the busy world, and in conjunction with the general work of a seminary of secular education. His first report to the annual court (1869) struck a new note—the authentic Barry-tone:

> The theological department of King's College possesses advantages second only to those which are the fruit of an university career. Its position in London gives it unusual opportunities not only for securing the services of professors of the highest class, but also for making its students familiar with the direction of modern thought, and practically acquainted with the duties and difficulties with which they are likely to meet in the present day. And the fact that this theological department

[1] The parts of Helen, Andromache, and Penelope were not after all taken by men. They were taken respectively by Mrs Beerbohm Tree, Mrs Andrew Lang, and Miss Jane Harrison. But they were taken not in the hall of King's College, but in a room at Cromwell House. A full account of a notable performance is given in the *King's College Ladies' Magazine* for April 1899.

does not exist in isolation, but in close connexion with the other branches of a great institution, general in its scope and presenting various forms of teaching and character, tends in the highest degree to preserve it from any professional narrowness or from devotion to any ecclesiastical party.

In spite of these numerous advantages—high-class professors, contact with modern thought, contiguity to the slums, association with medicals and engineers, freedom from sectarian narrowness—the theological department did not flourish. Perhaps some of these " advantages," and, in particular, its lack of " devotion to any ecclesiastical party," were regarded in some quarters rather as disadvantages. At any rate, the numbers of students in the department, which in 1853 had been at their maximum (78), were only 50 in 1868; and from this figure they steadily declined, until in 1876 they touched the bottom with 24—that is to say, with only three students to each teacher.

The starving members of the theological board were naturally much perturbed at this steady and rapid decline of their department, especially as it occurred at a time when, owing to the growth of population, the subdivision of urban parishes, the building of new churches, and the activity of missionary enterprise, the supply of candidates for holy orders hardly kept pace with the great and increasing demand. Often did they meet in anxious conclave to discuss the causes of this strange diminution. They came to the conclusion that the deplorable falling-off in the entries to the theological department of King's College was due mainly to two things— viz., (1) the new practice of admitting unattached or non-collegiate students to Oxford and Cambridge, and (2) the increase throughout the country of theological colleges which —because they were *not* in touch with the world, and *were* devoted to the interests of one or other of the sects in the church—attracted subscriptions and endowments so considerable as to enable fees to be reduced to a minimum. How did they propose to cope with this new and formidable rivalry? They did five things, four of which were not very effective, but the last of which was so successful that in 1881 they were able to announce triumphantly that the numbers in the department, viz., 79, were higher than they had ever been in the whole course of its history. What were these five things? First, they reorganized and improved the curriculum, adding new subjects (in particular mental and moral philosophy), systematizing the examinations, reducing the number of lectures, allowing more time for private reading, enlarging the library, and so on. Secondly, they tried to attract graduates from the universities by granting to them (July 1869) " the privilege of obtaining the associateship in one year, instead of two years, on condition of their passing at entrance the examination required of other students at the close of their first year." This concession was approved by the two archbishops, but not by Dr Jelf, who, from Oxford, vehemently denounced this curtailment of professional training. Thirdly, they secured from the university of Durham (December 1876) the reciprocal concession that theological associates of King's College should be qualified to attain its valuable degree in arts after a residence in Durham of one academical year, which (since the Durham terms are short) meant an actual period of about 180 days. Fourthly, they made efforts to secure an income independent of fees, realizing and admitting that " the department at present suffers from the competition of other colleges which, having some endowment, are able to receive students at a lower scale of payment." These efforts, however, were totally unavailing. The generosity of churchmen, both high and low, was flowing in the direction of those other colleges which did not offer the advantage of freedom from " professional narrowness or devotion to any ecclesiastical party." Then, fifthly and lastly, came Dr Barry's great and successful idea that the principle of the evening classes should be extended to the theological department. The realization of this idea not only resulted in the establishment of a new section of college activity; it also resulted (as a glance at the table at the end of this chapter will show) in a remarkable stimulus to the day classes.

On February 11, 1876,

the principal laid before the council the following resolution, which had been passed unanimously by the board of professors belonging to the theological department: (1) that it is desirable that classes should be open in the evening as part of the course of the theological department, attendance for two years in the evening to be reckoned as equivalent to one year in the department as at present constituted; (2) that the instruction given in the evening classes should be given either by the professors of the several subjects or by lecturers appointed by the council to teach under their direction.

The principal was asked to find out what the bishops thought of the proposal. On March 10 he reported that he " had had an interview with the archbishop of Canterbury on the subject of the proposed theological evening classes, and that his grace approved of the project." The bishop of London had already expressed his concurrence. Hence the council resolved that

> Subject to the approval of such other of the bishops as were connected with the neighbourhood of London, or with King's College, the principal was authorised to settle the scheme with the finance committee in time for the next council.

On April 7, 1876,

> the whole subject of the proposed new arrangements in the theological department was considered at full length, and it was resolved that the scheme proposed to the council by the theological board on February 11 be adopted and that the terminal fees be fixed at £6 6s.

This important innovation is referred to as follows in the annual report issued three weeks later. The attention of both the theological board and the council, it says,

> has been drawn to the fact that numerous applications are received from young men engaged in various professions who are desirous of entering holy orders, but are unable to give up for so long a period as two years the work by which they maintain themselves. Hence the theological board recommended that an option be given to students of taking a three years' course, during the first two years of which instruction shall be given in the evening, so that it will be necessary to give up other occupation only during the last year of their study. The council, finding that this proposal commended itself to the approval of the archbishops of Canterbury and York, and of the bishops of London, Winchester, and Rochester, have resolved to try the system as an experiment, beginning in October next. They trust it may do something to meet the present acknowledged difficulty of obtaining a sufficient number of well-qualified candidates for holy orders, and at the same time extend the advantages of the theological department to a larger number of students.[1]

Several important changes in the staff of the theological department occurred during this period of fifteen years. (1) In November 1874 Canon J. C. Robertson, professor of

---

[1] The first time-table for the evening classes in theology, October 1876, was as follows :

> Monday, 7–9 : Latin
> Tuesday, 7–9 : Old Testament and Hebrew
> Wednesday, 6–7 : Vocal Music
>   ,,   7–8 : Dogmatic Theology
>   ,,   8–9 : Public Reading
> Thursday, 7–9 : Greek Testament
> Friday, 7–8 : Ecclesiastical History
>   ,,   8 9 : Prayer Book

ecclesiastical history, because of continued ill-health, resigned the office which he had held with faithful efficiency for eleven years. The following January, out of nine applicants for the post, the council elected the Rev. Henry Wace, M.A., chaplain of Lincoln's Inn and an honorary fellow of King's College—which college he had entered as a student in 1853.[1] (2) In June 1877 the council, on the recommendation of Dr Barry, created a new professorship of logic and mental philosophy, and to this chair they appointed the Rev. H. W. Watkins of Balliol College, Oxford, who had been on the staff as chaplain and censor since 1875, and as lecturer in the exegesis of the New Testament (specially for evening students) since 1876. Mr Watkins retained the chair (the title of which was changed to "logic and metaphysics") even when, at the end of 1878, he was made warden of St Augustine's, Canterbury. "Moral philosophy," however, which had hitherto been included within its scope, was separated from it and assigned to Professor J. B. Mayor. In 1880 Mr Watkins was appointed archdeacon of Northumberland, and from that distance not even he could work a class at King's. Hence the Rev. A. W. Momerie (né Mummery), a brilliant but erratic fellow of St John's College, Cambridge, succeeded him in his chair, while Dr Maclear, headmaster of King's College School, took over the wardenship of St Augustine's. (3) In 1879 the professor of pastoral theology, the Rev. S. Cheetham, was appointed archdeacon of Southwark. For three years he succeeded in combining his archidiaconal with his professorial duties; but at the end of 1882 he resigned his chair, to which (January 12, 1883) the Rev. H. B. Swete was elected, with the Rev. H. C. Shuttleworth as lecturer under him. (4) Last, but most notable of all, on November 11, 1881,

> the principal informed the council that he had just received a letter from Professor Plumptre informing him that he had accepted the appointment of Dean of Wells, and that it would be necessary for him to resign the chair of exegesis of the New Testament at Christmas.

The council, while congratulating Dr Plumptre on his " well-earned ecclesiastical promotion," expressed

> their sincere regret at the approaching severance of his long connexion with the college, and their deep sense of obligation for the invaluable services rendered by him to the institution during the last thirty-five years, which have earned for him the respect and affection of all who have during that long period been

[1] See above, p. 272.

connected with the college, and which will still leave behind them the influence of a high example of ability, conscientiousness, and devotion.

As lecturer in divinity, 1847, professor of pastoral theology, 1854, and finally, in succession to Dr Ellicott, professor of exegesis since 1863, he had been connected with the department of theology almost from its start. Although his prolonged contiguity to the Thames never threatened to set that river on fire, his sound scholarship, his amiable disposition, his self-obliterating altruism, helped greatly to assuage the asperities which naturally arise in a college which enjoys the advantages of comprehensiveness. There were twelve candidates for the vacant chair of exegesis; four were summoned for interviews, and from among these, on December 9, 1881, the Rev. G. H. Curteis, M.A., Canon of Lichfield, was chosen.

Two minor matters of interest may be mentioned in conclusion. First, in October 1871, Archbishop Tait, knowing the urgent need of the theological department for a hall of residence for its students, generously offered to hand over the Lollards' and Chaplain's Towers at Lambeth Palace for the purpose. These venerable and appropriate buildings would, he said, provide thirteen sets of apartments, besides rooms for library, hall, and kitchens. Dr Barry was most anxious to accept the gracious offer, and to secure for the theological department of King's the advantages of residence, combined with the hall-mark of Lambeth, if not of Lollardy. The council, however, after appointing a committee to consider the proposal, felt compelled in the end (February 9, 1872) to decline it on account of (1) the expense that would be involved in fitting and furnishing the apartments, and (2) the impossibility of obtaining any security of tenure. A cordial vote of thanks, therefore, terminated the negotiations. Secondly, early in 1883, the council received a letter from the Rev. B. W. Gibsone, vicar of Wolvey in Warwickshire, offering to the college the half-advowson (the other half belonging to the see of Worcester) of his vicarage. In a picturesque passage explaining the causes and circumstances of his offer, he said:

> Wolvey, in Shakespeare's forest of Arden, is interesting for its Norman church, its Marian martyrdom, for a critical battle, for sites of an ancient hall, a hermitage, a preceptory of the Templars, for proximity to the Watling Street and the Fosse Way, which here cross, and as being the most central parish in England.

The council without hesitation accepted with thanks Mr

Gibsone's offer, which promised to place in their hands the alternate patronage of a living worth £300 a year.[1]

§ 9. *King's College School*

The principal feature that characterized King's College School during the headmastership of Dr Maclear—which almost synchronizes with Dr Barry's principalship of the college—was its growing autonomy and independence. It ceased almost entirely to perform its original function as a feeder of the college; and its multitudinous presence in the basement of that institution became an increasing inconvenience to itself and a swelling nuisance to its neighbour.

When Dr Maclear succeeded Dr Major in 1866 the fortunes of the school were at a very low ebb. Its numbers had fallen from over 500 to under 350; its discipline was bad; its moral tone unsatisfactory; its efficiency chequered. Dr Maclear, whose six years' experience as an assistant-master in the school had given him a thorough insight into its needs, was a man of great energy, lucid mind, strong will, quick conscience, and a man whose active piety contrasted sharply with the amiable formalism of his predecessor. He set to work with zeal and determination to reform and rejuvenate the school. Several venerable veterans, who but for poverty would long before have retired, were pensioned off; one reverend gentleman, whose failure to maintain order was notorious, was deprived of his boarding-house, and warned that unless he could secure control of his class he would have to depart; another reverend gentleman, the freedom of whose translations from, and disquisitions on, the more doubtful classics had long been a source of scandal, was summarily dismissed, in spite of the fact that he had served the school for thirty-two years and was over sixty in age. Among the new men brought in to take the vacant places were several destined to long and honourable connexion with the school—*e.g.*, Mr G. Wotherspoon (1878) and Mr W. J. Clarke (1880).

In the school itself many important changes were made. First and foremost, religion was made a much more vital matter than it had been for many preceding years. The scripture lessons (some of them conducted by Dr Barry) took on a new and more devotional tone; the hour of opening

---

[1] During the course of negotiations in 1884 it appeared that it would be necessary for the council to assist in the purchase of the advowson. This they declined to do. Hence, finally, in March 1886, the matter fell through.

school was shifted from 9 to 9.30, so that all boys could attend morning prayer in the college chapel; a confirmation class was instituted which in its very first year prepared 42 boys for the bishop's ministrations—the first confirmation service ever held in the chapel of King's—on March 25, 1867. Meantime, while piety was thus cultivated, naughtiness was held in check by the introduction of corporal punishment for small boys (November 1868) and for large ones (March 1869). About the same time—viz., in the school session 1867–68—a notable piece of reorganization took place. A "Lower School" was created as a separate administrative department. It consisted of the third, upper second, lower second, and first classes; and it was "intended to give to the pupils entering it a sound elementary and preparatory education, and to fit them for subsequently being moved to either of the higher divisions"— *i.e.*, classical or modern. This Lower School was placed under the authority of the Rev. George Rust, who for nineteen years had been a faithful and capable assistant-master in the school. In 1873, owing to rapid increase in numbers,

> the headmaster thought it well to make a further division of the school, and to create a Middle School, under the charge of Mr Rust, the master of the Lower School, subdivided like the Upper School into a classical and a modern department.

Mr Rust, however, unfortunately died, after an absence of only four days from his duties, in March 1874, and his post as "master of the middle and lower school" was not filled up, Dr Maclear himself undertaking the functions of the office.

By this time the numbers in the school were distinctly and rapidly on the up-grade once again. The 344 pupils whom Dr Maclear had taken over in 1866 had become 439 in 1871; and in two more years all previous records for the school were passed with a roll of 521. In this condition of things Dr Maclear prepared and presented to the council an important memorandum, dated March 3, 1873. He indicated, first, the causes of the gratifying return to prosperity, specially mentioning four—viz., (1) improved discipline; (2) better classification of pupils; (3) more masters; and (4) establishment of matriculation and other special classes. Secondly, he discussed and condemned a suggestion that numbers should be restricted. Thirdly, he vehemently opposed a proposal emanating from the under-employed professors upstairs that at a certain age —*e.g.*, sixteen—boys should be compelled to leave the school and enter the college. "During my own experience, which extends over thirteen years," he said,

I have never known an anxiety to proceed into the college evinced by any but two types of boys, *first*, diligent boys who wish to enter the medical or applied science departments; and, *secondly*, extremely idle boys who want to escape school discipline altogether.

Fourthly, he clearly proclaimed the independence of the school:

> Boys intending to go up to the universities prefer to go up from the school, and if they like the school and have confidence in its teaching and administration, it is but natural that they should do so.[1]

He had no intention of being a mere feeder to the college:

> As regards the general literature department, it is certain that the desire on the part of our boys to enter it is the exception rather than the rule.

Finally, since the school could not be restricted in numbers, and since no age limit could be imposed, all that remained was to say " let them all come " and " let them all stay." But in that case more accommodation was urgently needed.

The council accepted the policy so emphatically stated, and before the end of the year (December 1873) provided two new classrooms by cutting off a big slice from each end of the covered playground—which since 1870 had been fitted up as a gymnasium. But still the numbers grew. In 1874 there were 558 on the roll, and once again the council debated whether or not they should fix 600 as a maximum. Once again, however, they decided to let things take their course. The consequence was that in 1880 the numbers touched their high-water mark at 631. Hence still further classroom accommodation was required, and, at a cost of £750, two more rooms were thrown out in the area at the extreme north end of the basement corridor. The limits of expansion were reached.

While numbers were thus going up, the quality of the work done in the school was showing something of its old brilliance. In 1874 the council agreed to Dr Maclear's proposal that the better boys should be allowed to sit for the newly instituted joint board (Oxford and Cambridge) examinations. The results were remarkable. Within five years the school achieved distinctions which gave it a position in the educational world

---

[1] The tendency to keep boys at the school till the age of nineteen and then to send them direct to Oxford or Cambridge was further stimulated by the institution of a Salters' Exhibition (worth £80 a year for four years) open to all pupils of the school, but not to students of the college. It was established by the Salters' Company in October 1879 for the encouragement of natural science.

second only to that of Eton. Old boys, too, began once more to shed lustre on the school by the splendour of their attainments at the universities. This was the period of the triumphs of Sidney Low, F. H. Chase, J. Gow, A. W. Pollard, J. K. Wilson, A. C. Pearson, H. L. Withers, Reginald McKenna, and others. From among pupils of an earlier day, the Rev. William Ince was appointed Regius Professor of Divinity at Oxford (1877); the Rev. W. W. Skeat, Professor of Anglo-Saxon at Cambridge (1878); A. V. Dicey, Vinerian Professor of English Law at Oxford (1882); and W. H. M. Christie, Astronomer Royal (1883).

This cursory record is enough to show that the period of Dr Maclear's headmastership was a time of marvellous recuperation and recovery for the school. The doctor himself, however, was not a man of robust health, and after more than a dozen strenuous years the strain of his responsible office began to tell upon him. Hence in 1880, although with much regret, he felt it wise and right to take the chance of relief which the removal of Archdeacon Watkins to Northumberland gave him, and to accept the proffered wardenship of St Augustine's, Canterbury. He left the school at the end of the summer term, 1880. As a memorial of his most successful reign a sum of £200 was collected for the institution of the "Maclear Divinity Prizes." For the vacant headship there were nine applicants. Of these, four—all, of course, clergymen—were called up for interview, and from the four the one ultimately selected was the Rev. Thomas Henry Stokoe, D.D., of Lincoln College, Oxford, and lately headmaster of Reading School.

§ 10. *The College and the University*

Four things remain to be considered before we conclude this chapter—viz., (1) the constant modification of the college buildings; (2) the supersession of the original charter of 1829 by the statute of 1882; (3) the movement to secure a teaching university for London with King's College as one of its constituent members; and (4) Dr Barry's departure.

I. *The College Buildings.* During this period—as indeed during every period of the century of the existence of the college —the building between the Strand and the river was in a constant state of expansion and modification, alteration and repair. We have noted the two developments that followed the making of the Thames Embankment—viz., the opening up of a new southern approach to the college—an approach whose placidity was calculated to lessen the terrors of any lady students who at any time might be admitted to the college—and the new physiological laboratory. We have also remarked, in passing, the conversion of the covered playground of the school into a gymnasium, and the construction of four new classrooms. Further changes to be recorded were: first, the redecoration of the chapel in 1873, completed in time for a reopening sermon by that notable preacher, an old boy of the school, Canon H. P. Liddon, on November 9; secondly, the improvement of the residence of the clerk of works over the gateway, at a cost of £350, in 1874; thirdly, owing to increased demand for teaching accommodation, the conversion of seven sets of students' apartments at the top of the college into class-rooms, in 1878; and finally, the reseating of the large theatre, at a cost of £245, in 1881.

The conversion of students' apartments into classrooms was not at all due to any diminution in the demand for residence on the part of young men wishing to enter the college. It was due, as we have just said, to the superior claims of the staff for classrooms. A secondary cause was the realization—due to a disastrous fire which did much damage to the refectory in February 1878—that in case of a general conflagration the apartments would be death-traps. The council, therefore, felt it desirable to clear the residents out of the college, and secure accommodation for them elsewhere. At first they planned the building of a hostel—to be called King's College Hall—but the estimated cost of £7300 deterred them; nor did the architect's reduction of his estimate to £6500 lure them to proceed. Then, on March 8, 1878, "a letter was received from the Rev. Francis Grosvenor on the subject of opening a large boarding-house for King's College students at Sutton or the neighbourhood." The council, having through the principal instituted inquiries, granted Mr Grosvenor's request, and his house at Benhilton Park, Sutton, became a recognized hostel to the college. The accommodation provided, however, in this remote elysium was not nearly sufficient to meet the demand. Its expenses, moreover, together with that of daily travel, placed it beyond the means of the majority. Hence, in June 1880,

the secretary stated to the council the increasing difficulty found to arise with respect to the residence of students, and pointed out that the college was seriously suffering in all its departments from the want of a suitable house for young men coming to London from the country.

At the same time he submitted to the council an offer that had reached him of a delectable mansion, with nearly an acre of appurtenant land, close to Clapham Common. The council, however, had to decline the purchase of this rustic paradise, and to postpone the problem of hostel accommodation to more prosperous days.

Here, too, mention may be made of the fact that the old friction with Somerset House continued. For instance, toward the end of 1874 the authorities of Somerset House made some new windows in the east wall of their buildings overlooking King's College. The council wrote to the Board of Works to ask what right Somerset House had thus to intrude upon the privacy of the college. After meditating upon the matter for three months (and, incidentally, completing the windows) the Board of Works replied, February 8, 1875, that they

> were advised that the terms under which the college is held are not such as to enable the council to restrict Her Majesty from opening windows in Somerset House whenever she may think proper.

The matter having thus been made a personal one between the college and its august patron, the council ceased to pursue the question. They could not think of preventing Her Majesty from enjoying the benefit of fresh air, whether in Somerset House or elsewhere. Enough for them to make sure that whenever she should come and—as a relief from the asphyxiating atmosphere of the office of the supervisor of income-tax—open a window overlooking the quadrangle of King's College, she should behold therefrom behaviour on the part of both staff and students worthy of the institution which had the privilege of her patronage.

II. *The Act of Parliament, 1882.* We have noted that the adoption by the council of Dr Barry's scheme for a women's department of King's College, situated at the safe distance of three miles from the men's departments, involved the modification of the original charter of the college. The council resolved to secure the necessary changes by means of act of parliament. They further determined that, since the charter had to go into the melting-pot, the opportunity should be taken to effect a number of other alterations in the constitution of the college which either experience had shown to be desirable or lapse of time had rendered necessary. A small committee, under the chairmanship of Sir Edmund Beckett (later Lord Grimthorpe) was appointed to consider the whole problem of revision. It reported on June 17, 1881, advising new regulations respecting

(1) proprietors, (2) fellows, (3) life-governors, (4) nominations to the council, and (5) auditors, as well as the removal of " the doubt whether the college has the power to educate girls and women, and also to carry on its work in any other part of London." The report of the committee was in the main adopted by the council, and Sir E. Beckett was commissioned to draft a bill in accordance with its proposals. The bill, duly drafted, was approved by the council on July 15, 1881, and put into the hands of parliamentary agents. It ran an easy and uneventful course through the houses during the ensuing session, and received the royal assent on May 19, 1882. Its cost to the college was £423 19s. 8d.

The principal provisions of the new statute—apart from the express permission given to the college to try to educate women, and to make the attempt anywhere within a fifteen-mile radius of Somerset House—were, first, the abolition of all claims to dividends on the part of shareholders in the college; secondly, the admission of fellows of the college as members of the governing corporation; thirdly, the removal of the restriction that all life-governors must be laymen, so as to allow not more than four of the eight to be clergymen; fourthly, the simplification of the mode of nomination for the council; and finally, the excision of the requirement that auditors must be members of the college. In other respects the provisions of the charter were in substance reincorporated in the statute. In particular, the opportunity to relax the ecclesiastical test was lost. This test had been reduced in the case of laymen to the mere formal asking of the question " Are you a member of the Church of England? " And to be a member of the Church of England within the meaning of the question was primarily a negative thing: it consisted in *not* being an adherent of any other denomination. But even this mild negative test would have been enough to exclude Joseph Lister if he had remained a Quaker, or S. R. Gardiner if he had continued to be an active Irvingite. It was highly illogical and ridiculous to exact from medical men, or even from historians, a profession of conformity that was not demanded from teachers of oriental literature and modern languages. But this indefensible distinction between different types of teachers had been made in the charter of 1829, and it was felt, no doubt, that to attempt to modify what was regarded as the fundamental principle of the college would have been to cause alarm and agitation. The hope of the college still was fixed on the voluntary contributions of the Church rather than on

330

the dangerous subsidies of the State. It was therefore thought inadvisable to frighten the faithful. Hence the twelfth clause of the statute of 1882 was a virtual repetition of the twenty-fifth clause of the charter: it enacted that

> No person who does not declare himself to be a member of the Church of England shall be competent to act as a governor by virtue of his office, or to be a life-governor or a member of the council, or to fill any office in the college except professorships of oriental literature and modern languages.

Under this statute the college continued to be governed for twenty-one years, viz., until the passing of the King's College London Act of 1903.

III. *London University.* We have already remarked in passing that in 1858 the University of London, by abandoning the practice of affiliation, had become a mere examining body; and further that in 1878 it had begun to admit women to its examinations. We have also remarked that the standard of its examinations was so high, the status of its examiners so eminent, the mode of its inquisition so impersonal, so equitable, so searching, that the diplomas and degrees which it awarded had come to have a quite unique and peculiar value. True, they did not denote, like the degrees of Oxford and Cambridge, a certain period of residence amid academic surroundings, or an uncertain social status; but they did denote both considerable ability and sustained effort. In particular, the London medical degrees were recognized as incomparably the best in the kingdom; while its science degrees set upon their recipients the stamp of marked proficiency in subjects not cultivated extensively in the older universities. Its higher arts degrees (M.A. and D.Lit.), too, were valuable, since they indicated conspicuous merit, and not mere continuance of existence coupled with payment of fees; while even the humble B.A., the lowliest of its degrees, served to distinguish nonconformist ministers from their congregations, and to lure uncertificated schoolmasters along the paths of learning laid down by correspondence colleges.

Within the London colleges, however, and especially in University College and in King's, much dissatisfaction was felt because the syllabuses of the university examinations were wholly beyond the control of the college authorities, and because the professors of the colleges had, as such, no part or lot in the examination of their students. It was argued that teaching and examining ought not to be separated the one from the other; but that syllabuses should be framed by those who would have to work under them, and that examination papers should be set and marked by those acquainted with the courses pursued by the students. Hence in the seventies a fierce controversy developed between the " externals," or defenders of the existing examination university, and the " internals," or advocates of a new teaching university. Mr Robert Lowe (later Viscount Sherbrooke), member of parliament for the university (1868–80) and chancellor of the exchequer (1868–73), placed himself entirely on the side of the " externals." With that genius of his for saying what ought not to be said—a genius that made him the equal of Mrs Malaprop herself—he remarked: "What I mean by a university is an examining board"! This was not Newman's idea of a university; it was not the King's College idea; it was not even the idea of the philosophical radicals with whom Lowe was generally in accord. Professor Lyon Playfair (later Lord Playfair) was the first important person to express dissent from the chancellor's low ideal.[1] He was followed by Professors Croom Robertson, Goodwin, Karl Pearson, and others. Finally, Sir George Young, at the University College prize-giving of June 1877, clearly expressed the opinion that University College should emulate the new Owens College of Manchester in seeking to secure the privilege of conferring her own degrees. The suggestion was welcomed with enthusiasm in Gower Street. But what would be the attitude of King's? Would King's oppose the University College demand? Would she hold aloof? Would she make a similar demand on her own account? Or would she associate herself with University College and seek for joint control? Happily, she adopted the fourth and last of these possible courses. She, or rather her leading teachers, combined, with all those who were seeking to reunite education and examination, in establishing an "Association for promoting a Teaching University for London" (May 3, 1884). By this time, however, Dr Barry's principalship had come to an end, and the representatives chosen to consider the question from the King's College point of view were Sir Joseph Lister, Professor G. C. W. Warr, and a new principal—viz., the Rev. Henry Wace, D.D. Dr Barry had got his bishopric and gone.

IV. *The End of Dr Barry's Régime.* There can be no doubt that the fifteen years of Dr Barry's rule were a period of distinguished success and marked development. The technical laboratories, the medical school, the evening theological depart-

---

[1] Address on *Teaching Universities and Examining Boards*, delivered 1873, and subsequently republished in *Subjects of Social Welfare*, 1889.

ment, the civil service classes, and above all the lectures to ladies, stood as eloquent witnesses to his energy and initiative, and to his eminent faculty for getting the best out of his staff. He was also on very good terms with his students, who admired his manliness and vigour, respected his high abilities and fine character, and appreciated the breadth of his sympathies and the largeness of his tolerance. He encouraged their healthy activities, and became a ready supporter of their corporate adventures. Hence the decade and a half of his rule was rich in student organizations. The old Medical and Engineering Societies went on as usual, occasionally publishing transactions. A new Natural History Society was started in 1872, which in 1881 gave place to a more general Science Society. Various sectional literary and debating societies were amalgamated in 1878 to form a so-called King's College Union Society —quite unconnected with the present organization of the same name—whose modest purpose was " to hold debates, and to provide newspapers, periodicals, and writing materials for the use of members." Dr Barry and Professor J. B. Mayor (in whose room it met) were prominent on its prospectus as patrons. It was, of course, a voluntary society supported by the subscriptions of its members. By voluntary effort and sacrifice, moreover, another *King's College Magazine* managed to maintain a flickering existence for the four years 1877–81. The British Museum somehow failed to secure copies of it.

The council of the college were much impressed by Dr Barry's extreme competence. They found the institution running with admirable smoothness under his capable control, and through the agency of his newly constituted hierarchy of boards. Hence they left him very much in charge, and their attendance dropped to an average of little more than the quorum of five (which by the Act of 1882 was reduced to three). The new members of the council, moreover, who took the places of the veterans as they passed away, were by no means of the rank or standing of the founders of the college. The bishops almost ceased to come to council meetings; for the matters discussed there were nearly all related to machines, antiseptics, women, or other similar secularities which did not interest them; or else to finance which merely bothered them. For kindred reasons the visitor refrained from much visiting, and so King's College tended to lose its episcopal complexion. Its best friends on the governing body were content to serve it unostentatiously, working hard on its committees, and contributing with constant and lavish generosity to its pressing and incessant needs. Prominent among these benefactors, during Dr Barry's principalship, were Sir Edmund Beckett (Lord Grimthorpe), Sir William Bowman, Mr Robert Cheere, Sir J. T. Coleridge, Sir C. J. Freake, and Mr W. H. Smith.

Both Mr W. E. Gladstone and the Marquis of Salisbury were members of the governing body of the college; but, of course, both of them were far too busy with high politics to attend to the actual administration of college affairs. Both of them, however, were aware that Dr Barry wanted and expected a bishopric. He judiciously kept aloof from extreme party polemics, and was prepared to accept preferment from either liberals or conservatives. The one, indeed, gave him his canonry at Worcester in 1871, and the other his canonry at Westminster ten years later. His intense and notorious desire to secure a see, however, was the main cause of his recurring failure to obtain one. This was unfortunate; for he was eminently fitted in scholarship, character, and administrative ability to make a first-rate diocesan. Nevertheless, it must be admitted that—if we may be allowed to alter a single word in one of William Watson's flawless elegiacs—in his aspiring spirit

> Somewhat of worldling mingled still
> With saint and sage.

The methods of the importunate widow when applied to spiritualities savour too much of simony to be permitted to succeed. He that too ostentatiously asks, quite properly, does not receive. True, Dr Barry was offered the bishopric of Calcutta in 1876; but he did not share Disraeli's passion for the orient, and an episcopate *in partibus* with a temperature of over 90° in the shade made no appeal to him. In 1883, however, when it was clear that Gladstone had no intention of promoting his election to an English see, he decided to accept an invitation to become Bishop of Sydney, Metropolitan of New South Wales, and Primate of Australia and Tasmania. It was, indeed, a great position, giving ample scope for his educative and administrative powers. On August 10, 1883, he laid his resignation before the council; on November 16, his successor was appointed; on January 1, 1884, he was consecrated in Westminster Abbey, and soon afterward (February 14) he sailed away.[1]

[1] Dr Barry's subsequent career may be briefly summarized. In 1889 he resigned his antipodean see and returned to England. For two years he acted as suffragan to the bishops of Rochester and Exeter successively. In 1891 he was made a canon of Windsor, and this canonry he held till his death. During the five years 1895–1900 he was also rector of St James's, Piccadilly. He delivered the Bampton Lectures in 1892, and the Hulsean Lectures in 1894. He died in his sleep, at the age of eighty-four, at Windsor, in April 1910.

NOTE

I. Number of Students, 1868–83

SESSION	COLLEGE							SCH.	TOTAL
	REGULAR						Occ.		
	Gen.	Med.	Eng.	Theological		Even.			
				Day	Even.				
1867-68	66	130	88	50	—	630	55	344	1363
1868-69	52	140	73	49	—	537	47	353	1251
1869-70	56	138	66	42	—	561	54	385	1302
1870-71	68	141	57	46	—	519	45	439	1315
1871-72	68	154	55	41	—	484	61	456	1319
1872-73	64	150	58	33	—	563	45	521	1434
1873-74	51	161	59	32	—	488	50	558	1399
1874-75	51	151	66	34	—	514	81	544	1441
1875-76	47	135	70	24	—	533	38	553	1400
1876-77	38	127	90	39	6	534	58	541	1433
1877-78	43	121	89	52	13	493	59	606	1476
1878-79	45	160	78	56	15	487	70	575	1486
1879-80	39	185	65	58	16	477	58	631	1529
1880-81	45	210	53	61	18	479	81	611	1558
1881-82	42	215	69	66	8	430	113	612	1555
1882-83	41	206	91	60	9	424	142	561	1534
1883-84	39	223	103	55	14	384	114	572	1504

Extra-collegiate Classes

SESSION	CIVIL SERVICE		WORK-SHOP	PRACTICAL ART	GILBART LECTURES	TOTAL
	Male	Female				
1875-76	172	—	30	—	485 [1]	687
1876-77	300	—	38	—	432	770
1877-78	350	—	35	—	660 [2]	1045
1878-79	400	—	25	—	410	835
1879-80	464	—	32	31	454	981
1880-81	500	—	22	25	275	822
1881-82	677	105	22	25	230	1059
1882-83	866	178	38	10	372	1464
1883-84	799	192	53	15	390	1449

[1] The Gilbart Lectures had begun in the session 1871–72, but no exact figures for the attendances before 1875–76 are available. The reports merely say that the numbers at the first course were " fully 300," and that the second course was " even more successful."

[2] Including 400 who came to a " special course " on banking given this year only.

II. Distinguished Students

Among those who entered the college during the period 1868–83, and subsequently became distinguished, were the following:

Brodribb, Arthur Aikin (1868–69). Journalist; for fifty years a writer for the *Times* (1877–1927). The last of Delane's men.

Avory, Horace Edmund (1868–70). Lawyer; went to Cambridge from King's College; scholar and later honorary fellow of Corpus; called to the bar, 1875; recorder of Kingston-on-Thames; judge in King's Bench division of the High Court, 1910 to the present day.

Champion, John M. (1869). Student in the engineering department; later in the public works department of India; honorary adviser to the college on the admission of Indian students.

Bartlett, Charles Blakesley (1869–71). Pupil of the school; member of the council of King's College and of the finance committee from 1908 onward; member of the delegacy from its foundation in 1910; vicar of Yapton.

Milner, Alfred (later Viscount Milner) (1869–72). Journalist and statesman. After a brilliant career at King's and at Oxford (see above, pp. 304–305) he was called to the bar (1881), but devoted himself mainly to journalism. In 1887 he became private secretary to Mr Goschen, Chancellor of the Exchequer. Then, entering the public service, he was appointed successively under-secretary for finance in Egypt, 1889; chairman of the board of inland revenue, 1892; high commissioner for South Africa, 1897–1905. He was made K.C.B. in 1895; G.C.M.G. in 1897; a baron in 1901; and a viscount in 1902. Academic honours, too, were showered upon him. During the war he was invited to join the inner cabinet (1916) and two years later as secretary of state for war he was called upon to make the momentous decisions which finally gave victory to the allies.

Hammick, Murray (1869–73). Indian civil service, 1875; K.C.S.I., 1911; governor of Madras, 1912; member of the council of the secretary of state for India since 1915.

Fowler, James Kingston (1870–73). Medical student of King's College; Warneford scholar; house-surgeon and house-physician at King's College Hospital, 1874–76; house-physician, Addenbrooke's Hospital, Cambridge, 1877–79; president of the Medical Society of London; senator of the University of London; K.C.V.O., 1910; fellow of King's College, 1926.

Low, Sidney (1870–75). Publicist and journalist; Balliol College, Oxford; barrister of the Inner Temple; editor of *St James's Gazette*; lecturer in imperial history at King's College; fellow of King's College, 1907; knighted, 1918.

Lowther, James William (Viscount Ullswater) (1870–73). Came to King's from Eton, *æt.* fifteen; gained prizes in Latin, French, and German; A.K.C., 1873; went to Trinity College, Cambridge; honours in classics and in law; called to the bar, 1879; Member of Parliament, 1883; under-secretary for Foreign Affairs, 1891; chairman of committee, 1895–1905; Speaker of the House of Commons, 1905–21; raised to the peerage, 1921.

Robertson, Frederick Alexander (1870–73). Student in the general literature and science department; entered Indian Civil Service, 1876; director-general of agriculture in the Punjab, 1889–96; vice-chancellor of the Punjab University, 1909–10; fellow of King's College, 1915.

Soulsby, William Jameson (1870–73). For more than half a century secretary to the Lord Mayors of London, 1875 *et seq.* After leaving the City of London School, attended classes in law at King's College; called to the bar, Middle Temple, 1874; knighted, 1902; fellow of King's College, 1916; C.V.O., 1920.

Prince Imperial, son of Napoleon III (1871–72). The prince, soon after his arrival, with the other members of his exiled family, in England, came to King's College to attend the elementary lectures in physics given by Professor Grylls Adams. He was then fifteen years old, and distinctly backward for his age. The French tutor who accompanied him has left us an account of his advent to the college: " We had a disagreeable impression the first day we penetrated the corridors of King's College, filled with students who whistled incessantly. As in France I had never heard whistling except from the lower orders, for a moment I had some doubts as to the young gentlemen's designs; but almost immediately I became convinced that they were whistling for their own pleasure. ' It's not a school,' said the prince to me, ' it's a nest of blackbirds.' The prince never entered into conversation with any of them, and no one ever approached him. He would always have remained an alien in England if he had spent several years in those surroundings." In the long vacation, however, he got to know a former King's man, Henry de Worms, who taught him swimming at Cowes. After the vacation he was entered at Woolwich, to begin his military career, which was destined to end so tragically in 1881.

Clowes, William Laird (1872–76). Naval historian; naval correspondent to the *Times*, 1890–95; compiler of *The Royal Navy* (7 vols.), 1897–1903; helped to found the Navy Records Society, 1891; knighted, 1902; died 1905.

May, Arthur William (1872–76). Came to King's College from Sherborne School; student of the medical faculty; entered royal naval medical service, 1878; served in many expeditions,

1882–1913; director-general of the medical department of the royal navy, 1913–17; K.C.B., 1914; fellow of King's College, 1915.

Norman, William Henry (1873–77). Student of the medical faculty; entered the navy, 1882; director-general of the medical department of the navy, 1917–19; K.C.B., 1918; fellow of King's College, 1919; honorary surgeon to the King, 1920.

Hyde, Clarendon Golding (1874–78). Student in the faculty of law; called to the bar, Middle Temple, 1881; M.P., 1906–10; knighted, 1910; high-sheriff of Berkshire, 1918; fellow of King's College, 1927.

Sloggett, Arthur Thomas (1874–78). Student in the medical faculty; entered R.A.M.C., 1881; colonel, 1903; surgeon-major-general, 1908; lieutenant-general, 1914; director-general of the army medical service, 1914–18; honorary surgeon to the King; knighted, 1914; K.C.B., 1915; fellow of King's College, 1915; K.C.M.G., 1917.

Johnston, Harry Hamilton (1875–76). Traveller and administrator; gained a prize for Italian at King's, 1876; proceeded to Royal Academy of Arts, 1876–80; conducted many expeditions into Central Africa; commissioner and consul-general for British Central Africa, 1891; commander-in-chief and consul-general for Uganda, 1899; K.C.B., 1896; G.C.M.G., 1901; died 1927.

Dalton, Norman (1875–79). After early education in Queen's College, British Guiana, and Christ's College, Finchley, entered the medical department of King's College; held the Warneford scholarship, 1875–76; A.K.C., 1879; fellow of King's College, 1908; professor of pathological anatomy, and senior physician in the hospital; M.D.; F.R.C.P.

Northcote, the Hon. John Stafford (1876–78). Honorary chaplain to the King; vicar of St Andrew's, Westminster, 1889; prebendary of St Paul's, 1906. Entered King's College as a theological student, after an early education at Eton and after ten years spent as an engineer; A.K.C., 1878; fellow of King's College, 1913.

Claughton, Gilbert Henry (1876–79). Student of the applied science (engineering) department, after early education at Eton; chief mineral agent to the Earl of Dudley for twenty years; director of Barclays Bank; chairman of London and North-Western Railway Company; created baronet, 1912; fellow of King's College, 1917.

Pilditch, Philip Edward (1877–79). Architect and publicist; London county councillor, 1907–19; Member of Parliament since 1918; knighted, 1918.

Salter, Arthur Clavell (1877–80). Lawyer and politician; distinguished graduate in arts and in law of London University;

338

called to the bar, 1885; K.C., 1904; recorder of Poole, 1904–17; Member of Parliament, 1906–17; judge of the King's Bench division of the High Court, 1917; died 1928.

Adamson, John William (1878–81). Eminent educationist and historian of English education; A.K.C., 1880; head of the training department and master of method at King's College, 1890; lecturer in Education, 1901; professor, 1903; professor in the University of London, 1911. (See Appendix B.)

Atkinson, Llewelyn Birchall (1882–85). Eminent engineer; A.K.C., 1885; fellow of King's College, 1926.

Muntz, Gerard Albert (1882–83). Past president of the Institute of Metals; student of the engineering department; succeeded to baronetcy, 1908.

Thomas, William Henry Griffith (1882–85). Student of the theological department; A.K.C., 1885; proceeded to Christ Church, Oxford; vicar of St Paul's, Portman Square, 1896–1905; principal of Wycliffe Hall, Oxford, 1905–10; professor in Toronto, 1910–19; fellow of King's College, 1923; Doctor of Divinity.

Wordingham, Charles Henry (1882–85). Consulting engineer; student in the applied science department; Clothworkers' exhibitioner; pupil of Sir John Hopkinson; electrical engineer to Manchester Corporation, 1894–1901; electrical adviser to the Admiralty, 1903–18; fellow of King's College, 1912.

CHAPTER X

THE STRUGGLE FOR EXISTENCE

1883-97

§ 1. *The Sixth Principal: the Rev. Henry Wace*

THE council which on August 10, 1883, received Dr Barry's resignation of the office of principal resolved (1) to advertise the vacancy; (2) to continue the salary at £800, with capitation fees calculated to bring the total to about £1000 per annum; (3) to require the new principal to take up his abode in the house attached to the college—which, it will be remembered, had for ten years been sublet to the Statistical Society. Applications were to be in by October 13, and a strong committee of ten (including two bishops, three deans, and one doctor of divinity) was appointed to consider the applications and report. The committee on November 8 selected two candidates for interview by the council—viz., the Rev. F. J. Jayne, principal of Lampeter, and the Rev. Henry Wace, since 1875 professor of ecclesiastical history in the college. Never before had there been so keen a contest for the principalship. Both the committee and the council were sharply divided. Mr Jayne (*æt.* thirty-eight) had incontestably the better academic record. He had been, indeed, one of the most brilliant Oxford graduates of his time —triple first, double prizeman, fellow of Jesus, tutor of Keble, preacher at Whitehall from 1875 to 1877. Obviously he was marked out for high ecclesiastical office. Dr Wace (*æt.* forty-seven), on the other hand, had the advantage of being an old student of King's, a fellow of the college, and a successful teacher of eight years' standing. Moreover, if he had come down from Oxford with the modest achievement of two seconds to his credit, he had made up for academic mediocrity by subsequent successes in the city. He was a Londoner born and bred. After leaving the university he had held in turn three London curacies, and he had soon made a name as a preacher of striking pungency and power, a tremendous fighter for the faith, a master of terse and effective English. He had been appointed chaplain of Lincoln's Inn, 1872 ; Boyle lecturer,

340

HENRY WACE
Principal 1883–97

1874; select preacher at Cambridge, 1876; Bampton lecturer, 1879; select preacher at Oxford, 1880; prebendary of St Paul's, 1881. The degree of D.D. was conferred upon him in 1883. In his leisure moments he wrote leaders for the *Times*, and those who read that potent organ were able to recognize his utterances and to perceive in their anonymous but well-known author one of the ablest of the surviving champions of evangelical conservatism. As a professor of ecclesiastical history at King's he had been pronouncedly protestant, belabouring on the one hand sacerdotal superstition and on the other hand secularist scepticism.

The contest between the supporters of two such notable candidates was keen and prolonged. Finally, when the issue was put to the vote in a council meeting attended by no fewer than thirty members, Dr Wace received twenty votes and Mr Jayne ten.[1]

Dr Wace, on being summoned before the council and informed of his election, manifested the satisfaction of a successful combatant, and on receiving the congratulations of the chairman—Dr William Thomson, Archbishop of York—" returned warm thanks " to the electors. He was well aware, however, that the post to which he had been appointed was no sinecure mastership—like the headship of an eighteenth-century Oxford or Cambridge college, or the wardenship of a mediæval hospital, in whose serene altitudes, undisturbed by mundane cares, the character could mature, the spirit repose, the form develop, and the intellect subside, until revolving years should open the way to the still more eminent tranquillity of a deanery or a bishopric. His long connexion with King's—as student, 1853–56; as evening class lecturer, 1860–62; as fellow, 1873; and as professor of ecclesiastical history, 1875–83 —made him painfully alive to the fact that he was assuming responsibility for the administration of an institution which was still struggling for existence; an institution that had never recovered from the disasters of its infancy; an institution tottering on the verge of bankruptcy; an institution that had lost all sense of unity and had become a mere mass of disparate departments; an institution devoid of policy; a college at sea, vainly voyaging in search of a university. The fourteen years of his principalship constituted, indeed, a period of unparalleled *Sturm und Drang*. So serious, in fact, did the

---

[1] Mr Jayne remained at Lampeter till 1886; then for three years he was vicar of Leeds; in 1889 he was consecrated bishop of Chester, and at Chester he remained, honoured and beloved, until his death in 1919.

situation become that at one stage of its development—viz., in the years 1894–95—the prospect of closing down both college and school had seriously to be faced. In these circumstances of peril and anxiety Dr Wace proved himself to be an admirable pilot. He combined in a remarkable manner strength of character, clarity of mind, a high sense of honour, transparent integrity, fearless courage, and tireless energy. He was at the same time one of the strongest and also one of the most tactful and courteous of all the principals of King's. He knew his own mind; he formulated precise plans; he pursued his predetermined course with resolute will; and yet, such was the respect and admiration which he engendered, he made no enmities and he closed no doors to compromise. Only in one particular was he less well fitted than Dr Barry to guide and direct the course of King's through the crisis of the nineties: he was theologically much more rigid and unyielding than his predecessor. Indeed, as Barry was the disciple of Maurice, so was Wace the disciple of Jelf. He tended to tighten the tests on members of the staff; he re-enforced with vigour the compulsory attendance of matriculated students at chapel; he emphasized the fundamental Anglicanism of the college; and he did all this precisely at a time when the spirit of the age was opposed to religious exclusiveness, and when the council of the college was appealing to both the Government and the London County Council for public funds to save the institution from bankruptcy. Moreover, he engaged in acrimonious controversy with Professor Huxley and other agnostics concerning the Gadarene swine and similar unpropitious subjects, and displayed an uncompromising orthodoxy which made King's College appear as the last stronghold of English fundamentalism. Finally, in circumstances that painfully recalled the case of Professor Maurice, he secured in 1891 the dismissal of Professor Momerie for utterances which he considered heterodox and improper. Although Dr Momerie deserves much less sympathy than his distinguished prototype, and although he was dealt with by Dr Wace and Bishop Temple with a decisiveness and an ability that are in striking contrast to the fumbling ineptitude of Dr Jelf and Bishop Blomfield thirty-eight years earlier, nevertheless the whole unhappy episode did much to injure the college in the eyes of the public. It was undoubtedly one of the causes which made it difficult for it to get money, and impossible for it to secure the power to confer degrees. The matters of faith, however, for which Dr Wace contended were to him concerns of primary importance. Conscience and conviction were obvious in his every word and act. Much as he loved the college, and hard as he laboured for it, he was prepared to see it perish rather than connive at its abandonment of its basal principle—viz., the indissoluble union of religion with learning.

If, however, Dr Wace's ecclesiastical rigidity and pious pugnacity were detrimental to the secular interests of the college, in other respects he was one of its greatest developers and benefactors. He devoted much attention to the advancement of its engineering and technological work; he laboured hard and successfully in the business of the hospital and in the enlargement and improvement of the medical school; he saved the department of general literature and science from extinction by instituting within it a new day training school for elementary teachers, and by directing its activities to London University examinations; he fostered the civil service classes, brought them within the ambit of the college, and aided in the establishment of day classes for boys as a supplement to the prosperous evening classes for all and sundry that he found in existence; he greatly extended the scope of the "lectures for ladies," got them recognized as a college department, and converted their first lady superintendent, Miss C. G. Schmitz, into the second Mrs Wace. His most strenuous and persistent efforts were, however, directed first to the institution of a teaching university in London, and secondly to the placing of King's College on a sound financial basis. That he was not wholly successful in either of these big tasks was due partly to his fidelity to the foundation principle of the college, and partly to circumstances over which he had no control. So important, nevertheless, was his work in these two spheres that it is to these partial failures rather than to his numerous successes that we must first turn our attention.

§ 2. *The Move for a Teaching University* [1]

We have noted [2] that on May 3, 1884, was instituted an "Association for promoting a Teaching University for London," and that King's College was unofficially represented

---

[1] Full particulars of the early history of this complicated business, which spread itself over the fourteen years 1884–98, will be found in the three volumes of Dr W. H. Allchin's *Account of the Reconstruction of the University of London* (1905–1912). In the present section, of course, it is impossible to do more than note the major matters dealt with in detail in the 1288 pages of Dr Allchin's colossal work.

[2] See above, p. 332.

at its inaugural meeting by Dr Wace, Professor Warr, and Sir Joseph Lister. The objects of the association were avowedly (1) to organize a teaching university in and for London; (2) to associate university examination with university teaching, and to place both under the direction of the same authorities; (3) to confer a substantive voice in the government of the university upon those engaged in the work of teaching and examination. In December 1884 the association, after much negotiation and long deliberation, promulgated a " proposed plan of a teaching university for London," according to which the existing university, the two colleges, the two royal medical institutions, and the two great legal corporations, with many other similar bodies, located in London, would be federated to form one multi-facultied teaching and examining metropolitan university. In February 1885 an executive committee was appointed to further the realization of the plan, and to it were elected from King's College Dr Wace, Professor Warr, and Mr J. W. Cunningham; to whom, a year later, were added Professors Grylls Adams, Curnow, Hudson, and Gerald Yeo. Not, however, until June 11, 1886, did the council of King's College, after receiving a deputation from the association, resolve that " whilst reserving their opinion as to the details of the scheme laid before them for establishing a teaching university, they approve generally of the objects proposed by the association." A similar general approval was expressed by the council of University College a month later (July 10, 1886).

Not so successful, however, was the association in securing the acceptance of its plan from the other suggested constituents of the federal university. (1) Both the senate and the convocation of the existing university of London rejected the scheme, declining to entrust examinations to teachers, and insisting on the incorporation of provincial colleges; (2) the Royal Colleges of Physicians and Surgeons started a separate scheme of their own, the aim of which was to obtain the right to confer the doctor's degree on the results of their own examinations without reference to any university; (3) the Inns of Court and the Law Society declined to have anything to do with the movement. The plan of the association therefore broke down. In these circumstances University College (led by Sir George Young) and King's College (led by Dr Wace) drew together and determined that, as the wide federation envisaged by the association was impracticable, they would jointly on their own account seek from the crown a charter authorizing them to establish an entirely new university in and for London, empowered to confer degrees in arts, science, and medicine; leaving the existing university, to which the name of " London " had inappropriately become attached, to go its own way as an imperial institution conferring degrees on anyone from anywhere who could procure a certificate of good conduct, pay its fees, and pass its examinations. Hence was framed, mainly by Sir George Young and Dr Wace, the draft charter of the projected " Albert University of London," modelled upon that of the recently constituted Victoria University of the North. It was to be a purely metropolitan teaching university, dominated by its constituent colleges, organized in faculties, conducting its own examinations, and conferring its own degrees. It was to consist in the first instance of University College and King's College, but provision was made for the incorporation of other metropolitan colleges and schools of university rank if they should desire to come in. The council of King's College readily and enthusiastically supported the Albert University project, and on May 4, 1887, appointed a committee, with Lord Grimthorpe at its head, to co-operate with University College in petitioning the crown. The council of University College did not so easily concur; for University College had been from the first more closely associated than had King's College with the existing London University, and four prominent members of the college council were also members of the senate of the university, and were strongly opposed to the idea of the establishment of a second university in the metropolis. A keen debate, however, on May 21, 1887, resulted in the triumph of the Albertists, and the leading dissentients resigned their conciliar seats. The councils of the two colleges, having thus been brought into perfect harmony, joined in presenting to the crown in July 1887 a petition for the charter necessary for the realization of the Albert idea.

The petition of the two colleges let loose the deluge, and for the next six months the privy council was inundated by petitions in support, petitions in opposition, and cross petitions. In particular, the senate of the existing university implored the crown not to set up its Albertist rival; the medical colleges begged for the privilege of conferring degrees on their own account; provincial colleges, Scottish and Irish universities, and even private individuals swelled the flood of supplication, either asking for favours for themselves or objecting to favours sought by others. It was a horrible chaos of conflicting claims. Finally, the government, in sheer bewilderment, secured a period of tranquillity by appointing a royal commission " to inquire whether any and what kind of a new university or powers is or are required for the advancement of higher education in London" (May 1888). This was the so-called " Selborne Commission," named from its chairman, the Earl of Selborne, the other six members being three lawyers (Ball, Hannen, Brodrick) and three educationists (Thomson, Stokes, Welldon). The case for the new and separate Albert University was stated by Sir George Young and others from University College, while the point of view of King's was presented by Dr Wace, Professors Hudson and Thomson, Sir Joseph Lister, Dr Priestley, and the Bishop of London (Dr Temple). The main contentions of the King's representatives were (1) that the education given at King's was well up to university standard, but that the A.K.C. which it secured was not, in spite of its resplendent hood, regarded by the world as equal to a university degree; (2) that the degrees of the existing London University did not supply the need, because the syllabuses of the examinations on the results of which they were conferred, fixed entirely by extraneous authorities, did not at all accord with the King's curricula; (3) that degrees ought not to be conferred by examination alone, but ought also to denote a specific period of systematic study under qualified teachers at a recognized institution; and, finally, a point excellently stated and strongly emphasized by Bishop Temple, (4) that the existing " University of London has chosen an imperial in preference to a metropolitan position "; that " the two positions, the imperial and the metropolitan, cannot be combined "; and that, consequently, " it is impossible to adapt the University of London to the needs of the metropolis."

The Selborne Commission did not endorse the arguments of the two colleges. In a report dated April 29, 1889,[1] they declared themselves in favour of an extension of the existing university rather than the establishment of a second university in the metropolis. Their confused and hesitant conclusion runs as follows:

> We, therefore, humbly recommend to your Majesty that a reasonable time be allowed to the senate and convocation of the University of London to consider whether they will apply to your Majesty for a new charter extending the functions and duties of their university to teaching, associating with it teaching colleges and institutions, remodelling the constitution of its

[1] C. 5709.

senate. . . . In the event of their applying for and obtaining such a new charter, we recommend that no other university be now established in London, and that the prayer of the petition of University College and King's College be not granted.

Then, to make confusion worse confounded, three of the six who had signed this report—viz., Sir William Thomson, Mr G. G. Stokes, and the Rev. J. E. C. Welldon—added the totally contradictory rider:

> Considering that the London University has long ceased to be in any sense a teaching university and has become merely an examining board, that in this capacity it has established a high reputation, and is doing a useful work for the whole Empire; and considering the very large number of candidates who present themselves for the various examinations leading up to a degree, we doubt the possibility of effectually combining the functions of an examining and of a teaching as well as examining university in the University of London, and on this account we should have preferred the establishment of a new teaching university for London, leaving it to the London University to continue to discharge its present functions.

Rarely, indeed, can even a royal commission have propounded such incompatible futilities. The report, in fact, is quite the worst—the feeblest, least lucid, most self-contradictory—of all it has been my lot to examine. It left the situation infinitely more chaotic than it found it.

The two colleges (June 1889) submitted to the Lord President of the Council (Lord Cranbrook) a strongly worded protest against the main body of the report, pointing out that the commissioners had totally failed to see the point or appreciate the force of their contentions. This protest they followed up by sending a joint deputation—headed by the Bishop of London and Dr Wace for King's College, Sir George Young and Mr J. E. Erichsen for University College—which Lord Cranbrook sympathetically received on July 25, 1889. The government felt, however, that it must so far accept the findings of the commission as to allow the university a " reasonable time "—which it interpreted to mean twelve months—wherein to frame a scheme of reconstruction. The university accordingly set to work, and in November 1889 issued a draft scheme which provided that " if and when University and King's Colleges " should become constituent colleges of the reconstructed university they should each have one *ex officio* representative in a senate of thirty-eight! Strongly as the two colleges objected to this scheme—which not only left them an impotent minority in the senate, but also made no attempt to co-ordinate teaching with examination—they felt it necessary to enter into negotiations in order to see if the scheme could be amended. Hence the whole of the year 1890 was filled with conferences, confabulations, correspondences, and colluctations. Scheme after scheme was propounded and rejected by one side or the other. Finally, under great pressure from Birmingham and other distant centres of academic illumination, the senate proposed (March 1891) " to assign to the provincial colleges a position in the university analogous to that given to the London colleges." Thus on the teaching as well as on the examining side the local character of the reconstituted university was to be wholly obliterated. It was to be imperial, not metropolitan. The words of Bishop Temple were vindicated : " The imperial and the metropolitan cannot be combined : it is impossible to adapt the University of London to the needs of the metropolis."

The result of the senate's concession to the demand of the provincial academies, together with its unyielding attitude on various matters regarded as vital by the representatives of University College and King's College, constrained the two colleges to break off negotiations and to revert to the Albert scheme for a separate and purely metropolitan teaching university.[1] The council of King's College, after two protracted debates (March 3 and 20, 1891), resolved

> to appoint a committee to draw up a letter to the Lord President, representing the objections already recognised by the council to the revised scheme of the senate of the University of London, and expressing . . . their desire to be replaced in their original position as petitioners for the establishment in London of a teaching university upon the lines of their petition presented in 1887 and of the draft charter thereto appended.

The council of University College had already come to a similar determination. The King's College committee—consisting of Bishop Temple, Lord Grimthorpe, Dr Wace, Dr Priestley, and Mr C. P. Serocold—drew up and sent (with the sanction of the council), under the date April 29, 1891, a powerful letter to the Lord President stating under seven heads their objections to the senate's scheme, and begging him once again to give favourable consideration to their wishes as embodied four years earlier in the draft charter of the

---

[1] The resolution of the two colleges was strengthened when the convocation of the University of London itself rejected the senate's scheme by a majority of more than two to one.

Albert University. On June 12, 1891, Dr Wace was able to report to the governing body of King's College that

a letter had been received from the privy council office stating that the petitions sent in by University and King's Colleges would be forthwith heard, and that all papers connected therewith must be sent by June 22, and that the colleges would be heard by counsel. He had therefore conferred with Lord Grimthorpe, Mr Erichsen, and Sir George Young on the subject, and it had been agreed that one solicitor—viz., Mr Pennington, of Cookson, Pennington, and Co.—should act for both colleges, and on the advice of Sir R. Webster (who was unable himself to act as their counsel, as he would have to advise the government on the question and perhaps even sit on the committee) they had retained Mr Rigby, Q.C., to act for them, with Mr H. H. Cunynghame as junior counsel.

The papers having been duly sent in and counsel properly instructed, the case of the colleges was heard by a committee of the privy council, with Lord Cranbrook in the chair, on July 13, 1891. This amiable committee speedily brushed aside all the objections raised by the existing University of London against the Albert charter—except one. They agreed that "the name 'London' must be omitted from the title of the new university," which might be called either simply "The Albert University" or, more fully, "The Albert Metropolitan University." Apart from this matter of nomenclature, they were wholly in favour of granting the desire of the petitioning colleges. The problem seemed to be solved. On July 17 Dr Wace, in high delight, reported to the council the happy issue of their efforts, and that body resolved unanimously

That the warmest thanks of the council be presented to the Reverend the Principal for the zealous, untiring, and skilful labours during the last seven years in carrying thus far to a successful issue on behalf of the college the arrangements for the establishment of a teaching university in London.

The whole business had cost the college about £1200.

Those who are accustomed to follow the usual leisurely proceedings of the privy council will wonder how it came to pass that a matter of such moment should be begun, continued, and ended in the sacred precincts of Whitehall within the ridiculously minute space of three months. It may not be impertinent to suggest that the acceleration of the privy council's normal procedure was to some extent due to the fact that the prime minister (Lord Salisbury), the leader of the house of commons (Mr W. H. Smith), the attorney-general

(Sir R. Webster), and the home secretary (Mr Matthews) were all members of the governing body of King's College, and all of them ardent supporters of the policy of its council. It was not enough, however, in order to give effect to the newly drafted Albert University charter, that it should be approved by the privy council and passed by the law officers of the crown. Under the College Charter Act of 1871 it had to lie for thirty consecutive days upon the tables of both houses of parliament before being forwarded for the formality of the royal confirmation. Unfortunately, when it emerged from the hands of the law officers less than the required thirty days remained to the end of the summer session. Hence it had to be put away during an autumn recess that lasted nearly six months; and, as a matter of fact, not until February 19, 1892, did it commence its thirty days' vigil. During the disastrous interval the opposition had been organizing itself. The champions of the University of London denounced the Albert University scheme as a device of bankrupt colleges to attract students by offering them easy degrees; the provincial colleges condemned the exclusiveness of the charter and demanded equal privileges; the nonconformists and the radical politicians fastened upon the denominational character of King's as the most obnoxious feature in the new scheme. It is probable, however, that, if circumstances had remained unchanged, the charter would have survived the attacks of its numerous assailants. But one lamentable catastrophe wrecked its chance, and made all the labours of the two colleges and their friends of no effect. On October 6, 1891, Mr W. H. Smith died, and the leadership of the house of commons passed to Mr A. J. Balfour. Now Mr Balfour (who declined an invitation to join the council of King's College) was member of parliament for Manchester, one of the cities whose colleges were most vehemently opposed to the establishment of the new metropolitan university. Hence when criticisms of the charter were raised in the house of commons he showed no disposition to defend it or to facilitate its progress. His hostility was more than equalled by that of Mr Joseph Chamberlain, who represented the interests of the Mason College, Birmingham. An excellent excuse, moreover, for withholding assent had been furnished by an extremely injudicious act on the part of the supporters of the charter themselves. In the hope of securing the help of the city, and the money of its wealthy companies, they had agreed (January 1892) to alter the name of the projected university from

" Albert " to " Gresham," and to make the Gresham College, hitherto outside its ambit, the centre of the new institution. It was a fatal blunder, for which Dr Wace himself was primarily responsible. The matter being thus brought once more into the melting-pot, on March 10, 1892, Mr Balfour in the house of commons readily gave his assent to a motion that the whole question should once more be remitted to a royal commission.

The new commission—known alternatively as the "Cowper" or the " Gresham " commission—was issued on April 30, 1892. The question of the charter and of the objections thereto was placed before a body of fourteen experts chosen far more judiciously than the seven of the Selborne commission. In particular, all the leading interests were represented—Lord Reay, for instance, being taken from the council of University College and Bishop Barry from that of King's College.[1] The commission proceeded with great deliberation to collect information, hear evidence, weigh arguments, and form conclusions. From King's College no fewer than ten eminent men appeared before it—viz., Bishop Temple and Dr Priestley from the council, with Dr Wace and Professors Adams, Capper, Gault, Halliburton, Lister, Robinson, and Thomson from the staff. All the King's representatives pleaded hard for the Gresham scheme, stressing the impossibility of any effective yoking of a local teaching university with a cosmopolitan examining board. Most of the University College representatives did the same, although a few (led by Professor Karl Pearson) queered the pitch by contending for a more exclusively professorial university than the Gresham scheme envisaged. The spokesmen of the existing London University, of course, with renewed hope, urged vehemently that no second university should be established in London, but that the colleges should in some way be combined with that great institution which from offices in Burlington Gardens was controlling the Empire's cramming.

Not till the spring of 1893 did the Cowper commissioners cease from their heuristic labours and commence to collect their thoughts. And not until the beginning of 1894 did they complete their meditations and issue their report with its voluminous appendices of evidence.[2] Their recommendations

---

[1] The names of the commissioners were as follows : Earl Cowper (chairman), Lord Reay, Bishop Barry, Sir Lyon Playfair, Sir William Savory, Sir George Humphrey, Sir George Ramsay, the Rev. Canon Browne, Mr Henry Sidgwick, Professor John Scott, Mr Burdon Sanderson, Mr James Anstie, Mr E. R. C. Palmer, and the Rev. G. H. Rendall.

[2] C. 7259.

HISTORY OF KING'S COLLEGE

were a profound disappointment to both University College and King's College. The Gresham scheme for a new federal teaching university was emphatically rejected; as also was the scheme of Professor Karl Pearson and his friends for a unified professorial university. The commissioners reported in favour of one single institution—the existing University of London—with two sets of examinations, one internal and the other external, similar in standard, but differing in accordance with the varying needs of different classes of students. Individual teachers in the separate schools of the university would have to be recognized by the university itself, so that the exclusive authority of the college councils would come to an end. The colleges, as such, indeed, were to have very little weight on the new governing body of the remodelled university; but one-third of the senators were to be representatives of the recognized teachers, elected partly through the faculties and partly through an " academic council " which was now proposed for the first time. And the existing university was to be remodelled in this sense not by charter, but by legislative authority and a statutory commission. It is obvious that the *councils* of the two colleges stood to lose a good deal of their power under the projected constitution. On the other hand, the *teachers* stood to gain immensely both in independence and in influence; while the *students* were to receive the incalculable boon of "internal" examinations and degrees—controlled mainly by their teachers, but kept up to the required standard by "external" supervision. It is interesting to observe that Bishop Barry signed the report, but that he did so with a note to the effect that he doubted the possibility of combining or harmonizing the internal and external elements in the university, and that he would much have preferred the Gresham scheme.

There was another matter too concerning which Bishop Barry felt himself bound to express the strongest dissent from the findings of the majority of his fellow-commissioners. And that was the vital matter of religious tests. For the majority of the commissioners advised that there should be no

> grant of money out of university funds for any purpose in respect of which any privilege is conferred or any disability is imposed on account of religious belief.

This was a thunderbolt for the council of King's College; for it struck at the very foundation principle of their constitution. I shall have to return to this important topic in a moment,

352

under the head of finance; for simultaneous attacks upon this same fundamental principle came from two other quarters whither the desperate council was looking for pecuniary assistance—viz., Her Majesty's Treasury and the London County Council. It became clearly evident that retention of religious tests in any shape or form—for governors and councillors, or for teachers and students—would be incompatible with the receipt of public money, without which the college would have to close its doors. The alternatives were surrender or dissolution.

Leaving that supreme issue, however, for the moment, I will conclude this dull but necessary section by observing that the process of giving statutory effect to the findings of the Cowper commission was a much longer one than had been anticipated. Bills were introduced, by Lord Playfair in 1895 and the Duke of Devonshire in 1896, for the purpose; but both had to be withdrawn because of lack of parliamentary time. Meanwhile, there was immense activity behind the scenes, King's College in particular making strenuous endeavours—quite ineffective with Lord Rosebery, only partially effective with the Duke of Devonshire, distinctly more successful with Lord Salisbury—to secure support for some relaxation of the religious prohibition. Not, indeed, until 1898 did the University of London Bill, which implemented the recommendations of the Cowper report of 1894, pass the houses of parliament and receive the royal assent. By that time Dr Wace had resigned his principalship and departed to another sphere of activity. The transformation of King's from a denominational institution into a university college took place, therefore, during another *régime*, the story of which must be reserved for a later chapter.[1] We must now turn our attention to another arid but inevitable theme, closely associated with the struggle for the charter—namely, the question of finance.

§ 3. *Bankruptcy or Secularization*

One of the main causes that led Dr Wace and the council of King's College to struggle so hard to secure a charter empowering its holders to confer degrees was that they found their departments vanishing away, and their deficits swelling, under the competition of more fortunate rivals. Their medical school, for instance, sank from 223 in 1884 to 132 in 1897,

[1] See below, Chapter XI.

largely, they believed, because their students, unable to attain the extreme proficiency required for the London M.D., were migrating to Newcastle, Edinburgh, or Glasgow, where the coveted diploma could be obtained on easier terms. Similarly, the department of general literature and science almost disappeared. In 1884 it had but 39 students (with a staff of 23); while in 1893, when it reached its lowest depth, there were but 10 students (with a staff of 25)—apart from the subsidized day training students (soon to be dealt with) who had been imported in 1890 to save the department from sheer extinction. This decline was attributed to the rise of provincial colleges and municipal universities all over England and Wales, the more important of which began to obtain charters authorizing them to grant degrees. It was, in particular, the establishment of the Victoria University (Manchester, Liverpool, and Leeds) in 1880, followed by that of the University of Wales (Aberystwyth, Bangor, and Cardiff) in 1893, that made the London colleges realize that unless they became the constituent members of a university they would be lost.

By a disastrous coincidence—for the causes were wholly unconnected and different—at the same time as the leading departments of the college were withering away the school also was suffering a still more marked decline. The 612 boys whom Dr Maclear left on his retirement in 1880 sank to 538 in 1884, 432 in 1885, 349 in 1886, 294 in 1887, until finally in 1897 the numbers reached the abysmal depth of 166. This rapid and enormous decline (which we shall examine in a later section) meant a loss of thousands of pounds a year to the general funds of the college.[1] Instead of helping to carry the college, the school became an additional burden upon its scanty resources. The financial situation in the early nineties became desperate.

In 1884, the year in which Dr Wace took over the principalship, the college accounts for the last time in its history showed an excess of receipts from fees over expenditure: there was a profit on the preceding twelve months' working of £411 12s. 4d. The grateful and astonished council voted £100 to the secretary as a thank-offering, £96 to Dr Barry to assist him on his antipodean way, and carried the residue to reserve. They were well advised to do so, for the balance-sheet presented to the general court in May 1885 showed a deficit (January–December

---

[1] A very interesting and significant note in the council minutes of May 4, 1892, runs : " It may be doubted whether the college as apart from the school has at any time paid its own way."

1884) of £208 9s. 4d. Next year the deficit leaped to the alarming sum of £2052 8s. 3d.; and for the succeeding ten years it never sank below four figures. It will suffice to give the results in the form of a table: nothing could be more eloquent.

Year	Deficit		
	£	s.	d.
1885	2052	8	3
1886	1211	10	8
1887	1297	7	9
1888	2170	17	2
1889	3033	0	4
1890	2390	10	2
1891	3721	7	3
1892	c. 4826	0	0
1893	c. 2280	0	0
1894	6076	0	1
1895	7918	19	2

If we ask what was the explanation of this devastating declension from solvency toward bankruptcy, the answer is simple. On the one hand, income from fees was rapidly falling: it sank from £34,775 in 1881 to £27,485 in 1891. On the other hand, expenses were steadily increasing: the technological departments in particular were making demands that could not possibly be met out of students' payments. Physiological laboratories; bacteriological laboratories; public health departments; plumbing departments; dynamos for the electrical engineers; steam-engines for the mechanical engineers; surveying instruments and models for the civil engineers; apparatus for the chemists and physicists; microscopes for the biologists and geologists—these were the sorts of things that ran away with the money. The report of 1893 stated that "within the last ten years a sum of not less than £30,000 has been expended in the provision of new laboratories or in the improvement of old ones"; and, even so, equipment hardly kept pace with requirement.

How in these circumstances of cumulative adversity did the college carry on at all? The reply is, through the magnanimity of the bank, which allowed the college overdraft to run to the formidable sum of £28,000. In March 1894, however, the finance committee reported the ominous, but hardly surprising, news (reminiscent of Necker's communication to Louis XVI in 1788): "The borrowing powers of the council are exhausted."

355

Needless to say, during this dark decade (1884–94) the council resorted to many and various devices to redress the adverse balance. (1) First, of course, they made the customary levy on the portions of fees assigned to the staff—2 per cent. in 1886, 3 per cent. in 1887, rising to 10 per cent. in 1893 and the following years. But even a 10 per cent. levy did not realize so much as £2000, and it was so heavy a burden on the ill-paid professoriate as to make their posts almost worthless. (2) They sought counsel's opinion as to how far they were legally entitled to use their trust funds for the defraying of current expenses; but the sound response of the eminent lawyer whom they consulted did not encourage them to embark on a career of doubtful trusteeship (November 1893). (3) Then the council strove to reduce expenses, compelling each department to cut down its demands to a minimum, and introducing such boomerang economies as the disbanding of the chapel choir, the curtailment of prizes in the school, and the abolition of entrance scholarships. But economies in an already poverty-stricken institution merely meant lowered efficiency, discouraged teachers, disgusted students, accelerated decline. It was imperative to find new sources of revenue, hence (4) a special appeal was made to the city companies to place the college on a sound financial basis. The Clothworkers' Company promptly responded by voting (February 1889) a contribution of £200 a year for four years. Encouraged by this generous gift, the council resolved to issue a bold appeal for an endowment fund of £50,000 (October 1890); but this appeal yielded only £526 5s.—viz., £100 a year for five years from the Salters' Company and a donation of twenty-five guineas from the Coopers. Then (5), when the tests were attacked, and when public money was withheld because of the ecclesiastical demands made upon the staff and the religious duties imposed upon the students, the council made its last great general appeal to the Church (March 1894). The appeal was signed by the Bishop of London (Dr Temple) as chairman of the council, and he wrote to all the diocesan bishops, imploring their support. "Notwithstanding the badness of the times," ran one sentence of the letter,

> the council cannot allow this great institution to be ruined and abandoned without making a strong appeal to the friends of religious education; and particularly to churchmen, to save it from the consequences of an oppressive and illiberal policy, by raising either capital or income sufficient for the purpose, which it is impossible to estimate at less than £3000 a year, or £100,000.

The phrase " oppressive and illiberal policy " must have been painful reading to the prime minister, Mr Gladstone, a " proprietor " of the college from 1830, a life-governor, and one of the oldest members of its council: but the Mr Gladstone of 1894 was a very different person from the " stern and unbending " defender of the association of church and state of sixty years before. He was in 1894 at the mercy of his radical supporters, according to the principle " I am their leader, therefore I must follow them." At any rate, he made no response to the appeal. The other members of the council, however, headed by the Hon. W. F. D. Smith (later Lord Hambleden) with a donation of £5000—the first of a long series of noble benefactions to the college and its hospital—responded with splendid generosity, and gave the fund an excellent start. But their admirable lead failed to draw any considerable number of effective followers. True, the S.P.C.K. voted £5000 on condition that, " if the council of the college should ever consent to surrender the clause of the charter requiring membership of the Church of England from its teachers and governors," the grant should be repaid to the Society. The Clothworkers' Company gave £1000, and several gifts of £500 were made. Nevertheless, when Dr Wace resigned the principalship in 1897 the total amount contributed or promised was barely £25,000, and a large portion of that inadequate sum had had to be taken (with the consent of the donors) and used for the payment of current expenses, instead of being invested so as to provide a permanent endowment fund. The final appeal to the Church, in short, had failed to provide the sum—or anything approaching the sum—necessary to maintain the college in a state of independence and efficiency. Nothing remained except the painful alternatives of either the closing of the college altogether or the acceptance of grants from the public authorities—Her Majesty's Treasury and the London County Council—on such terms as they should dictate. The first alternative was seriously considered: the council sought legal opinion as to the personal liability of its members in the event of the bankruptcy of the institution; inquiries, too, were made as to the claims of the members of the staff " in case the college should unfortunately have to be closed and wound up " (May 1894). It was determined, however, that, before the desperate policy of dissolution was resorted to, the terms on which public money could be secured should be fully ascertained.

The move to obtain grants from the national exchequer for

higher education had started from the provincial university colleges in 1886, and in July of that year King's College had associated itself with eleven other similar institutions in an appeal to the Treasury for annual grants. The result of the appeal was a parliamentary vote in 1889 of a total sum of £15,000 a year for five years, to be divided among such of the colleges as had satisfied a board of five commissioners respecting their efficiency. King's College came within this favourable category, and in consequence received £1700 a year for the five years 1889–93 inclusive—a sum which, though useful, did not nearly suffice to wipe off her annual deficit. Nothing was said concerning the religious tests which distinguished King's College from all the other recipients of the bounty of the state. When the five years' period, however, came to an end, Lord Salisbury's government had given place to Mr Gladstone's; and when the renewal and increase of the grant came up for consideration by treasury and parliament, it speedily became evident that the ecclesiastical exclusiveness of King's would become a subject of formidable debate. In March 1892, in a treasury report, Professor Roscoe and Mr James Bryce had remarked that " King's College, being by its constitution a strictly denominational institution, stands in a position differing from that of the other colleges," and on September 16, 1893, a definite demand had been made in the house of commons that the grant to King's should be withdrawn. Hence Sir Albert Rollit, a member of the council of the college, on November 24, 1893, sought to anticipate further adverse criticism by moving in a special meeting of the council the following resolution :

> That in the opinion of the council it is expedient and necessary in the best interests of the college to modify its present constitution in relation to theological requirements made upon its students, professors, and governing body; and that with this object the question be referred to a committee for consideration and report.

The motion, as seconded by Mr William Stebbing, was long and seriously debated; but, though it received powerful support from Sir Owen Roberts, Sir Joseph Lister, and others, the general opinion was so strongly against it that Sir Albert Rollit withdrew it " for a time."

The time was not long in coming. In January 1894 the Board of Education and the Treasury made a formal inquiry respecting " the constitution and work of the college," and as a result issued on July 17, 1894, an intimation that they accepted the allocation of £1700 to King's College subject to the condition that it should obtain before March 31, 1895, the necessary alteration in Clause xii of the King's College Act, 1882, which imposes a religious test on officers of the college other than the professors of oriental literature and modern languages,

adding that

in the meantime no issue will be made to this college in respect of its provisional grant,

and that

should the existing tests not be removed from all its teachers, other than theological, before the date named, the provisional grant of £1700 will lapse.

Here, indeed, was an ultimatum from the government.[1] It compelled the council to face the final issue of secularization or bankruptcy—on the one hand, the abandonment of the fundamental principle of the college; on the other hand, the total closing of the college itself. The issue was faced at a special and unusually full meeting of the council held on October 25, 1894. After a detailed statement concerning the desperate financial condition of the college had been made, Sir Albert Rollit once more moved, and Mr Horton Smith seconded, the resolution,

That in the opinion of the council it is expedient and necessary in the best interests of the college to modify its present constitution in relation to theological requirements made upon its students and professors.

(The motion refrained from mentioning the governing body.) To this motion the treasurer (Mr C. P. Serocold) at once moved an amendment, which the Dean of St Paul's (Dr Robert Gregory) seconded:

That, considering the support which the college is now receiving from churchmen, it is not expedient to entertain a proposal for such an alteration in its constitution as the government require.

A prolonged debate took place, in which the Bishop of London, the Marquis of Salisbury, Bishop Barry, Sir John Mowbray, and Mr William Stebbing played the leading parts. In the course of the proceedings Dr Wace also spoke (in favour of the amendment), but he had to read a letter which he had that morning received from Professors Adams, Capper, Crookshank, Hales, Halliburton, Hudson, Huntington, Robinson, Seeley, Thomson, and Warr, together with the

[1] Lord Rosebery had succeeded Mr Gladstone as prime minister in March 1894.

headmaster of the school, "expressing their desire that all tests should be removed." When the question was put to the vote the amendment was carried by 15 to 8.[1] The immediate sequel to this heroic decision of the council was the resignation of Sir A. K. Rollit and Sir Owen Roberts, with Messrs Preece, Horton Smith, and Stebbing—that is, of all the defeated minority who had not at one time or other been members of the staff of the college.

It was at this juncture—*in hoc tanto cardine rerum*—that the purged and purified council, led by the Bishop of London, made that last frantic effort to rouse the faithful to a sense of their responsibilities which we have noted above. It was just becoming evident that the effort was doomed to failure when a brief respite was given to the despairing council by the fall of the Rosebery government and the return of the Marquis of Salisbury to power (July 1895). On October 23, 1895, the council received the welcome news that the treasury had decided to restore the grant of £1700 per annum for the remaining three years of the quinquennial period (1896–99) "without any stipulation as regards tests." At the same meeting, however, the principal reported an interview that he had had with the Chancellor of the Exchequer (Sir Michael Hicks-Beach) in which the chancellor had informed him that it would be impossible permanently to subsidize the college unless it should relax its religious requirements. The Dean of St Paul's then moved, and the council accepted, *nemine contradicente*, the following conscience clause for students:

> If the parent or guardian of any student shall state in writing that he has a conscientious objection to the attendance of such student at the divine service of the Church of England, or to his receiving religious instruction according to the principles of the Church of England, such student shall be exempted from attendance at chapel and at the divinity lectures, and shall not be debarred by reason of such exemption from any scholarship or exhibition, or from any privilege to which other students can be admitted by the council; but this regulation shall not apply to students of the theological faculty.

This concession left the disabilities of professors and councillors

---

[1] For the first time in the history of the college the voting list was recorded. It was as follows : (1) For the amendment : Marquis of Salisbury, Dean of St Paul's, Bishop Barry, Sir J. R. Mowbray, Bishop of St Albans, C. Awdry, G. W. Bell, Hon. and Rev. E. Carr Glyn, Canon Ince, C. Austen Leigh, Hon. R. C. Parsons, C. P. Serocold, Hon. W. F. D. Smith, J. G. Talbot, Rev. Professor Wiltshire. (2) Against the amendment : Sir George Johnson, Sir Joseph Lister, W. H. Preece, Sir W. O. Priestley, Sir Owen Roberts, Sir A. K. Rollit, R. Horton Smith, W. Stebbing.

intact; but it was hoped that it would be sufficient to pacify the nonconformist conscience, and satisfy the secularist demand. The question, however, was still in suspense when Dr Wace resigned the principalship.

Much the same story has to be told respecting the London County Council and its grants in aid of technical education. For two years (1894–95) the L.C.C. voted £1000 per annum to University College in aid of its technical instruction, but withheld the grant from King's College on the ground that it was a denominational institution. In December 1895 the council, fortified with its new conscience clause for students, renewed its application, and renewed it with success. King's College was placed on the same footing as University College. The council, however, were informed that as soon as the University of London should have been reconstructed according to the designs of the Cowper commission, whatever sums the L.C.C. might vote for technical education would be paid to the university, to be apportioned by the senate, and would not be paid direct to individual colleges. The council, therefore, had to face the prospect of the almost immediate loss of this grant if the senate of the university should, as the Cowper commissioners recommended, be precluded from making any assignment of money to any institution " in respect of which a privilege is granted or a disability imposed in respect of religious belief."

The council, therefore, realized that soon they would have to consider the question of tests for teachers as well as that of tests for students. For the Cowper commissioners had been more concerned with the former than with the latter. Sir Joseph Lister had been examined by them as to the operation of the inquisition, and had made light of the matter. It was, he thought, " a mild kind of test," which did not matter so long as the college did good work. He was, however, in favour of abolishing it. Not so Dr Wace. When the commissioners pressed him about it, he warmly defended it, and maintained that the intention of this statutory test was to exclude only those whose hostility to Christianity in general would destroy the confidence of parents in the college. Can he have known of the case of Professor Kerr, whose appointment to the engineering department had been postponed until he had transferred his sitting from a presbyterian to an anglican church; or of the similar case of Professor Leone Levi in the department of commerce; or of the case of Dr Cash, whose appointment in the medical school had been cancelled when it was found that he was a quaker? Can he, indeed, have remembered the following episode, which had occurred only six years earlier, in his own principalship? On July 15, 1887, when the health of Professor Delamotte was failing, Mr John Parker was elected joint professor of fine art in order to assist him. Mr Parker was duly informed of the appointment, and he wrote accepting it. The matter seemed to be settled. Then it occurred to the secretary of the college that Mr Parker had not been asked the usual question as to his ecclesiastical allegiance, and he accordingly wrote to him to make the inquiry. To his consternation he learned from Mr Parker, who called to see him, that he was a Roman Catholic. He sent him on to the principal, who, having heard the facts of the case, said that the matter would have to be remitted to the council for decision. On August 3 the council, " after full consideration," resolved :

> That the secretary address the following letter to Mr Parker : " I regret to have to inform you that the council, having considered the fact of your not being a member of the Church of England, of which they had not been informed, can come to no other conclusion than that they had no power to appoint you to the professorship of fine arts, so that your election was null and void under the terms of the Act of Parliament which governs the college."

Hence the appointment of Mr Parker was cancelled, the post was advertised as vacant, and another person was elected. If the facts of this case had been known or remembered, it would have been difficult for anyone to contend that the test was a " mild one," since it excluded a candidate who had presumably been chosen because he appeared best qualified technically for the post. Still more difficult would it have been for even so strong a protestant as Dr Wace to argue that a catholic was ineligible to a professorship of fine art merely because his " hostility to Christianity in general would destroy the confidence of parents in the college." It was evident, indeed, that the tests could not possibly be retained if the council were to continue to receive public money. The utterly illogical distinction between " professors of oriental literature and modern languages " (who had been free from tests since the foundation of the college) and professors of other subjects (on whom they had been imposed) would have to be swept away, and all teachers other than those of the theological department would have to be appointed on technical qualifications alone. Dr Wace, however, was not willing to accept this abandonment of the fundamental principle of the college as set forth in its charter of 1829, and as repeated in the statute of 1882. That the abandonment was inevitable, nevertheless, he must have perceived, and the recognition of this painful fact was probably one of the causes which led him to lay down his office in 1897.

Two years before Dr Wace resigned, Mr J. W. Cunningham, the old and faithful secretary of the college, terminated the fifty years of his strikingly efficient service. The council in accepting his resignation (April 5, 1895), and voting him a pension, passed a cordial resolution in which his great work for the college was summarized. There were a hundred and ten candidates for the vacant post, ten of whom were selected for interview. From the ten the one finally chosen was the admirably capable and zealous Mr Walter Smith, who for the next quarter of a century (1895–1919) continued to administer the affairs of the college with masterly skill, doing much to raise the institution from bankruptcy to solvency. No sooner was he installed in office than he undertook a drastic reorganization of the college finances. The deficit for the year 1894 (the treasury grant having been withdrawn) had been the appalling sum of £6076; and even when a 10 per cent. levy had been made on the staff an adverse balance of £4101 had remained. Mr Smith perceived that the whole system of deductions from fees and levies on salaries (which had become hopelessly complicated and grossly inequitable) would have to be abandoned in favour of a simpler and fairer plan. With infinite labour he examined the income and the expenditure of every department, the assets and the liabilities of every teacher, and on the basis of his findings he framed an exhaustive report and a wholly new scheme of payments. This scheme the council adopted on February 14, 1896—a questionable valentine for the staff! The opening sentence ran:

> The object of this scheme is to establish a system under which the annual expenditure of the college shall never exceed its annual income, and in which the expenses shall be borne in fair proportions by the various departments or chairs.

The general principle of the scheme was that each department should be treated as a financial unit; that the first charge upon its fees should be 25 per cent. for the general purposes of the college; that the second charge should be the amount of the departmental expenses; and that the whole of the remainder (if any) should be divided proportionally among the staff of the department. The application of this scheme (which postponed the period of Mr Smith's popularity with the professors) of course involved a considerable reduction in the already scanty sums paid to the teaching staff. It was estimated, indeed, that the immediate diminution in salaries was equivalent to a 24 per cent. deduction under the old system. In the year of its introduction, for instance, the sums payable to certain of the less fortunate professors were as follows: history, £67; literature, £56; geology, £25; comparative anatomy, £19; German, £17; ophthalmology, £14; neuro-pathology, £9; while the unhappy professor of public health found himself not only without any salary at all, but £8 in debt to the college in respect of the expenses of his department. The patient professoriate bore the shock astonishingly well; but most of its members had to seek supplementary occupation. Nay, more, they were compelled to look upon their college posts merely as visiting appointments and to concentrate their main energies elsewhere—medical men on their practices, engineers on their office work, clergymen on preaching or on parochial administration, literary men on journalism, linguists on private tuition, and so on. The vitality and efficiency of the college were drained to a low ebb. It lost corporate consciousness.[1] To all it became clear that unless the dwindling fees of the students and the inadequate donations of the pious could be supplemented by large grants of public money the staff would have to be disbanded and the college wound up. Mr Walter Smith's scheme of financial reorganization had rendered the council the inestimable service of making it face the stern facts of the situation. And the facts were sufficiently formidable. The loss on the working of the year 1895—the last year under the old system—reached the unprecedented figure of £7918 19s. 2d. This was the moment when the college most nearly touched the bankruptcy point. And at this moment the treasurer, Mr C. P. Serocold, resigned his thankless and laborious office. It was not easy to find a successor; but eventually (June 1896) the Hon. W. F. D. Smith, with self-sacrificing devotion, accepted the responsible and painfully exposed position. The story of the financial recovery of the college under what I may perhaps be allowed to call the *régime* of the two Smiths—the new treasurer and the new secretary—together with the story of the final removal of the religious tests, must be reserved for the next chapter.

---

[1] By a most remarkable concession the council (July 8, 1892) resolved " that each professor should be at liberty to advertise his own class at his own expense."

THE STRUGGLE FOR EXISTENCE

§ 4. *The Faculties of Arts and Science*

One of the incidental effects of Mr Walter Smith's financial reorganization scheme was a much sharper definition of the departments of the college, and a more clear-cut separation of the faculties from one another, than had been known before. In particular, the old department of general literature and science—the original nucleus of the college—ceased to exist under that name, being divided into the two respective faculties of arts and science. The bifurcation was gradual. So far back as 1887 a committee appointed to consider the causes of the ominous decline in the department, and to suggest remedies, had recommended

> that science should be altogether separated from general literature and be formed into a new department with the view of providing a systematic course in this subject, and affording such instruction as would meet the special requirements of candidates for the University of London science examination.

At the beginning of 1888, therefore, the division took place, and Professor J. M. Thomson became " first dean of the new department of science." The differentiation of teachers, however, was far from complete: science, for instance, shared mathematics with arts; chemistry with medicine; and geology with engineering. The second step was taken in 1893, when the council accepted a recommendation of the general (professorial) board that in future

> the designation of the great departments of the college should be changed to that of faculties, the name " department " being reserved for the subsidiary branches of the various faculties.

In accordance with this resolution the following five faculties were recognized : (1) the Faculty of Theology ; (2) the Faculty of Arts, with the Normal Department and the Department of Oriental Languages attached ; (3) the Faculty of Science, with divisions of (*a*) Natural Science and (*b*) Applied Science and Engineering ; (4) the Faculty of Medicine, with the Departments of Bacteriology and Public Health attached ; (5) the Faculty of Law. It will be observed that this change was much more than a mere change of name : the faculty of science was entirely dissociated from that of arts, and closely associated with that of engineering. It was left to Mr Walter Smith, however, in 1896, to complete the differentiation. Under his reconstruction engineering became a separate faculty, and science at last was liberated from all its old entanglements and made wholly independent.

365

Neither arts nor science, however, whether bound together or separate from one another, flourished during this distressful period. The "faculty of arts"—a sort of unattached classical sixth—having failed to secure affiliation with Oxford and Cambridge, being too proud to adapt its curriculum frankly to the syllabus of the external examinations of the University of London, and suffering from the successful rivalry of the progressive secondary schools (including the school in the basement of the college itself), dragged on a mournful existence, languishing for the Albert University which was to come as its deliverer and spouse. The "faculty of science" also failed to function effectively. Although it was specially constituted to prepare students for the London B.Sc., it did not succeed in attracting many students. Its lack of success was due partly to the imperfect adaptation of its courses to the university syllabus; partly to the inadequate equipment of its laboratories; partly to the high range of its fees; and partly to the uncertainty as to its future so long as the reports of the Selborne and Cowper commissioners were under discussion. Hence when Dr Wace's principalship came to a close there were no more than nine students in the faculty of science, and in the faculty of arts (apart from day training students) only eight.

The boards of the faculties, as well as the general board and the council, of course, from time to time discussed this lamentable failure. The dominant opinion was that no complete revival could be expected until King's College should have established its position as a constituent member of a new teaching and degree-conferring university in London. Meantime, however, while the college was waiting and striving for the Albert or the Gresham charter, various expedients were adopted to attract students and keep the departments and faculties in existence. In 1888, for instance, an effort was made to establish "commercial classes," in which modern languages, together with geography and political economy, would take the place of Latin, Greek, and other merely academic subjects. The budding merchants, however, did not come. In 1889 a serious attempt was made to revive the lethargic oriental section of the department.[1] An elaborate scheme was arranged in conjunction with University College and the newly founded Imperial Institute. In accordance with this scheme the Indian languages hitherto taught (or at

[1] How near to Nirvana the oriental section had approached may be gauged from the fact that in 1888 " it being reported to the council that the Rev. John Campbell, professor of Bengali, had been absent from the college and not heard of for some years, it was resolved to declare the professorship vacant."

any rate provided for) at King's College—Sanskrit, Bengali, Hindi, Hindustani, Tamil, and Telugu—were transferred to University College; while King's College undertook to give instruction in Chinese, Japanese, Burmese, Persian, Arabic, Turkish, Russian, and Modern Greek. The courses arranged were intended both for candidates seeking to enter the civil service and for those engaged in commerce with the east. Nothing much came of them, however, for a good many years. The civilians preferred the intensive culture of Wren and Gurney; and, as to the men of commerce, they thought it much more proper and reasonable that Asiatics who wanted English goods should learn to ask for them in English than that Englishmen should spend their time and money in acquiring a knowledge of the numerous and barbaric dialects of the Orient. The oriental section, therefore, during Dr Wace's term of office, did little to strengthen the dying faculty to which it was attached. The mere fact, however, that, for the first time, University College and King's College combined to produce a co-operative scheme of education, in which over-lapping was avoided, was significant of the cordial relations which had been established between the two quondam rivals in the course of their common effort to secure a charter and their common pursuit of public money.

The one successful device for the revivification of the faculty of arts adopted during this period was the institution within its borders of the day training department. To a brief sketch of this important innovation our next section will be devoted. Before closing the present section, however, we must note a few changes in the staff which occurred while Dr Wace was principal. (1) In 1885 Mr S. R. Gardiner moved to Oxford, and consequently resigned the chair of modern history which he had held since 1876; he was succeeded by Mr (later Sir) J. K. Laughton, the naval historian. (2) Two changes took place in the professorship of French. In 1885 M. Alphonse Mariette terminated a period of service to the college extending over thirty-one years. His immediate successor was Professor L. M. Moriarty, who, however, held the chair for four years only. Then, in 1889, came Professor Victor Spiers, who presided over a department that under him became one of the largest in the college until 1926. (3) In 1891 the sound and pacific Rev. Alfred Caldecott—one of the ablest and most devoted servants the college has ever known, destined to be the first independent dean of the college under the existing dual organization—succeeded the erratic and belligerent

Professor A. W. Momerie in the chair of logic and meta-physics. (4) In the same year the Rev. William Cunningham, of Cambridge, the pioneer in the study of English economic history, was appointed to the Tooke chair of economic science and statistics, in succession to Professor F. Y. Edgeworth, who himself, barely twelve months earlier, had taken over the post from its first holder, Professor Thorold Rogers (appointed 1859). (5) In 1892 Mr H. J. H. Mackay, the present dean of the faculty of law, began to teach his subject in the college. (6) In 1894 Mr (later Professor) J. B. Dale joined the mathematical department, followed in 1895 by Mr R. W. K. Edwards. Both of these brilliant Cambridge wranglers were destined to make service to King's College the staple of their life's work. (7) In 1895 Mr S. A. F. White, the present dean of the faculty of science, came from Oxford to assist Professor W. Grylls Adams in the teaching of natural philosophy. As we read of these appointments we begin to feel in touch with the current day, and to realize that we are passing out of the region of history into the region of living affairs.

§ 5. *The Day Training Department*

The sense that we are dealing not with records of the past but with realities of the present remains strongly upon us when we turn to treat of the founding of the day training department. For, although it was founded so far back as 1890, its beloved and revered founder, Professor J. W. Adamson, is still in our midst and, though nominally retired, still busy in countless good works in the cause of education. His admirable and authoritative sketch of his department, contributed as an appendix to this book, renders it needless for me to do more than cull a few specific notes from the council minute-books concerning its genesis.

On June 14, 1890:

> The principal reported that he had been in communication with the Education Department with respect to the college being recognised as a Day Training College under schedule 116, code 1890, and that, as an application had to be sent in at the beginning of the month, he had, after consultation with Canon Gregory and others, applied for leave to admit 80 students—40 first year and 40 second year—at a fee of £20 per annum, to be paid half by the student and half by the department. The council fully approved of the action of the principal, and authorised him to continue the necessary negotiations.

The outcome of the negotiations was that, not 80 as desired, but 50 students—25 first year and 25 second year—were assigned to King's College. They were attached to the faculty of arts, and for their academic studies they attended such lectures in the faculty as were suited to their needs. Some of the better equipped took the full course for the London pass degree. For their professional studies, and for the superintendence of their work in the practising schools,[1] a " normal master " had to be appointed, and for this important post the council, on October 10, 1890, elected Mr J. W. Adamson, a former distinguished evening student of the college. Under him the department, excellently administered, prospered greatly. The first report of the council (May 1892) said:

> The admission of Queen's Scholars has been hitherto well justified by the results, both their work and their conduct having been satisfactory, and some of them having distinguished themselves in the college examinations.

Later reports continued to speak well of the progress of the department. At the end of Dr Wace's principalship it constituted almost the whole of the faculty of arts, which but for it could hardly have survived at all.

In July 1892 arrangements were made by which the A.K.C. diploma could be obtained by day training students who, having completed their two years' educational course in the mornings, were prepared to return to college for a third year as evening students in order to take divinity and other necessary subjects.

In August of the same year a scheme was mooted according to which Mr Adamson and the arts professors of King's College would make themselves responsible for the training of fifty young women destined to teach in Church of England day schools, who would be lodged for the purpose of preparation for this work in the Wordsworth College, Kilburn, under the auspices of the Church Extension Association. The council gave its assent to the proposal; the Board of Education seemed favourable; but in the end the negotiations fell through.

Three years later—viz., on June 14, 1895,

> A scheme recommended by the principal and the board of the faculty of arts for starting a department for training teachers in secondary schools was submitted to the council.

[1] The first three " practising schools " placed at the disposal of the day training department were the Lambeth Schools, the St Martin's School, and the SS. James's and Peter's Schools.

The council referred the matter to a committee, and on receiving the report of the committee gave their approval to the project; but the necessary consent of the Board of Education was not secured. Hence the day training department remained, as it had begun, a department for the training of fifty young men for the work of teaching in the public elementary schools.

§ 6. *The Civil Service Classes*

Another department concerned with the public service, although definitely below university rank, and regarded rather as dependent on the college than strictly part of it, was that of the civil service classes. We have noted above [1] how in 1875 Mr Braginton had brought his classes for second-grade clerks within the ambit of the college; and further how in 1881 he had established at Exeter Hall, in association with the college, classes for young women aspirants to post-office employment—which classes the council had allowed to be transplanted to the college precincts before the close of that same year.

Both these sets of classes—male and female—prospered amazingly, under Mr Braginton's capable management, during the period of Dr Wace's principalship. Their success, indeed, in their lowly sphere was one of the few bright features in a gloomy era. One or two notable developments must be recorded. (1) The tables at the end of the chapter show sufficiently clearly the magnitude of the work that Mr Braginton organized and controlled. At their highest, which was precisely at the date of Dr Wace's departure, the classes numbered in all no fewer than 1657 persons; that is to say, they far exceeded in multitude the whole of King's College and King's College School put together. (2) At first the tuition was limited to evening classes, but in 1892 teaching by correspondence was introduced, and every year after that date saw, on the average, a couple of hundred students receiving guidance through the post. (3) At the same time a still more important innovation was made. In July 1892, at Mr Braginton's suggestion, the council decided to institute day classes, primarily for youths who wished to compete for what were called " boy clerkships " (pay, 14s. a week) or " boy copyistships " (pay, 4d. an hour) in the public offices. Since there was at that time no room available in the college for any more day classes,

---

[1] *Cf.* pp. 308–309, 310–312.

the council (October 1892) hired temporary premises at 4 Albion Place, Blackfriars Bridge, whence the classes a year later were transferred to more commodious and convenient quarters in 91A Waterloo Road, opposite the L. and S.W. railway terminus. In 1894 the rapid growth of these day classes necessitated alterations and additions to these premises that cost some £300. Very speedily the civil service day classes established themselves as what was virtually a high-grade commercial school. Their success, in common with that of the evening civil service classes, was most marked. Year after year Mr Braginton's pupils secured, against all the rest of the world, more than 50 per cent. of the appointments offered by the government for competition in the lower ranges of the public service—*i.e.*, boy clerkships, boy copyistships, telegraph learners, excise and customs appointments, assistant surveyorships of taxes, and so on.[1]

So important, indeed, did the civil service department become that in 1893 its teachers were formally recognized as belonging to the college staff. This elevation of status was not entirely due to a desire on the part of the council to reward distinguished merit and to acknowledge striking success. It rather resembled the emperor Caracalla's extension of the Roman citizenship to provincials. That is to say, it was done primarily in order that the teachers in the civil service classes might be subjected to the annual levies which at that time were being made on the salaries of the college staff. For, although the fees charged in the civil service classes were necessarily very low—ranging from £2 10s. to £5 per term—the numbers attending the classes were so large that it was far more profitable to be a teacher of these classes than a professor in the college.

For four years the civil service day classes flourished exceedingly in their Waterloo Road premises. Then, in 1897, King's College School migrated from the Strand to Wimbledon, leaving the basement of the college empty, swept, and garnished. In these circumstances the council sublet, on favourable terms, the Waterloo Road premises, and moved the day classes into the vacated schoolrooms, where they became known as the "Strand School."

[1] In 1894, for instance, 326 appointments were thrown open to competition. About 2400 candidates presented themselves, and Mr Braginton's pupils secured 190 out of the 326 prizes. In 1895 only 125 appointments were offered. The number of competitors was 1100. Mr Braginton's pupils secured 88 out of the 125.

§ 7. *King's College School*

Whilst the day classes of the civil service department took shape in Waterloo Road and prepared themselves for their transmigration to the north of the river and their reincarnation as the " Strand School," the old King's College School drooped and declined, until it seemed to be doomed to dissolution. We have already noted [1] the steady and rapid fall of its numbers from 612 in 1880 to 166 in 1897. The great slump curiously coincided with the headmastership of the Rev. Dr Stokoe (1880–89), but it would appear to have been due to circumstances over which he had no control. At any rate, the council, which had many and anxious deliberations concerning the matter, never suggested that he was in any way to blame; and when he resigned they expressed cordial appreciation of his efforts to restore the school to its old condition of prosperity. The causes of decline, as they appeared to the council, were three. First, the great schools which were the chief rivals to King's College School—*e.g.*, St Paul's School—were moving out of London into suburbs where they could have ample buildings and extensive playing-fields; secondly, the City of London School, established in its new premises on the Embankment, in close vicinity to King's College School, could offer incomparably better accommodation than the subterranean vaults of the Strand, and could place at the disposal of its pupils laboratories immeasurably better equipped; thirdly, lack of endowments handicapped King's College School, as compared with other schools, in the matter both of fees (which were high) and of scholarships (which were few and poor). On the top of these permanent and fundamental causes, a lamentable and discreditable tragedy in 1885 brought the school into an unenviable notoriety and a public disfavour which seriously accelerated its decline. On April 26 of that year a pupil of the school, aged twelve, C. F. Bourdas by name, died of concussion of the spine, and at the inquest it was proved that the cause of his death was grave injuries which he had received at the hands of a number of big bullies whose evil despotism had long maintained a reign of terror throughout the school. The *Times* took up the case with unwonted passion; victims of the bullies, freed from the incubus of fear, told horrid tales of tyranny, and revealed a grave lack of supervision during play hours; parliament took cognisance of the case and asked awkward questions; the home secretary, Sir William Harcourt

[1] See above, p. 354, and compare the table at the end of this chapter.

—although an *ex officio* governor of the college, and the son of one of its founders—passed severe censures upon the administration of the school, and ordered the public prosecutor to see to the due punishment of the murderers of the ill-fated boy, saying (house of commons, May 4, 1885):

> There are hundreds of boys sent to prison for offences trivial in comparison with crimes of this description. I think the time has come for dealing with this matter seriously, and when big boys guilty of offences of this kind are punished as they deserve to be, and when schools managed so as to allow a state of things of this sort to be possible are made to suffer, we shall then get to the end of a system which makes a number of innocent young lives miserable and intolerable.

The whole episode was extremely damaging to the name and reputation of the school; the council dealt with the matter in a hesitant, procrastinating, secretive, ineffective manner that roused intense resentment in the public mind; boys were removed from the school by scores. In vain did the headmaster frame new and stringent regulations respecting supervision during out-of-school hours. The damage was done beyond repair.

Dr Stokoe's period of headship, although it was signalized by this disastrous tragedy, and although it saw the school dwindle in numbers from 612 to 249, nevertheless was marked by some useful developments. In particular, in 1883 he secured for the school the use of a playing-field, albeit in the remote and not very salubrious suburb of Wormwood Scrubbs; in 1885 he persuaded the council to abolish the two half-holidays per week in favour of the whole day Saturday holiday; in 1886 he established a special "matriculation" class, and placed it in charge of a genial genius of amazing versatility, Mr C. D. Webb, who continued to conduct it with striking efficiency for nearly forty years; in 1888 he organized a new commercial department, in the hope of drawing a new class of boys to his depleted vaults. But nothing sufficed to recall prosperity to the doomed dungeons of the Strand. Necessity soon began to require diminutions of the teaching staff. Such of the masters as were clergymen sought livings, in order to avoid dyings: in May 1888 the Rev. John Twentyman, the vice-master for twenty-two years, resigned on being appointed rector of Ingoldsby; six months later the Rev. Blomfield Jackson, a still older member of the staff, and author of some of the best-known classical manuals of the day, secured the vicarage of St Bartholomew's, Moorfields; finally, in the summer of 1889 Dr

Stokoe himself withdrew from the unequal struggle with Giant Despair by accepting the rectory of Lutterworth, whence five centuries earlier John Wycliffe had waged his war on Giant Pope.

When the council met (May 10, 1889) to consider what should be done on the departure of Dr Stokoe, they came to the important decision that the new headmaster, although of course he must be a member of the Church of England, need not be in holy orders. And, as a matter of fact, when, in response to advertisement, applications came in, out of ten candidates a layman was chosen—viz., Mr Charles William Bourne, sometime scholar of St John's College, Cambridge (twenty-sixth wrangler and second-class classic in 1868), at the time headmaster of Inverness College, and formerly mathematical master at Marlborough.[1] When Mr Bourne, in the autumn of 1889, came to the Strand to take up his difficult duties he found that already (June 7, 1889) an epoch-making proposal had been debated by the council. It had been placed before the council by the finance committee, who had received it from Dr Wace, to whom it had been suggested by some person unnamed, but probably the Hon. R. C. Parsons. The proposal was none other than that the school should be moved from the Strand altogether, and replanted in the suburbs. After a long discussion the project was turned down for the time. It was decided to wait and see what the new head could do on the old site. Mr Bourne, when he had settled down, made valiant efforts to retrieve the situation. He improved the playground (which had been five feet higher at one end than the other!) at a cost of £650; he dismissed five superfluous masters; he reorganized the science teaching, substituting a regular tutor for the visiting professors of the college; he lowered the fees from £8 8s. per term to £7 7s. to boys entering the school under eleven years of age; he abolished entrance scholarships for the sake of economy in 1892, and reintroduced them for the sake of pupils in 1893; he made boys buy their own books, instead of hiring them from the school, in 1892; he arranged with the Temple and Lincoln's Inn to train their choir-boys at half-fees (1893); he managed to effect an exchange of rooms with the college in 1894, and so brought up some of his classes from the basement into the light of day. But all to no avail. The numbers continued to decline. True, the 249 whom he found in the school rose to 274 during his first year; but then the slump set in again more severely than ever, until fewer than 200 remained.

[1] Mr Bourne took orders in 1898.

Then it was seen clearly that, if the school were to survive at all, it would have to be removed. The question of removal, indeed, had never been allowed wholly to slumber. And Mr Bourne—ardently supported by Dr Wace in the college and by the Hon. R. C. Parsons on the council—had become its zealous advocate. Various possible sites had been considered. The favoured spot in 1889 had been Sutton; in June 1890 Clapham Junction had been suggested, but Mr Bourne had expressed a doubt as to whether that salubrious region would remain suitable for a public school; in July 1893 Mr Parsons was strongly urging the advantages of Putney. A year later Mr Bourne wrote a weighty letter begging that, even if the school as a whole could not be moved, the junior boys at least might be transplanted to " one of the southern suburbs." The council decided that they could not incur the expense of the transplantation, but that if Mr Bourne cared to open a suburban preparatory school at his own risk they would have no objection to his doing so. Finally, however, an intimation from the Surrey County Council (July 1896) that they would welcome a secondary school at Wimbledon, and would help to maintain it by grants, brought the matter to a head.

On July 17, 1896, a committee of the council was appointed to consider the problem of the removal to Wimbledon. On December 11, 1896, the report of the committee came before the council: it was emphatic in favour of removal, stating that the only alternative was closing down; it recommended Wimbledon as the site for the new establishment, because (1) the school had a large and loyal connexion in that locality, and (2) the Surrey County Council wished to have the school there. The council, after long debate, adopted the report, and expressed their

> desire and approval of the removal of the school to the neighbourhood of Wimbledon, provided that a sufficient amount of debentures, paying interest at the rate of 4 per cent., can be obtained to pay for the purchase of a suitable site and the erection of proper buildings.

Mr Bourne then set to work to explore the wilds of Wimbledon for sites, and on January 15, 1897, he presented a report respecting five that he had discovered. One of the five so far exceeded all the others in eligibility that it was at once selected. This was a house with six acres of land attached, known as South Hayes, facing Wimbledon Common. It was in the market, and procurable for the exceedingly reasonable sum of

£17,000. In February 1897 the property was purchased, the issue of debentures having speedily realized over £18,000. Since the house at South Hayes was sufficiently roomy to accommodate the 166 boys who then constituted the school, arrangements for the removal were speedily concluded. Soon after Easter 1897 the migration took place.

With the establishment of the school at Wimbledon a new era of prosperity began. The very first term saw a rise in numbers from 166 to 178. The next year witnessed the reaching of the 200 mark once more. Since then, under Mr Bourne, Mr Douglas Smith (1906–10), and Mr Lionel Rogers, all the old prosperity and glory have been recovered, and even surpassed. The removal of the school from the precincts of the college, however, marks the point where our detailed study of its fortunes must perforce cease.[1]

§ 8. *The Ladies' Department*

Whereas the tendencies of King's College School were centrifugal, those of the Ladies' Department were centripetal. While the school first ceased to feed the college, then ceased to support it financially, then ceased to occupy its cellars, and finally (1911) passed out of the jurisdiction of its council and set itself up as a completely independent institution, the ladies' department, on the other hand, drew toward the college. Not only, starting from Richmond, did it move to Kensington and, after a suitable period of probation in that elegant quarter, terminate its pilgrimage in the bosom of the college itself; it also continually strengthened its connexion with the college, and brought its curricula more fully into accord with those that prevailed in the Strand. Perhaps these two sharply contrasted movements—the outward movement of the school and the inward movement of the ladies' department—symbolize respectively the eternal conflict between youth and age and the perennial attraction of sex.

We left the "lectures for ladies" going on in temporary apartments in Observatory Avenue, Kensington, while the committee sought for a more permanent home for them in the vicinage. At the end of 1882 it had seemed certain that 13 Kensington Square—Talleyrand's old home—would be purchased for the sum of £7500; but in February 1883 the negotiations were broken off. The main cause of this rupture would seem to have been that certain members of the council,

---

[1] For its formal separation from King's College in 1911 see below, pp. 420–421.

headed by Sir Charles Freake, thought that it would be better to build a new college on an unoccupied site rather than buy an antiquated and inconvenient dwelling-house at an exorbitant price. At any rate, a search for sites began, and on May 9, 1884, a choice of three was laid before the council—viz., (1) in Cheniston Gardens, (2) in Young Street, and (3) in Kensington Court. The Kensington Court site was unanimously selected, and a provisional agreement for its purchase at £5300 was entered into by the council. On examination, however, the title of the estate proved to be defective, and after protracted controversy accompanied by a marked rise in temperature, negotiations were terminated (December 1884). The council then at once reverted to the scheme for the purchase of 13 Kensington Square, and early in 1885 secured it for £7500. Since at that time the special fund for the establishment of the ladies' institution amounted to no more than £5500, the sum of £2000 had to be borrowed to complete the transaction. Although the house was in good repair, extensive alterations had to be made in order to adapt it to the purposes of a college, and these cost an additional £1000 or so. Further borrowings had accordingly to take place, and when in October 1885 the new premises were formally opened by the Bishop of London they were burdened with a mortgage of £4000.

Before the formal opening took place—viz., in June 1885—an important change was made in the status of the ladies' organization: it was officially recognized as a department of King's College—just as a warship is regarded as a floating portion of the British Empire—and its government was remodelled. It was to be administered, under the council, by an executive committee consisting of seven members of council, seven members of the staff, and seven ladies. Three years later (June 1888) a slight change in constitution was made. The seven members of the staff left the executive committee and, with the other teachers of the college, formed a new advisory professorial board. The principal of King's College was, of course, *ex officio* head of the ladies' department. A " lady superintendent " (Miss Cornelia Schmitz), who in 1891 was elevated to the rank of " vice-principal," ruled as the principal's deputy in Kensington Square. When in 1894 Miss Schmitz consented to become the second Mrs Wace her place was taken by Miss Lilian Faithfull, selected out of thirty-nine candidates. " This lady," say the minutes, " had taken a first class in English at the Oxford University examination for women in 1887, and had been for five years lecturer in

English at the Royal Holloway College." Miss Faithfull soon made a notable change in the spirit and character of her department. Under Miss Schmitz it had been a pleasant meeting-place for leisured ladies, young and old, who wished by listening to popular lectures to keep up their education, to add to their accomplishments, and to pass the time. Miss Faithfull, with the traditions of Somerville and Egham behind her, added to the dilettante diversions of the department the stern and serious studies necessary for the securing of London University degrees and Oxford or Cambridge diplomas.[1]

§ 9. *The Theological Department*

The ladies' department of the college, situated in Kensington Square, under Miss Faithfull's able governance made the cultivation of the arts the main object of its activities. Under Miss Schmitz, supported by Dr Wace, theology had occupied a prominent position. Not only did the principal himself lecture twice a week—once on the scriptures and once on church history—to large and venerable classes, but the head-master of the school discoursed on the prayer-book; while, above all, the Rev. Professor A. W. Momerie (always immaculately clad and modestly wearing black kid gloves when lecturing) expounded to admiring multitudes of matrons and maids the mysteries of simplified metaphysics. Neither Miss Schmitz nor Dr Wace, however, wholly approved of Professor Momerie. He was too young, too well dressed, too popular, and, worst of all, too rash and rationalistic in his views to please them. Down at King's College he was giving a lot of trouble and causing much anxiety, and that at a time when the financial position of the college made it imperative that criticism and agitation should be avoided.

We have noted Professor Momerie's appointment in 1880 as successor to Archdeacon Watkins in the chair of logic and metaphysics. He was then but thirty-two years of age, and at the height of his effervescence. Brought up as an only child in the sternly puritanical home of a zealous dissenting minister and his still more zealous and dissident wife, he had after a crushed infancy, a subjugated boyhood, and a morbid adolescence risen in excessive revolt against the deadly dogmas and the rigid restrictions of the parental prison. At the City of London School and at Edinburgh University his powerful mind, too long repressed, exploded with destructive violence,

[1] See L. M. Faithfull, *In the House of my Pilgrimage* (1924), pp. 105 *sq.*

and, rejecting all the tenets of orthodox Christianity, he became a rationalist whose natural intellectual affinities were with Colonel Ingersoll and Mr Bradlaugh. But, though a rationalist in creed, his sentiments remained ardently religious. Hence, having distinguished himself in philosophy at Edinburgh, and having embarked on a brilliant career at Cambridge, he abandoned nonconformity and entered the Church of England, which he considered the most liberal church in Christendom. For, as he continually argued, since the Affirmation Act of 1865 (28–29 Vict., cap. 122)—the Magna Carta of ecclesiastical freedom—it was possible for a clergyman to express his sincere assent to the statement that " the doctrine of the Church of England is agreeable to the Word of God," while at the same time he totally denied the authority of the Word of God, and entirely disbelieved every specific article of the creeds. It was a position possible only to a logician; an early anticipation of the principle of relativity. In 1880, however, when he was appointed to King's College, he had been ordained but two years, and the lines of his latitude had not yet been revealed.

But the course of the next nine years displayed Professor Momerie not only as a thinker of originality and a writer of power, but also as a militant broad churchman whose most joyous assaults were delivered not on the infidel so much as on the high church sacerdotalist and the low church bibliolater. The faithful began to be scandalized, especially when, in the process of controversy, Professor Momerie's language lost the restraint usual with gentlemen, and he laid about him in sacred matters with an irreverence commonly associated rather with the rationalist press than with the utterances of a teacher in a theological faculty. The matter came to a head early in 1889 with the publication of a volume entitled *Inspiration and other Sermons*. In the council of King's College, on March 15,

> The principal mentioned the subject of the enquiry which he had intended to suggest respecting Professor Momerie's sermons, read a letter thereon from the Bishop of London, and stated that he had postponed bringing the matter forward because he had learnt from Professor Momerie last night that he much wished to send a copy of his sermons to each member of the council before the subject was considered.
>
> The council resolved to ask the Bishop of London to name a day for a special meeting respecting Professor Momerie's position, and that notices be then issued to consider Professor Momerie's volume of sermons entitled *Inspiration and other Sermons*.

379

The special meeting was held on Friday, April 5. Twenty-one members of the council were present, including Mr Gladstone, who must vividly have recalled the meeting (of which he was the sole survivor) held thirty-six years earlier to consider the analogous case of Professor Maurice. Mr Gladstone strongly advocated compromise, and urged that by all possible means a repetition of the tragedy of 1853 should be avoided. The result of a prolonged discussion was that the council " ultimately resolved that the question be adjourned till the Bishop of London has seen Professor Momerie." Dr Temple accordingly had two interviews with Professor Momerie, who seemed to be thoroughly enjoying the notoriety he was gaining. The bishop pointed out, among other things, the injury which was being done to the college, and particularly to its theological department, by Dr Momerie's violent anti-ecclesiastical philippics. This seemed to be an entirely new idea to the ardent belligerent, and, as he confessed, it " much impressed " him. The bishop then won his consent to the arrangement that the chair of logic and metaphysics should be removed from the department of theology to the department of general literature and science. When the council again met to consider the case (July 19, 1889) the transference was quickly effected. It meant that Professor Momerie lost 74 students, all of whom had been compelled to attend his lectures, and became a passenger in a department which numbered only 22 students, none of whom were constrained to attend his lectures, and few of whom wanted to attend them or had time to do so. He was extinguished without being made a martyr. His fees fell to less than £20 a year; he became a nonentity in the college; he contemplated early resignation.

In this, however, he was anticipated. The *Pall Mall Gazette* of December 12, 1890, contained a letter from his pen on doctrinal matters which even he himself was constrained later to confess was " flippant and sure to give needless offence." It formed the subject of anxious consideration on the part of the principal and the council as well as the Bishop of London and the Archbishop of Canterbury. Then, on May 25, 1891, he made his position in the college in any capacity impossible by delivering a lecture (subsequently published in pamphlet form) on " The Corruption of the Church," in which, according to the *Times* report of May 27, he characterized the fundamental doctrines of orthodox Christianity—including the doctrines of the atonement and the holy trinity—as "nonsense." This amazing utterance was examined at two successive council meetings (June 12 and 26, 1891), and strong disapproval was expressed at "the flippancy and virulence which characterize Dr Momerie's treatment of sacred subjects, and his general tone of irresponsibility and indiscretion." Finally, after two less drastic motions had been defeated, it was resolved (by 12 to 4) "that the chair of logic and metaphysics now held by Dr Momerie be declared vacant."

So ended Dr Momerie's unhappy connexion with King's College. His dismissal caused nothing like the sensation that Professor Maurice's eviction had caused thirty-eight years before. This was due partly to the fact that Dr Momerie had put himself entirely out of court by the extremity of his views and the violence of his language, and partly to the fact that public interest in theological controversy had markedly declined since the middle of the nineteenth century. Dr Momerie was intensely disgusted that no one seemed disposed to take up his case. As he said at the time, he would " much have preferred publicity." Publicity, however—that is to say, newspaper controversy and platform agitation—was the last thing that the council desired in the circumstances of 1891. Hence as unostentatiously as possible they got rid of their unprofitable servant, without assigning any reason for their act. There can be no doubt that this eviction of a professor of philosophy from his chair because of his utterances was a striking display of arbitrary authority, entirely incompatible with academic freedom. But it must be remembered that at that time King's College was not a public institution. It was an Anglican seminary, established by churchmen for ecclesiastical purposes. It was dominated by bishops and by the nominees of bishops, and it was pledged by its constitution to the maintenance of the doctrines and duties of Christianity as taught by the Church of England. Hence if a professor desired academic freedom beyond the very large limits allowed by this constitution King's College was not the place for him to come to; and if he took liberties beyond these limits it was the council's duty to dismiss him. Very different was the state of affairs when, the funds of the faithful having failed, the council had to come to the Government and the London County Council and beg for public money. And it was singularly unfortunate for those who, like Dr Wace, wished to secure public money while at the same time retaining the religious tests that at this precise juncture Dr Momerie's case should have called prominent attention to the fact that the fundamental principles of the college were incompatible with professorial freedom.

The whole college to some extent suffered because of this unfortunate episode, but the theological department suffered most. Its numbers fell from 74 in 1889 (when Dr Momerie's chair was transferred to the general department) to 56 in 1891 (when he was finally dismissed). Other causes, also, tended to depress it. First, Dr Wace was so deeply immersed in business relating to the reconstitution of the university and the securing of government grants that he was not able to give to it nearly so much attention as had been bestowed by his two predecessors. Secondly, it suffered from the increasing rivalry of the diocesan training colleges, which not only taught purer forms of partisanship, but also admitted students on much easier terms, both financial and intellectual. Thirdly, the establishment of Ridley Hall in Cambridge in 1881 drew to that abode of untainted protestantism and fervid piety many men of evangelical zeal who otherwise would have been attracted by the unquestionable orthodoxy of Dr Wace. Finally—and this was regarded at the time as the most serious handicap of the department—there was the old trouble of the lack of a residence for the students. Thus, on December 9, 1892,

> The principal stated that from various communications made to him from time to time he knew that many of the bishops felt great difficulty in accepting King's College students as candidates for ordination, on the ground that no sufficient arrangements were made for their superintendence when absent from the college.

The Archbishop of York and the Bishop of London, who were both present at the meeting, entirely concurred with the principal, and accordingly a strong committee was appointed to consider the problem. Several suggestions were examined. One of them was to remove the resident medicals from the college buildings to rooms near the hospital, and put the theologians in their places; but rooms fit for medicals in the vicinity of the hospital were unprocurable. Another proposal was (as of old) to hire or buy houses in the Strand abutting on the college. Inquiries were made, but prices were prohibitive. The owner of 161 Strand wanted £10,500 for the freehold of his property, and 158 Strand would cost still more, for there was an unexpired lease of sixteen years yet to run. So, once more, for a time, the hope of a theological hostel had to be postponed to a more propitious day.

In spite, however, of this disappointment, when the disturbance caused by Dr Momerie's ejection had subsided the department began to revive. The number of students, which had fallen to 56 in 1891, rose to 92 before Dr Wace retired, six years later. This recovery was due, in part, to improvement in the organization of the department. In July 1890, in order to leave Dr Wace free to fight his battles for the charter and the grant, the Rev. R. J. Knowling (since 1884 lecturer on the Greek Testament) was appointed vice-principal of the college and dean of the theological department. In seven strenuous years of office he was able to effect a marked amelioration of the administration. He was effectively assisted by several capable and energetic younger men who joined the staff during this period. In 1890, for instance, the Rev. H. C. Shuttleworth (lecturer since 1883) succeeded Dr H. B. Swete (who went to the Regius Chair in Cambridge) as professor of pastoral theology. He displayed much originality in the methods of tending spiritual sheep, and great skill in the exercises appropriate to the preparation for the pastoral office. In the long vacation of 1893 died the Rev. J. M. Fuller, who in 1884 had succeeded Dr Wace in the chair of ecclesiastical history. Extreme placidity had characterized the nine years of his inconspicuous exposition of the story of the church's evolution. His place was taken by a young professor (*æt.* twenty-six) of immense ability and consuming energy, a man of singularly fine presence and attractive disposition, the Rev. W. E. Collins, of Selwyn College, Cambridge—a man destined to become a bishop at the early age of thirty-seven, and, unhappily, to die prematurely in 1911, when only forty-four, leaving behind him, however, an amazingly large amount of excellent work.[1] In the following year, 1894, Canon Curteis, professor of New Testament exegesis, passed away, and to his vacant chair was elevated the vigorous vice-principal, the Rev. R. J. Knowling—the Rev. Harold Smith, of Cambridge, being appointed to take over some of the minor offices which he had held.

Other changes in the theological department during this period were as follows. First, in July 1887, in the interests of economy, the Sunday service in the college chapel was restricted to residents (and moved from 11 A.M. to 10), the choir was disbanded, and the salary of the organist reduced. Secondly, when in 1890 Mr D'Orsey resigned the post of instructor in public reading which he had held for twenty-six

---

[1] It was Dr Collins's predecessor in the see of Gibraltar who, having arrived in Rome on a visit, and having secured an audience with the great pope Leo XIII, was greeted by His Holiness with charming courtesy in the words, " I believe I have the honour to reside in your Lordship's diocese."

years the council decided not to appoint a successor, but to make the teaching of elocution one of the duties of the professor of pastoral theology. Thirdly, the bishops having decreed that, because of the new illiteracy that was beginning to permeate the priesthood,

> all non-graduates before entering upon their final course of two years in any theological college should be required to pass an examination, conducted by examiners appointed by the bishop, in Latin, Greek, History, and either Logic or Euclid,

a special preparatory class was instituted in the college, and (February 10, 1893) the Rev. J. H. Cheadle, minor canon of Westminster, placed in charge of it.

§ 10. *The Medical School and the Hospital*

Theology had played a considerable part in the education of the youthful medicos placed under the tuition of King's College in the early days of that institution. The urgent need of the profession, indeed, in that gross age had been the elevation of the moral and religious standards of the general practitioner. The task of the college in striving for this elevation had been a difficult one, proctorial supervision in London being an impossibility. Most of the grave disciplinary cases within the college during the first half-century of its existence came from the medical school, and a record of these cases would disclose violations of all the commands of the decalogue from manslaughter to sabbath-breaking. Every effort was made on the part of the council to have as many as possible of the medical students in residence within the college precincts, and these resident students were placed in charge of three potent officials—principal, vice-principal, and censor—who enforced a rigid and extensive set of rules which included prohibitions respecting the admission of dogs and ladies to the college, the employment of fire-arms, and the placing of flower-pots on the window-ledges.

Thanks to no small extent to the example and influence of King's, the Victorian era saw so marked an improvement in both the manners and the morals of the medical students of the metropolis that it was possible for all the great schools of physic and surgery to transfer their main efforts from the task of turning out decent general practitioners to the task of training highly skilled specialists in the many new departments of the medical profession which the rapid progress of science was opening up. In this work King's was again a pioneer. We have already noted how under Professor Lister's leadership (1877–92) the hospital became the headquarters in London of the new antiseptic method of surgical treatment. After Lister's retirement under the rule of the age limit in 1892, his work was ably carried on by such eminent disciples as Professor William Rose and Professor (now Sir) William Watson Cheyne. Closely associated with antiseptic surgery, of course, was the science of bacteriology, and at King's College there was established the first bacteriological laboratory in the country. Its establishment was the work of Dr Edgar Crookshank, an old student of the college, who in 1887 was appointed, first, lecturer in bacteriology, then professor. He himself, a man of independent means, contributed £1000 toward the equipment of the laboratory. Under his able and enthusiastic direction it speedily achieved striking success. In 1893, for instance, the council were in a position to report that it " had attracted a large number of zealous workers, not only from London and the provinces, but also from our colonies and from other countries," and that " from the foundation of this class six years ago the number of students who have entered for instruction or research has amounted to 419." It became the centre of a definite department of comparative pathology and bacteriology in the faculty of medicine.

In another important department of medicine also King's College led the way. That was the department of neuropathology, established in 1889 by the eminent Professor (later Sir) David Ferrier, who surrendered the chair of forensic medicine which he had held for seventeen years in order to devote himself to the study of diseases of the brain, toward which his special researches had long been leading him. For the conduct of his investigations, and for the preparation of the magnificent series of lantern slides and diagrams with which he illustrated his lectures, he too needed a laboratory, with money for its equipment and maintenance.

Shortly afterward—viz., in 1891—the department of hygiene, inaugurated twenty-two years earlier by Professor Guy, developed into a large and complex department of public health or " state medicine " under Professors Charles Kelly (hygiene) and W. R. Smith (forensic medicine). It was intended primarily for the training of medical officers of health; but it enlarged its scope to include courses for public analysts, sanitary inspectors, and even for plumbers who wished to know precisely what tools to leave behind for their mates to fetch. Here again laboratories were imperative, as well as a workshop for plumbers, which the worshipful company of that craft was good enough to fit up with all the latest traps in 1893.

Three new laboratories—bacteriology, neuro-pathology, and hygiene—soon followed by another required for researches in surgical pathology by Professor Watson Cheyne and his assistants, put a great strain on the accommodation of the college. Space was ultimately found only by the abolition of half the sets of rooms assigned on the top floor for students' residence—*i.e.*, fourteen sets out of twenty-eight—and the conversion of these rooms into scientific workshops. It meant much expense, and it involved a serious loss of annual revenue, to say nothing of the reduction of the resident portion of the college to depressing smallness. Still, the sacrifice had to be made (1891).

Meanwhile the well-established physiological laboratory in its building on the Embankment site was doing excellent work under Professor Gerald Yeo (1875–90). Even more successful, however, did it become under the eminent authority who came after him—viz., Dr W. D. Halliburton (1890–1923), author of the great *Handbook of Physiology* which for a whole generation has been the standard text-book on its subject. Dr Halliburton's appointment in May 1890 was followed almost immediately by a request from him to the council for £200 in order that he might bring his laboratory up to date. This request the council could not refuse, even though it meant a dangerous addition to its already heavy deficit.

The medical department in general at this time was, indeed, even more than usually, a serious burden upon the financial resources of the college. The hospital, too, was being run at so large an annual loss that in 1886 (March 12) a Mansion House meeting had to be held to raise funds in the City, while only two years later it was necessary to appeal to the West End by means of a bazaar, to which the Princess Louise lent her patronage. And the worst of it was that in spite of the money spent and the improvements made, and in spite of the eminence of the teachers and the excellence of the new laboratories, the department did not flourish. The number of students fell fairly steadily from 223 in 1883 to 132 in 1897. The medical professors, having considered at their board the possible causes of the unpopularity of their school, came to the conclusion in 1892 that compulsory divinity had something to do with it. They therefore, through their dean, addressed the following letter to the council (October 11, 1892):

THE STRUGGLE FOR EXISTENCE

At the meeting of the medical board in July it was unanimously resolved that in the opinion of the medical board the compulsory attendance at lectures on divinity is a bar to the entrance of medical students, and they recommend that in future it should be optional, and that no certificate of attendance at such lectures should be required for college scholarships.

The council, however, refused to relax the rule, arguing (1) that to do so would be inconsistent with the constitution of the college, and (2) that even if divinity were repellent to some students, it was attractive to the *parents* of others, and therefore that it probably brought as many students as it kept away. But more formidable as a barrier to prosperity than the compulsory divinity of the college was the prohibitive difficulty of the medical degrees of the University of London. Students were trooping away to Newcastle, Edinburgh, Glasgow, and other centres of medical education where they could secure the coveted and invaluable M.D. on easier terms. Hence the growing demand both from the royal colleges of physicians and surgeons, and from the university colleges of Gower Street and the Strand, for charters empowering them to confer the doctorate.[1] We have already traced the course of this struggle for the charters during the period of Dr Wace's principalship. The story of its concluding phases must be deferred until we come to the next stage of our work.

All that remains now to be done is to note a number of changes in the staff of the medical school and the hospital that occurred during the fourteen years under review. So many were these changes that, although some of them were of high importance, little more than a tabular record of them can be permitted. (1) In 1884 Dr E. B. Baxter resigned the professorship of *materia medica* and was succeeded by Dr N. I. C. Tirard. (2) In 1885 the offices of sub-dean and medical tutor (held since 1878 by Dr Tirard) were abolished, and in their place the very minor office of assistant-censor instituted, the remuneration of the assistant-censor to consist merely of free rooms in college and one free dinner a day. (3) In the same year the Sisterhood of St John's House relinquished the nursing of the hospital, which it had conducted, not without friction, for some forty years. The committee of the hospital then took the control of the nursing into their own hands,

---

[1] It should also be noted as a further cause of depression, although not peculiar to King's, that an important change in the course of medical education took effect on January 1, 1892. Hitherto four years' regular study had been required before a student could present himself for his final examination; but henceforth five years would be requisite.

made provision for the training of young women, and set apart a wing of the hospital for their accommodation. (4) In 1885, too, a new chair was established—another pioneer venture— when Dr Burney Yeo (who had been medical tutor from 1865 to 1871, and a physician at the hospital since 1869) was made first professor of clinical therapeutics. (5) Next year a still further innovation was made when Dr Urban Pritchard (aural surgeon at the hospital since 1876) was made professor of aural surgery in the college. (6) Two changes took place in the botanical department. In 1887 Professor Bentley resigned the chair which he had held for twenty-eight years, and was succeeded by Mr J. W. Groves. The new professor, however, kept his post for scarcely six years. At the end of 1892 he resigned, in order to travel to regions where vegetation flourished more luxuriantly than in the Strand. He broke the shock of his early departure from the college by presenting to the council " a life-sized female figure in plaster entitled *The First Plunge*," which either difficulties of transport or natural modesty prevented him from taking with him to the continent. He was succeeded by the genial Professor W. B. Bottomley, whose twenty-eight years' tenure of the chair (1893–1921) was marked by important discoveries of modes in which the bacteriologist can aid the market-gardener. (7) The year that saw the resignation of Professor Bentley saw also the death of one of the oldest of his colleagues—viz., Professor Bloxam, for thirty-three years head of the department of chemistry. His very able demonstrator, Mr J. Millar Thomson, was raised to the chair (December 1887), and Mr (now Sir) Herbert Jackson was appointed to assist him. (8) All the three surgical chairs changed their occupants— Professor Henry Smith resigned in 1888, Professor John Wood in 1889, and Professor Sir Joseph Lister in 1892. After various transmutations Professor W. Watson Cheyne undertook the teaching of the principles and practice of surgery, while the two clinical chairs were reunited and conferred upon Professor William Rose. (9) In 1890 Mr E. W. White, superintendent of the City of London Asylum, succeeded Dr E. Sheppard as professor of psychological medicine. (10) In 1896 Professor F. J. Bell terminated his eighteen years' tenure of the chair of comparative anatomy: no successor was appointed. (11) Later in the same year Professor Lionel S. Beale, one of the most eminent of the great physicians associated with King's College and its hospital, resigned the chair of medicine, thus bringing to a close a teaching career in the college extending

388

over forty-three years. He remained honorary consulting physician to the hospital until his death in 1906. Dr Burney Yeo succeeded him in the chair of medicine, and the separate professorship of clinical therapeutics was allowed to lapse. (12) In 1896 also Dr John Curnow was appointed to Sir George Johnson's old chair of clinical medicine, resigning his chair of anatomy, which was given to Mr Alfred W. Hughes. (13) Finally, in 1897 Dr Charles Kelly vacated the chair of hygiene, to which was appointed that eminent authority on tropical diseases Dr (now Sir) William J. R. Simpson.

§ 11. *Engineering and Technology*

Developments in medical and surgical science during the later decades of the Victorian era were equalled if not exceeded in magnitude by developments in engineering and technological science. In particular, the theory and practice of electricity made enormous advances during this period, and King's College played no unimportant part in the pioneer work. The college had from the very first been prominent in the field of electrical research. The names of the three great professors, Daniell, Wheatstone, and Clerk Maxwell, were, are, and always will be known wherever the progress of electrical science is studied. To these distinguished names, two more were to be added during the period of Dr Wace's principalship —viz., those of Dr John Hopkinson (too soon lost to science through his untimely death in the Alps in 1898) and Professor Ernest Wilson, his successor (still, happily, with us, and a continual source of joy to his colleagues and pupils), who was made demonstrator in 1891 and assistant-professor in 1897.

The great development in the sub-department of electrical engineering in King's College came in 1890, and was due to the munificence of Lady Siemens, widow of Sir William Siemens (1823–83), the famous metallurgist and electrician, for many years a devoted member of the council of King's College. On March 10, 1890, Lady Siemens addressed a long letter to Dr Wace, the opening paragraphs of which ran as follows:

> It has been my wish for some years past to perpetuate the memory of my husband, Sir William Siemens, by some memorial of a permanent nature. Hearing that the council of King's College have under consideration at the present time a scheme for increasing the instruction provided in electrical engineering, it

389

has occurred to me that such a memorial might take the form of an electrical engineering laboratory in the college, thoroughly equipped for practical teaching. Such a laboratory it will afford me sincere gratification to present to the college, provided that the council can find a suitable position for it within the college precincts. My husband took much interest in the electrical and metallurgical work carried on in the college, and I feel that the foundation of such a laboratory would form a memorial of a kind which would have been nearest to his own ideas. I should wish it to be called the " William Siemens Laboratory," and that a tablet indicating its origin and nature, together with a bust of Sir William Siemens, should be placed within it. I am prepared to expend £6000 for the above purpose. . . .

The council, of course, gratefully accepted Lady Siemens' splendid gift; at once established a new chair of electrical engineering, inviting Dr John Hopkinson to occupy it; and proceeded to search the college for a place in which to construct the new laboratory. Their final decision was to erect a new building over the entrance hall of the college. This they proceeded to do, at a cost of £4250; and this they succeeded in doing. But not until they had met and overcome a good deal of unexpected and most vexatious opposition from Somerset House, which not only objected to the addition to the height of the college, but also refused to evacuate some vaults under the slope to the Embankment wherein the council had intended to place the engines and dynamos.

The definition and development of the section of electrical engineering was accompanied by a necessary sharpening of the lines of demarcation of the other sections of the department. So early as 1886 the old and cumbersome titles " manufacturing art and machinery " and " land-surveying and levelling " gave place to the simpler designations " mechanical engineering " and " civil engineering " respectively; while the professor of " the arts of constructing " became primarily a " professor of architecture." This change of titles was ere long followed by important changes in personnel. At the end of 1889 the old, and somewhat antiquated, Professors Shelley (mechanical engineering) and Kerr (architecture) were pensioned off, and their places given respectively to the energetic and enterprising Mr David Sing Capper, who for thirty-one years (1890–1921) continued to control the constantly accumulating machines in the college underworld, and the eminent architect, pioneer of faience work in English street buildings, Mr Banister Fletcher. Movements of new life were immediately evident in the department. Professor Capper inaugurated a complete reorganization of the workshops; while Professor Banister Fletcher, mainly at his own cost, established an excellent architectural museum. And he did much more than this. He was a prominent member (ex-master) of the Carpenters' Company, and through his influence this wealthy and generous corporation established in the college a school of woodcarving, built a new room for its accommodation at the north-west corner of the top of the college, and (an entirely separate benefaction) opened, at a cost of £150, a new entrance to the subterranean engineering department from the ground floor of the college, close to the large lecture theatre. These works, undertaken in 1890, entailed a total expenditure of some £1250 in all. The council in their report for 1891 were able to say that " the engineering department is in a more prosperous condition than at any former time." The number of its students had jumped from 75 in 1890 to the record figure of 105; it had taken its place among the schools of the front rank in electrical engineering and architecture; it was drawing to its staff young men of outstanding ability, such as Ernest Wilson (electricity, 1891) and S. A. F. White (natural philosophy, 1894). The report of 1893, after saying that " the engineering department is in a most satisfactory condition," added the statement that " it is believed to be at present the largest school of engineering students in the kingdom." It was able further to announce, with pardonable pride, that

> this year the presidents of the three engineering institutions are former students of this department—viz., Mr Harrison Hayter (civil engineers), Dr William Anderson (mechanical engineers), and Mr W. H. Preece (electrical engineers).

In 1896, as a sequel to Mr Walter Smith's reorganization of the college finances, the department was entirely separated, under its own dean (Professor Robinson), from that of natural science. It was renamed as the division of " engineering, architecture, and applied sciences."

§ 12. *The Resignation of Dr Wace*

The success of the engineering department from 1890 onward was one of the few gleams of brightness that lightened the gloom of the closing years of Dr Wace's principalship. True, he was also, to some extent, cheered by the good repute of the medical school, by the revival of the theological department after the departure of Professor Momerie, by the swarming of the multitudes of little boys to Mr Braginton's classes in Waterloo Road, and by the ladylike behaviour of the polite students in Kensington Square. But these small beams of consolation did little to relieve the darkness caused by the rapid decline of the college toward bankruptcy, by the gathering certainty that grants from the public purse adequate to save the college from extinction could be secured only by a surrender of the fundamental principles of the founders of the institution, and by the failure of the college, in conjunction with University College and the Gresham Trustees, to obtain the charter for a new teaching university in London. Dr Wace had put up a magnificent fight; he had kept a brave face to the world; he had given no indication of either capitulation or defeat. Nevertheless, by 1896 he realized that, in regard to the three great matters that had occupied his attention—the securing of public money, the retention of religious tests, the establishment of a new teaching university with King's College as one of its main constituents—he had failed. Hence, being now sixty years of age, and therefore approaching the time of compulsory retirement, he decided to make a move, and to hand over the painful task of abandoning the tests and of adapting the constitution of King's College to the statutes of the reorganized University of London to a principal less committed to a side than himself.

On November 26, 1896, he addressed the following letter to the council:

My Lords and Gentlemen,

I am very sorry to be obliged to place in your hands my resignation of the office of principal of King's College. I have received the offer of the rectory of St Michael's, Cornhill, accompanied with the condition that I should resign the office of principal here; and I am not in a position to decline an offer which ensures me an honourable position and a competence at a time of life, not now far distant, when, by the rules of the college, my tenure of the post of principal would expire. I shall relinquish with deep regret an office and an institution with which the best years and deepest interests of my life have been bound up; but I hope that I may be only rendering another service to it by making way for a younger principal who will bring to it fresh energies and fresh connexions. I believe that, especially by the financial reorganization which was carried through last year, it will be left on a substantially sound footing, and in a condition in which it may be conducted with success by the new principal.

I beg leave to express my deep gratitude for the confidence which you have extended to me, without variation, since you elected me to my present office in 1883; for the constant support you have given me in my work, and for the generous construction you have always placed on my endeavour to serve the college. I beg your forgiveness for any errors, omissions, or faults I may have exhibited, and I beg you to be assured that I shall always be thankful if I can do anything to serve the college and its cause. I have the honour to remain [etc.].

The council, in regretfully accepting Dr Wace's resignation, expressed their strong sense of the services he had rendered to the college and their warm appreciation of his courage and loyalty. On April 9, 1897, they further signified their respect for him by electing him a member of their own body—to fill a vacancy caused by the death of Sir George Johnson—and by placing him on the finance committee and the committee of the ladies' department.

During so long a period as fourteen years changes on the council were, of course, numerous. Removals by death included Bishop Jackson of London in 1885; two Archbishops of York—Drs Thomson and Magee—together with Earl Powis and Mr W. H. Smith, in 1891, a peculiarly fatal year; in 1892 Bishop Harold Browne, formerly of Winchester, and Bishop Claughton, formerly of St Albans, together with the faithful and devoted Sir William Bowman, the great ophthalmic surgeon, whose association with King's College went back to 1839; and four years later that other notable medical man, Sir George Johnson, physician extraordinary to Queen Victoria, who during fifty-three years had filled almost every post in college and hospital open to a doctor, from medical student to councillor. Besides these removals by death, there were a number of resignations, of which the most significant were those in 1894 of the five dissentients from the council's determination to stick to the religious tests—viz., Mr (later Sir) W. H. Preece, Sir Owen Roberts, Sir A. K. Rollit, Mr R. Horton Smith, and Mr William Stebbing.

Among those who joined the council to take the vacant places were Bishop Barry (on his return from Australia in 1891), Mr J. W. Lowther (now Lord Ullswater), Sir Joseph Lister (who succeeded Sir William Bowman), Bishop Ellicott of Gloucester and Bristol (who was appointed a life governor in place of Bishop Claughton), and the Hon. W. F. D. Smith (son of Mr W. H. Smith and the Viscountess Hambleden), who joined the council in the dark days of 1894, and accepted the thankless and onerous office of treasurer in 1896, when the bankruptcy of the college seemed inevitable.

Although during Dr Wace's principalship the council continued to govern the college and to determine matters of general policy, it was content, on the one hand, to leave the details of administration to the principal and the secretary, and, on the other hand, to allow the departmental and other boards a large liberty in academic matters. And there can be no doubt that the professorial staff contained in those days men—such as Sir Joseph Lister among the medicals, Dr John Hopkinson among the engineers, Dr J. Millar Thomson among the men of science, and Professor Warr among the men of letters—of far vision and high practical ability. One feature in particular that marked the great teachers of this period was their gradual subordination of the lecture system to the tutorial system. They got on to more intimate and personal terms with their students; they grouped them in small companies for purposes of conversation and discussion; they set them to work in laboratories so that they might be trained in methods of originality and research. This bridging of the gulf which hitherto had separated professor from pupil made it possible to tighten up the discipline of the college without evoking rebellion. Students were made to understand that not only for moral offences would they be expelled from the college, but that mere laziness (as shown by failure to attend classes) or sheer incompetence (as shown by failure to pass examinations) would entail removal from the registers. In the evening classes, where the students were as a rule older and more mature than those of the day classes, the relations between teachers and taught were especially familiar and cordial. The evening classes, moreover, stood pre-eminent in social organization, in corporate activity, and in *esprit de corps*. A weekly dinner in hall (Wednesday, 6 P.M.); the use of one of the libraries as a common room; an annual commemoration reunion; a musical society; a literary society for old students, which maintained a vigorous existence for thirty-one years (1891–1922)—these were some of the features that testified to the vigorous vitality of this invaluable department.

As to the rest of the college, early in Dr Wace's principalship (1884) an athletic club was formed, of which every student of the college automatically became a member. For the purposes of the club the college shared with the school the seven-acre field which the council secured at Wormwood

394

THE STRUGGLE FOR EXISTENCE

Scrubbs, near the District Railway Station (1884). The old-established Engineering and Medical Societies continued to function, and intermittently to flourish. The " Union " Society and the " Science " Society were reconstituted in 1889 and renamed respectively the " General Literature Society " and the " Science Union." In 1894 a " Society of Education " was established. Two fleeting attempts to found a college magazine were made during this period: in 1888 the *King's College Gazette* began, continued, and ended its career; from 1889 to 1891 the *Kingsman* maintained a fitful struggle for existence. One gathers that the student life of the college pursued the by no means noiseless tenor of its way wholly unaffected by the battle for the charter or the flight from bankruptcy which disturbed the equanimity of the lofty regions where the principal incessantly worked and the council periodically met.

NOTE

I. Number of Students, 1883–97

SESSION	COLLEGE							Sch.	Total
	REGULAR						Occ.		
	Gen.	Med.	Eng.	Theological		Even.			
				Day	Even.				
1883–84	39	223	103	55	14	384	114	572	1504
1884–85	31	213	119	70	12	509	87	538	1579
1885–86	25	215	109	64	12	450	66	432	1373
1886–87	29	221	81	53	10	471	90	349	1304
1887–88	26	230	72	55	17	368	80	294	1142
1888–89	22	220	70	53	21	329	89	251	1055
1889–90	26	205	75	49	19	312	66	249	1001
1890–91	50	220	105	47	14	286	120	274	1116
1891–92	70	220	107	40	16	280	136	236	1105
1892–93	60	205	107	43	19	502	109	234	1279
	A^1 S^2								
1893–94	59 10	200	93	62	19	460	95	242	1240
1894–95	59 3	200	81	63	11	473	112	199	1201
1895–96	49 15	176	69	68	6	482	159	206	1230
1896–97	56 15	153	66	63	5	337	176	178	1049
1897–98	58 9	132	61	81	11	360	300	200	1212

¹ Arts. ² Science.

The Ladies' Department

Session	Number of Students	Session	Number of Students
1885–86	500	1892–93	430
1886–87	450	1893–94	384
1887–88	480	1894–95	392
1888–89	488	1895–96	392
1889–90	450	1896–97	350
1890–91	468	1897–98	429
1891–92	426		

Extra-collegiate Classes

Session	Civil Service		Workshop	Gilbart Lectures	Total
	Male	Female			
1883–84	799	192	68[1]	390	1449
1884–85	704	236	42	475	1457
1885–86	768	268	32	301	1369
1886–87	664	306	38	296	1304
1887–88	624	412	31	550	1617
1888–89	487	332	37	730	1586
1889–90	544	304	29	800	1677
1890–91	615	341	68	900	1924
1891–92	781	342	73	900	2096
1892–93	1042	386	115	1100	2643
1893–94	1216	299	— [2]	1150	2665
1894–95	1341	228	—	1100	2669
1895–96	1475	157	—	1200	2832
1896–97	1533	124	—	1200	2857
1897–98	1402	134	—	1000	2536

II. Distinguished Students, 1883–97

Among those who entered the College during the period 1883–97, and subsequently became distinguished, were the following : [3]

Alexander, Lieutenant-Colonel R. D. T., D.S.O., O.B.E.
Atkinson, Llewelyn B., Past President of the I.E.E.
Barth, Lieutenant-Colonel Sir Jacob W.
Bartley, Lieutenant-Colonel Bryan C.
Beale, Dr Peyton T. B.
Bell, Dr William Blair.
Bernhard-Smith, Dr William A. H.
Bidwell, Right Rev. Monsignor Manuel J., D.D., C.B.E.
Blades, Sir G. Rowland (Lord Ebbisham).
Blair, Sir Robert, LL.D.
Briscoe, Sir John Charlton, Bart., M.D., F.R.C.S.
Carr, Professor Herbert Wildon, D.Litt.

[1] Including 15 who took " Practical Art."
[2] Included henceforth under " Evening Classes " (see table on p. 395).
[3] For the preparation of this list, which has involved a lot of labour, I am indebted to Mr John Lester, head clerk, and Mr W. A. Campbell, his assistant. The list is necessarily incomplete. Notification of omissions will be welcomed.

THE STRUGGLE FOR EXISTENCE

Cheatle, Surgeon-General Sir George L., K.C.B.
Craufurd, Lieutenant-Commander Sir Charles W. F., Bart.
Crawfurd, Dr Raymond H. P., F.R.C.P.
Dalziel, James Henry (Lord Dalziel).
Day, Dr Harold Benjamin, F.R.C.S.
Dewrance, Sir John, G.B.E.
Doughty-Tichborne, Sir Henry A. J., Bart.
Fletcher, Sir Banister F., F.R.I.B.A.
Floud, Sir Francis Lewis Castle, K.C.B.
Gault, Professor James, M.A.
Gooch, George Peabody, M.A., D.Litt.
Gregory, Professor John Walter, D.Sc., F.R.S.
Hamilton, Professor Charles Joseph, M.A.
Heaton, Sir John Henniker, M.P.
Hewlett, Dr Richard Tanner, F.R.C.P.
Hibbert, William Nembhard, LL.D.
Hollander, Dr Bernard, M.D., F.R.C.P.
Kermode, Canon Robert D., M.A.
Kirkaldy, Professor Patrick Henry, F.I.C.
Kyd, Sir David H.
Le Quesne, Lieutenant-Colonel Ferdinand S., V.C.
Lyle, Dr Herbert Willoughby, F.R.C.S.
Mansbridge, Albert, M.A., LL.D.
May, Dr Otto.
Morley, Professor Edith.
Mowat, Brigadier-General M., C.B.E.
Newman, Sir George, M.D., F.R.C.P.
Parkins, James.
Pascoe, Sir Edwin H., M.A., D.Sc.
Perry, Colonel Frederick S., C.M.G., D.S.O.
Playfair, Hugh N., M.P.
Savile, Sir Leopold H., K.C.B.
Sikes, Dr Alfred Walter.
Snell, Sir John F. C., G.B.E.
Steele, Major William J., D.S.O.
Still, George Frederick, M.A., M.D.
Thompson, Miss Edith Marie, C.B.E.
Thorpe, Professor Jocelyn F., D.Sc., F.R.S.
Tritton, Sir William A.
Turner, Dr William, F.R.C.S.
Turtle, Dr Godfrey de Bec, M.R.C.S.
Veazey, Canon Harry G., M.A.
Waldo, Frederick Joseph, M.A., M.D.
Watson, Sir Duncan.
Williamson, Canon William, M.A.
Winchester, the (fifteenth) Marquis of.
Woodward, Sir Arthur Smith, LL.D., F.R.S.
Young, Dr Robert A., F.R.C.P.

PART IV

THE UNIVERSITY COLLEGE
1897–1928

CHAPTER XI

THE RECONSTITUTED UNIVERSITY
1897–1912

§ 1. *Two Academic Statesmen: Dr A. Robertson and Dr A. C. Headlam*

WE have now traced the development of the college throughout the first seventy years of its existence. We have been able by means of the admirably kept minute-books of its council to follow in some detail the story of its vicissitudes and the record of its resourceful struggle with persistent adversity. Thirty years more remain to be dealt with—viz., the thirty years which intervene between Dr Wace's resignation and the celebration of the college's centenary. This period will have to be sketched much more lightly and superficially than its predecessors; and that for several reasons. First, my space is limited. Secondly, the material for this last thirty years in council minutes, senate minutes, delegacy minutes, and minutes of numerous boards and committees is so vast and complicated that it would take months to digest it, and would require a section as large as the whole preceding part of this bulky volume to set it forth. Thirdly, the time for the printing of this centenary history is fully come. Fourthly, the events of these thirty years are too near our own day for us to see them in proper perspective; so many of the main actors are still living that it would be difficult to speak of these events with freedom; so large a number of the issues raised by them still remain controversial that due impartiality would be impossible. For sixteen of these thirty years I myself have been a lowly member of the college and a sharer of its life, and there is no period of its history that I find it so hard to deal with as that which has passed under my own eye. The detailed story, then, of the four principalships that have elapsed since Dr Wace's departure in 1897 I must leave to be told by the writer of the bicentenary history.

ARCHIBALD ROBERTSON
Principal 1897–1903

Dr Wace's letter of resignation came before the council on November 26, 1896. The writer had, however, a fortnight earlier, informally intimated to the council his intention to retire; hence that body was in a position to take immediate action. And it was necessary for it to do so, as Dr Wace wished to be released at the end of the Lent term (April 9, 1897). Accordingly, advertisements were at once issued; the conditions of appointment widely circulated; and applicants required to send in their papers before the end of December. Eight candidates presented themselves, and from these a special committee selected three who were invited to come before the full council for interview on January 15, 1897. Unfortunately, the *Times* got hold of the report of the committee, and caused great embarrassment to all concerned by publishing in its issue of Wednesday, January 13, the names of the selected trio—viz., the Rev. G. W. Gent, the Rev. L. M. Bebb, and the Rev. Dr A. Robertson. An acrimonious interchange of letters between Dr Wace and the editor preluded the meeting of the Friday. At the meeting itself a prolonged discussion as to the merits of the candidates took place, since it was realized that the college had come to a constitutional and financial crisis in which its very existence was at stake, and that upon the choice of a principal the question of its survival or extinction would very largely depend. During the course of the discussion a fourth eminent name was proposed for consideration. Finally, however, by a majority vote, the council decided to appoint Dr Robertson.

At the time of his election Dr Archibald Robertson was, and had been for fourteen years, principal of Bishop Hatfield's Hall, Durham, where he had acquired invaluable experience in the organization and development of a university founded about the same date as King's College, and faced by many of the same problems of government and finance. He had had a distinguished scholastic and academic career. Born in 1853, educated at Bradfield, he had passed to Trinity College, Oxford, where, having secured a first in Greats (1876), he became in turn fellow and dean. From Oxford he had been called to Durham in 1883. Thus when appointed to King's in 1897 he was forty-four years of age, and at the height of his great powers. It was in the main an immense advantage both to himself and to the college that—unlike Bishop Barry and Dr Wace—he was free from all previous association with King's; and this circumstance no doubt was one of the causes which determined the council in his favour. He was able to bring a wholly fresh mind to the consideration of the complicated problems he was called upon to face; he was not hampered by the traditions of the elders; he had not committed himself to any specific policy or attached himself to any sectional party. He was, moreover, a man of singular graciousness and tact; a loyal churchman, yet large and liberal in sympathy; wholly devoid of jealousy and suspicion, quick to see the good and to evoke the better in those with whom he had to do; kindly and conciliatory. At the same time, he was no weakling. He had a keen and penetrating intellect, a strong and courageous will, a sensitive conscience, and an immense fund of energy, which he lavishly expended in many good causes. He remained but six years at King's; for in 1903—and largely because of the high statesmanship that he had displayed during his tenure of the office of principal—he was elevated to the dignity and responsibility of the great bishopric of Exeter. But during his brief term of office he accomplished an all-important and permanently valuable work. Two tasks in particular he achieved, the first of which Dr Wace could hardly have performed, the second of which he would steadily have refused to attempt. The one was to effect the complete reconciliation of King's College with the reconstituted University of London; to lend his whole-hearted support to the university during the difficult days of its readjustment, and on the other hand to use to the full all the advantages that accrued to the college under the new constitution. So cordial were his relations with Sir Arthur Rücker, the first principal of the reorganized university, and so highly were his services regarded by the senate, that in 1902 he—the principal of King's College—received the remarkable distinction of being elected as the first vice-chancellor of the university under its revised statutes. The second and even more difficult task that he achieved—of which more anon—was the task of freeing the college, other than the theological department, from the incubus of the religious tests. Further, while he was heavily engaged in these absorbing and crucial matters of academic politics, he made time, and retained sufficient serenity, to do much other notable work. He acted as examining chaplain to the Bishop of Bristol (1897 *et seq.*); he delivered the Boyle lectures in 1900; he contributed learned articles to Smith's *Dictionary of the Bible*; above all, he published one of the ablest and most fascinating of the long series of Bampton lectures, entitled *Regnum Dei*, in 1901—a work displaying profound scholarship, lofty thought, wide acquaintance with Christian history, and penetrating insight into spiritual realities. When at the end of his eminently successful six years he received his well-merited promotion, the council passed the following resolution, which expressed their sense of the unique services that Dr Robertson had rendered to the college at one of the most critical junctures in its history:

The council have received with mingled feelings of satisfaction and profound regret the information that their principal, Dr Robertson, has been selected by His Majesty the King for the honour of being nominated for election to the see of Exeter, and therefore vacates the office of principal. The council are deeply sensible of the extraordinary services which, at a critical time in the history of the college, the principal has rendered to it during the comparatively short period of his tenure of the office. His distinguished ability, his combination of loyal churchmanship with largeness of heart, his great powers of organisation, the confidence which he has gained from men of various kinds, and his happy relation with council, staff, and students, have contributed to the high success of his principalship. In particular, the council remember with especial satisfaction the honour won for the college by Dr Robertson through his selection to be the first vice-chancellor of the new University of London. They believe that the college has before it a prospect of new and increased usefulness, which is largely due to his able administration, and they cordially wish him well in the high office to which he is now called.

This resolution was passed on February 27, 1903. On March 3 the principalship was advertised, applications to be sent in by the 20th of the month. Six candidates presented themselves; four were interviewed by a special committee; of these, two were selected to appear before the council, and of the two the Rev. Arthur Cayley Headlam, B.D., rector of Welwyn, was ultimately chosen (April 2, 1903). It was arranged that he should take up his duties and come into residence as soon after April 23 as possible. The new principal, although but forty-one years of age, was already recognized as among the ablest and best-equipped theologians of the Anglican communion. He had crowned a distinguished career as scholar of St Peter's College, Winchester, and of New College, Oxford, by winning a first in Greats and a fellowship at All Souls (1885). At Oxford he had remained for nearly a dozen years as lecturer in theology, and during this fruitful period of residence he had not only added immensely to his scholarship, but had also produced a number of works which had definitely established his position as a religious leader at once moderate yet progressive. In 1896 he had accepted the rectory of Welwyn, and in this Hertfordshire retreat he had continued with concentrated energy his theological labours. His treatise on *The Teaching of the Russian Church* (1897) materially assisted in that *rapprochement* between the English and Greek communions which has been so marked a feature of recent years; while his contributions to *Authority and Archæology* (1899), and to *New Testament Criticism* (1902), confirmed his influence with those who were interested in the reconciliation of the results of modern research with the venerable formularies of the faith. In all his works he showed a largeness of sympathy, a width of comprehension, a desire for mutual understanding and for unity, that marked him out as an ideal successor to the tolerant and catholic Dr Robertson.

As principal during the nine years 1903-12 he continued in the main to pursue the sound and statesmanly policy of his predecessor. That is to say, he made it his aim, on the one hand, to maintain the closest and most friendly relations with the University of London (to the senate of which he was at once elected a member); and, on the other hand, to convert King's College from a miscellaneous collection of incongruous departments—male and female, infantile and adult, day and evening, technical and academic, regular and occasional, anything and everything—into a unitary institution with a vigorous corporate life; in other words, to transform it from a universal provider into a university college. He had a high conception of the status and dignity of a university lecturer, and he never rested until he had secured for the teachers of King's far more adequate salaries, a greater security of tenure, and a better provision for old age than they had ever had before. Moreover, at the very beginning of his principalship he gained for them a new and important position in the administration of the college: on May 22, 1903, the council consented to the institution of an "education committee," of which, in addition to fourteen of their own body, the principal, the vice-principal, the deans of the various faculties, and the head of the women's department should all be members. So far he was but following the lines laid down by Principal Robertson. And he was doing no more than this when later in the same year (1903) he carried through to completion the measures necessary for the abolition of the religious tests from every department of the college save that to which they were proper—viz., the theological department. The first appointment, however, with which he had to do under the new regulations enabled him to display remarkable courage and

ARTHUR CAYLEY HEADLAM
Principal 1903–12, and Dean 1910–12   402

originality. The chair of English language and literature became vacant in July 1903, through the resignation of Professor J. W. Hales: to fill this vacancy he was bold and wise enough to nominate Mr (now Sir) Israel Gollancz. The council received with favour the nomination of this distinguished scholar and brilliant lecturer: he was invited to occupy the chair, and he accepted the invitation. The striking success of this first deviation from the old rule of religious exclusiveness was by itself a triumphant vindication of the charter of emancipation. Both Dr Robertson and Mr Headlam manifested perfect confidence in their professors and lecturers, feeling certain that no one of them would ever so abuse the position of trust in which he was placed as to use his rostrum as a vantage-ground for political or religious propaganda.

Principal Headlam, however, had not been long in office before he was called upon to face and to wrestle with problems some of which his predecessor had merely seen from a distance, others of which had been wholly beyond his ken. First, he had to tackle the tremendous problem of finance; that is to say, he had to find ways and means to make the college pay its way, to clear off the accumulated debt, to provide equipment for developing departments, to raise salaries, to enlarge the staff, to do a thousand and one things necessary to establish the old institution on its new university basis. It is not too much to say that in this department he showed himself a genius of the first order: he found a college in 1903 all but bankrupt; he left it in 1912 solvent and safe. In no period of the history of the college was so complete and enduring a transformation effected. A second problem, wholly unforeseen when the London University Act of 1898 was passed, and a problem of incredible complexity, was that of the incorporation of the college in the university. This problem was raised by the incorporation of University College under a Transfer Act of 1905. It was soon evident that if King's College were to maintain her rank and position in the university it would be necessary for her to follow the example of her sister-college. To do so involved not merely the paying off of her large accumulated debt, but also the separation from herself, and the placing under independent governing bodies, of a number of institutions which had hitherto been parts of her composite personality—the theological department, the hospital, the schools, the civil service classes, and what-not. It was a great achievement—the responsibility for which fell largely on Principal Headlam—to carry through with triumphant success this immense and manifold reconstruction. Finally, toward the end of his time, the difficult question of the future administration of the ladies' department—otherwise, King's College for Women—came up for settlement, and with it the still more critical question of the possible removal of both the women's college in Kensington and the men's college in the Strand to new sites. Well was it for King's that as one after another, in quick succession, these great matters emerged for consideration and decision the executive power was in the hands of so able, so strong, and so far-sighted a pilot as Principal Headlam.

§ 2. *The Dual University, 1898*

The first of all the great problems of this critical period that had to be faced was that of the reconstruction of the University of London. It will be remembered [1] that the Cowper commissioners had, in 1894, reported against the proposal to establish a new teaching university in the metropolis, and had advised the reorganization of the existing university on a dual basis—on the one hand an "internal" side (teaching and local), on the other hand an "external" side (examining and imperial). It will further be recollected that bills to give effect to the findings of the Cowper commissioners had been introduced in the House of Lords by Lord Playfair in 1895 and the Duke of Devonshire in 1896, but that both had lapsed for lack of time to debate them. Finally, it will be recalled that one of the main concerns of King's College in relation to the projected measure was to secure, if possible, some mitigation of the rigour of the commissioners' strict recommendation that there should be

> no grant of money out of university funds for any purpose in respect of which any privilege is conferred or any disability is imposed on account of religious belief.

The Cowper commission advised a scheme for the reconstruction of the university so different from that which King's College desired that the council for some time showed complete unconcern as to whether it were adopted by parliament or not. Their main preoccupations were to ensure that, if it were adopted and embodied in an act of parliament, first, the religious character of the college should be sustained; secondly, the control of the college over the curricula and the examinations of its students should be safeguarded; and, thirdly, that

---

[1] See above, p. 352.

the college should receive a due proportion of such grants of public money as might be placed at the disposal of the senate. As the years 1894–97, however, passed away the extreme inconvenience of having the constitution of the university chronically simmering in the crucible became painfully evident: public bodies withheld their grants; private donors closed their purses; teachers departed in disgust; students went elsewhere in despair—both education and administration were paralysed. Hence in December 1897, though still without enthusiasm, the council accepted an invitation from the registrar of the university to send representatives to a conference to promote the settlement of the twenty-year-old problem. The representatives chosen were the principal, the ex-principal, and Sir W. O. Priestley; and the same three representatives formed part of a deputation that waited on the Duke of Devonshire a month later (January 24, 1898). Both at the conference and on the deputation the spokesmen of King's made it clear that their council's support of the Cowper scheme was strictly conditional on the acceptance of their stipulations respecting religion, autonomy, and finance. Both the university and the government recognized the reasonableness of the council's demands, and went as far as they could to satisfy them. In particular, they agreed to the addition of the following proviso to the religious disability clause, which seemed at the time to be sufficient to furnish " a reasonable security for the interests of the college." It ensured that nothing, either in the ensuing act of parliament or in the statute made under its authority, should

> prevent the university from allocating funds for the payment of any person appointed or recognised by the university as a university teacher notwithstanding any conditions attached to any office held by him in any school of the university.

That was as near the wind of denominationalism as the Duke of Devonshire dared—and, perhaps, cared—to sail. And experience was later destined to show that it was not near enough to land the council's debt-logged bark in the safe harbour of state-and-rate maintenance. Meantime, however, it *was* enough to range the college by the side of the university and the other educational institutions of the metropolis in an urgent request to the lord president and the prime minister for early legislation.

The result of this pressing and unanimous appeal was the introduction of a third bill—similar in the main to those that had lapsed in 1895 and 1896 respectively—which rapidly passed both houses of parliament, and received the royal assent on August 12. This "University of London Act, 1898," which established the constitution whereunder both the university and the college as a constituent member of the university are still governed,[1] did two chief things: first, it formulated schedules of authoritative general principles for the reconstruction of the university; secondly, it appointed a board of seven commissioners,[2] whose function it was to frame detailed statutes for the application of these general principles. Of all the general principles the most fundamental was that of dualism: the university was to consist of two sections—viz., (1) an "external" section of unattached examinees maintaining the high traditions of the 1858 establishment, and (2) an "internal" section composed of students

> who have matriculated at the university, and are pursuing a course of study approved by the university in a school or schools of the university, or under one or more of the recognised teachers of the university.

The affairs of the examinees were to be administered by a "council for external students" (twenty-eight in number), and those of the internal *alumni* by an "academic council" (twenty in number). Both of these bodies were to be nominally committees of the one supreme governing authority of the university—viz., the "senate" (of fifty-six members), wherein, it was hoped, the conflicting interests of "externals" and "internals" would be harmonized and united. Beneath the senate and the two councils were to be, on the one hand, the "convocation" of graduates—at first, of course, wholly, and still dominantly, "external"—and, on the other hand, the "faculties" and "boards of studies" of the resident "internal" teachers. The chief officers of the dual university were to be a chancellor chosen for life by convocation and a vice-chancellor elected annually by the senate.

The commissioners appointed to draft the statutes under this complicated constitution set to work at once. But so many and varied were the interests that they had to consider, so vast and controversial the correspondence with which they had to deal, so numerous the deputations they had to receive, that not until February 1900 was their work completed and their seal affixed. The statutes numbered one hundred and

---

[1] Since the above was written a new constitution has come into force (May 1929).
[2] The commissioners were Lord Davey (chairman), Bishop Creighton, Sir William Roberts, Sir Owen Roberts, Professor Jebb, Professor Michael Foster, and Mr E. H. Busk.

thirty-six ; they were duly laid before parliament, and, having remained for the specified thirty days without criticism, at the end of that period became law. The council of King's, which had, through its special university committee, been very active in watching over the interests of the college during the year and a half of the commissioners' labours, reported as follows to the general court on May 11, 1900:

> The statutes have now been submitted to parliament for the prescribed time. Neither house has presented an address to Her Majesty in opposition. Unless any body or person affected petition Her Majesty in council to withhold her consent, the statutes and regulations will within a very few days pass into operation. The council received drafts of the statutes from the commissioners, and thus had the advantage of submitting suggestions for their amendment. Most of these have been practically adopted by the commissioners, and although in one or two cases of some importance the representations of the council have been unsuccessful, the council have every hope that on the whole the new scheme will work for the advantage of higher education in London, and for the benefit of its principal colleges. It should be observed that, together with University College, King's College gains direct representation on the new senate, while its professors form an important element in the different faculties which elect those members of the senate in whose hands the regulations for the studies and examinations of internal students will mainly reside.

A year later (May 10, 1901) they were able to announce that

> The reorganization of the University of London has now passed out of the hands of the statutory commissioners into those of the senate. The council is represented on that body by Dr Thomas Buzzard and the Principal. Sir John Wolfe Barry, a member of the council, was nominated to serve on the senate by the Crown. Professors Hudson, Halliburton, and Hewins have been elected members of the senate by the faculties, and are therefore members of the academic council, which is the advisory committee for the teaching work of the university; and Sir Albert Rollit, M.P., fellow of the college, and formerly a member of the council, is a representative of the graduates in arts.

We have already noted that (June 1902) Dr Robertson, principal of King's College, received the distinguished honour of being elected (by a unanimous vote of the senate) the first vice-chancellor of the reconstituted university. He clearly perceived the immense advantage that would accrue to the college, and particularly to its faculties of arts and science, from its new position as a constituent member of the university,

407

and he bent all his energies to the task of securing the smooth and efficient working of its novel and complicated machinery of government. He was loyally seconded by the council of the college and by the professorial board, who drew up revised courses of study for the approval of the senate, and began to direct their main attention to the preparation of candidates for the " internal " degrees of the university. Further, since now King's College was one of a group of associated university colleges, it became possible to arrange inter-collegiate courses of study, whereby overlapping was avoided and specialization encouraged. In pursuance of this inter-collegiate principle Professor D. S. Capper, of King's College, was appointed to a university chair of engineering (June 1902) and Professor H. G. Atkins to a university readership in German (October 1902). In 1903 the first special intermediate examinations were held in the college on behalf of the university; next year the council reported that " in various departments classes of students reading for honours have been formed," and that " more might be done in this direction if larger funds were available for the payment of salaries of professors."

The fact is that King's College had at last found herself. In association and co-operation with other colleges, and in particular with University College, a constituent and powerful member of a degree-conferring university, largely determining her own curricula and choosing her own teachers, and yet conforming to the regulations of a superior authority, she drew from the springs of a larger life, and began to manifest a vitality and a vigour such as she had never known before. Her venerable but almost moribund department of " general literature and science " in a special degree felt the urge of a new energy. So long as it was a mere unattached sixth form, " without pride of ancestry or hope of posterity," it languished and failed: it sprang no-whence; it led no-whither. Disliked by the public schools (including even the school in its own basement) because it sought to attract their elder boys, repudiated by Oxford and Cambridge because it wished to keep their freshmen away from them for a year, it had seemed likely in Dr Wace's days to perish of mere inanition. A glance at the tables given at the close of the last chapter will show that in 1888–89 its numbers had sunk to 22. An artificial revivification had come from the injection of fifty Queen's scholars, whose active principle was government grants, in 1890–91. But, even so, when Dr Wace resigned in 1897 there were but 56 matriculated day students reading for arts and 15 for science. So soon, however, as the courses in arts, in science, and in law (which was recognized as a faculty separate from arts in 1903) became university courses having a character and content of their own, and leading directly to a degree, an immense influx of students occurred. By 1912 the matriculated day students in arts numbered 104 and in science 74; while occasional and evening students swelled the totals to the large figures of 1160 in arts and 389 in science. The other departments of the college for the most part shared in the new prosperity. Taking the institution as a whole, the highwater mark of the period under review was the year 1906-7, when—including in the reckoning the pupils in the schools, the students in the civil service classes, and the ladies at Kensington—no fewer than 6897 persons were receiving instruction under the direction of the council of King's College.

§ 3. *The Abolition of Tests, 1903*

The great influx of students recorded in the last section, and in particular the institution of a growing number of specialized honours courses in arts and science, necessitated the appointment of many new professors and lecturers, and the consequent provision of considerable sums of money for the payment of the additional salaries. In order to attract good men it was necessary to offer some guarantee of adequate remuneration, and it was impossible to offer respectable sums to new professors while the old ones were perishing on the pitiful pittances enumerated above.[1] Further, an immense capital expenditure (some £15,000) was incurred during Dr Robertson's principalship on the necessary extension and progressive equipment of the scientific and technological laboratories and workshops. The income of the college from fees, although rapidly rising, was wholly insufficient to meet the new demands; the response to episcopal appeals for voluntary contributions from the devout had become negligible—and no wonder, since the money was required almost wholly for purely secular purposes. In vain was a " festival dinner " held, with Mr A. J. Balfour in the chair, in February 1900, in the hope of raising £14,000 to meet the heavy outlay on the building and its refitting. Equally ineffective was a still more ambitious appeal made in November 1902 at a meeting in the college presided over by Lord Selborne: toward £500,000 asked for in order to pay off the debt of the college and to endow its chairs rather less

[1] See above, p. 364.

409

than £30,000 was raised, and of this inadequate sum a large proportion came from members of the college council itself.

It had, in fact, become clear, even before this last desperate appeal for a modest half-million was made, that the rapidly increasing expenditure of the college precluded all possibility of keeping the doors open except by means of large, permanent, and calculable grants of public money. Nothing except regular contributions from the Treasury, the Board of Education, the London County Council, the Surrey County Council, and similar bodies could enable the council to provide the buildings, the apparatus, and the teachers necessary for the proper performance of educational work of a university standard. And all these eminent agencies for the dissemination of money extracted from the general payer of rates and taxes made it increasingly evident that they would not and could not contribute to any sort of denominational institution. It was even doubtful how far even the university itself could assign any portion of the funds at its disposal to a college whose teachers were tied by tests. For one of the fundamental principles of the Act of 1898 had been that

> No religious test shall be adopted or imposed, and no applicant for a university appointment shall be at any disadvantage on the ground of religious opinion.

True, as we have already noted,[1] the council had secured from the statutory commissioners the insertion of a proviso to the effect that nothing should

> prevent the university from allocating funds for the payment of any person appointed or recognised by the university as a university teacher, notwithstanding any conditions attached to any office held by him in any school of the university.

True, too, that under this proviso Professors Capper and Atkins of King's College were appointed to university posts. But, after all, that meant no more than that they were not placed " at any disadvantage on the ground of their religious opinions," the one in the department of mechanical engineering, the other in the department of German. The council found, however, a very different case would arise if the university were asked to endow any new chair, appoint any new teacher, or equip any new department. It would be totally impossible for the senate to make any inquiry as to any candidate's religious opinions. Hence it was obvious that if the college were to receive public money and were to share fully in

---

[1] See above, p. 405.

the life of the university it would be necessary for it to remove from teachers as well as from students the burden of the tests.

Other considerations, moreover, tended in the same direction. First, the members of the secular staff were unanimous in desiring emancipation. Not that they were not good churchmen, of unquestionable piety and orthodoxy. But they resented the imputation that they had secured their chairs only because the appointments were restricted to the members of one religious sect, and that they would not have got them in open competition. Again, the growing system of inter-collegiate lectures made the attempt to confine the instruction of any student to teachers attached to a particular church an absurdity. Finally—and this necessitated the extension of religious liberty to members of council as well as to teachers—the public bodies who voted money to the college were apt to insist that they should have a representative on the council, and it was manifestly impossible to dictate to the L.C.C. or the Surrey education committee and say that only a representative who was a member of the Church of England could be received.

All these considerations, financial, academic, constitutional, concurred to bring the great question to an issue in June 1902. A special meeting was called for the 13th, at which the treasurer of the college, the Hon. W. F. D. Smith (later Viscount Hambleden) proposed a motion which (as slightly amended in the meeting) read:

> That in view of the situation created by the University of London Act, 1898, the council, while determining to maintain the connection of the college with the Church of England, as set forth in section five of King's College London Act, 1882, resolves that so soon as may be every religious test as a qualification for office, position, or membership, in or under the council or college, other than professorships or lectureships in the faculty of theology, shall cease to exist, and, further, that all necessary and proper steps be taken to give effect to this resolution.

The meeting at which this revolutionary motion was debated was an exceptionally full one: twenty-five members were present, including five bishops, one of whom, the Bishop of London, was in the chair. Although the debate was a long and keen one—much of it centring round an amendment to exclude the council from the scope of the motion—the main issue was never in doubt. Only the two ex-students and ex-principals, Bishop Barry and Dr Wace, fought for the full retention of the tests. Dr Robertson spoke on the other side, and he fortified himself with a memorial from the staff of the college, who, faculty by faculty, beginning with the faculty of theology, unanimously implored the council to grant the desired and imperative emancipation. When, the amendment having been withdrawn, the motion as above drafted was put to the vote, Bishop Barry and Dr Wace found themselves with only one supporter—viz., the Rev. Dr Wiltshire, sometime professor of geology in the college. The remaining twenty-two members voted for the abolition of the tests for both councillors and teachers.

To give effect to this vote an Act of Parliament, repealing in part the Act of 1882, was necessary. This was at once promoted, and, since it met with general approval, its passage through the two houses was smooth and unobstructed. It received the royal assent on July 21, 1903. By this King's College London Act, 1903, it was stipulated that

> No religious declaration or test shall be imposed or required as a condition or qualification for any office, position, or membership in or under the college or the council thereof except for the office or position of a professor or lecturer in the faculty of theology in the college.

Advantage was taken of the occasion to effect two or three other changes of a minor character in the constitution: (1) to alter the dates of the college year so as to make them accord with the university year—viz., September 1 to August 31; (2) to move the meeting and the annual general court from the spring to the autumn; and (3) to place the audit of accounts in the hands of a professional accountant.

The abolition of the tests was followed immediately by the resignation of Dr Wace. He could no longer remain member of a council which had betrayed the solemn trust placed in their hands by the pious founders of the college. His example was imitated by Mr G. W. Bell, Mr H. W. Prescott, Sir Henry Harben, and the Bishop of Peterborough (Dr E. Carr Glyn). The vacant places were taken by Professor Rose, Sir Charles Lyall, Sir Albert K. Rollit, Mr John Wilson, and the Bishop of St Albans (Dr J. W. Festing).

§ 4. *Incorporation, 1908–10*

The council hoped that the London University Act of 1898, supplemented by the King's College Act of 1903, would complete the legislation necessary to establish the college as a full and entirely qualified member of the newly reconstituted

412

university. In some respects their anticipations were realized. The number of students rapidly increased: in 1898 the total was 1441; by 1904 it had become 2008; in 1907 it reached the unprecedented figure of 3145.[1] The staff, thanks to the removal of the tests, was reinforced by a succession of eminent scholars, led by Professor Israel Gollancz, whose work immensely added to the prestige of the college in the world of learning. Above all, the finances of the institution began to improve. The Treasury grants, flowing freely now that the religious obstacle was removed, rose from £2200 per annum in 1897 to £3900 in 1904, to £7800 in 1905, and to £8650 in 1907. At the same time, the contributions of the London County Council's Technical Education Committee were increased from £1500 per annum in 1897 to £3500 in 1906. As a result, buildings were improved; new laboratories constructed; up-to-date apparatus installed; salaries raised; the whole college converted from a condition of resigned adversity to progressive prosperity.

In one respect, however, the hope of the council was disappointed. The constitutional problem was not finally closed. In a surprisingly short period of time, indeed, two novel and unexpected questions presented themselves which required long and anxious consideration, and ultimately (1908) another Act of Parliament. These two questions arose out of (1) the incorporation of University College in the University of London, and (2) the establishment of a new Imperial College of Science at South Kensington. Let us briefly survey the two in turn.

I. *The Incorporation of University College.* So early as May 1902 the council of King's College reported to the annual court that

> the action of certain benefactors of University College, who have promised a sum amounting in all to £60,000 on condition of the transference of the buildings and endowments of that college to the university, has created a somewhat new situation,

and, they continued,

> in the probable event of the proposed transference being accepted by the senate of the university, an amendment of the University of London Act, 1898, will be necessary, and it remains to be seen how the position of the schools of the university will be affected in consequence.

[1] See the tables at the end of the chapter. These figures do not include the pupils of the school, or the students of the extra-collegiate courses whose numbers were also swelling enormously.

It appears that the University of London, which since its institution in 1836 had been lodged precariously in various government premises—first Somerset House in the Strand, later Burlington House in Piccadilly—was in urgent need of new and ampler accommodation. The addition to its secretarial staff and the increase of its academic duties consequent upon the reconstitution under the Act of 1898 were such as to render its old restricted offices wholly inadequate. Hence it seems to have occurred to some of the enterprising supporters of University College in Gower Street that here was an opportunity for recalling the university to its original home, for healing the schism of 1836, and for identifying University College with the University of London in a unique manner by making it the headquarters of the official organization. This suggestion raised a certain amount of alarm in the midst of the other colleges associated with the university: they feared lest their own position and status would be lowered if one of their number were thus peculiarly identified with the university. The immediate cause of anxiety was removed when the government placed a large part of the Imperial Institute in South Kensington at the disposal of the university for its administrative purposes. In spite of this, however, the council of University College decided to pursue the policy of surrender and incorporation: it seemed to promise an improved status for the college, a more assured rank for its teachers, a greater probability of favourable treatment on the part of the senate, and, above all, an unprecedented freedom from financial anxiety. The university, for its part, was disposed to accept the proposal of the college: it seemed likely to obviate friction, and in process of time to add considerable strength to the academic as distinct from the external side of the institution. The result was an agreement, conditional upon the preliminary liquidation of the large accumulated debt upon the college. The friends of the college rose to the occasion nobly: the Drapers' Company voted £30,000; Sir Donald Currie and other wealthy men made generous contributions, and in the course of a few years a total of some £200,000 was raised. Hence in 1905 the University College London Transfer Act was passed, and on January 1, 1907, the original corporation of the college ceased to exist, its functions being taken over by a committee appointed by the senate of the university.

The council of King's College watched this process of transformation and exaltation with keen attention and anxious interest. They were not eager to be incorporated and to lose their identity in the great leviathan. Moreover, in respect of King's College the difficulties of incorporation were greatly complicated by the religious problem: on the one hand the college was pledged by charter and statute to give in perpetuity instruction in " the doctrines and duties of Christianity as the same are inculcated by the Church of England "; while on the other hand the university was strictly precluded from imposing any theological test or imparting any denominational instruction. Nevertheless, it was generally felt from the first that if and when University College was incorporated it would be necessary, however great the difficulties might be, for King's College to follow suit. Principal Headlam in particular was a strong advocate of the policy of the maintenance of parity with University College. In an important and masterly memorandum laid before the council on June 22, 1904, he stated the considerations which seemed to him to make incorporation desirable, discussed the conditions that would have to be fulfilled to render incorporation possible, and estimated the consequences that would flow therefrom. Assuming that the incorporation of University College would shortly be consummated, he urged the expediency of a similar incorporation for King's College. First, the interests of the college demanded it; without it, the position of the staff of the college in the university would be adversely and most seriously affected; and, further, the college would probably suffer financially, both in respect of donations from the public and in respect of grants from the university itself. Secondly, the interests of the university demanded it; the incorporation of the two great colleges—which would probably be followed by the incorporation of all the rest—would greatly strengthen the university on its internal or teaching side, and " both the usefulness and the prestige of the college would be largely increased if the university as a whole should become a powerful and influential body." Dr Headlam, more consistently than any principal before or since, viewed college concerns from the university point of view, and realized that the future greatness and prosperity of King's were intimately bound up with the success and reputation of the University of London.

The council appointed a special committee to consider Dr Headlam's memorandum. The result of the committee's deliberations was that Dr Headlam was authorized to sound the university on the matter, which he did by means of a letter to the vice-chancellor (Dr P. H. Pye-Smith) dated July 15, 1904. The sequel was the appointment of a strong committee by the senate of the university to discuss the question with the council of King's College (November 1904). Conferences between this committee and representatives of the council of the college resulted (July 1905) in the formulation of a draft scheme for the consideration of the two governing bodies. Many and serious difficulties emerged in the process of discussion: they related especially to the position of the theological faculty, to the ownership of the site and the buildings of the college, to the government and discipline of the institution, to the status and powers of fellows and associates of the college, and to the future title of the principal of the college when he should pass from the service of the council to that of the senate. It would take more space than we have at our disposal to narrate the course of debate and negotiation from July 1905 to August 1908, when the King's College London Transfer Act, embodying the agreed terms of the university and the college, received the royal assent. Suffice it to say that agreement was virtually reached before the end of 1906, but that the securing of the necessary legislation had to be postponed until the debt of the college was wiped out. A special and pressing appeal for funds was issued by the council in February 1907, a total of £125,000 being asked for—viz., £22,000 to pay off the debt on the college, £37,000 to enable the school to be cut adrift unencumbered, and £66,000 to form an endowment fund. The appeal brought in about £32,000, mainly in the form of a few big subscriptions from devoted members of the council or beneficent city companies.[1] This sum, although only one-fourth of what had been asked for, sufficed to wipe out the college debt (as well as somewhat to reduce the burden on the school). Hence incorporation could be accomplished.

The significant terms of the Transfer Act of 1908, under which the college is still governed, were as follows. (1) The theological department of the college should be separated from the rest of the college, and should continue to be governed by the council, the constitution of which was slightly modified by the strengthening of the episcopal element and by the introduction of representatives of both staff and associates. Under the council its affairs should be administered by a dean, a theological committee, and a professorial board. (2) The secular departments of the college doing work of

---

[1] The largest donors were as follows : the Hon. W. F. D. Smith, £6000 ; the Clothworkers' Company, £5000 ; the Drapers' Company, £5000 ; the Goldsmiths' Company, £5000 ; Lord Grimthorpe, £2000 ; the Fishmongers' Company, £1000 ; Mr Charles Awdry, £1000.

university standard—that is, the faculties of arts, science, law, medicine, and engineering—should be transferred to the University of London, to be governed by its senate. Under the supreme authority of the senate, the actual administration should be in the hands of a principal,[1] a " delegacy " of the senate, and a professorial board. (3) The site of the college and the buildings thereon should remain the property of the old corporation of the college, but portions of them—all, indeed, except certain specified rooms reserved to the theological department—should be leased to the senate of the university for secular purposes.[2] (4) The hospital, with its advanced medical school, King's College School, the Strand School, and the civil service classes should all be severed as soon as possible from the college, and placed under separate governing bodies. (5) The women's department at Kensington should, as a separate institution, be transferred to the university on substantially the same terms as those arranged in respect of the men's departments in the Strand, except that in this case the property in the houses in Kensington Square should also pass to the senate (which should lease a room to the corporation of King's College for theological purposes). The women's department—to be called henceforth University of London King's College for Women—should be governed under the senate by a lady warden, a " delegacy," and a board of principal teachers.[3]

There were five schedules to the Transfer Act of 1908, relating respectively to the administration of King's College, the women's department, the hospital, the medical school, and the boys' school at Wimbledon. Besides these, an immense number of new statutes and regulations had to be framed by a body of commissioners in order to effect the great dispersion contemplated by the Act. Not until January 1, 1910, did " University of London King's College " under its new administration actually come into being and operation.

II. *The Imperial College of Science.* If imitation of University College was the original cause of the movement toward the incorporation of King's in the University of London, apprehension by the new Imperial College of Science was a secondary

[1] The title of " principal " was retained, although the university would have preferred the title of " warden " or " rector."
[2] This stipulation was a triumph for Dr Headlam's diplomacy. The senate had ardently desired the transfer to itself of the site and buildings. If it had attained its desire it is safe to say that the college would no longer be situated in the Strand.
[3] The " delegacy " at first was the same as that for King's College ; in 1913 a separate " delegacy " was instituted.

cause. In December 1903 the council of the college announced
to the general court of the corporation that

> A letter to the *Times* from Lord Rosebery on June 29 last put
> before the public the scheme for a higher scientific and technical
> college. A sum of £300,000 in subscriptions has been promised.
> The commissioners of the exhibition of 1851 are prepared to give
> a site of four acres still vacant at South Kensington, and the
> technical education committee of the London County Council
> . . . have promised a grant of £20,000 a year.

The new college, which was intended

> to give the highest specialised instruction, and to provide the
> fullest equipment for the most advanced training and research
> in various branches of science, especially in its application to
> industry,

was eventually constituted out of the already existing Royal
College of Science, Royal School of Mines, and the City and
Guilds Engineering College. Incorporated by royal charter in
July 1907, and established in its magnificent new buildings in
South Kensington, it was admitted as a school of the university
in the faculties of science and engineering in July 1908. Both
University College and King's College hoped that by sinking
themselves in the university they would, on the one hand,
strengthen their position in the face of a new and most formidable rivalry, and, on the other hand, would set an example
of self-immolation which the Imperial College would follow.
The Imperial College, however, did not follow; nor did any
other college in the university. The policy of incorporation,
in short, was a mistake.

§ 5. *The Great Dispersion*

However doubtful a boon it may have been to divide the
college into two sections, one sacred and the other secular—
divorcing, as it were, *sancte* from *sapienter* and merging the
second of the two in the university—there can be no question
that it was a great and necessary reform to free the college
from its association with numerous non-academic institutions
which had grown up within its borders during the course of
the eighty years of its existence. They had in their day
benefited by their connexion with the college ; they had,
moreover, for a time rendered benefits to the college either
(as in the case of the hospital) by providing a necessary supplement to the education given in the college, or (as in the case of
the schools and civil service classes) by providing funds essential

for the maintenance of the institution. But now that the college was receiving large grants of public money; now that it was a constituent member of a university; now that its advanced students were rapidly growing in numbers; now that the demand on its space for laboratories and research rooms was insatiable—now it was time for them to go, and for the college to devote itself exclusively to work of university rank.

I. *King's College Hospital.* The separation of the hospital, with its advanced medical school, from the college was facilitated (as well as rendered more necessary) by the removal of the hospital from its old site in Portugal Street, Westminster, to a new site on Denmark Hill, Camberwell. This removal had been effected under an Act of Parliament obtained in 1904. Its cause and process was, briefly, as follows. In 1903 the council noted with regret a diminution in the number of medical students. They attributed the decrease, not to any decline in the efficiency of the department, but to " the diminution of the number of patients, largely owing to the decrease in the density of the population surrounding the hospital." The clearance of the maze of mean streets between Holborn and the Strand for the making of Aldwych and Kingsway; the conversion of masses of tenements into offices and warehouses; the gradual shifting of the suburban middle class of London farther west, were leaving the hospital derelict and forlorn. On May 1, 1903, a long and detailed statement having been received from the joint medical boards, a special committee was appointed to survey the situation.[1] Its report, strongly urging removal, came before the council on July 6, 1903, and was by the council, after due discussion, unanimously accepted. The committee of management of the hospital was not unanimous in favour of the change; but the majority concurred with the council, as did a majority of a special court of governors summoned to decide the issue on October 12 of the same year.

In order to effect the removal an Act of Parliament was necessary, and here an unexpected obstacle presented itself. As the annual report of 1904 puts it:

> Unfortunately the opposition of the Westminster City Council had to be encountered. Efforts were made to compromise, but it was soon clear that this would be quite unsuccessful, and it

---

[1] The committee consisted of Sir Saville Crossley (chairman), Sir E. H. Currie, Messrs E. Nash, R. K. Causton, E. Tate, G. L. Hawker, with Mr Evan Spicer (London County Council), Mr J. King (Surrey County Council), and the Mayor of Camberwell.

was necessary to incur the expense of an opposed Bill. The result shewed that the position of the Westminster City Council would not bear examination. The cost, however, of meeting the opposition has been a very heavy drain on the funds of the appeal.

The special appeal here referred to ultimately brought in over £200,000; an excellent site on Denmark Hill, Camberwell, was secured, largely through the generosity and initiative of the Hon. W. F. D. Smith; in the spring of 1905 Mr W. A. Pike, of the firm of Pike and Balfour, was appointed architect, and his plans approved. The commencement of building was delayed until the appeal fund was large enough to justify the venture; difficulties respecting the plans caused further postponement; but on March 2, 1908, operations actually began, the first block consisting of the out-patient, casualty, dispensary, and bath departments. On July 20, 1909, the foundation-stone was laid by King Edward VII. Six weeks later (September 1, 1909), under the King's College London Transfer Act, the " appointed day " arrived, and the council of King's College handed over the government of the hospital to its new administrative authority.[1]

II. *King's College School.* Ten years before the hospital moved to Camberwell the school had moved to Wimbledon.[2] The removal was amply justified by its results: the number of boys on the rolls steadily rose, until in 1903 they once more exceeded 300. Long before this standard was reached new buildings had become necessary. These were planned by the distinguished architect, Mr Banister Fletcher, an old boy of the school, and they were opened by the Duke of Cambridge on July 6, 1899. In 1904 a new and ample playing-field was secured on the Woodhays estate adjoining the school at a cost of £8000—one-fourth part of which was raised by a special appeal for donations ; £6000, however, had to go to swell the already bloated debt on the school, which in 1909 stood at a sum not far short of £40,000. By this time the King's College London Transfer Act had been passed, and the council of the college were anxious to hand over the school to the new body of governors incorporated under the fifth schedule of the statute. It was impossible, however, to hand it over with so heavy an incubus of debt—a debt which tended to grow in spite of the prosperity of the school, because the interest upon it absorbed

[1] The constitution of the new governing body of the hospital and its medical school is laid down by the fourth schedule of the King's College London Transfer Act, 1908.

[2] See above, pp. 375–376.

more than all the annual profits. The " appointed day " for transfer, therefore, had to be postponed; strenuous efforts were made to reduce the liabilities of the school; during 1909 more than £10,000 was paid off, out of the proceeds of the incorporation fund, and finally, on January 1, 1911, the new governing body assumed control, coupled with responsibility for a residue of debt still exceeding £25,000.

Mr Bourne, headmaster since 1889, resigned in 1906, and was succeeded by Mr Douglas Smith. Mr Smith did excellent work for the school, but unfortunately his health could not stand the strain of labour and anxiety involved in the securing of pupils, the raising of money, and the changing of government under the Transfer Act, and in 1910 he was compelled to lay down his task. An extremely able and energetic successor was fortunately found in Mr Lionel Rogers.

III. *The Strand School.* It will be remembered [1] that in 1897 Mr Braginton's junior civil service classes had migrated from Waterloo Road, and had established themselves in the vaults vacated by King's College School, where they had assumed the name of the " Strand School." This school, an excellent one of its type, soon developed into a general commercial school. In 1900 it was recognized by the London County Council as a school in which intermediate county scholarships could be held, and five years later it was allowed to become a centre for the training of pupil teachers. Its numbers increased fabulously: 443 in 1900, they grew with epidemic rapidity, until in 1907 they reached their maximum inflation with 804. Never in the palmiest days of King's College School had such large classes of such little boys swarmed in the subterranean recesses of the basement of the college. Dr Headlam, who wanted to identify the college with the university, was horrified when he lifted up the lid and gazed down upon the seething masses of elementary infancy that congested his infernal regions. The Board of Education, too, perhaps not wholly of its own mere motion, intervened, with decisive effect. In 1907 it emphatically condemned the accommodation provided for the school, and threatened a withdrawal of the government grants unless the whole over-prosperous establishment were removed. In those circumstances the London County Council undertook to provide new buildings, and ultimately a site at Brixton was chosen. In 1909, in order to facilitate the transfer, the council handed over the government of the school to a committee, to which the London County Council added

[1] See above, p. 371.

representatives. In December 1910 Mr Braginton resigned the headmastership in which he had shown such striking initiative, such admirable energy, and such remarkable success. In 1911 Mr R. B. Henderson, mathematical scholar of New College, Oxford, and assistant master at Rugby School, was appointed in his place to be the Joshua of the exodus. Not, however, until 1913 were the buildings at Brixton finished and the school transferred to them. The release of so many classrooms was an immense boon to the college: it enabled a great and long-needed redistribution of lectures and seminars to take place. As an offset to this relief, however, the painful fact had to be faced that the college was losing a revenue of some £1500 a year. Its growing dependence upon grants of public money was accentuated.

IV. *The Civil Service Classes.* When Mr Braginton resigned the headship of the Strand School he still continued to preside over the civil service classes—mainly adult evening classes—which had been under his charge for over thirty-five years.[1] And the numbers attending these classes continued to be large.[2] The high-water mark was reached in 1905, when there were 1449 men and 147 women in attendance. One of the conditions under which the college was incorporated in the university was that within two years of the date of incorporation (*i.e.*, before December 31, 1911) these classes should be removed from the precincts of the college and placed under separate control. Mr Braginton himself agreed to lead them forth and rule them. In December 1909 he sent out the women as a vanguard under his daughter's command, and they took possession of new premises in Red Lion Square, off Holborn. Before the end of 1911 Mr Braginton placed himself at the head of his thousand men and established them in a commodious Canaan situated in Kingsway. To both establishments, male and female, he gave the name of " St George's College." Much consequent confusion ensued, which would have been avoided if the one section had been called " St George's " and the other " The Dragons' " !

Thus by the end of the year 1911 was King's College freed from association with its miscellaneous appendages—appendages which had at one time been indispensable supports, but which had become encumbrances. In place of a collection of varied and incongruous institutions governed by a single council there were henceforth seven separate corporations, each with its own governing body—viz., (1) University of

---

[1] See above, p. 370.   [2] See the tables at the end of this chapter.

London King's College; (2) the Theological Department of King's College; (3) King's College for Women; (4) King's College School, Wimbledon; (5) the Strand School ; (6) the Civil Service Classes; and (7) King's College Hospital. The transformation of the universal provider into the university college was complete.

§ 6. *University of London King's College*

We have already noted that the establishment of King's College as a constituent member of the University of London in 1898 was followed by an immense expansion in the work of the higher departments of the college, and particularly in the faculties of arts and science. The harmonization of the curricula of the college and the examinations of the university; the definite direction of the lectures of the professors and the labours of the students to the attainment of the valuable degrees bestowed by the senate; the development of the honours and post-graduate work in all departments powerfully attracted students, and soon filled the classrooms to overflowing.

To describe in detail the many activities of this period of remarkable expansion would require far more space than remains at our disposal. We must be content to note a few outstanding features in each of the main departments.

I. *The Day Training Department.* This excellently organized department continued to flourish. For the first half of the period under review it provided the majority of the candidates that the college sent in for the arts degrees of the university. Its devoted and capable head, Mr J. W. Adamson, was made lecturer in education in 1901 and professor in 1903. Three years later, when the development of the work of the department made assistance necessary, he was joined by one of the most zealous and brilliant of his former students, Mr A. A. Cock. So strong had the department become by this time that it was possible (1905) to lay down the stringent but salutary rule that no student should be admitted who had not passed the London matriculation examination and was not prepared to read for a London degree. The difficulty of combining degree work, however, with professional training was a formidable one, and no satisfactory solution was found until in 1911 the Board of Education sanctioned the " four-year course," according to which the first three years should be devoted to the reading for the degree, the fourth being reserved for professional training.

II. *The Faculty of Arts.* The first special intermediate arts examination for King's College, under the new university regulations, was held in the summer of 1903. Nine candidates entered, of whom eight were successful. Immediately afterward classes for honours degrees were instituted, Greek and Latin, mathematics, English, and French being the subjects first represented, to which history and philosophy were added a year or two later. The most popular honours subject proved to be English; in 1911 Professor Gollancz was able to report the presence of no fewer than 37 candidates in his class. In mathematics the numbers were so small that, since the same was the case at the other colleges of the university, in order to economize teaching power and encourage specialization an excellent inter-collegiate system of lectures was organized. A not less important piece of organization took place in the evening class department of the faculty. The college gradually dropped its more elementary work, leaving it to be performed by the polytechnics, which could do it more cheaply, and concentrated its attention upon degree work. In 1904–5 an excellent scheme of evening degree courses was arranged, the department of English once again leading the way in initiative and success. To this same energetic department in 1908 the London County Council began to make a special grant for the institution of an evening course for teachers. This course, under the inspiring guidance of Professor Gollancz and Mr A. C. Guthkeech, proved to be eminently attractive, drawing large companies of mature and serious students to the college. Definite research work was also extended in the various departments. On the one hand, members of the staff, under the easier conditions of salary, were able to give more adequate time to the proper task of the university teacher—viz., the enlargement of the bounds of knowledge. Year by year from 1901 the council, with its annual report, published a list of the contributions to learning made by professors and their colleagues. On the other hand, students who had taken high honours at their bachelor's examination were encouraged to proceed to the master's degree by way of research: in 1912 there were thirty-three of these post-graduate students in the faculty of arts alone. The developments of this honours and research work, of course, necessitated numerous additions to the staff. Of the older teachers Professor Buchheim (German) died in 1900, Professor Warr (Classics) in 1901, and Professor Perini (Italian) in 1903: while Professors Hudson (mathematics) and Hales (English) resigned in 1903. Their places were taken respectively by Professors H. G. Atkins, W. C. F. Walters, L. Ricci, S. A. F. White, and Israel Gollancz. Besides these, however, various specialists were appointed in the different departments—*e.g.*, in mathematics Mr S. T. Shovelton (1904), in classics Mr J. K. Fotheringham (1904), in Romance philology Mr A. V. Salmon (1905). In 1900 Assyriology began to be systematically taught in the college, which was fortunate in securing the services of Dr C. H. W. Johns, of Cambridge, as lecturer. On his resignation in 1910, owing to pressure of other duties, his place was taken by the eminent Dr L. W. King, of the British Museum.[1]

III. *The Faculty of Law.* When the University of London was reconstructed in 1898 it was hoped that a strong law school would become one of its leading features. The presence in London of the supreme tribunals of the empire, of the great inns of court, and of the headquarters of the law society, together with the fact that in the Public Record Office, the British Museum, and the libraries of the legal corporations all the main stores of materials for the advanced study of law were accumulated, seemed to mark out the metropolitan university as the predestined seat of the largest and most important seminary of jurisprudence in the world. The hope of 1898, however, was not realized. Both the barristers and the solicitors had their own systems of legal education, which they were not prepared to abandon or to merge in a common academic curriculum. Hence the law classes throughout the university remained small. At King's they were wholly evening classes, taken by working lawyers on their way home after the serious and remunerative toil of the day was done. The students were for the most part ambitious and energetic young men, by no means wholly from the legal profession, who wished to add degrees in law to their other qualifications. In 1904 the curriculum of the faculty of law was definitely directed to the LL.B. degree; in 1906, owing to the continued smallness of the classes, an inter-collegiate arrangement was made with University College and the new London School of Economics (founded 1895), which obviated a good deal of wasteful overlapping. The main teaching of the King's College portion of the scheme was done by Mr James Gault (1887), Mr H. J. H. Mackay (1892), Dr W. N. Hibbert (1898), and Mr W. H. Griffith (1911). The subjects taken at King's

---

[1] After Dr King's untimely death in 1919 the lectureship remained vacant for five years. In 1924 it was revived, its duties being divided between Mr C. J. Gadd (Sumerian) and Mr Sidney Smith (Accadian).

were jurisprudence for the intermediate; with laws of contract, tort, evidence, real and personal property, commerce, and private international law for the final. In 1912 there were 22 students registered at King's taking the degree course, while 46 students registered at the other colleges were in attendance.

IV. *The Department of Architecture.* This department from its institution in 1840 down to the year 1904 was associated with engineering as one of the applied sciences. In 1904, when Professor R. Elsey Smith was at its head, it was transferred to the faculty of arts. An important step in the development of the school was made in 1905, when the Royal Institute of British Architects recognized the certificate given by the college to successful students at the end of their second year as exempting candidates for admission to the institute from the usual intermediate examination. At this time there were 20 students of architecture in the day classes and 72 in the evening. By 1912 the day class had fallen to 11, while the evening class had risen to 116. Before that date, however—viz., in 1910— a fiat had gone forth from the senate of the university that, in order to avoid duplication and competition, the architectural school of King's College should be transferred to University College, where a new and commodious building was being erected through the generosity of Sir Herbert Bartlett. The delegacy of King's College agreed that " architecture is a subject which will be better taught in one strong department than in two weak ones." It was led to hope that if it consented without fuss to the surrender of its architecture it might hope for compensation in the form of a concentration of law at King's College. So the architecture went to Gower Street in 1913; but the compensating law never came to the Strand.

V. *The Department of Oriental Studies.* It will be remembered[1] that so far back as 1889 an inter-collegiate scheme for the teaching of the oriental languages had been drawn up by University College and King's College, in conjunction with the Imperial Institute. Nothing much had come of it, however, largely owing to lack of funds necessary to pay teachers and provide books. In 1907 an influential deputation drawn from many quarters waited on the prime minister to urge the importance of oriental studies and to ask for government endowment. The result of the deputation was the appointment of a committee of inquiry, under the chairmanship of Lord Reay. In 1909 this committee reported in favour of the concentration of the teaching of Asiatic and African

[1] See above, p 367.

languages, with the appurtenances thereof, in a new central School of Oriental Studies endowed with adequate funds—about £12,000 a year being suggested as necessary. Not till 1916, however, was the recommendation of the committee carried out, when the School of Oriental Studies was established in the fine buildings of the London Institution in Finsbury Circus. Meanwhile, King's College continued to provide instruction in Arabic, Chinese, Modern Greek, Japanese, Russian, Turkish, Hausa, and Zulu to such as aspired to an acquaintance with these tongues. The only classes that flourished, however, were those in Chinese and in Hausa: the former were filled by prospective bankers, commercial travellers, and missionaries to the celestial empire; the latter by would-be explorers, exploiters, and evangelists of darkest Africa. Sir R. K. Douglas, after thirty-four years' service, resigned the professorship of Chinese in 1907. For a short time Sir Walter Hillier (who had joined him in 1904) remained head of the department. But in 1908 he was recalled to China as adviser to the emperor, and the Rev. George Owen, a returned missionary, was appointed in his stead.[1] Hausa was taught by Mr W. H. Brooks, aided by an assistant.

VI. *The Faculty of Science.* In 1898 small results gave large satisfaction in the faculty of science. " The successes at the examinations of the University of London have been above the average," says the report of that year. " Five students gained the degree of B.Sc." As a matter of fact, although there were 253 students in the department, only 9 of them were matriculated, the remainder consisting of occasional students who came for such subjects as bacteriology or experimental psychology. The main feature of the period 1898–1912 was the steady increase of university work. Honours courses in all the main departments were instituted or developed; facilities for practical work were increased; research laboratories were provided. In 1912 successes at the intermediate examination numbered 27; the pass degree was secured by 6 candidates, while 15 achieved honours. Before this date, too, half a dozen doctorates by research had been secured. The development of this honours and post-graduate work had, of course, necessitated both considerable additions to the staff and large extensions to the laboratory accommodation of the

[1] In 1911 the China Society kindly deposited in King's College the 10,000 volumes of the *Chinese Encyclopædia*—the only copy in Britain outside the British Museum. It occupied the whole of one side of the gallery of the college library. In 1916 the King's College librarian gratefully transferred the deposit to the School of Oriental Studies.

college. In the annual report of May 1900 the most striking feature is the catalogue of vast and revolutionary changes made in the structure and arrangement of the building. The list concludes with the words:

> It may safely be said that the past year has seen more important and comprehensive additions to the teaching accommodation of the college than have ever been provided in a single year.

So far as the faculty of science was concerned, the most notable features of this great transformation were (1) the enlargement of the anatomical department, (2) the removal

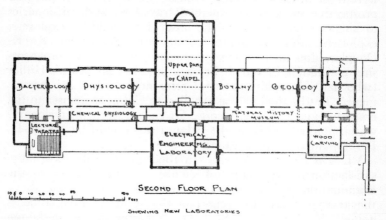

SECOND FLOOR PLAN

SHEWING NEW LABORATORIES

of the pathological museum to the vicinity of the dissecting rooms, (3) the provision of a new and excellent room for the public health laboratory, (4) the fitting-up of two new rooms for geology, (5) the equipment of a joint museum for geology, zoology, and *materia medica*, (6) the assignment of two new rooms to botany, and (7) the arrangement of a fine suite of contiguous rooms for physiology. The total cost of the reconstruction and reorganization was estimated at £14,000, for the raising of which a special appeal had to be made. The new laboratories were formally opened by Lord Lister on October 20, 1900. Very shortly afterward it became necessary to provide fresh accommodation for experimental psychology, for chemistry, for physics, for zoology. In respect of physics, something was done by the conversion of the white-elephantine George III Museum into a laboratory (1905), but the exhibits remained, and they occupied a lot of space.

Among the more important changes in the staff of the faculty of science during the fifteen years under review were the following. (1) In 1901 Professor E. M. Crookshank brought to an end his remarkable work as a bacteriologist in the college, and was succeeded by Dr R. T. Hewlett, senior bacteriologist of the Jenner Institute, a former student and demonstrator of King's. (2) Dr W. G. Smith was appointed lecturer in experimental psychology, and—in most inadequate accommodation, and with extremely scanty apparatus—he began the task of building up a psychological laboratory. In 1903 Dr C. S. Myers took over the task. In 1907 he was joined by Dr William Brown, who in 1909, on the failure of Dr Myers' health, became head of the department. (3) In 1905 Professor W. Grylls Adams terminated his forty years of distinguished service in the college. Some readjustment of the work of the department of " natural philosophy " was then made, applied mathematics being transferred to the charge of Professor S. A. F. White, while Dr H. A. Wilson, senior lecturer since 1904, became professor of physics. To the great regret of the college this distinguished physicist was lured away to McGill University, Canada, in 1909 by the attraction of a more adequate salary than King's could then afford. His place was taken by Professor C. G. Barkla. (4) Also in 1905 the chair of zoology, dormant since the early days of the college, was revived, and was bestowed on the brilliant and powerful Dr Arthur Dendy, who came to it rich in knowledge and experience gained in New Zealand and South Africa. (5) The chair of anatomy, held at the beginning of the period by Professor Arthur Robinson, passed in 1905 to Dr Peter Thompson, of the Middlesex Hospital, and from him to Dr David Waterston, of the University of Edinburgh. (6) In 1908 the department of geology was strengthened by the appointment of Dr T. F. Sibly to assist the venerable Professor H. G. Seeley. It was hoped that while Dr Sibly reintroduced discipline into the department his chief would be free " to carry on his researches in the fossil vertebrates," a subject on which his knowledge was unique. Unfortunately, however, Professor Seeley lived only a few months to enjoy the change from the turbulence of the un-fossilized to the tranquillity of the fossilized vertebrates. He died in 1909, and Dr Sibly became head of the department.

VII. *The Faculty of Medicine.* The removal of King's College Hospital from the vicinity of the Strand, and its establishment on Denmark Hill under entirely separate control, involved drastic changes in the medical school. In 1904 a broad general division was made. The purely scientific or preliminary portions of the curriculum—chemistry, physics, biology, elementary anatomy and physiology—were left in the hands of the professors at the college; the more advanced and specialized medical studies were transferred to the professional staff at the hospital. For some years (1904–8) there appeared to be a prospect that the preliminary scientific teaching of all the medical students of the university would be taken away from all the colleges and concentrated in a new special building at South Kensington; but the scheme fell through for lack of funds, and the two great colleges, University and King's, remained the chief seats of instruction. Some compensation for the transference of the advanced courses to the hospital was gained when the freshmen of Westminster and St George's medical schools (1905) and Charing Cross medical school (1911) began to come to King's for their preliminary scientific training. The rooms vacated at the Charing Cross Hospital by the classes transferred to King's were generously placed at the disposal of the overcrowded bacteriological and public health departments of the college, which were removed to these ampler and more convenient quarters in 1912. These two flourishing departments were at that time under the charge respectively of Dr (now Sir) W. J. R. Simpson, who in 1898 had succeeded Dr Charles Kelly as professor of hygiene, and Dr R. T. Hewlett, who, as we have noted above, had taken over Dr Crookshank's bacteriological work in 1901. Dr Crookshank himself displayed a warm and generous interest in the transmigration of his old department, and he gave it a send-off in its new home by presenting to it his valuable bacteriological library. The formal ceremony of transference was effected on October 30, 1912, when Professor Abraham Flexner, the Huxley Lecturer for the year, gave an address.

VIII. *Faculty of Engineering.* This faculty passed through striking vicissitudes during the period 1897–1912. Beginning strong with 324 students, it grew in multitude and vigour until in 1904, with 520 on its roll, it constituted more than one-fourth of the college proper. From 1904, however, a decline set in, and in 1912 only 150 names were on its books. This fall was a very serious matter for the delegacy to face: each student paid some £50 a year in fees; hence the loss of a couple of hundred engineering students meant a diminution of £10,000 in the gross annual revenue of the college. The cause of this decline in numbers was not at all any falling off in the efficiency of the department: never had its staff been more numerous and capable, its equipment so good, its standard

430

THE RECONSTITUTED UNIVERSITY

of achievement higher. It was due on the one hand to a
general and deep depression in the engineering world, which
affected alike all schools of engineering all over the country,
and on the other hand to the keen rivalry of the engineering
schools of University College and the new Imperial College
of Science at South Kensington. The Imperial College in
particular, with its abounding wealth, its magnificent buildings,
and its lavish equipment, naturally attracted many students
who would otherwise have gone to either Gower Street or the
Strand. It was hoped that if all three colleges were incorporated in the university the senate might so rule them all as
to prevent cut-throat competition; but the Imperial College,
having nothing to fear from its older and less powerful rivals,
refused to place itself under authority. The London County
Council, however, to which all three looked for technical
education grants, intervened and said that unless spheres of
influence could be marked out, overlapping stopped, and
unnecessary rivalry eliminated contributions to all three would
be suspended. Hence during the years 1911–12 a series of
conferences between representatives of the three colleges took
place, which happily ended in the substitution of a large
measure of co-operation in place of destructive antagonism.

The outstanding features in the history of the faculty during
these fifteen years were as follows. First, large additions
were made to the accommodation of the various departments,
particularly in that great year of reconstruction 1900, and
in 1905, when the electrical engineering laboratory was
moved from the roof to the basement. Secondly, equipment
was vastly increased and improved, especially by the installation of a gas-engine (presented by Professor Hopkinson) in
1898; a steam-engine (given by the Clothworkers' Company)
in the same year; electric apparatus to the value of £250
(through the generosity of Lady Siemens) in 1899; a con-
denser and air-pump (from Mr J. I. Thornycroft) in 1901;
some much-needed polyphase machinery, worth £300 (from
the Westinghouse Company), also in 1901. In 1905 two
anonymous donations amounting in all to £1500 enabled a
refrigerating plant, together with additional dynamos and
steam-engines, to be procured. In 1909 a liquid-air apparatus
was installed, so that henceforth the staff when in need of pure
refreshment were not compelled to cross the Strand to Shorts.
Thirdly, the institution of a new B.Sc. (Engineering) degree
by the University of London in 1901 caused the syllabus of the
college course to be revised in accordance with the regulations

of the examination. The teachers of the faculty, however, did not find the revised syllabus very satisfactory. In 1912 they complained that "too great stress is laid on book-work and too little on practical training," and they presented a memorial to the senate, through the delegacy, on the matter. Nevertheless, many of the students of King's College took excellent places in the engineering examinations of the university: in 1912, for instance, 18 passed the intermediate, 19 the ordinary B.Sc., and 3 the honours degree examination. Fourthly, a good deal of research work, both pure and applied, began to be done in the faculty, some of it leading to the doctorate. At one and the same time, for instance—viz., in 1907—investigations were going on in matters so varied as the critical velocity of water, the metacentric height of ships, the resistance of asphalt to wear, the strain on struts with lateral loads, the strength of reinforced concrete, the pheno-mena of alternate-current electrolysis, and the constitutional diseases of metals. The feverish excitement of the faculty in these circumstances can well be imagined. Fifthly, the retire-ment of Professor H. Robinson in 1903, after twenty-two years' service, enabled a certain reorganization to take place. The faculty was made entirely separate from that of science, and was more sharply subdivided than before into the three depart-ments of civil, mechanical, and electrical engineering. Sixthly, an experiment was tried in 1904 and the following years whereby, a fourth year having been added to the course, it became possible for a student to get part of his qualifying training at certain selected engineering works. The difficul-ties of organization, however, proved to be great, and at the end of the period the arrangement was undergoing reconsideration.

The faculty suffered a grave and unexpected loss when on August 27, 1898, the brilliant Dr John Hopkinson met his death in the Alps. His place was taken by his able and genial assistant, Professor Ernest Wilson, whose popular personality still continues in the centenary year of the college to enliven and enlighten the community. In 1902 Professor D. S. Capper was appointed to a university chair in mechanical engineering, and the money released by this honourable appointment enabled the college to provide several much-needed assistants. At the end of 1912 civil engineering received a most capable head in Professor A. H. Jameson.

§ 7. *The Theological Department*

When last we surveyed the history of the theological department of King's College [1] we observed that during Dr Wace's
principalship a serious decline in numbers had marked the
years 1883–92, and that there was general agreement among
both the members of council and the staff that one of the prime
causes of the fall was the lack of a hostel wherein the domestic
virtues and the social graces of the would-be curates might be
cultivated. Parents did not like to expose their sensitive
theological sons to the chilly or infected airs of lodging-houses;
still less did bishops care to ordain young men, even when
guaranteed by the A.K.C., who had passed so large a part of
the three most critical years of their lives in circumstances
wherein no supervision of either their manners or their morals was
possible. We observed, too, that, although in 1892–93 strenuous
efforts had been made to find some solution of the hostel
problem, the desperate condition of the college finances had prevented anything from being done. We have now to see how,
ten years later, under Principal Robertson, the long-standing
difficulty was settled. On March 14, 1902, in the council,

> The principal reported that certain members and friends of
> the theological faculty of the college were prepared, if the amount
> necessary to provide for furnishing and for two years' rent could
> be obtained, to open as an experiment a house in a central part
> of London as a hostel for theological students. The Bishops of
> London, Rochester, and St Albans had expressed approval of
> the scheme, and there was every prospect of a fair number of
> students taking advantage of it. It was not proposed that the
> college should incur any expense or liability in connection with
> the hostel. The principal mentioned that Mr Newsom, the vice-
> principal, had been most energetic in making the necessary
> enquiries and in enlisting influential support for the project.
> The council were asked to express approval of the proposal before
> any definite steps were taken.
>
> The proposal was approved and the principal was requested
> to convey to Mr Newsom the council's thanks for the trouble he
> had taken in the matter.

The Mr Newsom referred to here is, of course, the Rev. G. E.
Newsom, who later (1903) became professor of pastoral
theology in the college; who left the college in 1916 in order
to be vicar of Newcastle-on-Tyne and canon of its cathedral;
and who at the moment of writing is the recently appointed
master of Selwyn College, Cambridge. He had joined the

[1] See above, pp. 378–384.

2 E

staff of King's in 1897 in the composite capacity of vice-principal, censor, chaplain, and lecturer in theology. A man of abounding geniality and friendliness, he had soon won a secure place in the affections of his colleagues and his students. Throwing himself with untiring energy and inextinguishable enthusiasm into the many and various duties of his four unremunerative offices, he soon realized the nature of the needs of his department and determined to do what in him lay to meet them. To him, above all others, the establishment of the hostel was due. He it was who sought and found the suitable houses in the proper situation; and he it was who finally became the first warden of the hostel and the organizer of its success.

The site chosen for the hostel was Mecklenburgh Square, close to the Foundling Hospital. Here two excellent houses— numbers 42 and 45—were secured, the lease of one being purchased, the other being rented. The initial cost was some £1600, toward which about £1000 was raised by subscription —the bishops of London and Rochester assisting from their diocesan funds. In the hostel some 26 students could be accommodated, and before the end of 1903 the place was full to overflowing. Nevertheless, mainly because of the burden of debt hanging about it, it could not be made entirely to pay its own way. In 1905, by a new and strenuous effort, the debt (then exceeding £800) was cleared off, the main contributors to the extinction fund being the staff of the theological faculty, the ecclesiastical commissioners, and the trustees of the parochial charities fund. Notwithstanding this relief, however, ends could not be made to meet: even when the hostel was full, and even when extreme economy was practised, the annual deficit amounted to about £170. The fact was that the fees of students who were in residence only thirty-three weeks a year could not be made to cover the cost of maintaining the establishment for fifty-two weeks. Annual subsidies had to be sought, until, in 1910, the council found itself in the fortunate position of being able to assume financial responsibility, together with administrative control. The hostel, in fact, although not self-supporting, was a most valuable asset to the theological department. It brought students to the college. Numbers flew up. The 85 students in the department at the end of 1902 had become 190 in 1910, and the following year there were well over 200. Fees flowed in.

Another source of financial prosperity, moreover, was the King's College Transfer Act of 1908; the separation of the theological department from the secular departments revealed the fact that divinity had for some time been bearing more than its proportionate share of the general cost of college administration. Now that it was able to use all its revenues for its own purposes; and now that new revenues were coming in from the rent of rooms let to " University of London King's College," divinity began to enjoy an unprecedented financial prosperity. Still further, in 1903 the good offices of the bishops secured from the administrators of the City Parochial Charities an annual grant of £1500 for the endowment of several chairs, and a further £500 a year to provide a fund for exhibitions. The money released by these generous contributions was used not only to secure more adequate salaries for the staff, but also to effect material reductions in the fees of the students and to found bursaries for the impecunious.

Thus for the theological department, even more than for the college generally, the period 1897–1912 saw the definite turn from adversity to prosperity, from struggle to security, from weakness to strength. Dr Headlam, in particular, placed the department in an impregnable position when, instead of surrendering the site and buildings of the college to the senate of the university, he achieved the statutory confirmation of their ownership by the old (and now exclusively theological) council and corporation. Real and personal property, however, were not the only bases of the striking increase and development of the department under Dr Robertson and Dr Headlam. Tranquillity and harmony succeeded the dissension and unrest which the controversy between Dr Wace and Professor Momerie had caused. Toleration, mutual respect, liberality, amiability prevailed. Lions lay down with lambs, and all combined to further the interests of their common fold. Besides these general conditions of prosperity, however, four more particular causes must be mentioned. (1) Early in the century the university instituted the B.D. degree, and the council at once (1902) determined to take advantage of it. The main difficulty in the way of doing so was due to the fact that the course required three years of study instead of the two customary for the A.K.C. In spite of this difficulty, however, the theological curriculum was reorganized so as to provide for the extra year, and promising students were enabled by the aid of exhibitions and bursaries to afford it. The intellectual standard of the school was speedily and steadily raised: the very first year (1903) the number of matriculated students increased by fourteen. From 1904 onward a regular feature of the council's annual reports was a record of university degrees and distinctions gained. The first great triumph of the new curriculum was achieved in 1908, when the Rev. W. R. Matthews (the present dean of the college) gained first-class honours at the B.D. examination in the philosophy of religion. (2) In 1906 an admirable tutorial system was introduced into the department. Each student was placed under the special charge of one of the members of the staff. " Each," reported the council,

is thus enabled to feel that there is some one in the college who is able to take a personal interest in his career, and on the other side it is possible for the college to give the bishops valuable information as to the character and capacity of those who are desirous of being ordained.

(3) The bishops' " central examination " for prospective theological students, instituted in 1893, had proved unsatisfactory. Preparation for it had passed too much into the hands of the crammers, and young men who got through it frequently entered college in an extremely unsatisfactory mental and moral condition. Hence in 1908 the council secured the consent of the bishops to the substitution of a special " preliminary course," normally of one year, within the college itself. The course consisted of " a thorough instruction in Greek, Latin, and logic," together with some training in the Old and New Testaments, English literature, history, and science. At the end of the year an examination was held, the staff being assisted in judging the results by external examiners appointed by the central board. But the chief advantages of this preliminary course over the central examination were, on the one hand, that it co-ordinated the work of the preparatory year with the work of the subsequent years spent in the theological faculty, and, on the other hand, that it enabled the tutors to estimate the moral and social fitness of candidates for the ministry. That the tests imposed by the preliminary course and examination were severe is indicated by the fact that at the end of the first year, out of 27 members of the class, only 10 were passed on for admission to the faculty; and at the end of the second year only 20 out of 45.[1] (4) But without question one of the prime causes of the success of the theological department of the college during this period was the eminence and ability of its teachers. Both Dr Robertson and Dr Headlam were men of outstanding rank, both as scholars and as teachers. Mr Newsom, as vice-principal, warden of

[1] In 1911 the number was 27 out of 48 ; in 1912 it was 16 out of 42.

the hostel, and professor of pastoral theology, obtained an immense hold over his men, and inspired them with enthusiasm for their work and vocation. True, the department suffered serious loss through the deaths of such notable members of its staff as Professors Leathes and Shuttleworth (1900); but as the older teachers died, or were called to higher offices in the church, their places were taken by scholars and divines not less eminent than themselves. Among these notable new-comers were Dr Alexander Nairne (now regius professor of divinity in Cambridge and canon of Windsor), 1899; the Rev. H. C. Beeching (later dean of Norwich), 1900; Dr E. W. Watson (now regius professor of ecclesiastical history in Oxford), 1904; the Rev. C. H. W. Johns (later president of Queens' College, Cambridge), 1904; Dr H. J. White (now dean of Christ Church), 1905; the Rev. Clement Rogers (now professor of pastoral theology), 1907; the Rev. W. R. Matthews (the present dean of King's College), 1908; Dr J. P. Whitney (now Dixie professor at Cambridge), 1908; Dr G. H. Box (now university professor of Hebrew), 1911; and Dr Claude Jenkins (now Canon of Canterbury, Lambeth librarian, professor of ecclesiastical history in the college, reader in palæography in the university, chairman of the board of studies in history, etc.), 1911. No wonder that with such a succession of professors and lecturers the department flourished like a green bay-tree.

One further matter should be noted. With the abolition of tests in 1903, compulsory attendance at chapel and at divinity lectures ceased save for members of the theological faculty. It was remarked, however, that neither chapel nor lecture-room suffered from the withdrawal of constraint. The services of the chapel gained in reverence from the absence of involuntary non-worshippers; the lecture-rooms became fuller than ever. In 1905 the hour of the weekly divinity lecture, which hitherto had fallen within the luncheon interval, was fixed at 10–11 on Wednesday, and it was arranged that no other lecture in any faculty should be held during that period. By the Transfer Act of 1908 (Schedule I, § 40) this arrangement was made statutory, and it was further stipulated (Schedule I, § 42) that the A.K.C., which hitherto had been a general college diploma, should be restricted to (1) theological students, and (2) to

students of other departments who have obtained a degree of the university and have also attended such courses of instruction in theology and passed such examinations in theology as may from time to time be prescribed by the council.

437

The new arrangements worked well. In December 1911 the theological committee reported that

> about 150 students have registered themselves as candidates for the A.K.C., and 104 took the examinations in the summer of 1911. The majority of these—especially in the faculties of arts and science—did well, and so good a general level of work was attained as to show evidence, not only of ability, but of real interest in the subject. The number of students in the first year who are beginning their course is about the same as last year. The result of the transition to the voluntary system shows, as far as it is possible to judge, that neither the attendance nor the interest has suffered by the change.

§ 8. *King's College for Women*

The general prosperity that characterized the theological department of King's College during this period was almost equalled by that of the women's department. The women's department, however, went through far more rapid and revolutionary changes than did the theological, and these, although treated fully by Miss Oakeley (under whom they were in part effected) in her appendix to this volume, must be briefly sketched here from the point of view of the Strand.

When last we observed the progress of the polite community in Kensington Square we left the new vice-principal, Miss Lilian Faithfull, hard at work converting it from a "ladies' department" to a "women's department," the difference between ladies and women being that the one class did not pass examinations, while the other did.[1] From 1897 onward the reports of the department year by year tell of increasing successes in the universities—in the Cambridge higher locals, in the Oxford honours schools, in the London degree examinations: in 1899 two ex-students got firsts at Oxford; in 1907 four students gained firsts in London; in 1908 four attained the M.A. degree. Distinctions of another kind, but even more gratifying, came when in 1902 lectureships at Bedford College and at Reading University College fell to candidates trained in Kensington Square. Further incentives to effort and emulation were provided by the Merchant Taylors' and the Skinners' Companies, both of whom established entrance scholarships (1899 and 1903); by the college council, who opened the A.K.C. to women in 1899, and numerous college prizes four years later; and by the

---

[1] See above, p. 378. The change of title from "ladies' department" to "women's department" first occurs in the Calendar for 1902–3.

Board of Education, which in 1903 authorized the introduction
of day training students.

The development of work of a university standard, and the
increase of regular full-time matriculated students, necessitated
improvement in accommodation and equipment. The capacities of the two old houses in Kensington Square were soon
taxed to the uttermost, as were the financial resources of the
council. In 1904 the vice-principal, who had hitherto lived
in college, was moved to a house in Sussex Villas, and the
space thus vacated was used to provide a new physics laboratory, an extension of the botanical department, and a common
room for the staff. Next year a biological laboratory was
fitted up, and, that having been done, the council announced:

> The whole of the existing buildings are now utilised, and no
> further accommodation can be provided without extending the
> premises, or making very considerable structural alterations.
> The department has now reached the limit of its space.

It had not, however, by any means reached the limits of its
expansion. Its numbers, which in 1905 stood at 367, were
over 500 in 1906, and over 600 in 1908. Congestion could be
carried no further; comfort had long since vanished. Hence
in 1908 the council was constrained to purchase two new
houses, 11 and 12 Kensington Square, and incorporate them
in the department. Owing to lack of funds and to changes
in the constitution of the college, however, the new premises
were not fully brought into use until 1911. The immediate
gains that accrued from their utilisation were better library
accommodation, larger common rooms for both staff and
students, more numerous class and tutorial rooms, and " a
very simple refectory." In spite, however, of this addition,
the housing of the department was very unsatisfactory. No
conceivable number of antiquated suburban residences, no
matter how ingeniously knocked into unity, can adequately
accommodate a modern university college. Palatial drawing-
rooms make cramped and inconvenient lecture theatres;
low-pitched bedrooms cannot be converted, however many
partitions may be removed, into cheerful or healthy laboratories; labyrinths of winding staircases and narrow passages
are no effective substitutes for lifts and airy corridors.

That the joining of house to house in Kensington Square
would be no more than a temporary expedient was speedily
made evident by the development of the home science section
of the department. This was a novelty in which King's
College was again a pioneer. In 1907, in addition to the

regular courses of study, special lectures were given, as an experiment, in subjects relating peculiarly to women's life and work—viz., " economics of health " by Miss Ravenhill, " women and the land " by Mr Gwyer, and " industrial problems " by various lecturers from the women's industrial council. The course was so strikingly successful, and it aroused so widespread an interest, that the committee of management decided to organize more permanent and systematic instruction in the household and social sciences, knowledge of which seemed to be so generally desired. The new course was instituted in 1908, and it not only drew many students, but also attracted money in sums far exceeding those that flowed in for any mere general appeal. When it became known that building and equipment were necessary to enable the new school to realize itself contributions poured in. In 1911 one anonymous donor (Lord Anglesey) gave £20,000 for laboratories, and another anonymous donor (Sir Richard Garton) £20,000 for a hostel, while £10,000 was raised during the course of the year for the endowment of chairs. Here was £50,000 within twelve months; and before many more months had passed the total contributions exceeded £100,000. This lavish response made to the appeal for funds to develop " household and social science," as contrasted with the scanty contributions that accrued in answer to appeals for the maintenance of religious education, showed that for the time being sanitation took precedence of salvation. The governing body were positively embarrassed by the riches showered on their Cinderella; both her mother in the Strand and her sisters in Kensington Square were poverty-stricken as compared with her. Wooed as she was by many academic princes, would she be content to remain in tutelage ? The answer to this question—which was in the negative—was deferred until after the departure of Dr Headlam.

The policy of the ultimate separation of the women's department from King's College in the Strand, and of establishment as an independent King's College for Women in Kensington, was distinctly the policy favoured and fostered by Dr Headlam. That, too, was the policy supported by Miss Hilda D. Oakeley, the scholarly and philosophical vice-principal who in 1907 succeeded Miss Faithfull as chief of the Kensington Square staff: she clearly avowed her dislike of large co-educational institutions, and proclaimed her preference for small, separate colleges, " each having a vivid life of its own." [1] But, of

[1] Haldane Commission Report (Cd. 5528), Appendix to second report, p. 193.

course, neither Dr Headlam nor Miss Oakeley contemplated the disintegration of the women's college into two sections and the setting-up of the household and social science section as a college in itself. Dr Headlam in particular strongly disapproved of sectional institutions, holding (like the founders of King's College) that the essence of a university is the close association of all branches of knowledge, and the intimate inter-communion of the teachers and students in all the faculties: he even went so far as to disapprove of the isolation of such institutions as the School of Economics and the School of Oriental Studies. In 1908, however, when the Transfer Act was passed, and when the status of the women's department of King's College had to be determined, the establishment in Kensington Square was a miniature university college. All the faculties were represented, and some of them were doing work of a high order. Nothing except more money and new buildings seemed to be necessary in order to establish a great college in Kensington similar to Bedford College in Marylebone, Westfield College in Hampstead, or Holloway College in Egham. It therefore seemed natural and proper that under the Act of 1908 the women's department should be incorporated in the University of London as a distinct " King's College for Women," that it should be placed under separate administration from the mother-college in the Strand, and that it should begin to receive grants of its own directly from the Board of Education, the London County Council, and the university. Early in 1910 a special committee of the senate was appointed to examine fully the position and prospects of the newly recognized, semi-independent King's College for Women. It reported emphatically in favour of the continuance and development of its work as a complete and separate institution. Separation and autonomy seemed to be advanced one stage further when in March 1913 a special delegacy for King's College for Women was constituted by the senate. The very same month, however (March 27, 1913), the dream of a composite and complete university college for women in Kensington was shattered by the report of the unhappy Haldane commission.

§ 9. *Paying the Piper and Calling the Tune*

That King's College for Women would have to move from its congested and incommodious quarters in Kensington Square to an ampler site and more appropriate buildings had

441

long been evident, and long ardently desired. Funds for the purpose of migration were accumulating, and, although a disproportionate share of these was ear-marked for the special development of the home science section, a donation of £10,000 from the Goldsmiths' Company to the general building fund in 1912 did something to redress the balance and to render possible a speedy and simultaneous removal of all the departments of the college. In March 1913—the very month in which a separate King's College for Women delegacy was constituted—an excellent site was secured on Campden Hill,[1] and plans were framed for the erection on one-half of the site of buildings for the general work of the college and on the other half of buildings reserved for the exclusive use of the opulent home science establishment. Everything seemed to be moving toward the end desired by the delegacies, the staffs, and the senate when the Haldane commissioners' bombshell fell and shattered the scheme. Without any preliminary intimation, and in direct opposition to the expressed wishes of all the King's College witnesses, in the most approved manner of Continental bureaucracy, the commissioners (1) recommended the establishment in Kensington of a university department of household and social science, but (2) denounced the design of developing in that region, remote from the site suggested for the future university building, of a college of general education in arts and sciences. This deplorable pronouncement meant on the one hand the schism of King's College for Women and the complete reversal of its normal plan of development, and on the other hand the virtual severance of the household and social science department from all connexion with King's College.

When this bombshell fell Dr Headlam had just (December 1912) resigned his principalship. Hence we must reserve the rest of the story of King's College for Women for the next chapter. The remainder of the present chapter must be devoted to a survey of the circumstances that led to Dr Headlam's resignation and the causes which compelled him to lay down his command. Suffice it to say here that the wholly unexpected recommendations of the Haldane report—which the university and the college (since they were dependent on the government for funds) had no option but to obey—entirely confirmed his contention that the universities of the country were in imminent peril of losing their freedom.

It is a principle generally recognized as equitable that he

[1] The Blundell House estate of two and a half acres.

who pays the piper should call the tune. Hence when the London County Council and the Surrey County Council began to make grants to King's College it was eminently proper that these fiduciary bodies should have representatives on the council or delegacy whose duty it should be to see that the ratepayers' money was properly spent. Similarly, grants from the Board of Education justified regular inspection of the teaching and equipment of the college, while the large subventions of the Treasury necessitated the quinquennial visitation of financial and academic experts. Inspection and visitation involved reports, and reports involved both recommendations and condemnations. In other words, the government, naturally and inevitably as trustee of public funds, began to exercise considerable control over university and college administration. The question was: How far should government control go, and what were the proper limits (if any) of its sphere of influence? That was, and is, an extraordinarily difficult question. On the one hand, not to go far enough is to condone inefficiency and to connive at the waste of public money. On the other hand, to go too far is to suppress academic freedom and to mould the universities to a bureaucratic uniformity.

In the main, the periodical inspections and visitations made during the principalships of Dr Robertson and Dr Headlam were valuable and beneficent. They were carried out by able and sympathetic men of high eminence in the worlds of learning and administration; and they resulted in vast improvements in the buildings, equipments, and staffing of the college, generously assisted by increased or supplementary grants. Even when in 1907 the Treasury commissioners on their quinquennial round condemned in no measured terms the accommodation provided for the women's department in Kensington Square, nothing but satisfaction was felt. For the college authorities were saying the same thing, and they were delighted to have their inaudible utterances amplified by the government's loud-speakers. Their appeal for a building fund was carried into quarters where it would not otherwise have been heard, and it was enabled to penetrate pockets impervious to unofficial persuasions.

Very different, however, was the condition of things when in 1912 the Board of Education—which had acquired control of the Treasury grants—acting on the motion of its advisory committee, without consultation with the authorities of either King's College or the University, condemned the buildings

443

in the Strand and intimated a withholding of subsidies unless a new site were found and a new college erected. The communication of the Board ran:

> In connection with the application made by King's College for further assistance in respect of the maintenance of additional buildings, the committee do not think that the present site admits of such an extension as would enable the college to take its proper place in the university; and in this opinion the Board fully concur.

The college at the time, thanks to the removal of the civil service classes and in anticipation of the speedy departure of the Strand School, was busily engaged in framing plans for the rearrangement and rehousing of its departments. A skilled architect, Mr Rowland Plumbe, had been employed, his drawings were completed, and all was ready for the commencement of work. Only the sanction of the Board, with the guarantee of the necessary funds, was wanting; and no difficulty beyond the usual governmental delay was anticipated. Hence the ultimatum of October 1912, with its unheralded notice to the college to quit the Strand site, came as a thunderbolt out of the blue books. Dr Headlam's worst fears of bureaucratic interference were realized. Only ten months earlier (December 1911) he had written in his annual report to the senate, with reference to the transference of the administration of the Treasury grant to the Board of Education,

> The result is to give the Board control over all university education, and to deprive the universities of the position of independence which they formerly occupied. The Board controls also the distribution of the technical grants, and the grants for day training students. The result is to create opportunities for taking part in the internal affairs of universities and colleges in many directions.

When he wrote this he can have had little anticipation that within a year so enormous a demonstration of the danger of departmental dictation would be provided. He realized, however, that as a result of the pronouncement of the Board of Education a tremendous fight for freedom and for self-determination was likely to arise. And he felt that he himself was not the commander who should wage it. He was involved in other and complicated controversies in the senate, arising out of the mistaken policy of incorporation. He was overwhelmed with the labours entailed by the threefold office he held—viz., principal of the college, dean of the theological department, and professor of dogmatic theology. He was anxious for leisure in which to think and to write. Hence

444

on October 11, 1912, he sent to the chairman of the council the following letter (which was also communicated to the press [1]):

My dear Lord Bishop,

I am writing formally to announce to your lordship what I have already intimated to you privately, that I propose shortly to resign my position as principal and dean of King's College, and to request you to inform the council of my intention. You may be quite sure that I would not take such a step without the most serious consideration, and I feel it due to you and to the council, which has always treated me with such uniform kindness, that I should state at some length the reasons that have led me to this decision.

My principal reason, and the one that has weighed with me most, is a personal one. I am anxious to obtain leisure for literary and theological work, and that I feel is quite impossible in my present position. I have reached an age when I cannot any longer postpone a decision in this matter. If I retire now, I may reasonably hope to have the strength, if I have the ability, to do what I wish; if I wait any longer I shall find myself too old for effective work.

But there are other reasons which have weighed with me that I desire to have an opportunity of stating publicly. The Board of Education has recently, through the control of what was formerly the Treasury grant to universities and university colleges, obtained some authority over universities, and it has informed the college that its present site is inadequate, and that it will have to be removed. It seems to me most unfortunate that the Board should have initiated its control over universities by peremptory and arbitrary action such as would not be possible in dealing with the smallest national school. Even ordinary courtesy should have demanded some preliminary conference with the college, and with the university which is now responsible for carrying it on. The committee on whose advice the Board acted considered the most cursory visit to the college all that was necessary. A scheme for the improvement of the present buildings, and for the extension of the college on the present site, has been worked out with great labour, and very great expense has been incurred in obtaining expert advice. Only one member of the committee cared to examine the scheme, and he considered five minutes sufficient time to devote to it.

It is admitted that the present site is confined, but its position makes it of the greatest value as a centre for university teaching; and, while I have always kept in mind the possibility of removing the college to another site, such a course would be justified only as part of a coherent and well-thought-out scheme for the unification of the University of London. There is no evidence that

[1] See the *Times*, October 31, 1912.

the Board of Education has formed any such scheme, and their whole action is an instance of arbitrary administrative interference of a character such as seriously militates against those conditions of freedom and independence under which alone a university is able to perform its functions effectively.

As regards myself, I must honestly say that the position of head of a college exposed to such methods of interference is not one which I desire or am qualified to hold; and it is clear also to me that, in the interests of the college, I should resign now, unless I am prepared to continue as principal for another ten years. A new policy will have to be formulated. That will mean either a long and difficult controversy with the Board of Education, or the building of a new college. I do not feel that I should now care to embark on either: I must leave to others the carrying out of whatever scheme is decided upon, and I think that whoever has to carry out the future policy of the college should have a considerable voice in formulating it.

A further reason that has prompted me in deciding to resign is that I do not feel that I could much longer stand the strain of my present office. In any case the combination of the three offices of head of one of the largest university colleges, head of a theological college, and professor of theology, is too much for one person. Were it not for the loyal and ungrudging assistance that I have received from many members of the staff, it would have been impossible for me to carry out my duties, and I am glad to think that my present work will, in the interests of the college and of themselves, be divided among at least two successors. But the strain of the position has been very materially increased during the period of nearly ten years that I have held it by the constant opposition to which the college has been exposed, and by what has been, in my opinion, the unfair treatment that it has received. Many difficulties have been brought before the council and the delegacy, but there are many others that have been dealt with privately, and I do not think that there is anyone who quite realises how great the opposition to be encountered has often been.

The situation has been equally difficult in dealing both with outside bodies and with the senate of the university. While some members of the senate seem to consider that the well-being of the university is injured by the prosperity of its colleges, there have been other and more serious causes of friction. All my experience has shown me that the assistance of members of the professorial staff in the government of a university institution is essential to its well-being; but I am not equally convinced that it is desirable to place professors of one college in a position to interfere with the internal government of another college. Again and again schemes for the development of King's College—schemes which in some cases have been ultimately most successful

—have needed the most strenuous efforts to carry them through the academic council and the senate. Looking back on the time that I have been connected with the college, I cannot help feeling astonished at the opposition which has so often been exhibited to the efforts made for its development, and I can honestly say that the strain that it has caused has been at times almost intolerable.

In conclusion, I am glad to have an opportunity of expressing my gratitude for the great kindness and consideration that have been shown me throughout by the council of the college, and for the continuous loyalty of the staff, for whose unselfish work in the service of the college I have always had the greatest admiration.

As regards the time of my resignation, I should, of course, be anxious to accommodate myself in every way to the convenience of the college. My purpose at present is, however, to resign on December 31 of this year.

I am, my Lord Bishop,

Yours very sincerely,

ARTHUR C. HEADLAM

To the RIGHT HON. AND RIGHT
REV. THE LORD BISHOP OF LONDON

NOTE

NUMBER OF STUDENTS, 1897–1912 [1]

College

SESSION	FACULTIES					LADIES' DEPARTMENT	TOTAL
	Theol.	Arts and Law	Science	Eng.	Med.		
1897–98	92	189	253	324	154	429	1441
1898–99	102	206	171	304	151	381	1315
1899–1900	110	197	158	299	159	370	1293
1900–1	101	340	188	329	173	406	1537
1901–2	93	280	197	340	186	289	1385
1902–3	85	347	286	344	194	263	1519
1903–4	120	331	260	520	359	418	2008
1904–5	155	713	287	295	349	367	2166
1905–6	162	435	193	215	397	525	1927
1906–7	173	1329	692	196	293	462	3145
1907–8	171	849	586	168	191	608	2573
1908–9	196	591	761	207	188	331	2274
1909–10	190	804	704	190	196	408	2492
1910–11	239	959	376	218	338	428	2558
1911–12	229	1160	389	150	231	341	2500

[1] From 1897 a new method of tabulating the number of students in the college was adopted. The Occasional Students and Evening Class Students of the earlier tables were included under their various " faculties." Fuller details will be found in the college Calendar.

Extra-collegiate Classes

Session	School	Civil Service		Female	Gilbart Lectures	Total
		Male				
1897–98	200	1402		134	1000	2736
1898–99	228	1491		151	1100	2970
		School [2]				
1899–1900	261	443	1006	153	1130	2993
1900–1	265	498	984	121	1160	3028
1901–2	250	520	970	108	1200	3048
1902–3	264	544	980	65	1210	3063
1903–4	316	731	1446	110	1210	3813
1904–5	342	733	1449	147	1220	3891
1905–6	352	799	1356	182	1208	3897
1906–7	336	804	1268	144	1200	3752
1907–8	310	757	1201	152	1200	3620
1908–9	317	593	1157	235	800	3102
1909–10	307	603	926	294	800	2930
1910–11	— [1]	— [1]	— [1]	— [1]	800	800
1911–12	—	—	—	—	800	800

[1] No longer reckoned as part of King's College, owing to the incorporation of the college in the university.

[2] The so-called " Strand School."

CHAPTER XII

THE CLOSE OF THE CENTURY
1912–28

§ 1. *Dr Ronald Burrows and the Haldane Commission*

IN October 1912 the delegacy and the council of King's College received with expressions of profound regret Dr Headlam's resignation of the two offices of principal and dean.[1] In conveying their thanks to him for his great work during the preceding ten years they paid a well-merited tribute to " his indefatigable energy, clear grasp of principle, and extraordinary mastery of detail." His outstanding achievements appeared to them to be, first, the incorporation of the secular departments of the college with the university; secondly, the removal of the hospital to Camberwell; thirdly, the establishment of the women's department at Kensington as a separate institution; fourthly, the transference of the school at Wimbledon to a separate governing body; fifthly, the extrusion of the civil service classes and the Strand School; and, finally, the assumption of

> the additional task of bringing the studies and arrangements of the college into greater harmony with the new conditions, and the salaries of many of the teaching staff into juster accord with obvious deserts.

Anyone who has ever attempted to bring the salaries of professors into accord with their obvious deserts will realize that this alone is a full-time task for any principal: its theoretical difficulties are as great as those that face the mathematician who tries to square the circle; its practical problems are as formidable as those that confront the film-maker who seeks to discover the secret of perpetual emotion. No wonder that Dr Headlam sought release from an intolerable burden.

One of the most deplorable consequences of the incorporation effected under the Act of 1908 had been the severance of the theological department of King's from the rest of the college, and one of the most dangerous innovations of the

---

[1] At the urgent request of the council and his colleagues he consented to retain the chair of dogmatic theology, which chair he continued to hold until 1918.

statutes necessitated by that incorporation had been the transference of the appointment of the principal from the council of the college, not to the delegacy or even the senate, but to the crown. The reason for the transference of the appointment to the crown is indeed obvious: the principal, under the new constitution, was to exercise disciplinary control over all the students of the college whether secular or spiritual; hence it was appropriate that some authority superior to both delegacy and council should nominate him. But why was not the power conferred upon delegacy and council meeting in joint session? The rule actually laid down, however, ran: "The principal officer of the college shall be called 'the principal' and shall be nominated and if necessary removed by the crown." [1] Nomination by the crown means, of course, in practice appointment by the prime minister or by the president of the board of education; and the peril of placing the power of appointment in the hands of these eminent politicians is that party considerations may enter into the determination of their choice. Hitherto, it is true, the crown nominations have been of the happiest and most fortunate kind. But if in the course of time the extraneous and inaccessible authority through whom the crown acts should send to the college a principal who does not regard the Church of England with the domestic tenderness of Dr Burrows or the neo-platonic love of Dr Barker the dual constitution will prove entirely unworkable. That it has not already broken down, indeed, is due primarily to the cordial personal relations that have prevailed between the successive principals and deans: even so, however, in 1919 the difficulties of adjusting the finances of the two sides of the college were so serious that the matters in dispute had to be settled by arbitration.

The dean, of course, continued to be elected by the council. The new statutory regulation ran:

> The council shall appoint a head of the theological department who shall be called "the dean of King's College," and shall have power to remove the dean from his office.

In accordance with this regulation the council met on November 27, 1912, and elected the Rev. Dr Alfred Caldecott, professor of mental and moral philosophy, to be dean of King's College in place of Dr Headlam as from January 1, 1913.

The crown was slower about the business of appointing a principal. The mysteries of its operations are of course veiled;

---

[1] King's College London Transfer Act, 1908, Schedule I, Stat. 20.

RONALD MONTAGU BURROWS
Principal 1913-20

but not until January 1913 was it announced that Mr Asquith had offered the principalship to Dr R. M. Burrows, and that the offer had been accepted. Dr Burrows was the first lay principal of King's; but, though a layman and unfettered by tests, he was a good churchman. He was, moreover, bound by unusually numerous family ties to the Anglican episcopate: his brother was Bishop of Lewes, his cousin Bishop of Truro; while Mrs Burrows was daughter of the Bishop of Chichester and niece of the Bishop of Salisbury. In matters ecclesiastical, therefore, his hands were supported and controlled by four Aarons and Hur. He was an accomplished classical scholar —an Oxford double first—who, having lectured in Glasgow University (1891–97) and in Cardiff (1898–1908), was at the time of his appointment to King's the Hulme professor of Greek in the University of Manchester. He had also made a name for himself in the world of scholarship by his explorations of Pylos and Sphacteria and by his masterly epitome of the story of the recent *Discoveries in Crete* (1907). His interests, however, were by no means limited to the academic world. He was a man of boundless energy, overflowing vitality, infectious enthusiasm, and widespread sympathy. A keen politician, a first-rate business man, a capable financier, an ardent social worker, an administrator of restless activity, a leader with vision and ideas, he touched life at many points, and identified himself with countless causes—good, bad, and indifferent. During his principalship King's College became a miniature of the world and the underworld. At the time of his appointment no man could have been more ideally fitted to serve the best interests of the institution. Friction was rife; a conflict with the Board of Education seemed pending; the relations between the college and the university were strained. As Sir Henry Miers, the principal officer of the university, said in a letter to him:

> You will find a hard task before you, especially at the outset; a difficult financial position, a great many misunderstandings and prejudices to be cleared up.

Sir Henry, however, added:

> But I am convinced that you will be able to grapple with all the difficulties, and work King's College into its right position.[1]

He was justified in his conviction. Dr Burrows played a conspicuous part in helping to ease the financial stringency; he

[1] G. Glasgow, *Ronald Burrows : a Memoir* (1924), p. 181, where Sir Henry Miers is erroneously described as " vice-chancellor " of the University.

cleared up misunderstandings by his irresistible geniality and obvious sincerity; he removed prejudices by his patent and patient unselfishness, as well as by his evident desire to further the general good and to live amicably with his neighbours. His joyousness, his sense of humour, his love of fun, his broad tolerance, his keen interest in people, his kindly humanity, his sociability, his easy good-fellowship, his self-forgetfulness—all his admirable and fascinating qualities enabled him without apparent difficulty to face and to solve problems of administration and organization that would have been impervious to mere logic.

He was appointed, as we have observed, in January 1913, but it was of course impossible for him to divest himself instantly of his duties in the University of Manchester. It was necessary, indeed, for Dr Headlam to continue to act as principal of King's until well on in March. And even then, when Dr Burrows had come into residence in the Strand, he felt bound right up to the end of the session to pay a weekly visit to Manchester in order to complete the courses of some of his more advanced students.

In the very month in which Dr Burrows actually assumed his duties as principal of King's College—viz., March 1913—the Haldane Commission issued its sixth and final report.[1] However admirable its recommendations in respect of the university as a whole may have been, in respect of King's College they more than realized Dr Headlam's gloomiest apprehensions. The commissioners advised three things, each of which was destructive; three things which in combination, if they had been carried out, could hardly have failed to effect the ruin of the college. They advised, first, that, without any sort of compensation, King's College should abandon its prosperous evening class degree work, in order that this work might be concentrated in the Birkbeck College. They advised, secondly, that King's College for Women in Kensington should no longer be recognized as a teaching institution in the faculties of arts and science; that women who wished to study in these faculties should go either to Bedford College or to University

[1] The Haldane Commission had been appointed in 1909. Its prime purpose had been to determine the relation of the new Imperial College of Science to the University. But the terms of reference were wide and general : they included authority to make a comprehensive inquiry into the working of the Act of 1898 and power to frame recommendations involving a complete reconstitution of the University. Its reports were issued as follows : first (Cd. 5165), 1910 ; second (Cd. 5527), 1911 ; third (Cd. 5910), 1911 ; fourth (Cd. 6015), 1912-13 ; fifth (Cd. 6311), 1912-13 ; sixth (Cd. 6717), 1913. Each report had supplementary volumes of evidence.

College; that " lectures for ladies " in Kensington, if required at all, should be provided by the University Extension Board; and that only the household and social science department (now richly endowed) should be allowed to survive and to continue in Kensington. They advised, thirdly, that King's College itself should be removed from the Strand and located in " the neighbourhood of University College," where possibly " some economies might be introduced into the staffing and library arrangements of both "! Said the commissioners:

> We are convinced that the present buildings are unsuitable for the purposes of a university college of the first rank, and, what is more serious, that they cannot be rendered suitable for such a college, still less for an institution which is to form such an important part of the University of London itself.

Here was a devastating programme of dispersion, dissolution, and migration. And, owing to incorporation and its consequences, the college had to face it not as a unit, but as three separate institutions, under three different governing bodies, two of which were mere delegacies of the senate of the university. No wonder that Dr Burrows, when he first met his staff at dinner on February 25, 1913—a dinner at which the present writer was himself a guest—spoke of the almost insuperable difficulties of the task he was taking up.[1]

§ 2. *Making the Best of Things, 1913-14*

The Haldane Commission was dominated and controlled by a small group of able and resolute men who were filled with that admiration and envy of Germany (mingled with fear of her) which prevailed in high places in the days before the war. They believed in bureaucracy; they worshipped organization; they loved system and consistency; they longed for centralization and co-ordination; they loathed overlapping, reduplication, and all the defects displayed by products of nature as distinct from products of logic; they were inspired by the confidence that comes from philosophical doubtlessness, and they were prepared for the ruthlessness which the enforcement of rigid principle requires. They had little respect for history or tradition; they tended to despise the antecedents and associations of the various colleges of the heterogeneous university; they envisaged everything from

---

[1] At this memorable dinner the writer sat next to Mr John Cutler, K.C., who had been professor of law in the college since 1865—*i.e.*, since the thirty-fourth year of the existence of the institution.

the central and official point of view; they dreamed of a "university quarter" wherein, regardless of convenience or accessibility, offices, colleges, institutes, and laboratories would be concentrated. In particular, they lacked sympathy with King's, and were ready to sacrifice her on the altar of organization.

After the publication of the final report of the commission in the spring of 1913 a departmental committee was set up "to enquire and report after consultation with the bodies and persons concerned as to the steps by which effect shall be given to the scheme of the report." Strong representations were made to this committee by the various authorities of King's College with a view to saving the evening class work from extinction, preserving the women's college in Kensington from disintegration, and ensuring that if King's College itself had to leave its old home in the Strand it should secure an adequate site, and a roof to cover it, in the Babylon to which it was to be exiled. Two of these three crucial problems still remained unsettled when, a year later, the great war intervened and put a stop to deputations and departmental committee alike. (1) The evening classes for degrees continued to be held at King's. On the one hand the Birkbeck College was not ready to receive them; on the other hand they continued to flourish and expand so remarkably in their old quarters that the idea of transplanting them, in the interests of an abstract unification, became unthinkable. That portion of the commissioners' ideology passed out of the sphere of practical academics. (2) The question of a new site to which both King's College from the Strand and the university offices from South Kensington should be transported was long and anxiously debated. The delegacy and the theological committee in joint session on September 24, 1913, passed the following resolution:

That King's College is willing to consider any proposal to remove to a new site which would further the main objects set forth in the report, provided that (a) King's College be permanently maintained as an administrative unit; and (b) not less than six acres be reserved for University of London King's College and the theological department of King's College.

Various possible sites were discussed. First it was suggested that the government should surrender Somerset House to the university; that King's College should add the east wing to the existing college buildings; and that the university should take the rest for offices and institutes. The government went so far as to have Somerset House valued; but when the valuation was found to be some £3,000,000 they intimated their inability further to consider the matter. Secondly, a site on the south bank of the river was proposed, and in particular it was said that the London County Council would be glad to house both university offices and college on a plot of land contiguous to their own new buildings near Westminster Bridge. Thirdly, the site of the Foundling Hospital was advocated. Finally the Bloomsbury site—the oasis amid the desert of decayed lodging-houses behind the British Museum—was brought forward; and this alone—owing to its nearness to University College—satisfied the requirements of the commissioners as tending to the concentration of colleges and the establishment of a university quarter. Hence for King's College the alternatives gradually declared themselves to be *either* to move to Bloomsbury *or* to remain in the Strand. This issue was alone to be faced when the war broke out and postponed further consideration of the question for another six years.

Before the war interposed its tremendous veto upon civilian controversies, however, the third great problem had been settled, and the fate of King's College for Women had been decided. We have seen that from the date of the Transfer Act (1908) down to the moment when the final Haldane report was issued (March 1913) the steady policy of King's College for Women—in which both the delegacy of King's College and the senate of the University concurred—was to establish on a new site in Kensington a complete university college for women similar to Bedford, Westfield, or Holloway. Large sums of money had been presented, mainly for the home science department of the college; the Blundell House estate on Campden Hill had been procured; plans had been prepared; all was in readiness to proceed. So late as the beginning of 1913 the senate of the university had instituted a delegacy for King's College for Women separate from that for King's College in the Strand. Everything pointed toward integrity, autonomy, prosperity. Then came the shattering Haldane recommendation that, on the one hand, arts and sciences should cease to be taught in King's College for Women, and that, on the other hand, its home science section should be converted into a university department. This recommendation meant the total reversal of the policy of both college and university; and it involved the destruction of King's College for Women as it had hitherto existed. The new King's College for Women delegacy made strenuous efforts to ward off the impending doom of their college: they sent a deputation to the departmental committee, and implored its permission to continue to live and to retain their integrity. The old students of the college rallied loyally to its side, and presented petitions begging for a reprieve. The senate was asked to sanction a widespread appeal for funds, so that the financial objection to continuance in Kensington might be removed. But here the fatal barrier of incorporation blocked the way: the senate could not sanction an appeal for funds the object of which was to reverse the recommendation of the Haldane Commissioners: and without the consent of the senate the King's College for Women delegacy could not act. Finally, the departmental committee delivered its judgment, announcing that it

> saw no reason to depart from the conclusion of the royal commission, that the work of the arts and science faculties in Kensington should be discontinued.

What then should be done with the arts and science faculties? The Haldane report had contemplated their transference to Bedford College or University College. The King's College for Women delegacy, however, with the cordial support of the King's College delegacy, suggested that the extruded faculties might be allowed to migrate to the Strand, and that King's College (like University College) might be converted into a co-educational institution. This suggestion the departmental committee were constrained to admit would be " not inconsistent with the recommendations of the royal commission "; and, since it did not clash with this inspired authority, they gave their consent to the great trek. Hence in September 1914 His Majesty in Council sanctioned the necessary change in the statutes of the college, and on January 1, 1915, King's College for Women took up its abode in the premises of King's College in the Strand.[1] On March 1, 1915, its own separate delegacy ceased to exist, and the delegacy of King's College resumed its sway. Nevertheless, King's College for Women still remained—and at the present moment still remains—a separate legal entity. Act of Parliament alone can undo the work of the Transfer Act of 1908. But for practical purposes King's College for Women has been absorbed in, and has become an integral part of, King's College. The student societies were amalgamated from the start. Next, when Miss Oakeley resigned her wardenship in December 1915 her place was taken, not by another warden, but by an " administrative

---

[1] *Cf.* G. Glasgow, *Ronald Burrows*, pp. 196 and 205, where Kensington Square is erroneously called Campden Hill.

officer " with far less independence. After 1920 King's College for Women ceased to send up a separate report to the senate. Its board of principal teachers, though it still has a ghostly existence, has long since ceased to meet, all its business being transacted in and by the professorial board of King's College, on which all its members have seats.

What makes this condition of things constitutionally so anomalous is that the opulent and flourishing household and social science institution on Campden Hill still remains in theory a mere department of this spectral and vanished King's College for Women in the Strand. That curious anomaly, however, is being removed at the moment of writing (1929). It has for some years caused considerable inconvenience. For the great department on Campden Hill has in the course of years wholly drifted away from King's College and become an independent institution. The foundation-stones of its new buildings were laid on June 11, 1914, by the Princess Christian; in October 1915 residence and work were begun. Since then it has continued to flourish under a succession of able heads. It has, however, severely felt the disadvantages of separation from the other faculties of a complete university college. It has lacked the larger life and the wider culture that come from the intermingling of minds engaged in the pursuit of varied branches of knowledge.

While these important constitutional changes were taking place under the skilful and conciliatory direction of Dr Burrows, under the same inspiring leadership notable developments were taking place in the work and organization of the college. In the summer of 1913 the Strand School moved to its new buildings on Brixton Hill, and the rooms thus vacated were— thanks to a special grant of £3000 from the L.C.C.—fitted up for college use. One of them in particular was assigned to Professor Gollancz as the " Skeat and Furnival Library "—a room wherein the books of two famous English scholars, generously bequeathed to the college, could be kept together and used for the furtherance of advanced linguistic and literary research. In the same year, moreover, under the fiat of the senate, and in accordance with the principle of concentration, the department of architecture was taken away from King's College and added to that of University College. It was expected that, in compensation for this deprivation, the faculty of law would be concentrated in King's College; but this expectation was not realized. Nor was any compensation given for the large amount of valuable material that was transferred with the department. King's was now an incorporated college, and it was open to the senate of the university to shift its own property and the appendant staffs from one place to another as it saw fit. The transfer was effected in the summer of 1914. The fine room at King's which had been the architectural museum was converted into the college library, the former library being fitted up as a common room for the women students pending their arrival from Kensington Square in January 1915.

This same period, moreover, saw a noteworthy advance in the provision of hostel accommodation for students of the college who could not live at home. The theologians, as we have seen,[1] already had their hostel in Mecklenburgh Square. For ten years (1902–12) it served an invaluable purpose ; but it was obviously a mere makeshift. It was too small; it was inconvenient; it was not well situated. Hence the council rejoiced when in 1912 they received from the ecclesiastical commissioners the offer, on very favourable terms, of an excellent plot of land in Vincent Square, Westminster. The offer was accepted; plans were prepared by Mr Arthur Martin; a Mansion House meeting for the raising of a building fund was held on November 4, 1912, and speedily £7000 was contributed—a small sum compared with the lavish wealth that flowed in the direction of home science, but enough to warrant a start. The foundation-stone of the building was laid on May 6, 1913, by the Princess Louise, and so rapid was the progress made that on November 8 of the same year fifty-two students were able to go into residence. The formal opening took place on February 26, 1914, when the Bishop of London presided over a distinguished assembly. Of course only a portion of the projected building was then completed, and even this cost £4000 over and above the subscriptions in hand; the estimated cost of the whole was over £28,000. The completion of the architect's fine design has had to wait for sixteen years: it is one of the outstanding features of the centenary alterations.

The pioneer energy of the theological department in providing hostel accommodation for its students stirred up the secular side of the college to activity. There was a pressing demand from medicals, engineers, and others for some convenient place of residence wherein college discipline could be maintained. Inquiries were made, and in December 1914 the delegacy were able to report that

> the friends of King's College and King's College Hospital have formed a limited company to adapt and furnish as a hostel for

[1] *Cf.* above, p. 434.

New Wing, 1929

THE THEOLOGICAL HOSTEL
A. C. Martin, F.R.I.B.A., Architect

medical and other students a large and commodious house, called "The Platanes," standing in its own grounds of about one and a half acres on Champion Hill, S.E., close to King's College Hospital.

This excellent home at once provided lodging for thirty students. Since 1914 various extensions have enabled it to house eighty. The current prospectus states that

> in addition to eighty comfortable bed-sitting-rooms there are several excellent common rooms, including a billiard-room, dining-room, and reading-room. All the rooms are lighted by electricity, and the house is centrally heated.

Women students had to wait rather longer for adequate hostel accommodation. All that could be said during Dr Burrows' time was that in the Queen Mary's Hostel on Campden Hill "the women students of King's College are given priority of admission immediately after those of the home science department itself." This proved to be totally insufficient to meet the growing demand, and Dr Barker during his principalship had to tackle the problem afresh.

Another striking feature in Dr Burrows' time was the remarkable development of the system of free public lectures provided by the college. The situation of the college in the Strand, one of the greatest of all the highways of the larger London, made it admirably fitted to attract and secure audiences. In particular, it was found that lectures arranged for 5.15 or 5.30 drew notable assemblies of lawyers, bankers, and city men generally, on the way from their offices to their homes. The rapid growth, indeed, of this section of the activity of the college became one of the many causes which led the delegacy and the council firmly to resolve not to consent to the removal of the college from the Strand to any less central site. To have uprooted the college and replanted it in the obscure solitude behind the British Museum would have been to destroy all this efflorescence at a stroke. Occasional public lectures and even short courses had been given from time to time since the college was opened. The first systematic attempt, however, to provide popular instruction of the modern type seems to have been made in 1912, when the department of theology arranged a course of eight lectures by eminent experts on "Christian Art." The success of this course was such that in 1913 the Rev. Dr Whitney, professor of ecclesiastical history, suggested to the present writer that a similar course in the faculty of arts might prove to be attractive. Dr Burrows welcomed the suggestion, and gave it his cordial

459

support. The powerful aid of Mr (now Sir) Sidney Low—an old student and lecturer of the college—was secured, and a course (which drew large and distinguished audiences) was provided for the autumn of 1913 on " Colonial and Imperial Problems." [1] The system thus inaugurated was adopted by other departments and faculties, and rapidly a lecture connexion with London and Westminster was formed that proved of the utmost interest and value. Year by year, as the knowledge of the existence of these lectures extended, the numbers in regular attendance grew: from a few hundreds in 1913 they increased to over 33,000 in 1928–29. During the war, when many of the ordinary activities of the college had to be suspended, the system of public lectures on current affairs was among the most important of its surviving functions.

§ 3. *The Great War, 1914–18*

When in the long vacation of 1914 the great war broke out the college was busy adapting its premises for the reception of the women students from Kensington Square. Their advent at that particular juncture was indeed a godsend. But for their presence the college could barely have maintained a continuity of existence; while the coming of the women members of the staff released many of the male lecturers for military service of one kind or another. From the very first call of the government for volunteers there was a prompt and noble response on the part of both teachers and taught. In particular, the officers' training corps (established 1909), under its capable colonel, Professor D. S. Capper, responded with ready loyalty. Before the end of 1915 more than three hundred students had gone. It is true that their places were partially filled by refugee students who poured into this country from Belgium, Russia, and other allied lands. In 1915 there were more than a hundred of them about the premises ; they were, however, a source of embarrassment rather than of strength to the college, since they generally paid no fees, observed no rules, did no work, and showed no gratitude. Many of them were evading military service, and some of them were discovered to be spies. One of the most attractive was a Russian Jew who, while receiving free medical tuition (from the college), free books (from a special Jewish fund), and free meals (from a fund provided by the college staff), was found to be making a quite respectable income as a member of a

[1] Subsequently published as a book by Messrs G. Bell and Sons (1914).

Russian ballet company, in which his duties were on some
days so engrossing as to allow him no time to come to college

Соломон Ханинов

Храмченко

Яковъ Китайгородский

[Bengali/Devanagari signature]

[Devanagari signature]

[Arabic signature]

[Arabic/Urdu signature]

[Japanese signatures]

श्रीविद्यानन्द छूबर ।

Израиль Урмунуку

Iaд Iaдnтु।

Gaston Devos.

at all except for food. Some, however, were more satisfactory.
In particular, Professor Ernest Wilson in 1915–16 had an
excellent electrical engineering class. He gave me at the

time a sheet containing the signatures of all the members of the group completing their courses that year. It seems worth while to reproduce it: the signatures are, in order, Russian, Hebrew, Bengalese, Arabic, Chinese, Japanese, Assamese, Russian, and Siamese.

The question whether or not the students of the theological department should offer themselves for military service was one that caused the council much concern. On the one hand was the call of the country; on the other hand was " the high question of fulfilment of vocation." The bishops were discouraging the clergy from becoming combatants; but theological students, and, *a fortiori*, prospective theological students, were not yet clergy. Hence their duty was less clear. The professorial board of the department held three meetings " to consider how students should be advised who might desire guidance as between offering for military service or continuing their studies." They finally " came unanimously to the conclusion that in this great national emergency . . . each student must make the final decision for himself." This conclusion was conveyed in two letters to all students whose course was unfinished. Thus the valuable advice, already impressive because of its unanimity, was rendered doubly impressive by being administered twice. The government, however, did not long leave the decision in this vital matter to the individual choice of youthful students. In 1916 compulsory military service was introduced, and the theological department, already depleted of its volunteers, was reduced to 25 in 1917 and to 19 in 1918.

In both secular and theological departments, indeed, little beyond continuity was retained. Fees, of course, fell off, and, in spite of the fact that about half the staff departed on war work of one sort or another, financial embarrassment became extreme. Special grants from the treasury to the delegacy, and from the ecclesiastical commissioners to the council, alone saved the college from bankruptcy. The theological hostel in Vincent Square was requisitioned as a hospital for nurses, and such it remained for the four years 1915–19. The college itself barely escaped seizure by the war office; but Dr Burrows was able to save it by demonstrating to the government the importance of the war-work that was being done by the surviving members of the staff.

To give even a summary of the war-work done in the college during the years 1914–18 would require immeasurably more space than remains at my disposal. The following brief indication of some of the leading items must suffice. (1) Professor Sir Herbert Jackson and Dr Merton made researches into the manufacture of glass which enabled English firms to supply glass for lenses and other purposes hitherto procurable only from Germany; (2) Professor Kirkaldy with Messrs Collins and Hinkel conducted analyses of tar with a view to the extraction of its toluene content; (3) in the engineering department, under Professor Jameson, between one and two thousand munition workers were trained; (4) in the same department 410 aeronautical inspectors were equipped for their important and responsible duties; (5) in the electrical department Professor Ernest Wilson conducted valuable researches on insulating materials; (6) in the physics department Professor Richardson, with the assistance of Dr Cox, Mr Robertson, Mr Wells, and Mr Williamson, tested on behalf of the government about fifteen hundred optical instruments—field-glasses, telescopes, etc.—for use in naval and military operations; (7) in the same department useful work was done at the special request of the Admiralty in effecting improvements in wireless receivers; (8) in the department of botany Professor Bottomley was able to demonstrate the practical value of his bacteria in increasing the output of the land—a work of national service in days when submarine warfare threatened the isolation of Britain; (9) in the department of zoology Professor Dendy and Mr Row sought means to combat the insect pests that destroyed grain and the malarial germs that destroyed man; (10) in the department of physiology Professor Halliburton and Dr Rosenheim investigated the nutritive properties of the various edible substitutes for food on which a patriotic populace was endeavouring to assuage the pangs of hunger.

Besides this scientific war-work, much work of national importance was done in other departments of the college. Worthy of special mention are the " intensive courses " of linguistic instruction by means of which interpreters and *liaison* officers were prepared for their duties in three months of concentrated cramming. Another branch of the activity of the college which was immensely stimulated by the war was that of the public lecture department. A large section of intellectual London came to look to King's College for guidance and information respecting the many and intricate problems raised by the great conflict. The college calendars must be consulted for details of the multitudinous courses that were given. Here it must suffice to enumerate the following as typical: 1915, " The Spirit of the Allied Nations " and

" International Problems "; 1916, " Aspects of the War "
and " The War and the Problems of Empire "; 1917, " The
University and the Nation " and " The Sentiment of Empire ";
1918, " The Empire and the Outer World " and " The Visions
of a World Peace." The report of December 1918, commenting on this remarkable development, said:

> The policy of providing public lectures has now been adopted
> for three years, and it has been justified by success. Very large
> audiences have been gathered week by week throughout each of
> the winter terms for lectures in each of the faculties of arts,
> science, and theology; and considerable numbers of the educated
> public have learnt to look to the college as a means of keeping
> in touch with the intellectual problems of the day. During the
> war the more important lectures have naturally dealt with
> historical and political questions, but the audiences (amounting
> in the aggregate to 3700) that gathered to the course arranged
> by Professor Dendy during the spring term [on " Animal Life
> and Human Progress "] show that there is a wide demand for
> similar lectures in natural science. It would seem that we cannot
> do better than continue this work on the lines hitherto laid down,
> and at the same time make an attempt to supply public lectures
> in each department of a much more technical character, which,
> although attracting smaller audiences, would fill the gap that at
> present exists between the detailed systematic lectures of the honours
> courses and the advanced papers read before the learned societies.

So much for the war-work done in and by the college.
Besides and beyond this there was an infinitude of activity on
the part of members of the college, both students and staff, in
the world outside. Before the termination of the war the
number on actual military service reached the total of 1567;
further, many gave their services to various government
offices. Dr Burrows became the energetic agent and emissary
of M. Venizelos, and did not a little to bring Greece into the
war on the side of the allies.[1] Professor R. W. Seton-Watson
established that influential magazine *The New Europe*, and
carried it on from King's College, largely by the aid of his
colleagues there. Professor T. G. Masaryk, exile from
Bohemia, was appointed to a chair of Slavonic studies in King's
College, and from its safe obscurity was able to foster the
creation of the Czecho-Slovak republic, of which at the close
of the war he became the first president.

King's College became a sort of international clearing-house
during the war. In Dr Burrows' drawing-room, in particular, besides the principal's numerous episcopal relatives and

[1] See G. Glasgow, *Ronald Burrows*, pp. 226-269.

ALFRED CALDECOTT
Dean 1913–18

464

socialistic friends, could be seen a vast multitude, whom no man could number, drawn from every nation, kindred, people, and tongue, except (pending the conclusion of the war) those of the Germanic group. One permanent result of this polyglot internationalization was of prime importance. It was the founding of no fewer than four new departments of linguistic study—viz., Slavonic, Spanish, Portuguese, and Modern Greek. (1) Concerning the founding of the first of these, Professor Sir Bernard Pares, the present head of the school, sends me the following valuable note:

> The School of Slavonic Studies at King's College was instituted in 1915. It was inaugurated in November of that year by a lecture by Professor Thomas G. Masaryk, one of the first members of the staff, who has since become president of the Czecho-Slovak Republic. The college is proud to have sheltered at the time of his exile this conspicuous European scholar, who was a teacher of civic effort for thousands not only in his own country, but in other Slavonic countries, notably Jugoslavia. Professor Masaryk remained at the college until he became president of the Czecho-Slovak Republic. Since then he has given constant help to the development of the school, and has always devoted to it his care and affection. Dr R. W. Seton-Watson became honorary lecturer in the history of the Danubian and Balkan area; Mr M. Trofimov, now professor in the University of Manchester, was lecturer in Russian, and was assisted by Mr A. Raffi. Among other teachers in the school were Mr August Zalewski, later foreign minister of the Polish Republic; Mr Bogdan Popović, afterwards professor of literature in Belgrade University, and Mr Pavle Popović, subsequently rector of Belgrade University.

In 1918 Professor Pares himself came from the University of Liverpool to organize the school, a task on which he has been engaged ever since. (2) The University of Liverpool also provided the first head of the School of Spanish Studies. Early in the war the desirability of instituting classes in Spanish became evident, and Dr Burrows prepared to appoint a lecturer. Sir Israel Gollancz, a man full of ideas and possessed of wide influence, suggested that the Cervantes tercentenary in 1916 presented an opportunity for the realization of a more ambitious scheme. Hence, under his inspiration, a powerful committee was formed—including the Spanish ambassador and the ministers for Chile, the Argentine, and Bolivia—and speedily some £24,000 was raised. Hence in 1916 Professor James Fitzmaurice-Kelly, most eminent of British authorities on Spanish literature, was invited to become the first occupant of the Cervantes chair. Concerning this distinguished man Dr A. R. Pastor, the present head of the school, sends me the following interesting note :

In the year 1916 Professor Fitzmaurice-Kelly resigned the Gilmour chair of Spanish in the University of Liverpool in order to occupy the Cervantes chair of Spanish founded in King's College, University of London. This position he held for four years, retiring in 1920 because of ill-health. Although these four years were beset with difficulties, which did not encourage literary production, it is a happy circumstance that the origin of the new centre of Hispanic studies should have been associated with the personality of so great a scholar.

(3) The great success of the appeal for funds to found a Spanish chair suggested to Sir Israel Gollancz and others that a companion chair of Portuguese would be appropriate. The project was welcomed by the Portuguese and Brazilian ministers; a committee was formed, and before the end of 1918 over £8000 was contributed. A further intermittent grant from the Portuguese government made it possible to establish the Camoens chair in 1919. Mr George Young was appointed as the first professor in 1919. In 1923 he was succeeded by the present distinguished holder of the position, Dr Edgar Prestage. (4) The chair in which Dr Burrows himself took the keenest personal interest was the Koraïs chair of Modern Greek. He himself in the delegacy report of December 1918 thus describes its inauguration:

As long ago as October 1, 1915, Monsieur Venizelos, who is the real founder of the chair, cabled that he intended to introduce a bill in the Greek parliament to grant a sum of money for the purpose. Immediately afterwards he was driven from office. The scheme, however, was not allowed to fall through, for a number of Greeks and Anglo-Greeks set to work to raise the necessary money. With the unfailing support of Mr Gennadius, the Greek minister in London, they succeeded in raising a sum of £12,200. When he returned to power in Greece, one of M. Venizelos's first acts was to revive his project, and the Greek government has voted an annual grant which at the present rate of exchange will amount to about £300 a year. The subscribers have decided to call the chair after Koraïs, the Greek scholar who was the intellectual father of the war of independence in which Byron fought and fell.

The fact that governments and politicians were interested in these modern linguistic chairs had advantages in securing money and promises of money for their inauguration and maintenance —although the actual payment of foreign government grants

466

proved to be liable to frequent interruption by revolution or change of administration. It carried with it, however, that grave disadvantage that the holder of these subsidized seats found his academic freedom compromised. He was expected to teach what was agreeable to his patrons. The first holder of the Koraïs chair, for instance, appointed in 1919, became embroiled on political grounds with the Greek government and the Greek committee in London, and his position became an intolerable one. He resigned in 1924 ; and before a successor was elected the conditions of tenure had to be radically altered.

By this time, however, the war was over, and the college was beginning to resume its normal course of existence. The warriors returned; but, alas! not all of them. Of the 1567 King's men who had served, 239 had been called upon to lay down their lives.[1]

> Blow out, you bugles, over the rich Dead !
>   There's none of these so lonely and poor of old,
>   But, dying, had made us rarer gifts than gold.
> These laid the world away ; poured out the red
> Sweet wine of youth ; gave up the years to be
>   Of work and joy, and that unhoped serene,
>   That men call age ; and those who would have been,
> Their sons, they gave, their immortality.
>
> Blow, bugles, blow ! They brought us, for our dearth,
>   Holiness, lacked so long, and Love, and Pain.
> Honour had come back, as a king, to earth,
>   And paid his subjects with a royal wage ;
> And Nobleness walks in our ways again ;
>   And we have come into our heritage.
>
>   RUPERT BROOKE [2]

§ 4. *The Peace Settlement, 1918–20*

The most conspicuous feature of the two years that followed the armistice of November 1918 was, in respect of King's College, the enormous influx of students. The tables at the end of this chapter will show how a total of 1775 in the session 1917–18 rose to 2831 the following year, and to 3879 in 1919–20. Almost as remarkable, however, as the increase in numbers was the change in the character of the students. The men who came back from the war were on the average

---

[1] Of King's men who served in the war 2 gained the V.C.—viz., Captain A. C. T. White and the Rev. E. N. Mellish, C.F. ; 18 were awarded the D.S.O. ; 20 were mentioned in dispatches ; 64 received the M.C.

[2] Quoted by kind permission of Rupert Brooke's literary executor and Messrs Sidgwick and Jackson, Ltd.

considerably above the normal age, and many of them had gone through experiences that had made them mature beyond their years. One student, for example, who entered the history department, and joined the officers' training corps as a recruit, was found to have been an acting lieutenant-colonel (M.C. and D.S.O.) who at one time had been in command of 1000 men on the Belgian front, and at another time of 10,000 native troops in India. Men such as this gave a new tone of virility to the college. Never had there been so much smoking in forbidden places; never had faculty dances been so popular; never had the periodical battles with the students of University College respecting the possession of mascots and trophies been so sanguinary or so expensive.[1] Among the newcomers in 1919 were 130 American soldiers sent by the American Army Headquarters. They included men of many different ages, ranks, classes, and colours. In college, however, a remarkably complete equality prevailed among them: the spectacle of white colonels and black privates seated side by side taking down notes dictated to them by a female assistant lecturer younger than any of them made one imagine that the prophecy of Isaiah xi, 6, was being evidently fulfilled before one's eyes.

The immense and rapid increase of numbers during the sessions 1918–20 strained beyond breaking-point the accommodation of the college. The departments of chemistry, physics, botany, geology, zoology, pharmacology, and electrical engineering had to be extended. The demand for the use of the larger lecture-rooms became too incessant to be fulfilled. The principal had to allow classes to be held in his house; temporary structures had to be erected on the roof; a big new building, intended primarily as a laboratory for hydraulics and testing machines, was erected on what had been the playground of the school; a large ex-army hut was hired in Aldwych. It soon became evident, however, that these extemporized expedients would not be enough ; but that permanent additions to the lecture and laboratory accommodation of the college would have to be made. Could they be made on the existing site ? Dr Burrows at first ardently hoped that the government would cede Somerset House to the university, and that King's College would be enabled to annex its eastern wing. When this hope was found to be illusory, he veered to the opinion that the college would have to move, with the

[1] The biggest battle occurred on December 4, 1922, when University College came for Phineas ; when the traffic of the Strand was completely held up ; when casualties were conveyed to the hospital on stretchers, and when damage to the amount of £200 was effected.

university, to the Bloomsbury site. Not he, however, but his successor, had to face the great decision.

The congestion in the college during the sessions 1918–20 was rendered more severe than it normally would have been by various new developments. First, the department of public health and bacteriology, which had been housed at the Charing Cross Hospital since 1912,[1] came back to the college and had to be accommodated.[2] Secondly, new departments of study, with new lecturers attached to them, were continually being opened up—Slavonic studies, Spanish studies, Portuguese, Modern Greek, and many others. In 1919, too, the Rhodes Trustees generously offered a sum of £575 a year to aid in the founding of a chair of imperial history, the first holder of which was the energetic Professor A. P. Newton, who required a lot of space. To his enterprise was largely due the revival of the department of geography. At this time, moreover, the university had the happy inspiration of establishing a diploma in journalism, and King's College played a leading part in providing the necessary courses. The following interesting note is furnished by Mr H. R. W. Wiltshire, a distinguished King's College student and one of the earliest university exhibitioners:

The University of London courses for journalism may be regarded as one of the most interesting developments of the modern system of education, and as King's College is the headquarters of the courses it can claim to be the first acre of the large field involved in this development.

The courses for journalism were commenced in 1919, and London was the first great academic body to give a place to journalism in its curriculum of studies. The suggestion was made by the Institute of Journalists, and the late Sir Sidney Lee, who was dean of the faculty of arts in the university at that time, framed a scheme of courses which was adopted forthwith by the senate. A strong committee of acting journalists and of university teachers was nominated at the outset, and Sir Sidney Lee was appointed its first chairman. In 1922 Sir Sidney, owing to the pressure of his other duties, was compelled to relinquish his direction of the courses, and, at his suggestion, Mr Valentine Knapp was appointed.

At the present time there are classes for journalism at King's College, University College, Bedford College for Women, and the London School of Economics. King's College takes first place, because it has a larger number of journalism students than any other college, and it is at King's that the lectures in connexion with the practical side of the courses are given. Until the

[1] See above, p. 430.   [2] Until 1925, when it was closed down.

beginning of the academic year 1925–26 lectures upon the various branches of practical work were given to first-year students by leading journalists from Fleet Street and the provinces weekly throughout the terms, while Mr E. G. Hawke, M.A., lectured second-year students on " Writing for the press." Now, however, Mr Hawke lectures first-year students on practical journalism, and second-year students are supervised in their practical studies by Mr F. J. Mansfield, of the *Times* editorial staff.

The journalism courses at King's College are very liberal, and the students were fortunate to have as their first tutor Dr A. W. Reed, M.A., who was ably assisted by Mr G. B. Harrison, M.A. (the present tutor), and Mr J. Isaacs, B.A.

Another striking and space-absorbing feature of this vivacious period was the increase in the number of students' societies, the improvement of the organization of the students' union, and the enormous expansion of the aggregate demand of the students for victuals and drink—a demand which necessitated a great extension of the refectory accommodation.

A further important matter primarily affecting the students that had to be dealt with at this time was the question of securing a new athletic ground. The old hired field at Wormwood Scrubbs was required for building purposes in 1919. An exhaustive search amid the rapidly vanishing suburbs of London resulted in the discovery of " an ideal site of fifteen acres at Mitcham." It was decided that the purchase and equipment of this site should be the college war memorial. The cost of the land was £6000; its laying out involved an expenditure of another £2200. Toward the £8200 thus required nearly £5000 was raised by subscriptions; the delegacy made a grant of £1000, and the rest was provided by loan. The projected pavilion still exists only in the architect's idea, a couple of army huts serving as temporary substitutes. In the college itself the memory of the war, and of the part which the men of King's played in its conduct, is perpetuated by a fine new doorway to the chapel, flanked by tablets inscribed with the names of the 239 fallen ; it was dedicated by the Bishop of London on June 8, 1922. The athletic ground at Mitcham had been brought into use during the spring of the preceding year.

The close of the war brought a number of changes in the college staff. The most numerous and important occurred in the department of theology. Toward the end of 1918 the dean of the department, Dr Alfred Caldecott, having reached the age of retirement, terminated his twenty-six years of loyal and able service. The council in its resolution of gratitude

470

and regret recognized the benefits that had accrued, not only from his scholarly teaching, but also from the " conspicuous fairness and patience " with which he had discharged his administrative duties and from the kindliness and friendliness that had always marked his relations with his colleagues and his students. Dr Headlam at the same time resigned his chair of dogmatic theology in order to leave a free hand to the council in appointing a new dean.[1] The same year also saw the departures of Professors A. Nairne (Hebrew) and J. P. Whitney (ecclesiastical history), with Messrs S. C. E. Legg (Syriac) and S. K. Knight (New Testament). The office of dean was filled by the election of the Rev. W. R. Matthews, one of the most distinguished of all the theological students of King's College, and since 1908 a lecturer on the staff.[2] As to the other vacancies: the Rev. Canon G. H. Box, assisted by the Rev. F. J. Hollis, undertook the teaching of Hebrew and Syriac; the Right Rev. Bishop Charles Gore, assisted by the Rev. Dr Maurice Relton, assumed Dr Headlam's work; the Rev. Claude Jenkins succeeded Professor Whitney in the chair of ecclesiastical history, while the Rev. D. Bruce-Walker was engaged to assist Dr H. J. White in the exegesis of the New Testament. In the following year (1919) the Rev. Clement Rogers' lectureship in pastoral theology was raised to the rank of a professoriate; a new chair of ecclesiastical art was established and conferred upon the Rev. Dr Percy Dearmer; a chair of ecclesiastical music was designed, but could not be created through lack of funds.

On the university side of the college, Sir Herbert Jackson in 1918 resigned his position as Daniell professor of chemistry on being appointed director of the British Scientific Research Association; he was succeeded by Dr A. W. Crossley, who was in 1919 joined by Dr A. J. Allmand. Dr Crossley, however, was shortly afterward made director of the British Cotton Research Association, and in the early part of 1920 his place as Daniell professor was taken by Dr S. Smiles. In 1920, too, a most useful and mutually advantageous exchange was effected between King's College and the London School of Economics—a neighbour with whom friendship and co-operation were becoming increasingly close: the readership in palæography (held at the school by Dr Hubert Hall) was transferred to the department of history at the college, and in

---

[1] Dr Headlam was shortly afterward made Regius Professor of Divinity in the University of Oxford.
[2] Lecturer in mental and moral philosophy, 1908 ; dogmatic theology, 1909.

return the college surrendered the Tooke professorship of economics (then in the hands of Professor E. J. Urwick). About the same time Mr Walter Smith, the able and devoted secretary of the college, terminated his twenty-four years of service and retired. Both delegacy and council in wishing him godspeed expressed cordial appreciation of his work in helping to restore the finances of the college, in superintending the remodelling of the college buildings, in facilitating the incorporation of the college and in adjusting its relations to the university, in effecting the separation of the college from its appendant institutions, and particularly in assisting the development of the engineering department.

All the changes and exchanges of 1920, however, were thrown into the shade by the lamentable death of the beloved and revered principal, Dr Ronald Burrows, which occurred on May 14. Early in 1919 the enormous pressure of his multiform work began to tell upon him, and Professor H. G. Atkins was appointed assistant-principal in order to relieve him of some of the routine duties of his office. Frequent illnesses, however, made inroads upon his strength, and in the autumn of the year it was discovered that an operation was necessary. The present writer, in common with many of his colleagues, has a vivid recollection of the noble cheerfulness and courage with which, right up to the eve of the ordeal, he continued his labours and drew up directions for the continuance of his work during the period of his enforced absence. On November 3, 1919, he wrote:

> If all goes well to-morrow, and I take the necessary interval for recovery, you ought to have me back at the beginning of January a fitter man than I have been for years.

Alas; all did not go well on that 4th of November. The evil was deeper-seated and wider-spread than had been suspected. In a few weeks a second operation became essential. This too was unsuccessful, and then nothing more could be done. In growing weakness, and in constant pain, he lingered, with unbroken bravery and with complete submission to what he regarded as the divine will, until the end came. The grief of the college was intense, and its consciousness of loss overwhelming. It was realized then, and it has more than ever been realized since, that Dr Burrows was a great principal. He accomplished much himself; but even more conspicuous than his own achievement was the self-effacing way in which he encouraged and stimulated the activities of others. He was a source of limitless energy and enthusiasm.

472

WALTER ROBERT MATTHEWS
Dean 1918–

472

§ 5. *Dr Ernest Barker and the Site Question, 1920–24*

The lamentable death of Dr Burrows on May 14, 1920, was necessarily followed by an interregnum or interval during which the choice of a successor was pondered by those responsible for the action of the crown. This interval, which extended till July 12, was used by the professorial board as a convenient occasion on which to bring forward a proposal that had long been in their minds. It was to the effect that henceforth the principal's house, with its extensive basement, its convenient dining-room, its luxurious drawing-room, and its numerous attics, should be absorbed into the college, and that the principal should receive in lieu of it such an increase of salary as should enable him to live in proper style elsewhere. This proposal, mooted by the board of June 2, was adopted by the delegacy and the council, and was readily accepted by the new principal when he was appointed. By this simple means nearly a score of excellent rooms were added to the accommodation of the college, and the immediate pressure on space was sensibly relieved.

The new principal placed over the college by the crown—which probably at this time meant Mr Lloyd George (prime minister) and Mr H. A. L. Fisher (president of the board of education)—was Mr (later Dr) Ernest Barker, fellow and tutor of New College, Oxford. Mr Barker had had an academic career of remarkable distinction. A Balliol scholarship obtained from the Manchester Grammar School had been followed by a triple first in the University of Oxford, and by successive fellowships at Merton (1898–1905), St John's (1909–13), and New College (1913–20). He was known as one of the most brilliant lecturers and most successful teachers in the university, while his writings on political theory had given him a world-wide reputation.[1]

He took up his work in King's College at a critical moment. For on April 7, 1920, the government had offered to the senate for the use of the university and of King's College a site of about $11\frac{1}{2}$ acres in Bloomsbury, at the back of the British Museum. The offer was subject to the conditions that the university should vacate its quarters in the Imperial Institute and that King's College should surrender its site and buildings in the Strand. The government's offer was therefore not a " gift " (as it has sometimes been called), but a suggestion for

[1] *The Political Thought of Plato and Aristotle* (1906) and *Political Thought in England from Herbert Spencer to To-day* (1915).

an exchange extremely profitable to itself. For the purchase price of the Bloomsbury site which it offered was £425,000, while (apart altogether from the Imperial Institute, which was a white elephant) the value of the site and buildings of King's College, as estimated by an L.C.C. valuer, was £1,500,000. It was known that Somerset House, extremely cramped for room, was burning with desire to recover its lost backyard, with the appurtenances thereof, and if it could have recovered them in this way it would have achieved a crowning and exceedingly lucrative victory. On the other hand, the university, as represented by the majority of the senate, was anxious to leave South Kensington and to establish a close association with University College and the transplanted King's College, the visionary " university quarter " of the Haldane report. Hence the university was much more willing than was King's College to accept the unprofitable exchange proposed by the government. The college, however, did not incontinently reject the bad bargain, as it might well have done, but, eager to move in line with the university, it resolved fully to explore the possible advantages of removal. Hence, says the annual report of December 1920,

> Representatives of the delegacy and also of the council of the college conferred in May and June with members of the senate in regard to the offer of His Majesty's government to provide a new site for the headquarters of the university and for King's College, and in regard to the compensation which King's College should receive if it were moved from its present site. Later the representatives of the delegacy and the council, accompanied by the vice-chancellor, interviewed the president of the board of education, and discussed with him the terms of the removal of the college to the new site, should the offer be accepted by the senate.

Within King's College itself, the council (controlling the theological department) was much less attracted than was the delegacy (administering the secular side under the control of the senate of the university) by the prospects of removal. It had nothing to gain and much to lose by the change. It was the legal possessor of both the site and the buildings in the Strand; it was entirely satisfied with its position and its accommodation; it had little hope of being placed in nearly so good a situation in any new college established by either the government or the university. Hence at a special meeting, held on July 23, 1920, it passed the following resolution:

> That in any proposals for the removal of King's College from its present site, the council reserves and insists upon the legal

right of the corporation to deal directly with the government and any other body or bodies concerned in the matter, and to exercise all the powers conferred upon it by the Act of 1882 and Amending Acts.

The senate of the university recognized the independent rights of the council of the college, and when, on October 20, 1920, it accepted the government's offer of the Bloomsbury site it did so on five conditions, of which one was:

> That the terms of the removal of King's College from the Strand to the Bloomsbury site shall be a matter of subsequent negotiation between His Majesty's government, the council of King's College, and the senate of the university, and that an agreement shall be concluded between the said parties.

The negotiations concerning this and the other conditions specified in the senate's provisional acceptance of the Bloomsbury site on October 20, 1920, proved to be extremely protracted and difficult, the main crux being the problem of how to secure funds wherewith to erect the new buildings on the desert offered by the government. In December 1921 the council of King's College reported as follows:

> No perceptible progress has been made in this matter [of a new site for the college] during the past year. The council has taken legal opinion with a view to safeguarding the interests of the corporation and of the theological department, and is carefully considering the conditions which it must lay down before consenting to the removal. The council wishes to reaffirm the statement which was made in the last annual report, that it sees no advantage, from the point of view of the theological department, to be gained by giving up the present site. It desires, however, to facilitate the development of the college as a whole, and will be prepared to co-operate in the establishment of the college on a new site, provided that they can obtain a reliable assurance that the position of the theological department will not be injured, and that no financial obligations will be imposed upon them.

The council's view that " no advantage was to be gained " by removal was becoming increasingly the view of the delegacy, of the professorial board, and of Dr Barker himself. The college was asked to surrender one of the finest sites in London, together with buildings on which some £500,000 had at one time and another been spent, in return for six acres of an arid waste in an obscure and decaying suburb, off all the main lines of traffic and difficult of access. It realized that its removal would involve the breaking of its association with South London; the severing of its connexion with the great hospitals it served; the hampering of its growing co-operation with the School of Economics and the Birkbeck College; and the ruin of its system of public lectures. It was felt, moreover, that on the new site the college would be inconveniently and even dangerously near to University College; and that speedily, under the dominating authority of the contiguous university in which both were incorporated, whole departments would be closed down, numerous transferences of staffs and students would be made, frightful co-ordinations would be accomplished, and that ultimately a fusion of the two colleges would be effected in which each would lose its individuality. Hence, as the months of fruitless negotiation passed away, the attitude of the college as a whole began to stiffen: it resolved not to move unless it found the government prepared to give such ample compensation for its site and buildings in the Strand as would enable it to restart in far more favourable conditions on the new site.

As King's College became less and less inclined to migrate from the Strand to Bloomsbury the dominant party in the university became more and more anxious that it should do so. For unless the government got King's it would not hand over the new site—the university being allowed to the end of March 1926 to decide whether or not it would make the exchange. For the dominant party in the university, although it was unable to say whether or not the five conditions of exchange enumerated in October 1920 would be fulfilled, had in 1921 heavily committed itself to the acceptance of the site. With extreme rashness, and with the very improper connivance of the government, it had placed on a large plot of the site in question an Institute of Historical Research costing well over £20,000. Unless, therefore, the site were secured before April 1926 this large sum of money would be sunk. From this date, therefore, the communications of the university with the college on the site question assumed a more minatory tone. On October 19, 1921, for instance, the vice-chancellor (Sir Sidney Russell-Wells) wrote to the council:

> You are aware that under an arrangement with H.M. government the University of London intends to acquire a new site in Bloomsbury. It is the intention of the university to provide for the removal of King's College to this site, and it will in due course undertake negotiations with the government with reference to certain matters relating thereto.

After inviting the council to take notice of this intention, he continued:

476

The university will be glad to receive any representation which the council may desire to make with reference to the theological department, and any points relating thereto which the council would like the university to bring forward in its further negotiations with the government.

It was incorporation, and incorporation alone, which made it possible for such a tone to be assumed toward the college by what had been till 1908 an extraneous authority. The council, through the Bishop of London, very properly replied (1) that it claimed to negotiate with the government directly, and not via the university, and (2) that the university could not move King's College from the Strand without the council's consent. The university then proceeded to take legal opinion on the question " how far it has power to arrange for the transfer of King's College without the consent of the council." The answer of counsel (Messrs T. J. C. Tomlin and Warwick Draper), dated January 16, 1922, was discouraging:

We do not think that the university has any power to remove King's College as a whole, or the theological department, from the Strand site.

On which answer the principal officer (Sir E. Cooper Perry) regretfully commented:

If counsel's opinion is accepted it is clear that the removal of King's College as a whole, and the removal of the theological department of King's College from the Strand site, can be effected only with the consent of the delegacy and the council; and though the appointment of the delegacy is ultimately in the hands of the senate, the senate has no means of imposing its will on the council.

It is clear that the spirit of coercion was in the air; it is clear that the delegacy, if it had stood alone, would have been coerced; it is clear that the council, and only the council, strong in its legal possession of the site and the buildings of the college, prevented the forceful eviction of the college from the Strand and its establishment in servitude in Bloomsbury.

Since coercion was impossible, it was necessary for negotiations to be resumed. A joint conference between the university, the delegacy, and the council was held on October 25, 1923, and after some subsequent correspondence it was agreed that a joint deputation should be sent to the chancellor of the exchequer to find out what sum he would be prepared to grant to King's College as compensation for the surrender of its site and buildings in the Strand and as an aid toward the erection of the new buildings (estimated to cost £1,000,000) on the Bloomsbury site. The joint deputation waited on the chancellor (Mr Philip Snowden) on March 14, 1924. The chancellor's definitive answer to the deputation's inquiry was delayed until the following August. When it came it finally, and most happily, closed the question of the possibility of the removal of King's College: for the sum offered

> as compensation for the existing site and buildings of the college, if it should be moved to Bloomsbury, and the site and buildings should be taken over by His Majesty's government, was— £370,000!

The absurd inadequacy of this sum was such that not even the university could urge its acceptance. Hence, when it was found that no increase in the amount was to be hoped for, nothing remained but the rejection of the offer of the Bloomsbury site altogether. The rejection was conveyed to His Majesty's Treasury in a letter from Sir E. Cooper Perry, on behalf of the university, dated June 24, 1925. The central paragraph ran:

> As it is certain that the expense of rebuilding King's College on the Bloomsbury site . . . would far exceed the sum of £370,000, and as the Lords Commissioners of H.M. Treasury are not able to hold out any hope that parliament could be asked to contribute a larger sum than £370,000 as representing the commercial value of the site and buildings of King's College in the Strand in the event of King's College removing to Bloomsbury, and the Strand site reverting to the crown, the senate find themselves compelled to decline the offer contained in Mr Fisher's letter of April 7, 1920, conditionally accepted by the senate on October 20, 1920.[1]

The long and short of the matter—which cannot here be laboured—is that the council of King's College had saved the college as a whole, and not merely its own department, from a move that must almost inevitably have been fatal to its individuality and even to its own separate existence.

The further history of the site question does not directly concern King's College. Suffice it, then, to say that on March 31, 1926, the offer of the government lapsed, and the Bedford trustees (under the terms of the original agreement) were required to resume the site and refund to the treasury the £425,000 paid for it. Having resumed the site, they promptly gave notice to the university to clear from it the Institute of Historical Research and other encumbrances injudiciously and improperly erected thereon. The university

[1] See the *Times*, June 25 and 26, 1925.

was placed in a painful and ridiculous situation. It managed, however, to secure a short moratorium, and during the interval of respite succeeded in securing (mainly from the Rockefeller Foundation) gifts of money which enabled it to purchase the site on its own account, free from all those inequitable conditions which had burdened the offer of the government in 1920. Hence it was able to proceed to develop the site in its own way. There can be no doubt that it is admirably suited to be the abode of academic offices where quietude, obscurity, and inaccessibility are the prime requisites of the life of supreme felicity.

§ 6. *The Great Expansion*

The laying of the bogey of eviction which for twelve years (1912–24) had haunted the college enabled both delegacy and council to proceed with cheerfulness and confidence to develop their still extensive resources. The possibilities of the old site were by no means exhausted. At the very moment, indeed, when the board of education launched its original ultimatum, important schemes of construction and reconstruction were under consideration. It was now, after more than a decade of delay, feasible to take them up again. In 1923 a number of internal rearrangements were made, one of which enabled the old council room to be converted into a staff refectory, wherein both men and women teachers could lunch. During the long vacation of 1925, when it had been finally decided that the college was to stay in the Strand, the structural changes were commenced. An additional storey was erected on the top of the north-west side of the college buildings, providing a couple of laboratories for the zoologists and three research rooms for the physiologists. At the southern end of the building, further extensive accommodation for the geologists was supplied by constructing three rooms on the roof of the central corridor. The closing of the department of bacteriology and public health enabled space to be found for the teaching of bio-chemistry. The total expenditure on new buildings and alterations in 1925 amounted to over £8000. In 1926 a mezzanine floor was run across the Wheatstone laboratory and the George III museum, thus providing an honours laboratory for physics students, as well as a lecture-room and various private rooms for the department.[1] At

[1] The valuable but cumbrous contents of the George III Museum were removed, with the consent of the Government, to the Science Museum at South Kensington.

the same time the top floor of the house formerly occupied by the principals of the college was converted into a laboratory of experimental psychology. The total cost of these alterations was £1200. More extensive and expensive alterations of the college, however, were effected in 1927. Two new floors were built in the lofty entrance-hall, the lower one providing an invaluable lecture-room capable of holding a couple of hundred students; the upper one divided into rooms for botanists, zoologists, and photographers. Secondly, an additional refectory was provided by the incorporation of the women's common room looking on to the Embankment, fresh accommodation for the women being found in a couple of lecture-rooms on the basement floor. Thirdly, by mezzanining part of the long corridor on the ground floor large expansions of the Skeat and Furnival library and of the college office were rendered possible. Finally, a lift (the first of its kind) was constructed connecting the sub-basement with the roof; and the large theatre (the scene of much silent suffering) was reseated. The cost of these numerous and important works was £14,746. For the centenary year, however, still larger plans were formed. A site was acquired on the roof of the Aldwych station of the Piccadilly tube railway—contiguous to the college, on the east side of Strand Lane. On this site a fine five-storeyed building was projected to provide accommodation for geology, geography, history, education, and classics. At the time of writing (March 1929) this excellent and roomy building is nearing completion. Its inauguration will be one of the leading features of the centenary celebrations. The payment of its cost, moreover, will be one of the first charges made upon the centenary fund. Later on, it is hoped, if money is forthcoming, to rebuild the ugly south-east block of the college overlooking the Embankment: the estimated expense of this, however, is some £125,000.

It may be reckoned that with the opening of its second century the college has got nearly all the accommodation it wants, as well as nearly all it can easily get on its old site. It has got nearly all it wants; for it is realizing that beyond a certain calculable limit increase in numbers is not a blessing, but a curse. If particular classes grow too large, the masses of students become mere audiences, and the teacher loses that personal touch with his pupil from which springs half the virtue of a university education. It is arguable that in the session 1927–28, when 57 students were reading for final honours in chemistry, 75 in English, 78 in history, 82 in physics,

480

ERNEST BARKER
Principal 1920–28

and 88 in French, the *optimum* point had been reached and even passed. So, too, in respect of the college as a whole: just as there are certain dimensions beyond which a ship ceases to be a ship and becomes an unnavigable monstrosity, so there are certain numerical bounds beyond which a college ceases to be a college and becomes an unmanageable mob, devoid of organic unity and corporate consciousness. It was Dr Barker's deliberate opinion that, for King's College, at any rate, the maximum beyond which it was undesirable to go was 1500 full-time day students, divided as evenly as might be between the five faculties of arts, science, medicine, engineering, and theology. For that number the accommodation already provided, together with that contemplated as the result of the centenary appeal, is ample. Should, however, further demands for new departments arise, there are still some possibilities of internal rearrangements, as well as of loftier elevations toward the sky.

The rapid post-war increase in the number of students had the happy effect of re-establishing the college finances on a satisfactory basis. In the session 1927–28, for instance, the income from fees alone amounted to £50,919; government grants came to £49,000, and income from other sources brought up the grand total to £125,112. This large sum not only allowed the college to be run without undue parsimony; it also provided a credit balance of £1240 to be transferred to the building fund. How such figures would have amazed the older principals who struggled year by year with devastating poverty!

Increase in numbers and stabilization of finance were accompanied during Dr Barker's principalship by a wide extension of college activities—an extension in which both staff and students played a prominent part. The work of the students (more fully described in an appendix by Mr C. H. Driver) included the inauguration of an annual " commemoration week " in December 1920, wherein, lectures being relegated to limbo, the students surrender themselves to a programme such as only they could either conceive or survive, consisting of a sermon, an oration, a reception, a dinner, a dance of eight hours' duration, a play, a football and hockey contest with University College, and a final enormous supper. What this all " commemorates," unless it be the eternal miracle of youth, has never been made clear. King's men, and women too, were active in aiding the formation of a University of London Union Society in 1921 and a National Union of

Students in 1922; the latter organization, indeed, found its first president, secretary, and treasurer all in this college. The social gatherings which the students of King's College for Women had introduced into the austere precincts of the Strand in 1915 developed after 1920 into "faculty dances," whose frequency and intensity became such that the committee of deans had to impose strict limits upon their periodicity: the great hall of the college, originally intended for examinations, was in 1922 fitted with a dance-floor. New clubs and societies—literary, scientific, social, religious, political, too numerous even to mention—sprang up like mushrooms, flourished like green bay-trees, and occasionally perished like gourds. They had (and have) this supreme advantage, that they cause the fusion of the faculties, cut across the divisions of departments, and tend to bind the college in organic unity. In connexion with the political societies—conservative, liberal, socialist—it became the practice from 1922 onward to invite prominent statesmen and would-be statesmen to address the college during the lunch-hour. These addresses continued until the habit of expressing dissent from the opinions of the distinguished speakers by means of musical instruments, fireworks, sawdust, confetti, and smoke bombs became so alarming as to cause the Union Society to decree their discontinuance.

In respect of the more strictly academic work of the college, the following outstanding features of the last seven years of the first century may be noted. First, during the sessions 1921–23 the School of Oriental Studies (established in 1916) moved into the buildings of the London Institution in Finsbury Circus, taking over the fine but antiquated library of that institution. King's College then transferred the whole of its teaching of Asiatic and African languages to the school, and handed over (on permanent loan) the oriental books of the Marsden library, as well as the 10,000 volumes of the *Chinese Encyclopædia*, receiving in return a very valuable collection of historical and other works. Secondly, in 1921 and the following sessions a new department of geography was organized in conjunction with the London School of Economics, for several years the new department being worked by the existing teachers of the college without any addition to the staff. At the time of writing the great success and popularity of the department points to a separate organization and a staff peculiar to itself. Finally, in almost all departments of the college post-graduate and research work enormously increased, and year by year a growing volume of publications revealed the fact that important results were being achieved. In the closing session of the century (1927–28) no fewer than 238 advanced students on the university side were endeavouring to extend the bounds of knowledge and improve their own chances of getting good appointments; [1] while in the department of theology a dozen bold speculators (hoping to become doctors of divinity, or at any rate of philosophy) were seeking to solve such mysteries respecting the relations of God to Man as had eluded the notice of the Apostles.

The period of Dr Barker's principalship saw some important changes in the staff. During the long vacation of 1920 Dr H. J. White received the great distinction of appointment to the deanery of Christ Church, Oxford. His chair of New Testament exegesis was held successively by Dr H. L. Goudge (1921–23), Mr F. R. Barry (1923–28), and Dr E. J. Bicknell. In 1923 Professor W. D. Halliburton, the eminent physiologist, terminated his thirty years of successful teaching in the college, and was followed by Dr R. J. S. MacDowall, from the University of Leeds. During the same year Professor W. C. F. Walters, who had held the chair of classical literature since 1901, was compelled by ill-health to retire[2]; his place was taken by Professor J. A. K. Thomson, of the universities of Aberdeen and Oxford, whose *Studies in the Odyssey* and other works had given him an established reputation both with lovers of Greek poetry and with admirers of good English (or Scottish) prose. In 1923, too, the department of Portuguese language and literature passed into the charge of that admirable scholar and fine gentleman, Professor Edgar Prestage, of Balliol College, Oxford, and of the Lisbon Academy of Science.

The year 1924 saw the close of Professor J. W. Adamson's thirty-four years of devoted and most efficient service as head of the department of education. The report of the delegacy, in mentioning his retirement, said with justice and propriety:

> The services which he has rendered to the college and to the cause of learning are of the very highest order. He has guided his department with a quiet sagacity; he has thrown an abundant light on the history of education, and made himself perhaps the foremost authority in the country in that subject.

The chair of education vacated by Professor Adamson was conferred on Mr (later Dr) Dover Wilson, the celebrated

---

[1] The post-graduate students of 1927–28 were classified as follows : science, 103 ; arts, 101 ; engineering, 27 ; law, 7.
[2] Professor Walters died on March 18, 1927.

Shakespearean scholar, who was able with unfailing charm and delightful humour to apply to the problems of modern pedagogy all that was relevant to them in the writings of the Tudor dramatists. In the same year Professor O. W. Richardson, since 1914 head of the physics department, was appointed to a research professorship of the Royal Society. He was, fortunately for the college, able to continue to direct the work of some of the advanced students of his department; but his place as Wheatstone professor was taken by Mr E. V. Appleton, of St John's College and the Cavendish Laboratory, Cambridge, who strengthened the connexion between the college and the Heavyside layer. The kindred department of mathematics, moreover, saw an important change at the same date: Professor C. B. Jeffery, who in 1922 had come as colleague to Professor S. A. F. White, was appointed to the Astor chair at University College; he was succeeded at King's by Professor A. E. Jolliffe, for many years a distinguished mathematical tutor at Corpus Christi College, Oxford, and, since 1920, professor at the Royal Holloway College, Egham.

In 1925 the college suffered a distressing loss in the unexpected death, on March 24, of its brilliant zoologist, Dr Arthur Dendy, who, after twenty years of efficient teaching and fruitful research in the college, was just beginning to put into permanent form the results of the labours of a lifetime. Professor Julian Huxley, of New College, Oxford, grandson of the old antagonist of Dr Wace, was appointed to succeed him. He held the chair, however, for two years only, being lured away in 1927 to join Mr H. G. Wells in the great task of lightening the biological darkness of the human race by means of an excellently illustrated periodical published in fortnightly parts. The less sensational task of teaching biology as professor at King's fell to Dr Doris Mackinnon, who for eight years had with marked ability filled the second place in the department.

The year 1926 saw the departure of two old yet ever young servants of the college. Professor Victor Spiers retired after having occupied the chair of French for thirty-seven years; the versatile Dr C. D. Webb gave up the mastership of the preliminary class which he had held from the old days when it was part of the school—viz., since 1886. Each of the two continued to display his perpetual juvenility in characteristic fashion: Professor Spiers by attending all the faculty dances; Dr Webb by taking up the study of Chinese and by winning, in open competition, at the age of seventy-five, the Gilchrist scholarship in that language at the School of Oriental Studies. Dr Denis Saurat, director of the French Institute, South Kensington, became professor of French; while charge of the preliminary class was entrusted to the skilled hands of Mr Hubert Brinton, formerly of Eton College.

The summer of 1927 brought to an end the professoriate of Dr E. Barclay-Smith, who for twelve years had occupied with great distinction the chair of anatomy: Dr D. M. Blair came from Glasgow to succeed him. The same year saw the establishment by the university of a new chair of military studies, particularly attached to King's College. The college welcomed as the first occupant of this chair the eminent soldier Major-General Sir Frederick Maurice, the eldest grandson of Professor F. D. Maurice, whose connexion with King's College had been so conspicuous in the early years of the theological department (1846–53). Sir Frederick, on his appointment, generously presented to the college library 353 volumes from his grandfather's collection—many of them memorial volumes given by admirers to the professor on his retirement in 1853. The grateful, and apparently penitent, theological department decided to make one of the features of its centenary celebration the establishment of a Frederick Denison Maurice chair of theology.[1]

Toward the end of the year 1927 the college was perturbed to hear that Dr Barker was likely to leave it. A new chair of political science had been established in the University of Cambridge, and he had been invited to be its first occupant. For long he had desired to have more opportunity for teaching and more leisure for writing; for some time, too, he had felt the burden of administrative work necessitated by his office of principal to be excessive. Hence, after much hesitation and with obviously sincere regret, he intimated his intention to resign his office on December 31. The report for 1928 notes that

> The delegacy recorded their great regret at receiving Dr Barker's resignation, and their deep appreciation of his services to the college and to the cause of education during his seven years' tenure of the office of principal. The chairman referred to the administrative ability with which Dr Barker had steered the college successfully through the great difficulties with which it was faced when he became principal, and to the regret which all members of the college would feel on losing a chief whom some would miss as scholar, some as administrator, but all as a friend with the gift of sympathy and a sense of humour.

[1] *Cf.* Luke xi, 47.

485

The report went on to announce that Dr W. R. Halliday, Rathbone professor of ancient history in the University of Liverpool, had been appointed principal in succession to Dr Barker, and that he had taken up his duties in January 1928.

The chairman mentioned in the above extract from the annual report was, of course, Lord Hambleden. Never did the college have a stauncher friend, a more generous supporter, or a more laborious and devoted leader. For thirty-four years he was a member of the council. In 1896 he undertook the thankless and extremely expensive office of treasurer, at a time when, owing to the suspension of government grants, the bankruptcy of the college seemed imminent. He had been chairman of the delegacy from its inauguration in 1910. Alas, that within six months of Dr Barker's resignation Lord Hambleden should have died! He passed away, at the comparatively early age of fifty-nine, on June 16, 1928. Thus on the eve of the centenary celebrations the college lost both the principal and the chairman to whom it had looked for leadership on the great occasion. Institutions, however, have a way of surviving catastrophes, and not infrequently the passing away of one great leader reveals the fact that another, with different but not inferior powers, is ready to carry on his work. Dr Halliday with quick enthusiasm and marvellous resource took up the work of Dr Barker; while the delegacy found a new chairman of tried ability in the famous lawyer Lord Blanesburgh.

§ 7. *Conclusion*

Thus we come to our centenary. The hundred years that lie behind us—as all will realize who have managed to wade through this dull and inadequate record—have been a period full of strange vicissitudes, but on the whole a period of constant development and remarkable achievement. The recurrent burden throughout the whole existence of the college has been financial stringency: the initial misfortune which deprived the founders of a large portion of their expected funds was never wholly redressed. True it is that in recent years increases in the number of students, generous government grants, subventions from the county councils, and private donations have freed both the delegacy and the council from pressing pecuniary anxiety, and have enabled the work of the various faculties to be carried on with unprecedented efficiency.

486

WILLIAM REGINALD HALLIDAY
Principal 1928–

Nevertheless, the conduct of the college is still hampered by the inadequacy of some of the buildings, by the lack of endowments for its chairs, by the scantiness of the funds available for scholarships and bursaries, and by the insufficiency of its hostel accommodation.

Hence the authorities are making a joint centenary appeal for the sum of £350,000—a very modest sum, not far exceeding a two years' total income of the college—for four main purposes —viz., first, to reconstruct the south-east block of the college buildings which at present is both ugly and uneconomical; secondly, to provide endowments for the chairs of English language and literature, physics, physical chemistry, electrical engineering, and physiology, as well as various chairs in the department of theology; thirdly, to establish an adequately supplied fund for scholarships and bursaries, so as to enable the clever children of the poor to enjoy the advantages of the higher education; and, finally, to extend the hostel accommodation for both men and women students, and in particular to complete the fine theological hostel in Vincent Square. If these modest requirements are satisfied the college will be able to start its second century well equipped for the great educational tasks that lie before it, and confident that, great as have been its achievements in the past, they will be exceeded by those of the future. It is the fervent hope of the writer of this history that even this imperfect record of the doings of the college to which he is proud to belong will render some small assistance toward the attainment of the end in view. He feels that he cannot more fitly bring his work to a close than by quoting the last paragraph of a fine letter addressed by Dr Barker to the *Times* on June 26, 1925:

> We have now been on our present site for nearly a hundred years. It was about 1828 that the foundation of King's College was first mooted; it was on August 14, 1829, that we received our charter; it was in the autumn of 1831 that the work of the college began. In 1929 we shall be celebrating our centenary; and we hope to make our appeal for the better endowment of the college—it has been all too poorly endowed from its first beginnings—to all friends of the principle on which the college is based—viz., the principle of the union, under a system of free toleration, between the full advancement of all knowledge and the profession and teaching of Christian doctrine. We hope in that day to receive the aid of those who believe that in this quarter of London and this City of Westminster, a college of limited size, bound together by the personal contact of its members, and seeking to hold together religion and science—

sancte et sapienter, as it is expressed in our motto—has a place to fill and a work to do.

NOTE

I. NUMBER OF STUDENTS, 1912–28

SESSION		Theol.	Arts	Laws	Sci.	Med.	Eng.	Gilbart Lects.	K.C.W.	TOTAL
						FACULTIES				
1911–12		229	1087	73	389	231	150	800	341	3300
1912–13		202	956	119	210	371	141	800	212	3011
1913–14		153	981	105	194	480	135	1000	225	3273
1914–15	*During the War*	100	884	53	90	204	59	575	112	2077
1915–16		91	613	19	69	220	34	600	99	1745
1916–17		25	620	23	52	313	196[1]	914	70	2213
1917–18		19	504	18	65	369	127	592	81	1775
1918–19		90	798	49	240	391	292	853	118	2831
1919–20		200	1277	49	401	458	269	1040	185	3879
1920–21		257	1239	47	463	427	247	1140	—[2]	3820
1921–22		230	1221	47	413	504	240	1165	—	3820
1922–23		213	1185	46	432	499	189	1193	—	3757
1923–24		204	1185	64	410	520	150	1785	—	4318
1924–25		245	1124	43	418	493	140	1800	—	4263
1925–26		306	1216	60	433	408	164	1900	—	4487
1926–27		295	1255	68	431	425	147	1800	—	4421
1927–28		354	1348	87	336	442	138	2000	—	4705

II. DEGREES AND DIPLOMAS GAINED 1912–28

1912–13 89		1920–21 163
1913–14 120		1921–22 296
1914–15 70		1922–23 299
1915–16 *During the War* 78		1923–24 . . . . . . 519[3]
1916–17 84		1924–25 295
1917–18 52		1925–26 325
1918–19 57		1926–27 345
1919–20 81		1927–28 317

[1] Including special war classes for aeroplane inspectors.

[2] From 1920 the King's College for Women students were included in the faculties.

[3] Owing to the alteration of the date of the final examinations from October to June, two examinations fell within this session. The number of successes were respectively 273 and 246.

APPENDIX A

KING'S COLLEGE FOR WOMEN

By Miss Hilda D. Oakeley, M.A.

INTRODUCTORY. The history of the women's side of King's College in its different phases is representative in a remarkable way of the changes and developments in the mind of the educational public on the subject of women's education during the last fifty years, as well as in the ideals and aims of succeeding generations of women. It is not that the tale can be simply told as of one of those dramatic advances from a position not of rights, but of kindly toleration, on the outskirts of a system to which they did not belong to the winning of full membership of an ancient university, as in the history of women at Oxford. Such a story does not belong to London, whose university has since 1878 treated women as having the same status as men within its system. The special interest of the history of women in connexion with King's College has lain rather in the very various views and conceptions of the needs and aims of women which it has reflected, its relation to the social changes of the period and to the distinctive character of the college, which in an idealistic spirit was led in the first place to take up a task not originally contemplated in its constitution without fully foreseeing the final outcome. Other special circumstances contributed to the determination of the peculiar atmosphere of ideas in which the women's college had its origin, especially the fact that, founded by King's College, it was established in Kensington Square, with associations still suggestive of leisure and literature and old-world memories, and that it welcomed local interest. An important feature of the early years is the influence upon the curriculum of the students. Many of these were mature women who, in the more leisured life of middle-class girlhood in the seventies and eighties, had found out the subjects in which they were keenly interested, and, unable to leave home for their more thorough study, seized with an enthusiasm akin to that of the pioneer women at Cambridge and Oxford the opportunity of listening to scholars and masters in a college set down in their midst. We find in the early records a number of instances of lectures instituted at the desire of students, as, for example, a set by Miss Jane Harrison, also courses in Spanish, architecture, etc. At a later date Mrs Fawcett was similarly invited. At this halcyon period, in fact, as some might regard it, the young life of the Ladies' Department was free from the iron hand of examinations, and some subjects insinuated themselves into the state, such as music and fine art, which Socrates, in the guise of the spirit of professional education, found it necessary later to expel, without giving them so flattering a farewell as the philosopher of the *Republic* accorded to the poets.

The connexion with King's College ensured that here, for the first time, women had the opportunity of advanced education in theological subjects, and the rare opening of this avenue made the department a centre for a valuable group of students whose appreciation of their privileges was extremely keen. On the other hand, it was natural that the elastic system and comparative absence of strict organization with which the Kensington Square College began should have encouraged an openness to new ideas and possibilities which continued to characterize it after it had been brought more into line with other university colleges. Thus those desirous of attempting a new adventure in education at a later date were led to turn to King's College women's department for their field, and as King's College for Women it became the scene of the struggle to give a more scientific basis to domestic science and to raise the subject to a university standard. Here, then, was fought out one of the keenest conflicts of principles and methods which have occurred in the movement for the higher education of women.

In another aspect of interest, not many institutions can have had a more chequered constitutional history. From its position in relation to the parent college which, whilst actually close, was loose constitutionally, it grew to the status of a department analogous to the departments of engineering, medicine, etc. Then, after being for a short span of years constitutionally independent, as King's College for Women separately incorporated in the University, though always closely linked to its eponym founder, the women's side was to all intents and purposes combined with King's College in a co-educational whole, while the household and social science department of King's College for Women [1] alone remained a geographically and practically distinct institution, in its

[1] Now King's College for Household and Social Science.

fine buildings on Campden Hill, inheriting some slight portion of the memories of Kensington Square, though in soul as well as body a new thing, with an interesting new history before it.

The Ladies' Department. King's College had earlier displayed a considerable interest in the higher education of women, especially shown in the assistance given to the teaching at Queen's College and also Bedford College in early stages of their history. The idea that it should make an original contribution of its own to this cause appears to have been formed in the mind of Dr Warr, the distinguished professor of classics at King's College. Professor Warr, hearing that Mrs William Grey, a leader in women's education, was in search of an institution willing to organize lectures for ladies in the West End, resolved that this institution should be King's College. That the project was immediately set on foot was due to the welcome accorded it by Dr Barry, the principal, in whose library the preliminary conference on the subject was held in 1877. It was his energy, together with the assistance of Mrs Grey, Miss Emily Shirreff, Miss Mary Gurney, Mrs G. A. Spottiswode, Mrs Edward Garston, Miss C. G. Schmitz (afterward Mrs Wace), lady superintendent and first vice-principal, and also of Dr Maclagan, then Vicar of St Mary Abbot's, Kensington, which ensured its rapid progress.

The lectures were originally held in the old Town Hall, where the vestry granted the use of large rooms for the classes. These details are taken from the *King's College Ladies' Magazine*, 1898, which records an observation of Bishop Barry that " There are more young ladies in Kensington than in any other fashionable quarter of London." These young ladies, including some no longer young, evidently appreciated the recognition of their existence as an educational constituency, for they appear to have poured into and filled to overflowing the lecture-rooms, which were soon removed to a house in Observatory Avenue. It is worthy of note that the women's college did not originate merely as a growth from King's College, but that it arose in part to meet the vital needs of women in Kensington as perceived by such women as Mrs Grey and Miss Gurney, while its educational character and high standard were in essential respects due to its adoption by King's College, and the fact that leading members of King's College, as well as a succession of distinguished principals and professors, threw themselves with remarkable zeal into the new development.

The most picturesque illustration of the efforts on behalf of the new venture is found in the performance of Dr Warr's *Tale of Troy, or Scenes and Tableaux from Homer,* given at Cromwell House in 1883, and at the Prince's Hall in 1886, under the direction of Sir Charles Newton, Sir Edward Poynter, P.R.A., and Professor George Warr. The event seems to deserve some notice, if only in the impression it gives of a cultural effort of Victorian society in London. The scenery was painted from designs by Sir E. Poynter, Mr Walter Crane, and Mr Henry Halliday, the opening tableaux designed by Lord Leighton. The music was by Sir Walter Parratt, Mr Otto Goldschmidt, and others; Mr George Alexander was stage-manager at the first performance; and amongst the performers were Mrs Beerbohm Tree (Helen, and Andromache), Mrs Andrew Lang, Miss Jane Harrison (Penelope), Mr J. K. Stephen (Hector), Mr Beerbohm Tree, Mr W. Benson, Mr Lionel Cust, Mr Lionel Tennyson (Ulysses), Mr Rennell Rodd (Emmæus). As Professor Warr narrates,[1] it was owing to the special interest of Sir Charles Freake, a member of King's College council, in the new extension of King's College in Kensington that the *Tale of Troy* (which had its rise in a Braemar Hotel party in the summer of 1883) was given for the ladies' department. When Professor Warr first offered it for this purpose to the council, a difficulty arose, as no ladies could be permitted to appear on a stage at the college. Sir Charles and Lady Freake then threw open the Odeum at Cromwell House for the performance. Sir Charles Newton, keeper of the classical antiquities at the British Museum, took up the Homeric drama *con amore,* and enlisted the help of Lord Leighton, Sir E. Poynter, who designed the architectural backgrounds, and Sir Walter Parratt. Far from being interested only in the artistic and classical form of the effort, Lord Leighton told Professor Warr that the chief inducement for him was the idea of installing the ladies' department in a house of its own. There were two performances of the Greek and two of the English version. Mr W. E. Gladstone was present on one of the Greek evenings. On the closing evening Ruskin, " with a tribute to the beauty of the festival couched in words as beautiful, presented to Mr Alexander a superbly bound Shakespeare, the gift of the company." Professor Warr modestly observes that this event " for a whole London season put my name on a level with Homer's."

For the fund of the ladies' department there was a balance of £650. As regards the chief supporter, Dr Warr writes:

[1] *King's College Ladies' Magazine,* 1899.

What Sir Charles Freake's goodness would have done for King's College, had he lived, I can say perhaps better than anyone else. He had taken up our educational enterprise in such practical earnest that he drove about Kensington with me to select the site for a building which would probably have been close to the houses at present (1899) rented by the department, and then went down to the college office to learn for himself just what was wanted. He spoke of his intention of attending the next monthly meeting, to offer what appeared requisite for a permanent ladies' college, but he was taken away by a sudden illness only a few days before the council met.

We may speculate whether the history of the college might have been different but for this grievous loss.

Turning to the beginnings of the educational life of the ladies' department, the first records available of lectures and numbers attending are for Lent 1879. In these we find that Dr Barry's course in scripture and church history had an attendance of 145, Professor Hales' lectures on English literature 79, Professor Buchheim's on German 53. Courses in modern history by Professor Gardiner, ancient history by Professor Warr, and chemistry by Professor Thomson had also very fair attendances. Amongst other subjects added in the course of the next year or two were mathematics, ethics, and constitutional history. In 1887 Dr Momerie's course on moral philosophy had an audience of 81, members of which can still be found who recollect the profound impression he made. His little idiosyncrasies—e.g., the black kid gloves he never took off when lecturing—are also recalled. Samuel Rawson Gardiner continued to lecture in the ladies' department till 1895. Amongst the students of the early years the poet Miss Mary Coleridge is remembered, also two daughters of De Quincey.

An important stage in the constitutional history of the institution was reached in 1885, when the council of King's College adopted a report of a committee " recommending that the council take over the work now being carried on in the ladies' classes at Observatory Avenue, and constitute them a department of King's College." The new conditions included the institution of a committee, with the principal as chairman, the other members being seven ladies, seven members of the staff, and seven members or nominees of the council. All lecturers were to be appointed by the council. The ladies' department was inaugurated on Monday, October 12, 1885, by a special service in St Mary Abbot's,

Kensington, at which the Bishop of London gave an address, afterward proceeding to the new centre, 13 Kensington Square (two houses in one), which he formally opened. This was to be the home of the college till 1915, two other houses, numbers 11 and 12, being added in 1911. The charm and peaceful gravity which in those days belonged to Kensington Square, as well as the literary memories which lingered about its houses, were appreciated by successive generations of students. The square dates from the seventeenth century. It was completed, and its houses filled with courtiers and royal officials, when William III brought his Court to Kensington. The Mills—James and John Stuart—Addison, and Thackeray were amongst its former inhabitants; also the Earl of Shrewsbury, Lord Chamberlain in 1698, Nassau Senior, the political economist, and Talleyrand in exile in 1793. The total number of students in 1886 was 500. In that year the title of lady superintendent was given to the secretary, Miss Schmitz. In 1887 the Princess of Wales consented to become patroness of the department. In 1888 the council decided that this department should be organized like the other departments of the college. A board was constituted, consisting of the whole body of professors and lecturers, while the committee of management was to consist henceforth only of members of the council of King's College and ladies appointed by them. It may be noted that it was recognized in 1889 that the ladies' branch had materially contributed to the total receipts of the college, on which the government grant was based.

Throughout these developments there does not seem to have been any important change in the original character of the institution from the point of view of the students. The educational atmosphere, the type of thought it represented, not less liberally educational than that of other contemporary institutions, but different, the needs it met, and the spirit in which it met them, continued to be fundamentally the same. At the best it was the love of learning and desire to realize the intellectual life which brought the students to its doors. At the worst their studies were somewhat unsystematic and disconnected. Its special function was as yet not to prepare women for definite professional careers, but to give them a taste of a liberal education, which might, for some, mean that turning of the eye of the mind to the light which transfigures for them the world. In days when to go to Oxford or Cambridge was to be a " blue stocking " those who attended the lectures in Kensington Square were sensible neither of the romance nor of the pleasing singularity of this character in the play of women's progress. It must not, however, be supposed that the spirit and methods of collegiate education were not beginning to show themselves at this stage. It was recognized by the committee when Miss Schmitz resigned in 1894—on the occasion of her marriage with Dr Wace—that it was in great measure due to her work during the six years previous to 1884 that the classes were brought into a condition which justified their being taken over by the council of King's College. "Do not imagine," it is said in an article on the education of London girls,

> that the council of King's College thought to lure the *débutantes* of Belgravia and Kensington and Bayswater from their existence in a victoria or a drawing-room by offering them spoonfuls of jam in the shape of diluted science, or lollipops in the form of silver-gilt formulæ. No one knows better than what we call the "leisured student" when science unbends to her level, and no one resents it more deeply.[1]

Amongst the subjects which were independently developed in Kensington, the chief in the early nineties was music, which at this period promised to become a strong feature. Various distinguished musicians were amongst the teachers—as, for instance, Mrs Hutchinson (singing), Mme Haas and Mr Dykes (piano)—whilst classes in harmony and lectures on great composers were instituted.

King's College Women's Department. With the appointment of Miss Lilian Faithfull as vice-principal in 1894 the department entered upon a new phase of its history. Under her statesmanlike guidance it steadily developed the character of a university college, retaining, however, some of the valuable features belonging to the first stage of its growth. It continued to be distinguished by the variety of needs which it met. The musical department still flourished, an art school of a high standard grew up, whilst the movement for university education in home science was beginning before Miss Faithfull left, in 1907, for Cheltenham, although the courses were not actually inaugurated. Systematic work for examinations in arts and science as well as in divinity soon began, and King's College threw open to women some of its prizes and scholarships. The institution in Kensington before long took its place amongst the centres of education for internal students of the University of London, whilst also sending women up for the final honours

[1] Mrs Stephen Rawson, 1898.

examinations of Oxford, a policy at that time permissible.[1] A corporate spirit, to which the earlier conditions had naturally not been so favourable, began to develop, and became a striking characteristic of the college. Literary and athletic societies were soon active. The changing phases of the department under the influence of the new spirit are well reflected in a college magazine, of a somewhat higher literary order than these publications commonly attain, started in 1896.[2] In 1897 Dr Robertson succeeded Dr Wace, as principal of King's College.

In order to give an impression of the progress of the department in its chief activities, now that these are becoming more differentiated, it seems best to record briefly, first, the steps of general advance toward a more definite collegiate status, and, secondly, the most important events in the various special branches of its work. In 1898 the application of the committee for the admission of women to the King's College associateship was granted by the council. In the same year the Merchant Taylors' Company allotted a scholarship for a student reading for her degree at Kensington Square. In 1899 the prospectus contained notice of preparation for the London degrees and certain public examinations of the University of Oxford. The Clothworkers' Company in the same year asked that their two science scholarships tenable at King's College should be opened to women. Amongst a number of distinguished men who gave inaugural addresses for the department we note (in 1899) the honoured name of Professor Pelham, President of Trinity College, Oxford, and one of the best friends of women's education in Oxford. Miss Edith Morley (now Professor of English in the University of Reading) and Miss Caroline Spurgeon (now Professor of English in the University of London, Bedford College), who had both obtained first classes in the Oxford English honours schools, were the first students of Kensington Square to be awarded the King's College associateship. In 1900 Miss Tinkler gained first-class honours in English at Oxford. In this year women were first admitted to the King's College science laboratories. In 1902 Miss Helen Fraser, now Dame Helen Gwynne-Vaughan, was awarded the Carter medal and prize for Botany, and Miss Olive Bray was the only

---

[1] This alternative continued to be possible till 1910, when on representations of friends of women's education in Oxford it was decided to omit from the calendar the announcement that students were prepared for the Oxford Honours Schools, as being possibly unfavourable to the cause of residential students at Oxford.

[2] A bound volume of which (1897–1907) has been kindly lent to us by Miss Faithfull.

woman placed in the first class of the Oxford Honours English school. The name of the department was at this time changed to that of "women's department." It was observed by an old student, as recorded in the magazine, that she had at least at college lived and died a lady!

In 1903 Dr A. C. Headlam, now Bishop of Gloucester, had succeeded Dr Robertson as Principal. An important event in the process of assimilating the work of the department to that of other London colleges was the announcement of the London County Council in 1903 that its scholarships for King's scholars were tenable at this centre. Some students appear to have entered at once, as the grant was received in 1904. More accommodation for the college in its expanding needs being now essential, the vice-principal ceased to reside at Kensington Square, a separate house being found for her. About this time a tutorial system was inaugurated, the idea being derived from the Oxford system, with modifications required by the different conditions. Inter-collegiate courses were attended in 1905, at King's, University, and Bedford Colleges and the London School of Economics. Some idea of the university work at this date may be given by noting that amongst students working for examinations were three preparing for Oxford honours, thirteen for London B.A. honours, twelve for B.A. pass, three for M.A., sixteen for the intermediate examination, thirteen for the Archbishop's diploma in divinity, and a few others for matriculation and Oxford Higher Local.

Whilst the institution was thus, so to speak, finding itself, or learning to perform its function as an element in the teaching University of London, we may ask whether it was also playing its original part in the educational life of Kensington. There is no doubt that in some directions at least it was still doing very valuable service for the constituency for the sake of which it was first called into existence—in so far as the members of this constituency had not also accepted the principle:

Tempora mutantur, nos et mutamur in illis.

In the subject of English literature, in which, in addition to the strength given by the King's College professor, the department possessed a brilliant staff of its own in Miss Faithfull herself, Miss Morley, and Miss Margaret Lee, large numbers of students, though they had fallen on days when all who were not preparing for examinations must submit to classification as "occasional," attended the lectures; the same was true, though to a less extent, of the courses in history, languages, and other subjects. The art school and the department of music were also mainly, though not entirely, for the benefit of students in the neighbourhood. The former was, indeed, for some years a source of pride to the department, with its staff of distinguished teachers, including Mr Byam Shaw, Miss Eleanor Brickdale, and Mr Vicat Cole, whilst leading artists, such as Mr Seymour Lucas, Mr David Murray, and Mr Henry Tuke, acted at different times as honorary visitors and inspectors. Some of the work done in the life-class was very serious, and was highly praised by the inspectors, but there was not much room for expansion, and the school does not appear to have been at any time pervaded by the professional spirit belonging, for instance, to the Slade School, nor to have aimed at this.

The lectures in divinity by the eminent principals of King's College, who from the beginning had been generous in giving their time, and by such theological scholars as Professor H. J. White, Professor Nairn, Professor Caldecott, and Canon Newsom, were very highly valued by many serious non-examination students, as well as by those preparing for the Archbishop's diploma. The biblical study scheme was instituted in response to appeals to the college, coming from such bodies as the St Paul's Association, to enlarge its work for teachers of divinity. It steadily became more systematic, and in 1904 attracted 145 students.

With reference to the service done by the college in its own neighbourhood, the question arises whether a stronger local interest would have affected the history of the institution. At a public meeting held on behalf of the college in 1904 it was pointed out (by Mr Bousfield) that it was especially important that Kensington should possess an adequately equipped centre of university education for women that should carry on the work done in its schools. Kensington, it was argued, ought to be the home of culture in the broadest sense, for it contained within a limited area more educated people than any other district of the same size in London. The recognition of this point of view, however, did not make itself felt very effectively.

As regards the social side of the college, a corporate life was made possible by the institution of a common room in 1897— " an inestimable boon," the magazine tells us—dramatic and literary societies, and other clubs. The literary and debating society soon had a membership of 50, and organized itself in accordance with parliamentary forms. "Party spirit," we are told, runs very high. The liberals are particularly enthusiastic in their applause, and occasionally have to be suppressed. However, the prepared speeches are usually very serious, and bristling with facts and figures.

In 1901 a society for scientific discussion was meeting, the secretary being Miss Helen Fraser. An association for old students had been earlier formed, also a college guild in aid of the women's settlement at Stratford, which continued to exist until the removal of the college from Kensington Square. Nor ought the athletic side to be forgotten. The vice-principal in this activity also was a leading spirit. She was president of the English women's hockey team during all her time at King's. Miss Edith Thompson, who often led the King's team to victory, is now (1928) president of the All-England team. Miss Faithfull and Miss M. A. Julius, later organizing secretary of the home science department, were made life members of the latter team, in recognition of their services to the game, a distinction they shared with three others. A hall of residence closely connected with the college, though not governed by it, was instituted as King's Hall, under the principalship of Miss Evelyn Faithfull.

Signs of growing importance and prosperity may be seen in the increase in 1905 in the share of the Treasury grant allotted to the women's department—a recognition that the numbers and successes of matriculated students in Kensington were taken into account by the commissioners—and in the enlargement of the botanical laboratory and the increase in the library.

Transition to Incorporation. A new phase in the history of the institution as a university college was brought about by the policy of incorporation in the university, determined upon by King's College during the principalship of Dr Headlam. This constitutional change, which at first led to the assumption by the college in Kensington of a more important and independent position in the university, was ultimately one of the factors which helped to bring about its final union with the parent college as a co-educational institution. The question how incorporation would affect the department was considered by a sub-committee in 1906, and amongst the notes on the preamble of incorporation to be sent up to the university the following provision is found—that

With regard to the women's department of King's College, the university shall, so far as its means and other duties permit, maintain and develop the women's department, which shall continue to be located in the South-West district of London,

499

separate and distinct from the college in the Strand, and as an institution in which wide academic culture may be secured by the variety of subjects taught in different faculties, including theology.

And in May 1906 the committee passed a resolution that the department should not be moved so long as a university college for women was required in Kensington. Details of the various proposals in regard to the special policy of the women's department at this juncture would not be of great interest at the present time, unless to those who take delight in constitutional subtleties. The most important issue was decided in favour of giving to the institution a distinct existence as King's College for Women, the vice-principal to have in future the title of warden. The government was to be in the hands of a committee, or delegacy, of the senate, separate from the delegacy of King's College, though closely connected with it, a certain proportion of the members being members of both. The department of divinity was excepted from this arrangement, and was to be directed by the council of King's College, whose officer at King's College for Women would be the sub-dean. Attendance at a weekly lecture in divinity open to all students would qualify degree students for the King's College associateship. Although the main principles of incorporation had been laid down in Miss Faithfull's time, the change was not actually carried out till January 1910, when the then vice-principal, Miss Oakeley, became warden.

Miss Faithfull resigned her office on her appointment in 1907 as principal of the Ladies' College, Cheltenham, having accomplished a remarkable work in the building up, out of the organization for higher education by means of an excellent system of lectures to which she came in 1894, a college for women which was in 1907 already known for the good standing of its students in university examinations and for its strong community spirit.

King's College for Women. The period of seven years from 1907 to 1914, when the decision was made to leave Kensington Square, was a period of much change and development from almost every point of view, whether we look at the constitutional evolution and the strengthening of the university character of the college naturally following on incorporation, the considerable growth in activities through the vigorous beginnings of the movement for university education in home science, or the expansion in buildings by taking into the college two more houses. There was also some inevitable loss in the abandonment, first of the music, later of the art department. To certain of these aspects reference must be made in some detail. But, with a view to indicating what may be called the drama of the college history in these years, it may be well to say a few words at this point in regard to the general direction in which it appeared to be moving and the special place it might have seemed destined to fill. To anyone familiar with its history and continuous evolution toward a more definitely academic and collegiate type its future might now seem to be assured as an important women's college in a district of London particularly well suited to be a centre of university education, with its great museums and the Imperial College of Science, as well as the university administrative buildings, not far off. In virtue of its special association with King's College and other aspects of its history it had a distinctive character of its own. The connexion with King's College gave it very great educational advantages in proportion to its size, since the professors had always been generous in their services, and the women's college had thus distinguished heads in all the chief subjects undertaken. With incorporation the policy of appointing university readers attached to King's College for Women in the main arts subjects was entered upon, the first to be appointed being in the subjects of history and French. Through King's College, again, it was possible to offer women instruction in theological subjects of a character not obtainable elsewhere. The history of the college had favoured a spirit of enterprise and adventure, the most striking illustration of which was perhaps its readiness to adopt the home science scheme, which in its early days might be termed the Cinderella of university movements, destined to captivate the prince—in the form of public interest. The increasingly academic atmosphere was, however, not altogether favourable to the maintenance of the original function of the Kensington Square lectures, the provision of higher education for non-examination students—amongst the most distinguished of whom in the later years of the women's department was Miss Evelyn Underhill (Mrs Stuart Moore). Yet there was good reason to hope that the presence of a number of these— a larger number than would be found in other colleges—would always be a distinctive and valuable feature of the college in Kensington. The chief difficulties ahead which might have suggested themselves to anyone familiar with the position of the institution were, in the first place, the question whether the system by which the King's College professoriate in all the principal arts subjects undertook to lecture in Kensington as well as in the Strand could be permanent in view of the continually increasing needs of the parent college, and, in the second place, the inadequacy of the buildings for the women's college. The latter difficulty was considerably eased by the acquisition of the adjoining houses, numbers 11 and 12, which were adapted to the use of the college for the session 1911–12. This was a picturesque addition, for they were two of the most interesting houses of the Square, once a retreat for Talleyrand, within living memory a home where Thackeray might be met at tea. The result of throwing the two houses into one was to provide charming common rooms for staff and students, rooms for administrative offices, and additional lecture-rooms, which made possible the extension of the library in the original houses. This now became a really adequate reading-room. Had it not been for the continuous growth of the home science department, and the large aims of its chief promoters, as well as the munificent gifts for laboratory accommodation which it attracted, the college with this extension might have looked forward to a few more years of successful development in Kensington Square, though the addition was never regarded as more than a temporary relief.

It is necessary, then, at this point to refer more particularly to the beginnings of the latest branch of the college activities, the most original of the educational developments to which it contributed. The origin of the movement for a university standard in home science seems to have lain in two distinct sources of interest. One of these was the aim of supplying an intellectual and scientific foundation for the pursuits of women as home-makers and housekeepers, or to provide as highly cultural and scientific a basis for this life and profession as for any other. Closely allied to, but distinct from, this was the object of those supporters who wished to raise to a higher level the whole teaching of domestic science by providing a system of education in which the sciences concerned would be studied up to the degree standard and in which the application of chemistry to food, the knowledge of biology, physiology, and bacteriology in connexion with sanitation and hygiene, would be understood by teachers in a much deeper way. It is evident that the hope of creating a more widespread and intelligent interest in health questions, and so contributing to reforms which would be of incalculable benefit to the nation, was associated with both these points of view. The movement thus aroused keen interest in a wide circle. There were other aspects which appealed to some amongst those who greeted it as a great cause, and worked for it with disinterested and self-sacrificing labours—as, for instance, the idea of attracting to higher education women to whom it might not have appealed in the hitherto recognized curricula, or of training scientific investigators in directions not yet very fully explored—but the central aims have been indicated.

The scheme thus aroused much enthusiasm; it also led to such acute controversies as usually attend upon the history of a novel and vital movement. A few words upon this part of its early adventures may be of interest to those who have come to know it only as an accepted fact in the London system. It was from the first very fortunate in the support and devoted efforts on its behalf of men eminent in the fields which were most closely related to its purpose. Sir Arthur Rücker, then principal of the university, was a convinced believer in the possibility of a genuinely scientific education of this kind, and gave valuable aid in defending it from criticism on this score. In this connexion we may be permitted to mention also the names of Sir Herbert Jackson, then professor of chemistry at King's College, and Professor Smithells, of Leeds University, who gave the inaugural lecture for the college session in 1908, the year in which the courses actually started, on the subject of " A University Standard in Home Science," and acted for several years as honorary director. From another side, Miss Maude Taylor, a leading authority on domestic science education, who had long cherished the hope of a more scientific training in this field, warmly espoused the cause from the outset, as also did Miss Alice Ravenhill, to whom it appealed from the standpoint of education in knowledge of hygiene and sanitation. Guidance in regard to the kind of economics relevant to the aims of the course was given by Sir Halford Mackinder, then director of the London School of Economics. As regards the benefit to the cause derived from the constant interest of Dr (now Sir John) Atkins, who saw its immense practical potentialities, it would be hardly possible to overestimate this.

It is unnecessary for the purposes of the present sketch, which is concerned only with the early development of the course in close connexion with King's College for Women, and its relation to the history of the latter, to describe in detail its constitutional position when it was a department of the college, though not yet of London University, and might be considered in some respects independent. The warden acted as its chief executive officer, but a special organizing secretary was appointed for its executive committee, which had as its first three chairmen successive principals of the university, Sir Arthur Rücker, Sir Henry Miers, and Sir Cooper Perry. Munificent donations for the forwarding of the movement were given by Lord Anglesey (for laboratories), Sir Richard Garton (for a hostel, in 1911, which was to be also a school for training in domestic arts), Sir Thomas Dewey, and others. Many gifts have since flowed in; it is the earliest to which reference is here made.

In spite of the somewhat complicated system of relations between the home science department, which was at the time referred to outside the university, and the incorporated college to which it was attached, the actual working of the scheme was very smooth, and harmonious with that of the other departments. The students joined in the general college life, and were a welcome addition, even when their numbers were small. For there was something of the pioneering spirit amongst them, always a healthy quality in a college atmosphere. The first student for the three-year course entered in 1908, but there were also seven for the one-year post-graduate course, including graduates of Cambridge and London. Others came for special subjects, and a course for L.C.C. teachers, in applied chemistry, was held on Saturday mornings.

As already mentioned, the inauguration of the course aroused keen controversy among educationists, and members of the committee were much engaged in its defence in the early years. The chief criticisms proceeded on the one hand from some leaders of the women's movement, who regarded the institution of a course intended especially for women (though men were not necessarily excluded) as a retrograde step. On the other hand, there was some opposition from the point of view of domestic science education, since it was held by some experts in this subject that the actual practical side of domestic arts would inevitably suffer when combined with so much science, and, moreover, that the science taught in the best domestic science institutions was already adequate. There was also, for authorities in the various sciences taught, the issue whether it would be possible to bring these to a university standard in a course so heavily weighted with practical subjects and originally also including the arts subjects of ethics and psychology. The importance of winning over such opponents was recognized, and those concerned were much called upon for speaking, debate, and written argument. At King's

College and King's College for Women there were ready defenders who were convinced that the college was making a valuable contribution to the furtherance of women's education in co-operating in this movement and that it would have good fruits in educational and also social spheres. Other interesting problems arose in connexion with the struggle of subjects for a place in the course. The attempt to include some elements of an arts education by finding a place for ethics and psychology was inevitably defeated when the course had to be constituted with a view to the university degree. The scheme gained steadily in educational as well as general support. The London County Council had shown approval from an early stage, the Head Mistresses' Association agreed to appoint representatives on the committee, some of the domestic science schools testified to their keen interest, and the attitude of the university became more favourable.

Reference should perhaps be made at this stage to the prospects of the special subjects outside the academic system, inherited from the early period of the college history. When plans for extension were first considered in 1908 (with the idea of rebuilding on the same site) provision was to be included for a strong, though not large, art school. The school had done excellent work in inadequate accommodation, and it was felt that the association of a school of art with a university institution had advantages for both sides. On the other hand, the study of music was very difficult to develop to a high standard, except in an institution solely devoted to it, and it had already been necessary to seek rooms outside. Nor did it appear to be so much required in view of the proximity of the Royal College of Music. It was decided, therefore, that the college could not permanently provide for a musical department. The art school continued to flourish, though there was a slight decrease in numbers, till 1910. It then received a severe blow in the resignation of Mr Byam Shaw and Mr Vicat Cole in order to set up a school of their own. After considerable efforts, not attended with much success, to revive it under another gifted teacher it was finally decided that, in view of the number of independent art schools not far off, there was no obligation on the college to maintain under difficulties this part of the work, and it was closed in 1911.

The question of the rebuilding of the college or of its removal to another site became more and more pressing in view both of the rising standards in regard to the requirements of an incorporated college and still more of the rapidly growing needs of the home science department and enlarging conceptions of its future. Its endowments for laboratories and hostel pointed to the necessity for a larger site, whilst it was intended to make an appeal to the public, especially of Kensington, for a fund which, together with the value of the existing site, would enable the main part of the college to combine with it in obtaining a site and buildings adequate for all purposes. After prolonged consideration and negotiation for sites in different parts of Kensington the beautiful grounds now occupied by King's College for Household and Social Science were secured, and Mr Percy Adams, A.R.I.B.A., was appointed architect to plan a complete college, including the hostel for the home science students, which, by the gracious consent of Her Majesty the Queen, was to be called Queen Mary's Hostel. These preparations for the new college appeared to be proceeding under highly favourable auspices. A royal commission on the University of London was sitting, but there was no reason to suppose that any recommendations of a startling character in regard to King's College for Women would be included in the report. When, therefore, on the publication of the report in 1913, it was found that the recommendation of the commissioners in respect to this college was that the home science department alone should be developed in Kensington, this came as a bolt from the blue, and brought about an extraordinarily difficult crisis. The site had been acquired, and it could hardly be confidently anticipated at that time that the department of household and social science could make use of the whole of it. Moreover, the promoters of the scheme had generally conceived of it as working in close association with a complete university college. It was, of course, by no means certain that the report of the royal commission would be adopted.

The idea that the continued life of the college in Kensington was endangered aroused strong feeling amongst the old students, and they began to organize an appeal for its support in the borough. It was found, however, that there were constitutional reasons which prohibited the sending out of a public appeal which would be inconsistent with a recommendation of the royal commission. The question, therefore, whether there would have been strong enough interest in Kensington to produce sufficient financial support was never tested. The further existence of the college as a whole in Kensington seemed, then, to be almost impossible, though many ways were explored, and much anxious consideration given to the problem for many months, during which there was much consultation with the educational authorities concerned. An alternative policy was suggested by the attitude of the King's College delegacy and the principal, Dr Ronald Burrows, who had succeeded Dr Headlam in 1913. He was a whole-hearted believer in university co-education, and strongly favoured the policy of amalgamating King's College for Women, as regards the arts and science departments, with King's College, and making provision for a growing women's side in any plans for the future extension of the college. He also foresaw clearly the difficulty which would almost certainly arise in the future in continuing the arrangement by which the staff gave some of their time to an institution at some distance from the Strand. As regards the problem of the site on Campden Hill, the executive committee for the household and social science department felt that they had reason to believe that in time their department would expand to the point of requiring the whole site. In adopting this view they could count upon the approval of weighty educational authority, though some of the friends of the movement might regret that in this parting of the ways the principle of a close living association of their faculty and students with others of a different type and purpose had to be sacrificed. With the intricate constitutional and financial problems to be solved this history need not concern itself. Enough that they were in time solved by the long-continued efforts of administrators on both sides and the generosity of supporters of the household and social science movement.

In the face of all the factors to which reference has been made, and especially, on the one hand, the welcome of King's College and, on the other, the impossibility of an appeal to Kensington, King's College for Women thus had in the end little doubt as to the wisdom of the final decision. And many of its friends could feel that, in the transition to the last stage of its evolution, there was, if some inevitable loss in continuity and associations, also a gain even weightier in joining the wider life of a greater institution. It is idle now to speculate whether a college free from the dignity and restrictions of incorporation could have won through its difficulties and fulfilled the other destiny to which its earlier history seemed on the whole to point—of a university college in arts and science for Kensington. The die had been cast before the outbreak of the great war. The grounds for the change were, of course, strengthened by this event, both because of the importance of economizing resources in teaching and in other ways and because a public appeal, even if it had been sanctioned, would now have been wholly inopportune. The actual move took place in January 1915. The separate staff of the women's college was welcomed as an addition to that of King's College. Amongst them, it may be noted, was the first of the women students to gain the London D.Lit. degree, Dr Clara Knight, whilst one of the students in the final year, Miss Edna Purdie (now head of the German department of Bangor University College), was to be the second. The students accepted the decision which caused so great a change in their college life with remarkable loyalty, though doubtless there were some seniors whose feelings on their uprooting could be rendered only in Browning's words:

Nothing can be as it has been before,
Better so call it, only not the same.

The majority, nevertheless, recognized that in essential respects they belonged to the same college.

King's College for Women in the Strand remained constitutionally a distinct body, though for all practical purposes the system was henceforth entirely co-educational. The student body at King's, with striking openness of mind, from the outset—and before, in October 1914, their numbers were seriously diminished by enlistment for the war—determined to act on strictly co-educational principles and admit the women to their union. A constitution was worked out in which adequate representation of the women on the executive committee of the union was secured. A fine common room was allotted to them, and they settled down very contentedly, taking, moreover, in some seriousness their position as pioneers in the new departure.

At this point, as we commemorate the farewell of the women's college to Kensington Square, we may recall the names of some of those distinguished men who gave inaugural addresses in succeeding generations for the college in the Jehanghir Hall of the University—men such as Dr (afterward Sir) Adolphus Ward of Peterhouse, Bishop Robertson of Exeter, Frederick Myers, Canon Beeching, Sir W. Richmond, Sir George Parkin, Sir Alfred Lyall, Sir Charles Loch, Dr Bernard Bosanquet, Principal Ronald Burrows, and Professor Pelham.

The foundation-stone of the new buildings on Campden Hill to be occupied by the household and social science department of King's College for Women (the name it continued to use till 1928) was laid by Princess Christian on June 11,

1914, and it was possible to begin work there before October 1915. The department now required a special executive officer of its own, and the first dean, Miss Rosamund Shields, was appointed and took up the work in October 1914. In its fine new position and buildings it began to make rapid progress, and in the time of the second dean, Dr Janet Lane-Claypon, it soon became evident that the institution would not find the accommodation too ample for its needs. It is not for us, however, to pursue here further the special and interesting history of this important offshoot of King's College. Nor need much more be said of the further development of the women's side at King's College itself, apart from the general history, since its progress may be described as henceforth one with that of the whole college, though the women will no doubt always have a social life of their own. Whether there is anything distinctive in this, resulting from the unusual history of the women's department (whether kept alive or not in memory) is a matter on which the students themselves are probably best qualified to pronounce. The only other facts which appear to call for mention in this appendix are as follows. The first important development (already considered before the migration actually took place) was the opening to women of the medical faculty in 1916, the immediate occasion of which was the increasing need for doctors on account of the war. On the resignation of Miss Oakeley in 1915, in order to take up social work as warden of a settlement during the war, a special administrative officer (now called tutor) was appointed, and Miss Plumer, old student and secretary of King's College for Women, was the first to occupy this position. The number of women students soon began rapidly to increase, especially those from the country, and in 1921 a development which owed much to Miss Plumer's efforts took place in the institution of the hostel in Bayswater, known as King's College Hostel for Women. This has been able to expand from time to time by taking in the adjoining houses.

APPENDIX B

THE DEPARTMENT OF EDUCATION

By PROFESSOR J. W. ADAMSON, B.A.

THE unsatisfactory administration of public elementary education led to the appointment in 1886 of a royal commission, which reported two years later. Amongst its less striking proposals the commission recommended that, by way of supplementing the existing residential training colleges for teachers, training departments, to be aided by government grants, should be opened at the universities and university colleges. Effect was given to the recommendation by the institution in 1890 of " day training colleges," as these departments were somewhat unhappily named by the Education Department, the public office which controlled elementary education until 1900, when its functions passed to the Board of Education. Amongst the first of these departments to be instituted was the " London (King's College) Day Training College," which opened in October 1890.

In common with all such departments, the early career of that of King's College was marked by straitened means, by an insufficiency of suitably prepared candidates, and by the handicap usually attaching to novel schemes, which arouse prejudice and seem to demand caution in accepting them. The ablest and best-equipped students continued to go to the old-established residential training colleges of good repute; those of even moderate attainments viewed askance a new-fangled mode of educating and training teachers. King's College was authorized by the Education Department to receive for training twenty-five men, termed " Queen's Scholars," to be followed by a second twenty-five a year later; as the course was for two years, the full strength was therefore fifty. It took six weeks to recruit twenty-five students.

The course, chiefly selected from the college classes in arts, included English, French, Latin, geography, history, and physics; the purely professional instruction, which was given entirely apart from the general studies of the college, always presented some aspects of educational history. Members of

510

the Church of England " kept chapels " and attended the principal's weekly divinity lecture to the college at large; others were exempt. For many years after 1891 the department had Jewish students—sometimes a large number of them; in their interest instruction in divinity and Hebrew was given within the college by Mr Israel Abrahams, afterward reader in Talmudic and Rabbinic literature at Cambridge. As Dr Wace once expressed it, "We have no conscience clause, but we have consciences." Until 1897 College chapel began daily at 10 o'clock, and was followed by two lectures only between 10.20 and 1 P.M., without an interval; during the afternoon lectures ran on continuously. There was no half-holiday, and on Saturday morning the Queen's scholars had lectures from 10 (there being no " chapel " on that day) till 1 o'clock. Opportunity to use the ground at Wormwood Scrubbs was very limited. A successful attempt to bring a social element into the department's life was made in 1893 by the founding of the Society of Education, open to past and present students, for periodical social gatherings and the discussion of matters of interest to teachers.

The first aim of the authorities was to secure better-prepared candidates, and with that in view the standard of admission was steadily raised. In 1893 the Day Training Colleges were permitted to retain for a third year students who were likely to profit from an extended academical and professional course, these two parts of the training being pursued concurrently, to the disadvantage of both. King's College had three of these third-year men in the year 1893–94, and always thereafter numbered some of these abler students in its department. At the end of this session University College closed the Day Training Department which it had opened in October 1891, and its two remaining students were transferred to King's College. One of the two passed in the following session to Professor Rein's Pedagogic Seminar at Jena; the Education Department at that time permitted suitably qualified students to spend their third year abroad, on condition that they maintained a close correspondence with the college at home. During the early years any candidate who passed the government's " Queen's Scholarship examination " was admitted to the department; a step forward was taken in 1897 by restricting admissions to those who passed this examination in the first class; those who had passed in the second class were required to pass in addition a college entrance examination in elementary Latin, French, and mathematics. At the first test of this kind only six candidates out of fifteen were successful. Nevertheless, able students were not entirely wanting. In 1899 Queen's scholars won both the Inglis scholarship in English and the Brewer prize in modern history. Up to that date seven Queen's scholars had gained one or other of these distinctions, and two had been Inglis modern history exhibitioners.

The imposition of an entrance test was at once followed by a drop in the number of students, with a corresponding fall in the government grant, the department's chief source of revenue; in 1899 the shortage of students amounted to 20 per cent. The college suggested to the Education Department that other examinations than the Queen's Scholarship examination should qualify for admission to a government-aided training college.

The reorganization of the University of London in the years following 1898 had an immediate and important effect upon the fortunes of the department. In 1900 a conference representing University, King's, and Bedford Colleges and the College of Preceptors urged upon the commissioners who were making new statutes for the university that a board of studies in pedagogy should be formed and a one-year post-graduate course of teachers' training be instituted. The new statutes in due course created this board amongst others, and included amongst the recognized teachers of pedagogy the head of the training department of King's College, who became the first honorary secretary of the board of studies in pedagogy. In this year (1901) nearly half of the 46 King's Scholars were reading for university examinations; the official report of his Majesty's inspector noted that " the students take a creditable position in university examinations and enter into the life of the college as a whole."

In September 1902 the London County Council opened its Day Training College, sending its students for academic studies to University, King's, and Bedford Colleges, and segregating them for professional studies in temporary premises in Southampton Street, Bloomsbury. The arrangement produced this anomaly: King's Scholars from the County Council's college, who themselves paid no fees, sat side by side with King's Scholars of King's College, who paid £10 per annum in the faculty of arts and £20 in that of science. But by this time the department's position as a national and not a purely local institution was well established, and there was no diminution in the demand for admission from the provinces, although that from London itself virtually ceased for some years. In 1903 only those candidates were accepted who before their admission had passed the university's matriculation examination; the rank of professor was accorded to the head of the department; and its university history had fairly begun. In the session 1903–4 three of its students were reading for honours; six years later more than half of the second- and third-year men were honours men, and their number grew rapidly, until it was very exceptional for a King's Scholar to take a pass degree in either faculty, arts or science.

Almost from the first it was felt that the function of the training department ought not to be limited to the field of elementary education; and the conviction was strengthened by the twenty-year-old agitation for a reorganization of London University. So early as 1894 a scheme of secondary training was propounded by the college, to be followed by yet other schemes in the succeeding years; but they attained no material realization. While there was a fairly general agreement, after the publication of the Bryce report in 1895, that training for secondary school teachers should not be conducted after the government pattern, but that technical training should follow and not be concurrent with general education, there was want of agreement as to what was to be regarded as a token that the secondary teacher's general education had been, comparatively speaking, completed. Should it be a university degree, something less, or something merely different? The first schemes framed by King's College were based on the post-graduate plan, but they required two years of study at correspondingly high fees, the first year being devoted to the studies belonging to general education. This seemed necessary, since in 1899 32 per cent. of certain secondary schools, public and private, which had responded to a government inquiry were staffed exclusively by non-graduates, to which category it was believed half the secondary school teachers of the country belonged. For reasons easily understood, women at this time were much more ready to take a course of training than were the men who proposed to teach. There was no compulsion to train, although the trend of opinion was revealed in the Duke of Devonshire's Registration of Teachers Bill (1898), which required as a qualification for enrolment a university certificate of the applicant's competent knowledge of education, theoretical and practical. At the close of 1901 Oxford, Cambridge, and six university colleges (of which King's College was one) were offering secondary training to men, with preparation for a university diploma. Four of these eight had twenty students between them, two colleges made no return, one had just launched its scheme. King's College had no secondary students in training, but it had a plan both ambitious and expensive, asking in fees twice and even five times as much as some of the others.

But the reorganization of London University, the movement for registering teachers, and a clearer conception of what should constitute secondary or, indeed, all teachers' training at length made it possible to frame a practicable scheme. In 1905–6 there were two graduates in the department following the course of training directed by the university, whose successful completion was rewarded by the Teacher's Diploma. In the same session the department was formally recognized by the Board of Education as giving such a training as was required for registration as a qualified teacher in secondary schools. From that time onward the department has continued to train secondary teachers in gradually increasing numbers, the present arrangement for the purpose dating from 1907–8.

The session 1905–6 was a critical one for the elementary side of the department. Of its 42 King's Scholars 39 were internal students of the university, the remainder being men who had entered before 1903, when matriculation had been made a necessary qualification for admission. In July 1905 the Board of Education issued a circular, which required from all training college students who proposed to study for degrees that before admission they must pass in a specified manner the Board's "preliminary certificate examination," the successor of the old King's Scholarship examination. The Board was moved to take this course by noting that in 1904–5 in the day training colleges the failures at university examinations were a little under 20 per cent., in residential colleges for women about 30 per cent., in those for men 40 per cent. By requiring a high standard of passing the "preliminary" from these candidates, in addition to the matriculation examination, the intention seemed to be to diminish very considerably, if not to eliminate altogether, the number of King's Scholars permitted to undertake university courses. The authorities of the training colleges, residential and day, were agreed as to the tendency of the circular, and conferences with each other and deputations to Whitehall followed. The immediate result was small, but in the end the Board was content to require

514

that matriculation examinations should include certain specified subjects and be passed at a level more or less defined.

From the year 1900–1 until the interruption caused by the
war the department took part in the scheme of free Saturday
morning lectures to London teachers which King's College
had initiated a year or two earlier. The lecture courses of
this nature, subsequently financed by the London County
Council and extended to several colleges and other institutions
of the university, originated in the King's College scheme,
which was wholly carried out at the expense of the college and
of the teachers who gave the lectures.

The separation of technical training from general education
was a procedure which the college desired to apply to all its
students in training, irrespective of the grade of school in
which they would teach. In 1904 it was suggested that King's
Scholars should, before admission, have passed the intermediate examination in arts or science, that the first two
years of the course should be spent in completing the degree
course, and the third or final year be reserved for technical
training and preparation for taking the Teacher's Diploma as
well as the certificate of the Board of Education. The university made such an arrangement of studies possible, and, as
circumstances favoured, it became the department's settled
policy. In 1912–13 a considerable proportion of the King's
Scholars were following this course, taking their third year
with the secondary students, since by the regulations of the
Board of Education they were eligible to teach in secondary
as well as in elementary schools. But the Board raised the
objection that grants were paid in respect of King's Scholars
in order that they might be prepared for elementary school
service, and that under such an arrangement this was not
being done. Then came the war, and the department's
students were reduced to one or two men and two or three
women. From October 1915 to the following June the hospitality of the London Day Training College was extended to
these students and to the staff of the department. In 1917 the
Board of Education lengthened the course of King's Scholars
(the term had become obsolete by this time) studying at
universities from three to four years, stipulating that the
academic course should be completed before the final year,
and that this year should be devoted to professional training.
Thus the Board adopted for its own the policy which it had
condemned at King's College only a few years earlier.

In January 1914 a course of lectures on the history of

education was thrown open by the college to all internal students of the university, irrespective of the colleges of which they were members and without payment of fees. In the following October it was arranged that the department should be responsible for teaching this part of the Teacher's Diploma syllabus throughout the university. Since that date this duty has always been discharged by the department, the number of women students in the university making its continuance throughout the duration of the war necessary.

In the session 1911–12 the university had established a higher diploma in pedagogy; but in 1915 the M.A. was thrown open to students of education, and the higher diploma was abolished. Students of the department, men and women, were the first amongst internal students to obtain both the higher diploma and the M.A. degree in education. Beginning in the session 1916–17, tutorial classes for the latter have contained an increasing number of pupils engaged upon research in educational problems, their goal being the degrees of M.A. and Ph.D. The only internal student who at present has gained the degree of D.Lit. for a thesis on an educational subject was a student of this department.

Former students are engaged in all the continents upon all grades of educational work. Four occupy professorial chairs in the British Isles, one in America; two are directors of education, one in an Indian native state, one in Polynesia. But the great majority are serving as head or assistant masters in elementary and secondary schools. The war brought to some the M.C., to one the D.S.O., to another the V.C., to a great but uncertain number that even greater distinction which their friends are nevertheless constrained to regret.

[The foregoing history of the department is written by the hand that guided its destinies for the whole period it describes, a term of thirty-four years. The writer's modesty, however, has prevented him from mentioning that for which the department has been most famous—famous, indeed, throughout the world of scholarship—namely, his own publications. After Arthur Leach, and following in his steps, Professor J. W. Adamson has probably done more in this country for the study of the history of education than any other man, and his *Short History of Education* (1922) is now the standard work on the subject. This, together with the chapters on " Education " in volumes ix and xiv of the *Cambridge History of English Literature* and the valuable bibliographies accompanying them,

THE DEPARTMENT OF EDUCATION

constitutes perhaps his best-known publication. But he has also done valuable work in the more restricted field of seventeenth-century education in a volume entitled *Pioneers of Modern Education*, while it is known that he is at present engaged upon a history of education in England during the nineteenth century, a task which his former colleagues and his successor wish him many years of health and strength to complete.—J. D. W.]

APPENDIX C

THE COLLEGE BUILDING

1894–1919

By WALTER SMITH

The Buildings of King's College as they were in 1894

Office. The secretary's offices were located in the basement, at the north-west end of the building, immediately under the present office. King's College School, which had hitherto occupied the basement, was at this time in a critical financial position, and, amongst other changes which were made in the endeavour to improve the school accommodation and equipment, the senior classes were moved to the rooms on the ground floor formerly occupied by the secretary's office and the office descended to the basement. The approach was by a wooden covered staircase from the quadrangle. The school retained the greater part of the remainder of the basement, which was approached by a flight of stone steps from the quadrangle at the north end. Incidentally it may be mentioned that the office establishment consisted of the secretary, head clerk, two junior clerks, and the accountant, an old man who was so deaf that all communications had to be made to him in writing.

Basement. The basement was mainly occupied by the school class-rooms, which were the opposite of cheerful. In the winter old gas pendants and brackets gave the necessary light. The corridor was decidedly cold. Still, the old boys always maintained that the school was extremely healthy! The gymnasium occupied the space under the great hall, and astride the east side and extending from the chapel to the wall bounding the Strand building was the playground, with fives courts.

The remaining part of the basement on the west side consisted of vaults, used for stores and wine-cellars, unlighted, and, beyond them, a room used by the professor of anatomy and a larger room which formed a dining-room for the staff. The school dining-hall was the room under the terrace looking over the Embankment.

518

King's College, London

THE COLLEGE BUILDING

On the east side of the corridor, beyond the gymnasium, were some school class-rooms and the college chemical laboratory.

The areas on the north and west sides had not then been built over, except at the end near the principal's house, and that at a low level—viz., that of the sub-basement.

Under the basement was this sub-basement, extending from the entrance hall to the south end of the college. In this was situated the metallurgical department, on both sides of the corridor, with a building in the area, top-lighted, and containing the professor's private room. Vaults at the north end were used as storerooms for the engineering department, and access was gained to the engineering laboratory and workshops, which were situated the former south of the chapel and the latter in vaults under the hall and chapel. Some small amount of daylight was obtained from half-windows, heavily grated, looking on to the playground, but work had generally to be carried on by the aid of gas brackets over the benches, lathes, etc.

Beyond the main building came the kitchen and offices on the Embankment level, and above that the dining-room of the school, the roof of which was the terrace. This roof, by the way, leaked considerably, and it was one of my first jobs thoroughly to renew the asphalt. East of these buildings were the dissecting-room and physiological laboratory, built on land leased from the Office of Works. The entrance was from the basement corridor by steps leading into an area, and thence through vaults to the dissecting-room and the physiological laboratory, and also to the anatomical theatre, built outside the college main building and abutting on Strand Lane. The mortuary was at a lower level still: it was a gruesome place to visit.

The physiological laboratory occupied a part separated from the dissecting-room. Here a small chamber used for stores was frequently flooded during high tides in the Thames, owing to the failure to work of a flap-valve leading to the Embankment sewer.

The electrical engineering laboratory for heavy machines was, as at present, under the quadrangle, but new and better entrances were made later.

Finally, of the underground parts of the building, vaults under the quadrangle at the north end were used for the instruction of plumbers, being fitted up by the Plumbers' Company, which carried on the classes and gave certificates of proficiency.

519

Ground Floor. This part of the building was much as it appears at present, but the rooms were differently occupied. At the north end of the entrance hall were the class-rooms of the school. On the other side of the hall were the large lecture theatre and a smaller theatre and class-rooms, and at the south end the college refreshment room, under the manciple and " John." There was a passage from the hall leading to the engineering department. The great hall was used in the day-time for civil service classes for girls under Mr Harcourt, and in the evening by classes under Mr Braginton. There was a separate entrance to the hall for the girls' classes by a covered way from Strand Lane. The King's College School rooms were also used in the evening for civil service classes under Mr Comyn and others.

First Floor. The rooms were occupied by the library (now the Council Room), the Wheatstone laboratory of physics, and the George III museum. In the centre was the chapel, and next to it—the chief structural difference from the present—came the natural history museum, now the library : this had no floor above it, and was lighted from the roof. The class-rooms were used by all faculties as required.

Second Floor. Shortly before my appointment the scheme of adding to the buildings by raising the height began. Under Professor Banister Fletcher as architect, the floor at the northern half of the college was built over the first floor main corridor and rooms on the east side and at a level above that of the resident students' chambers, which ran the whole length of the building except where intercepted by the Siemens electrical engineering laboratory, over the entrance hall.

One side of the new floor was allotted to the bacteriological laboratory and the architectural department. On the other side of the corridor was built a lecture theatre used by several departments. I think that at the same time the room at the south end (now a lecture theatre for botany and biology) was built; it was used as a school of woodcarving. It should be noted that the architectural department and the school of woodcarving were maintained by the generous assistance of the Carpenters' Company. The resident students' chambers were, as mentioned, on the west side of the building. They were approached from the south staircase, and a wooden-floored corridor ran from end to end. There were twenty-five rooms, all occupied.

South-east Block. The block at the south-east corner of the college, overlooking the Embankment and Strand Lane, which has been a source of much controversy and which undoubtedly spoilt the façade, was built before my time. The building was stopped by the Office of Works, but in the dispute which followed the council won. The block was formerly occupied by resident students' chambers, but owing to decrease in numbers they were being used for various departments— chemistry, public health, etc. Above the roof of the block was the structure used for botany and biology classes; it was approached by the main south staircase.

Other Departments outside the College. In addition to the multifarious classes and the school in the college in the Strand the council controlled the work of the civil service day classes which Mr Braginton carried on in a good-sized building in Waterloo Road, originally, I believe, a chapel, and now incorporated in the Union Jack Club.

There was also a " ladies' department," then located in Kensington Square, but a constituent part of King's College. This was carried on by a committee of management, on which were representatives of the council.

Changes from 1894 Onward

Such, without entering into details, is a short account of the buildings of the college when I was appointed. Owing to lack of funds nothing much had been done lately by way of maintenance and decoration of the rooms, or improving the equipment. The general impression given was depressing. Before anything could be done it was necessary to reorganize the finances as far as possible. The government grant had been withheld on the question of the tests for the staff, and there was a large deficit in the revenue and expenditure account and a heavy debt due to the bankers. An attempt had been made to help matters by imposing a 10 per cent. tax on the emoluments of the staff, which were, even for those days, miserably inadequate. The school was a heavy drain on the resources of the council. The main income from fees was from the civil service department. It seemed to me that the only way of stopping the annual deficit was to pool the fees in each faculty and department, to deduct a fixed proportion (25 per cent.) for administration and the actual departmental expenses, and then to divide the residue between the staff in proportion to definite shares to each. This abolished the unpopular 10 per cent. deduction. The council accepted the scheme, and matters began to improve. All possible economy

521

in administration was made. The secretarial staff was reduced and reorganized; the dining was put on a profit-making basis instead of a losing one; savings were effected in the works department, etc. Some additional revenue was obtained from a grant from the old technical education committee of the L.C.C., and gifts for equipment were received from some of the city companies and other donors. As far as funds would allow, small improvements in the existing rooms were gradually carried out. The name of the college and its work were advertised at the entrance gate in the Strand. Until then the London cabman did not know of the situation of the college, and if told to drive there invariably took his fare to the King's College Hospital in Portugal Street.

The first real effort to improve the position was made when, by the enthusiasm and energy of Mr Bourne, the head-master of the school, debentures were issued to friends of the college and school in order to raise sufficient funds to purchase a large house and grounds facing Wimbledon Common to which to move the school. This move was accomplished, the school vacating the Strand in 1897, and thereafter the number of boys increased slowly but steadily. The school continued under the government of the council of the college until it was transferred under the King's College Transfer Act of 1908 to a new corporation on January 1, 1911. During this time on the Wimbledon site the great hall, with class-rooms below on the ground floor, was built, and new science laboratories erected in the grounds close to the main building. An adjoining vacant piece of land was also purchased as an extension to the playing-field on the school property.

College Buildings. Immediately on the removal of the school the secretarial office was retransferred to its old quarters on the ground floor. It was felt that it was important that the office should be easily accessible to the public and should create a favourable impression. The rooms freed by the removal of the school were quickly occupied by the civil service day classes, and the Waterloo Road building was vacated. This department, under the efficient direction of Mr Braginton as headmaster, was reorganized on the lines of a good secondary school, and was named the "Strand School." Its extra-ordinary efficiency was shown by the large number of successes in civil service examinations gained by the boys working under the curriculum of an ordinary day school, without undue specialization or cramming.

Similar classes for girls seeking appointments in the civil

service were carried on under the able headship of Miss Braginton in two of the large class-rooms in the basement, approached by a separate entrance from the quadrangle.

The new buildings necessitated by the expansion of the Strand School were (1) chemical and physical laboratory, formed by roofing in the area at the north end of the college. These were fitted up with the usual benches and equipment for school laboratories, and were, in fact, used later by the college department of physics when the Strand School was removed to Brixton and taken over by the L.C.C. For the overflow of pupils and for certain special work the vaults used for plumbers' classes were by arrangement also utilized.

(2) Two new class-rooms were in a similar way built in the area on the west side as far as the entrance hall. These again were later used by the college, and ultimately became research laboratories for physics. It may be mentioned that in carrying out the above works the old brick barrel drains were dealt with and new pipe drains laid—a most necessary but difficult business.

(3) The end room adjoining the new laboratories was converted into a proper science theatre.

(4) New laboratories were provided in the playground, which was redrained and asphalted.

All these improvements, although made in the first place for the Strand School, were permanent additions most useful for the college work proper at a later date.

Consequent on the removal of the school the dining-hall became vacant, and was taken over by the staff for a luncheon and common room. It was an enormous convenience and was a real asset to the college owing to the opportunities it gave to the members of the staff to meet together. The next large improvement was the addition of a second floor at the south end of the college, continuing, in fact, the floor built previously at the north end. This was carried out by Mr (now Sir) Banister Fletcher, then a member of the architectural staff. This addition gave much-needed relief to several departments and opportunity of expansion. (a) The architectural department was removed to the room formerly the natural history museum, now the library, on the first floor. The contents of the museum were distributed amongst the various departments of the faculty of science. (b) Following on this change, the physiological department was transferred from its restricted quarters adjoining the dissecting-room on the Embankment level to the fine rooms vacated by the architectural department on the second floor.

The new floor contained four lecture-rooms and a fine corridor paved with marble slabs. It was connected by a narrow passage behind the organ-loft with the corridors on the north side. The new rooms were allotted to geology and botany, geology obtaining a fine large combined laboratory and lecture-room. In the corridor were the larger natural history specimens from the old museum, together with objects suitable for teaching collections. These latter were supplemented and brought up to date by Professors Dendy, Gordon, and Bottomley. The room previously used as a woodcarving school was fitted up as a lecture theatre for biology and botany. The woodcarving was discontinued.

Anatomy Department. The transfer of the physiological laboratory enabled much-needed improvements to be carried out in the anatomy department. (1) The dissecting-room obtained the space vacated by physiology. The old stone flags were taken up, the drainage remodelled, and a good asphalt floor laid down. The area between the dissecting-room and the main building was roofed in, and converted into a museum of anatomical specimens, collected by Professor Hughes. A new and more convenient access was provided to the department. A portion of the dissecting-room was partitioned off for a demonstrator's room. Minor improvements were made in the anatomical theatre, lavatories, cloak-rooms, etc.

Changes in the Residential Students' Rooms. Further expansion was provided by ceasing to take resident students and gradually utilizing the chambers for teaching work. The changes began at the north end, when several rooms and a part of the corridor were allotted to pharmacology and fitted up with modern apparatus. Later the zoological department obtained a series of rooms and the corridor. By removing partition walls between the old chambers and the wall of the corridor very considerable space was obtained, and by removing the low ceilings and inserting top-lights good laboratories and research rooms were provided, together with a professor's private room. The corridor space was used for the fine teaching specimens brought together by the late Professor Dendy, to whose efforts in building up a school of zoology the changes were due.

At the south end, beyond the entrance hall, the chambers were converted in a similar way to house the botanical department, additional research laboratories and a professor's private room being provided. Beyond these, again, were two rooms allotted and fitted up for research laboratories in geology.

Finally, the end room, formerly the censor's room, was given over to the School of Slavonic Studies; it was reached from the south staircase.

South-east Block. The changes made here were (1) the closing down of the fine art studio and its conversion into a chemical laboratory, raising the number of the main teaching laboratories to three; (2) the transfer of the public health laboratory to the second floor, next to the bacteriological laboratory; (3) the conversion of some smaller rooms into another chemical research laboratory; (4) the provision of a laboratory of spectroscopy; (5) the arrangements for a private room and laboratory for the professor of anatomy. Access to the dissecting-room was provided by a special staircase.

Mezzanine Rooms. All spare space in areas and odd corners having been utilized, further accommodation was obtained by inserting mezzanine floors, which the loftiness of the old rooms allowed. In this way several departments in arts benefited, while the secretary's office obtained additional space by flooring over the accountants' room.

Engineering Department. The improvements made were in internal construction and in equipment. The floor over the engineering laboratory used as a drawing office was cut away, leaving only a gallery sufficient for a few drawing-tables: this enormously improved the light of the laboratory. The drawing office was removed to a large room on the ground floor. Small improvements were constantly being made, and larger schemes of building in the playground were contemplated, but had to be postponed on the outbreak of the war. During the war the engineering department, including the electrical engineering section, vigorously carried on classes for munition workers. The buildings were constructed under Professor Jameson after my retirement. The department has to thank him for enormous progress in the engineering school.

Students' Dining and Refreshment Room. The conversion of the college kitchen and cook's room into a refreshment room for students was about the last change in which I was concerned. It involved cutting off the greater part of the kitchen, altering the entrance from the college, and making a new entrance from the bottom of the slope to the Embankment. Suggestions for glazing in the arches on the Embankment were, I am glad to say, rejected by the Office of Works, for this would have spoiled the façade. I believe this refreshment room is still used, and that it has been greatly added to by an ingenious scheme proposed by Mr Shovelton.

Heating. There were no funds to lay out on a complete system of central heating, but by degrees matters were improved by taking up a section at a time, improving or replacing old boilers and pipes, and adding radiators where possible.

Finally, during Mr Headlam's principalship bold schemes for reconstruction and rebuilding were thought out, and the late Mr Rowland Plumb, F.R.I.B.A., was commissioned to prepare plans and approximate estimates. These were deposited in the secretary's office, and tracings also were made. It is understood that these have been of great assistance in working out and starting as parts of a whole scheme the alterations now in hand.

APPENDIX D

THE LITERARY AND DEBATING SOCIETY

By James Parkins

In the comparatively early days of King's College the social side of its life was not very prominent, and old calendars make little mention of students' common rooms or college societies. The latter, however, receive nearly fifteen pages of mention in the calendar for the present year. Amongst other societies which began to be formed in later times, the old evening department was represented by a literary and debating society which flourished for many years. Known, during its thirty years of life, as the King's College Literary and Debating Society, it started in 1891, and lasted until 1922, during which time it certainly accomplished what it set out to do. In its origin it was strongly supported by the principal and staff, and the college authorities were at all times exceedingly kind and helpful.

It consisted of former students and associates, and the calendar states that it was formed in the first instance for the purpose of affording past students an opportunity of meeting together occasionally during the winter session and maintaining an interest in the college and the hospital. For some years the meetings were held in the old Marsden Library—now the principal's private room—on Wednesday evenings in the Michaelmas and Lent terms, when papers and lectures on subjects of literary and general interest were read and discussed. The principal and vice-principal and members of the staff frequently attended, and contributed their share to the proceedings of the society.

At the time it started there was a daily dinner in college at 6 P.M., which was always attended by the resident students, and the new society sometimes made the hall dinner a feature of their proceedings. Those of them who were associates exercised their privilege of dining at the high table. The meeting was held directly after dinner, at 7 P.M., and was generally followed by attendance at the chapel service for students, which was then held on Wednesday evenings at

527

8 P.M. After chapel some of the members were often invited for coffee, etc., to the rooms of the vice-principal or of the resident chaplain and censor of the students. The evening was thus rendered a very delightful one, and was a source of much real refreshment and enjoyment. The ideal of service was always strongly upheld, and several members became governors of the hospital, then in Lincoln's Inn Fields, or helped it in other ways. In the hospital report for 1892 special mention is made of the assistance thus rendered.

The society was also more or less responsible, with college assistance, for the annual festival dinner of old students, which, with its long list of stewards and eminent chairmen, was for many years a notable feature of college life.

That interest in the college should be maintained was one of the cardinal objects of the society, and its realization took many forms. The members present at the meetings seldom failed in their attendance at the chapel service, and for some years, with the approval of the professor of music and chapel organist, the musical part of the service was assisted by the members, the president or some other qualified person officiating at the organ. During the life of the society every principal in turn afforded it his cordial support, and contributed lectures or addresses at the meetings.

There are in existence two large and interesting photographs taken by flashlight in which those who were present are grouped with the vice-principal of the time and a predecessor in that office.

Occasionally former members of the college, holding important public positions, were good enough to attend and encourage by their presence as lecturers, or otherwise, the work in which the society was engaged, while an occasional combined gathering with other college societies would result in a large and happy united meeting in the large theatre, with the president in the chair and the college principal as the lecturer of the evening.

In this connexion it is interesting to note that the recent foundation of an old students' association of both sexes, and of all the faculties, which desires to co-operate with sectional societies without in any way interfering with their special work, is an augury of good for the future. While it will afford an opportunity of fostering and developing that spirit of loyalty which animates many former and present students of King's College, it will, if wisely guided, not only contribute to the happiness of its members, but may result in real usefulness to our Alma Mater.

THE LITERARY AND DEBATING SOCIETY

The outbreak of the war in 1914, which altered so many things, had its effect on the fortunes of the society, and there were many internal changes in the college, which opened out other avenues of action and service.

The society had existed without a break for thirty-one winter sessions: it held its final meeting on March 22, 1922, after more than thirty years of happy and useful life.

The few original members who remained had the satisfaction of knowing that the literary side of their work was being carried on probably more effectively by a new society, bearing a similar name, which was formed in 1915, under the able presidency of Sir Israel Gollancz, and they can only hope that this society in its pursuit of the most delightful of all studies may meet with the success which attended their own humble efforts.

APPENDIX E

THE UNION SOCIETY

By C. H. DRIVER, M.A.

I. *Early Attempts to found a Society, 1873–1908.*[1] The birth of the Union Society is given as December 1873. True it is that previous to that date attempts had been made to constitute a similar club. Apparently, however, our predecessors of the days of general literature and applied sciences, though fully recognizing the possibilities of such a club, withheld their support, probably on account of the scanty benefits which it afforded. Thus, when on December 2, 1873, Professor Mayor generously offered his room—No. 7—for use as a common room, the advantages so proffered soon cemented all departments into one body.

The common room was managed by a committee of twelve, who chose as their chairman and honorary secretary Messrs F. Finch and E. L. Hesketh. For a time it was known as the common room, and was furnished as a reading- and writing-room. Periodicals were taken in, and writing material supplied. The initial membership was 41. In 1874 both the debating and engineering societies were granted the use of the room for their debates and papers. In 1875 the latter society joined as a body, and was followed in 1877 and 1878 by the medical and theological societies. Thus in five years the common room cemented together all departments, and facilitated free intercourse between all students. The membership rose to 120, and the financial aspect was correspondingly sound. This period saw the institution of a library, and justified further expenditure in furnishing the common room.

On November 15, 1878, the amalgamation of the debating society and common room was officially confirmed. It was arranged that the rules should be modified, and the club called the Union Society of King's College. The membership was again largely increased, and an unsuccessful attempt was made to secure better accommodation. In the same month Professor Mayor was made the first honorary member. To his name

[1] Reprinted from the *Union Society Handbook*, 1912.

THE UNION SOCIETY

were added, in 1879, those of Messrs Guinness, Cunnington, Lambert, Norvill, Paley, and Slater.

Unfortunately, in 1880 the lack of room caused the medical department to accept the offer of special accommodation. Later in the year the theological department acted similarly. The immediate result was felt by the treasurer, who in 1881 presented a most unsatisfactory report.

In 1882 the Union Society was dissolved and the common room constitution reverted to. The finances, however, did not improve, and in May 1885, in order to clear the debt, the engineering society took over the common room at the request of the committee of the latter.

Shortly after the dissolution of the Union Society, in May 1884, a new club was formed. This, formed at the instigation of the principal and several members of the staff, sought to combine the offices of the Union with those of an athletic club. Its constitution was drawn up by members of the staff, and it was given the name of " The King's College, London, Athletic Club." Its first work was to lease a piece of ground at Wormwood Scrubbs of about 7½ acres, the council kindly coming forward and lending £500. The management fell into the hands of the principal, the headmaster, several members of the staff, and representatives of all college teams. The annual sports, first organized in 1869, were taken over in a flourishing condition. Indeed, of all sports these were the best supported. As early as 1872 they numbered among their staunch friends and supporters H.R.H. the Duke of Cambridge, the Earl of Derby, Earl Powis, Lord Hatherley, Sir H. C. Daubeney, Sir R. Wilbraham, Sir J. T. Coleridge, and Sir W. Fergusson.

The Athletic Club continued to foster the sports and athletic teams till 1908, in which year it was taken over by the Union Society of 1905. In March 1905, at a general meeting of the regular students, the reformation of the Union Society was discussed and approved. The objects as set down at that meeting were:

1. To obtain Union Common Rooms, to be open to all members of the Union.
2. To take steps to form a college debating society, a gymnastic and other clubs.
3. To provide entertainments.
4. To promote the success of college clubs and students generally.

The Union was formally acknowledged by the principal,

and progressed rapidly. Financial support was granted by the council in the form of a sum deducted from every student's fees.

II. *1908–29*. In 1908 the Union Society appears to have been completely reorganized at a general meeting held on Friday, December 4, and to have taken over both the athletic club and all social activities of the college. The minutes of this meeting constitute the first entry in the present minute-book of the society. The minutes of the earlier societies seem to be lost, but from this time onward the record is unbroken.

In the years before the war the society and the staff worked in closer co-operation than in the period 1919–29. The very first entry in the minute-book is interesting both as exemplifying this fact and also as revealing some of the oldest friends of the Union:

> The President (Mr F. J. C. Hanson) in the chair. The following members of the college staff were present: Professors Sir John K. Laughton, Herbert Jackson, and G. E. Newsom; the Revs. H. F. B. Compston and W. R. Matthews; and Mr P. H. Kirkaldy. Letters and messages of goodwill to the society were reported from the following members of the staff who were unavoidably prevented from attending: the Rev. the Principal; Mr Walter Smith; Professors S. A. F. White, Ernest Wilson, Peter Thompson, D. S. Capper, A. Caldecott, and W. C. Flamstead Walters, and the Rev. C. F. Rogers.

The present Bishop of Gloucester when principal seems frequently to have attended and addressed Union Society meetings, and on several occasions to have superseded the president in the chair. Only once since the war has a principal presided at a Union meeting: Dr R. M. Burrows took the chair at an extraordinary general meeting on March 6, 1919; but he not infrequently attended meetings as an ordinary member of the College.

The Union Society seems to have had very little history from 1908 to 1918, though it was developing a system and procedure of its own capable of the enormous development it underwent from 1919 onward. Meetings of the Union Society were infrequent: apparently only once a term, though even that was uncertain, for the minute-book records that: "On June 14 and 19, 1913, general meetings of the Union Society were called, but at neither was a quorum present, so that no business was transacted." It is interesting to note that the sorrowful secretary who penned those words (A. C. T. White) was wounded at Suvla Bay within two years of that date; and

532

Officers of the Union Society, 1908–29

Year	President	Vice-President	Vice-President	Hon. Secretary	"Review" Editor
1908–9	F. J. C. Hanson	J. Hunter Watts	F. E. Laughton	A. Macnamara	R. W. K. Edwards, Esq., M.A.
1909–10	A. Welby-Solomon	A. Macnamara	F. J. C. Hanson	S. H. White	R. W. K. Edwards, Esq., M.A.
1910–11	F. E. Laughton / S. H. White	M. K. Ingoldby	H. I. Piper	C. Brailsford	R. W. K. Edwards, Esq., M.A.
1911–12	N. H. W. Burke / C. Brailsford	M. K. Ingoldby	J. C. White	J. Rowbotham	F. W. Walton, Esq., M.A.
1912–13	J. W. Fitkin	A. D. Young	J. Rowbotham	H. F. Peerless / O. H. Harland	F. W. Walton, Esq., M.A.
1913–14	A. R. Hart	W. A. Bass		A. C. T. White	O. H. Harland
1914–15	S. W. Card / A. N. M. Davidson	L. H. Reakes	J. A. Moskovitch	E. Teasdale / D. H. Dyer	A. N. M. Davidson
1915–16	E. C. G. Hull	H. T. Rymer	R. G. Browning and Kathleen Spicer	M. A. Pink	D. G. E. Hall
1916–17	D. G. E. Hall	G. F. Burnell	—	F. L. Hussey	G. R. A. de N. Rudolf
1917–18	C. F. Burnall	A. Weston	Gladys M. Greenwood	Nora Edmed	G. R. A. de N. Rudolf
1918–19	Arnold Weston	Miss N. Thomson	K. M. King / — Goodman	D. L. G. Joseph	R. W. K. Edwards, Esq., M.A.
1919–20	B. D. Godfrey / R. C. Lightwood	Miss P. M. Bailey / H. A. Peyton-Bruhl	E. E. Ayling / A. S. W. Joseph	J. R. C. Bartlett	C. H. Driver
1920–21	D. A. Stevens / R. C. Rham	C. M. Scott / P. R. Howe	E. G. Steler	J. R. C. Bartlett	Miss K. M. Leake
1921–22	I. S. Macadam	R. J. Huntley	C. A. Risbridger	R. C. Howard	Miss Yvonne Mayer
1922–23	S. J. Worsley	A. M. Bannatyne	H. C. Green	B. H. Colquhoun	Miss M. Lyttelton
1923–24	A. M. Bannatyne	W. D. Matthews	Miss A. P. H. Ellis	P. E. James	Miss D. S. Sillavan
1924–25	G. C. Olver	Miss M. R. J. Edwards	Miss D. Barter	L. H. S. Bagshaw	Miss N. Selman
1925–26	L. H. S. Bagshaw	A. Craven	C. E. Steward	G. W. Lanyon	Miss I. J. Todd-Naylor
1926–27	G. W. Lanyon	A. Craven	J. V. Alexander	G. W. Nightingale	J. W. Smith
1927–28	L. L. Barnes	H. W. Beck	F. C. Bailey	N. C. B. Brierley	Miss E. Brown
1928–29	D. M. Robinson	Miss E. Halpin	F. F. Cartwright	T. E. V. Snelling	J. A. Bramley

within three years had been awarded the V.C. for an act of gallantry which was hailed all over the Empire.

Since the war the Union Society has developed out of all recognition, both in size and organization. Whereas the average attendance at a debate before the war was 40, the attendance at the annual commemoration debate is now nearly always about 400. It is impossible to give even a sketch of this development—that awaits its own volume; for the truth has yet to be told in full concerning some of the more historic struggles of 1919–24, the Pussyfoot Rag, the Phineas War, and other episodes that will live long in the memories of those who were members at the time.

INDEX

By ELIZABETH S. HEARNSHAW

[*The Table of Contents should also be consulted.*]

INDEX

539

INDEX

INDEX